Lecture Notes in Computer Science 14892

Founding Editors

Gerhard Goos
Juris Hartmanis

The series Lecture Notes in Computer Science (LNCS), including its subseries Lecture Notes in Artificial Intelligence (LNAI) and Lecture Notes in Bioinformatics (LNBI), has established itself as a medium for the publication of new developments in computer science and information technology research, teaching, and education.

LNCS enjoys close cooperation with the computer science R & D community, the series counts many renowned academics among its volume editors and paper authors, and collaborates with prestigious societies. Its mission is to serve this international community by providing an invaluable service, mainly focused on the publication of conference and workshop proceedings and postproceedings. LNCS commenced publication in 1973.

Christian Wallraven · Cheng-Lin Liu · Arun Ross
Editors

Pattern Recognition and Artificial Intelligence

4th International Conference, ICPRAI 2024
Jeju Island, South Korea, July 03–06, 2024
Proceedings, Part I

 Springer

Editors
Christian Wallraven ⓘ
Korea University
Seoul, Korea (Republic of)

Cheng-Lin Liu
Chinese Academy of Sciences
Beijing, China

Arun Ross
Michigan State University
Michigan, MI, USA

ISSN 0302-9743   ISSN 1611-3349 (electronic)
Lecture Notes in Computer Science
ISBN 978-981-97-8701-2   ISBN 978-981-97-8702-9 (eBook)
https://doi.org/10.1007/978-981-97-8702-9

This Springer imprint is published by the registered company Springer Nature Singapore Pte Ltd.
The registered company address is: 152 Beach Road, #21-01/04 Gateway East, Singapore 189721, Singapore

If disposing of this product, please recycle the paper.

Preface

These proceedings contain the scientific output of the Fourth International Conference on Pattern Recognition and Artificial Intelligence (ICPRAI 2024), held from July 3–6 at the Jeju Conference Center in South Korea. This fourth edition of ICPRAI followed the previous, successful iterations of ICPRAI 2022, held in Paris, France, ICPRAI 2020, held in Zhongshan, China, and ICPRAI 2018, held in Montréal, Canada.

ICPRAI 2024 received kind endorsement by the International Association for Pattern Recognition (IAPR) and was sponsored by the Korea University Institute for Artificial Intelligence and the Korea Brain Education Society, whose grateful support we acknowledge.

We received a total of 135 submissions, which were critically reviewed by our program committee - at this point again, we would like to sincerely thank all the reviewers for putting in the time to provide us with their reviews. Following the general review process, the program chairs conducted a final arbitration process, resulting in a total of 69 accepted papers (28 oral presentations, 33 poster presentations, and 8 work-in-progress poster presentations), equivalent to an overall acceptance rate of 51.1%. Papers spanned a wide range of state-of-the-art topics, including advanced deep learning approaches for image and document processing, generative AI, novel analysis methods for medical data, and biometrics, to name just a few.

This conference also marked the introduction of the "work in progress" category for papers. With this, we invited authors to submit papers meant to showcase new results and current work. We hope that with this category authors get an opportunity to discuss and receive feedback for their ideas at the conference.

We gratefully acknowledge our two keynote talks by world-renowned experts in the field: Jun Zhu (Department of Computer Science and Technology at Tsinghua University) on Diffusion Models, and Bastian Leibe (Department of Computer Science, RWTH Aachen University) on Mask Transformers for Segmentation and Tracking.

In addition, we would like to thank our tutorial speakers for organizing two excellent tutorials (Chang D. Yoo and Haeyong Kang: "Continual Learning"; Zuchao Li, Zhuosheng Zhang, and Yao Yao: "On the Shoulders of LLMs: From LLM Optimization to LLM Agents").

We would like to also thank the local organization team for their help for a smooth organization, as well as all members of the organization committee and authors and attendees for helping to make ICPRAI 2024 another success.

July 2024

Cheng-Lin Liu
Arun Ross
Christian Wallraven

Organization

Honorary Chair

Ching Y. Suen   Concordia University, Canada

General Chairs

Mohamed Cheriet   ETS, Canada
Seong-Whan Lee   Korea University, South Korea
Klaus-Robert Müller   TU Berlin, Germany

Program Chairs

Cheng-Lin Liu   Chinese Academy of Sciences, China
Arun Ross   Michigan State University, USA
Christian Wallraven   Korea University, South Korea

Publication Chairs

Camille Kurtz   Université Paris Cité, France
Unsang Park   Sogang University, South Korea
Vishal Patel   Johns Hopkins University, USA
Kiran Raja   Norwegian University of Science and Technology, Norway

Publicity Chairs

Umapada Pal   Indian Statistical Institute, India
Christian Rathgeb   Hochschule Darmstadt, Germany
Stephanie Schuckers   Clarkson University, USA
Imran Siddiqi   Bahria University, Pakistan

Tutorial Chairs

Guo-Sen Xie	NJUST, China
Chang D. Yoo	KAIST, South Korea

Financial Chair

Dong-Gyu Lee	Kyungpook National University, South Korea

Local Organizing Chairs

Heung-Il Suk	Korea University, South Korea
Dong-Ok Won	Hallym University, South Korea

Web Master

Hyung-Seok Oh	Korea University, South Korea

Program Committee

Sudipta Banerjee	New York University, USA
Jenny Benois-Pincau	LABRI, Bordeaux University, France
Jean-Christophe Burie	La Rochelle University, France
Chee Seng Chan	Universiti Malaya, Malaysia
Cunjian Chen	Michigan State University, USA
Farida Cheriet	Polytechnique Montréal, Canada
Anurag Chowdhury	3M, USA
Florence Cloppet	Université Paris Cité, France
Runmin Cong	Shandong University, China
Brian DeCann	Systems & Technology Research, USA
Rita Delussu	University of Cagliari, Italy
Jing Dong	Chinese Academy of Sciences, China
Mounim A. El Yacoubi	Télécom SudParis, France
Andreas Fischer	University of Fribourg, Switzerland
Giorgio Fumera	University of Cagliari, Italy
Guangwei Gao	Nanjing University of Posts and Telecommunications, China
Shizhe Hu	Zhengzhou University, China

Kaizhu Huang	Duke Kunshan University, China
Xiaoyi Jiang	University of Münster, Germany
Lianwen Jin	South China University of Technology, China
Tae-Eui Kam	Korea University, South Korea
Harkeerat Kaur	IIT Jammu, India
Sangpil Kim	Korea University, South Korea
Sungwoon Kim	Korea University, South Korea
Camille Kurtz	Université Paris Cité, France
Byung-Jun Lee	Korea University, South Korea
Hae-Na Lee	Michigan State University, USA
Chenglong Li	Anhui University, China
Hongjun Li	Nantong University, China
Xiao-Hui Li	National Laboratory of Pattern Recognition, Institute of Automation of Chinese Academy of Sciences, University of Chinese Academy of Sciences, China
Josep Llados	Computer Vision Center, Spain
Daniel Lopresti	Lehigh University, USA
Huimin Lu	Kyushu Institute of Technology, Japan
Jiwen Lu	Tsinghua University, China
Emanuela Marasco	George Mason University, USA
Jean-Marc Ogier	University of La Rochelle, France
Wataru Ohyama	Tokyo Denki University, Japan
Srikanta Pal	BIT Mesra, India
Umapada Pal	Indian Statistical Institute, India
Shivakumara Palaiahnakote	University of Salford, UK
Nicolas Passat	Université Reims Champagne-Ardenne, France
Marius Pedersen	NTNU, Norway
Hanyang Peng	Peng Cheng Laboratory, China
Sandip Purnapatra	Clarkson University, USA
Lorenzo Putzu	University of Cagliari, Italy
Ajita Rattani	University of North Texas, USA
Kaushik Roy	WBSU, India
Tonghua Su	Harbin Institute of Technology, China
Heung-Il Suk	Korea University, South Korea
Dapeng Tao	Yunnan University, China
Da-Han Wang	Xiamen University of Technology, China
Qiufeng Wang	Xi'an Jiaotong-Liverpool University, China
Xiao-Jun Wu	Jiangnan University, China
Guosen Xie	Nanjing University of Science and Technology, China
Jian Xu	Casia, China

Contents – Part I

Oral Session: Knowledge Representation

Oral Session: Explainability and Uncertainty

Oral Session: Applications

Poster Session

Contents – Part II

Work-in-Progress Session

Oral Session: Deep Learning

SwInception - Local Attention Meets Convolutions

David Hagerman[1]([email]) [iD], Roman Naeem[1] [iD], Jakob Lindqvist[1] [iD],
Carl Lindström[1,2] [iD], Fredrik Kahl[1] [iD], and Lennart Svensson[1] [iD]

[1] Chalmers University of Technology, 412 96 Gothenburg, Sweden
david.hagerman@chalmers.se
[2] Zenseact, Lindholmspiren 2, 417 56 Gothenburg, Sweden

Abstract. Sparse vision transformers have gained popularity as efficient encoders for medical volumetric segmentation, with Swin emerging as a prominent choice. Swin uses local attention to reduce complexity and yields excellent performance for many tasks but still tends to overfit on small datasets. To mitigate this weakness, we propose a novel architecture that further enhances Swin's inductive bias by introducing Inception blocks in the feed-forward layers. The introduction of these multi-branch convolutions enables more direct reasoning over local, multi-scale features within the transformer block. We have also modified the decoder layers in order to capture finer details using fewer parameters. We demonstrate a performance improvement on eleven different medical datasets through extensive experimentation. We specifically showcase advancements over the previous state-of-the-art backbones on benchmark challenges like the Medical Segmentation Decathlon and Beyond the Cranial Vault. By showing that the existing inductive bias in Swin can be further improved, our work presents a promising avenue for enhancing the capabilities of sparse vision transformers for both medical and natural image segmentation tasks. Code and pre-trained weights can be accessed at https://github.com/Eiphodos/SwInception.

Keywords: Vision transformers · Medical images · Convolutional Neural Networks

1 Introduction

Vision Transformers (ViTs) [5] have emerged as a promising alternative to convolutional neural networks (CNNs) for many vision tasks. It is based on the transformer architecture and uses attention [26] mechanisms to capture long-range dependencies and global context in images. A ViT model can be pre-trained in a self-supervised fashion using masked image modeling [10], but the architecture suffers from long convergence times, large data requirements, and high computational complexity.

Supplementary Information The online version contains supplementary material available at https://doi.org/10.1007/978-981-97-8702-9_1.

Various attempts have been made to mitigate the limitations of ViT, including the introduction of sparse attention mechanisms such as in the Swin Transformer (Swin) [19]. The local attention used in Swin reduces the computational complexity and yields an inductive bias by only attending to nearby features. Swin also utilizes a shifted window scheme to enable cross-windows connections over the local windows. Compared to ViT, sparse transformers generally perform better on moderate-sized datasets. Nonetheless, the inherent inductive bias is limited to the attention windows, which in domains like medical volumetric segmentation are often restricted to a small size due to the high GPU memory requirements.

In this paper, we introduce an encoder architecture dubbed SwInception that attempts to alleviate these weaknesses. SwInception is a hybrid model that combines the strengths of transformers and convolution layers in a multi-branch approach. The use of convolutions provides a stronger local inductive bias that leads to faster convergence, more accurate predictions, and reduced data requirements. Additionally, incorporating branches with receptive fields of multiple scales enhances the capacity of transformer blocks to process features of different sizes effectively. We also modify the decoder in the previous state-of-the-art model to more efficiently utilize the feature vectors from the encoder. Extensive experiments conducted on a range of medical datasets representing various modalities demonstrate a substantial advancement over the preceding state-of-the-art methodologies.

The main contributions can be summarized as follows:

1. We show that the inductive bias of the sparse transformer Swin can be improved further by introducing convolutions in the feed-forward blocks.
2. We present a novel encoder architecture based on these findings named SwInception that has an improved inductive bias, a larger receptive field, and sub-layer multi-scale features.
3. We improve upon an existing decoder for medical volumetric segmentation, resulting in a model with fewer parameters and better performance.
4. Experimental results demonstrate improved performance compared to the previous state-of-the-art on two publicly available benchmarks, the Medical Segmentation Decathlon (MSD) and Beyond the Cranial Vault (BTCV).

2   Related Work

Efficient Vision Transformers. The ViT suffers from quadratic complexity and there are various methods to reduce it to linear complexity to enable larger inputs. Some works [2,15] approximate the attention operation with a less computationally expensive one. While, others [27,29] approximate the softmax operation inside the attention operator by replacing the key and value matrices with a low-rank approximation.

Sparse Vision Transformers. The predominant approach, also employed in our paper, involves reducing complexity through sparse attention. Extensive efforts [4,12,19,30] have been dedicated to linearizing the attention operation by incorporating sparseness, with each work employing different selection methods for tokens to attend to. Among these methods, sparse local attention stands out for vision tasks due to its inductive local bias. However, enlarging their window size is costly and the receptive field can often be relatively small. Among sparse transformers, Swin is widely adopted, primarily for its shifted window strategy that enhances the receptive field. While state-of-the-art vision models pre-trained on massive datasets like JFT [32] often use some kind of ViT variant as encoders, Swin-based models are frequently preferred in domains with smaller datasets, such as medicine.

Transformer-Convolution Hybrid Models. Considering the complementary properties of CNNs and transformers, it is natural to want to combine the two architectures. Several studies have investigated using depth-wise convolutions in the feed-forward layer [7,29,31] within a ViT. Depth-wise convolutions have also both been used to project attention matrices [28] and to directly produce attention weights [8]. Depth-wise convolutions are cheap but lack the ability to use information from different channels, limiting their expressiveness. In [21,33], convolutions are explored using a separate parallel branch to the multi-head self-attention, similar to Inception [23]. However, in both works, the interlayer fusion between the CNN and transformer features is applied to downsampled features due to the full attention.

Medical Volumetric Segmentation. Until recently, the state-of-the-art in medical volumetric segmentation were models identified using network search [11,14]. While vision transformers have become state-of-the-art for image classification, medical volumetric segmentation cannot utilize full attention as easily. The extra dimension introduces an order of magnitude more input tokens, which is problematic for models with quadratic computational complexity. The complexity can be alleviated by using smaller models and larger patch embeddings [9], but most medical segmentation tasks require voxel-level precision where large patches are counter-productive. Newer models, therefore, use transformers with some way of enforcing locality [13,20] and most of them [16,18,25,34] use a Swin-based encoder due to its lower computational complexity. Recent research [16,18] has examined the combination of Swin and convolutions; however, this exploration has been limited to parallel integration with transformer blocks, which prevents the localized enhancement of features within the blocks. The top ranking architecture on MSD, the Universal Model [17], utilizes SwinUNETR [25] as the base segmentation model and improves performance by significantly increasing the size of the pre-training dataset through the use of CLIP embeddings.

3   Methodology

In this section, we introduce the SwInception architecture, which uses a UNet structure with multi-scale features. An overview of the proposed architecture is shown in Fig. 1, and additional details about the SwInception encoder and decoder are given below.

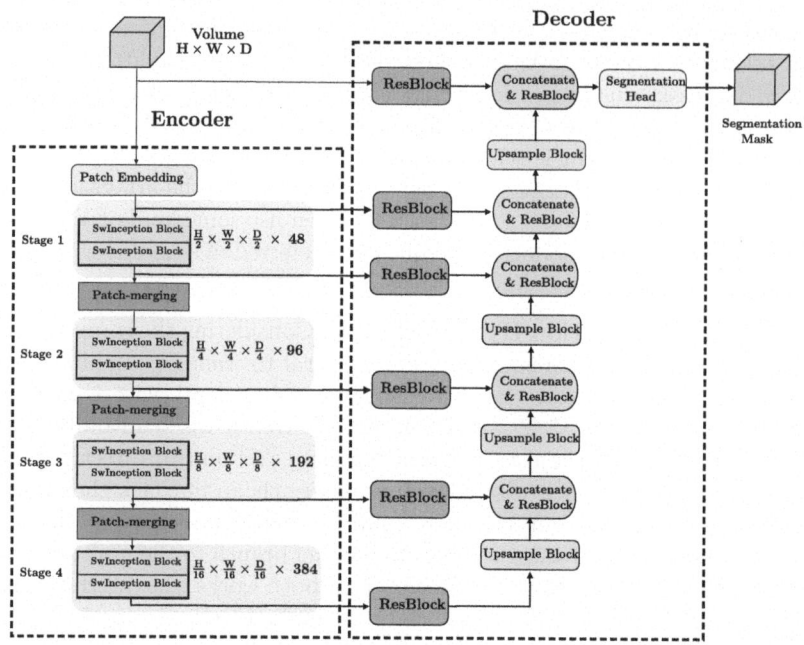

Fig. 1. An overview of the SwInception architecture for volumetric segmentation.

3.1 The SwInception Encoder

As illustrated in Fig. 1, the SwInception encoder consists of a patch embedding layer and four stages of SwInception blocks. The patch embedding layer is implemented as a convolutional layer comprising 48 filters, with both the stride and patch size set to two and no activation function. Each stage consists of two sequential SwInception blocks and maintains the same resolution throughout the entire stage. Between each stage, a patch merging block is used to downsample the resolution with a factor of 8 while doubling the output dimension. The patch merging block differs from the original Swin by utilizing a convolutional layer with overlapping filters as proposed in [34], which allows for stronger representations at the subsequent stages.

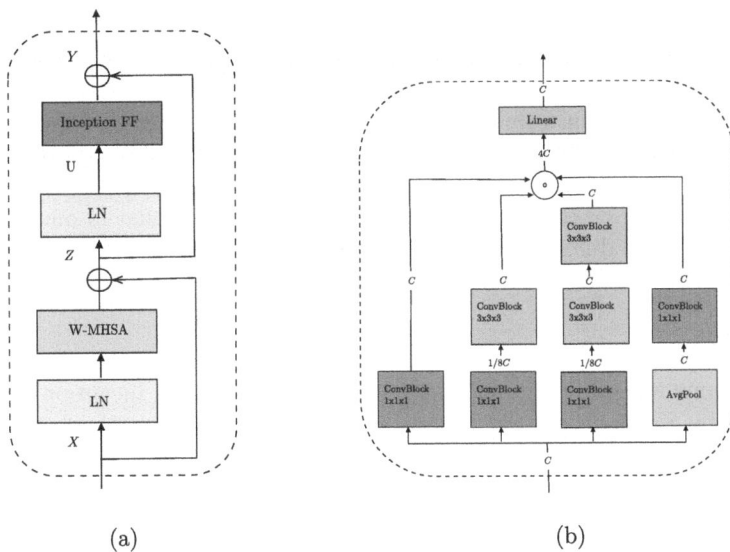

(a)   (b)

Fig. 2. (a) A SwInception block with layer normalization (LN), windowed multi-head self-attention (W-MHSA), and the Inception feed-forward block. (b) The Inception feed-forward block. Here C denotes the number of channels.

The SwInception Block. SwInception is the first model that incorporates convolutions directly into the window multi-head self-attention (W-MHSA) mechanism from the Swin transformer [19]. The convolutions are introduced in the feed-forward layer of the transformer block and can therefore improve the features used in later attention operations. More specifically, SwInception uses Inception [22,23] blocks as illustrated in Figs. 2 and 2b.

Incorporating the Inception block in the Swin transformer introduces several advantageous features. First, convolutions enforce a stronger inductive bias toward locality in the architecture, reducing convergence time and lowering data requirements, which is particularly relevant for transformers. Second, convolutions increase the receptive field of the Swin transformer by expanding the number of tokens that communicate in each block. Third, convolutions in a transformer-based architecture can provide a stronger positional encoding and improve translation-equivariance, as shown in [3]. Incorporating the Inception block into the Swin transformer architecture results in enhanced performance and efficiency, albeit with a slight increase in parameter count. This is alleviated using bottlenecks at the beginning of the more expensive Inception branches.

The Inception block serves as an intermediate solution between basic convolutional layers and depth-wise convolutional layers. While depth-wise convolutions are computationally inexpensive and less prone to overfitting, they cannot capture features that require input from multiple channels. In contrast, regular convolutions offer high capacity but can be expensive to use in transformer architectures. The Inception block strikes a balance by incorporating branches that operate on a subset of input channels, similar to depth-wise convolutions while retaining the ability to capture multi-channel features. By incorporating kernels of different sizes in the branches, our model can utilize features at varying scales within each transformer block, which proves advantageous for tasks like tumor detection involving objects of diverse sizes. Furthermore, both the pooling and convolution branches have local invariance to translations, enhancing this property of sparse vision transformers. It should be noted that in our research, we explored many different variations of Inception branches, convolutions, and depth-wise convolutions, but we are presenting the one we deemed best.

SwInception Block Implementation. The output of SW-MHSA is reshaped into a volume and processed in parallel by each of the four Inception branches employed by SwInception. Let us recall that the MLP used in the feed-forward layer of Swin and most other transformer architectures utilize two sequential linear layers with an inverted bottleneck ratio of 4. From Fig. 2b, we observe that if the number of filters in the $1 \times 1 \times 1$ branch is set to 4C and the number of filters in every other branch is zero (meaning that those branches are not used), we obtain the regular Swin MLP. By adjusting the number of filters in each branch, we can adjust how much relative weight to give each branch and thus how similar the SwInception block is to an MLP. In our research, we explored several types of weightings and found that equal branch weightings gave the strongest performance.

Each Inception branch consists of convolutional blocks that include a convolutional layer with stride 1 and no dilation, batch normalization layer, and a GELU activation layer. The $1 \times 1 \times 1$ branch comprises a single $1 \times 1 \times 1$ convolutional block. The $3 \times 3 \times 3$ branch first bottlenecks the feature channels by $\frac{1}{8}$ via a $1 \times 1 \times 1$ convolutional block before applying a $3 \times 3 \times 3$ convolutional block. The $5 \times 5 \times 5$ branch has the same bottleneck as the $3 \times 3 \times 3$ branch, followed by two $3 \times 3 \times 3$ convolutional blocks. The pooling branch incorporates a $3 \times 3 \times 3$ average pooling layer followed by a $1 \times 1 \times 1$ convolutional block. The output of each branch is concatenated and reshaped into tokens before a final linear layer reduces the dimensionality back to the original size.

The output $\boldsymbol{Y}$ of a SwInception block can be written as follows. Let $\boldsymbol{X}$ be the input to a SwInception block, LN the layer normalization, and B_i, the ith Inception branch with $i \in \{1, 2, 3, 4\}$. The shifted window multi-head self-attention is denoted by SW-MHSA and shifts the windows every other block. Then, according to Figs. 2 and 2b,

$$\boldsymbol{Z} = \text{SW-MHSA}(\text{LN}(\boldsymbol{X})) + \boldsymbol{X}, \tag{1}$$

$$\boldsymbol{U} = \text{LN}(\boldsymbol{Z}), \tag{2}$$

$$\boldsymbol{V} = \text{Concat}(\text{B}_1(\boldsymbol{U}), \text{B}_2(\boldsymbol{U}), \text{B}_3(\boldsymbol{U}), \text{B}_4(\boldsymbol{U})), \tag{3}$$

$$\boldsymbol{Y} = \text{Linear}(\boldsymbol{V}) + \boldsymbol{Z}. \tag{4}$$

3.2   The SwInception Decoder

The SwInception decoder is based on the decoder used in SwinUNETR [25] but introduces a few important modifications. A complete diagram of the decoder model can be found in Fig. 1. The decoder produces a segmentation map by utilizing the multi-scale features obtained from the encoder through the lateral skip connections. Each feature is first fed through a residual block using two $3 \times 3 \times 3$ convolutional layers and concatenated with the features from the layer below. The resulting volume is upscaled with an upsampling block and then sent through a second residual block. This process is repeated for every layer $l_i, i \in \{0, 1, 2, 3, 4\}$ where l_0 is the patch embedding layer. The residual convolutional block comprises two $3 \times 3 \times 3$ convolutional layers and a residual connection. The upsampling block utilizes a single $2 \times 2 \times 2$ transposed convolutional layer. Instance normalization and PReLU activation are also employed in both block types.

What differentiates the SwInception decoder from the SwinUNETR decoder is that the extracted features are taken prior to the patch-merging step. This yields higher resolution features, obviates one upsampling step in the decoder, and eliminates the patch-merging step after the final SwInception block. Due to this reduction in the number of patch-merging operations, we also utilize a more expensive but efficient convolutional patch-merging strategy as mentioned in Sect. 3.1. The decoder still works on multi-scale features but at a higher resolution, which is beneficial for segmenting small objects. Additionally, the extracted feature vectors from the encoder are lower-dimensional, resulting in fewer decoder parameters as the convolutional filters become smaller.

4   Experiments and Results

For an extensive evaluation of the capabilities of the SwInception architecture for medical volumetric segmentation, we utilize the Beyond the cranial vault (BTCV) [6] dataset as well as all ten datasets in the Medical Segmentation Decathlon challenge (MSD) [1].

We present results from two SwInception versions. One uses the hyperparameters, pre-trained weights, and code from SwinUNETR [25], and we refer to that paper for details. As SwInception has several additional layers not included in the SwinUNETR pre-trained weights, they have been loaded in a non-strict fashion and frozen for the first 25 epochs. The other version, denoted by SwInception*, is an optimized SwInception model that utilizes pre-trained SwInception weights and hyperparameters optimized specifically for SwInception. The pre-training was performed using the same methodology and datasets as presented in the SwinUNETR paper but using a SwInception encoder. Detailed hyperparameters can be found in Appendix 1.2 in the supplementary material.

We compare our work to the top three ranked models in the MSD challenge, SwinUNETR [25], nnUNet [14] and DiNTS [11]. We also perform a comparison using the number one ranked solution, the Universal Model [17], with both SwInception and SwinUNETR as the base segmentation model. All models used for comparison have been trained using their respective shared code, weights, and optimal hyperparameters. The parameter counts for the respective networks are as follows: nnUNet has 30M, SwinUNETR and SwInception each contain 63M, and DiNTS holds 152M.

The comparisons of architectures for medical volumetric segmentation in Sects. 4.2 and 4.1 use averaged 5-fold cross-validation while the ablation studies are done on single folds. We have not compared performance on test data for two main reasons. First, the challenges is now closed and does not accept new submissions. Second, SwinUNETR [24,25] and other models use extensive post-processing. The details regarding their post-processing steps are often unknown and, therefore, not reproducible. Considering that we want to compare model performance and not post-processing performance, we have opted for cross-validation as our method of choice.

All models are implemented in Python using the open-source libraries PyTorch and MONAI. Models have been trained with 4 A100 GPUs on a single node using mixed precision.

4.1   Medical Segmentation Decathlon

The MSD challenge [1] contains 6 CT datasets and 4 MRI datasets. Each dataset/task has its own training and test data, and the challenge covers a wide range of segmentation tasks for organs and lesions. The number of samples in the training sets ranges between 20 volumes (Heart) to 484 volumes (Brain).

We compare SwInception, SwInception*, and the top three models in the challenge: SwinUNETR, nnUNet, and DiNTS. For each task, we evaluate the models through 5-fold cross-validation over all training data. The averaged results across all folds can be found in Table 1; for detailed results and the specific hyperparameters used by SwInception* we refer to the supplementary material. For MRI tasks, no pre-trained weights are used for any model. No post-processing has been used for any of the listed models.

The results show that even the baseline SwInception model outperforms the previous state-of-the-art models when looking at average performance over all tasks. In particular, a significant increase can be observed both at MRI tasks such as prostate segmentation and CT tasks like lung cancer.

The optimized SwInception* increases the gap further with large increases at several tasks. Using SwInception's pre-trained weights grants major improvements on CT tasks, possibly due to the transformer block weights being properly optimized to leverage the locally enhanced features. The difference is particularly clear on cancer segmentation tasks such as colon, liver, and pancreas, which are some of the most difficult segmentation tasks in the challenge.

Table 1. Cross-validation performance on MSD from SwInception, SwinUNETR, nnUNet, and DiNTS.

Task	Brain Tumour	Heart	Liver	Hippocampus	Prostate
Metric	Mean Dice				
DiNTS	72.63	92.20	72.21	88.13	70.60
nnUNet	74.03	**93.30**	76.84	89.04	71.72
SwinUNETR	74.26	90.78	78.69	87.08	71.59
SwInception	74.49	92.57	79.22	87.34	73.01
SwInception*	**74.57**	92.60	**82.19**	**89.06**	**74.77**

Task	Lung	Pancreas	Hepatic Vessel	Spleen	Colon	All
Metric	Mean Dice					
DiNTS	60.35	57.98	59.94	94.68	37.54	70.63
nnUNet	64.09	66.58	**66.58**	95.35	41.53	73.91
SwinUNETR	64.68	62.97	62.72	95.66	42.74	73.12
SwInception	66.73	64.57	64.10	96.24	43.73	74.20
SwInception*	**68.03**	**67.03**	66.33	**96.39**	**48.19**	**75.92**

4.2 Beyond the Cranial Vault

BTCV [6] is an abdomen multi-organ segmentation dataset first released in conjunction with MICCAI 2015 comprised of 30 volumes, and the data is collected from patients with either colorectal cancer or ventral hernia.

We perform a 5-fold cross-validation comparison between SwInception, SwInception*, SwinUNETR, nnUNet, and DiNTS. The results can be found in Table 2. For detailed per-organ segmentation results, we refer to Appendix 1.1 in the supplementary material.

The experiments show that SwInception* outperforms all other models on average. The nnUNet architecture also shows great performance, indicating the importance of larger crops for multi-organ segmentation in large volumes. The experiments suffer from a large variance with big differences in performance between different folds due to the small size of the dataset.

Table 2. BTCV results from SwInception and SwinUNETR.

Fold	1	2	3	4	5	All
Metric	Mean Dice					
DiNTS	77.11	72.49	76.57	75.78	71.04	74.60
nnUNet	82.91	**79.33**	81.32	82.15	73.57	79.86
SwinUNETR	80.64	71.78	79.19	78.01	77.75	77.14
SwInception	82.53	71.61	80.49	80.06	**78.67**	78.67
SwInception*	**84.15**	73.00	**82.45**	**83.14**	77.82	**80.11**

4.3   Ablation Study on Encoder and Decoder Combinations

We investigate the effect the separate parts of the SwInception architecture have on performance by comparing different combinations of the encoder, decoder, and encoder patch-merging strategy. The experiments are all performed on the Decathlon Prostate dataset, which is a challenging task with very large inter-subject variability. All models have been trained from scratch without pre-trained weights. For a fair comparison between the Swin and SwInception encoders, we also include experiments where the inverted bottleneck ratio for the feed-forward layer in Swin has been increased from 4.0 to 7.0 such that the number of parameters is roughly equal for both models.

From the results in Table 3, it can be observed that changing the encoder from Swin to SwInception always increases performance, even when compared to a Swin model with the same number of parameters in the feed-forward layer. The experiments also show that the proposed decoder improves performance for all encoder types with the added benefit of a lowered parameter count. The convolutional patch-merging strategy, described in Sect. 3.1, generally performs better but at the cost of more parameters, specifically when using the Swin-UNETR decoder, due to the final patch-merging operation being performed on feature maps with many channels.

Table 3. Ablation study over encoder, decoder, and patch-merging strategies on MSD Prostate.

Encoder	Decoder	Patch-Merging	MLP-ratio	Params	Mean Dice
Swin	SwinUNETR	Linear	4.0	62.8M	72.17
Swin	SwinUNETR	Linear	7.0	65.2M	72.36
SwInception	SwinUNETR	Linear	4.0	64.9M	**72.81**
Swin	SwinUNETR	Conv	7.0	72.6M	73.48
SwInception	SwinUNETR	Conv	4.0	72.3M	**74.97**
Swin	SwInception	Linear	4.0	59.2M	73.99
Swin	SwInception	Linear	7.0	61.6M	72.38
SwInception	SwInception	Linear	4.0	61.3M	**75.20**
Swin	SwInception	Conv	7.0	63.4M	72.99
SwInception	SwInception	Conv	4.0	63.1M	**75.33**

4.4   The Choice of Inception Block

We investigate the difference between adding an Inception block and depth-wise convolutional blocks to a Swin encoder. The architecture denoted as SwinDepth has two blocks of depth-wise convolutions, batch norms, and GELU activations in between the two linear layers in the Swin feed-forward layer, similar to [7,29,31]. All models were trained on single folds from three challenging MSD datasets with the SwinUNETR decoder and the linear patch merging strategy. All models were trained from scratch without pre-trained weights. The inverted bottleneck ratio in the MLP was increased to 7.0 for Swin and SwinDepth to make the parameter count equivalent for all models.

The results in Table 4 show that introducing depth-wise convolutions can improve performance for the baseline Swin encoder on specific datasets. However, the improvements for the SwInception encoder are both larger and more consistent while introducing only a minor increase in parameter count.

Table 4. A comparison between Swin encoders with feed-forward layers using Inception and Depth-Wise convolutions.

Task	Liver	Pancreas	Colon
Metric	Mean	Dice	
Swin	83.84	76.02	73.55
SwinDepth	84.25	75.78	76.14
SwInception	**84.84**	**77.40**	**77.08**

4.5   Visual Comparison

To further analyze the differences between SwInception* and the models evaluated on MSD, we present a visual comparison in Table 5. We can see that while organ segmentation results are very similar regardless of the model, SwInception improves the rate of true positives for cancer segmentation without adding any false positives. In general, the segmentations from SwInceptions are smoother and less fragmented, which improves the segmentation accuracy and reduces the need for post-processing.

4.6   Model Performance on Smaller Datasets

In Table 6, a comparison between SwinUNETR and SwInception on several differently sized subsets of Decathlon training data can be found. All the data that was not used in the subset has been utilized as validation data. Both models have been trained as in Sect. 4.1 using SwinUNETR hyperparameters and no pre-trained weights. The results demonstrate that SwInception outperforms SwinUNETR on all subset sizes. Notably, the relative difference grows significantly for the smaller datasets, especially for the more difficult task of segmenting colon cancer. From an 11.8% relative increase on the colon subset containing half of the dataset to a 34.5% relative increase on the smallest colon subset with only 10% of the data. As one effect of a stronger inductive bias is to reduce the data required to train models to convergence, these results align with the theorized advantages that the multi-branch convolutions bring to the Swin encoder.

14   D. Hagerman et al.

Table 5. Visual comparison using examples from MSD. A. Liver cancer. B. Colon cancer. C. Pancreatic cancer. Green denotes organ segmentation, and yellow denotes cancer segmentation for all examples.

Ground Truth   SwInception*   SwinUNETR   nnUNet   DiNTS

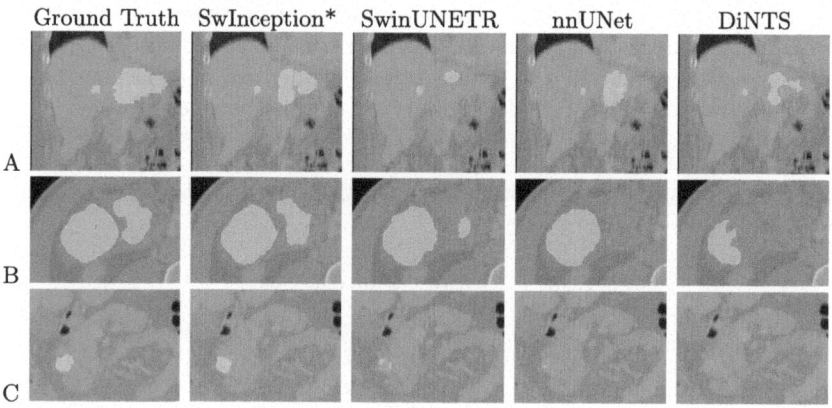

Table 6. A comparison between SwInception and SwinUNETR on small datasets.

Task	Hippocampus			Colon		
Subset size	50%	25%	10%	50%	25%	10%
Metric	Mean Dice			Tumor Dice		
SwinUNETR	91.09	90.67	90.15	38.64	27.05	15.18
SwInception	**91.71**	**91.41**	**90.95**	**43.23**	**34.02**	**20.42**

4.7   SwInception as a Backbone in UniversalModel

The UniversalModel, utilizing upon the CLIP framework [17], introduces a pre-training strategy that facilitates the integration of multiple diverse medical datasets in a supervised pre-training phase. Utilizing SwinUNETR as its backbone segmentation model, it currently stands as the SOTA method for the Medical Segmentation Decathlon. Table 7 presents extensive cross-validation results across all MSD CT tasks and BTCV, employing SwinUNETR and SwInception backbones. The models were pre-trained following the methodology outlined in the paper, excluding any dataset containing MSD or BTCV data. The codebase and hyperparameters remain consistent with the original paper, with two modifications: post-processing was disabled, and learning rates were optimized for specific tasks due to the smaller volume of pre-training data.

Our findings consistently demonstrate that employing SwInception as the base segmentation model outperforms SwinUNETR across diverse tasks. This performance improvement is particularly evident in challenging tasks that require the segmentation of small cancerous regions, such as those found in the Lung and Colon. Some of the cancer tasks show worse performance compared to the results in Table 1. This could be attributed to the fact that the pre-training data now contains very low number of cancer annotations after the exclusion of MSD data. Conversely, tasks such as Spleen and BTCV showcase substantial performance enhancements, aligning with the prevalence of general organ segmentation data in the majority of the pre-training datasets.

Table 7. UniversalModel with SwinUNETR and SwInception as backbones on Decathlon CT tasks and BTCV

Task	Liver	Lung	Pancreas	Hepatic Vessel	Spleen	Colon	BTCV
Metric	Mean Dice						
UM-SwinUNETR	76.13	57.07	62.55	62.49	96.63	43.01	82.60
UM-SwInception	**77.40**	**60.06**	**64.39**	**63.73**	**96.83**	**46.12**	**82.93**

5   Conclusion

In this paper, we have investigated the effect a stronger local inductive bias can have on the Swin architecture for small and medium-sized datasets and how to efficiently utilize encoder features for volumetric semantic segmentation. These investigations have resulted in a backbone encoder and a segmentation decoder that we name SwInception. This hybrid transformer-convolution architecture outperforms the previous state-of-the-art methods on competitive medical image segmentation challenges. Finally, we observe significant increases in performance on tiny datasets, possibly due to the stronger inductive bias introduced by the convolutional branches.

Acknowledgements. The computations were enabled by resources provided by the National Academic Infrastructure for Supercomputing in Sweden and the Swedish National Infrastructure for Computing at Chalmers Centre for Computational Science and Engineering partially funded by the Swedish Research Council through grant agreements no. 2022-06725 and no. 2018-05973. The computations were also enabled by the Berzelius resource provided by the Knut and Alice Wallenberg Foundation at the National Supercomputer Centre.

References

1. Antonelli, M., et al.: The medical segmentation decathlon. Nat. Commun. **13**(1), 4128 (2022)
2. Choromanski, K.M., et al.: Rethinking attention with performers. In: ICLR (2021)
3. Chu, X., et al.: Conditional positional encodings for vision transformers. In: ICLR (2023)
4. Dong, X., et al.: Cswin transformer: a general vision transformer backbone with cross-shaped windows. In: CVPR, pp. 12124–12134 (2022)
5. Dosovitskiy, A., et al.: An image is worth 16x16 words: transformers for image recognition at scale. In: ICLR (2021)

6. Gibson, E., et al.: Automatic multi-organ segmentation on abdominal CT with dense v-networks. IEEE Trans. Med. Imaging **37**(8), 1822–1834 (2018)
7. Guo, J., et al.: CMT: convolutional neural networks meet vision transformers. In: CVPR, pp. 12175–12185 (2022)
8. Guo, M.H., et al.: SegNeXT: rethinking convolutional attention design for semantic segmentation. In: NeurIPS, vol. 35 (2022)
9. Hatamizadeh, A., et al.: UNETR: transformers for 3d medical image segmentation. In: WACV, pp. 574–584 (2022)
10. He, K., Chen, X., Xie, S., Li, Y., Dollár, P., Girshick, R.: Masked autoencoders are scalable vision learners. In: Proceedings of the IEEE/CVF Conference on Computer Vision and Pattern Recognition (CVPR), pp. 16000–16009 (2022)
11. He, Y., Yang, D., Roth, H., Zhao, C., Xu, D.: Dints: differentiable neural network topology search for 3d medical image segmentation. In: CVPR, pp. 5841–5850 (2021)
12. Ho, J., Kalchbrenner, N., Weissenborn, D., Salimans, T.: Axial attention in multi-dimensional transformers. arXiv preprint arXiv:1912.12180 (2019)
13. Huang, X., Deng, Z., Li, D., Yuan, X.: Missformer: an effective medical image segmentation transformer. arXiv preprint arXiv:2109.07162 (May 2021)
14. Isensee, F., Jaeger, P.F., Kohl, S.A., Petersen, J., Maier-Hein, K.H.: nnU-Net: a self-configuring method for deep learning-based biomedical image segmentation. Nat. Methods **18**(2), 203–211 (2021)
15. Kitaev, N., Kaiser, L., Levskaya, A.: Reformer: the efficient transformer. In: ICLR (2020)
16. Lin, A., Xu, J., Li, J., Lu, G.: Contrans: improving transformer with convolutional attention for medical image segmentation. In: MICCAI, pp. 297–307. Springer (2022)
17. Liu, J., et al.: Clip-driven universal model for organ segmentation and tumor detection. In: ICCV, pp. 21152–21164 (2023)
18. Liu, W., et al.: Phtrans: Parallelly aggregating global and local representations for medical image segmentation. In: MICCAI, pp. 235–244. Springer (2022)
19. Liu, Z., et al.: Swin transformer: hierarchical vision transformer using shifted windows. In: ICCV, pp. 10012–10022 (2021)
20. Rahman, M.M., Marculescu, R.: Medical image segmentation via cascaded attention decoding. In: WACV, pp. 6222–6231 (2023)
21. Si, C., Yu, W., Zhou, P., Zhou, Y., Wang, X., Yan, S.: Inception transformer. NeurIPS **35**, 23495–23509 (2022)
22. Szegedy, C., Vanhoucke, V., Ioffe, S., Shlens, J., Wojna, Z.: Rethinking the inception architecture for computer vision. In: CVPR (2016)
23. Szegedy, C., et al.: Going deeper with convolutions. In: CVPR. pp. 1–9 (2015)
24. Tang, Y.: Private communication (2023)
25. Tang, Y., et al.: Self-supervised pre-training of swin transformers for 3d medical image analysis. In: CVPR, pp. 20730–20740 (2022)
26. Vaswani, A., et al.: Attention is all you need. In: NeurIPS, vol. 30 (2017)
27. Wang, S., Li, B.Z., Khabsa, M., Fang, H., Ma, H.: Linformer: self-attention with linear complexity. arXiv preprint arXiv:2006.04768 (2020)
28. Wu, H., et al.: CVT: introducing convolutions to vision transformers. In: ICCV, pp. 22–31 (2021)
29. Xie, E., Wang, W., Yu, Z., Anandkumar, A., Alvarez, J.M., Luo, P.: Segformer: simple and efficient design for semantic segmentation with transformers. NeurIPS **34**, 12077–12090 (2021)

30. Yang, J., et al.: Focal attention for long-range interactions in vision transformers. NeurIPS **34**, 30008–30022 (2021)
31. Yuan, K., Guo, S., Liu, Z., Zhou, A., Yu, F., Wu, W.: Incorporating convolution designs into visual transformers. In: ICCV, pp. 579–588 (2021)
32. Zhai, X., Kolesnikov, A., Houlsby, N., Beyer, L.: Scaling vision transformers. In: CVPR, pp. 12104–12113 (2022)
33. Zhang, Q., Xu, Y., Zhang, J., Tao, D.: Vitaev2: vision transformer advanced by exploring inductive bias for image recognition and beyond. Int. J. Comput. Vis. 1141–1162 (2023)
34. Zhou, H.Y., et al.: nnformer: volumetric medical image segmentation via a 3d transformer. IEEE Trans. Image Process. (2023)

FMM-Head: Enhancing Autoencoder-Based ECG Anomaly Detection with Prior Knowledge

Giacomo Verardo[1]([⊠]) [iD], Magnus Boman[2,3] [iD], Samuel Bruchfeld[2] [iD],
Marco Chiesa[1] [iD], Sabine Koch[2] [iD], Gerald Q. Maguire Jr.[1] [iD], and Dejan Kostic[1] [iD]

[1] KTH Royal Institute of Technology, Stockholm, Sweden
{verardo,mchiesa,maguire,dmk}@kth.se
[2] Karolinska Institutet, Stockholm, Sweden
{magnus.boman,samuel.bruchfeld,sabine.koch}@ki.se
[3] MedTechLabs, Stockholm, Sweden

Abstract. Detecting anomalies in electrocardiogram data is crucial to identify deviations from normal heartbeat patterns and provide timely intervention to at-risk patients. Various AutoEncoder models (AE) have been proposed to tackle the anomaly detection task with machine learning (ML). However, these models do not explicitly consider the specific patterns of ECG leads, thus compromising learning efficiency. In contrast, we replace the decoding part of the AE with a reconstruction head (namely, FMM-Head) based on prior knowledge of the ECG shape. Our model consistently achieves higher anomaly detection capabilities than state-of-the-art models, up to 0.31 increase in area under the ROC curve (AUROC), with as little as half the original model size and explainable extracted features. The processing time of our model is four orders of magnitude lower than solving an optimization problem to obtain the same parameters, thus making it suitable for real-time ECG parameters extraction and anomaly detection. The code is available at: https://github.com/giacomoverardo/FMM-Head.

Keywords: Machine Learning · ECG anomaly detection · AutoEncoders

1 Introduction

Cardiovascular conditions are the main causes of death worldwide [13]. Tools such as electrocardiogram (ECG) measurements are utilized to monitor and identify these conditions. An ECG records the heart activity by detecting electrical signals. Electrodes positioned on different parts of the body measure the signal propagation through different planes (*i.e.*, *leads*), thus allowing the analysis of multiple heart sections. Collecting ECG data is standard procedure for both hospitalized patients and outpatients since it allows detection of various cardiovascular conditions, such as myocardial infarction and arrhythmia. In recent years, the amount of available ECG data has increased considerably due to wearables (*e.g.*, smart, low-powered, ECG-capable devices (*e.g.*, smartwatches and wearable smart textiles [18])), institutional databases, and continuous ambulatory monitoring of high-risk patients. Continuous ambulatory monitoring produces a huge quantity of data, whose analysis can be difficult since it requires expert

C. Wallraven et al. (Eds.): ICPRAI 2024, LNCS 14892, pp. 18–32, 2025.
https://doi.org/10.1007/978-981-97-8702-9_2

knowledge of cardiac conditions and their related effect on ECG measurements [25, 26]. This increase in available data moves the bottleneck from *monitoring* to **processing** the collected data. Given the vast amount of available data, (*deep learning (DL)*) has been employed to tackle multiple ECG-related tasks. We propose including ECG prior knowledge in neural networks to improve anomaly detection and explainability in ECGs.

Anomaly detection through deep learning and (*ML*) models is a promising technique to improve care by spotting health records that deviate from the patterns of normal data *without* any knowledge of what the underlying conditions might be. Anomalies may be symptoms of major heart issues, like heart muscle failure [27]. In contrast, ML *classification* requires labeled data from different health conditions (*i.e.*, classes) that are used to train the model. AutoEncoders (AEs) are a family of ML models trained to reconstruct the original input signal. AEs are trained only on data which show no anomaly, so that during the testing and inference phases an anomaly alert is raised if the input sample is not normal. An anomaly can be detected when the reconstruction loss between original and predicted data is high [9]. Multiple rule-based ECG anomaly detection methods have been proposed [4]. Unlike ML models, these techniques rely on extracting well-known indicators for specific heart conditions. However, these methods lack generalization capabilities since they rely on strong *a priori* knowledge of what these parameters are; therefore, these assumptions hinder their usability for anomaly detection of *unknown diseases*, *i.e.*, there is no *a priori* knowledge of them.

Although the most prominent strength of AEs is the lack of assumptions regarding the classes and shapes of different inputs, the inclusion of *a priori* information about the structure of input data may be beneficial for the learning procedure. While ECG signals demonstrate different patterns depending on the underlying heart condition, their shape is composed of five waves (shown in Fig. 1a), which correspond to different instants of the heart's electrical signal, as measured via the electrodes. For different heart conditions, the shape of these waves change, but the number of waves and their general structure are steady. This *weak a priori* knowledge is valid for almost all ECG classes, but this knowledge is currently not exploited by state-of-the-art anomaly detectors.

Recently, [23] proposed *Frequency Modulated Möbius (FMM)* waves to provide explainable parameters for ECG data [24]. They proposed an optimization algorithm to iteratively compute the amplitude, position, direction, and frequency parameters for the five waves composing the ECG signal through a cycle of polarization and depolarization. However, this optimization takes tens of seconds to be solved for a single heartbeat, thus making it unsuitable for real-time monitoring of critical patients and processing of voluminous quantities of ECG data. [31] have shown that a neural network (NN) can be used to approximate the FMM coefficients and correctly classify heartbeats, but did not apply it for anomaly detection.

Our contributions are threefold. Firstly, we develop FMM-Head, a first approach for incorporating *weak a priori* knowledge of the ECG leads' structure into an AE model. In particular, FMM-Head replaces the decoding sub-model of AEs, provides an explainable representation of the FMM parameters, and reconstructs the signal accordingly (see Fig. 1b). We design a generic pooling layer to adapt FMM-Head to different hidden dimensions of the AE encoder. Secondly, we demonstrate FMM-Head's ease of

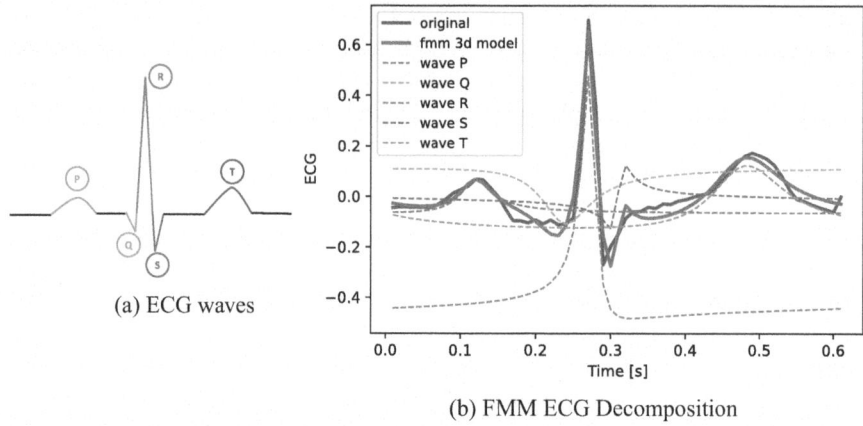

(a) ECG waves

(b) FMM ECG Decomposition

Fig. 1. (a) Shows the ECG shape, (b) shows the FMM decomposition of an ECG wave

use by incorporating it into five baseline AEs models, thus showing that our layer is flexible enough to handle the output of different kinds of encoders. FMM-Head significantly enhances the performance of these AEs. Moreover, as shown in Fig. 2a, even low-performing models such as EncDecAd can be enhanced to be on par with other models. At the same time, FMM-Head outperforms baselines based on Generative Adversarial Networks (GANs) [8] and diffusion models [3], as shown in Fig. 2b. Thirdly, we evaluate and compare our enhanced models to the baselines. Replacing the decoder with the FMM-Head almost halves the total number of trainable parameters of the AEs and leads to up to -77% reduction in inference time and -47% memory required to store the model. Using a fully connected AE with 6 layers, the execution time is 21 thousand times lower than the optimization solution to the FMM problem using the [23] code, which was not designed to perform anomaly detection. The 4 orders of magnitude lower time to process batches of heartbeats enables real-time anomaly detection and is suitable for analyzing huge amounts of ECG data. Our model also provides coefficients that are highly correlated with the original FMM coefficients, thus making its output more transparent than blackbox AEs, whose extracted features are not explainable. Although training for anomaly detection reduces the output similarity to the real FMM coefficients, it improves the *detection of anomalies* of five baseline models.

2 Background

2.1 Electrocardiograms

For over a hundred years, ECGs have been used to detect heart conditions, such as myocardial infarction and arrhythmia [2]. The main idea behind ECG monitoring is to repeatedly measure the electrical polarization and depolarization waves that propagate through the heart muscles and cause rhythmic contraction and relaxation. A standard 12-lead ECG machine uses 10 electrodes, which are combined in different pairwise

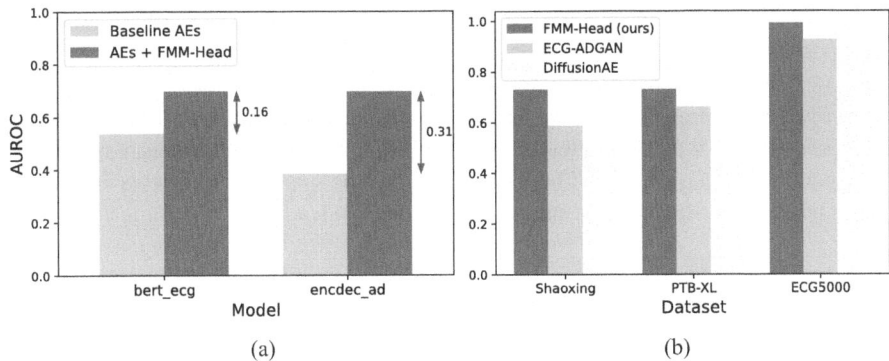

Fig. 2. (a) FMM-Head improves anomaly detection for transformer and LSTM-based models and (b) shows better performance than GANs and diffusion models

combinations to measure the voltage through planes that intersect the heart with different orientations, thus giving insights into various parts of the heart (*e.g.*, inferior, superior anterior, posterior leads). In contrast, smartwatches produce one ECG lead, *i.e.*, the plane intersecting the heart through the arm, similarly to having 2 electrodes.

Figure 1a shows the shape of an ECG, composed of 5 waves corresponding to rhythmic polarization and depolarization phases. The P wave corresponds to the depolarization of the atria. The QRS complex depends on depolarization of ventricula before their contraction, whereas the T wave is determined by ventricular repolarization. Detecting a cardiac disturbance in conductance may involve different features of the ECG, such as the interval and slope between the peaks, their amplitude or underlying area. Depending on the task, a cardiologist uses this information to identify conditions and diseases. Instances of such conditions with relative ECG change are nodal tachycardia (hidden P-wave), sinus tachycardia (visible P wave with higher rate), hypertrophic cardiomyopathy (deep and narrow Q waves in specific leads), myocardial infarction (ST segment elevation or depression), and atrial fibrillation (wide QRS complex, absence of P wave).

Given the bulk of possible heart conditions and their corresponding relevant ECG features, anomaly detection and classification of ECG data requires *strong* a-priori knowledge [13]. The problem is exacerbated in real-time monitoring of patients [25,26]; hence, it requires automatic processing to scale with the quantity of available data.

2.2 FMM Waveforms

To provide a comprehensive way to parameterize the rhythmic behavior of the hearth, [24] proposed modeling each individual heartbeat as the sum of 5 FMM waves [23]. Each wave is modeled as per the following equation:

$$W(t_i) = \mu(t_i) + e(t_i) = M + A\cos(\varphi(t_i)) + e(t_i) \tag{1}$$

$$\varphi(t) = \beta + 2\arctan(\omega\tan(t - \alpha)) \tag{2}$$

$$\mathbf{e} = (e(t_1), \dots, e(t_n))^T \sim \mathcal{N}(\mathbf{e}; 0, \sigma^2 \mathbf{I}) \tag{3}$$

where, $A \in \mathbb{R}^+$ is the amplitude of the wave, $\alpha \in [0, 2\pi)$ represents the position of the peak, $\beta \in [0, 2\pi)$ is the peak direction, $\omega \in [0, 1]$ parametrizes the lobe width of the peak, $M \in \mathbb{R}$ is the constant offset of the wave, t_i is the timestep index. The tuple $\theta = (A, \alpha, \beta, \omega, M)$ represents the encoded parameters necessary to represent each wave. Their proposed 3D model includes the FMM waves formulation but makes assumptions of the parameters that are shared between leads, $i.e.$, the α and ω coefficients are shared among leads while A, β, and M are not. Therefore, the lead vector X for lead L is:

$$X(t_i)^L = M^L + \sum_{j \in \{P, Q, R, S, T\}} W(t_i, A_j^L, \alpha_j, \beta_j^L, \omega_j) + e^L(t_i); \qquad (4)$$

To estimate the optimal parameters, the following objective function is used:

$$\theta^* = \min_\theta \sum_L \sum_i (X^L(t_i) - \hat{X}^L(t_i, \theta))^2; \qquad (5)$$

The estimated best tuple θ^* is obtained by repetitively iterating a fitting and wave assignation phase. During fitting, optimization is performed over a single FMM wave, and the single-lead parameters are extracted by solving a linear regression problem. More than 5 waves might be obtained. During wave assignation, a choice of the best ones is made: each peak (P, Q, R, S, T) is selected based on the α coefficient and thresholds on the main model's parameters. The proposed algorithm is inherently sequential, not parallelizable and it often requires minutes-order of magnitude of execution time.

2.3 AutoEncoders

AEs (Fig. 3a) are a family of self-supervised NN models [9]. AEs have a dumbbell structure ($i.e.$, wide-narrow-wide as in Fig. 3a), sequentially combining (i) an encoder, which transforms the inputs' features into a lower-dimensional latent representation, and (ii) a decoder, that reconstructs the input from the latent space. The loss function measures the error between original and output data. Hence, the aim of an AE is to exactly reconstruct the inputs. However, due to the dumbbell shape, irrelevant information is lost, thus enforcing a compact, semantically meaningful latent space.

AEs are state-of-the-art models for anomaly detection [5]. AEs are trained on normal data so that abnormal samples during test phases can straightforwardly be recognized. Samples unseen during training, so-called holdout data, will be wrongly encoded and decoded, thus causing a large loss. Different kinds of NN models have been proposed to tackle ECG anomaly detection, including Long-short term memory (LSTM)-based models [6,10,16,17,22], transformers [1] and variational AEs [12,14].

2.4 Circular Variables

A representation of circular data [15] is necessary whenever the direction of a measure is a crucial feature to understand the correspondent phenomenon. ECGs are intrinsically circular since the electrical signal passing through the heart is quasi-periodic and can be modeled as an oscillator. In the FMM formulation, α and β are circular variables since they respectively represent a position and a direction within the $[0, 2\pi]$ interval.

The circular mean of a circular random variable θ can be computed as: $\bar{\theta} = \arctan 2\left(\sum_{i=1}^{n} \sin(\theta_i), \sum_{i=1}^{n} \cos(\theta_i)\right)$. The correlation between circular variables should be computed differently than linear correlation. For instance, the linear Pearson coefficient ρ between two random variables x and y, for whom we extracted n samples, can be computed as: $\rho = \dfrac{\sum_{i=1}^{n}(x_i - \bar{x})(y_i - \bar{y})}{\sqrt{\sum_{i=1}^{n}(x_i - \bar{x})^2 \sum_{i=1}^{n}(y_i - \bar{y})^2}}$. However, using the Pearson coefficient between two circular variables will return an incorrect estimate of the correlation. For example, a realization of $x, y = \epsilon, 2\pi - \epsilon$ should positively contribute to the correlation coefficient. To solve this problem, circular correlation [11] can be computed by using the circular mean instead of the linear mean:

$$\rho = \frac{\sum_{i=1}^{n} \sin(\theta_{1i} - \bar{\theta}_1) \cdot \sin(\theta_{2i} - \bar{\theta}_2)}{\sqrt{\sum_{i=1}^{n} \sin^2(\theta_{1i} - \bar{\theta}_1) \cdot \sum_{i=1}^{n} \sin^2(\theta_{2i} - \bar{\theta}_2)}}.$$

3 Methodology

Our FMM-Head layer reconstructs the original ECG input and provides the corresponding explainable FMM coefficients. To do so and maintain FMM parameter explainability, we split the training procedure into a warm-up regression phase and an anomaly detection training phase. Combined with constraints imposed inside the NN, this two-phase approach provides meaningful FMM coefficients.

3.1 Preprocessing

We preprocess the ECGs to extract heartbeats and provide correctly structured input data. We build on top of the preprocessing in [24], whose pipeline consists of (i) low pass filtering to remove baseline wandering, a common artifact in ECGs due to patient's breathing or movement, (ii) application of the Pan-Tompkins algorithm [19] to detect R-peaks, (iii) extraction of ECG heartbeats' interval around the R-peak with 40% of the distance from the previous peak and 60% from the next one. Additionally, we zero-pad each sequence to a constant length in order to be able to feed the input samples to the evaluated models. The original coefficients of the FMM-model are also preprocessed. In particular, circular variables such as α and β are split into their cosine and sine, so that they can be easily learnt by the NN. Also, the parameters are sorted according to the α parameter, so that the P wave corresponds to the first coefficients, etc.

3.2 FMM-Head

We design a novel layer, which we name FMM-Head since it resides on top of the NN and draws inspiration from the FMM formulation detailed in Sect. 2.2. As depicted in Fig. 3b, the main idea behind FMM-Head is that any hidden representation encoded into the latent space can be mapped to meaningful FMM coefficients. This mapping is provided by a non-linear function that is implemented through one pooling layer and two fully connected layers, followed by suitable activation functions that produce parameters in the correct range for the FMM formulation. The parameters obtained after the activation function are used to reconstruct an ECG time-series $\hat{X}$ for anomaly detection. We leverage this weak *a priori* knowledge drawn from the FMM formulation to better reconstruct the input ECG signal.

The main drawback of standard anomaly detection through FMM waves is that the reconstruction might not reflect the original meaningful pattern of the FMM optimization. Although it is straightforward to obtain FMM waves that approximate an ECG signal, obtaining peaks with meaningful shapes is challenging. Hence, we propose an initial warm-up regression phase using the original FMM coefficients. This procedure constrains the output of the NN to be in the range of the original FMM coefficients, thus steering the anomaly detection phase to correct and meaningful patterns.

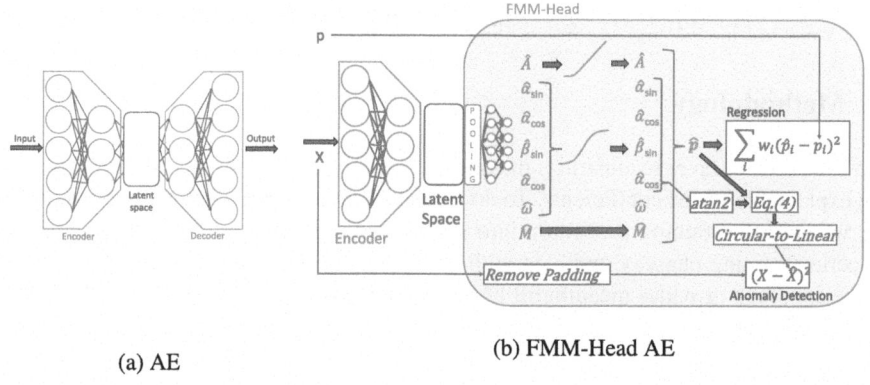

(a) AE

(b) FMM-Head AE

Fig. 3. *(a)* Structure of standard AE and *(b)* AE with the FMM-Head decoder. The FMM-Head is usually smaller than the baseline decoders.

Pooling Layer. Depending on the employed AE, the encoder produces a latent space with different shapes. To handle different dimensions of hidden representations, a layer that maps them to a common output is needed. The pooling layers take as input the latent representation and generate a 2D output, which can be used as input to the following fully connected layers. The pooling layer is, in general, different for each encoder. Transformer and LSTM-based networks have output shapes consisting of a batch, time step, and feature dimension, which can be reduced to two by applying a linear transformation to each time step feature. For fully connected AEs and LSTM layers with state output (such as [17]) there is no need for pooling since the output is already 2D. For convolutional networks, we flatten the 3D output space into a 2D representation.

Fully Connected Layers. Two fully connected layers are used to map the output of the pooling layer to the size of the FMM parameters. The first layer utilizes a non-linear function with tanh activation, while the second layer employs a linear activation. While the second layer has a fixed size (depending on the number of parameters N), the number of units of the first layer can be flexibly chosen. We tested multiple options (64,

128, and 256 units), and found only slight differences in performance. When the size is too small, there is a drastic decrease in performance. Hence, we chose one hidden layer composed of 256 units and a second layer with N units for the fully connected network.

Activation Functions for FMM Coefficients. The output of the fully connected network is unsuitable for direct generation of FMM waves since different parameters have different range requirements. We handle this by selecting an appropriate activation function for each parameter. In particular, a non-negative amplitude is obtained by applying *softplus*, while restricting the ω parameter to the range $(0, \omega_{max})$ with a sigmoid-like function. The sine and cosine components of the circular variables are also mapped to the $(0, 1)$ interval: $\hat{A}' = \ln(1 + e^{\hat{A}})$, $\omega' = \dfrac{\omega_{max}}{1 + e^{-\omega}}$, and $\alpha'_{\text{sin/cos}} = \dfrac{2}{1 + e^{-\alpha_{sin/cos}}} - 1$. The predicted α and β are obtained by computing the angle that corresponds to the predicted sines and cosines. The use of ω_{max} instead of the original unitary limit reduces the possibility of non-meaningful waves with good reconstruction. With high ω values, peaks can be too wide and hence negatively influence the pattern of other peaks.

The output of the layer includes parameters that may be shared or not between leads. We exploit the formulation from Sect. 2.2 to identify such parameters and provide single and multiple layer output variables for shared and not shared coefficients respectively. Hence, FMM-Head can inherently support multi-leads ECG inputs.

Regression and Anomaly Detection. The predicted parameters can be used to directly compute the mean squared error loss. We directly inject the original FMM parameters, obtained by running FMM optimization, to compute the error and back-propagate it to train the AE. We employ the cosine and sine circular parameters to compute the loss and also apply a weight to each parameter to produce better alignment with the original time series. Specifically, we apply a $10\times$ higher weight for the parameters of the R-peak to obtain well-separated waves in the QRS complex. This specific multiplying factor was selected empirically, but it is not crucial to correctly perform warm-up, since lower values still provide distinct QRS waves. We perform a warm-up regression phase on the original coefficients by training the AE to produce results closer to the original optimized ones. Hence, although such a network cannot be employed for anomaly detection, the NN provides a prediction of the FMM coefficients.

After warm-up regression, the NN is trained as a standard AE. We employ Eq. (4) to generate the 5 ECG waves, sum them, and obtain a reconstructed signal in the $[0, 2\pi)$ domain. We then map the signal to the original length through a linear transformation and compute the mean squared error between the input ECG, stripped of the zero-padding, and the predicted sum of waves. We point out that the original FMM coefficients are only needed to perform regression in the training phase, where time is not a constraint. In contrast, the time-critical testing phase does not require computing them.

4   Experimental Results

We evaluate the performance, inference time, and model size of our FMM-Head on three datasets: Shaoxing [32], PTB-XL [30], and ECG5000 [7]. We compare to seven baselines: five AEs (ECG-NET [22], CVAE [12], EncDecAD [17], a transformer model referred as BertECG [1], a fully connected AE), an ECG-specific GAN (ECG-ADGAN [21]) and one diffusion-based model (DiffusionAE [20]). The non-AE baselines were motivated by reviews from ICLR2024. Although FMM-Head can handle more than one lead, we use lead 2 to train the NNs on normal data and then test the anomaly detection performance on a holdout set that includes both abnormal and normal classes, as done for the provided baselines. We run 5 experiments for multiple learning rates and report the one with the highest average area under the ROC curve (AUROC). If applicable, we ran the training session for 500 warm-up epochs followed by 500 epochs. For ECG-ADGAN we instead train for 20000 epochs, as in [21]. We set ω_{max} to 0.2 according to the distribution of the original ω_i. For AEs we perform early-stopping based on the validation loss. Our code is available at [29]. To enhance reproducibility, we provide the FMM coefficients for PTB-XL and Shaoxing at the same link, which were obtained by solving the FMM optimization problem [24].

With Warm-up Regression, FMM-Head Consistently Enhances the Anomaly Detection Capabilities of the Baseline Models by up to 0.31 of AUROC. Table 1 shows the AUROC for the evaluated models and datasets and the gains compared to baselines for the different models. For the Shaoxing and PTB-XL datasets, our pipeline consists of warm-up regression followed by anomaly detection training. In these cases, the performance increase is consistent for all combinations of datasets and models. The AUROC enhancement is more evident for low-performant baselines, such as EncDecAd and BertECG, where the evaluated AUROC can increase by up to 0.31. The main reason some baselines perform poorly is the complexity of the task. Compared to simple datasets (such as ECG5000), PTB-XL and Shaoxing are among the largest publicly available ECG datasets, consisting of multiple patients and labeled conditions. We experimentally determined that one of the major sources of complexity is the variable length of the ECG time series. While most models do not consider this factor, our FMM-Head inherently maps the time series to the $[0, 2\pi)$ interval, thus equalizing the lengths of the samples in the last layer. Therefore, even low-performant baselines can achieve considerable AUROC for variable-length training sets.

The benefits of FMM-Head are noticeable for high-performing baselines, such as ECG-NET and CVAE. Replacing the decoder with a head based on prior knowledge better exploits the features extracted from the encoder. One exception is FMM-CAE, whose baseline counterpart CVAE performs slightly better for the PTB-XL dataset. We argue that convolutional AEs are mostly focused on recognizing patterns between adjacent time steps, therefore being less suitable for the extraction of features for FMM coefficients. Our belief is confirmed by the 0.02 decrease in AUROC for FMM-CAE in the Shaoxing dataset, which is the largest decrease in performance of all of the model-dataset combinations. However, for the ECG5000 dataset the AUROC is already very high and the addition of the FMM-Head makes little (at most 1.7%) difference.

Baselines with Integrated FMM-Head can Extract Coefficients that are Highly Correlated with those Extracted by Solving an Optimization Problem in less than $\frac{1}{20000}$ **of the Time.** Although our model is built for anomaly detection and *not* to exactly reproduce the FMM coefficients, we can nevertheless produce coefficients correlated

Table 1. Highest AUROC values for best learning rate and gains compared to baselines. Our FMM-Head enhanced models produce consistently better results compared to the baselines when the warm-up regression is employed (*i.e.*, for Shaoxing and PTB-XL)

Model	Shaoxing		PTB-XL		ECG5000	
	AUROC	Gain	AUROC	Gain	AUROC	Gain
ecgnet	0.575		0.661		0.993	
fmm_ecgnet	0.659	**0.084**	0.731	**0.070**	0.988	−0.005
encdec_ad	0.461		0.384		0.982	
fmm_encdec_ad	0.617	**0.156**	0.695	**0.311**	0.988	**0.006**
bert_ecg	0.545		0.536		0.971	
fmm_bert_ecg	0.650	**0.105**	0.697	**0.161**	0.989	**0.017**
dense_ae	0.653		0.691		0.992	
fmm_dense_ae	0.699	**0.046**	0.698	**0.007**	0.990	−0.002
cvae	0.749		0.693		0.992	
fmm_cae	0.729	−0.020	0.727	**0.034**	0.990	−0.002
ecg_adgan	0.587		0.662		0.927	
diffusion_ae	0.491		0.464		0.919	

with those obtained with the original FMM optimization. Thus, our method provides explainability by means of the interpretability benefits discussed in [24].

Figure 4a shows the linear or circular correlation between the coefficients extracted by [24] and those obtained after warm-up. The extracted parameters are usually highly correlated (*i.e.*, value greater than 0.4). Noteworthy is that the P and T waves manifest in general high correlation to the optimized ones. This is due to the two peaks being spaced apart by the QRS complex, thus making them more straightforward to extract. In contrast, the waves belonging to the QRS complex are close, thus enabling the same reconstructed time series through possibly non-ideal wave combinations. For instance, the same ECG pattern could be obtained through the sum of three wide extracted waves instead of three narrow peaks. Therefore, the inference of the QRS complex with a NN is less correlated to the original when compared to the P and T wave. The results for PTB-XL are similar to those for Shaoxing, except for the inference time gains for the LSTM-based models, which are lower due to the smaller input size.

Figure 4b shows the decrease in inference time compared to baseline models for the Shaoxing dataset. Compared to the original FMM optimization problem, which takes in average 38 s, AEs with FMM-Head reduces the computation time by more than four orders of magnitude. Compared to the baseline AEs, the benefits of FMM-Head varies from −30% to −91%, with the exception of DenseAE. The main reason behind this is that although FMM-Head is small, it is still more complex than most state-of-the-art layers. For DenseAE, replacing the fully connected 3-layer decoder with FMM-Head does *not* reduce the inference time but actually increases it by +169%. However, dense, convolutional, and LSTM layers have been extensively researched and optimized in the last decades; hence, we argue that FMM-Head execution times could be further improved by optimizing the code.

By Replacing Standard Decoders with FMM-Head, the Model Size is Nearly Halved for the non-LSTM Evaluated Models, Greatly Reducing the Storage Requirements on Mobile and Wearable ECG Monitoring Devices. Figure 5a shows the reduction in model size obtained by replacing each baseline's decoders with FMM-Head. In most cases, the file size of the obtained models is nearly halved. The large decrease in model size on BertECG is due to a reduction in the encoder, which we experimentally showed did not produce a relevant impact on the performance of the correspondent model integrated with FMM-Head. Noteworthy is that LSTM-based models such as ECG-NET and EncDecAD gain the least benefits from FMM-Head in terms of model size. This is due to the inherent design of LSTM layers, which favor minimizing model size over training and inference time; hence, the gains of FMM-Head are less prominent. In particular, the size of ECG-NET is 51% higher when FMM-Head is employed since the long inputs of Shaoxing increase the size of the pooling layer and consequently increase the size of the first fully connected layer.

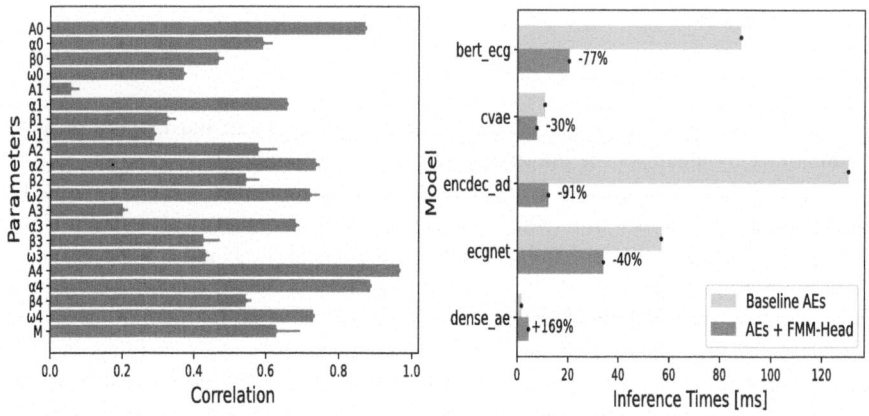

(a) Correlation between FMM coefficients for Shaoxing   (b) Inference Times for Shaoxing

Fig. 4. Despite not being built for FMM coefficient extraction, FMM-Head produces FMM parameters that are highly correlated with those extracted by the original method (see FMM-DenseAE in *(a)*). *(b)* Compared to the baselines, our NN-based models provide lower inference, except for models with low-complexity such as DenseAE.

Figure 5b shows the epoch duration of each model on the Shaoxing dataset. As expected, the reduced model size enables faster training than the baselines. Similarly to Fig. 4b, the only exception is DenseAE, which trades off the model size with the additional complexity of FMM-Head, thus showing an increase in the epoch duration.

Warm-up Regression is Essential to Maximize the Benefits of the FMM-Head. Column 3 in Table 1 shows the performance of different models on the ECG5000 dataset.

Whereas for EncDecAd and BertECG the AUROC is slightly better, for the other baselines we notice a decrease instead. We claim that this is due to the fact that we did not perform any warm-up regression on ECG5000, thus not exploiting the prior knowledge of the ECG shape. Without warm-up, the waves are not constrained in a meaningful position and the increase in AUROC is consequently less prominent.

Compared to State-of-the-Art GAN and Diffusion-Based Models, FMM-Head Enhanced AEs Increase Anomaly Detection Performance. The last two rows of Table 1 show the AUROC of baseline ECG-ADGAN [21] and DiffusionAE [20]. Whereas the two models produce acceptable performance on the small ECG5000 dataset, they struggle to perform well in more complex scenarios, such as in PTB-XL and Shaoxing. In particular, ECG-ADGAN shows the well-known mode collapse issue [28]: the generator produces outputs that belong to a single mode, thus being unsuitable for the normal samples with high complexity and variability in the bigger datasets. Moreover, ECG-ADGAN shows limited robustness to hyper-parameters, such as the learning rate, as shown in the appendix. DiffusionAE has been proposed to tackle anomaly detection on time series with anomalies in seasonality and trends, thus different inputs compared to ECG shapes during a single heartbeat, on which it performs poorly.

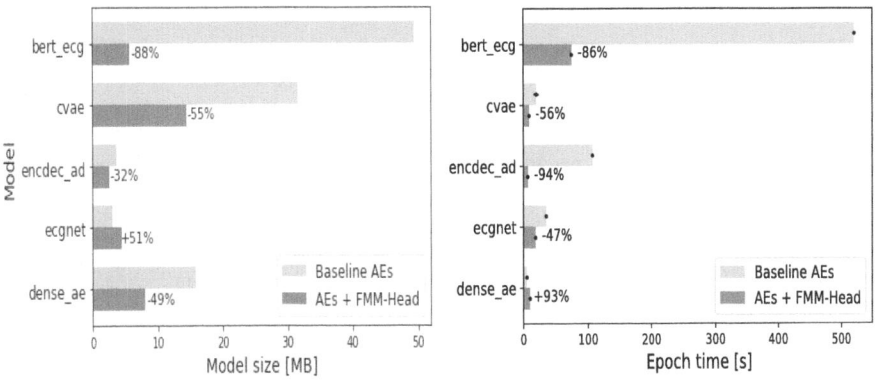

(a) Model sizes for Shaoxing dataset   (b) Epoch duration for Shaoxing dataset

Fig. 5. *(a)* FMM-Head has negligible size compared to most decoders, and thus one can considerably reduce the amount of file storage and memory needed to compute training and inference for neural network models. *(b)* shows the epoch duration for different models during training.

Compared to [31], FMM-Head can be Applied to Multiple Baseline NNs for Anomaly Detection and Not Just Classification. [31] provides a way to estimate 12-leads FMM coefficients by means of a custom NN and use them for ECG classification with SVM or logistic regression. In contrast, FMM-Head can be applied to multiple AEs for anomaly detection instead of classification with a single model. In [31] the waves are centered into the correct position by adding a loss regularization term, which is based on 100 random samples, whose coefficients are obtained through the non-ECG specific code from [23]. We instead perform warm-up on *all* the coefficients, obtained from the ECG-specific R code from [24]. Moreover, we explicitly consider α and β as circular variables, thus correctly estimating their values and correlations.

5   Conclusion and Future Works

We introduced a novel way to insert *a priori* knowledge into AEs for anomaly detection applied to ECG data. Our FMM-Head increased the AUROC of five baselines and reduced model size and inference time, thus allowing to perform real-time, explainable anomaly detection for continuously monitored patients. As future work, we will vary the regression loss function to provide more precise FMM coefficients and better exploit parallel operations in TensorFlow to decrease the inference time.

Acknowledgements. This work was supported by the Swedish Research Council (project "Scalable Federated Learning", no. 2021-04610) and by the King Abdullah University of Science and Technology (KAUST) Office of Research Administration (ORA) under Award No. ORA-CRG2021-4699.

References

1. Alamr, A., Artoli, A.: Unsupervised transformer-based anomaly detection in ECG signals. Algorithms **16**(3) (2023). https://doi.org/10.3390/a16030152, https://www.mdpi.com/1999-4893/16/3/152
2. AlGhatrif, M., Lindsay, J.: A brief review: history to understand fundamentals of electrocardiography. J. Community Hosp. Intern. Med. Perspect. **2**(1), 14383 (2012). https://doi.org/10.3402/jchimp.v2i1.14383
3. Atwood, J., Towsley, D.: Diffusion-convolutional neural networks. In: Proceedings of the 30th International Conference on Neural Information Processing Systems, pp. 2001–2009. NIPS 2016, Curran Associates Inc., Red Hook (2016). https://doi.org/10.5555/3157096.3157320
4. Bortolan, G., Christov, I., Simova, I.: Potential of rule-based methods and deep learning architectures for ECG diagnostics. Diagnostics **11**, 1678 (2021). https://doi.org/10.3390/diagnostics11091678
5. Chalapathy, R., Chawla, S.: Deep learning for anomaly detection: a survey. CoRR **abs/1901.03407** (2019). http://arxiv.org/abs/1901.03407
6. Chauhan, S., Vig, L.: Anomaly detection in ECG time signals via deep long short-term memory networks. In: 2015 IEEE International Conference on Data Science and Advanced Analytics (DSAA), pp. 1–7 (2015). https://doi.org/10.1109/DSAA.2015.7344872
7. Chen, Y., Keogh, E.: ECG5000 dataset (2000). http://www.timeseriesclassification.com/description.php?Dataset=ECG5000
8. Goodfellow, I., et al.: Generative adversarial networks. Commun. ACM **63**(11), 139–144 (2020). https://doi.org/10.1145/3422622
9. Hinton, G.E., Salakhutdinov, R.R.: Reducing the dimensionality of data with neural networks. Science **313**(5786), 504–507 (2006). https://doi.org/10.1126/science.1127647
10. Hochreiter, S., Schmidhuber, J.: Long short-term memory. Neural Comput. **9**(8), 1735–1780 (1997). https://doi.org/10.1162/neco.1997.9.8.1735

11. Jammalamadaka, R., Sarma, Y.R.: Correlation coefficient for angular variables. In: Statistical Theory and Data Analysis II: Proceedings of the Second Pacific Area Statistical Conference, pp. 349–364. Pacific Area Statistical Conference, North-Holland, Amsterdam; New York City (1988). https://archive.org

12. Jang, J.H., Kim, T.Y., Lim, H.S., Yoon, D.: Unsupervised feature learning for electrocardiogram data using the convolutional variational autoencoder. PLOS ONE **16**(12), 1–16 (2021). https://doi.org/10.1371/journal.pone.0260612

13. Kaplan Berkaya, S., Uysal, A.K., Sora Gunal, E., Ergin, S., Gunal, S., Gulmezoglu, M.B.: A survey on ECG analysis. Biomed. Signal Process. Control **43**, 216–235 (2018). https://doi.org/10.1016/j.bspc.2018.03.003

14. Kingma, D.P., Welling, M.: Auto-encoding variational Bayes (2022). https://doi.org/10.48550/arXiv.1312.6114

15. Lee, A.: Circular data. WIREs. Comput. Stat. **2**(4), 477–486 (2010). https://doi.org/10.1002/wics.98

16. Liu, P., Sun, X., Han, Y., He, Z., Zhang, W., Wu, C.: Arrhythmia classification of LSTM autoencoder based on time series anomaly detection. Biomed. Signal Process. Control **71**, 103228 (2022). https://doi.org/10.1016/j.bspc.2021.103228

17. Malhotra, P., Ramakrishnan, A., Anand, G., Vig, L., Agarwal, P., Shroff, G.: LSTM-based encoder-decoder for multi-sensor anomaly detection. CoRR **abs/1607.00148** (2016). http://arxiv.org/abs/1607.00148

18. Nigusse, A.B., Mengistie, D.A., Malengier, B., Tseghai, G.B., Langenhove, L.V.: Wearable smart textiles for long-term electrocardiography monitoring–a review. Sensors **21**(12) (2021). https://doi.org/10.3390/s21124174, https://www.mdpi.com/1424-8220/21/12/4174

19. Pan, J., Tompkins, W.J.: A real-time QRS detection algorithm. IEEE Trans. on Biomed. Eng. **BME-32**(3), 230–236 (1985). https://doi.org/10.1109/TBME.1985.325532

20. Pintilie, I., Manolache, A., Brad, F.: Time series anomaly detection using diffusion-based models. In: 2023 IEEE International Conference on Data Mining Workshops (ICDMW), pp. 570–578 (2023). https://doi.org/10.1109/ICDMW60847.2023.00080

21. Qin, J., et al.: A novel temporal generative adversarial network for electrocardiography anomaly detection. Artif. Intell. Med. **136**, 102489 (2023). https://doi.org/10.1016/j.artmed.2023.102489

22. Roy, M., Majumder, S., Halder, A., Biswas, U.: ECG-NET: a deep LSTM autoencoder for detecting anomalous ECG. Eng. Appl. Artif. Intell. **124**, 106484 (2023). https://doi.org/10.1016/j.engappai.2023.106484

23. Rueda, C., Larriba, Y., Peddada, S.D.: Frequency modulated Möbius model accurately predicts rhythmic signals in biological and physical sciences. Sci. Rep. **9**, 18701 (2019). https://doi.org/10.1038/s41598-019-54569-1

24. Rueda, C., Rodríguez-Collado, A., Fernández, I., Canedo, C., Ugarte, M.D., Larriba, Y.: A unique cardiac electrocardiographic 3D model. toward interpretable AI diagnosis. iScience **25**(12), 105617 (2022). https://doi.org/10.1016/j.isci.2022.105617

25. Sampson, M.: Continuous ECG monitoring in hospital: part 1, indications. Br. J. Card. Nurs. **13**(2), 80–85 (2018). https://doi.org/10.12968/bjca.2018.13.2.80

26. Sampson, M.: Continuous ECG monitoring in hospital: part 2, practical issues. Br. J. Card. Nurs. **13**(3), 128–134 (2018). https://doi.org/10.12968/bjca.2018.13.3.128

27. Shan, L., et al.: Abnormal ECG detection based on an adversarial autoencoder. Front. Physiol. **13**, 961724 (2022). https://doi.org/10.3389/fphys.2022.961724

28. Srivastava, A., Valkov, L., Russell, C., Gutmann, M.U., Sutton, C.: Veegan: reducing mode collapse in GANs using implicit variational learning. In: Proceedings of the 31st International Conference on Neural Information Processing Systems, pp. 3310–3320. NIPS 2017, Curran Associates Inc., Red Hook, NY, USA (2017). https://doi.org/10.5555/3294996.3295090

29. Verardo, G.: Fmm-head (2023). https://github.com/giacomoverardo/FMM-Head
30. Wagner, P., et al.: PTB-XL, a large publicly available electrocardiography dataset. Sci. Data **7**(1), 154 (2020). https://doi.org/10.1038/s41597-020-0495-6
31. Yang, Y., Rocher, M., Moceri, P., Sermesant, M.: Explainable electrocardiogram analysis with wave decomposition: application to myocardial infarction detection. In: Statistical Atlases and Computational Models of the Heart. Regular and CMRxMotion Challenge Papers, pp. 221–232 (2022). https://doi.org/10.1007/978-3-031-23443-9_21
32. Zheng, J., Zhang, J., Danioko, S., Yao, H., Guo, H., Rakovski, C.: A 12-lead electrocardiogram database for arrhythmia research covering more than 10,000 patients. Sci. Data **7**(1), 48 (2020). https://doi.org/10.1038/s41597-020-0386-x

Hierarchical Attention Decoder
for Solving Math Word Problems

Jiajia Li[1], Letian Peng[3], Ping Wang[1,2(✉)], and Hai Zhao[4]

[1] School of Information Management, Wuhan University, Wuhan, China
{cantata,wangping}@whu.edu.cn
[2] Center for the Studies of Information Resources, Wuhan University, Wuhan, China
[3] Department of Computer Science and Engineering, University of California,
San Diego, USA
lepeng@ucsd.edu
[4] Department of Computer Science and Engineering, Shanghai Jiao Tong University,
Shanghai, China
zhaohai@cs.sjtu.edu.cn

Abstract. To answer math word problems (MWPs), models must formalize equations from the source text of math problems. Recently, the tree-structured decoder has significantly improved model performance on this task by generating the target equation in a tree format. However, current decoders usually ignore the hierarchical relationships between tree nodes and their parents, which hinders further improvement. Thus, we propose a structure called a hierarchical attention tree to aid the generation procedure of the decoder. As our decoder follows a graph-based encoder, our full model is therefore named Graph to Hierarchical Attention Tree (G2HAT). We show that a tree-structured decoder with hierarchical accumulative multi-head attention leads to a significant performance improvement and reaches a significant improvement on various strong baselines on both English MAWPS and Chinese Math23k MWP benchmarks. For further study, we also apply a pre-trained language model to G2HAT, which even results in a new higher performance.

Keywords: Math Word Problems · Hierarchical Attention · Encoder-Decoder Model

1 Introduction

Math Word Problems (MWPs) require models to automatically provide an answer to a mathematical problem described by natural language text, which is referred to as the word context in a formal MWP. As shown in Fig. 1, given a word context, models must infer an equation from it and calculate the final solution. Since the introduction of machine learning methods in the field of Natural

This work was supported by the National Natural Science Foundation of China [No. 72074171] [No. 72374161].

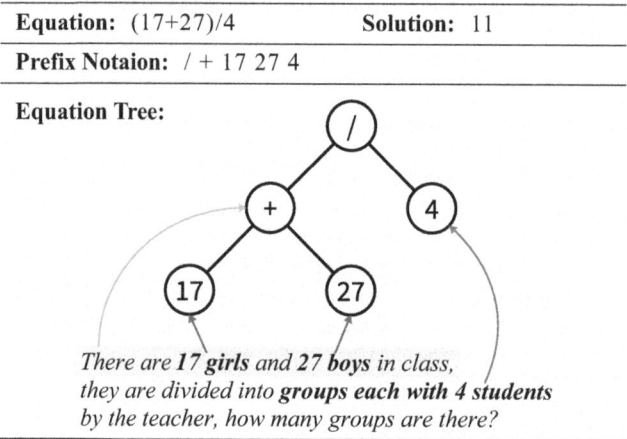

Word Context: There are 17 girls and 27 boys in class, they are divided into groups each with 4 students by the teacher, how many groups are there?

Equation: (17+27)/4   **Solution:** 11

Prefix Notaion: / + 17 27 4

Equation Tree:

There are 17 girls and 27 boys in class,
they are divided into groups each with 4 students
by the teacher, how many groups are there?

Fig. 1. An example for MWP.

Language Processing (NLP), much effort has been put into designing features to train models to solve MWPs [7,13,14]. However, these models are not very scalable, as they require features to be hand-crafted by humans.

In recent years, there has been a booming trend of the application of deep learning methods to MWP, among which seq2seq models apply an encoder to encode the word context into an intermediate representation for a decoder to sequentially generate parts of the equation. To take advantage of the tree-structured nature of equations for MWP, [16] introduces a tree-structured decoder that significantly improves model performance. Their tree-structured decoder generates a tree for prefix notation by generating tree nodes recursively while considering their parents and siblings.

Efficient though the tree-structured decoder is, it ignores the hierarchical nature of nodes in the generated equation tree. Consider the equation tree from Fig. 1 for example. To induce the + operator, the model should pay attention to "There are 17 girls and 27 boys in class," to induce the addition operation. When inducing the 17 and 27 as figures for + to operate on, the model has to pay attention to "17 girls" and "27 boys".

From the example above, two conclusions may be reached. Firstly, more attention should be given to parent nodes than to their children, as greater contextual comprehension of words is necessary for the induction of nodes in higher hierarchies. We refer to this property of equation trees as **hierarchical attention decay**. Secondly, the context covered by children's attention is included in the context covered by the parent's attention. We call this property in an equation tree **hierarchical attention succession**.

Previous tree-structured models have overlooked two key properties of parent-child relationships in the equation tree: they score attention based solely on the input features of the current predicting node, without considering the attention score of the parent node. To address this, we propose the Hierarchical Attention Tree (HAT) decoder, which is able to implement hierarchical attention on both hierarchical decay and hierarchical succession. Specifically, this allows nodes in the decoded tree to succeed attention from their parents, and also to complement any attention loss during succession. Our full model incorporates a graph-based encoder with the HAT decoder, forming a Graph to Hierarchical Attention Tree model that solves MWPs using an encoder-decoder framework.

We conducted experiments on two MWP benchmarks for English and Chinese, MAWPS and Math23k, respectively. We incorporated multi-head attention to improve information extraction from the context via an attention mechanism. Our model outperformed the strong baselines by 1.7 solution matching accuracy scores on MAWPS and 2.6 on Math23k, thus setting a new competitive baselines for both MWP benchmarks. Moreover, with further improvement from the application of a pre-trained language model, G2HAT achieved a remarkable 3.3 score improvement on MAWPS and a 3.2 score improvement on Math23k.

2   Related Work

Early works on machine learning for mathematical word problems (MWPs) concentrate on statistical models [3,7,11,13,18] and semantic information [4,6,12,14,19] for sequence construction and solution inference. [18] models MWPs as path searching problems for token sequences and uses a statistical model to solve this modified problem. [19] models MWPs as semantic parsing tasks and defines special operators to build a Text-Math Tree, which is then interpreted into a common equation to produce the final solution.

The encoder-decoder structure has become the dominant approach in solving mathematical word problems (MWPs) with deep learning. An early study [15] directly applied a Seq2Seq scenario to generate a sequence representing an equation from a given context. [8] added multi-head attention to MWP solvers for further improvement. Tree-structured decoders [16], which exploit the structural nature of MWPs, have recently been introduced and significantly improve model performance. [2] proposed a weakly supervised model that corrects the generation process by back-searching for faults from the result node. [1] introduced a DAG-structured decoder. Furthermore, [10] applied hierarchical attention for the encoder and sequential additive clause attention and word attention were added. Finally, [17] implemented a dependency-based graph encoder (Fig. 2).

3   Our Model

3.1   Graph Encoder

For the encoder, we follow [17] to use a quantity graph to encode word context of MWP by constructing a quantity graph based on it. Specifically, for a sentence $W = \{w_1, w_2, \cdots, w_n\}$, we first use rules to extract quantity tokens $Q = \{q_1, q_2, \cdots, q_m\}$ from it. Then a dependency parser is used to extract related non-quantity tokens and connect them to quantity tokens in the graph. A quantity token and its related tokens with edges between them are called a quantity cell, which is used when building quantity graph for encoding in graph encoder.

With quantity cells extracted, we build two quantity graphs:

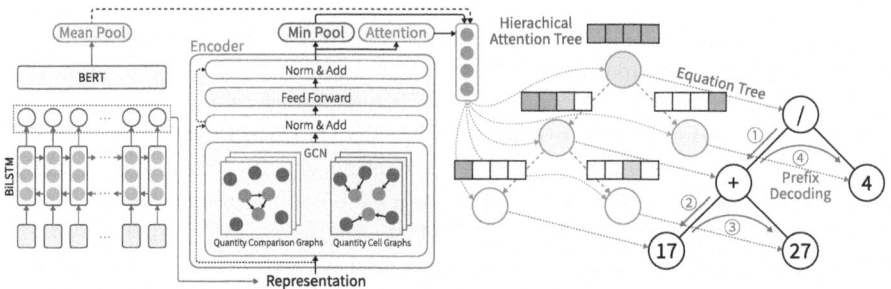

Fig. 2. Our G2HAT model.

- **Quantity Cell Graph** is a combination of graphs of all cells that are isolated from each other.
- **Quantity Comparison Graph** only contains quantity tokens as nodes. Edges are built based on partial ordering relations between quantity nodes. Specifically, a directed edge $e = (q_1, q_2)$ is built when $q_1 > q_2$.

Based on Quantity Cell Graphs $G^{Qcell} = \{G_i^{Qcell}\}$ where $i = 1, 2, \cdots, k_{Qcell}$ and Quantity Comparison Graphs $G^{Qcomp} = \{G_i^{Qcomp}\}$ where $i = 1, 2, \cdots, k_{Qcomp}$, A represents the adjacent matrix for a certain graph G where $A_{i,j} = 1$ notating there is an edge from i to j and $A_{i,j} = 0$ otherwise. The encoding procedure for MWP context is formulated as follows,

$$
\begin{aligned}
&X = \text{Embed}(W); \\
&X := \text{RNN}(X); \\
&X := \text{TransLayer}_i(X) \ for \ i = 1, 2, \cdots N; \\
&H = \text{MinPooling}(X)
\end{aligned}
\tag{1}
$$

Here, the sentence is first embedded via an embedding layer before it is fed into a recurrent neural network, such as a bidirectional long short-term memory (BiLSTM) network or a gated recurrent unit (GRU) network for contextual representations. Then the sentence is further processed by multiple Transformer layers which are defined as follows,

$$
\begin{aligned}
&TransLayer(X) = GCN(X) + LN(GCN(X)); \\
&GCN(X) = FFN(\underset{A \ for \ G}{||} (LN(AX) + X)); \\
&G = G^{Qcell} \cup G^{Qcomp}
\end{aligned}
\tag{2}
$$

where LN refers to layer normalization. Finally, the output $Y \in \mathbb{R}^{n \times d}$ from graph encoder is pooled into hidden representation $H \in \mathbb{R}^d$ by token-level min pooling for decoder to process and generate the equation tree.

3.2   Hierarchical Attention

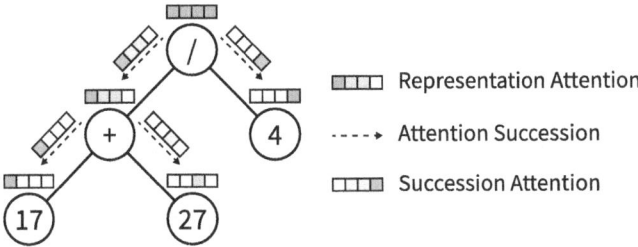

Fig. 3. The procedure of attention succession from top to bottom in hierarchical attention tree.

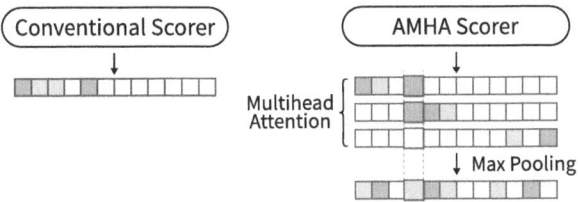

Fig. 4. Comparison between the conventional attention scorer and our accumulative multi-head attention scorer.

We give an elaborate description for our hierarchical attention mechanism in the HAT-structured Decoder in this section. Our decoder generates an equation tree following a hierarchical structure from top to bottom with attention succeeded from parent to child. In practice, we first generate the root operator node, then its left sub-tree and right sub-tree, each with part of its parent's attention on the encoded representation. This procedure recurses for each sub-tree until the sub-tree is a single quantity node.

As in Fig. 3, the root operator node attends fully on the whole encoded representation. When we build the left and right sub-tree, we pass the representation down to them via an attention succession process. However, the sub-trees will only attend on part of the representation from its parent based on attention scores (succession attention) which are calculated during the succession process. Thus we can see how our hierarchical attention mechanism satisfies the two key properties for better equation tree construction.

- **Hierarchical Attention Decay** A child node in a hierarchical attention tree can only focus on part of the encoded representation that is attended by its parent. As a result, the attention will decay hierarchically during the succession from top to bottom.
- **Hierarchical Attention Succession** Likewise, the partial attention of child nodes will always be covered by their parents, which leads to succession relationships.

3.3 Accumulative Multi-head Succession Attention

To better exploit the hierarchical attention mechanism, we apply a novel attention mechanism which we call accumulative multi-head attention (AMHA) to score succession attention to pass representation attention. As shown in Fig. 4, different from conventional attention scorer, the AMHA scorer will use a multi-head input to score multiple attention scores for all heads. Then, those attention scores are accumulated together via a max pooling process.

$$A_i^k = \frac{\exp(\text{Scorer}^k(X_i^k))}{\sum_{j=1}^n \exp(\text{Scorer}^k(X_j^k))}, \quad A_i = \max(A_i^1, A_i^2, \cdots, A_i^n) \tag{3}$$

where $X_i^k \in$ refers to the hidden representation of word in i-th position and k-th head. Each scorer passes X_i^k through a linear layer and then uses a softmax function to get attention A^k on k-th head. These attention scores are finally pooled via max pooling to get our AMHA score.

AMHA is intuitively better than conventional attention mechanism for MWP solving due to the following two reasons:

- **Multiple Concentration** When constructing an equation tree, an operator node should not only contain information to induct its type, but it should also integrate information for its children, the nodes in its left sub-tree and right sub-tree. Thus, AMHA is a better vector for trees' information as different heads are responsible to attend to different parts of the encoded representation.
- **Steady Attention Decay** For hierarchical attention tree building, attention succession is a key procedure for better performance. However, using conventional attention mechanism will lead to an attention succession that decays too fast for performance improvement.

Here is an easy example: suppose there are two positions i and j for which a parent node wants to memorize for its children. This parent node will be encouraged to assign attention score close to 1 for them. However, conventional attention mechanisms only allow attention score with sums of 1, which means at least half of the attention will decay for either position. This will certainly hurt the efficiency of attention succession. AMHA can easily fix this problem by applying two heads for both positions for a parent node to succeed an integrative attention for its children. This allows AMHA to preserve attention succession which is critic for hierarchical attention tree building.

3.4   Complement Attention

To capture all necessary information for building trees and further improve the capacity of our model, we introduce another complementary attention mechanism to replenish attention scores that are dropped in previous rounds of attention succession. We once again apply AMHA for attention scoring. For a node during tree building, A^{parent} refers to attention of the node's parent, and X refers to the input representation to induct succession and complement attentions.

$$SA = \text{AMHA}^{succession}(X); \quad CA = \text{AMHA}^{complement}(X) \qquad (4)$$

We then use max pooling to get the final attention on the child node.

$$A_i^{child} = \max(SA_i * A_i^{parent}, CA_i) \qquad (5)$$

Integrating complement attention can lead to further improvement compared to using only succession attention as complement attention allows child nodes to replenish their information to themselves without harming the hierarchical attention decay or succession properties. Also, application of complement attention can prevent node attention from degrading to zero, which guarantees a slower attention decay for better tree building.

3.5   HAT-Structured Decoder

Our HAT-structured decoder decodes the encoded representation H following the tree-structured decoder's [16] with accumulative multi-head attention based attention succession process. Starting with a root representation q^{ROOT} initialized based on H and an all-ones root attention vector a^{ROOT}, we predict the label of the root node and generate the rest equation tree via four sub-modules of decoder, the Left Label and Attention Scorer (LLAS), Right Label and Attention Scorer (RLAS), Sub-Tree Encoder (STE) and Node Classifier (NC).

Here, LLS and RLS use AMHA to score succession attention. LLAS and RLAS are of gated structures to process input representations while NC applies a linear classifier for operator and constant label and pairwise classifier for pairs between the input representation and encoded quantity representations. These details are omitted in this paper since they are not contributions of this paper and can be found in detail in the implementation of tree-structured decoder of [16].

Step 1. Representation Attention Integration. With current root representations and attention, we first use element-wise multiplication to integrate attention scores with encoded representations.

$$\hat{H}_i = H_i \times a_i^{ROOT} \qquad (6)$$

Step 2. Left Sub-tree Generation. LLAS generates the label representation, node representation, and succession attention for the left child node of the current root node. Then, NC is used to classify the label of the left child node.

$$e^l, q^l, SA^l, CA^l = \text{LLAS}(q^{ROOT}, \hat{H});$$
$$a_i^l = a_i^{ROOT} \times SA_i^l + CA_i^l; \quad c^l = \text{NC}(e^l) \tag{7}$$

If e^l is classified to be an operator label, jump to **Step 1** with current root node representation set to q^l and root representation attention set to a^l to generate the left sub-tree. This procedure returns when the left sub-tree is completely constructed.

Step 3. Right Sub-tree Generation. We first integrate representation of the left sub-tree with the root representation via STE. The label representation, node representation, and succession attention are then generated by RLAS for the right child node of the current root node. The same NC for the left child node is applied to finally label the right child node.

$$t^l = \text{STE}(e^l, q^l);$$
$$e^r, q^r, SA^r, CA^r = \text{RLAS}(q^{ROOT}, \hat{H}, t^l); \tag{8}$$
$$a_i^r = a_i^{ROOT} \times SA_i^r + CA_i^r; \quad c^r = \text{NC}(e^r)$$

Likewise, if e^r is classified to be an operator label, jump to **Step 1** with current root node representation set to q^r and root representation attention set to a^r to generate the right sub-tree. The procedure ends when the right sub-tree is completely constructed.

3.6   Pre-trained Language Model

For encoding word context, we first encode the sentence with the pre-trained language model (PLM) and then pool it into a context representation Q with mean pooling on the word level.

$$P = \text{PLM}(W), \qquad Q = \frac{1}{n}\sum_i^n (P_i) \tag{9}$$

Finally, Q from PLM and H from graph encoder are added together to get the final context representation.

$$H' := H + Q \tag{10}$$

4   Experiment

4.1   Experimental Setting

Dataset. We conduct experiments on two MWP datasets: MAWPS and Math23K. MAWPS is an English MWP dataset comprised of 2373 problems, for which both the template equation and final solution are provided for training and testing. Math23K, a Chinese MWP dataset, contains 23162 problems, where only equations for real quantities within the context are provided.

Model. We employ an embedding size of 128 dimensions and a hidden size of 512 dimensions for word representation. For RNNs, we use a 4-layer LSTM or GRU for encoding. When calculating AMHA for succession attention, we utilize 4 attention heads to aggregate attention scores. The beam size is set to 5 in order to search for the most likely equation and induce a more plausible solution.

Pre-trained Language Model. We apply BERT-base-cased and BERT-base-Chinese as PLMs for MAWPS and Math23k, respectively. We do not fine-tune the PLMs during training, as the training datasets are rather small. To ensure a fair comparison with stronger pre-training methods, we also replace BERT with MWP-BERT [9].

Training and Evaluation. We utilize cross entropy loss for model optimization. The batch size for training is set to 64, and we utilize the Adam optimizer [5] with an initial learning rate of $1e^{-3}$ and a decay rate of $1e^{-5}$ for parameter updating. We train the model for 200 epochs in each experiment and save the model with the highest solution accuracy on the development sets. Equation Matching Accuracy (EMA) and Solution Matching Accuracy (SMA) are two metrics adopted in MWPs evaluation. Equation matching accuracy measures how well the model's generated equation matches the reference equation, while solution matching accuracy evaluates the alignment between the model's generated solution and the reference solution.

4.2   Result

Tables 1 and 2 show the comparison between our proposed G2HAT model and previous strong models. We re-implemented the Graph2Tree model [17], and found the results to be slightly lower than the reported results but still competitive for comparison. We then ran our G2HAT on MWP datasets for GRU and LSTM encoders and found that our AMHA-based HAT-structured decoder led to a significant improvement on both the English and Chinese datasets. For solution matching accuracy, our model resulted in a 1.7 accuracy score improvement on the English MAWPS dataset and a 2.6 accuracy score improvement on the Chinese Math23K dataset.

The equation matching accuracy results in Table 2 demonstrate the effectiveness of our G2HAT model, which boosts the baseline G2T model by 1.7 accuracy score on MAWPS and 2.6 accuracy score on Math23K. This improvement is due to the hierarchical attention decay and succession for hierarchical tree building, which enables the production of better equation trees and higher solution matching accuracy. Furthermore, the results of the 5-fold validation on Math23k show the robustness of our model, as G2HAT outperforms G2T by 1.9 accuracy score on solution matching and 1.4 accuracy score on equation matching.

Table 1. Comparison of solution matching accuracy on MWP datasets. †: Result of GTS from G2T. ‡: Result of GTS from HMS. *: Re-implementation of previous model.

Model	MAWPS	Math23K	
		Test	5-fold Valid
DNS	59.5	–	58.1
Math-EM	69.2	66.7	–
T-RNN	66.8	66.9	–
S-Aligned	–	–	65.8
GROUP-ATT	76.1	69.5	66.9
AST-Dec	–	69.0	–
IRE	–	76.7	–
HMS	80.3	–	76.1
GTS	$82.6^\dagger$/$78.6^\ddagger$	75.6	74.3
G2T [17]	83.7	77.4	75.5
G2T*	83.7	77.0	75.3
G2HAT(GRU)	85.2(↑1.5)	**80.0(↑2.6)**	76.6(↑1.3)
G2HAT(LSTM)	**85.4 (↑1.7)**	79.2 (↑1.8)	**77.4(↑2.1)**
G2HAT+BERT	**87.0 (↑3.3)**	**80.9 (↑3.5)**	**78.0(↑2.7)**
MWP-BERT	87.3	84.7	82.4
G2HAT+MWP-BERT	**88.5 (↑1.2)**	**85.4 (↑0.7)**	**83.2 (↑0.8)**

Table 2. Comparison of equation matching accuracy on MWP datasets. *: Re-implementation of previous model.

Model	MAWPS	Math23K	
		Test	5-fold Valid
G2T*	82.8	65.8	64.3
G2HAT(GRU)	84.3	**68.0**	65.6
G2HAT(LSTM)	**84.4**	67.3	**65.7**
G2HAT+BERT	85.7	69.0	66.5

For encoder choice, we can observe that LSTM outperforms GRU on MAWPS, yet performs worse on Math23k. We attribute this to the difference in vocabulary. MAWPS has a smaller vocabulary, thus most words in the training dataset will still occur in the test dataset. A more precise encoder like LSTM will better capture details of the training data. On the other hand, Math23k covers problems in various mathematics applications, resulting in a much larger and unusual vocabulary, which makes LSTM prone to overfitting. GRU, with its simpler structure than LSTM, can resist this overfitting risk.

After incorporating features from BERT for context representations, the G2HAT model achieved an improvement of 3.3 on the English MAWPS dataset and 3.5 on the Chinese Math23k dataset for solution matching. Correspondingly, the MAWPS and Math23k datasets experienced respective improvements of 2.9 and 3.2 for equation matching, demonstrating the effectiveness of BERT features in language understanding.

When replacing the generalized pre-trained BERT with MWP-BERT, which specifically uses numeracy-augmented pre-training, we found that the results of MWP-BERT greatly surpassed the BERT-based system without G2HAT enhancement. This demonstrates that task-specific pre-training is more beneficial for task-specific understanding. On adding our G2HAT to MWP-BERT, the performance of MWP was further improved, confirming the generalization capacity of our proposed G2HAT decoder.

5   Analysis and Discussion

5.1   Ablation Study

Table 3. Ablation studies on MWP datasets with only succession attention, CA: complement attention. SA: succession attention. G2T equals to G2HAT with all these mechanisms removed.

Model	MAWPS		Math23K	
	EMA	SMA	EMA	SMA
G2HAT	**84.4**	**85.4**	68.0	**80.0**
SA-only	84.3	85.1	**68.8**	79.1
CA-only	83.7	84.4	67.6	78.7
-AMHA	83.2	84.1	66.9	77.7
G2T	82.7	83.7	65.8	77.0

Table 3 shows the results of the ablation study for our G2HAT model. We found that both succession attention (SA) and complement attention (CA) contribute to the model performance. The comparison also shows that SA makes a larger contribution than CA. Moreover, SA-only G2HAT achieves a higher equation matching accuracy score, but a lower solution matching accuracy than the full model. This indicates that SA-only G2HAT better reconstructs equation trees as taught by the training dataset, but is not flexible enough when facing new MWP problems.

We also trained a model without Accumulative Multi-Head Attention (AMHA) and, unsurprisingly, encountered a drop in performance; although there was still improvement on the baseline G2T model. Thus, it is evident that AMHA is a critical attention mechanism that supports the efficacy of our Sentiment Analysis and Content Analysis procedure by avoiding a too-fast attention decay, which may hinder parent-child attention succession.

Table 4. Performance (Equation Matching) comparison between G2T and G2HAT on constructing equations with certain operator. †: Linear Equation ‡: Non-linear Equation

Operator	G2T			G2HAT		
	Root	Tree	Only	Root	Tree	Only
+	73.9	79.8	75.9	**86.6**	**85.7**	**88.8**
−	88.1	85.8	86.0	**88.3**	85.8	**85.4**
*	71.6	69.0	75.0	**74.1**	**71.4**	**80.0**
/	82.7	78.5	76.5	**85.3**	**81.0**	**85.2**
+&−	80.7	81.0	81.8 †	**86.0**	**84.6**	**87.1**†
*&/	76.9	75.5‡	71.8	**79.5**	**78.0**‡	**78.2**

5.2 Source of Improvement

To make the improvement of our G2HAT clear, we compare model performance on equation trees with different operators as the root node or a tree node. To ensure fairness, we do not apply PLM for either model. Equation matching accuracy is used as the metric for equation construction comparison. The results presented in Table 4 show that G2HAT outperforms G2T on almost all types of equation trees by a large margin, except when the subtraction operator − is a tree node.

We then group operators (+ and −, * and /) together to test the construction capability of models for linear or non-linear equations. Our G2HAT is convincingly more powerful than the G2T baseline, as it performs better on both linear operator-only (87.1 vs. 81.8) and non-linear operator-involved (78.0 vs. 75.5) equation construction. Thus, our model is verified to be more competent in capturing word context information about both linear and non-linear relationships among quantities.

5.3 Attention Distribution Learning

Focusing on modeling hierarchical attention with attention succession and complementing, we next explore how our model learns to pass the attention score from parent nodes to child nodes. To evaluate the attention distribution learning of our G2HAT model, we conduct an experiment on MAWPS and compare it with the G2T baseline. We use the Kullback-Leibler (KL) divergence to represent the variation between the attention distributions in two sibling nodes. A good learning process for attention distribution should present a steady increase, as sibling nodes should attend to related, yet distinct, information. Since attention scores on deeper nodes become relatively small due to hierarchical attention decay, we first normalize the attention distribution and then compute the KL divergence:

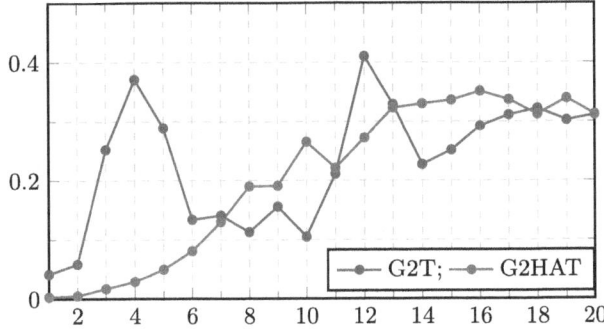

Fig. 5. KL Divergence between Siblings vs. Training Epoch

$$a_i^{left} := \frac{a_i^{left}}{\frac{1}{n}\sum_{j=1}^{n} a_j^{left}}; a_i^{right} := \frac{a_i^{right}}{\frac{1}{n}\sum_{j=1}^{n} a_j^{right}};$$

$$D = D_{KL}(a^{left}||a^{right}) + D_{KL}(a^{right}||a^{left}) \qquad (11)$$

$$= \sum_{i=1}^{n} \log(a_i^{left}) \log(\frac{a_i^{left}}{a_i^{right}}) + \sum_{i=1}^{n} \log(a_i^{right}) \log(\frac{a_i^{right}}{a_i^{left}})$$

From Fig. 5, we can observe the learning curves of KL divergence for the G2T baseline and our G2HAT model. It is evident that both converge to approximately 0.3 KL divergence. However, the training of G2T model fluctuates significantly, which may impede the decoder's ability to accurately allocate attention to sibling nodes. In contrast, our G2HAT model maintains a steadier learning curve due to its two attention mechanisms, resulting in superior model performance when constructing equation trees.

6   Conclusion and Future Work

In this paper, we propose a novel HAT decoder that satisfies two intuitive properties for equation tree building. The HAT-structured decoder allows child nodes to access attention via a succession attention scorer. This scorer selects the parent's attention representation of the child, enabling hierarchical attention decay and succession in the tree structure. Furthermore, accumulative multi-head attention is incorporated to avoid a too rapid attention decay, allowing for better attention succession. Experiments on MWP benchmarks demonstrate that the use of our HAT decoder yields a large performance gains on strong baselines with equation matching accuracy, accompanied by a substantial improvement in solution matching accuracy. In the future work. the HAT Decoder we have proposed can be applied to many languages and structures generation tasks, such as machine translation, semantic parsing, and text-to-sql generation.

References

1. Cao, Y., Hong, F., Li, H., Luo, P.: A bottom-up DAG structure extraction model for math word problems. In: AAAI, pp. 39–46 (2021)
2. Hong, Y., Li, Q., Ciao, D., Huang, S., Zhu, S.: Learning by fixing: Solving math word problems with weak supervision. In: AAAI, pp. 4959–4967 (2021)
3. Hosseini, M.J., Hajishirzi, H., Etzioni, O., Kushman, N.: Learning to solve arithmetic word problems with verb categorization. In: Moschitti, A., Pang, B., Daelemans, W. (eds.) EMNLP, pp. 523–533 (2014)
4. Huang, D., Shi, S., Lin, C., Yin, J.: Learning fine-grained expressions to solve math word problems. In: Palmer, M., Hwa, R., Riedel, S. (eds.) EMNLP, pp. 805–814 (2017)
5. Kingma, D.P., Ba, J.: Adam: a method for stochastic optimization. In: Bengio, Y., LeCun, Y. (eds.) ICLR (2015)
6. Koncel-Kedziorski, R., Hajishirzi, H., Sabharwal, A., Etzioni, O., Ang, S.D.: Parsing algebraic word problems into equations. Trans. Assoc. Comput. Linguist. **3**, 585–597 (2015)
7. Kushman, N., Zettlemoyer, L., Barzilay, R., Artzi, Y.: Learning to automatically solve algebra word problems. In: ACL, pp. 271–281 (2014)
8. Li, J., Wang, L., Zhang, J., Wang, Y., Dai, B.T., Zhang, D.: Modeling intra-relation in math word problems with different functional multi-head attentions. In: Korhonen, A., Traum, D.R., Màrquez, L. (eds.) ACL, pp. 6162–6167 (2019)
9. Liang, Z., Zhang, J., Wang, L., Qin, W., Lan, Y., Shao, J., Zhang, X.: MWP-BERT: numeracy-augmented pre-training for math word problem solving. In: Findings of the Association for Computational Linguistics: NAACL 2022 (2022)
10. Lin, X., Huang, Z., Zhao, H., Chen, E., Liu, Q., Wang, H., Wang, S.: HMS: a hierarchical solver with dependency-enhanced understanding for math word problem. In: AAAI, pp. 4232–4240 (2021)
11. Mitra, A., Baral, C.: Learning to use formulas to solve simple arithmetic problems. In: ACL (2016)
12. Roy, S., Roth, D.: Solving general arithmetic word problems. In: Màrquez, L., Callison-Burch, C., Su, J., Pighin, D., Marton, Y. (eds.) EMNLP, pp. 1743–1752 (2015)
13. Roy, S., Roth, D.: Mapping to declarative knowledge for word problem solving. Trans. Assoc. Comput. Linguist. **6**, 159–172 (2018)
14. Shi, S., Wang, Y., Lin, C., Liu, X., Rui, Y.: Automatically solving number word problems by semantic parsing and reasoning. In: Màrquez, L., Callison-Burch, C., Su, J., Pighin, D., Marton, Y. (eds.) EMNLP, pp. 1132–1142 (2015)
15. Wang, L., Wang, Y., Cai, D., Zhang, D., Liu, X.: Translating a math word problem to an expression tree. CoRR **abs/1811.05632** (2018)
16. Xie, Z., Sun, S.: A goal-driven tree-structured neural model for math word problems. In: Kraus, S. (ed.) IJCAI, pp. 5299–5305 (2019)
17. Zhang, J., et al.: Graph-to-tree learning for solving math word problems. In: Jurafsky, D., Chai, J., Schluter, N., Tetreault, J.R. (eds.) ACL, pp. 3928–3937 (2020)
18. Zou, Y., Lu, W.: Quantity tagger: a latent-variable sequence labeling approach to solving addition-subtraction word problems. In: Korhonen, A., Traum, D.R., Màrquez, L. (eds.) ACL, pp. 5246–5251 (2019)
19. Zou, Y., Lu, W.: Text2math: end-to-end parsing text into math expressions. In: Inui, K., Jiang, J., Ng, V., Wan, X. (eds.) EMNLP-IJCNLP, pp. 5326–5336 (2019)

Enhancing Output Diversity Improves Conjugate Gradient-Based Adversarial Attacks

Keiichiro Yamamura[1]($\boxtimes$) (iD), Issa Oe[1] (iD), Hiroki Ishikura[1] (iD), and Katsuki Fujisawa[2] (iD)

[1] Graduate School of Mathematics, Kyushu University, Fukuoka, Japan
`keiichiro.yamamura@kyudai.jp`
[2] Institute of Mathematics for Industry, Kyushu University, Fukuoka, Japan

Abstract. Deep neural networks are vulnerable to adversarial examples, and adversarial attacks that generate adversarial examples have been studied in this context. Existing studies imply that increasing the diversity of model outputs contributes to improving the attack performance. This study focuses on the Auto Conjugate Gradient (ACG) attack, which is inspired by the conjugate gradient method and has a high diversification performance. We hypothesized that increasing the distance between two consecutive search points would enhance the output diversity. To test our hypothesis, we propose Rescaling-ACG (ReACG), which automatically modifies the two components that significantly affect the distance between two consecutive search points, including the search direction and step size. ReACG showed higher attack performance than that of ACG, and is particularly effective for ImageNet models with several classification classes. Experimental results show that the distance between two consecutive search points enhances the output diversity and may help develop new potent attacks. The code is available at https://github.com/yamamura-k/ReACG.

Keywords: Adversarial attack · Computer vision · Robustness

1 Introduction

Szegedy et al. [33] noted that the output of deep neural networks (DNNs) can be significantly altered by small perturbations imperceptible to the human eye. These perturbed inputs are referred to as adversarial examples, and it is well-known that this is a crucial vulnerability of DNNs. Addressing this vulnerability is crucial because DNNs have safety-critical applications such as automated driving [16], facial recognition [2], and cyber security [22]. Several defense mechanisms have been proposed to improve the robustness of DNNs against adversarial examples. The most fundamental approach is adversarial training [25], which requires several adversarial examples. The rapid generation of adversarial examples is expected to reduce the computation time for adversarial training and improve the robustness of the obtained DNN.

Adversarial attacks are methods used to generate adversarial examples. If the purpose is better robustness evaluation and improving robustness, the white-box attack, which optimizes the objective function L using the gradient of the DNN to generate adversarial examples, is one of the most promising approaches. Untargeted attacks, in which attackers do not specify a misclassification class, are often used for robustness evaluations and adversarial training. This study focuses on untargeted white-box attacks against image classifiers.

Targeted attacks have also been studied [6,19,38], in which attackers specify the misclassification class, in contrast to untargeted attacks. Different adversarial examples with different predictions can be generated through targeted attacks on a single input. The difference in their predicted classes implies differences in the model outputs. The success of existing untargeted attacks that consider output diversity [15,34,37] suggests that enhancing the output diversity results in higher attack performance.

We focus on the Auto Conjugate Gradient (ACG) attack [37], which is based on the conjugate gradient method and has a high diversification performance. ACG does not assume any restarts, and is advantageous over restart-based approaches in terms of the computation time [15,34]. Restart-based techniques can also be combined with ACG. The search points of ACG move more in each iteration than those of Auto-PGD (APGD) [9], which is based on the momentum method. Additionally, ACG shows a higher diversity of second likely predictions (CW target class, CTC) than that in APGD. We hypothesized that increasing the distance between two consecutive search points would enhance CTC diversity.

To validate this hypothesis, we propose Rescaling-ACG (ReACG), which modifies the search direction and step size control of ACG, as described in Sect. 3. The search direction and step size significantly affected the distance between two consecutive search points. ReACG determines whether the coefficient $\beta^{(k)}$ should be modified based on the ratio of the gradient to the conjugate gradient (Sect. 3.1). If $\beta^{(k)}$ must be modified, $\beta^{(k)}$ is calculated using the gradient normalized by its Euclidean norm. Although ACG has different characteristics that those of APGD, it updates the step size using the same rule as that in APGD. By contrast, as described in Sects. 3.2 and 4.1, ReACG controls the step size with appropriate checkpoints determined through multi-objective optimization using Optuna [3].

Section 4.2 presents the empirical evaluation of ReACG on 30 robust models trained on the CIFAR-10, CIFAR-100 [18], and ImageNet [30] datasets. ReACG showed a higher attack performance than that of the state-of-the-art (SOTA) methods APGD and ACG for more than 90% of the 30 models, including a wide range of architectures. Particularly, ReACG exhibited the highest attack performance for all models trained on ImageNet, which has several classification classes. ReACG showed a higher attack performance than those of APGD and ACG, with approximately 0.4 to 0.9% and 0.1 to 0.4%, respectively. Considering the recent advances in adversarial attacks based on nonlinear optimization methods, such as PGD [25], APGD, and ACG, significant performance improvement was achieved.

The analyses in Sects. 4.3 and 4.4 show that modifying $\beta^{(k)}$ and step size control increases the distance between two consecutive search points and the CTC diversity, which leads to the high attack performance of ReACG. This relationship is beneficial for the development of novel and potent attacks. The contributions of this study are summarized below.

1. We propose ReACG, which automatically modifies $\beta^{(k)}$ based on the hypothesis that increasing the distance between two consecutive search points enhances output diversity.
2. ReACG showed a higher attack performance than those of SOTA attacks on more than 90% of the 30 robust models trained on three representative datasets.
3. Our analysis suggests that increasing the distance between two consecutive search points enhances CTC diversity. This relationship is beneficial for the development of novel and potent attacks.

2 Preliminaries

2.1 Problem Setting

Let $f : D \to \mathbb{R}^C$ be a locally differentiable function that serves as a C-classifier. Assume that the input $\boldsymbol{x}_{\mathrm{org}}$ is classified into class c using classifier f. Given a positive number ε and distance function $d : D \times D \to \mathbb{R}$, we define an adversarial example $\boldsymbol{x}_{\mathrm{adv}} \in D$ as an input satisfying the following conditions

$$\arg\max_i f_i(\boldsymbol{x}_{\mathrm{adv}}) \neq c, \quad d(\boldsymbol{x}_{\mathrm{org}}, \boldsymbol{x}_{\mathrm{adv}}) \leq \varepsilon. \tag{1}$$

Generally, an adversarial example is generated by maximizing the objective function L within the feasible region $S = \{\boldsymbol{x} \in D \mid d(\boldsymbol{x}_{\mathrm{org}}, \boldsymbol{x}_{\mathrm{adv}}) \leq \varepsilon\}$. This problem is formulated as follows:

$$\max_{\boldsymbol{x} \in S} L(f(\boldsymbol{x}), c) \tag{2}$$

The condition $\arg\max_i f_i(\boldsymbol{x}_{\mathrm{adv}}) \neq c$ can be rephrased as $\max_{i \neq c} f_i(\boldsymbol{x}_{\mathrm{adv}}) - f_c(\boldsymbol{x}_{\mathrm{adv}}) \geq 0$. Hence, objective functions such as the CW loss (L_{CW}) [7] and Difference of Logit Ratio (DLR) loss (L_{DLR}) [9] are commonly used. Let $\boldsymbol{z} = f(\boldsymbol{x})$ and π_k be the index of the k-th largest element of $\boldsymbol{z}$. The CW loss and DLR loss are denoted as $L_{\mathrm{CW}}(\boldsymbol{z}, c) = -\boldsymbol{z}_c + \max_{i \neq c} \boldsymbol{z}_i$ and $L_{\mathrm{DLR}}(\boldsymbol{z}, c) = \frac{L_{\mathrm{CW}}(z,c)}{z_{\pi_1} - z_{\pi_3}}$, respectively. $\arg\max_{i \neq c} f_i(\boldsymbol{x})$ was referred to as CTC in [37]. We define output diversity as the variation of CTC during the attack procedure.

For adversarial attacks on image classifiers, the input space is $D = [0, 1]^n$. Additionally, the Euclidean distance $\| \cdot \|_2$ or uniform distance $\| \cdot \|_\infty$ is often used as the distance function d. This study focuses primarily on ℓ_∞ attacks that use $d(\boldsymbol{u}, \boldsymbol{v}) = \|\boldsymbol{u} - \boldsymbol{v}\|_\infty$ as a distance function.

2.2   Related Work

Szegedy et al. [33] suggested the existence of adversarial examples, and several gradient-based attacks have been proposed subsequently [7,9,20,25,37]. Among these, a promising approach is to consider the diversity in the output space. MT-PGD [15] achieves diversification in the output space by sequentially performing targeted attacks using different misclassified target classes. Output Diversified Sampling [34] and its variants [24] randomly sample the initial point, considering the diversity in the output space by maximizing the inner product of a random vector w and logit $f(x)$. These methods assume several restarts based on the changes in the target class or initial points. By contrast, ACG improves the output diversity by moving to the sign of the conjugate gradient. ACG is advantageous in terms of the computational time because output space diversification can be achieved without restarts. Additionally, an ensemble of attacks, such as AutoAttack [9], has attracted research attention in recent years [23,26]. Although ensemble-based attacks are stronger than simple attacks, such as PGD, their performance depends on the individual attacks in the ensemble. Therefore, it is important to develop individualized attacks.

2.3   Auto Conjugate Gradient Attack

ACG Step. ACG attack [37] is based on the conjugate gradient method, which updates search points using the following formulas:

$$g^{(k)} \leftarrow \nabla L\left(f(x^{(k)}), c\right), \tag{3}$$

$$y^{(k-1)} \leftarrow g^{(k-1)} - g^{(k)}, \tag{4}$$

$$\beta_{HS}^{(k)} \leftarrow -\frac{\langle -g^{(k)}, y^{(k-1)} \rangle}{\langle s^{(k-1)}, y^{(k-1)} \rangle}, \tag{5}$$

$$s^{(k)} \leftarrow g^{(k)} + \beta_{HS}^{(k)} s^{(k-1)}, \tag{6}$$

$$x^{(k+1)} \leftarrow P_S\left(x^{(k)} + \eta^{(k)} \text{sign}(s^{(k)})\right), \tag{7}$$

where $\langle \cdot, \cdot \rangle$ is the inner product and $P_S(\cdot)$ is a projection onto the feasible region S. $x^{(k)}$ is referred to as the search point, and $s^{(k)}$ is referred to as search direction.

Step-Size Updating Rule. ACG controls the step size using the same rule as that in APGD. APGD halves the step size and moves to the incumbent solution x_{adv} if conditions C1 and C2 are satisfied at the precalculated checkpoints $w_j \in W$.

C1 $\displaystyle\sum_{i=w_{j-1}}^{w_j-1} \mathbb{1}_{L\left(f(x^{(i+1)}),c\right)>L\left(f(x^{(i)}),c\right)} < \rho \cdot (w_j - w_{j-1})$

C2 $L_{\max}\left(f(x^{(w_{j-1})}), c\right) = L_{\max}\left(f(x^{(w_j)}), c\right)$ and $\eta^{(w_{j-1})} = \eta^{(w_j)}$,

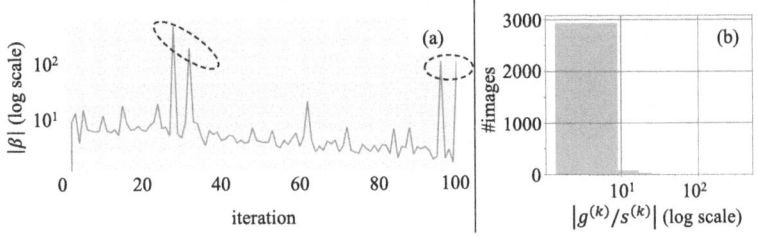

Fig. 1. (a) Transition of $|\beta_{HS}^{(k)}|$. (b) Distribution of $|g^{(k)}/s^{(k)}|$.

where $\rho \in [0, 1]$ denotes a parameter with a default value of 0.75. The following gradual equation determines the checkpoints w_j:

$$p_0 = 0, \ p_1 = 0.22, \ q = 0.03, \ q_{min} = 0.06 \tag{8}$$

$$p_{j+1} = p_j + \max(p_j - p_{j-1} - q, q_{min}), \ w_j = \lceil p_j N \rceil. \tag{9}$$

3 Rescaling-ACG

This section describes the ReACG attack, a modification of ACG aimed at increasing the distance between two consecutive search points and enhancing output diversity. ReACG automatically modifies its search direction and controls the step size using the appropriate checkpoints obtained through multi-objective optimization. Section 3.1 describes the modification of the search direction, and Sect. 3.2 provides the checkpoints used for step size calculation. The pseudocode for ReACG is described in Algorithm 1.

3.1 Search Direction

Motivation. Search direction such as $s^{(k)}$ or $g^{(k)}$ is one of the main factors affecting the distance between two consecutive search points. Conjugate gradient methods are characterized by the coefficient $\beta^{(k)}$ used to calculate the conjugate gradient. The preliminary experiment conducted by Yamamura et al. [37] suggests that $\beta^{(k)}$ significantly affects attack performance. Figure 1(a) depicts the average transition of $|\beta_{HS}^{(k)}|$ over 10,000 images. Although $|\beta_{HS}^{(k)}|$ was less than 10 in several iterations, it reached approximately 500 in other iterations. Additionally, Fig. 1(b) shows that most elements of $|g^{(k)}/s^{(k)}|$ averaged over 10,000 images are less than 10. Equation 6 indicates that if $|\beta_{HS}^{(k)}|$ is extremely larger than each element of $|g^{(k)}/s^{(k)}|$, $s^{(k+1)}$ and $s^{(k)}$ are likely to be the same vector. These results imply that an ACG search may be redundant.

Rescaling Condition. Equation 6 suggests that $s_i^{(k)}$ and $s_i^{(k-1)}$ are likely to take approximately the same values for the index i such that $\left| g^{(k)}/s^{(k-1)} \right|_i \ll |\beta^{(k)}|$. If the following inequality holds, ReACG modifies the coefficient $\beta^{(k)}$:

Algorithm 1. ReACG

Input: f, L, S, c, $\boldsymbol{x}^{(0)}$, $\eta^{(0)}$, N, $W = \{w_0, \dots, w_n\}$

Output: $\boldsymbol{x}_{adv}$

1: $\boldsymbol{x}_{adv} \leftarrow \boldsymbol{x}^{(0)}; \beta^{(0)} \leftarrow 0; \boldsymbol{s}^{(0)} \leftarrow \nabla L(f(\boldsymbol{x}^{(0)}), c); \boldsymbol{x}_{pre} \leftarrow \boldsymbol{x}^{(0)}; \boldsymbol{s}_{pre} \leftarrow \boldsymbol{s}^{(0)}$

2: **for** $k = 0$ to N **do**

3:     Compute $\boldsymbol{x}^{(k+1)}$ (7); $\eta^{(k+1)} \leftarrow \eta^{(k)}$

4:     **if** $L(f(\boldsymbol{x}^{(k+1)}), c) > L(f(\boldsymbol{x}_{adv}), c)$ **then**

5:         $\boldsymbol{x}_{adv} \leftarrow \boldsymbol{x}^{(k+1)}; \boldsymbol{x}_{pre} \leftarrow \boldsymbol{x}^{(k)}; \boldsymbol{s}_{pre} \leftarrow \boldsymbol{s}^{(k)}$

6:     **end if**

7:     **if** $k \in W$ and (C1 or C2 hold) **then**

8:         $\eta^{(k+1)} \leftarrow \eta^{(k)}/2; \boldsymbol{x}^{(k+1)} \leftarrow \boldsymbol{x}_{adv}; \boldsymbol{x}^{(k)} \leftarrow \boldsymbol{x}_{pre}; \boldsymbol{s}^{(k)} \leftarrow \boldsymbol{s}_{pre}$

9:     **end if**

10:    /* The difference to ACG is highlighted in blue. */

11:    Compute $\beta^{(k+1)}$ (5) and $\tilde{\beta}^{(k)}$ (12)

12:    **if** $|\tilde{\beta}^{(k)}| < |\beta^{(k)}|$ and (10) hold **then**

13:        $\beta^{(k)} \leftarrow \tilde{\beta}^{(k)}$

14:    **end if**

15:    Compute $\boldsymbol{s}^{(k+1)}$ (6)

16: **end for**

$$\mathbb{E}\left[\left|\frac{\boldsymbol{g}^{(k)}}{\boldsymbol{s}^{(k-1)}}\right|\right] < |\beta^{(k)}| \tag{10}$$

The severity of this condition can be adjusted by multiplying the right side of Eq. 10 by a constant. However, we did not consider this extension to maintain a number of hyperparameters similar to those of ACG.

Rescaling Method. When Eq. 10 holds, the coefficient $\tilde{\beta}_{HS}^{(k)}$ is calculated using $\tilde{\boldsymbol{g}}^{(k)} = \boldsymbol{g}^{(k)}/\|\boldsymbol{g}^{(k)}\|_2$ instead of $\boldsymbol{g}^{(k)}$. More precisely, Eqs. 11 and 12 are used to calculate the coefficients instead of Eqs. 4 and 5.

$$\boldsymbol{y}^{(k-1)} \leftarrow \tilde{\boldsymbol{g}}^{(k-1)} - \tilde{\boldsymbol{g}}^{(k)} \tag{11}$$

$$\tilde{\beta}_{HS}^{(k)} \leftarrow -\frac{\langle -\tilde{\boldsymbol{g}}^{(k)}, \tilde{\boldsymbol{y}}^{(k-1)}\rangle}{\langle \boldsymbol{s}^{(k-1)}, \tilde{\boldsymbol{y}}^{(k-1)}\rangle} \tag{12}$$

If $|\tilde{\beta}_{HS}^{(k)}| < |\beta_{HS}^{(k)}|$ holds, $\boldsymbol{s}^{(k)}$ is calculated using $\tilde{\beta}_{HS}^{(k)}$ in stead of $\beta^{(k)}$.

3.2   Rethinking the Step Size

ACG uses precalculated checkpoints to control the step size. The three magic numbers p_1, q, and q_{min} that appear in the checkpoint calculation affect the obtained checkpoints. We searched for the appropriate values of these parameters through multi-objective optimization using Optuna. Based on the experimental results in Sect. 4.1, we set $p_1 = 0.43, q = 0.24$, and $q_{min} = 0.08$.

Table 1. The results of step size optimization using Optuna. The lowest robust accuracy for each model and loss is in bold, and the second lowest is underlined.

Loss			CW					DLR				
p_1	q	q_{min}	[31]	[36]	[1]	[4]	[14]	[31]	[36]	[1]	[4]	[14]
0.22	0.03	0.06	56.47	45.07	53.08	45.47	59.73	56.34	45.04	52.92	45.28	59.67
0.43	**0.24**	**0.08**	56.48	**45.00**	<u>53.06</u>	**45.31**	**59.65**	**56.23**	44.83	**52.89**	<u>45.10</u>	59.47
0.26	0.04	0.08	**56.41**	45.07	53.08	45.43	59.73	56.38	45.01	52.92	45.21	59.58
0.31	0.28	0.09	56.47	45.06	53.12	45.41	59.71	<u>56.26</u>	44.91	<u>52.91</u>	45.25	59.62
0.42	0.25	0.10	<u>56.44</u>	<u>45.01</u>	**53.05**	<u>45.32</u>	59.66	**56.23**	44.82	52.94	45.12	<u>59.44</u>
0.69	0.69	0.05	56.57	45.19	53.19	45.35	<u>59.66</u>	56.27	**44.81**	52.96	**45.06**	**59.41**

4 Experiments

This section describes the results of comparative experiments on ℓ_∞-robust models trained on CIFAR-10, CIFAR-100, and ImageNet. The attacked models were in RobustBench [8], which is a well-known benchmark for adversarial robustness. The performance evaluation was based on robust accuracy, defined as follows:

$$\frac{\# \text{ correctly classified adversarial examples}}{\# \text{ test samples}} \times 100. \tag{13}$$

A low robust accuracy indicates a high misclassification rate and high attack performance. As with the RobustBench leaderboard, we used 10,000 images and $\varepsilon = 8/255$ for CIFAR-10/100, and 5,000 images and $\varepsilon = 4/255$ for ImageNet. The experiments were conducted using an Intel(R) Xeon(R) Silver 4214R CPU at 2.40 GHz and NVIDIA RTX A6000. We chose APGD and ACG as the baseline. Both typically perform better for adversarially robust models than early techniques such as FGSM [12] and PGD [25].

4.1 Experiments on Step Size Control

This experiment used five robust PreActResNets [1,4,14,31,36] trained on CIFAR-10. Optuna [3] searched for appropriate parameters through multi-objective optimization, which minimized robust accuracy and maximized the average CW loss value. In each optimization iteration with Optuna, ReACG with CW loss was executed starting at the input points for different values of $0.01 \le p_1 \le 0.9$, $0.01 \le q \le 0.5p_1$, and $0.01 \le q_{min} \le 0.1$. To make the step size sufficiently small, the objective function of this multi-objective optimization problem was designed to return a tuple $(\infty, -\infty)$ when the number of checkpoints was less than four. Optuna requires 100 iterations per model. Table 1 shows the obtained parameters and robust accuracy. The obtained p_1 values tend to be larger than those in the APGD setting. The experimental results indicate that $p_1 = 0.43, q = 0.24$, and $q_{min} = 0.08$ are effective in several models.

Table 2. Comparison in robust accuracy. Δ is the difference in robust accuracy between ACG and ReACG. The lowest value for each model and loss is in bold.

CIFAR-10 ($\varepsilon = 8/255$)			CW loss				DLR loss			
Defense	Model	clean	APGD	ACG	ReACG	Δ (↑)	APGD	ACG	ReACG	Δ (↑)
Peng [28]	WRN70-16	93.27	71.92	71.66	**71.60**	0.06	71.99	71.53	**71.41**	0.12
Wang [35]	WRN70-16	93.25	71.57	71.25	**71.17**	0.08	71.58	71.32	**71.13**	0.19
Bai [5]	RN152+ WRN70-16	95.23	**69.42**	69.78	70.10	−0.32	**69.38**	69.86	69.72	0.14
Wang [35]	WRN28-10	92.44	68.28	68.02	**67.77**	0.25	68.30	67.97	**67.80**	0.17
Rebuffi [29]	WRN70-16	92.23	67.71	67.54	**67.45**	0.09	67.85	67.38	**67.24**	0.14
Cui [10]	WRN28-10	92.17	68.57	68.34	**68.24**	0.10	68.63	68.21	**68.06**	0.15
Huang [17]	WRN-A4	91.58	66.79	66.52	**66.41**	0.11	67.02	66.52	**66.34**	0.18
Gowal20 [13]	WRN70-16	91.10	66.76	66.48	**66.47**	0.01	66.89	66.40	**66.31**	0.09
Gowal21 [14]	WRN70-16	88.74	67.75	67.26	**67.19**	0.07	68.33	67.21	**67.00**	0.21
Rebuffi [29]	WRN106	88.50	65.57	**65.35**	65.38	−0.03	65.60	65.26	**65.07**	0.19
CIFAR-100 ($\varepsilon = 8/255$)										
Bai [5]	RN152+WRN70-16	85.19	**40.70**	41.64	41.60	0.04	**40.78**	41.60	41.66	−0.06
Bai [5]	RN152+ WRN70-16	80.20	**37.47**	37.66	37.48	0.18	37.82	37.81	**37.58**	0.23
Debenedetti [11]	XCiT-L12	70.77	36.75	36.15	**35.88**	0.27	37.21	36.30	**35.91**	0.39
Debenedetti [11]	XCiT-M12	69.20	35.75	35.16	**34.91**	0.25	36.05	35.19	**34.80**	0.39
Gowal20 [13]	WRN70-16	69.15	38.77	38.27	**38.19**	0.08	38.93	38.02	**37.80**	0.22
Pang [27]	WRN70-16	65.56	34.14	33.77	**33.61**	0.16	34.22	33.82	**33.64**	0.18
Rebuffi [29]	WRN70-16	63.56	36.06	35.62	**35.53**	0.09	36.09	35.30	**35.22**	0.08
Wang [35]	WRN70-16	75.22	43.84	43.55	**43.47**	0.08	43.83	43.63	**43.32**	0.31
Cui [10]	WRN28-10	73.85	40.28	**39.93**	39.96	−0.03	40.29	40.13	**39.78**	0.35
Wang [35]	WRN28-10	72.58	39.58	39.29	**39.20**	0.09	39.60	39.41	**39.27**	0.14
ImageNet ($\varepsilon = 4/255$)										
Peng [28]	WRN101-2	73.10	50.92	50.40	**50.20**	0.20	51.32	50.36	**50.06**	0.30
Liu [21]	Swin-B	76.16	57.80	57.26	**57.12**	0.14	58.04	57.12	**56.96**	0.16
Liu	Swin-L	78.92	61.34	60.84	**60.74**	0.10	61.76	60.78	**60.56**	0.22
Liu	ConvNeXt-L	78.02	60.56	59.96	**59.78**	0.18	60.94	59.96	**59.54**	0.42
Liu	ConvNeXt-B	76.70	58.06	57.44	**57.18**	0.26	58.56	57.26	**57.06**	0.20
Singh [32]	ViT-B+ ConvStem	76.30	56.74	56.04	**55.78**	0.26	57.30	56.22	**55.82**	0.40
Singh	ConvNeXt-B +ConvStem	75.88	58.04	57.38	**57.18**	0.20	58.56	57.64	**57.48**	0.16
Singh	ConvNeXt-S +ConvStem	74.08	54.34	53.78	**53.56**	0.22	54.90	53.82	**53.38**	0.44
Singh	ConvNeXt-T +ConvStem	72.70	51.66	51.04	**50.70**	0.34	52.04	50.82	**50.56**	0.26
Singh	ConvNeXt-L +ConvStem	77.00	59.16	58.80	**58.70**	0.10	59.78	58.68	**58.50**	0.18
Summary	CIFAR-10 (#**bold**)		1	1	**8**		1	0	**9**	
	CIFAR-100 (#**bold**)		2	1	**7**		1	0	**9**	
	ImageNet (#**bold**)		0	0	**10**		0	0	**10**	
	Total (#bold)		3	2	**25**		2	0	**28**	

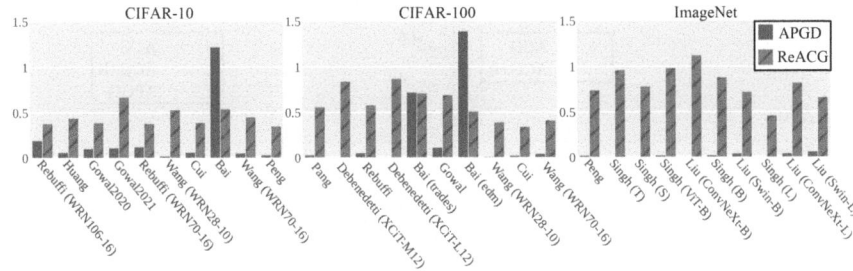

Fig. 2. The percentage of images where APGD/ReACG found adversarial examples but ReACG/APGD did not.

4.2   Experiments on ReACG

ReACG was compared with APGD and ACG. This experiment used 30 models, including the top 10 for each dataset listed on the RobustBench leaderboard as of October 1, 2023. All compared methods used the input point as the initial point, $N = 100$ as the total number of iterations, and CW/DLR loss as the objective function. Table 2 shows the robust accuracy obtained by each attack. Δ represents the difference in robust accuracy between ACG and ReACG. From the "CW loss" columns in Table 2, ReACG showed lower robust accuracy for 90% of the 30 models than that in APGD and ACG. With DLR loss, ReACG showed a higher attack performance than APGD and ACG for 93% and 97% of the 30 models, respectively. ReACG showed lower robust accuracy than APGD and ACG by approximately 0.4 to 0.9% and 0.1 to 0.4%, respectively. Additionally, the difference in robust accuracy among APGD, ACG, and ReACG was higher with DLR loss than that with CW loss. These improvements are sufficient considering the recent advances in adversarial attacks based on nonlinear optimization methods.

Figure 2 shows the percentage of images where APGD/ReACG attacked successfully and ReACG/APGD attacked unsuccessfully. APGD exhibited a lower robust accuracy than that of ReACG for the models proposed by Bai et al. [5]. However, Fig. 2 shows that ReACG successfully perturbs the images for which APGD fails. This result suggests that the ensemble of ReACG and APGD is likely to exhibit a high attack performance.

4.3   Effect of Rescaling

Figure 3(a) and (b) show the transitions of $|\beta^{(k)}|$ and $\|x^{(k)} - x^{(k-1)}\|_2$, respectively. ACG+R adopts $\beta^{(k)}$-rescaling. Figure 3(a) demonstrates that ACG+R has smaller $|\beta^{(k)}|$ than that of ACG, which indicates that our rescaling method reduces $|\beta^{(k)}|$. Additionally, Fig. 3(b) shows that the search points of ACG+R move more than those of ACG. These results suggest that our rescaling method enhances the search efficiency by resolving the issue caused by a large $|\beta^{(k)}|$.

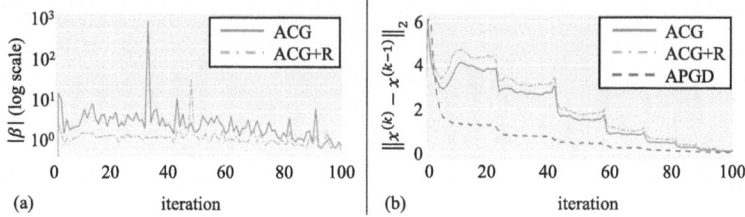

(a)   iteration   (b)   iteration

Fig. 3. (a) Transition of $|\beta_{HS}^{(k)}|$. (b) Transition of the moving distance per iteration.

4.4 Difference in CTC Variation

In Sect. 4.3, we discussed the effect of our rescaling method in the input space. This section highlights one reason for the high performance of ReACG by focusing on the difference in the output diversity of ACG and ReACG. Analysis of Sect. 4.3 implies that ReACG performs a more diversified search than that of ACG using appropriate step-size control in addition to rescaling $\beta^{(k)}$. The analysis in this section is based on CTC variation. Let $c^{(k)} = \arg\max_{i \neq c} f_i(\boldsymbol{x}^{(k)})$ be the CTC at the kth iteration. The number of CTCs that appear during an attack #CTC, is defined as #CTC := $|\{c^{(i)} \mid i = 1, \dots, N\}|$. The left/right of Fig. 4 show the percentage of images in which #CTC = K during an attack with ACG/ReACG. Figure 4 shows that ReACG has a smaller percentage of images where #CTC = 1 than that in ACG and a larger percentage of images where #CTC ≥ 2. Additionally, ReACG has a larger maximum number of #CTCs than that in ACG. These results suggest that ReACG enhances the output diversity compared to that with ACG.

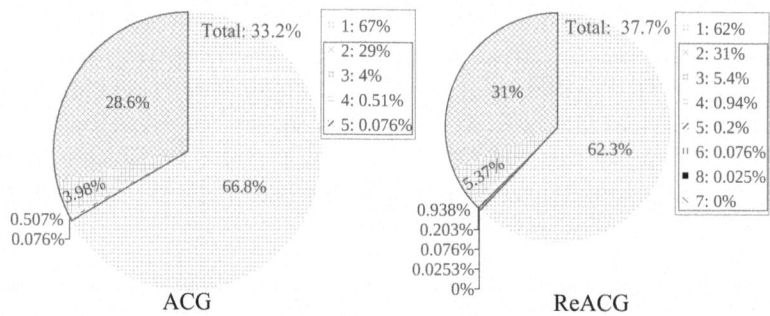

ACG   ReACG

Fig. 4. Comparison in CTC variation. Let $c^{(k)} = \arg\max_{i \neq c} f_i(\boldsymbol{x}^{(k)})$ be a CTC at k-th iteration. The number of CTCs appeared during an attack, #CTC, is defined as #CTC := $|\{c^{(i)} \mid i = 1, \dots, N\}|$. In the legend, "$K$: P%" means that the percentage of images for which #CTC = K is P%.

Table 3. The results of the ablation study. Δ is the difference in robust accuracy between ACG and ReACG. The lowest value for each model and loss is in bold.

CW loss

Dataset	CIFAR-10 ($\varepsilon = 8/255$)			CIFAR-100 ($\varepsilon = 8/255$)			ImageNet ($\varepsilon = 4/255$)		
Defense	Peng [28]	Wang [35]	Bai [5]	Wang [35]	Cui [10]	Wang [35]	Liu [21]	Liu [21]	Singh [32]
Model	WRN 70-16	WRN 70-16	RN-152+ WRN-70-16	WRN 70-16	WRN 28-10	WRN 28-10	Swin-L	Conv-NeXT-L	ConvNeXt-L +ConvStem
clean	93.27	93.25	95.23	75.22	73.85	72.58	78.92	78.02	77.00
APGD	71.92	71.57	**69.42**	43.84	40.28	39.58	61.34	60.56	59.16
ACG	71.66	71.25	69.78	43.55	39.93	39.29	60.84	59.96	58.80
ACG+R	71.66	71.22	69.83	43.52	39.96	39.27	**60.74**	59.86	58.72
ACG+T	71.68	71.23	70.04	**43.42**	**39.88**	39.24	60.80	59.84	58.74
ReACG	**71.60**	**71.17**	70.10	43.47	39.96	**39.20**	**60.74**	**59.78**	**58.70**
Δ (↑)	0.06	0.08	−0.32	0.08	−0.03	0.09	0.10	0.18	0.10

DLR loss

APGD	71.99	71.58	**69.38**	43.83	40.29	39.60	61.76	60.94	59.78
ACG	71.53	71.32	69.86	43.63	40.13	39.41	60.78	59.96	58.68
ACG+R	71.52	71.21	69.56	43.55	39.96	39.35	60.74	59.82	58.66
ACG+T	71.55	71.24	69.91	43.52	39.96	**39.25**	60.66	59.74	58.62
ReACG	**71.41**	**71.13**	69.72	**43.32**	**39.78**	39.27	**60.56**	**59.54**	**58.50**
Δ (↑)	0.12	0.19	0.14	0.31	0.35	0.14	0.22	0.42	0.18

4.5 Ablation Study

Effects of Rescaling and Step Size Optimization. Table 3 describes the robust accuracy for nine models, including the top three for each dataset listed in the RobustBench leaderboard. This experiment used the same initial points, total number of iterations, and objective functions as those in Sect. 4.2. ACG+T is ACG that uses the parameters p_1, q and q_{min} selected in Sect. 4.1.

In Table 3, ACG+R and ACG+T show lower robust accuracies than that of ACG in many cases. This result indicates that rescaling $\beta^{(k)}$ and step size optimization can improve attack performance. Additionally, ACG+T showed the same or slightly lower robust accuracy than that of ACG+R, and ReACG showed a lower robust accuracy than that of ACG+R and ACG+T in several cases.

Relationship Between the Number of Total Iterations and Robust Accuracy. Figure 5 shows the transition of the robust accuracy of ACG and ReACG with $N = 50, 100, 200, 400,$ and 1000. The dashed line in the figure represents the ACG, and the solid line represents the ReACG. The left figure shows the typical results for CIFAR-10/100, and the right figure shows the typical results for ImageNet. As shown in the figure on the left, the decrease in robust accuracy by ReACG was slower than that by ACG for CIFAR-10/100. At approximately $N \leq 200$, ReACG recorded a lower robust accuracy than that of ACG; however, at $N \geq 400$, ACG showed a lower robust accuracy than

ReACG. As shown in the figure on the right, the decrease in robust accuracy by ReACG was faster than that by ACG for ImageNet. Additionally, ReACG exhibited a lower robust accuracy than that of ACG for all N. Similar trends were observed in the remaining models.

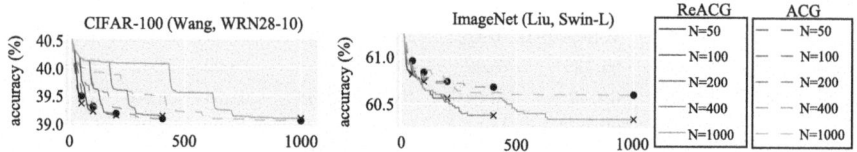

Fig. 5. ACG vs. ReACG for different maximum numbers of iterations N.

Relationship Between the Number of Restarts and Robust Accuracy.
This experiment investigated the effect of random restarts on the attack performance of ACG and ReACG. The initial points were sampled uniformly from a feasible region. The left part of Fig. 6 shows the typical results for models trained on CIFAR-10/100, and the right part shows representative results for models trained on ImageNet. Figure 6 shows that the robust accuracy decreases as the number of restarts increases. Additionally, ReACG showed a lower robust accuracy than that of ACG, even with multiple restarts. The same trend was observed in the other models.

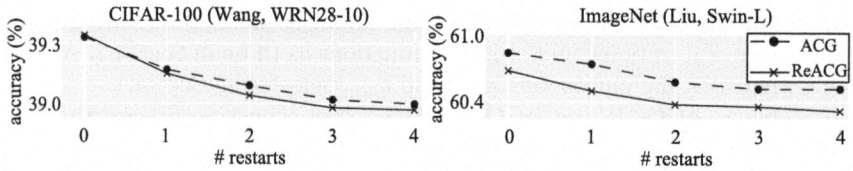

Fig. 6. ACG vs. ReACG for different numbers of restarts.

5   Conclusion

We hypothesized that increasing the distance between two consecutive search points would enhance the output diversity, resulting in high attack performance. We propose ReACG with an improved ACG search direction and step-size control to test our hypothesis. ReACG automatically modifies $\beta^{(k)}$ when $|\beta^{(k)}|$ exceeds the average ratio of the gradient to conjugate gradient. Our analyses show that modifying $\beta^{(k)}$ and step size control increased the distance between two consecutive search points and CTC diversity, which led to the high attack performance of ReACG. ReACG showed better attack performance than the baseline methods APGD and ACG for 90% of the 30 SOTA robust models trained on the three representative datasets. The differences in the robust accuracy between APGD and ACG were approximately 0.4 to 0.9% and 0.1 to 0.4%, respectively. These are sufficiently large considering the recent advances in adversarial attacks based on nonlinear optimization methods. Additionally, ReACG demonstrated particularly promising results for ImageNet models with a large number of classification classes. This result supports the claim that the output diversity contributes to high attack performance. Increasing the distance between two consecutive search points to enhance the output diversity may be beneficial for developing new potent attacks.

Acknowledgments. This research project was supported by the Japan Science and Technology Agency (JST), Core Research of Evolutionary Science and Technology (CREST), Center of Innovation Science and Technology based Radical Innovation and Entrepreneurship Program (COI Program), JSPS KAKENHI Grant Numbers JP16H01707 and JP21H04599, Japan.

Disclosure of Interests. The authors declare no competing interests relevant to the contents of this article.

References

1. Addepalli, S., Jain, S., Radhakrishnan, V.B.: Efficient and effective augmentation strategy for adversarial training. In: NeurIPS (2022)
2. Adjabi, I., Ouahabi, A., Benzaoui, A., Taleb-Ahmed, A.: Past, present, and future of face recognition: a review. Electronics **9**(8), 1188 (2020)
3. Akiba, T., Sano, S., Yanase, T., Ohta, T., Koyama, M.: Optuna: a next-generation hyperparameter optimization framework. In: SIGKDD (2019)
4. Andriushchenko, M., Flammarion, N.: Understanding and improving fast adversarial training. In: NeurIPS (2020)
5. Bai, Y., Anderson, B.G., Kim, A., Sojoudi, S.: Improving the accuracy-robustness trade-off of classifiers via adaptive smoothing. arXiv preprint arXiv:2301.12554 (2023)
6. Carlini, N., Wagner, D.: Audio adversarial examples: targeted attacks on speech-to-text. In: SPW (2018)
7. Carlini, N., Wagner, D.A.: Towards evaluating the robustness of neural networks. In: SP (2017)
8. Croce, F., et al.: Robustbench: a standardized adversarial robustness benchmark. In: NeurIPS (2021)
9. Croce, F., Hein, M.: Reliable evaluation of adversarial robustness with an ensemble of diverse parameter-free attacks. In: ICML (2020)
10. Cui, J., Tian, Z., Zhong, Z., Qi, X., Yu, B., Zhang, H.: Decoupled Kullback-Leibler divergence loss. arXiv preprint arXiv:2305.13948 (2023)
11. Debenedetti, E., Sehwag, V., Mittal, P.: A light recipe to train robust vision transformers. In: SaTML (2023)

12. Goodfellow, I.J., Shlens, J., Szegedy, C.: Explaining and harnessing adversarial examples. In: ICLR (2015)
13. Gowal, S., Qin, C., Uesato, J., Mann, T.A., Kohli, P.: Uncovering the limits of adversarial training against norm-bounded adversarial examples. CoRR abs/2010.03593 (2020)
14. Gowal, S., Rebuffi, S., Wiles, O., Stimberg, F., Calian, D.A., Mann, T.A.: Improving robustness using generated data. In: NeurIPS (2021)
15. Gowal, S., Uesato, J., Qin, C., Huang, P., Mann, T.A., Kohli, P.: An alternative surrogate loss for pgd-based adversarial testing. CoRR abs/1910.09338 (2019)
16. Gupta, A., Anpalagan, A., Guan, L., Khwaja, A.S.: Deep learning for object detection and scene perception in self-driving cars: survey, challenges, and open issues. Array **10**, 100057 (2021)
17. Huang, S., Lu, Z., Deb, K., Boddeti, V.N.: Revisiting residual networks for adversarial robustness: an architectural perspective. arXiv preprint arXiv:2212.11005 (2022)
18. Krizhevsky, A., Hinton, G., et al.: Learning multiple layers of features from tiny images (2009)
19. Li, M., Deng, C., Li, T., Yan, J., Gao, X., Huang, H.: Towards transferable targeted attack. In: CVPR (2020)
20. Lin, W., Lucas, K., Bauer, L., Reiter, M.K., Sharif, M.: Constrained gradient descent: a powerful and principled evasion attack against neural networks. In: ICML (2022)
21. Liu, C., et al.: A comprehensive study on robustness of image classification models: benchmarking and rethinking. arXiv preprint arXiv:2302.14301 (2023)
22. Liu, R., Lin, Y., Yang, X., Ng, S.H., Divakaran, D.M., Dong, J.S.: Inferring phishing intention via webpage appearance and dynamics: a deep vision based approach. In: USENIX Security (2022)
23. Liu, S., Peng, F., Tang, K.: Reliable robustness evaluation via automatically constructed attack ensembles. In: AAAI (2023)
24. Liu, Y., Cheng, Y., Gao, L., Liu, X., Zhang, Q., Song, J.: Practical evaluation of adversarial robustness via adaptive auto attack. In: CVPR (2022)
25. Madry, A., Makelov, A., Schmidt, L., Tsipras, D., Vladu, A.: Towards deep learning models resistant to adversarial attacks. In: ICLR (2018)
26. Mao, X., Chen, Y., Wang, S., Su, H., He, Y., Xue, H.: Composite adversarial attacks. In: AAAI (2021)
27. Pang, T., Lin, M., Yang, X., Zhu, J., Yan, S.: Robustness and accuracy could be reconcilable by (proper) definition. In: ICML (2022)
28. Peng, S., et al.: Robust principles: architectural design principles for adversarially robust CNNs. In: BMVC (2023)
29. Rebuffi, S., Gowal, S., Calian, D.A., Stimberg, F., Wiles, O., Mann, T.A.: Data augmentation can improve robustness. In: NeurIPS (2021)
30. Russakovsky, O., et al.: ImageNet large scale visual recognition challenge. Int. J. Comput. Vis. **115**(3), 211–252 (2015). https://doi.org/10.1007/s11263-015-0816-y
31. Sehwag, V., et al.: Robust learning meets generative models: can proxy distributions improve adversarial robustness? In: ICLR (2022)
32. Singh, N.D., Croce, F., Hein, M.: Revisiting adversarial training for imagenet: architectures, training and generalization across threat models. arXiv preprint arXiv:2303.01870 (2023)
33. Szegedy, C., et al.: Intriguing properties of neural networks. In: ICLR (2014)
34. Tashiro, Y., Song, Y., Ermon, S.: Diversity can be transferred: output diversification for white- and black-box attacks. In: NeurIPS (2020)

35. Wang, Z., Pang, T., Du, C., Lin, M., Liu, W., Yan, S.: Better diffusion models further improve adversarial training. In: ICML (2023)
36. Wong, E., Rice, L., Kolter, J.Z.: Fast is better than free: revisiting adversarial training. In: ICLR (2020)
37. Yamamura, K., et al.: Diversified adversarial attacks based on conjugate gradient method. In: ICML (2022)
38. Yao, Q., He, Z., Han, H., Zhou, S.K.: Miss the point: targeted adversarial attack on multiple landmark detection. In: MICCAI (2020)

Open-World Visual Reasoning
by a Neuro-Symbolic Program
of Zero-Shot Symbols

Gertjan J. Burghouts[✉], Fieke Hillerström, Erwin Walraven, Michael
van Bekkum, Frank Ruis, Joris Sijs, Jelle van Mil, Judith Dijk,
and Wouter Meijer

TNO, 2597 AK The Hague, The Netherlands
gertjan.burghouts@tno.nl

Abstract. We consider the problem of finding spatial configurations of
multiple objects in images, e.g., a mobile inspection robot is tasked to
localize abandoned tools on the floor. We define the spatial configuration of objects by first-order logic in terms of relations and attributes.
A neuro-symbolic program matches the logic formulas to probabilistic
object proposals for the given image, provided by language-vision models by querying them for the symbols. This work is the first to combine neuro-symbolic programming (reasoning) and language-vision models (learning) to find spatial configurations of objects in images in an open
world setting. We show the effectiveness by finding abandoned tools on
floors and leaking pipes. We find that most prediction errors are due to
biases in the language-vision model.

Keywords: Neuro-Symbolic Programming · Open World Robotics ·
Zero-shot Models · Language-Vision Models · Knowledge
Representation

1 Introduction

Finding spatial configurations of multiple objects in images is a very relevant
capability. For instance, a mobile inspection robot is tasked to localize situations
of interest on an industrial site, such as abandoned tools on the floor, because
they may pose a hazard to the personnel and robot itself. Once such a spatial
configuration is found, proper action can be taken, such as reporting it to the
operator or removing the object using the robot. On such sites, there may be
many activities; as a consequence, the objects, their position, and the environment may change constantly and this may differ per site. Therefore the robot
may encounter new objects, e.g., a new type of tool; new environments, e.g., the
floor is made of a different material; and new relevant situations, e.g., a leaking
pipe. This is a challenge of the open world: handling previously unseen objects

Supported by TNO ERP APPL.AI program.

and configurations. We consider the problem of localizing spatial configurations of interest in an open world, with a focus on situations that require an action of some kind.

To identify situations of interest, which deviate from the normal, a common approach is to use a statistical model of the sensory data [3,17,18]. However, the robot's goal, its context and explicit prior knowledge are not taken into account. As a consequence, the detected anomalies are not necessarily relevant for the robot's mission. Another drawback of statistical models is that they do not generalize well to new observations in the open world. They cannot be adapted quickly, because it requires a significant amount of training samples to adjust the statistical model.

We take a different approach by leveraging prior knowledge, in this case knowledge about spatial configurations of objects. This knowledge can be adapted quickly during operation and via generic definitions it can generalize better to new situations. An example of a spatial configuration is a tool that is left behind on the floor. A tool can be one of many types, such as a hammer, screwdriver, wrench, and many more. Likewise, floors can be composed of different materials with various appearances. Our goal is to find spatial configurations in images, based on a high-level definition of the involved object (categories) and the spatial relations between them, with the ability to define the object or its category, and without learning dedicated models for each of them. The rationale is that such an approach has a broader applicability, because it can generalize better across similar configurations and is adaptable to new configurations by formulating a new definition.

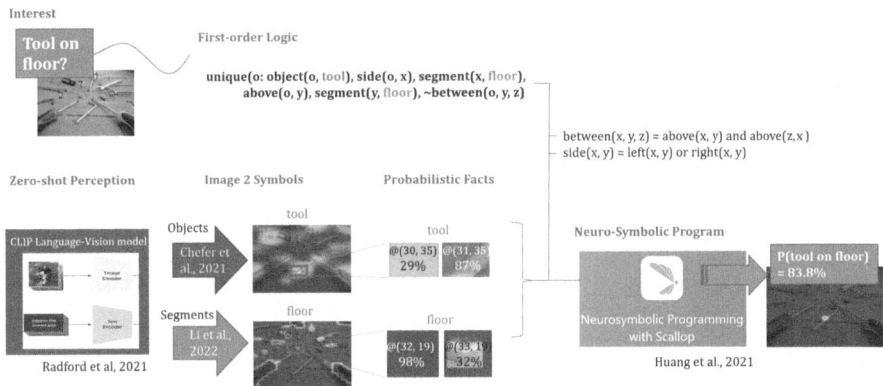

Fig. 1. Finding spatial configurations of object categories in an open world. A configuration is specified by first-order logic. The symbols relate to (possibly novel) objects that are extracted from images in a zero-shot, probabilistic manner. A neuro-symbolic program validates hypotheses.

We start by defining the configuration of interest by first-order logic. Logic formulas specify the object categories and their spatial configuration in terms of relations between them. For flexibility and generalization, the logic formulas may entail the categories of the objects (tool), instead of the specific objects (hammer, screwdriver, etc.). This reduces the amount of human effort. The logic formulas are symbolic, where each relation and object (category) is expressed as a symbol. Each symbol is used as a query to generate object proposals for the current image. Object proposals are generated from language-vision models [9,19,20], by querying them for the symbols that are in the logic formulas. In the image, there may be many objects and their proposals will be imperfect, leading to many possible hypotheses. Therefore, a multi-hypothesis framework is required. A natural choice is to leverage a neuro-symbolic program [5,6,8] for this purpose, as it validates the logic formulas against many hypotheses about the object proposals and the relations between them. Our method is outlined in Fig. 1. Our contribution is the integration of the neuro-symbolic programming (reasoning) with the language-vision models (learned) for the purpose of finding spatial configurations of objects. We show the effectiveness on real-world images by finding specific situations in a robotic inspection setting.

2   Related Work

To operate in an open world, it is essential to interpret situations well. One aspect of such interpretation is to analyze configurations of objects in the scene. A typical approach is to incorporate prior knowledge when analyzing images [15]. Connecting knowledge representation and reasoning mechanisms with deep learning models [5] shows great promise for learning from the environment and at the same time reasoning about what has been learned [6]. Previous reasoning methods based on logic, such as DeepProbLog [11,12], were limited in terms of scalability when there were many possible hypotheses. For instance, a task such as industrial inspection involves many possible objects and relations and therefore many possible hypotheses. Therefore, such methods were ill-suited for real-world applications. A more efficient variant of DeepProbLog was proposed [13]. Recently, a framework was proposed that further improved the efficiency: the neuro-symbolic programming framework called Scallop [8]. Scallop is based on first-order logic and introduces a tunable parameter k to specify the level of reasoning granularity. It restrains the validation of hypotheses by the top-k proofs. This asymptotically reduces the computational cost while providing relative accuracy guarantees. This is beneficial for our purpose, as we expect many possible hypotheses in complex environments with many objects and imperfect observations. In [8], the neuro-symbolic programming framework was used to reason about visual scenes using a pre-defined set of classes of objects. End-to-end learning between objects and a neuro-symbolic program was proposed to jointly learn visual concepts, words and semantic parsing [14]. Both approaches rely on a fixed set of visual concepts, since a vocabulary, knowledge graph, or learning scheme are involved. We aim to generalize to the open world, extending the vocabulary of logical symbols to previously unseen objects, and enabling one to define symbols at the category level instead of the class level.

For open world settings, perception models have to be applicable for a wide variety of tasks in a broad range of settings. General-purpose vision systems have been proposed, e.g., [7], that are trained on a large set of datasets and tasks. Because some of these models can solve various tasks at the same time, these are coined foundation models [2]. An example of such a complex task is where the model provides answers to textual questions about images [1,15]. Large progress has been achieved in language-vision tasks. Language-vision models learn directly from huge datasets of texts describing images, which offers a broad source of supervision [9,16,19,20]. They have shown great promise to generalize beyond crisp classes and towards semantically related classes. This so-called zero-shot capability is beneficial for recognizing the object categories that are involved in the spatial configuration of interest. Recently, these models were extended with capabilities to localize objects in images via co-attentions [4] and to segment parts of the scene based on textual descriptions [10]. We adopt both methods to relate image parts to respectively objects and segments from the environment, which are relevant for the configuration at hand.

The abovementioned works in language-vision models have made huge progress in learning visual concepts in relation to language and semantics. However, they have not considered a combination with reasoning. We integrate neuro-symbolic programming with language-vision models. To the best of our knowledge, this work is the first to combine neuro-symbolic programming and language-vision models to find spatial configurations of objects in images in an open world setting.

3 Method

We find spatial configurations of object categories, based on prior knowledge about the involved objects and their relations. An overview of our method is shown in Fig. 1. At the top, it shows how a configuration of interest, such as our working example 'tool on floor', is translated into symbolic predicates such as $object(o, tool)$, $segment(x, floor)$ and $above(o, x)$. At the bottom left, the figure shows how the symbols from the predicates, such as 'tool' and 'floor', are measured from images by language-vision models. These measurements are transformed into probabilistic facts, e.g., $P(tool|image)$ and $P(floor|image)$, which are provided to the neuro-symbolic program which validates them against the logic (bottom right). Each component is detailed in the following paragraphs.

3.1 First-Order Logic

The configuration of interest is defined by logic formulas and predicates. The symbols in the predicates are about the objects and segments in an image. For a tool that is left on the floor, the formulas are:

$$\exists o : object(o, tool) \wedge side(o, s_1) \wedge$$
$$segment(s_1, floor) \wedge above(o, s_2) \wedge \qquad (1)$$
$$segment(s_2, floor) \wedge \neg between_{vert}(z, o, s_2)$$

This defines that a tool on the floor is defined by seeing the tool above and aside the floor. For a robot, its perspective is oblique downward, i.e., the floor will be visible at the bottom of the tool and on the side of the tool. We also define that the tool should be on the floor, without anything (z) in between. Otherwise, a tool that is on a cabinet standing on the floor, would also fulfil the definition. The helper predicates are:

$$between_{vert}(o_1, o_2, o_3) = above(o_1, o_2) \wedge above(o_3, o_1)$$
$$side(o_1, o_2) = left(o_1, o_2) \vee right(o_1, o_2) \tag{2}$$

to express that some o_2 is vertically between o_1 and o_3. Finally, these are the predicates for positioning of one object relative to the left, right and above another object:

$$left(o_1, o_2) = pos_x(o_1) < pos_x(o_2)$$
$$right(o_1, o_2) = pos_x(o_1) > pos_x(o_2) \tag{3}$$
$$above(o_1, o_2) = pos_y(o_1) < pos_y(o_2)$$

Another example of a spatial configuration is a leaking pipe. Analogous to the abandoned tool, it can be formulated by predicates that relate objects and segments:

$$\exists o : object(o, pipe) \wedge neighbor(o, s) \wedge$$
$$segment(s, leakage) \tag{4}$$

An additional helper predicate is needed to express that one object is neighboring another object:

$$neighbor(o_1, o_2) = |pos_x(o_1) - pos_x(o_2)| \leq 1 \wedge$$
$$|pos_y(o_1) - pos_y(o_2)| \leq 1 \tag{5}$$

We refer to the set of logic formulas as L.

3.2   Image to Symbols

To find a specified configuration in the current image, the symbols from the logic formulas are used to initiate corresponding image measurements. From the image, measurements are taken that are an estimate of the symbols. We refer to this process as 'image to symbols'. For each logical symbol, we produce a probabilistic fact about that symbol for the given image, e.g., $P(tool|image)$ and $P(floor|image)$. The probabilistic facts are input to the neuro-symbolic inference process (next subsection).

Each symbol generates probabilistic proposals for the image by prompting a language-vision model. For our purpose, we adopt CLIP [19] because we found its performance to be solid for various symbols, even for niche objects (i.e., zero-shot performance [16]). We query CLIP by a text prompt of the symbol, e.g. 'tool'. CLIP operates on the image level, i.e., matching a prompt to the full image. Our objective is different: we aim to localize the symbols, such that we can analyze their spatial configurations within the image. We adopt recent extensions of CLIP that can generate attention maps [4] and segmentation maps [10] for text prompts. The attention maps show where the model is activated regarding objects, as the model is specialized to learn the important objects in images. Hence we use them to localize objects (e.g., tool). However, this model is object-specific and not suitable for environmental elements such as walls and floors. For this purpose, we leverage a segmentation model to segment scenes, in order to localize environmental segments (e.g., floor). In this way, we obtain probabilistic symbols.

The attention maps for the CLIP model are obtained by [4]:

$$\overline{A} = \mathbb{E}_h((\nabla A \odot A)^+) \tag{6}$$

where $\odot$ is the Hadamard product, $\nabla A = \frac{\partial y_k}{\partial A}$ is CLIP's output for a textual prompt T_k, $\mathbb{E}_h$ is the mean across CLIP's transformer heads, and $\cdot^+$ denotes removal of negative contributions [4].

$\overline{A}$ is an attention map and therefore it is not calibrated to probabilistic values. For that purpose, we scale $\overline{A}$ to the range $[0, 1]$ by dividing by its maximum value, thereby we obtain $\overline{A}'$. The values of $\overline{A}'$ are not probabilities. That is, the values are uncalibrated for the prompt T_k, since the maximum value is always 1. To calibrate $\overline{A}'$ for a prompt T_k, we weight $\overline{A}'$ with the confidence for T_k, Y_k: $G(k) = \overline{A}' \odot Y_k$, with $Y = softmax(\{y\})$ for CLIP's outputs $\{y\}_{1:N}$ for the respective set of prompts $\{T\}_{1:N}$. We consider a set of prompts that contrast the objects of interest (e.g., tool) with irrelevant negatives (e.g., wall, floor, closet, ceiling, etc.): $T = \{tool, ..., ceiling\}$. Since $G(k)$ is calculated for an image I at its pixels (i, j), we rewrite: $G(I, i, j, k)$. To obtain a proxy for the probability for the object of interest o at index k from set T, we take: $G(I, i, j, k_o)$. For the full image, we denote the probability map shortly as $G(I, o)$.

To segment image I at image location (i, j), the response to a textual prompt T_k from the set of prompts $\{T\}_{1:N}$ is given by [10]:

$$f(I, i, j, k) = I'(i, j) \cdot T_k', \ k \in \{1, ..., N\} \tag{7}$$

where I' is the visual encoding of image I, T' the textual encoding of prompt T and $\cdot$ is the dot product. The vector f is transformed by the softmax operator to obtain values in the range of $[0, 1]$: $F(I, i, j, :) = softmax(f(I, i, j, :))$. We consider a set of prompts that contrast the segments of interest (e.g., floor) with irrelevant negatives (e.g., wall, ceiling, etc.): $T = \{floor, ..., ceiling\}$. To obtain the proxy of a probability for the segment of interest s at index k from set T, within image I at pixel (i, j), we take: $F(I, i, j, k_s)$. For the full image, we denote the probability map shortly as $F(I, s)$.

Using $F(I, s)$ and $G(I, o)$, we obtain a probability for each symbol from the logic formulas, where for each pixel of image I the probability is stored:

$$\begin{aligned} P(object = o \,|\, I, o) &= G(I, o), \ o \in \{tool, pipe, etc.\} \\ P(segment = s \,|\, I, s) &= F(I, s), \ s \in \{floor, leakage, etc.\} \end{aligned} \tag{8}$$

3.3 Neuro-Symbolic Inference

Inference of the probability for the (spatial) configuration C as defined by L, in the image I is performed by the neuro-symbolic program. This program operates on probabilistic facts [8] which we derive from the symbolic heatmaps $P(s)$ and $P(o)$ (Eq. 8). We consider various spatial scales to infer C, because the distance between the robot and the scene may differ from time to time. As a consequence, the amount of pixels on the objects may vary. The original heatmaps $P(s)$ and $P(o)$ are finegrained. For multi-scale analysis, we add down-sampled versions of them, $P(s, \sigma)$ and $P(o, \sigma)$ at spatial scales $\sigma \in \{1, 2, .., 32\}$ to indicate the down-sampling factor. This enables both finegrained and coarser inference, to accommodate for varying distances from camera to the relevant objects. To achieve scale-invariant inference, we select the scale σ that maximizes the probability $P(C)$ for the spatial configuration C in the current image I given the logic L and its symbols S and O:

$$P(C) = \underset{\sigma \in \{1, 2, 4, 8, 16\}}{\arg\max} \; P(C \mid I, L, \{P(s, \sigma)\}_{s \in S}, \{P(o, \sigma)\}_{o \in O}) \qquad (9)$$

Note that this can be generalized to an optimal scale σ specifically for each segment s and object o in Eq. 9. However, this requires that all possible combinations of s and o at all scales σ are analyzed by the neuro-symbolic program P. This will cause a computational burden. For computational efficiency, we optimize a single scale σ for all s and o.

4 Experiments

To analyze the performance of our method, we collected a wide variety of test images to find various spatial configurations of objects. The configurations are about undesired situations that require action: finding an abandoned tool on the floor inside a factory, and detecting a leaking pipe on an industrial site. We evaluate our method in a zero-shot manner: we use the models without any retraining so they have not been optimized for the tested situations. The purpose of this setup is to validate the method in an open world.

4.1 Abandoned Tool on Floor

We collected 31 test images about an abandoned tool on the floor. To validate how well the method generalizes to various tools, we include images with hammers, screwdrivers, wrenches, etc. For the same reason, we include various floors, with different materials, textures and colors. Moreover, the viewpoint and zoom are varied significantly. There are 9 images of tools on floors. These are the positives which should be detected by our method. To verify true negatives, we include 8 images where there is a both a tool and a floor, but the tool is not on the floor (but on a cabinet, wall, etc.). There are 5 images with only a floor (no tool) and 4 images with only a tool (no floor). To verify true negatives, there are also 5 images where there is no tool and no floor.

There are 9 positives, from which we detect 7 cases. Figure 2a–2d shows 4 out of those 7 cases. Each case is illustrated by showing the original image in the top left and the result of the neuro-symbolic program in the top right. The involved symbols are shown in the lower left and right. The visualizations are heatmaps, where a high probability is red, whereas blue indicates a low probability. For the symbols (lower rows), the full heatmap is shown. For the result of the neuro-symbolic program (top-rights), only the most likely location is shown.

The resolution of the heatmaps indicates the granularity of the reasoning, as it reflects the optimal spatial scale which maximized the resulting probability (Eq. 9). In Fig. 2, most spatial scales are relatively small, indicated by the fine-grained heatmaps. Since the symbols are predicted well (often the tools and floors have a high probability at the respective symbols), the reasoning is able to pinpoint a place in the image where the spatial configuration is fulfilled mostly (a peak in the neuro-symbolic output). In the case of a negative, the probability is typically much lower, as shown in the next paragraph.

Out of the 17 negatives, there are 8 hard cases, as these images contain both a tool and a floor, but not in the defined configuration: the tool is not on the floor. Out of these 8 negatives, 6 are correctly assessed as such. The two errors (i.e., false positives) are shown in the next subsection. Figure 2e and 2f show 2 out of 6 true negatives. Although there are both a floor and tools, the reasoner correctly finds that the spatial configuration is not a tool that is on the floor.

The two false positives are shown in Fig. 3a and 3b. The neuro-symbolic program incorrectly reasons that these cases are a tool left on the floor (false positives). This is due to errors in the symbols. There is a wrong association of the symbol tool in both images. On the left, the Gazelle logo is associated with a tool. We hypothesize that the reason for this flaw is that Gazelle is a manufacturer of bicycles: many images on the web about this brand involve tools. The language-vision model probably has learned a bias to associate Gazelle with tools. On the right, the duct tape is considered to be a tool. From a semantic point of view this makes sense. These symbol errors propagate into the reasoner's outputs. Refining the prompts that we pose to the language-vision models, may overcome such errors in the symbols.

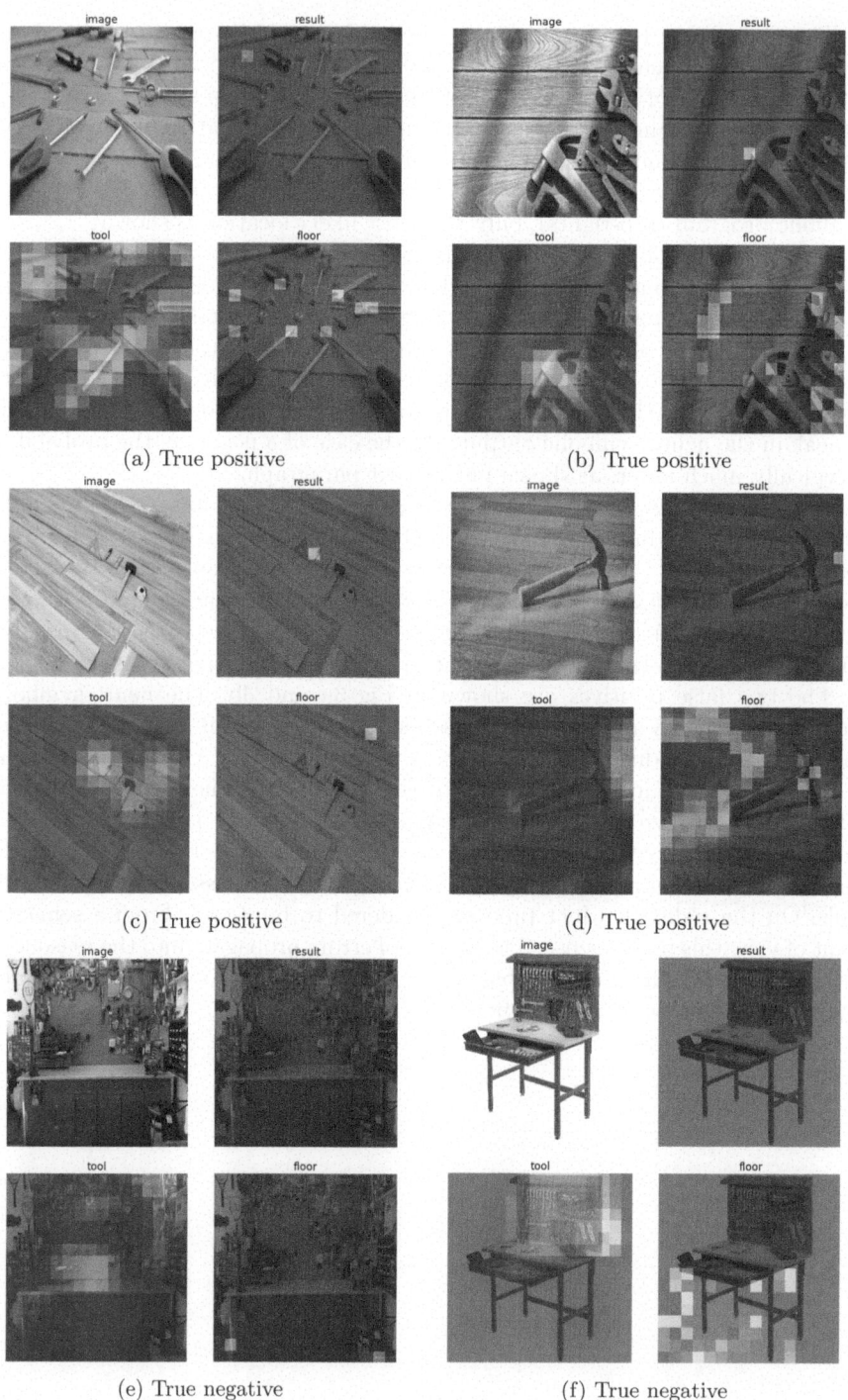

Fig. 2. Tool on floor: good predictions.

Figure 3c and 3d show missed cases (false negatives). Again, the source of the errors is in the symbols. On the left, the tool (a grinder) is not recognized as such. This is a flaw in the language-vision model, probably because this tool does not appear often in everyday images and language. On the right, the floor is not recognized as such. We hypothesize that this is due to a lack of context within the image: it could also be a wooden plate. Without the proper evidence for each involved symbol, the reasoner cannot assess these configurations correctly. The computation time per image is approximately 1 s on a standard CPU without any optimization of efficiency.

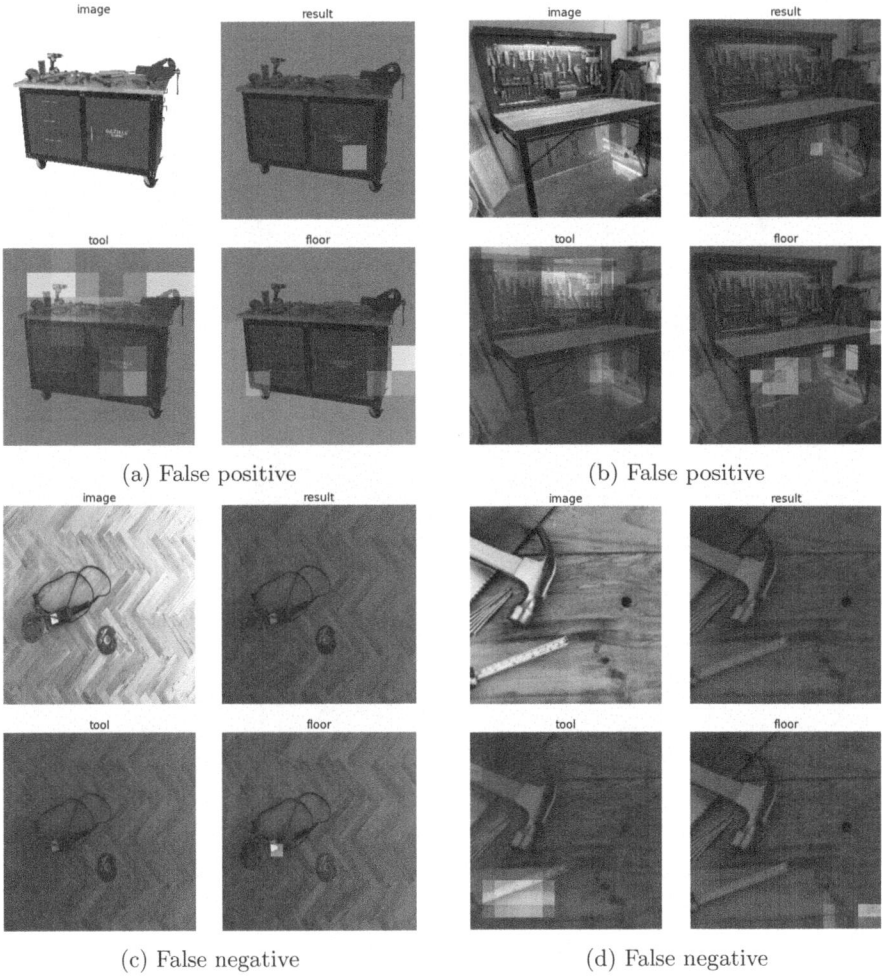

(a) False positive   (b) False positive

(c) False negative   (d) False negative

Fig. 3. Tool on floor: errors.

4.2   Leaking Pipe

The second experiment is about another task: to find a leaking pipe. We collected 15 images of very different cases with various pipes and leaking fluids. Likewise the abandoned tool, we include various viewpoints and distances to the scenes.

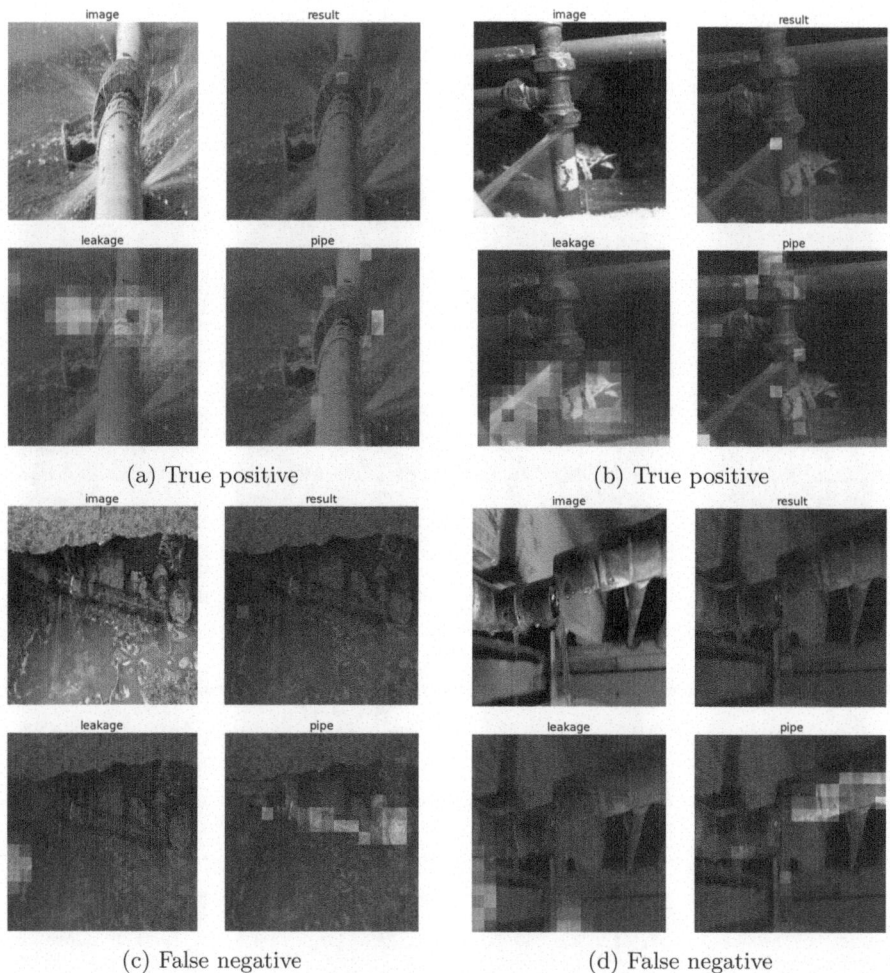

(a) True positive   (b) True positive

(c) False negative   (d) False negative

Fig. 4. Leaking pipe.

There are 15 positives, from which we detect 13 cases. Figure 4a and 4b show 2 out of those 13 cases. The organization of the figure is the same as previous result figures. Although the scenes are very different, the symbols are predicted well. Often the pipes and leakages have a high probability at the respective symbols. The neuro-symbolic program is able to pinpoint a place in the image where the spatial configuration is fulfilled (bright spot in the heatmap).

Out of the 15 actual cases, 2 were considered to be a negative (miss). Figure 4c shows a false negative where the leakage was localized too far away from the pipe. Hence the spatial arrangement did not fulfil the definition and therefore it was not assessed as a leaking pipe. In Fig. 4d there is a false negative, because the left part of the broken pipe was not assessed as such. Therefore the leakage is not close to a part in the image that was considered as a pipe.

4.3 Performance and Ablations

The performance is evaluated by ROC curves as shown in Fig. 5. Our neuro-symbolic program is compared against baselines that use partial information (only the tool or only the floor) and a baseline that uses the same information (tool and floor) but without the spatial configuration. For ablation, three variants of the neuro-symbolic program are evaluated, each having more contextual knowledge and multi-scale reasoning.

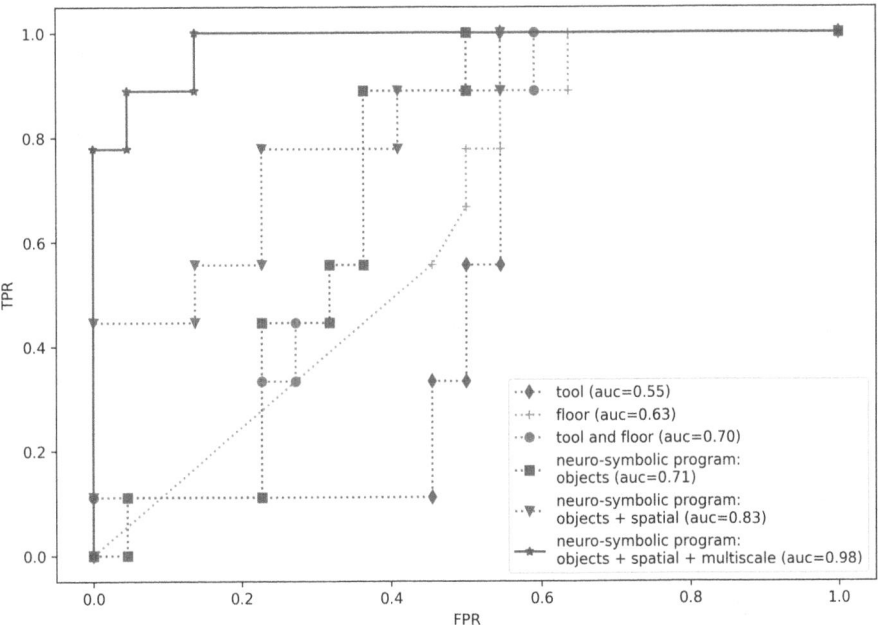

Fig. 5. ROC curves for abandoned tool on floor. The neuro-symbolic program is more effective than alternative combinations of tool and floor. Spatial information and multi-scale reasoning are helpful.

It can be concluded that both tool and floor are required, and the spatial configuration is also essential. With only tool and floor as inputs, the performance becomes almost random, resp. AUC = 0.55 and AUC = 0.63. With both inputs, yet without spatial configuration, the performance increases only slightly:

$AUC = 0.70$. Including tool and floor in the neuro-symbolic program, without taking their spatial relations into account, is equally ineffective: $AUC = 0.71$. When the spatial configuration is considered by the neuro-symbolic program, the performance increases significantly: $AUC = 0.83$. Including multi-scale makes the neuro-symbolic program very effective: $AUC = 0.98$. Most of the situations of interest can be detected without false positives, whereas the alternatives produce many false positives.

5   Conclusions

For open world settings, we proposed a method to find spatial configurations of multiple objects in images. It enables expert-driven localization of new or unseen object configurations. Our method is able to find situations of interest in a robotic inspection setting: abandoned tools on floors and leaking pipes. The tools, floors, pipes and leakages have not seen before and no task-specific training was performed. Most of the situations of interest were correctly localized. A few false positives occurred, due to erroneous object proposals. This was caused by a bias in the language-vision model, e.g., a logo of a tool that was considered to be a tool. A few false negatives happened, due to missed object proposals. A typical example is a close-up image of a floor, which was missed because context was lacking. Our method avoids the necessity of learning dedicated models for each of the involved objects, which makes our method flexible and quickly operational in an open world.

References

1. Antol, S., et al.: VQA: visual question answering. In: Proceedings of the IEEE International Conference on Computer Vision, pp. 2425–2433 (2015)
2. Bommasani, R., et al.: On the opportunities and risks of foundation models. arXiv preprint arXiv:2108.07258 (2021)
3. Chandola, V., Banerjee, A., Kumar, V.: Anomaly detection: a survey. ACM Comput. Surv. (CSUR) **41**(3), 1–58 (2009)
4. Chefer, H., Gur, S., Wolf, L.: Generic attention-model explainability for interpreting bi-modal and encoder-decoder transformers. In: Proceedings of the IEEE/CVF International Conference on Computer Vision, pp. 397–406 (2021)
5. De Raedt, L., Dumančić, S., Manhaeve, R., Marra, G.: From statistical relational to neuro-symbolic artificial intelligence. In: International Joint Conference on Artificial Intelligence, pp. 4943–4950 (2020)
6. Garcez, A., Gori, M., Lamb, L.C., Serafini, L., Spranger, M., Tran, S.N.: Neural-symbolic computing: an effective methodology for principled integration of machine learning and reasoning. J. Appl. Logics **6**, 611–632 (2019)
7. Hu, R., Singh, A.: Unit: multimodal multitask learning with a unified transformer. In: Proceedings of the IEEE/CVF International Conference on Computer Vision, pp. 1439–1449 (2021)
8. Huang, J., et al.: Scallop: from probabilistic deductive databases to scalable differentiable reasoning, vol. 34, pp. 25134–25145 (2021)

9. Jia, C., et al.: Scaling up visual and vision-language representation learning with noisy text supervision. In: International Conference on Machine Learning, pp. 4904–4916. PMLR (2021)

10. Li, B., Weinberger, K.Q., Belongie, S., Koltun, V., Ranftl, R.: Language-driven semantic segmentation. In: International Conference on Learning Representations (2022)

11. Manhaeve, R., Dumancic, S., Kimmig, A., Demeester, T., De Raedt, L.D.: Neural probabilistic logic programming. Adv. Neural. Inf. Process. Syst. **31**, 3753–3763 (2021)

12. Manhaeve, R., Dumančić, S., Kimmig, A., Demeester, T., De Raedt, L.: Neural probabilistic logic programming in deepproblog. Artif. Intell. **298**, 103504 (2021)

13. Manhaeve, R., Marra, G., De Raedt, L.: Approximate inference for neural probabilistic logic programming. In: Proceedings of the 18th International Conference on Principles of Knowledge Representation and Reasoning, pp. 475–486. IJCAI Organization (2021)

14. Mao, J., Gan, C., Kohli, P., Tenenbaum, J.B., Wu, J.: The neuro-symbolic concept learner: interpreting scenes, words, and sentences from natural supervision. In: International Conference on Learning Representations. In: International Conference on Learning Representations, ICLR (2019)

15. Marino, K., Rastegari, M., Farhadi, A., Mottaghi, R.: Ok-VQA: a visual question answering benchmark requiring external knowledge. In: Proceedings of the IEEE/CVF Conference on Computer Vision and Pattern Recognition, pp. 3195–3204 (2019)

16. OpenAI (2021). https://openai.com/blog/clip/

17. Pang, G., Shen, C., Cao, L., Hengel, A.V.D.: Deep learning for anomaly detection: a review. ACM Comput. Surv. (CSUR) **54**(2), 1–38 (2021)

18. Paschalidis, I.C., Chen, Y.: Statistical anomaly detection with sensor networks. ACM Trans. Sens. Netw. (TOSN) **7**(2), 1–23 (2010)

19. Radford, A., et al.: Learning transferable visual models from natural language supervision. In: International Conference on Machine Learning, pp. 8748–8763. PMLR (2021)

20. Yuan, L., et al.: Florence: a new foundation model for computer vision. arXiv preprint arXiv:2111.11432 (2021)

The Hidden Influence of Latent Feature Magnitude When Learning with Imbalanced Data

Damien A. Dablain and Nitesh V. Chawla[(⊠)]

Department Computer Science and Lucy Family Institute for Data and Society,
University of Notre Dame, Notre Dame, IN 46553, USA
{ddablain,nchawla}@nd.edu

Abstract. Machine learning (ML) models have difficulty *generalizing* when the number of training class instances are numerically imbalanced. The problem of generalization in the face of data imbalance has largely been attributed to the lack of training data for under-represented classes and to feature overlap. The typical remedy is to implement data augmentation for classes with fewer instances or to assign a higher cost to minority class prediction errors or to undersample the prevalent class. However, we show that one of the central causes of impaired generalization when learning with imbalanced data is the *inherent* manner in which ML models perform inference. These models have difficulty generalizing due to their heavy reliance on the *magnitude* of encoded signals. During inference, the models predict classes based on a combination of encoded signal *magnitudes* that linearly sum to the largest scalar. We demonstrate that even with aggressive data augmentation, which generally improves minority class prediction accuracy, parametric ML models *still* associate a class label with a limited number of feature combinations that sum to a prediction, which can affect generalization.

Keywords: Machine Learning · Imbalanced Data · Deep Learning

1 Introduction

Biological systems transmit neural signals through *spikes*, where *timing* is a key component of the selection and movement of signals through the network [1,32]. In contrast, during inference, many modern ML models, such as convolutional neural networks (CNN), support vector machines (SVM) and logistic regression (LG) classifiers, rely on latent signal *magnitude* to arrive at decisions [25]. We refer to these signal magnitudes, in the final layer of ML models, and before they are summed into scalars or logits for prediction, as *classification embeddings (CE)*. The impact of signal magnitude on model decisions and generalization is often *hidden* because the activation of individual latent features during inference is masked by summation and thresholding operations.

C. Wallraven et al. (Eds.): ICPRAI 2024, LNCS 14892, pp. 76–91, 2025.
https://doi.org/10.1007/978-981-97-8702-9_6

An important problem of ML models is their perceived difficulty in generalizing to imbalanced data (see Supplemental Section S1 for a quantitative analysis) [5,6,23]. To that end, we investigate the importance of latent feature magnitude during the inference phase of supervised classifiers as a potential culprit in generalization for imbalanced data. We select three representative algorithms from the class of parametric ML models: CNN, SVM and LG. We demonstrate the importance of feature magnitude in parametric ML prediction and that these models rely on only a handful of features to predict classes for individual instances in both image and tabular data. In the case of imbalanced classes, the reliance on a few features with out-sized magnitudes prevents adequate generalization. This reliance on a few features for prediction persists even when classes with fewer instances are augmented through several widely used over-sampling techniques.

In this paper, we make the following contributions to the study of imbalanced data:

The importance of latent feature magnitude during inference. We show that parametric ML models rely on a few, high magnitude latent features to predict individual class instances. This observation applies to both majority and minority classes. In the case of image data, a CNN requires approximately 12% of classification embeddings to predict either majority or minority classes. **Minority class over-sampling does *not* meaningfully change the ratio of latent features required for prediction.** Even though we augment minority classes with several over-sampling techniques, the number of latent features required for majority and minority class prediction do not meaningfully change.

Latent feature *magnitude* is directly related to the *frequency* with which the features appear in the training set for image data. This relationship applies in the case of majority and minority classes, and with and without over-sampling.

The number of latent features required to predict an entire class is much larger than the number of features required to predict a single class instance. This implies that parametric ML models learn different *combinations* of latent features for a class.

2   Related Work

Imbalanced learning focuses on how a disparity in the number of class instances affects the training of supervised classifiers. The classes are colloquially referred to as the majority class(es) (with more samples) and the minority class(es) (with fewer samples). Class numerical sample differences may be due to: (1) step imbalance (cliff effect disparity in class samples), or (2) exponential imbalance (a graduated difference in the number of instances in a multi-class setting).

Much of the research on generalization in parametric ML models has been conducted outside of imbalanced learning and has mainly focused on CNNs [2,14,26,27,33,37], where classifiers have difficulty generalizing to slightly harder images than those found in the original dataset [31] and to small changes in model inputs (adversarial examples), without explicit training [18,19,22,36]. In contrast to these approaches, which mainly focus on weight regularization and data augmentation to improve generalization, we focus on the *magnitude* of the feature embeddings learned by parametric ML models as the central culprit in generalization.

Within imbalanced learning, the reason why ML classifiers have difficulty generalizing to classes with fewer instances has been attributed to: numerical class imbalance [23], class overlap [3,11,13,30], subconcepts, and disjuncts [21, 35]. Instead of searching for the problem of generalization in class overlap or numerical class imbalance, we focus on the *summation* function in supervised ML models.

When training ML models with imbalanced data, common techniques that improve generalization with respect to the minority class include: cost-sensitive approaches that increase the penalty of minority class misclassification, ensemble methods, and oversampling the minority class, which is a form of data augmentation [15,20,23]. Oversampling balances the number of class training instances by synthetically increasing the number of minority class instances.

Three representative oversampling techniques that use data augmentation (DA) are: SMOTE [6], ADASYN [16], and REMIX [4]. SMOTE and ADASYN draw samples from the same class (minority class) for augmentation; although ADASYN specifically samples hard-to-classify instances. REMIX integrates mixup [38], which is widely used in balanced image training, into imbalanced learning. It samples instances for augmentation from both the majority and minority classes and uses label smoothing. SMOTE, ADASYN and REMIX all implement DA for class imbalance at the front-end of model training (i.e., on raw input features).

In addition to these methods, we examine two DA techniques that improve generalization for minority classes that work on *latent* features: EOS [8] and DSM [10]. EOS draws samples from adversary classes to synthetically augment minority classes. DSM is based on DeepSMOTE [7], except that it draws same class latent features from the model itself, instead of using a separate auto-encoder.

3   Classification Embedding Motivation

To motivate the importance of signal magnitude to the classification process of parametric ML models, we first define the latent features, or classification embeddings (CE), used in our experiments for LG, CNN, and SVM models. We describe how parametric ML models require that the magnitude of CE for the predicted class be greater than the competing class(es). In this environment, it is possible for only a few latent features (CE) to dominate class prediction, and hence limit model generalization capacity. To simplify our discussion, we assume that LG and SVM models perform binary classification and that CNNs perform multi-class classification. We also assume that inference is performed on each instance, instead of in batches.

LG Classifier. During inference, a LG classifier can be described as:

$$y = \phi(\sum_{i=0}^{F_D} CE_i + b)$$

(1)

where y is a binary label ($y \in \{0,1\}$), ϕ is a thresholding function described below, F_D is the dimension of the features, $\sum CE_i$ is the summation of a vector of classification embeddings and b is a bias term. CE can be described as:

$$CE_i = FE_i \cdot W_i$$

(2)

where the FE is a vector of features and W is a vector of learned weights. For LG models, the real determinant of label prediction during inference is the *summation* of the CE. If the sum of CE plus bias is negative, then the sigmoid and rounding functions will produce a 0 value (class prediction). It will produce a value of 1 (class prediction) if the sum of the CE plus bias term is positive. Thus, the prediction of the LG model is highly dependent on the linear sum of the magnitudes of features contained in a vector of CE, plus a bias term, during inference.

CNN Classifier. The final classification layer in a CNN can be described by Eq. 1; however, there are important differences in ϕ and how FE are encoded for CNNs. For a CNN classification layer, the *argmax* function can be substituted for ϕ so that Eq. 1 becomes:

$$y = argmax(_{c=0}^{C}(\sum_{i=0}^{F_D} CE_i + b_i))_c$$

(3)

where C is the number of classes and the *argmax* returns the index (label) of the class with the largest sum. In a CNN, the FE are described as:

$$FE = pool(f(\cdot))$$

(4)

where *pool* is a pooling function and $f(\cdot)$ is the embedding output of multiple convolution layers [9]. Although FE and related weights are determined through different operations in the LG and CNN models, the *final prediction* is based on the *summation of CE plus a bias term.*

SVM Classifier. For SVMs, Eq. 1 can be rewritten as:

$$y = Sign(\sum_{i=0}^{F_D} CE_i + b)$$

(5)

The Sign function returns a label based on whether the summation is negative (label: 0) or positive (label: 1). During the SVM inference process, the components of CE - FE and W - are also computed differently. In a SVM classifier, FE can be expressed as:

$$FE = K(SV, I_t) \tag{6}$$

where SV are support vectors, I_t is a test instance, and K is a kernel function. Kernel functions can consist of the dot product, polynomial functions, or radial basis functions, which are standard approaches to compute the similarity of two vectors.

Conclusion. In all three models, prediction, and hence generalization, depends on the sum of latent features (CE). In this environment, it is possible for only a handful of CE to dominate, which may limit the ability of the models to generalize to instances not observed during training. This limitation is especially pronounced in the case of imbalanced learning because minority classes, which have a decreased number of training examples, do not contain a sufficient number of instances to ensure class feature diversity. In the following sections, we show that, even with data augmentation to supplement the number of minority class instances, parametric ML models continue to rely on a limited number of CE for prediction, which can limit their generalization capacity when learning with imbalanced data.

4   Experimental Study

We investigate the role of the magnitude of the latent feature (CE) magnitude during the inference process of LG, SVM, and CNN models when learning with imbalanced data. We demonstrate, through our experiments, that regardless of *where* DA is performed (e.g., at the front end of training or in latent space) to improve minority class generalization, ML models still rely on a limited number of CE for prediction when learning with imbalanced data. We base our investigation on the following research questions (RQs):

– **RQ1:** Do parametric ML models rely on a *limited number* of latent features (CE) to predict a *single* instance? If models only rely on a handful of features for single instance predictions, do these features have larger *magnitudes* than nonrelevant features?
– **RQ2:** Do parametric ML models rely on a larger number of CE than in RQ1 to predict a *entire* class? Does this imply that these models rely on any linear combination of CE that sum to a requisite threshold vs. learning invariant features that describe all class instances?
– **RQ3:** Is there a relationship between the latent characteristic *magnitude* and the *frequency* that CE occur in a training set?

For a CNN, we use Resnet-32 and Resnet-56 architectures [17]. We test the LG and SVM classifiers using tabular data and a CNN using image data. For tabular data, we select 5 imbalanced binary classification datasets: Ozone, Scene, Coil, Thyroid and US Crime from the UCI Machine Learning library [12]. For image data, we use 3 imbalanced datasets: CIFAR-10 [24], Places [39], and INaturalist [34]. For tabular data, we compare a baseline model trained with imbalanced data with 3 methods that employ DA at the front end of model training

(SMOTE, ADASYN, and REMIX). For image data, we compare a baseline model trained with imbalanced data with a method (REMIX) that employs DA at the front-end of model training and two that implement DA in latent space (DSM and EOS).

4.1 Image Data Details

This section provides details of the three image datasets: CIFAR-10 [24], Places [39], and INaturalist [34]. The number of class instances in CIFAR-10 is initially balanced, and we imbalance them exponentially, with a 100:1 maximum level. We follow Cao et al.'s [5] exponential imbalance formula for CIFAR-10 (5000, 2997, 1796, 1077, 645, 387, 232, 139, 83, 50). We select five classes from the Places dataset: airfield, amusement park, acquarium, baseball field and barn. The number of class instances is also initially balanced. We employ 10:1 step imbalance (airfield and amusement park with 5K training samples and the rest with 500). We randomly select samples from five classes with the INaturalist dataset: plant, insect, bird, reptile and mammal, with 5:1 step imbalance (plant and insect are the majority classes; bird, reptile and mammal are the minority). We use datasets with 5 to 10 classes because fewer classes allows us to visualize feature distributions. We report our results based on the average of three random permutations of the training sets. Table 1 contains more details of the image training and test sets.

Table 1. Image Datasets

Dataset	# Class	Imbal Type	Max Imbal Level	# Train Maj	# Train Min	# Test Maj	# Test Min
CIFAR-10	10	Expon	100:1	5000	50	1000	1000
Places	5	Step	5:1	2500	500	250	250
INaturalist	5	Step	5:1	6250	1250	500	250

4.2 Tabular Data Details

For tabular data, our dataset selection criteria are: imbalance ratio greater than 10:1, number of samples greater than 1,000, number of features greater than 50, and datasets containing only non-categorical features (i.e., integer and real numbers). The key details of the datasets are summarized in Table 2. We report our results based on the average of 5 randomly drawn splits of the datasets, with a 70:30 training to test split. We select our datasets from the UCI Machine Learning Library [12]

Table 2. Tabular Datasets

Dataset	Imbalance Ratio	# Samples	# Features
Ozone	34:1	2,536	72
Scene	13:1	2,407	294
Coil	16:1	9,822	85
Throid	15:1	3,772	52
US-crime	12:1	1,994	100

4.3   Model Training

For LG and SVM (RBF kernel) models, we use standard classifiers that are publicly available from the SK Learn library with default hyperparameters [29]. For CNN training, we employ the CNN training regime for imbalanced data established by Cao et al. [5], with the following modifications. For CIFAR-10, we train for 200 epochs and for Places and INaturalist, we train for 40 epochs. We use a standard Resnet-32 architecture [17] for CIFAR-10 and a standard Resnet-56 architecture for Places and INaturalist. We use a single NVIDIA 3070 GPU with PyTorch [28].

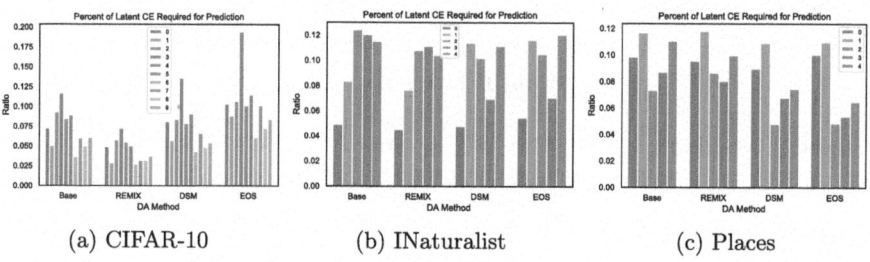

(a) CIFAR-10   (b) INaturalist   (c) Places

Fig. 1. This figure displays the percentage of *CE* (y-axis) that are required to predict a label for a single instance for 3 image datasets. Classes with more samples (majority) have lower class labels (e.g., 0), with the imbalance increasing from left to right, depending on exponential or step. A base model is trained with imbalanced data and 3 models are trained with over-sampling methods (x-axis). With a few exceptions, 12% or fewer *CE* are needed to predict a single instance of a minority or majority class. This holds whether the models are trained with or without minority class DA.

5   Results

5.1   RQ1: Number of Latent Features to Predict an Instance

Figure 1 shows the number of *CE* that are required to predict true positive (TP) instances in 3 image datasets. The results are shown as a percentage of the dimension of the classification embeddings (e.g., dimension of 64 for a Resnet-32). For this purpose, the number of CE needed to exceed the sum of CE of the next largest predicted class for each TP instance was determined. The average number of required CE was then calculated based on 3 splits of each dataset.

In Fig. 1, each class is represented by a different color bar. The bars (classes) are grouped by DA method, with a base model trained on imbalanced data and 3 models for DA methods (REMIX, DSM and EOS). In all cases, only a small percentage of CE are required to predict a label for an instance of a class. With the exception of a single class in CIFAR-10 (class #3 - cats), fewer than 12% of CE are required to predict a TP instance for a class, when averaged over three splits for each method and each dataset. These results hold whether models are trained on imbalanced or augmented data, and whether DA occurs in real or latent space.

Figure 2 shows the percentage of latent features (CE) that are required to correctly predict an instance in 5 tabular datasets using LG models. Here, a model is trained on baseline, imbalanced data and with 3 DA methods (SMOTE, ADASYN and REMIX). Overall, the percentage of CE required to predict an instance ranges from a low of 2.5% to just over 40%. We hypothesize that LG

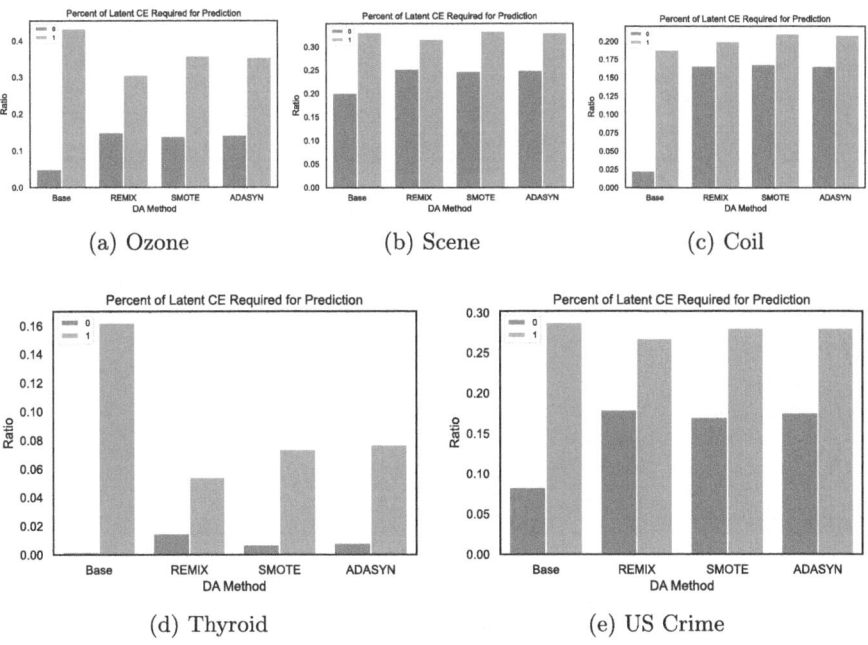

(a) Ozone   (b) Scene   (c) Coil

(d) Thyroid   (e) US Crime

Fig. 2. This figure displays the percentage of CE (y-axis) required to predict a *single instance* for LG models on 5 tabular datasets. Class 0 (blue) denotes the majority and class 1 (brown) is the minority. A base model is trained on imbalanced data and 3 models are trained with over-sampling. For all datasets, more CE are required to predict minority classes, both with and without over-sampling. (Color figure online)

models generally require more *CE* to predict an instance than CNN models because deep CNNs learn a more compact embedding of the input than single layer LG models.

For all datasets in the case of LG classifiers, more *CE* are required to correctly predict minority class instances (class #1, with brown bars) than majority class instances (class #0, with blue bars).

In the case of base models trained on imbalanced data, there is a wide gap; however, DA methods narrow the gap such that the number of *CE* required to predict the two classes is more evenly balanced. We hypothesize that the reason why over-sampling narrows this gap is because single layer LG models have more difficulty predicting majority classes when the number of minority class instances is augmented; hence, they require more *CE* for majority class instances.

Figure 3 displays the percentage of *CE* that are required, on average, to correctly predict a class using SVM models for 5 tabular datasets. The models are trained with base, imbalanced data and 3 different DA methods. In contrast to the CNN and LG examples presented above, SVM models rely on a much larger percentage of *CE* (and support vectors) to correctly predict class labels.

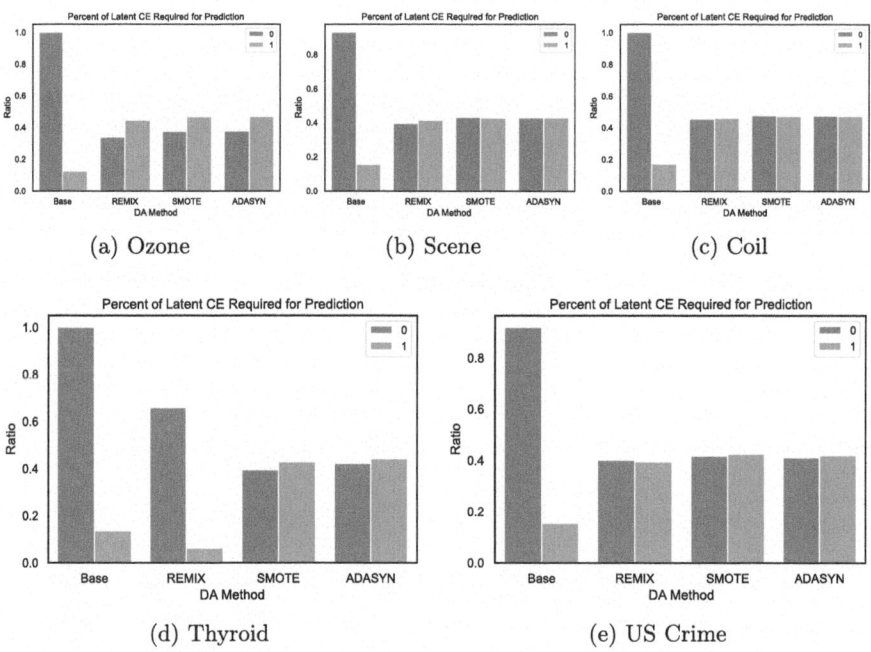

Fig. 3. This figure displays the percentage of *CE* required to predict a single instance using SVM models for 5 UCI tabular datasets. Blue bars denote majority, and brown bars denote minority, classes. When training with base (imbalanced) data, majority class instances require, on average, almost all *CE* for prediction; however, when trained with SMOTE and ADASYN, and in some cases with REMIX, the percentage of *CE* falls to approx. 40% for both majority and minority classes. (Color figure online)

In the base, imbalanced models, nearly 100% of CE are required to predict the majority class, which may be indicative of a high degree of memorization and a less efficient encoding.

In SVM models, with the exception of REMIX in the Thyroid dataset, DA causes the number of CE required to predict majority and minority classes to be more evenly balanced - at ≈40% for models trained with DA.

Figure 4 compares the number of CE required to predict a single instance versus the number of CE required to predict an entire class. The number of CE to predict an entire class is the number of unique CE indices compiled from the top-10 CE for each TP instance in a class. For multi-class datasets, such as CIFAR-10, Places and INaturalist, we split the datasets into the majority class(es) and minority class(es). The majority class is the class with the most instances (two classes in the case of Places and INaturalist, which have step imbalance and one class in the case of CIFAR-10). The minority class(es) are all other classes. In cases where multiple classes are combined, we average the

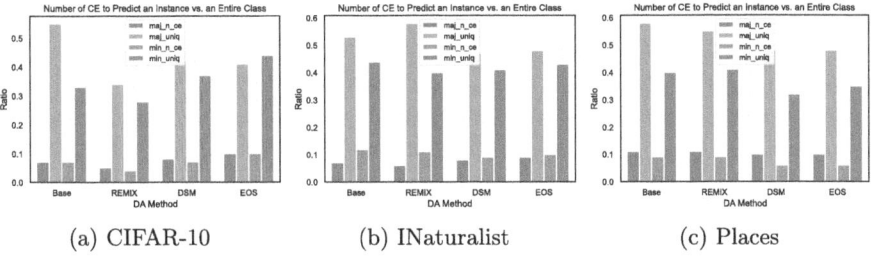

(a) CIFAR-10   (b) INaturalist   (c) Places

Fig. 4. This figure compares the number of CE or features required to predict an *instance* versus the number of CE required to predict an *entire class*.

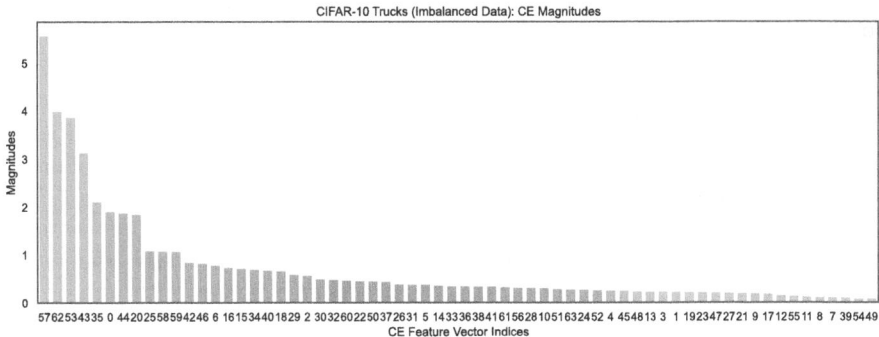

Fig. 5. This figure illustrates that, out of a total of 64 latent features in a Resnet-32 model trained to predict the CIFAR-10 truck class, only a handful of features have large feature magnitudes (y-axis). This figure depicts the minority class (class #9 - trucks). The indices of the latent features are shown on the x-axis.

number of *CE* required to make predictions. We express the number of *CE* as a percentage of the total dimension of the classification embeddings. In the figure, the number of *CE* required to predict a majority instance is denoted in blue and a minority instance in green. The number of unique latent features (*CE*) needed to predict *all* instances in a class is denoted in orange for majority classes and red for minority classes. In all cases, a relatively low number of *CE* are required to predict an individual class *instance* (blue and green for majority and minority classes, respectively) and more are required to define *all* class instances (orange and red for majority and minority classes, respectively). This implies that the *identity* of the features (*CE*) required to predict individual instances varies across all class instances.

5.2   RQ2: Importance of Feature Magnitude

Figure 5 visualizes the importance of feature magnitude to label prediction during the inference process of parametric ML models. Here, the mean magnitudes averaged across all class instances represent the output of the feature maps that serve as latent input to the final classification layer in a CNN. In this figure, the model is trained with imbalanced CIFAR-10 data (trucks are the class with the fewest number of training instances). The mean magnitudes of the pooled feature maps are sorted to show their relative size and are averaged across all instances in the truck class. We can see that the magnitude of only a few feature indices dominate, with the vector locations of the features listed on the x-axis.

Figure 6 shows the percentage that the *CE* with the largest magnitudes contribute to correct predictions (true positives). For CNN classification, the percentage is expressed as the sum of the top-10% of *CE* (i.e., the 10% of *CE* with the largest magnitude) divided by the sum of all positively signed *CE* (i.e., *CE* with a magnitude greater than zero). For LG and SVM models performing binary classification, the percentage is expressed as the sum of the top-10% of *CE* divided by the sum of the appropriately signed *CE* (i.e., negative for 0 label and positive for 1 label). We report the percentages for models trained with imbalanced data (base) and DA methods.

For the LG and CNN models, on average, the top-10% of *CE* contributed between 40% and over 80% toward the class prediction (summation). For all image datasets, the average contribution of the top-10% of *CE* was 66.7% and for LG models trained on tabular data, the average was 62.8%. These percentages include both models trained with imbalanced data and synthetically augmented data. In the case of SVM models, the percentages were lower, with an average of 31.6% for the top-10 *CE*.

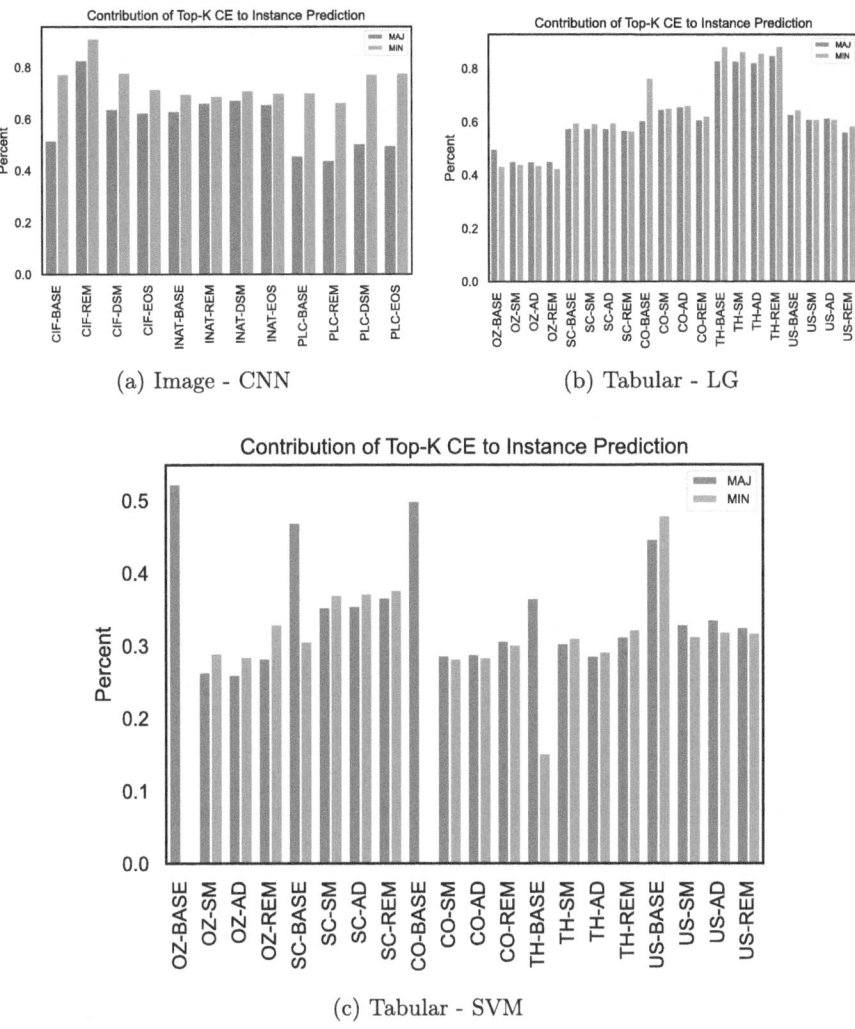

(a) Image - CNN   (b) Tabular - LG

(c) Tabular - SVM

Fig. 6. This figure displays the contribution of the top-10% of CE with the largest average magnitudes. Here, the majority class(es) are blue and minority class(es) are orange. On the x-axis, the models trained with the respective data are presented and the ratio of the contribution of the top-10% of CE with the largest average magnitudes to the total average class CE is shown on the y-axis.

These results confirm that the final prediction in these models is based on the propagation of high-valued (magnitude) signals through one-layer (LG and SVM) or multi-layer (CNN) networks. Only a handful of features matter to the final prediction and those features have larger magnitudes than the features that contribute little to the final prediction.

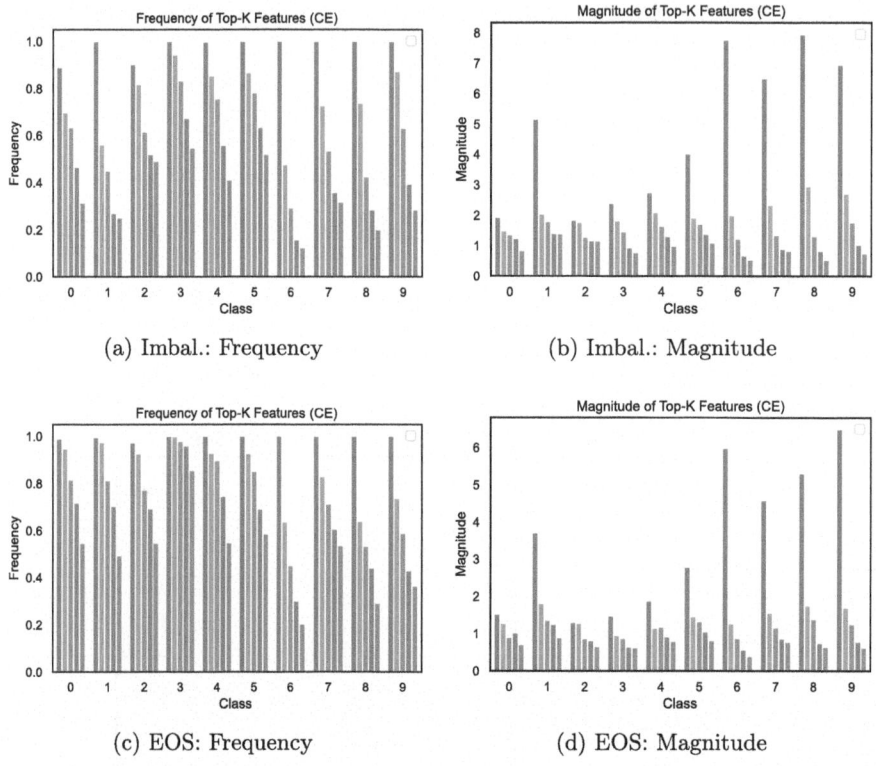

(a) Imbal.: Frequency

(b) Imbal.: Magnitude

(c) EOS: Frequency

(d) EOS: Magnitude

Fig. 7. This figure illustrates the relationship between the frequency with which features (CE) are used to predict instances in a class and their magnitude for CIFAR-10. It illustrates a base model trained with imbalanced data and a model trained with augmented minority latent features using EOS. It shows the top-5 features with the highest mean magnitude for each class and the corresponding frequency with which those CE appear in the training set. For all classes and with and without over-sampling, there is a clear relationship between magnitude and frequency - the magnitude of the feature declines as the frequency of that feature declines.

5.3   RQ3: Feature Frequency and Magnitude

Figure 7 illustrates the relationship between the frequency with which CE are used to predict instances in a class and their magnitude. For CIFAR-10, we show the frequency and the magnitude of the top-5 CE for each class for a model trained with imbalanced data. The CE with the highest frequency are sorted and displayed and then the magnitudes of the respective CE are shown. In the case of CIFAR-10 CE, there is a clear correspondence between frequency and magnitude. In other words, the CE, or encoded features, that occur with the highest frequency in each class also have the largest magnitudes. There is a clear matching of declining frequency and declining magnitude. In the figure, this relationship exists in CNNs trained with imbalanced and augmented data (EOS).

This relationship is evident in other tested image datasets (Places and INaturalist) and DA methods; but not in tabular data. For more details, see https://github.com/dd1github/Hidden_Influence_Magnitude.

6   Conclusion

In this paper, we investigate the importance of latent signal magnitude to generalization. We show that generalization depends on the linear summation of latent features in classification layers. In this environment, it is possible for only a few latent features to dominant class prediction, which can limit the ability of ML models to generalize for classes with fewer, less diverse, training examples. Thus, the difficulty that parametric ML models have with minority class generalization can be traced, in part, to the inherent nature in which these models predict. Through our experiments, this study contributes an important, although often overlooked and hidden, factor that limits the ability of parametric ML models to generalize in the face of class imbalance.

References

1. Abeles, M., et al.: Spatiotemporal firing patterns in the frontal cortex of behaving monkeys. J. Neurophysiol. **70**(4), 1629–1638 (1993)
2. Arpit, D., et al.: A closer look at memorization in deep networks. In: International Conference on Machine Learning, pp. 233–242. PMLR (2017)
3. Batista, G.E., Prati, R.C., Monard, M.C.: A study of the behavior of several methods for balancing machine learning training data. ACM SIGKDD Explor. Newsl. **6**(1), 20–29 (2004)
4. Bellinger, C., Corizzo, R., Japkowicz, N.: Remix: calibrated resampling for class imbalance in deep learning. arXiv preprint arXiv:2012.02312 (2020)
5. Cao, K., et al.: Learning imbalanced datasets with label-distribution aware margin loss. arXiv preprint arXiv:1906.07413 (2019)
6. Chawla, N.V., et al.: SMOTE: synthetic minority over-sampling technique. J. Artif. Intell. Res. **16**, 321–357 (2002)
7. Dablain, D., Krawczyk, B., Chawla, N.V.: DeepSMOTE: fusing deep learning and SMOTE for imbalanced data. IEEE Trans. Neural Netw. Learn. Syst. (2022)
8. Dablain, D., et al.: Efficient augmentation for imbalanced deep learning. In: IEEE 39th International Conference on Data Engineering (2023)
9. Dablain, D., et al.: Understanding CNN fragility when learning with imbalanced data. Mach. Learn. (2023)
10. Dablain, D.A., Chawla, N.V.: Towards understanding how data augmentation works with imbalanced data. arXiv preprint arXiv:2304.05895 (2023)
11. Denil, M., Trappenberg, T.: Overlap versus imbalance. In: Canadian Conference on Artificial Intelligence, pp. 220–231. Springer (2010)
12. Dua, D., Graff, C.: UCI Machine Learning Repository (2017). http://archive.ics.uci.edu/ml

13. Garca, V., Sánchez, J., Mollineda, R.: An empirical study of the behavior of classifiers on imbalanced and overlapped data sets. In: Iberoamerican Congress on Pattern Recognition, pp. 397–406. Springer (2007)
14. Geirhos, R., et al.: Shortcut learning in deep neural networks. Nat. Mach. Intell. **2**(11), 665–673 (2020)
15. He, H., Garcia, E.A.: Learning from imbalanced data. IEEE Trans. Knowl. Data Eng. **21**(9), 1263–1284 (2009)
16. He, H.: ADASYN: adaptive synthetic sampling approach for imbalanced learning. In: IEEE International Joint Conference on Neural Networks (IEEE World Congress on Computational Intelligence), pp. 1322–1328. IEEE (2008)
17. He, K., et al.: Deep residual learning for image recognition. In: Proceedings of the IEEE Conference on Computer Vision and Pattern Recognition, pp. 770–778 (2016)
18. Hendrycks, D., Dietterich, T.: Benchmarking neural network robustness to common corruptions and perturbations. arXiv preprint arXiv:1903.12261 (2019)
19. Huber, L.S., Geirhos, R., Wichmann, F.A.: A four-year-old can outperform resnet-50: out-of-distribution robustness may not require large-scale experience. In: SVRHM 2021 Workshop@ NeurIPS (2021)
20. Japkowicz, N., Stephen, S.: The class imbalance problem: a systematic study. Intell. Data Anal. **6**(5), 429–449 (2002)
21. Jo, T., Japkowicz, N.: Class imbalances versus small disjuncts. ACM SIGKDD Explor. Newsl. **6**(1), 40–49 (2004)
22. Kolesnikov, A., et al.: Big Transfer (BiT): general visual representation learning. In: Vedaldi, A., Bischof, H., Brox, T., Frahm, J.-M. (eds.) ECCV 2020. LNCS, vol. 12350, pp. 491–507. Springer, Cham (2020). https://doi.org/10.1007/978-3-030-58558-7_29
23. Krawczyk, B.: Learning from imbalanced data: open challenges and future directions. Progress Artif. Intell. **5**(4), 221–232 (2016)
24. Krizhevsky, A., Hinton, G., et al.: Learning multiple layers of features from tiny images (2009)
25. Maass, W.: Networks of spiking neurons: the third generation of neural network models. Neural Netw. **10**(9), 1659–1671 (1997)
26. Neyshabur, B., Tomioka, R., Srebro, N.: In search of the real inductive bias: on the role of implicit regularization in deep learning. arXiv preprint arXiv:1412.6614 (2014)
27. Neyshabur, B., et al.: Exploring generalization in deep learning. In: Advances in Neural Information Processing Systems, vol. 30 (2017)
28. Paszke, A., et al.: Automatic differentiation in PyTorch (2017)
29. Pedregosa, F., et al.: Scikit-learn: machine learning in Python. J. Mach. Learn. Res. **12**, 2825–2830 (2011)
30. Prati, R.C., Batista, G.E., Monard, M.C.: Class imbalances versus class overlapping: an analysis of a learning system behavior. In: Mexican International Conference on Artificial Intelligence, pp. 312–321. Springer (2004)
31. Recht, B., et al.: Do imagenet classifiers generalize to imagenet? In: International Conference on Machine Learning, pp. 5389–5400. PMLR (2019)
32. Sejnowski, T.J.: Time for a new neural code? Nature **376**, 21–22 (1995)
33. Shah, H., et al.: The pitfalls of simplicity bias in neural networks. Adv. Neural. Inf. Process. Syst. **33**, 9573–9585 (2020)
34. Van Horn, G., et al.: The inaturalist species classification and detection dataset. In: Proceedings of the IEEE Conference on Computer Vision and Pattern Recognition, pp. 8769–8778 (2018)

35. Weiss, G.M.: Mining with rarity: a unifying framework. ACM SIGKDD Explor. Newsl. **6**(1), 7–19 (2004)
36. Yalniz, I.Z., et al.: Billion-scale semi-supervised learning for image classification. arXiv preprint arXiv:1905.00546 (2019)
37. Zhang, C., et al.: Understanding deep learning (still) requires rethinking generalization. Commun. ACM **64**(3), 107–115 (2021)
38. Zhang, H., et al.: Mixup: beyond empirical risk minimization. arXiv preprint arXiv:1710.09412 (2017)
39. Zhou, B., et al.: Places: a 10 million image database for scene recognition. IEEE Trans. Pattern Anal. Mach. Intell. (2017)

AM-SORT: Adaptable Motion Predictor with Historical Trajectory Embedding for Multi-Object Tracking

Vitaliy Kim⬤, Gunho Jung⬤, and Seong-Whan Lee[✉]⬤

Department of Artificial Intelligence, Korea University, Seoul, Republic of Korea
{vitaliy,gh_jung,sw.lee}@korea.ac.kr

Abstract. Many multi-object tracking (MOT) approaches, which employ the Kalman Filter as a motion predictor, assume constant velocity and Gaussian-distributed filtering noises. These assumptions render the Kalman Filter-based trackers effective in linear motion scenarios. However, these linear assumptions serve as a key limitation when estimating future object locations within scenarios involving non-linear motion and occlusions. To address this issue, we propose a motion-based MOT approach with an adaptable motion predictor, called AM-SORT, which adapts to estimate non-linear uncertainties. AM-SORT is a novel extension of the SORT-series trackers that supersedes the Kalman Filter with the transformer architecture as a motion predictor. We introduce a historical trajectory embedding that empowers the transformer to extract spatio-temporal features from a sequence of bounding boxes. AM-SORT achieves competitive performance compared to state-of-the-art trackers on DanceTrack, with 56.3 IDF1 and 55.6 HOTA. We conduct extensive experiments to demonstrate the effectiveness of our method in predicting non-linear movement under occlusions.

Keywords: Multi-object tracking · Adaptable motion predictor · Non-linear motion · Historical trajectory embedding

1 Introduction

Motion-based multi-object tracking (MOT) approaches [2,3,17,22,23,29,31,36] utilize a motion predictor to extract spatio-temporal patterns and estimate object motion in future frames for subsequent object association. The original Kalman Filter [13] is widely employed as a motion predictor, which operates under assumptions of constant velocity and Gaussian-distributed noises in the prediction and filtering stages, respectively [2]. Constant velocity postulates that object speed and direction remain consistent over a short period, and Gaussian distributions assume constant error variance in both estimations and detections. While these assumptions result in resource efficiency for the Kalman Filter by simplifying mathematical modeling, they are only valid for a specific scenario where the object displacement remains linear or consistently small at each time

© The Author(s), under exclusive license to Springer Nature Singapore Pte Ltd. 2025
C. Wallraven et al. (Eds.): ICPRAI 2024, LNCS 14892, pp. 92–107, 2025.
https://doi.org/10.1007/978-981-97-8702-9_7

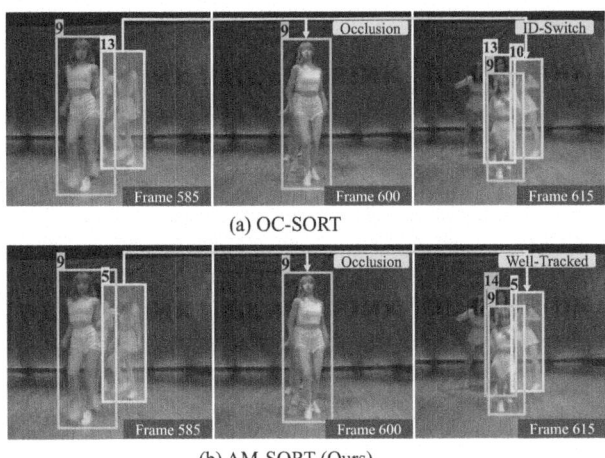

(a) OC-SORT

(b) AM-SORT (Ours)

Fig. 1. Results on *dancetrack0004* sequence from DanceTrack for (a) OC-SORT and (b) AM-SORT (Ours). The object, marked in yellow, moves to the left and becomes occluded in the middle frame. Then, the yellow object changes the movement direction to the right after occlusion, and OC-SORT does not capture this sudden directional shift, causing an ID-switch from 13 to 10. (Color figure online)

step [31]. Due to the neglect of scenarios with non-linear motion and occlusions, the Kalman Filter inaccurately estimates object locations in complex situations.

To address the limitations of the original Kalman Filter, alternative estimation algorithms were proposed, such as Extended Kalman Filter (EKF) [26] and Unscented Kalman Filter (UKF) [12]. EKF linearizes object motion modeling, and UKF estimates non-linear transformations by employing the first and third-order Taylor series expansions, respectively. However, both methods are still conditioned on linear approximations for non-linear systems and assume Gaussian-distributed noises. On the other hand, particle filters [11] avoid linearization by utilizing a set of discrete particles to handle non-linearity and non-Gaussian noises, yet require expensive computational resources. Recent OC-SORT [3] improved the original Kalman Filter by placing a greater emphasis on observations rather than estimations to reduce noises in motion prediction. While this approach allows for tracking objects with linear motion during occlusions, OC-SORT still faces challenges with non-linear motion. When the lack of observations occurs caused by non-linear motion or occlusions, OC-SORT relies on its linear estimations, formulated upon the linear assumptions inherent to the Kalman Filter. Consequently, this linear assumption-based modeling accumulates errors in motion prediction leading to significant trajectory deviations.

We argue that the linear assumptions inherent to the Kalman Filter lead to inaccurate motion estimations and false identity matches when objects involve non-linear uncertainties characterized by sudden speed changes, directional shifts and occlusions. Due to these assumptions, the accumulated errors in motion

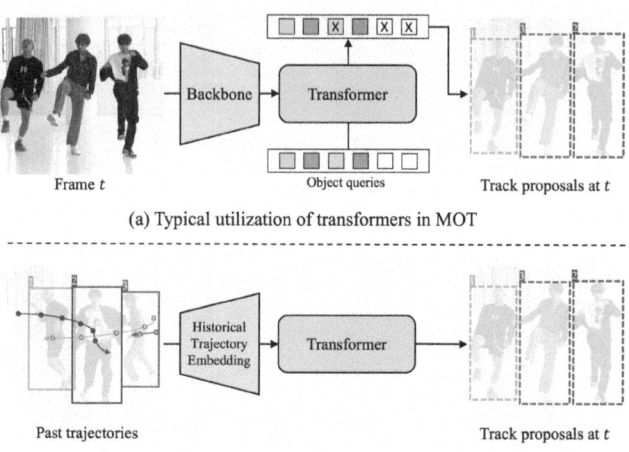

(a) Typical utilization of transformers in MOT

(b) Our utilization of the transformer as an adaptable motion predictor

Fig. 2. Comparison of (a) conventional transformer-based MOT and (b) our frameworks. The key difference lies in the input feature level: typical transformer-based approaches take frames as input and primarily utilize appearance information, whereas AM-SORT processes bounding boxes and solely relies on motion information.

estimations restrict the Kalman Filter-based approaches in handling non-linear uncertainties. Figure 1 shows tracking results in a non-linear motion scenario under occlusion using (a) OC-SORT and (b) our AM-SORT. As illustrated in Fig. 1(a), the identity switch occurs for the yellow object after an occlusion event. The linear motion assumptions in the Kalman Filter cause directional errors in motion estimations that the yellow object continues moving to the left. As a result, the Kalman Filter relies on these linear estimations with accumulated directional errors, failing to predict the directional shift to the right.

In this paper, we propose an adaptable motion predictor with historical trajectory embedding for MOT that addresses the limitations of the linear assumptions inherent to the Kalman Filter. The adaptation ability releases the motion predictor from the constraints of linear assumptions, allowing it to estimate uncertainties related to non-linear motion. Inspired by transformer architectures [6,10,30], known for their ability to capture complex dependencies in sequence data, we explore the utilizing of a transformer encoder as an adaptable motion predictor. In contrast to conventional transformer-based MOT approaches, we leverage the transformer to encode only motion information without visual features for object association, as shown in Fig. 2. Utilizing bounding boxes as input features provides a limited object representation compared to appearance information but significantly reduces computational complexity. To maintain simplicity and resource efficiency comparable to the Kalman Filter, we focus on the transformer encoder to learn object discrimination features exclusively from object trajectories.

Furthermore, our adaptable motion predictor derives benefits from analyzing and observing longer object trajectories compared to the Kalman Filter, which predicts object motion solely based on estimations from the previous time step. To enhance the representation of long object trajectories, we present historical trajectory embedding that encodes the spatio-temporal information from the sequence of bounding boxes. Consequently, we concatenate the embedded bounding boxes with a prediction token that functions as an embedded bounding box of the current frame. The encoder extracts the spatio-temporal features from the historical trajectory embedding, enabling the prediction token to estimate the bounding box in the current frame. Notably, AM-SORT utilizes sequences of bounding boxes as input, omitting the visual features of objects, which enables the model to process with low computational cost.

Our contributions are summarized as follows:

- We propose a novel SORT-series tracker with an adaptable motion predictor, called AM-SORT, which provides non-linear motion estimations without linear assumptions;
- We introduce historical trajectory embedding to effectively capture motion features from a sequence of bounding boxes;
- The qualitative results show that AM-SORT accurately predicts the non-linear changes in object motion, demonstrating its competitiveness with state-of-the-art approaches.

2 Related Work

2.1 Motion-Based Methods in Multi-Object Tracking

DanceTrack [28] reveals the limitations of appearance-based MOT methods in distinguishing objects that share highly similar visual features. This motivates the development of motion-based and hybrid methods that leverage both appearance and motion information. [1–4,16,24,29,31,36] propose trackers that solely employ motion features without appearance information. CenterTrack [36] introduces an efficient tracker that represents each object as a single point and predicts their associations with minimal input as detections from a pair of frames. PermaTrack [29] addresses the limitations of CenterTrack in recovering objects after occlusions. It assumes object permanence under occlusions and continues modeling the spatio-temporal movement of lost objects. LGM [31] proposes a motion-based model for the vehicle tracking task, leveraging both local and global motion consistencies to track and recover vehicles after occlusions. However, its applicability is limited to tracking vehicles with linear motion, lacking robustness in handling objects with non-linear motion.

Along with these works, the SORT-series trackers [2,3,32,35] utilize the Bayesian estimation [18] as a motion model. For instance, SORT [2] employs the original Kalman Filter [13] with linear assumptions for object motion estimation and the Hungarian matching algorithm [15] to match predictions and

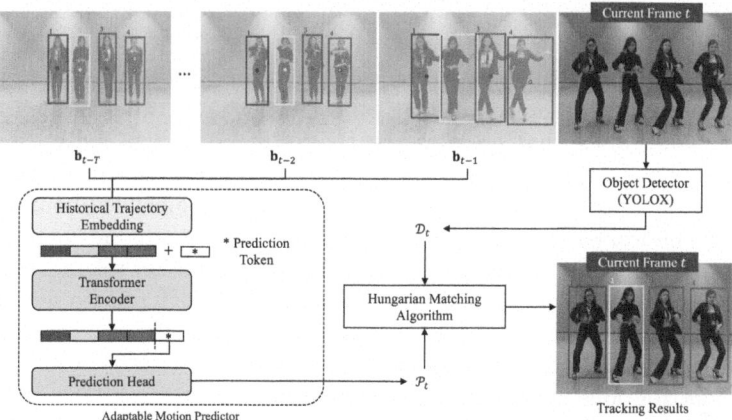

Fig. 3. Illustration of the AM-SORT overall pipeline. The historical trajectory of length T is fed into the transformer encoder to estimate the track predictions $\mathcal{P}_t$. Through utilizing an off-the-shelf detector, detections $\mathcal{D}_t$ are obtained. Subsequently, the Hungarian matching algorithm associates $\mathcal{D}_t$ with $\mathcal{P}_t$, resulting in the final output tracks.

detections. However, as motion features alone offer limited information, Deep-SORT [32] and ByteTrack [35] propose a hybrid method by incorporating the visual features with the Kalman Filter predictions to enhance object discrimination. On the other hand, OC-SORT [3] improves robustness in handling occlusions without appearance information by prioritizing observations instead of linear estimations, but still struggles in recovering lost objects under non-linear motion and long-term occlusions.

2.2 Transformers in Multi-Object Tracking

In scenarios involving non-linear motion and occlusions, transformers demonstrate promising results for their inherent power to model complex interactions and adaptively process sequential information. As shown in Fig. 2(a), the existing transformer-based MOT approaches learn object queries to capture mainly appearance information [8,20,27,34,37]. In particular, TransTrack [27] utilizes the transformer to extract the object-level appearance features and learn the aggregated visual embedding of each object for subsequent IoU-based matching. Since appearance information is sensitive to occlusions, TrackFormer [20], MOTR [34] and MeMOTR [8] jointly model both motion and appearance by representing each object as an autoregressive track query and recurrently propagating them to associate with identical instances across subsequent frames.

In contrast, AM-SORT only leverages motion information, employing simple and lightweight bounding boxes. To the best of our knowledge, AM-SORT stands out as the first successful application of transformers in purely motion-based methods. We believe that AM-SORT will encourage further research on adaptable motion predictors.

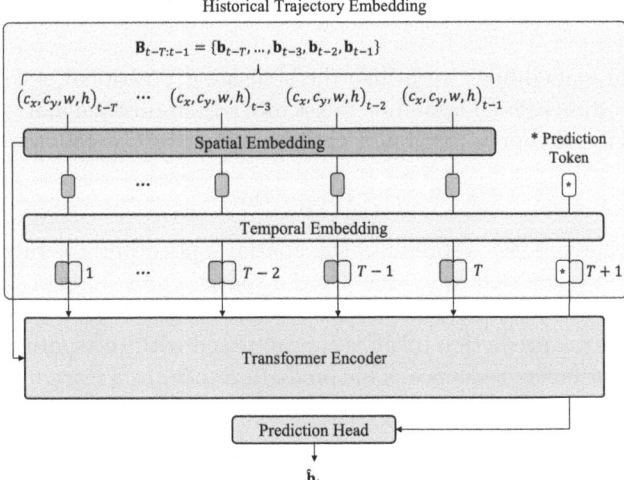

Fig. 4. Illustration of our historical trajectory embedding in the motion predictor. The historical trajectory embedding encodes a comprehensive representation of a bounding box sequence by jointly considering spatio-temporal information.

3 Proposed Method

AM-SORT leverages motion cues to robustly track objects with non-linear motion patterns. Our primary focus is on achieving accurate estimations of non-linear uncertainties by introducing an adaptable motion predictor based on the transformer encoder which supersedes the Kalman Filter. Figure 3 shows the overall pipeline of AM-SORT. Specifically, we input the historical trajectory of an individual object containing a sequence of bounding boxes in the previous frames, denoted as $\mathbf{B}_{t-T:t-1} = \{\mathbf{b}_{t-T}, \ldots, \mathbf{b}_{t-2}, \mathbf{b}_{t-1}\}$, where T is the pre-defined historical trajectory length. The bounding boxes are represented as $\mathbf{b} = (c_x, c_y, w, h)$, where (c_x, c_y) is the center coordinate of the object in the image plane, w and h stand for width and height, respectively. The transformer encoder produces the refined prediction token, which is subsequently converted into a bounding box $\hat{\mathbf{b}}_t$ through the prediction head. The estimated bounding boxes generate a set of track predictions for the current frame, denoted as $\mathcal{P}_t$. Subsequently, detections in the corresponding frame, referred to as $\mathcal{D}_t$, are associated with $\mathcal{P}_t$ based on Intersection-over-Union (IoU) using the Hungarian matching algorithm [15].

3.1 Historical Trajectory Embedding

Historical trajectory embedding jointly encodes the spatial and temporal information from a sequence of bounding boxes and consists of three operations: spatial embedding, prediction token concatenation, and temporal embedding.

Figure 4 illustrates the structure of our historical trajectory embedding in the motion predictor.

For spatial embedding, we utilize the sinusoidal positional encoding [30] to transform low-dimensional bounding boxes into a high-dimensional space to facilitate a fine-grained representation of each bounding box as follows:

$$\mathbf{x}_{t-T} = \text{PE}_{\text{spat}}(\mathbf{b}_{t-T}), \tag{1}$$

where $\text{PE}_{\text{spat}}: \mathbb{R}^4 \to \mathbb{R}^D$ represents the spatial embedding operation, D is an embedding dimension and $\mathbf{x}_{t-T}$ denotes the spatial embedding of the bounding box.

Subsequently, a prediction token is concatenated with the spatial embeddings at the end of the entire sequence. This prediction token is a learnable embedding that functions as a bounding box in the current frame t. The mathematical formulation is as follows:

$$\mathbf{X}_{t-T:\text{pred}} = \text{Concat}(\mathbf{x}_{t-T}, \ldots, \mathbf{x}_{t-1}, \mathbf{x}_{\text{pred}}), \tag{2}$$

where $\mathbf{X}_{t-T:\text{pred}}$ denotes the spatial embedding of the historical trajectory, obtained through the concatenation $\text{Concat}(\cdot)$ of spatial embeddings and the prediction token $\mathbf{x}_{\text{pred}}$.

For temporal embedding, we employ positional encoding similar to spatial embeddings. In contrast, we encode natural numbers which assign serial numbers to each spatial embedding in the sequence in reverse order from $T+1$ to 1, starting from the last element. This ensures that the model prioritizes the terminal part of the historical trajectory embedding, even for objects with historical trajectory lengths less than T. Thus, the historical trajectory embedding is as follows:

$$\mathbf{Z}_{t-T:\text{pred}} = \mathbf{X}_{t-T:\text{pred}} + \text{PE}_{temp}(\mathbb{N}_{T+1:1}), \tag{3}$$

where $\mathbf{Z}_{t-T:\text{pred}}$ represents our historical trajectory embedding, $\text{PE}_{\text{temp}}: \mathbb{R} \to \mathbb{R}^D$ denotes the temporal embedding and $\mathbb{N}_{T+1:1}$ is a sequence of natural numbers from $T+1$ to 1.

Notably, in the context of bounding box prediction where object localization is crucial, we enrich the historical trajectory embedding with additional spatial information before passing it through each encoder layer.

3.2 Adaptable Motion Predictor

We utilize the transformer encoder as an adaptable motion predictor, which contains multi-head self-attention (MHSA) [30] layers and feed-forward neural networks. MHSA facilitates interactions among each bounding box within the historical trajectory extracting their non-linear relationships. This process refines the prediction token with sufficient information for precise localization of the object bounding box in the current frame, formulated as:

$$\hat{\mathbf{Z}}_{t-T:\text{pred}} = \text{Enc}(\mathbf{Z}_{t-T:\text{pred}}), \tag{4}$$

where $\text{Enc}(\cdot)$ represents the transformer encoder operations, with $\hat{\mathbf{Z}}_{t-T:\text{pred}}$ denoting the refined historical trajectory embedding. The prediction head receives only the prediction token $\hat{\mathbf{z}}_{\text{pred}}$, which is the last element in the refined historical trajectory embedding, and utilizes it to generate the bounding box coordinates as follows:

$$\hat{\mathbf{b}}_t = \text{Head}(\hat{\mathbf{z}}_{\text{pred}}), \tag{5}$$

where $\text{Head}(\cdot)$ denotes the prediction head and $\hat{\mathbf{b}}_t$ is the estimated bounding box in the current frame. The prediction head is composed of three linear layers each accompanied by a ReLU activation function, and the last layer utilizes a Sigmoid activation function to convert the bounding box coordinates in the range between 0 and 1.

3.3   Training

We train our adaptable motion predictor by comparing the predicted bounding boxes with the ground truth. We extract all the trajectories in an entire tracking video and segment them into bounding box sequences of length $T + 1$. The beginning bounding box sequence of each trajectory segment is utilized as a historical trajectory to estimate $\hat{\mathbf{b}}$ at the frame $T + 1$, while the last bounding box $\mathbf{b}$ in the segment is considered as the ground truth. We adopt the L1 loss function as the prediction loss to enhance robustness to outliers, such as errors in object detection and track prediction. Specifically, the estimated attributes $(\hat{c}_x, \hat{c}_y, \hat{w}, \hat{h})$ of bounding box $\hat{\mathbf{b}}$ are compared to the respective attributes of ground truth $\mathbf{b}$ with L1 loss and our total prediction loss $\mathcal{L}_{\text{pred}}$ is computed as the mean value:

$$\mathcal{L}_{\text{pred}}(\hat{\mathbf{b}}, \mathbf{b}) = \frac{1}{4} \sum_i |\hat{b}_i - b_i|, \quad i \in (c_x, c_y, w, h). \tag{6}$$

Masked Tokens. We employ masked tokens as an augmentation strategy to simulate the effect of non-linear motion and occlusions. We mask bounding boxes within historical trajectories with a probability p. Subsequently, the masked bounding boxes are replaced by masked tokens to prevent the encoding of their spatial information. These masked tokens are represented as learnable embeddings, that are initialized with random values and optimized during training. In this manner, we enhance our model to gain a clear comprehension of missing trajectory segments. Our augmentation strategy with masked tokens facilitates effective masking operations, ensuring robust training in complex scenarios.

Additionally, we utilize masked tokens to handle padding in historical trajectory embeddings during inference. We fill the historical trajectory embedding with masked tokens to maintain the constant length for newborn objects with past bounding boxes fewer than T.

4   Experiments

4.1   Datasets and Evaluation Metrics

We provide experimental results on DanceTrack [28], MOT17 [21] and MOT20 [5]. DanceTrack mainly consists of dance videos featuring objects with similar appearances. DanceTrack provides scenarios characterized by non-linear object motion and occlusions, thereby posing significant challenges for motion-based tracking approaches. MOT17 and MOT20 contain pedestrian tracking videos in public spaces, where object motion is represented by slow and smooth movements, approximately linear. However, these datasets are still challenging due to highly crowded scenes with dense object populations.

We use the evaluation metrics including HOTA (Higher Order Tracking Accuracy) [19], AssA (Association Accuracy) [19], DetA (Detection Accuracy) [19], IDF1 [21] and MOTA (Multi-Object Tracking Accuracy) [21]. HOTA offers a balanced evaluation of both detection and association accuracy, in contrast to MOTA or DetA which is biased toward measuring detection. IDF1 and AssA are used to demonstrate the association performance.

4.2   Implementation Details

We train our adaptable motion predictor on the corresponding tracking datasets without incorporating extra samples from other datasets. To ensure a fair comparison, we utilize the publicly accessible YOLOX [9] detector weights developed by ByteTrack [35] for object detection following the baselines. The transformer encoder is comprised of 6 layers with the multi-head self-attention employing 8 heads. The embedding dimension D is set to 512. We use the Adam [14] to optimize the network with a learning rate of 0.0001 for 50 epochs and set the batch size to 512. The historical trajectory embedding length T is predefined as 30. The masking probability p is selected as 0.1. Analysis of the choice of T and p can be found in Sect. 4.4. All experiments were conducted on a single NVIDIA TITAN XP.

4.3   Benchmark Results

Table 1 shows the benchmark results on the DanceTrack test set. AM-SORT achieves competitive performance compared to the appearance-based and hybrid trackers, and state-of-the-art results among motion-based MOT approaches. It obtains 56.3 IDF1 and 55.6 HOTA, outperforming the baselines. It is important to note that a significant gain of 1.7 is observed for IDF1, which measures association performance and re-identification accuracy.

Table 2 shows the tracking performance on the MOT17 and MOT20 test sets to verify the generalizability covering linear object motion. AM-SORT achieves higher results compared to state-of-the-art MOT approaches. As mentioned earlier, MOT17 and MOT20 are designed for tracking pedestrians, where motion patterns are generally linear and do not contain non-linear scenarios. Despite

Table 1. Tracking results on the DanceTrack test set.

Tracker	Appear.	Motion	HOTA↑	IDF1↑	MOTA↑	AssA↑	DetA↑
DeepSORT [32]	✓	✓	45.6	47.9	87.8	29.7	71.0
ByteTrack [35]	✓	✓	47.3	52.5	89.5	31.4	71.6
MOTR [34]	✓	✓	54.2	51.5	79.7	40.2	73.5
MeMOTR [8]	✓	✓	68.5	71.2	89.9	58.4	80.5
TransTrack [27]	✓		45.5	45.2	88.4	27.5	75.9
GTR [37]	✓		48.0	50.3	84.7	31.9	72.5
QDTrack [7]	✓		54.2	50.4	87.7	36.8	80.1
GHOST [25]	✓		56.7	57.7	91.3	39.8	81.1
CenterTrack [36]		✓	41.8	35.7	86.8	22.6	78.1
TraDes [33]		✓	43.3	41.2	86.2	25.4	74.5
SORT [2]		✓	47.9	50.8	**91.8**	31.2	72.0
OC-SORT [3]		✓	54.6	54.6	89.6	40.2	**80.4**
AM-SORT (Ours)		✓	**55.6**	**56.3**	89.6	**40.4**	80.3

Table 2. Tracking results on the MOT17 and MOT20 test sets under private detection protocols.

	MOT17				MOT20			
	HOTA↑	IDF1↑	MOTA↑	AssA↑	HOTA↑	IDF1↑	MOTA↑	AssA↑
Hybrid								
MOTR [34]	57.2	68.4	71.9	55.8	57.8	68.6	73.4	/
MeMOTR [8]	58.8	71.5	72.8	58.4	54.1	66.1	63.7	55.0
DeepSORT [32]	61.2	74.5	78.0	59.7	57.1	69.6	71.8	55.5
ByteTrack [35]	63.1	77.3	80.3	62.0	61.3	75.2	77.8	59.9
Appearance-based								
QDTrack [7]	53.9	66.3	68.7	52.7	60.0	73.8	74.7	58.9
TransTrack [27]	54.1	63.9	74.5	47.9	48.9	59.4	65.0	45.2
GTR [37]	59.1	71.5	75.3	57.0	/	/	/	/
GHOST [25]	62.8	77.1	78.7	/	61.2	75.2	73.7	/
Motion-based								
SORT [2]	34.0	39.8	43.1	31.8	36.1	45.1	42.7	35.9
CenterTrack [36]	52.2	64.7	67.8	51.0	/	/	/	/
TraDes [33]	52.7	63.9	69.1	50.8	/	/	/	/
PermaTrack [29]	55.5	68.9	73.8	53.1	/	/	/	/
OC-SORT [3]	63.2	77.5	**78.0**	63.4	**62.1**	75.9	**75.5**	**62.0**
AM-SORT (Ours)	**63.3**	**77.8**	**78.0**	**63.5**	62.0	**76.1**	**75.5**	61.3

Table 3. Analysis at various association cost matrices.

IoU	$\Delta\theta$	L1	IDF1↑	
			OC-SORT	AM-SORT (Ours)
✓			51.1	54.3
✓	✓		**54.1**	52.1
✓		✓	53.4	**56.5**
✓	✓	✓	53.2	53.2

these different conditions, AM-SORT still demonstrates consistent improvements, even though it does not align with primary issues.

4.4 Ablation Study

Association Cost in Hungarian Matching Algorithm. During inference, the SORT-series trackers utilize the Hungarian matching algorithm for object association. To show the impact of the association costs in the Hungarian matching step, we compare OC-SORT and AM-SORT at different combinations of association costs including IoU, motion direction difference $\Delta\theta$ and L1 distance. Motion direction difference calculates the direction similarity between existing tracks and new observations. AM-SORT with IoU alone as in Table 3 Row 1 outperforms OC-SORT with IoU alone as in Table 3 Row 1 by 3.2 IDF1 and achieves an increase of 0.2 IDF1 compared to OC-SORT with the best settings as in Table 3 Row 2. On the other hand, motion direction difference degrades the tracking performance of our model. The reason is that the motion direction cue, which is incorporated in OC-SORT to compensate for the approximately estimated bounding boxes in non-linear scenarios, is not suitable for AM-SORT. Our adaptable motion predictor already captures non-linear directional shifts in the prediction step making location-based matching sufficient. Furthermore, incorporating location-based association costs, IoU and L1 distance as in Table 3 Row 3, gains an extra 2.5 IDF1 compared to OC-SORT with the best settings.

Reliability of Bounding Box Predictions. To verify the reliability of bounding box predictions, we evaluate OC-SORT and AM-SORT at progressively increased IoU thresholds. The higher IoU threshold requires a larger overlap to associate detections with predictions. Table 4 demonstrates that AM-SORT with IoU alone outperforms OC-SORT with the best settings at IoU thresholds greater than 0.4, while AM-SORT with the best settings achieves superior performance across all IoU threshold values. The higher IDF1 demonstrates that AM-SORT has a larger number of positively matched tracks with the ground truth. This indicates that our adaptable motion predictor captures more accurately the object area, which serves as strong evidence for the higher reliability of the bounding box predictions.

Table 4. Analysis on prediction reliability at varying IoU thresholds.

IoU threshold	IDF1↑					
	0.3	0.4	0.5	0.6	0.7	0.8
OC-SORT	54.1	51.5	46.9	38.7	25.5	15.8
AM-SORT (IoU)	54.3	51.2	48.4	40.4	27.0	16.4
AM-SORT (IoU+L1)	**56.5**	**53.6**	**50.7**	**42.2**	**28.9**	**17.0**

Table 5. Impact of the historical trajectory embedding length T.

T	IDF1↑					
	5	10	20	30	40	50
AM-SORT (Ours)	52.9	53.5	55.2	**56.5**	55.0	54.3

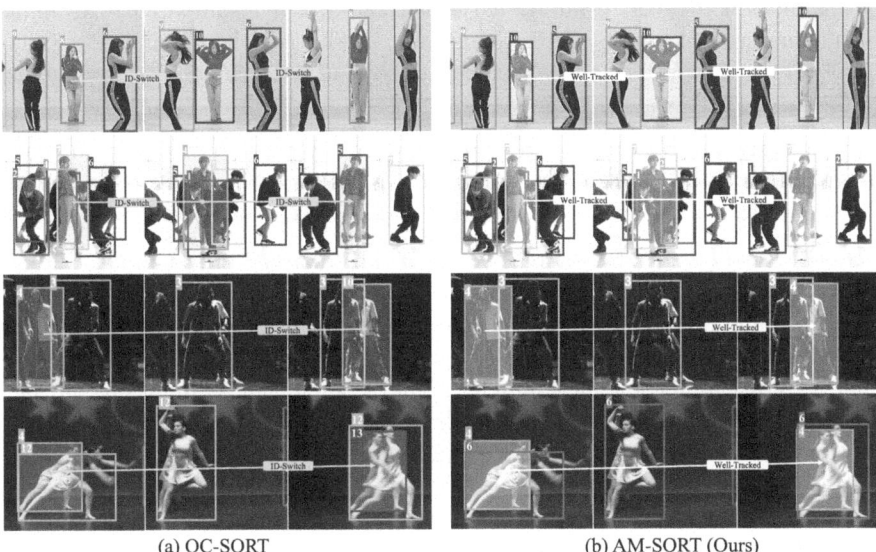

(a) OC-SORT   (b) AM-SORT (Ours)

Fig. 5. Qualitative comparison of OC-SORT and AM-SORT (Ours). The first and second rows show the tracking results in scenarios with non-linear changes of the bounding box for *dancetrack0010* and *dancetrack0058* sequences, respectively; the third and fourth rows in scenarios with non-linear object movement during occlusions for *dancetrack0018* and *dancetrack0019*, respectively.

Impact of Historical Trajectory Embedding Length. To demonstrate how tracking performance varies with the historical trajectory embedding length, we evaluate AM-SORT at different T values. Table 5 shows that performance increases with a longer historical trajectory and decreases when T is greater than 30. We conclude that a longer historical trajectory provides more comprehensive spatio-temporal information about object motion up to $T = 30$. In contrast,

Table 6. Impact of masked tokens at varying probabilities p.

p	IDF1↑					
	0	0.05	0.1	0.2	0.3	0.4
AM-SORT (Ours)	55.1	56.1	**56.5**	54.7	53.2	51.9

overly old bounding boxes of the historical trajectory can provide noises and thus negatively impact the overall tracking performance. We set $T = 30$, which covers 1.5 s of object trajectory in a 20 FPS video.

Impact of Masked Tokens. To show the effectiveness of utilizing masked tokens during training, we provide the tracking results for mask probabilities p ranging from 0 to 0.4. Table 6 demonstrates that employing masked tokens with a probability of $p = 0.1$ results in a 1.4 increase in IDF1 compared to training without masked tokens at $p = 0$. Conversely, masking with probability $p \geq 0.2$ slightly drops the performance. We suggest that utilizing moderate masking of $p = 0.1$ provides robust training to occlusions.

4.5   Qualitative Results

Figure 5 shows a qualitative comparison of OC-SORT and AM-SORT. These examples illustrate identity switches of the yellow-marked object in OC-SORT. In Fig. 5 Row 1 and Row 2, due to the linear assumptions inherent to the Kalman Filter, OC-SORT estimates a thin-shaped bounding box for the marked object in the middle frame. It is unable to predict the sudden change in a wide-shaped bounding box leading to a false match. Similarly, the linear assumptions prevent the capture of the directional shift to the right after occlusion in Fig. 5 Row 3 and Row 4. In contrast, AM-SORT maintains consistent identities under these non-linear object motions and occlusions.

5   Conclusion

In this paper, we propose AM-SORT, a motion-based tracker with an adaptable motion predictor, that effectively addresses non-linear motion and occlusion. We introduce historical trajectory embedding to encode spatio-temporal information in bounding box sequences for a comprehensive representation of object trajectory. We leverage the ability of transformers to model long-range dependencies in object trajectory, enabling our motion predictor to adapt to complex motion patterns. As a result, AM-SORT achieves competitive performance compared with state-of-the-art methods and outperforms existing motion-based approaches.

Future Work. The primary limitation of our work is that AM-SORT exhibits inferior object tracking speed compared to the baselines. Hence, in future works, our objective is to enhance our adaptable motion predictor to sustain optimal performance, particularly for tracking objects within large crowds.

Acknowledgments. This work was supported by the Institute of Information & communications Technology Planning & Evaluation (IITP) grant funded by the Korea government (MSIT) (No. 2019-0-00079, Artificial Intelligence Graduate School Program (Korea University); No. 2022-0-00984, Development of Artificial Intelligence Technology for Personalized Plug-and-Play Explanation and Verification of Explanation).

References

1. Ahmad, M., Lee, S.-W.: Human action recognition using multi-view image sequences. In: Proceedings of the International Conference on Automatic Face and Gesture Recognition (ICAFGR), pp. 523–528 (2006)
2. Bewley, A., Ge, Z., Ott, L., Ramos, F., Upcroft, B.: Simple online and realtime tracking. In: Proceedings of the IEEE International Conference on Image Processing (ICIP), pp. 3464–3468 (2016)
3. Cao, J., Pang, J., Weng, X., Khirodkar, R., Kitani, K.: Observation-Centric SORT: rethinking sort for robust multi-object tracking. In: Proceedings of the IEEE/CVF Conference on Computer Vision and Pattern Recognition (CVPR), pp. 9686–9696 (2023)
4. Cho, N.-G., Yuille, A., Lee, S.-W.: A novel linelet-based representation for line segment detection. IEEE Trans. Pattern Anal. Mach. Intell. **40**(5), 1195–1208 (2018)
5. Dendorfer, P., et al.: MOT20: a benchmark for multi object tracking in crowded scenes. arXiv preprint arXiv:2003.09003 (2020)
6. Dosovitskiy, A., et al.: An image is worth 16×16 words: transformers for image recognition at scale. arXiv preprint arXiv:2010.11929 (2020)
7. Fischer, T., et al.: QDTrack: quasi-dense similarity learning for appearance-only multiple object tracking. arXiv preprint arXiv:2210.06984 (2022)
8. Gao, R., Wang, L.: MeMOTR: long-term memory-augmented transformer for multi-object tracking. In: Proceedings of the IEEE/CVF International Conference on Computer Vision (ICCV), pp. 9901–9910 (2023)
9. Ge, Z., Liu, S., Wang, F., Li, Z., Sun, J.: YOLOX: exceeding YOLO series in 2021. arXiv preprint arXiv:2107.08430 (2021)
10. Giuliari, F., Hasan, I., Cristani, M., Galasso, F.: Transformer networks for trajectory forecasting. In: Proceedings of the IEEE International Conference on Pattern Recognition (ICPR), pp. 10335–10342 (2021)
11. Gustafsson, F., et al.: Particle filters for positioning, navigation, and tracking. IEEE Trans. Signal Process. **50**(2), 425–437 (2002)
12. Julier, S.-J., Uhlmann, J.-K.: New extension of the kalman filter to nonlinear systems. In: Proceedings of the Signal Processing, Sensor Fusion, and Target Recognition VI, vol. 3068, pp. 182–193. Spie (1997)
13. Kalman, R.-E., et al.: Contributions to the theory of optimal control. Boletín de la Sociedad Matemática Mexicana **5**(2), 102–119 (1960)
14. Kingma, D.-P., Ba, J.: Adam: a method for stochastic optimization. arXiv preprint arXiv:1412.6980 (2014)
15. Kuhn, H.-W.: The hungarian method for the assignment problem. Nav. Res. Logist. Q. **2**(1–2), 83–97 (1955)

16. Lee, D.-G., Suk, H.-I., Park, S.-K., Lee, S.-W.: Motion influence map for unusual human activity detection and localization in crowded scenes. IEEE Trans. Circuits Syst. Video Technol. **25**(10), 1612–1623 (2015)
17. Lee, M.-S., Yang, Y.-M., Lee, S.-W.: Automatic video parsing using shot boundary detection and camera operation analysis. Pattern Recogn. **34**(3), 711–719 (2001)
18. Lehmann, E.-L., Casella, G.: Theory of point estimation. Springer Science & Business Media (2006)
19. Luiten, J., et al.: HOTA: a higher order metric for evaluating multi-object tracking. Int. J. Comput. Vis. **129**, 548–578 (2021)
20. Meinhardt, T., Kirillov, A., Leal-Taixe, L., Feichtenhofer, C.: TrackFormer: multi-object tracking with transformers. In: Proceedings of the IEEE/CVF Conference on Computer Vision and Pattern Recognition (CVPR), pp. 8844–8854 (2022)
21. Milan, A., Leal-Taixé, L., Reid, I., Roth, S., Schindler, K.: MOT16: a benchmark for multi-object tracking. arXiv preprint arXiv:1603.00831 (2016)
22. Park, U.-S., Choi, H.-C., Jain, A.-K., Lee, S.-W.: Face tracking and recognition at a distance: a coaxial and concentric ptz camera system. IEEE Trans. Inf. Forensics Secur. **8**(10), 1665–1677 (2013)
23. Roh, M.-C., Kim, T.-Y., Park, J., Lee, S.-W.: Accurate object contour tracking based on boundary edge selection. Pattern Recogn. **40**(3), 931–943 (2007)
24. Roh, M.-C., Shin, H.-K., Lee, S.-W.: View-independent human action recognition with volume motion template on single stereo camera. Pattern Recogn. Lett. **31**(7), 639–647 (2010)
25. Seidenschwarz, J., Brasó, G., Serrano, V.-C., Elezi, I., Leal-Taixé, L.: Simple cues lead to a strong multi-object tracker. In: Proceedings of the IEEE/CVF Conference on Computer Vision and Pattern Recognition (CVPR), pp. 13813–13823 (2023)
26. Smith, G.-L., Schmidt, S.-F., McGee, L.-A.: Application of statistical filter theory to the optimal estimation of position and velocity on board a circumlunar vehicle, vol. 135. National Aeronautics and Space Administration (1962)
27. Sun, P., et al.: TransTrack: multiple object tracking with transformer. arXiv preprint arXiv:2012.15460 (2020)
28. Sun, P., et al.: DanceTrack: multi-object tracking in uniform appearance and diverse motion. In: Proceedings of the IEEE/CVF Conference on Computer Vision and Pattern Recognition (CVPR), pp. 20993–21002 (2022)
29. Tokmakov, P., Li, J., Burgard, W., Gaidon, A.: Learning to track with object permanence. In: Proceedings of the IEEE/CVF International Conference on Computer Vision (ICCV), pp. 10860–10869 (2021)
30. Vaswani, A., et al.: Attention is all you need. In: Advances in Neural Information Processing Systems (NeurIPS) (2017)
31. Wang, G., et al.: Track without appearance: learn box and tracklet embedding with local and global motion patterns for vehicle tracking. In: Proceedings of the IEEE/CVF International Conference on Computer Vision (ICCV), pp. 9876–9886 (2021)
32. Wojke, N., Bewley, A., Paulus, D.: Simple online and realtime tracking with a deep association metric. In: Proceedings of the IEEE International Conference on Image Processing (ICIP), pp. 3645–3649 (2017)
33. Wu, J., et al.: Track to detect and segment: an online multi-object tracker. In: Proceedings of the IEEE/CVF Conference on Computer Vision and Pattern Recognition (CVPR), pp. 12352–12361 (2021)
34. Zeng, F., et al.: MOTR: end-to-end multiple-object tracking with transformer. In: Proceedings of the European Conference on Computer Vision (ECCV), pp. 659–675 (2022)

35. Zhang, Y., et al.: ByteTrack: multi-object tracking by associating every detection box. In: Proceedings of the European Conference on Computer Vision (ECCV), pp. 1–21 (2022)
36. Zhou, X., Koltun, V., Krähenbühl, P.: Tracking objects as points. In: Proceedings of the European Conference on Computer Vision (ECCV), pp. 474–490 (2020)
37. Zhou, X., Yin, T., Koltun, V., Krähenbühl, P.: Global tracking transformers. In: Proceedings of the IEEE/CVF Conference on Computer Vision and Pattern Recognition (CVPR), pp. 8771–8780 (2022)

Character Identifying Video Language Alignment Network for Weakly-Supervised Video-Subtitle Moment Retrieval

Donghoon Lee, Jun Yeop Shim, Sun-Jae Yoon, and Chang D. Yoo[(✉)]

Korea Advanced Institute of Science and Technology (KAIST),
Daejeon, South Korea
dh_lee99@kaist.ac.kr

Abstract. This paper introduces the Character Identifying Video Language Alignment Network (CIVLAN), a labor-efficient approach for weakly-supervised Video-Subtitle Moment Retrieval (VSMR). CIVLAN efficiently localizes pertinent temporal moment in untrimmed videos or subtitles by responding to natural language queries. It addresses three key limitations of previous methods: the extensive need for fully supervised training with labor-intensive annotations, underutilization of auxiliary modalities like subtitles and audio, and the neglection of character identification in dialogues. CIVLAN comprises two main components: the Modality Alignment Network (MAN), which aligns queries to video/subtitle content through contrastive loss minimization, and the Character Identifying Network (CIN), which associates on-screen characters with their references in subtitles and queries. This method eliminates the need for ground-truth temporal moment, significantly reducing manual annotation efforts. Our experiments demonstrate that CIVLAN surpasses previous state-of-the-art methods on the TVR benchmark dataset under weakly-supervised conditions. The paper also includes comprehensive ablation studies and qualitative analyses to showcase the effectiveness of CIVLAN's components.

Keywords: Video-Subtitle Moment Retrieval · Multi-Modal Alignment · Deep Learning · Weakly-supervised learning · Video Understanding

1 Introduction

Recent research has contributed to bridging computer vision and natural language processing, especially regarding the task of image/video-grounded question answering [1,3,15], image/video captioning [26,29], activity localization [8,17], video moment retrieval [2,34], weakly-supervised video language tasks

---

D. Lee and J. Y. Shim—Denote equal contribution.

C. Wallraven et al. (Eds.): ICPRAI 2024, LNCS 14892, pp. 108–123, 2025.
https://doi.org/10.1007/978-981-97-8702-9_8

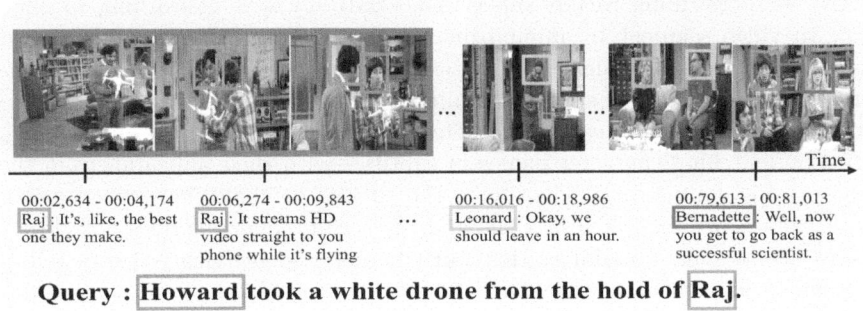

00:02,634 - 00:04,174
Raj : It's, like, the best
one they make.

00:06,274 - 00:09,843
Raj : It streams HD
video straight to you
phone while it's flying

...

00:16,016 - 00:18,986
Leonard : Okay, we
should leave in an hour.

00:79,613 - 00:81,013
Bernadette : Well, now
you get to go back as a
successful scientist.

Query : Howard took a white drone from the hold of Raj.

Fig. 1. Illustration of character matched video-subtitle moment retrieval. The characters in video and names in language with same color-box represent the character matching for VSMR

[23, 27]. Among these tasks, Video Moment Retrieval (VMR) is a task that identifies video segments referenced by text query based on a common understanding of video and language. Recently, the use of additional modalities such as subtitles and audio in untrimmed video has prompted a higher level of interpretability between video and language. As an extension of VMR, the task to localize the temporal video-subtitle moment pertinent in responding to the query in the untrimmed video and subtitle will henceforth be referred to as video-subtitle moment retrieval (VSMR).

One significant challenge in VSMR is conducting moment retrieval in a weakly-supervised manner to mitigate for the labor-intensive annotations and susceptibility to annotation noise. Another challenge is effectively utilizing auxiliary modalities to boost moment retrieval performance. This paper will focus on improving the retrieval performance on the TVR dataset, which consists of video and subtitle information of the TVQA dataset and a temporal scene description in relation to the two modalities. In summary, we propose to perform VSMR in a weakly-supervised manner by taking advantage of the information provided by the additional auxiliary subtitle modality.

VSMR necessitates the integration of auxiliary modalities with video scenes involving one or more characters, making the identification of characters crucial for enhancing retrieval accuracy. To localize the moment with query such as "Raj was talking to Howard before Leonard walked in?" requires character identification, and it would be worthwhile for a VSMR algorithm to learn to associate names in the script with the characters in the video without any direct annotations. Moreover, it was found from our analysis that the subtitles in our dataset included at least one character name 70% of the time, indicating the need for character identification for a successful result.

In this paper, we address the aforementioned objective with our proposed Character Identifying Video Language Alignment Network (CIVLAN). CIVLAN is composed of the following two main modules: (1) Modality Alignment Network

(MAN) for performing weakly-supervised VSMR by way of learning to align query to video segment by minimizing contrastive loss between positive and negative video samples, and (2) Character Identifying Network (CIN) for performing character identification by learning to associate speaker name referenced in the subtitle with the speaking character appearing in the video. Our approach begins by matching character names in subtitles with their appearances in the video. As Fig. 1 illustrates, identifying the speaker is challenging when multiple characters are present in a scene and the script's dialogue does not clearly specify the speaker. To address this, our Character Identifying Network (CIN) identifies speaking characters by analyzing their repeated appearances across different scenes and dialogues. This method enables CIVLAN to accurately match characters in the video with their names in the script, mimicking human reasoning processes. Figure 1 depicts 'Raj' in both the first and third scenes, each time accompanied by a different set of individuals. By analyzing the commonality across these scenes, it is possible to deduce Raj's identity in the context of the scene. Following character identification, our Modality Alignment Network (MAN) performs weakly-supervised video-subtitle alignment. Once characters in the video and script are matched and identified, MAN generates character-weighted cumulative video proposals that are used as candidates pertinent to respond to the query. Where the character in the query exists in the video, several cumulative proposals are generated, and where there is not, relatively few proposals are generated.

To summarize, our main contributions include: (1) VSMR is executed in a weakly-supervised manner, eliminating the need for labor-intensive annotations and reducing issues related to annotation noise. (2) We propose Character Identifying Video Language Alignment Network (CIVLAN) to identify characters in video with the character name referred in the script. (3) Experimental results show that CIVLAN outperforms the previous state-of-the-art on weakly-supervised setting of TVR benchmark.

2   Related Works

2.1   Video Moment Retrieval

Video Moment Retrieval (VMR) is a task focused on localising the temporal moment that is semantically aligned with a given language query. Various innovative methods [2,8,28,31,32,34] have emerged, each introducing a novel approach to tackle the challenge. Xu et al. [28] proposes a model that performs a fine-grained multi-modal feature fusion, where it combines video and language information a the word level. In contrast, Zhang et al. [34] introduces a Moment Alignment Network (MAN) that considers the relationship between proposals as a structured graph, unifying the candidate proposal encoding and temporal structural reasoning in a single-shot feed-forward network. Further more, Hendricks et al. [2] and Gao et al. [8] proposes methods that involves sampling moment proposal candidates with sliding windows of various lengths and applying multi-modal fusion to estimate the correlation between the queries and video moments. However, despite the effort to propose methods to align video and language, the task of VMR still faces significant challenges due to the labour-intensive annotation problem.

2.2 Weakly-Supervised Video Moment Retrieval

The field has recently shifted towards weakly-supervised Video Moment Retrieval (VMR) to reduce the extensive labeling required by fully-supervised methods. Mithun *et al.* [23] developed the Text-Guided Attention (TGA) method, which creates a joint embedding space between video and language queries, enhancing the alignment by focusing on semantically similar language queries. Lin *et al.* [18] introduced the Semantic Completion Network (SCN), which selects the top-K proposals rather than just the top one, allowing for more thorough exploration and utilization of video content. Additionally, Ma *et al.* [20] proposed the Video Language Alignment Network, which reduces redundant proposals early in the process by employing surrogate proposal selection. These methods not only advance weakly-supervised VMR but also integrate additional modalities like audio and subtitles, improving the interpretability between video and language content (Fig. 2).

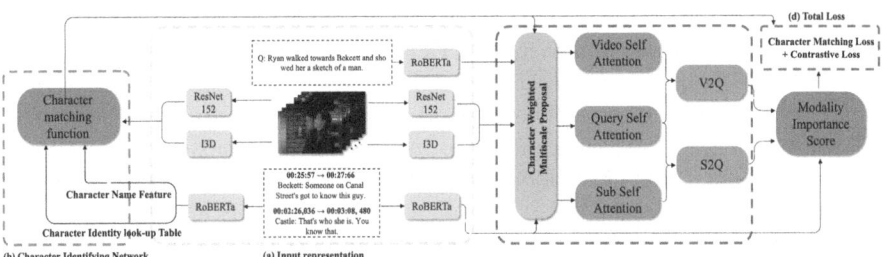

Fig. 2. Illustration of our Character Identifying Video Language Alignment Network (CIVLAN). CIVLAN is composed of the following: (a) ResNet-152, I3D, and RoBERTa for video and text embeddings (b) Character identifying network to identify all characters in video and subtitle (c) Modality alignment network for query-to-video/subtitle alignment in a weakly-supervised manner (d) Modality importance score to weight the output video and subtitle proposals.

3 Method

The architecture of the proposed Character Identifying Video Language Alignment Network (CIVLAN) is illustrated in figure two. CIVLAN is composed of two main modules, the Character Identifying Network (CIN) and the Modality Alignment Network (MAN). Such foundational architectural principal derived from the following key observation: The discernment of characters through their names elevates the perception within the captured video narrative. Concurrently, the synchronisation of the queries with the video subtitles becomes notably straightforward in a weakly-supervised setting, assuming an accurate character discernment. CIN handles the task of character discernment, engaging in a matching process that aligns the character names with the corresponding character portrayed in the video sequence. MAN then generates character weighted cumulative proposals to be sued as candidate moments for minimising the contrastive loss. Both proposals are attended by a Modality Importance Score (MIS) which contributes to the final selection of the proposal. CIVLAN is learned in weakly-supervised and end-to-end manner without ground truth temporal moment.

3.1 Input Representation

We use the same appearance, motion, and textual features as in the previous work [15]. We extract 2048 dimensional appearance features using ResNet-152 [10] at 3FPS and max-pool the features every 1.5 s to get a clip-level feature, while we extract 1024 dimensional motion features using I3D [5] every 1.5 s. The ResNet152 model is pre-trained on ImageNet [6] for image recognition, and the I3D model is pre-trained on Kinetics-600 [12] for action recognition. The final video representation is the concatenation of the two features after L2-normalization, and it is denoted as $V \in \mathbb{R}^{l \times 3072}$, where l is the number of clips. For the query features, we extract the 768 dimensional contextualized token features from pre-trained RoBERTa [19]. The query feature is denoted as $Q \in \mathbb{R}^{l_q \times 768}$. For the subtitle features, we first extract the same 768 dimensional token features and max-pool them every 1.5 s to get a 768 dimension clip-level features, which is aligned with the video representation. The subtitle feature is denoted as $S \in \mathbb{R}^{l \times 768}$. Three modality features are projected on to a d dimensional embedding space and the positional encoding [25] is applied with layer normalization [4]. The processed features are mathematically summarized below

$$\mathbf{E}^v = \mathrm{LN}(V + \mathrm{PE}(V)) \in \mathbb{R}^{l \times d}, \tag{1}$$

$$\mathbf{E}^s = \mathrm{LN}(S + \mathrm{PE}(S)) \in \mathbb{R}^{l \times d}, \tag{2}$$

$$\mathbf{E}^q = \mathrm{LN}(Q + \mathrm{PE}(Q)) \in \mathbb{R}^{l_q \times d}. \tag{3}$$

3.2 Character Identifying Network

For identifying the speakers in the subtitle, we build a binary character identity look-up table $T \in \mathbb{R}^{l \times N}$, where a total of N characters are recorded in a single video. We also define the N characters name features $E^n \in \mathbb{R}^{N \times d}$. If the j-th character appears in i-th subtitle clip, we define $T_{ij} = 1$; otherwise, $T_{ij} = 0$. For example, the final character identity look-up table T is constructed as follows:

$$T = \begin{bmatrix} 1 & 0 & 1 & 0 & \cdots & 0 \\ 1 & 0 & 1 & 1 & \cdots & 1 \\ 0 & 1 & 1 & 0 & \cdots & 0 \\ \vdots & & & \ddots & \\ 0 & 0 & 1 & 1 & \cdots & 1 \end{bmatrix}. \tag{4}$$

With the character identity table T, the character matching loss is defined as:

$$\mathcal{L}_{char} = -\sum_{j=1}^{N}\sum_{i=1}^{l} max[\Delta_r, T_{ij}M_{ij}(E^v, E^n)], \tag{5}$$

$$M_{ij}(E^v, E^n) = ReLU(Pool(\sigma([E_i^v||E_j^n]W_h)W_s)), \tag{6}$$

where the ranking threshold $\Delta_r = 0.2$. Here $ReLU$ denotes Rectified Linear Unit [24], $Pool$ denotes mean-pooling, and σ denotes the sigmoid function. Here, M_{ij} is defined as character matching function, which projects the concatenated visual context features E_i^v and character name features E_j^n onto a joint embedding space. Here, the character identity value T_{ij} filters out visual context features where the j-th character does not exist. $W_h \in \mathbb{R}^{2d \times d}$ and $W_s \in \mathbb{R}^d$ are learnable parameters. With the character matching loss, the character identifying network (CIN) learns recognizability of characters in visual context by the name of character in subtitles. The character matching matrix $M \in \mathbb{R}^{l \times N}$ is used for character weighted cumulative proposal generation module in the following section.

3.3   Modality Alignment Network

Modality alignment network (MAN) is introduced to consider the alignment query with video and subtitle. Based on the characters identified in the query, character weighted cumulative candidate proposals are generated. Each proposal is attended by query guided attention, where the proposals related to the query are highlighted. All proposals in each modality are recalibrated by modality importance score and the final moment is selected by pooling all proposals.

Character Weighted Cumulative Proposal. We first investigate the characters' names in given query and make the one-hot character vector $\mathbf{v}_{name} \in \mathbb{R}^N$. If the first and third character name are in the query, then $\mathbf{v}_{name} = [1, 0, 1, ..., 0]$. We define character matching score $\mathcal{R}^{score} \in \mathbb{R}^l$ along the l length video using character matching matrix M and character vector $\mathbf{v}_{name}$ as follows:

$$\mathcal{R}^{score} = M \times \mathbf{v}_{name}. \tag{7}$$

To generate cumulative character weighted proposals (CCWP) using $\mathcal{R}^{score}$, we calculate the integral of the character matching score over l axis as follows, where n is the frame index up to which the cumulative sum is calculated:

$$\mathcal{G}(n) := \sum_{i=1}^{n} \mathcal{R}_i^{score}. \tag{8}$$

Figure 3 shows the character weighted cumulative proposal generation. The (a) of Fig. 3 is the distribution of character matching score over l axis, and (b) of Fig. 3 is the integral of character matching score. We generate the new video

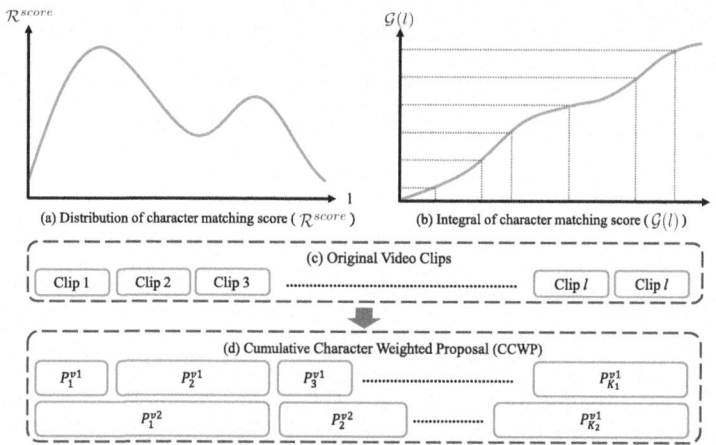

Fig. 3. Illustration of Cumulative Character Weighted Proposal (CCWP). CCWP is composed of the following process: (a) Character matching score estimated by CIN, (b) The integral of character matching score is induced, (d) CCWP is generated by (c) linear combination of original video clips under character matching score.

proposals in (d) of Fig. 3 by linear combination of original l video clips in (c) of Fig. 3. In the (d) of Fig. 3, the K proposals in the first layer were reconstructed using the inverse function of $\mathcal{G}(n)^{-1}$ which is defined as:

$$L_k = \mathcal{G}(y_k)^{-1}, \tag{9}$$

$$P_n^{v1} = L_{n+1} - L_n, (1 \leq n \leq K), \tag{10}$$

where $y_k \in \{y_1, ..., y_{K+1}\}$ is a value obtained by equally dividing the y-axis by K segments and L_k is matched location on x-axis in (b) of Fig. 3. The character weighted K proposals are generated by Equation (10). The original video clips in (c) of Fig. 3 are combined to make the $P^1 = \{P_1^{v1}, ..., P_K^{v1}\}$ in first layer of (d) of Fig. 3. The proposals in second layer (d) of Fig. 3 are combined by adjacent P^{v1} proposals and total proposal $P^v = P^{v1} \cup \cdots \cup P^{vT}$ is union of T layers proposals, while the number of proposals N_p is calculated by $N_p = K + \frac{K}{2} + \cdots + \frac{K}{2^T}$. Therefore, the Cumulative Character Weighted Proposal (CCWP) $P^v \in \mathbb{R}^{N_p \times d}$ performs to make more cumulative video proposals in the proximity of the characters in query, where not, it makes fewer proposals. The subtitle proposals $P^s \in \mathbb{R}^{N_p \times d}$ is also reconstructed to fit the video proposals.

Query Guided Attention. Multi-head attention from the Transformer [25] is applied to all proposals in the d-dimensional feature space, providing self-attention across characters in the query, video, and subtitle as shown below:

$$P^v \leftarrow MultiHead(P^v, P^v, P^v), \tag{11}$$

$$P^s \leftarrow MultiHead(P^s, P^s, P^s), \tag{12}$$

$$E^q \leftarrow MultiHead(E^q, E^q, E^q). \tag{13}$$

The video proposals and subtitle proposals are again attended by their semantic similarity to the query:

$$\alpha_i = \sum_{j=1}^{N_q} (P_i^v W_P)(E_j^q W_E)^T, \tag{14}$$

$$P^v \leftarrow softmax([\alpha_1, \alpha_2, \cdots, \alpha_{N_p}]) P^v + P^v. \tag{15}$$

where the $W_P \in \mathbb{R}^{d \times d}$ and $W_E \in \mathbb{R}^{d \times d}$ are high-level feature embedding matrices and $softmax$ of α performs element-wise multiplication with P^v. The same process is repeated for subtitle proposals P^s.

Modality Importance Score. The Modality Importance Score (MIS) measures how important each modality is in finding the moment related query. The modality-level importance score α^v and α^s is obtained by summing all the proposal-level importance scores α_i^v and α_i^s in each modalities. The proposal-level importance score is also calculated by summing all the single MLP layer outputs, where the MLP receives word features of query and proposal features as inputs like below:

$$\alpha_i^v = \sum_{j=1}^{N_q} MLP(P_i^v || E_j^q), \tag{16}$$

$$\alpha^v = \sum_{i=1}^{N_p} \alpha_i^v. \tag{17}$$

With the MIS, final modality alignment features $\mathcal{A} \in \mathbb{R}^{2N_p \times d}$ are produced by concatenating each modality. Again, the same attention mechanism in Equation (14,15) is applied for attending the final feature $\mathcal{A}$ as shown below:

$$\mathcal{A} = [\alpha^v P^v || \alpha^s P^s], \tag{18}$$

$$\beta_i = \sum_{j=1}^{N_q} (\mathcal{A}_i W_P)(E_j^q W_E)^T, \tag{19}$$

$$\mathcal{A} \leftarrow softmax([\beta_1, \beta_2, \cdots, \beta_{2N_p}]) \mathcal{A} + \mathcal{A}. \tag{20}$$

The mean-pooling $\mathcal{A}_p \in \mathbb{R}^d$ over proposal axis and mean-pooling $E_p \in \mathbb{R}^d$ over word axis are produced for the weakly-supervised learning using the contrastive loss like below:

$$\mathcal{A}_p = Pool_{mean}(\mathcal{A}), \tag{21}$$

$$E_p = Pool_{mean}(E), \tag{22}$$

$$\mathcal{L}_{contrastive} = max[0, \Delta_c - MLP(\mathcal{A}_p^+ || E_p) + MLP(\mathcal{A}_p^- || E_p)] \tag{23}$$

Here, the same parameters for the MLP are used in both the Modality Importance Score (MIS) and $\mathcal{A}^+$ represents the positive pair while $\mathcal{A}^-$ represents the

Table 1. Performance comparison of CIVLAN to the related methods on TVR dataset. Model references: MCN [2], CAL [7], MEE [21], ExCL [9], XML [16] TGA [23], VLANet [20], SAN [13], CTDL [30], SQuiDNet [31]. ⋆: denotes pre-trained on large scale dataset [22]. The highest scores for each type are highlighted in bold in the results.

Type	Method	IoU=0.5				IoU=0.7			
		R@1	R@5	R@10	R@100	R@1	R@5	R@10	R@100
Chance	Random	0.00	0.01	0.04	0.32	0.00	0.00	0.01	0.05
Fully	MEE+MCN	1.15	4.50	5.32	19.74	0.65	2.16	3.21	11.32
	MEE+CAL	1.04	5.91	6.81	20.26	0.57	1.89	3.58	10.44
	MEE+ExCL	0.96	3.63	4.89	6.02	0.45	1.24	2.52	3.61
	XML	**5.14**	**11.62**	**15.89**	**36.26**	2.51	**6.84**	9.29	24.07
	SAN	–	–	–	–	3.64	–	15.32	34.73
	CTDL⋆	–	–	–	–	10.02	–	30.08	43.52
	SQuiDNet⋆	–	–	–	–	**10.09**	–	**31.22**	**46.05**
Weakly	TGA	1.14	2.94	4.84	10.23	0.38	1.52	2.51	5.75
	VLANet	2.47	4.58	7.47	18.33	0.76	2.80	3.87	8.32
	CIVLAN (ours)	**3.82**	**6.14**	**8.46**	**21.64**	**1.12**	**3.04**	**4.48**	**12.14**

negative pair in the same batch. Δ_c is the margin for MIS of positive pair to be higher than the negative pair. The final loss is defined by adding character matching loss from character identifying network and contrastive loss from modality alignment network like below:

$$\mathcal{L}_{total} = \gamma\mathcal{L}_{contrastive} + \delta\mathcal{L}_{char}, \qquad (24)$$

where the γ and δ are a hyperparameter that tunes the degree to which each loss contributes to the final loss. Based on the character matching loss and contrastive loss, our proposed character identifying video language alignment network (CIVLAN) performs query to video-subtitle alignment in weakly-supervised manner.

4   Experiments

4.1   Datasets

TVR dataset [16] is constructed based on the TVQA [15] dataset which is used for the video question answering task under human annotated multiple-choice question-answer pairs for short video clips from 6 long running TV shows. TVR is a modified version of the TVQA dataset for Video-Subtitle Moment Retrieval task that replaces the orginal questions with natural language queries that describes the situation in the temporal moment. TVR contains 109K queries from 21.8K videos. Due to the absence of the test dataset, we repurposed the provided validation set to serve as our test set. Additionally, we designated 10%

of the training set to function as our validation set. This adjustment in the data partitioning necessitated the re-evaluation of several models to ensure their performance integrity under the new setup.

4.2   Experimental Details

We adopted the average recall at K (R@K) as our metric, following [7,8,16]. A correct prediction requires a matched video and high overlap between prediction and ground truth measured by IOU. We set our model's hidden layer dimension to $d = 128$ and attention heads to $h = 4$. The margin for contrastive loss is $\Delta_c = 0.2$, and the ranking threshold for the character identifying network is $\Delta_r = 0.15$, all optimized through grid-search on the validation set.

For training, we used an NVIDIA TITAN V GPU, employing the Adam optimizer [14] with specified with $\beta_1 = 0.9, \beta_2 = 0.98$, and $\epsilon = 10^{-9}$, and followed a learning rate strategy similar to [25]. The model trained for up to 20 epochs, with a batch size of 32 and a dropout rate of 0.3, selecting the best model based on the highest R@K on the validation set.

Inference utilized the highest β index over modality importance scores for temporal moments and selected videos with the largest β sum. The the framework was implemented in PyTorch [16].

4.3   Results on TVR Benchmark

Table 1 presents experimental results on the TVR dataset, comparing our CIVLAN model with previous methods in both weakly-supervised and fully-supervised settings. The first section in Table 1 sets the baseline by selecting a video randomly from the selected random moment from the test dataset. For a fair comparison, six metrics from recently published methods on the TVR dataset was reproduced. Of the weakly-supervised methods, CIVLAN achieves the state-of-the-art performance in most metrics. Similar to the first section, metrics from four recent models that showed high performance in VMR tasks was reproduced, as shown in the second section of the same table. MEE [21] was used to retrieve 100 videos for each query as candidates and performed single video moment retrieval task on MCN [2], CAL [7], and ExCL [9] as in [16]. Both MCN and CAL evaluate all proposals, while ExCL adapts for single video moment retrieval. SQuiDNet and CTDL show more high performances, but these are attributed to pre-trained knowledge [22].

For weakly-supervised models, we replicated TGA, which uses text-guided attention, and VLANet, introducing a surrogate proposal selection to reduce redundancy. However, TGA showed relatively low performance in the overall metric, indicating the complexity of VSMR. VLANet, employing Cascaded Cross Attention and Surrogate Proposal Selection, outperforms TGA by improving attention efficiency. Our CIVLAN, focusing on character-relevant proposals, minimizes unnecessary proposals, aligning modalities more effectively. The results suggest that early character matching and character-weighted proposal generation enhance interpretability across modalities.

4.4 Ablation Studies

Ablation Study on Model Variants. Table 2 summarizes the ablation analysis on model variants of CIVLAN on the validation set of TVR in order to measure the effectiveness of the proposed key components. The first section of Table 2 provides the ablation results of Character Identifying Network (CIN) to the overall performance. Without CIN, accuracy is 18.34%. The CIN performs character matching between character name and visual context of the character. Without the CIN, character matching is performed only for subtitles. For video proposal, we generate cumulative proposals uniformly across the video. The results without CIN indicate that matching the character name with the visual context enhances common understanding between modalities. The second section of Table 2 provides the ablation results on cumulative character weighted proposal (CCWP). Without the CCWP on modality alignment network, there is the highest performance drop of 5.02%. As an alternative to CCWP, cumulative proposals like [20] were uniformly generated for both video and subtitles. Attention is blurred due to redundancy proposals, which seem to have weakened alignment. Therefore, CCWP plays an important role in a proposal-based framework. Modality importance score also contributes to selecting the moment in the modality by attending to each proposal according to the importance of modality. Without the MIS, there is 1.08% of performance drop. For the MIS, we assign ground truth information of which modality should be chosen for retrieval. An increase of 5.71% in performance indicates that valid modality selection can improve performance.

Table 2. Ablation study on model variants of CIVLAN on the validation set of TVR for IoU=0.5, R@10. The last column shows the performance drop compared to the full model of CVLAN.

Methods	valid Acc.	Δ
CVLAN w/o CIN	18.34	-3.3%
CVLAN w/o CCWP	16.62	-5.02%
CVLAN w/o MIS	19.56	-1.08%
CVLAN w GT modality	27.35	+5.71%
CVLAN	21.64	0

Ablation Study on CCWP. The Table 3 summarizes the ablation analysis on cumulative character weighted proposal (CCWP) generation. The hyperparameter K is the number of segments in the first proposal layer P^1 and T is the number of proposal layers. When the K is 8, the CIVLAN showed the highest performance with 3 proposal layers. Other options show performance drop, and the CIVLAN is performed to select the final moment under the proposal consisting of a total of 3 layers, with 8 proposals in the first layer.

Table 3. Ablation study on the number of segments K and the number of proposal layer T in CCWP on the validation set of TVR for IoU=0.5, R@10.

K=# of segments T=# of Layers	valid Acc.	Δ
K=8, T=2	20.74	−0.9%
K=8, T=3	21.64	0%
K=8, T=4	19.41	−2.23%
K=16, T=2	19.2	−2.44%
K=16, T=3	18.1	−3.54%

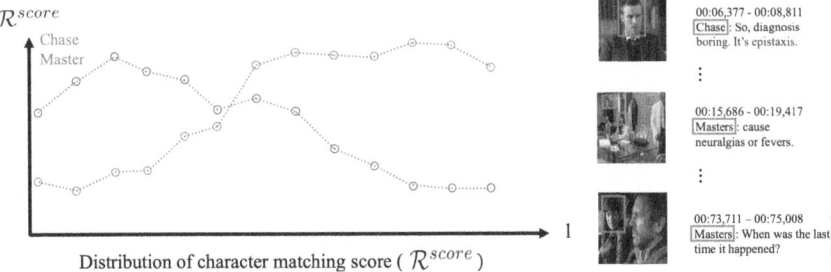

Fig. 4. Character matching score according to the appearance of characters. As Chase appears, the character matching score for Chase is high and the same in the Masters.

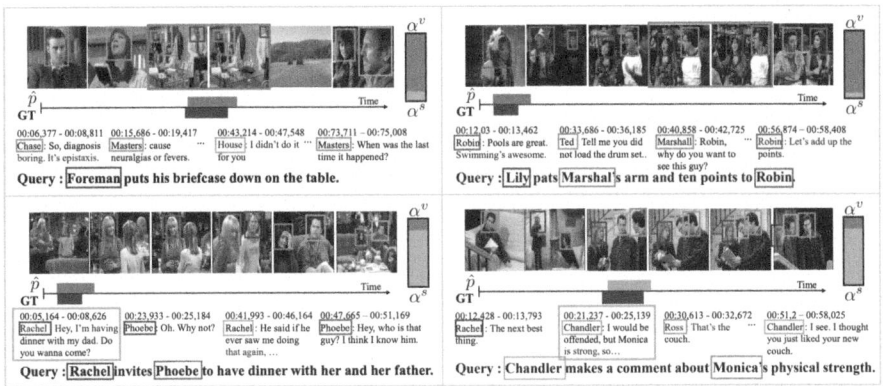

Fig. 5. Visualization on the inference path of CIVLAN. Each example provides MIS weights, the localized temporal moment, and ground-truth (GT) temporal moment. Video and subtitle modality are represented in orange and yellow respectively. CIVLAN dynamically modulates both modalities and identifies the characters according to the input query. This figure is best viewed in color. (Color figure online)

4.5   Qualitative Analysis

Character Matching Score. Figure 4 shows the character matching scores, with 'Chase' scoring highly when present in both the scene and subtitle. Conversely, the appearance of other characters in scene or subtitle reduces 'Chase's' matching score. These results suggests that the Character Identifying Network has effectively learned to correlate character names with their visual contexts.

Moment Retrieval and Modality Importance Score. Figure 5 shows the examples of Moment Retrieval and the modality importance score (MIS) between video and subtitles according to the given query on validation set. The bar on the right of each example means which modality is weighted with different colors and the timeline includes ground truth moment and predicted moment from CIVLAN. The first and second examples in the figure show that the MIS is weighted on video than on subtitles and also the query is related to the situation in the video. The third and fourth examples, on the contrary, show that the MIS puts weight on the subtitle, and we can confirm that the query is also related to the subtitle. Other options show performance drop, and CIVLAN is performed to select the final moment under the proposal consisting of a total of 3 layers, with 8 proposals in the first layer. In the fifth and sixth case, the MIS has similar weights for both modalities and MIS attend video and subtitle modality with similar size, where CIVLAN applicably performs moment retrieval.

5   Limitation

This study presents technical contributions to utilize paired information on the identity of character faces and the names of characters presented in subtitles. However, our proposed character-matching approach has difficulties in operating with scenes of a single subtitle and many characters. Therefore, our future work is to incorporate the method of estimating scene complexity knowledge [33] into our system and apply this to adaptively process scenes according to the scene complexity. Furthermore, employing specific characteristics of characters' pose and motion [11] is also an interesting approach for Future work.

6   Conclusion

In this study, we introduce the Character Identifying Video Alignment Network (CIVLAN) for video-subtitle moment retrieval, addressing three main challenges: extensive labelling requirements of prior methods, underutilization of auxiliary modalities such as subtitles, and the overlooking of character identification in dialogues. CIVLAN integrates a Modality Alignment Network for weakly-supervised learning and a Character Identifying Network to align character names across video, subtitles, and queries. The accompanying experimental results demonstrates superior performance of CIVLAN on the TVR benchmark, surpassing existing methods. The effectiveness of CIVLAN's components is further substantiated through ablation studies and qualitative analysis.

Acknowledgement. This work was supported by the Institute of Information & Communications Technology Planning & Evaluation (IITP) grant funded by the Korea government (MSIT) (No. 2022-0-00184, Development and Study of AI Technologies to Inexpensively Conform to Evolving Policy on Ethics), and the Institute for Information & Communications Technology Promotion (IITP) grant funded by the Korea government (MSIT) (No. 2021-0-01381, Development of Causal AI through Video Understanding and Reinforcement Learning, and Its Applications to Real Environments).

References

1. Anderson, P., et al.: Bottom-up and top-down attention for image captioning and visual question answering. In: Proceedings of the IEEE Conference on Computer Vision and Pattern Recognition, pp. 6077–6086 (2018)
2. Anne Hendricks, L., Wang, O., Shechtman, E., Sivic, J., Darrell, T., Russell, B.: Localizing moments in video with natural language. In: Proceedings of the IEEE International Conference on Computer Vision, pp. 5803–5812 (2017)
3. Antol, S., et al.: VQA: visual question answering. In: Proceedings of the IEEE International Conference on Computer Vision, pp. 2425–2433 (2015)
4. Ba, J.L., Kiros, J.R., Hinton, G.E.: Layer normalization. arXiv preprint arXiv:1607.06450 (2016)
5. Carreira, J., Zisserman, A.: Quo vadis, action recognition? A new model and the kinetics dataset. In: Proceedings of the IEEE Conference on Computer Vision and Pattern Recognition, pp. 6299–6308 (2017)
6. Deng, J., Dong, W., Socher, R., Li, L.J., Li, K., Fei-Fei, L.: Imagenet: a large-scale hierarchical image database. In: 2009 IEEE Conference on Computer Vision and Pattern Recognition, pp. 248–255. IEEE (2009)
7. Escorcia, V., Soldan, M., Sivic, J., Ghanem, B., Russell, B.: Temporal localization of moments in video collections with natural language. arXiv preprint arXiv:1907.12763 (2019)
8. Gao, J., Sun, C., Yang, Z., Nevatia, R.: Tall: temporal activity localization via language query. In: Proceedings of the IEEE International Conference on Computer Vision, pp. 5267–5275 (2017)
9. Ghosh, S., Agarwal, A., Parekh, Z., Hauptmann, A.: Excl: extractive clip localization using natural language descriptions. arXiv preprint arXiv:1904.02755 (2019)
10. He, K., Zhang, X., Ren, S., Sun, J.: Deep residual learning for image recognition. In: Proceedings of the IEEE Conference on Computer Vision and Pattern Recognition, pp. 770–778 (2016)
11. Hong, J.W., Yoon, S., Kim, J., Yoo, C.D.: Joint path alignment framework for 3d human pose and shape estimation from video. IEEE Access (2023)
12. Kay, W., et al.: The kinetics human action video dataset. arXiv preprint arXiv:1705.06950 (2017)
13. Kim, D., Yoon, S., Hong, J.W., Yoo, C.D.: Semantic association network for video corpus moment retrieval. In: ICASSP 2022-2022 IEEE International Conference on Acoustics, Speech and Signal Processing (ICASSP), pp. 1720–1724. IEEE (2022)

14. Kingma, D.P., Ba, J.: Adam: a method for stochastic optimization. arXiv preprint arXiv:1412.6980 (2014)
15. Lei, J., Yu, L., Bansal, M., Berg, T.L.: Tvqa: localized, compositional video question answering. In: Proceedings of the Conference on Empirical Methods in Natural Language Processing (2018)
16. Lei, J., Yu, L., Berg, T.L., Bansal, M.: TVR: a large-scale dataset for video-subtitle moment retrieval. In: Proceedings of the European Conference on Computer Vision (ECCV) (2020)
17. Lin, T., Zhao, X., Su, H., Wang, C., Yang, M.: BSN: boundary sensitive network for temporal action proposal generation. In: Proceedings of the European Conference on Computer Vision (ECCV), pp. 3–19 (2018)
18. Lin, Z., Zhao, Z., Zhang, Z., Wang, Q., Liu, H.: Weakly-supervised video moment retrieval via semantic completion network. In: Proceedings of the AAAI Conference on Artificial Intelligence, vol. 34, pp. 11539–11546 (2020)
19. Liu, Y., et al.: Roberta: a robustly optimized bert pretraining approach. arXiv preprint arXiv:1907.11692 (2019)
20. Ma, M., Yoon, S., Kim, J., Lee, Y., Kang, S., Yoo, C.D.: Vlanet: video-language alignment network for weakly-supervised video moment retrieval. In: European Conference on Computer Vision, pp. 156–171. Springer (2020)
21. Miech, A., Laptev, I., Sivic, J.: Learning a text-video embedding from incomplete and heterogeneous data. arXiv preprint arXiv:1804.02516 (2018)
22. Miech, A., Zhukov, D., Alayrac, J.B., Tapaswi, M., Laptev, I., Sivic, J.: Howto100m: learning a text-video embedding by watching hundred million narrated video clips. In: Proceedings of the IEEE/CVF International Conference on Computer Vision, pp. 2630–2640 (2019)
23. Mithun, N.C., Paul, S., Roy-Chowdhury, A.K.: Weakly supervised video moment retrieval from text queries. In: Proceedings of the IEEE Conference on Computer Vision and Pattern Recognition, pp. 11592–11601 (2019)
24. Nair, V., Hinton, G.E.: Rectified linear units improve restricted boltzmann machines. In: Proceedings of the International Conference on Machine Learning (2010)
25. Vaswani, A., et al.: Attention is all you need. In: Advances in Neural Information Processing Systems, pp. 5998–6008 (2017)
26. Venugopalan, S., Rohrbach, M., Donahue, J., Mooney, R., Darrell, T., Saenko, K.: Sequence to sequence-video to text. In: Proceedings of the IEEE International Conference on Computer Vision, pp. 4534–4542 (2015)
27. Wang, L., Xiong, Y., Lin, D., Van Gool, L.: Untrimmednets for weakly supervised action recognition and detection. In: Proceedings of the IEEE conference on Computer Vision and Pattern Recognition, pp. 4325–4334 (2017)
28. Xu, H., He, K., Sigal, L., Sclaroff, S., Saenko, K.: Text-to-clip video retrieval with early fusion and re-captioning. arXiv preprint arXiv:1804.05113 (2018). 2(6), 7
29. Xu, K., et al.: Show, attend and tell: neural image caption generation with visual attention. In: International Conference on Machine Learning, pp. 2048–2057 (2015)
30. Yoon, S., et al.: Counterfactual two-stage debiasing for video corpus moment retrieval. In: ICASSP 2023-2023 IEEE International Conference on Acoustics, Speech and Signal Processing (ICASSP), pp. 1–5. IEEE (2023)
31. Yoon, S., et al.: Selective query-guided debiasing for video corpus moment retrieval. In: European Conference on Computer Vision, pp. 185–200. Springer (2022)
32. Yoon, S., Kim, D., Kim, J., Yoo, C.D.: Cascaded MPN: cascaded moment proposal network for video corpus moment retrieval. IEEE Access **10**, 64560–64568 (2022)

33. Yoon, S., Koo, G., Kim, D., Yoo, C.D.: Scanet: scene complexity aware network for weakly-supervised video moment retrieval. In: Proceedings of the IEEE/CVF International Conference on Computer Vision, pp. 13576–13586 (2023)
34. Zhang, D., Dai, X., Wang, X., Wang, Y.F., Davis, L.S.: Man: moment alignment network for natural language moment retrieval via iterative graph adjustment. In: Proceedings of the IEEE Conference on Computer Vision and Pattern Recognition, pp. 1247–1257 (2019)

Oral Session : Computer Vision

Spiral Patch Exemplar-Based Inpainting of 3D Colored Meshes

Olivier Lézoray$^{(\boxtimes)}$ (ID) and Sébastien Bougleux (ID)

Normandie Univ, UNICAEN, ENSICAEN, CNRS, GREYC, Caen, France
`olivier.lezoray@unicaen.fr`

Abstract. 3D colored meshes are becoming popular in many computer graphics applications. However, they may contain many color defects due to the scanning process. We present an exemplar-based framework for color completion in 3D colored meshes, as an adaptation of the approach of Criminisi *et al.* proposed for images [5]. To exploit the self similarity of the vertices, a spiral patch is defined to represent the local neighborhood of vertices, as well as how to compare two spiral patches. A dedicated priority term is used to define the filling order, so that patches close to the inpainting boundary with specific continuity properties are inpainted first. The proposed approach is tested on several meshes for different correction tasks and shows good performances in terms of visual reconstruction of the inpainted areas.

Keywords: Inpainting · 3D Colored mesh · Spiral patch

1 Introduction

3D acquisition techniques have recently undergone a number of advances and developments. The latter include 3D laser scanners, structured light cameras and photogrammetry. While these techniques initially only captured the 3D coordinates of the points to represent the object, it has now become common practice to also acquire the color of each 3D point. The 3D data then takes the form of a 3D colored point cloud or a 3D colored mesh (a triangulated surface). 3D color data has thus come to the forefront in a wide range of new application fields: digital forensics, digital cultural heritage, digital twins. However, while it is now easy to acquire 3D data, editing them is much more difficult, even though users demand it. In particular, consolidating colored 3D meshes from scans is essential for fixing geometric or color defects of the mesh surface. This problem, known as 3D data completion or inpainting, can be carried out at either the geometric or colorimetric level.

The completion of the geometry of surfaces represented by meshes has received much attention. Many methods have been proposed for filling holes in 3D meshes [8,19,22] or in 3D point clouds [6,7,10]. Some of these methods

---

This work received funding from the Normandy region under the COSURIA emergent project.

C. Wallraven et al. (Eds.): ICPRAI 2024, LNCS 14892, pp. 127–141, 2025.
https://doi.org/10.1007/978-981-97-8702-9_9

are extensions of the image inpainting algorithm proposed by Criminisi *et al.* [5]. More recently some deep learning approaches have also been proposed [9], they operate directly on meshes eliminating the need for conversion to point clouds or voxel grids [20].

In contrast, for the completion of color on 3D meshes, almost no approach has been proposed so far. We can nevertheless quote some close works. In [14] an approach was proposed for the colorization of meshes. In [16] an approach was proposed for the inpainting of texture on the faces of 3D textured meshes by manipulating the associated 2D texture map image. Our objective is to establish an approach that performs the completion of the missing color information on 3D colored meshes (where one has a color per vertex). Indeed, colored meshes might be preferred to textured meshes as the latter can introduce mapping discontinuities and limitations for model editing [21]. To do so, we propose an adaptation of the approach of Criminisi *et al.* proposed for images [5]. As the latter relies on the notion of similarity between patches that are subsequently pasted to fill in the inpainting area, a similar notion of patches is needed for meshes. However, this is difficult as the number of neighbors of each vertex is not always the same. To cope with this, a spiral patch is defined to represent the local neighborhood of vertices, as well as how to compare two spiral patches. A dedicated priority term is used to define the filling order that permits to reconstruct first the patches near the inpainting boundary and that exhibit specific properties in terms of density, variance and continuity.

In the next section, we introduce some notations. In Sect. 3 we describe the notion of spiral patch, at the core of our adaptation of [5]. Section 4 presents the proposed 3D colored mesh inpainting and its details. Then we present some results and conclude.

2   Notations

A mesh M is represented by a graph $\mathcal{G} = (\mathcal{V}, \mathcal{E})$ that consists in a finite set $\mathcal{V} = \{v_1, \ldots, v_m\}$ of vertices and a finite set $\mathcal{E} \subset \mathcal{V} \times \mathcal{V}$ of edges. We assume $\mathcal{G}$ to be undirected, with no self-loops and no multiple edges. Let (v_i, v_j) be the edge of $\mathcal{E}$ that connects two vertices v_i and v_j of $\mathcal{V}$. The notation $v_i \sim v_j$ is used to denote two adjacent vertices. The set $\mathcal{N}(v_i) = \{v_j, v_j \sim v_i\}$ gives the set of all the adjacent vertices to v_i within a 1-hop (vertices that can be reached in one walk). We define a graph signal $\mathbf{F}$ on $\mathcal{G}$, as a function that assigns vectors to vertices $\mathbf{F} \colon \mathcal{V} \to \mathbb{R}^d$. We will consider three different graph signals on vertices:

1. $\mathbf{S} \colon \mathcal{V} \to \mathbb{R}^3$ that provides the coordinates at a vertex v_i,
2. $\mathbf{N} \colon \mathcal{V} \to \mathbb{R}^3$ that provides the normal at a vertex v_i,
3. $\mathbf{C} \colon \mathcal{V} \to \mathbb{R}^3$ that provides the color at a vertex v_i.

Vertices' normals $\mathbf{N}(v_i)$ are computed as a weighted average of incident face normals with angle-based weighting [1].

3   Spiral Patch

To be able to perform exemplar-based inpainting on 3D colored meshes, we need a definition of patches on meshes (mainly for search and copy of similar patches). In [15], Lim *et al.* proposed local spiral hop operators. The principle is that the surrounding vertices of one vertex can be enumerated by following a spiral, as illustrated in Fig. 1. We propose to use this principle to define patches on 3D meshes.

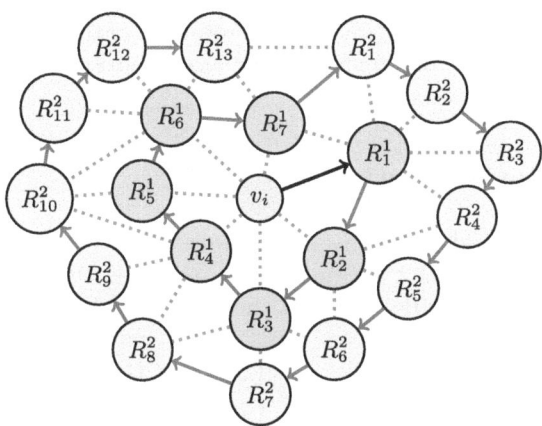

Fig. 1. Example of a spiral patch $\text{Sp}(v_i, 2)$ for a node v_i of a mesh.

First, we introduce the following definitions for local spiral hop operators:

$$R^0(v_i) = \{v_i\}$$

$$R^{k+1}(v_i) = \mathcal{N}(R^k(v_i)) \setminus k\text{-disk}(v_i)$$

$$k\text{-disk}(v_i) = \bigcup_{l=0,\ldots,k} R^l(v_i)$$

$$k\text{-ring}(v_i) = k\text{-disk}(v_i) \setminus \{v_i\}$$

Given a vertex v_i and a radius size k, a k-disk(v_i) is the set of vertices that can be reached from v_i in 0 to k walks. As this includes v_i, the set k-ring(v_i) is the same set without v_i. $R^k(v_i)$ is the k-ring: an ordered set of vertices whose shortest path to v_i is exactly k hops long. Then, $R^{k+1}(v_i)$ is the set of vertices that can be reached in 1 walk from $R^k(v_i)$ without going through its k-disk (that contains vertices that can be reached from v_i in 0 to k walks). $R_j^k(v_i)$ denotes the j-th element in the k-ring. Obviously one has $R^1(v_i) = \mathcal{N}(v_i)$ and $R_1^0(v_i) = v_i$. From these operators, we can define a spiral patch $\text{Sp}(v_i, k)$ as an ordered sequence from the concatenation of the elements of the ordered rings:

$$\text{Sp}(v_i, k) = (v_i, 1\text{-ring}(v_i), \ldots, k\text{-ring}(v_i))$$

$$= \left(R_1^0(v_i), R_1^1(v_i), R_2^1(v_i), \ldots, R_{|R^k|}^k(v_i) \right)$$

This operator has two degrees of freedom: the direction (clockwise or counterclockwise) of the rings and the first chosen vertex $R_1^1(v_i)$ (shown by the black arrow in Fig. 1). The remaining vertices are ordered inductively. To suppress both freedom degrees, we fix the orientation to clockwise and choose the initial vertex $R_1^1(v_i)$ as the one in the direction of the shortest geodesic path to v_i [18]:

$$R_1^1(v_i) = \arg \min_{v_j \in \mathcal{N}(v_i)} d_{\mathcal{G}}(v_i, v_j)$$

where $d_{\mathcal{G}}$ is the geodesic distance between two vertices on the graph $\mathcal{G}$. This enables the operator to become invariant to rotations of the neighborhoods. Such a choice has also been considered in [3] for the definition of spiral convolution on graphs.

4   Mesh Color Inpainting

Given a Mesh M and its associated graph $\mathcal{G} = (\mathcal{V}, \mathcal{E})$, the area to be inpainted is denoted as $\Omega \subset \mathcal{V}$ and its boundary is $\partial\Omega = \{v_i \in \Omega | \exists v_j \in \mathcal{N}(v_i)$ with Marked$(v_j) = 0\}$. We mark the vertices to be inpainted by the following function:

$$\text{Marked}(v_i) = \begin{cases} 1 \text{ if } v_i \in \Omega \\ 0 \text{ if } v_i \notin \Omega \end{cases}$$

For vertices v_i in Ω, their color is considered as unknown and set to $\mathbf{C}(v_i) = (0, 0, 0)^T$. The objective of the inpainting is to recover the color of these vertices by pasting the color of vertices from surrounding spiral patches.

4.1   Algorithm Flowchart

The outline of the algorithm is similar to the one proposed by Criminisi et al. for images [5], but we adapt it for the special case of 3D color meshes inpainting. A pseudo-code description of the algorithmic steps is shown in Algorithm 1. At each iteration, the priority of the vertices is computed, and the vertex v_{target} with the highest priority is selected as the one to be filled. The vertex v_{best} having the most similar spiral patch $\text{Sp}(v_{best}, k)$ to $\text{Sp}(v_{target}, k)$ is then searched within the set of vertices that belong to γ-ring(v_{target}). The algorithm has therefore two parameters: the size k of spiral patches and the ring search size γ for similar patches. The search is restricted to spiral patches that are fully defined (they have no vertex in Ω). The color values of $\text{Sp}(v_{best}, k)$ are pasted on the patch $\text{Sp}(v_{target}, k)$ for its vertices included in Ω. The boundary $\partial\Omega$ is then updated and the algorithm iterates until there are no more vertices to inpaint. In the sequel we provide details on the steps involved in this algorithm.

Algorithm 1. 3D Colored mesh spiral patch exemplar-based inpainting

---

Input: Mesh M and associated graph $\mathcal{G} = (\mathcal{V}, \mathcal{E})$, inpainting area $\Omega \subset \mathcal{V}$

Set the size k of spiral patches and γ the ring search size

Compute Spiral patches $\mathrm{Sp}(v_i, k)$ of size k, $\forall v_i \in \Omega \cup \{v_j \in \gamma\text{-ring}(v_i)\}$

Mark vertices to be inpainted : $\mathrm{Marked}(v_i) = 1$, $\forall v_i \in \Omega$

while $\partial\Omega \neq \emptyset$ **do**

    1) Compute $\mathrm{Priority}(v_i)$, $\forall v_i \in \partial\Omega$

    2) Find the spiral patch $\mathrm{Sp}(v_{target}, k)$ with the maximum priority i.e., $v_{target} = \arg\max\limits_{v_i \in \partial\Omega} \mathrm{Priority}(v_i)$

    3) Find the fully-defined exemplar $\mathrm{Sp}(v_{best}, k)$ (with $v_{best} \in \mathcal{V} \setminus \Omega$) that minimizes $d(\mathrm{Sp}(v_{target}, k), \mathrm{Sp}(v_{best}, k))$ with $\mathrm{Confidence}(v_{best}) = 1$ in $\gamma\text{-ring}(v_{target})$

    4) Copy colors from the spiral patch $\mathrm{Sp}(v_{best}, k)$ to $\mathrm{Sp}(v_{target}, k)$, $\forall v_i \in \mathrm{Sp}(v_{target}, k)$ with $\mathrm{Marked}(v_i) = 1$

    6) Update $\mathrm{Marked}(v_i)$ and $\partial\Omega$ for all inpainted vertices

end while

4.2 Spiral Patch Comparison

In step three of Algorithm 1, one needs to find in $V \setminus \Omega$ the spiral patch that is the most similar to a given one located on $\partial\Omega$. Therefore, we have to properly define how to compute distances between spiral patches. Local hop spiral operators have been used in [3, 15] and provided competitive results for shape correspondence. However, as the size of the operator $\mathrm{Sp}(v_i, k)$ varies for the vertices (as all the vertices do not have the same number of neighbors), both these approaches have considered only fixed-size spiral. They either truncate or zero-pad each spiral depending on its size. This obviously doesn't adequately capture the similarities between different spirals, and is totally unsuitable for examplar-based inpainting. Therefore, we proceed differently. We define the difference between two spiral patches of two vertices as the sum of the differences between their respective k-rings:

$$d(\mathrm{Sp}(v_i, k), \mathrm{Sp}(v_j, k)) = \sum_{l=0}^{k} d(R^l(v_i), R^l(v_j))$$

Two k-rings are compared by mapping the vertices of the largest ring to the smallest one:

$$d(R^l(v_i), R^l(v_j)) = \sum_{n=0}^{|R^l(v_i)|} d(R_n^l(v_i), R_{n'(n, v_i, v_j)}^l(v_j))$$

with $n'(n, v_i, v_j) = \left\lfloor \frac{n \cdot |R^l(v_j)|}{|R^l(v_i)|} \right\rfloor$ and $|R^l(v_i)| > |R^l(v_j)|$. The distance between two vertices is then the distance between their color graph signal vectors:

$$d(R_n^l(v_i), R_m^l(v_j)) = \|\mathbf{C}(R_n^l(v_i)) - \mathbf{C}(R_m^l(v_j))\|_2$$

Finally, this distance definition between spiral patches exactly recovers that of images patches represented as 8-adjacency grid-graph meshes.

4.3   Priority Computation

Algorithm 1 is similar to the one proposed in [5] and performs the inpainting through a best-filling strategy that depends on priority values assigned to each spiral patch of the front boundary $\partial\Omega$. In [5], the priority is based on the product of two terms: confidence and data terms. The confidence term measures the amount of known information around one pixel and the data term encourages linear structures to be inpainted first. These two terms cannot be directly used for 3D color meshes (e.g., there is no definition of isophotes for meshes), so we propose a priority term dedicated to 3D colored meshes that is the product of four terms. The priority term is used in steps one and two of Algorithm 1.

Confidence: The confidence term is similar to the one used for images. Its objective is to fill first the spiral patches that have most of their vertices' colors already known. The confidence is defined as

$$\text{Confidence}(v_i) = \frac{\sum\limits_{v_j \in \ k\text{-disk}(v_i)} (1 - \text{Marked}(v_j))}{|k\text{-disk}(v_i)|}$$

This measures the proportion of known vertices' colors within the spiral patch $\text{Sp}(v_i, k)$. It is close to 1 if most of the vertices' colors of the spiral patch are known, and close to 0 for spiral patches that contain few known vertices' colors (see Fig. 2(c)).

Density: The density term aims at favoring dense spiral patches to be filled first. Indeed, in meshes, the spatial coverage of a patch can be very different from one part of the mesh to another. It is preferable to inpaint first small spiral patches. The density is defined as

$$\text{Density}(v_i) = \frac{|k\text{-ring}(v_i)|}{\sum\limits_{v_j \in \ k\text{-ring}(v_i)} \|\mathbf{S}(v_i) - \mathbf{S}(v_j)\|_2}$$

This measures the average spatial dispersion of the vertices of the spiral patch $\text{Sp}(v_i, k)$ with respect to its center v_i. It is high if the spiral patch is small and low otherwise (see Fig. 2(d)).

Variance: The variance term aims at favoring the filling of spiral patches that exhibit strong geometrical variations. We measure the latter by the total variance of the vertices' normals of a spiral patch $\text{Sp}(v_i, k)$. If its value is high this means that there are variations in the surface of the spiral patch (see Fig. 2(e)). The variance term is defined as

$$\text{Variance}(v_i) = \sum_{j=1}^{3} \sigma_j^2(\mathcal{N}(v_i, k))$$

where $\mathcal{N}(v_i, k)$ is the set of vertices' normals for vertices in $\text{Sp}(v_i, k)$.

Continuity: The continuity term is similar to the data term used for images. Its aim is to encourage the inpainting of spiral patches where a strong variation in color is present. The spiral patches that lie on the continuation of color structures will then be filled first. For images, this was motived by the notion of isophotes. As there is no equivalent notion for meshes, we consider the Structure Tensor Total Variation (STTV) [13]. Moreover, a similar SSTV has already been used for image inpainting in [4] and showed good results. The structure tensor $\mathbf{J}$ is the outer product of the gradient: $\mathbf{J}(v_i)=\nabla^T \mathbf{f}(v_i) \cdot \nabla \mathbf{f}(v_i)$. We define the gradient at a given vertex v_i as the vector of all the distances between the spiral descriptors of v_i and its neighbors within its k-ring(v_i):

$$\nabla \mathbf{f}(v_i) = [d(\mathrm{Sp}(v_i, k), \mathrm{Sp}(v_j, k)), v_j \in k\text{-ring}(v_i)]^T$$

The structure tensor summarizes the dominant directions of the gradient in the k-ring(v_i) of a vertex v_i. The importance of the structure tensor lies in its eigenvalues that provide a rich and discriminative description of the local geometry by summarizing the distribution of the gradients in the k-ring(v_i) neighborhood. Its spectral decomposition is $\mathbf{J}(v_i) = \mathbf{U}\Lambda\mathbf{U}^T$ with $\mathbf{U}$ its eigenvectors and Λ its eigenvalues. This leads us to define the continuity from the STTV as:

$$\mathrm{Continuity}(v_i) = \sqrt{\sum_{j=1}^{|k\text{-ring}(v_i)|} \lambda_j^2}$$

with $\lambda_j = \Lambda(j, j)$. If its value is high this means that there are color variations on the surface around the spiral patch (see Fig. 2(f)).

Priority: The priority is then defined as

$$\mathrm{Priority}(v_i) = \mathrm{Confidence}(v_i) \cdot \mathrm{Density}(v_i) \cdot \mathrm{Variance}(v_i) \cdot \mathrm{Continuity}(v_i)$$

Its objective is to favor the inpainting of spiral patches that: 1) have few missing information (Confidence term), 2) have a small spatial range (Density term), 3) are located at strong geometric features (Variance term), 4) are located at strong color structures (Continuity term). Figure 2 shows these terms for a zone to be inpainted. One can see that the selected target patch of highest priority is the one that makes the most of these four terms.

4.4   Copying One Spiral Patch on Another

In step four of Algorithm 1, once the best matching spiral patch $\mathrm{Sp}(v_{best}, k)$ of $\mathrm{Sp}(v_{target}, k)$ has been identified. Its content must be pasted on the missing parts of $\mathrm{Sp}(v_{target}, k)$. This means that only the vertices $v_j \in \mathrm{Sp}(v_{target}, k)$ with $\mathrm{Marked}(v_j) = 1$ will have their color inpainted. To perform this, we rely on the matching we have defined between rings to compare two spiral patches. The color of a vertex $v_m = R^l_{n_m}(v_{target}) \in l\text{-ring}(v_{target})$, with $\mathrm{Marked}(v_m) = 1$ is filled by the average of the colors of all the vertices $v_p = R^l_{n_p}(v_{best}) \in l\text{-ring}(v_{best})$ such that $n'(n_p, v_p, v_m) = n_m$. The indexes of v_m and v_p in their respective l-ring are n_m and n_p. In other words, the colors of all the vertices from $l\text{-ring}(v_{best})$ that are matched to a vertex v_m are averaged to fill $\mathbf{C}(v_m)$.

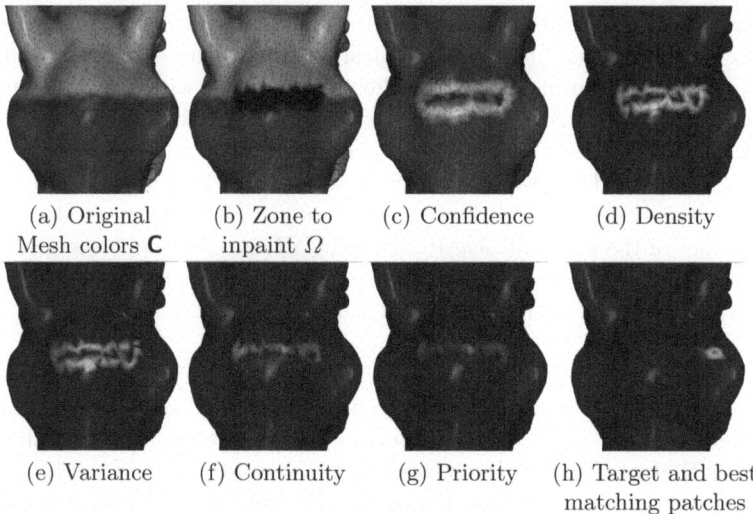

(a) Original   (b) Zone to   (c) Confidence   (d) Density
Mesh colors **C**   inpaint Ω

(e) Variance   (f) Continuity   (g) Priority   (h) Target and best
matching patches

Fig. 2. From left to right, top to bottom: an original part of a 3D colored mesh, the selected zone to inpaint Ω, the computed Confidence, Density, Variance, and Continuity terms that are combined to obtain the Priority (warm colors mean highest priority). Final image shows the target spiral patch $\mathrm{Sp}(v_{target}, 1)$ of highest priority (shown in red) and its best matching spiral patch in a 3-ring (shown in green). (Color figure online)

5 Results

In this section we provide examples of 3D colored mesh inpainting with the proposed approach[1]. We start with an example that shows the benefit of the approach. Figure 3 presents a 3D colored mesh (A gargoyle mesh on which the lena image has been projected) where three areas have been suppressed. The latter are shown in yellow and each area is about 200 vertices insize. In the first pair of images of Fig. 3, the area that has been suppressed is on the continuity of a linear color structure separating two colored areas. Our approach has successfully succeeded to reconstruct the missing part while preserving the continuation of the linear structure. This shows the quality of our proposed priority computation. The preservation is not (and cannot be) perfect as the patches are not all of the same sizes in this part of the mesh. In the second pair of images of Fig. 3, the area that has been suppressed is located in a textured area. We can see that our approach has managed to reconstruct the missing part without any visible artifacts. In the last pair of images of Fig. 3, the area that has been suppressed is located in a zone of subtle color and texture changes. The reconstructed area appears to be very coherent with its surrounding. The PSNR between the inpainted area in the original mesh and the inpainted mesh is of

---

[1] Complementary videos can be found at https://lezoray.users.greyc.fr/projects/ ICPRAI-2024/.

33.24db assessing that our approach can well restore both homogeneous or textured areas. These examples show the interest of our approach that is able to reconstruct complex missing color structures on 3D colored meshes. The parameters were the following. Spiral patches $\mathrm{Sp}(v_i, 2)$ are extracted on 2-rings for each vertex v_i. The search area for finding the most similar spiral patch (step three in Algorithm 1), is fixed as being the 5-ring(v_i). The parameters are therefore $k = 2$ and $\gamma = 5$.

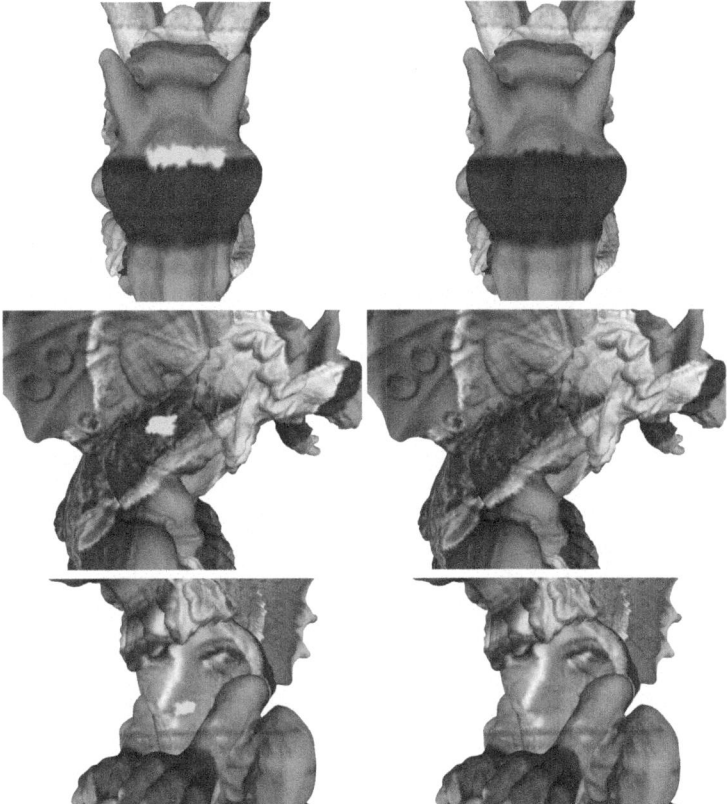

Fig. 3. Examples of 3D colored mesh inpainting. Images (before/after inpainting) are presented in pairs by rows. The areas to be inpainted appear in yellow. (Color figure online)

In Fig. 5, we present results on real scanned meshes. The first two meshes are from the GREYC 3D colored mesh database [17]. They present some color scanning defects on the surface that have to be corrected. These defects correspond mainly to colors that have been wrongly captured during the scanning process. The objective is therefore to define inpainting areas (shown in yellow in the second column of Fig. 5) where the color has to be corrected. One can

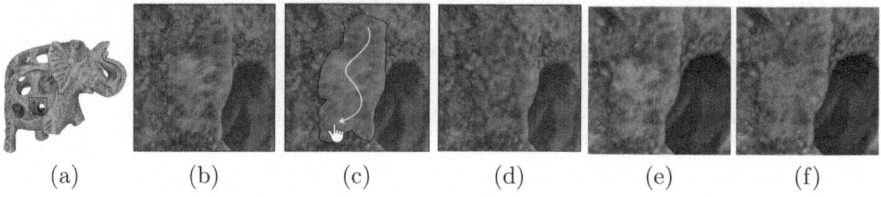

(a)   (b)   (c)   (d)   (e)   (f)

Fig. 4. Inpainting comparison with the approach of [16] with from left to rigth, (a) Elephant Mesh, (b) Texture defect: 90.26, (c) Inpainting area, (d) Result of [16]: 96.33, (e) Ours ($k = 1$, $\gamma = 15$): 69.11, (f) Ours ($k = 2$, $\gamma = 15$): 68.40. Values correspond to the BRISQUE IQA.

see in the third column of Fig. 5 that our approach has managed to reconstruct the color from these missing areas (mostly homogeneous) without any visible artifacts, even if the missing area can be large. The parameters were $k = 1$ and $\gamma = 3$, meaning that we used 1-ring spiral patches with a search area in 3-ring(v_i). These parameters will be used for all other experiments, if not stated otherwise. The last rows of Fig. 5 present scans from cultural heritage objects downloaded from sketchFab[2]. The areas to be inpainted have been selected to either be in homogenous, transition or textured areas. The reconstruction is of good visual quality for all these situations even when the underlying texture is complex. There doesn't exist any no-reference quality metrics for 3D colored meshes (in contrast to uncolored 3D meshes [11]), so we have measured the BRISQUE Image Quality Assessment (IQA) of the rendered images before and after inpainting (first and last columns of Fig. 5). Indeed, inpainting quality evaluation is a well-known problem, and BRISQUE is frequently used to that aim [12] (the lower the better). In Fig. 5), the inpainted images always show a lower BRISQUE value with an average gain of 0.13, showing that inpainted results have a slightly better perceptual quality.

In Fig. 4 we present a comparison with the recent approach of Maggiordomo *et al.* [16]. They do not inpaint the vertices' colors but the faces' textures. The latter being stored in a 2D image that is mapped onto the triangles of the mesh, it can be processed by usual deep learning approaches that operate on images. To compare our approach with theirs, we have considered a model they used from sketchfab (Broken Stone Elephant, see Fig. 4(a)). To have color per vertices, we have remeshed the model and transferred the color from the faces' texture to the vertices. The mesh has some acquisition defects (Fig. 4(b)). A user has delineated the zone to inpaint (Fig. 4(c), around 2000 vertices to inpaint). Figure 4(d)-(f) presents the result of [16] and of our approach with two different spiral patch sizes. Whatever the patch size, it is easy to see that our approach produces visually competitive results that are not blurry (as we copy/paste patches) in contrast to [16]. Indeed we obtain much better BRISQUE quality values, and with larger spiral patches, the completion looks more realistic.

---

[2] https://sketchfab.com/, used models are under CC BY-NC 4.0 Licence.

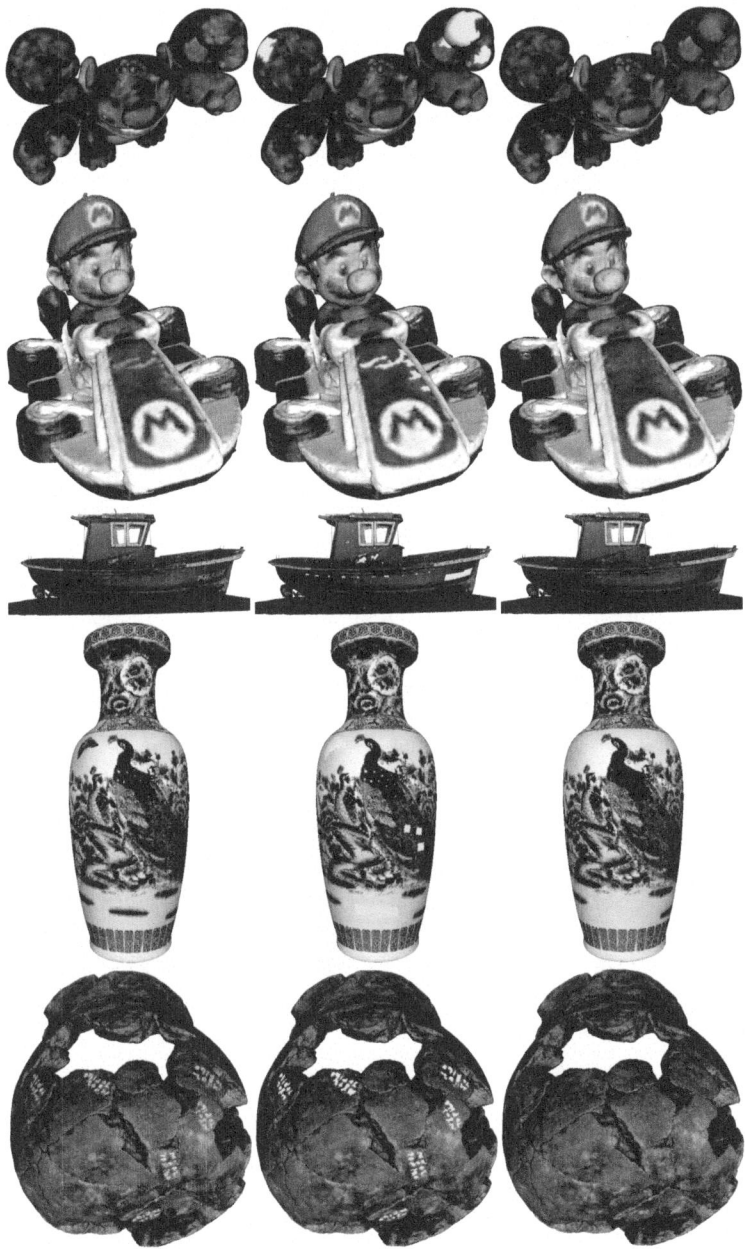

Fig. 5. Examples of 3D colored mesh inpainting (best viewed zoomed). Each row presents an original mesh (first column) where some defects appear and have to be corrected. These zones are marked in yellow (second column) and have to be inpainted. Last column presents the inpainting results. First row mesh has 83063 vertices, 166118 edges and 459 vertices to inpaint. Second row mesh has 216375 vertices, 432706 edges and 236 vertices to inpaint. Third row mesh has 514806 vertices, 1028551 edges and 3092 vertices to inpaint. Fourth row mesh has 336053 vertices, 672098 edges and 1750 vertices to inpaint. Last row mesh has 770354 vertices, 1540772 edges and 1182 vertices to inpaint. (Color figure online)

In Fig. 6, we present a practical situation where our inpainting algorithm can be very useful. The presented 3D colored mesh is a scan of a person. Such models have recently received much attention as they can be used to virtually represent scanned persons as realistic avatars in virtual reality environments. Here we use our approach in a similar way that image inpainting algorithms are used by photographs in order to remove unpleasant elements in faces' images such as acne marks and freckles, moles, or rashes. We have manually selected such elements to inpaint on the person head scan (second column of Fig. 6). The number of vertices to be inpainted is 18906. Last column of Fig. 6 presents the results. One can see that the inpainted areas are almost indistinguishable from their surroundings assessing the fact that our inpainting performs very well (as assessed by he BRISQUE values) and can be beneficial for such practical applications.

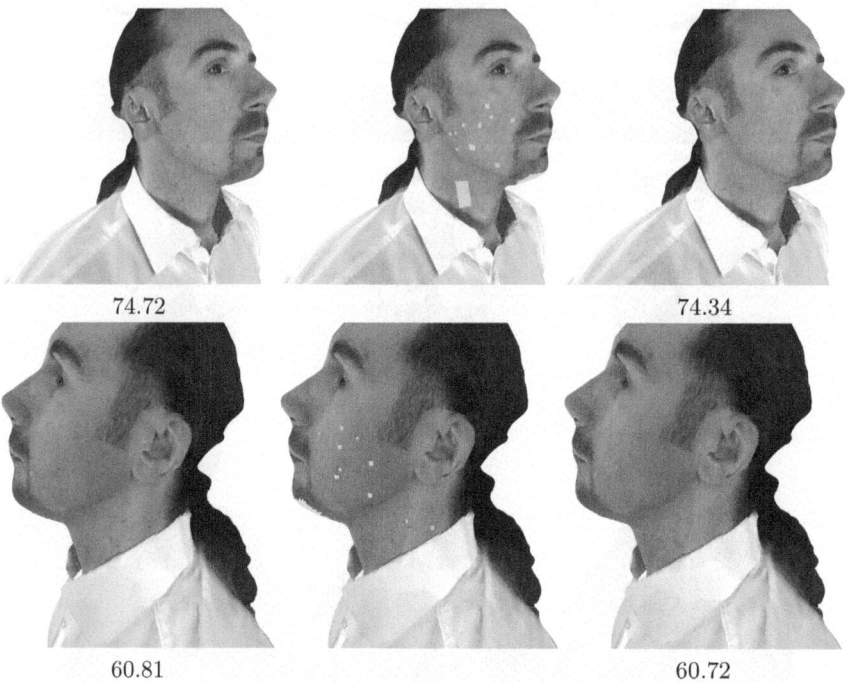

74.72   74.34

60.81   60.72

Fig. 6. Inpainting of acne marks and freckles, moles, or rashes on the scan of a person face (1928258 vertices and 3856512 edges). Provided values are the BRISQUE IQA.

Finally, Fig. 7 presents a mesh of a scan of a Nefertiti bust statue (also from sketchfab). A large part of the antique hat presents defects (first column of Fig. 7). This area has been marked to be inpainted (second column of Fig. 7). The reconstructed area looks plausible (last column of Fig. 7, see the BRISQUE IQA) but is not totally satisfactory when examined closely. This illustrates a

16.52   16.22

Fig. 7. Nefertiti bust statue inpainting (993434 vertices and 1986864 edges). Provided values are the BRISQUE IQA.

limitation of our approach. We considered a fixed search area in the 3-ring of each vertex. So, as the reconstruction progresses, there may be a progressive copy of patches that were reconstructed from the previous iteration. A solution could be to enlarge the search area but this comes with higher computational costs. The best way to cope with this problem would be to have a smarter similar patch search such as the PatchMatch algorithm [2], which we should adapt to 3D meshes.

6   Conclusion

We have proposed an approach for the exemplar-based inpainting of 3D colored meshes. The objective is to reconstruct the missing color for vertices of the mesh. An equivalent of patches on meshes has been defined as spiral patches. Then, a specific adaptation of the algorithm of Criminisi *et al.* for images [5] has been proposed. Critical parts concerned the definition of the priority of the filling order and the comparison and copying of spiral patches. Several results have been presented that show the benefit of the approach that is able to well reconstruct missing colored areas in 3D colored meshes. A limitation of the approach is the simple patch search strategy. Replacing it with an adaptation of the PatchMatch algorithm [2] to 3D meshes could improve results in certain situations.

References

1. Bærentzen, J.A., Aanæs, H.: Signed distance computation using the angle weighted pseudonormal. IEEE Trans. Vis. Comput. Graph. **11**(3), 243–253 (2005)
2. Barnes, C., Goldman, D.B., Shechtman, E., Finkelstein, A.: The patchmatch randomized matching algorithm for image manipulation. Commun. ACM **54**(11), 103–110 (2011)
3. Bouritsas, G., Bokhnyak, S., Ploumpis, S., Zafeiriou, S., Bronstein, M.M.: Neural 3d morphable models: spiral convolutional networks for 3d shape representation learning and generation. In: ICCV, pp. 7212–7221. IEEE Computer Society, Los Alamitos, CA, USA (2019)
4. Buyssens, P., Daisy, M., Tschumperlé, D., Lézoray, O.: Exemplar-based inpainting: technical review and new heuristics for better geometric reconstructions. IEEE Trans. Image Process. **24**(6), 1809–1824 (2015)
5. Criminisi, A., Pérez, P., Toyama, K.: Region filling and object removal by exemplar-based image inpainting. IEEE Trans. Image Process. **13**(9), 1200–1212 (2004)
6. Dinesh, C., Bajic, I.V., Cheung, G.: Adaptive nonrigid inpainting of three-dimensional point cloud geometry. IEEE Signal Process. Lett. **25**(6), 878–882 (2018)
7. Fu, Z., Hu, W., Guo, Z.: Point cloud inpainting on graphs from non-local self-similarity. In: 2018 IEEE International Conference on Image Processing. ICIP 2018, Athens, Greece, 7–10 October 2018, pp. 2137–2141. IEEE, Piscataway, NJ, USA (2018)
8. Gisbert, G., Chaine, R., Coeurjolly, D.: Inpainting holes in folded fabric meshes. Comput. Graph. **114**, 201–209 (2023)
9. Hattori, S., Yatagawa, T., Ohtake, Y., Suzuki, H.: Learning self-prior for mesh inpainting using self-supervised graph convolutional networks (2023)
10. He, J., Fu, Z., Hu, W., Guo, Z.: Point cloud attribute inpainting in graph spectral domain. In: ICIP, pp. 4385–4389 (2019)
11. Ibork, Z., Nouri, A., Lézoray, O., Charrier, C., Touahni, R.: No reference 3d mesh quality assessment using deep convolutional features. In: IEEE (ed.) International Symposium on Image and Signal Processing and Analysis (ISPA - IEEE), pp. 1–6 (2023)
12. Kong, D., Kong, K., Kim, K., Min, S., Kang, S.: Image-adaptive hint generation via vision transformer for outpainting. In: IEEE/CVF Winter Conference on Applications of Computer Vision, WACV 2022, Waikoloa, HI, USA, 3–8 January 2022, pp. 4029–4038 (2022)
13. Lefkimmiatis, S., Osher, S.J.: Nonlocal structure tensor functionals for image regularization. IEEE Trans. Comput. Imaging **1**(1), 16–29 (2015)
14. Li, B., Lai, Y., Rosin, P.L.: Sparse graph regularized mesh color edit propagation. IEEE Trans. Image Process. **29**, 5408–5419 (2020)
15. Lim, I., Dielen, A., Campen, M., Kobbelt, L.: A simple approach to intrinsic correspondence learning on unstructured 3d meshes. In: ECCV. LNCS, vol. 11131, pp. 349–362. Springer-Verlag, Berlin, Heidelberg (2018)
16. Maggiordomo, A., Cignoni, P., Tarini, M.: Texture inpainting for photogrammetric models. Comput. Graph. Forum **42**(6), e14735 (2023)
17. Nouri, A., Charrier, C., Lézoray, O.: Greyc 3d colored mesh database. Technical Report hal-01441721 (2017)
18. Surazhsky, V., Surazhsky, T., Kirsanov, D., Gortler, S.J., Hoppe, H.: Fast exact and approximate geodesics on meshes. ACM Trans. Graph. **24**(3), 553–560 (2005)

19. Wu, X., Lin, X., Li, N., Li, H.: Patch-based mesh inpainting via low rank recovery. Graph. Models **122**, 101139 (2022)
20. Yuan, W., Khot, T., Held, D., Mertz, C., Hebert, M.: PCN: point completion network. In: 3DV, pp. 728–737 (2018)
21. Yuksel, C., Keyser, J., House, D.H.: Mesh colors. ACM Trans. Graph. **29**(2), 15:1–15:11 (2010)
22. Zhao, W., Gao, S., Lin, H.: A robust hole-filling algorithm for triangular mesh. Vis. Comput. **23**(12), 987–997 (2007)

BEVFormer's Plugin: Integrating Historical Detection Data, BEV-Level Information, Time Information, and Depth Information

Zeen Pan, Zongyang Tong, and Yuhan Dong[✉]

Shenzhen International Graduate School, Tsinghua University, Shenzhen, China
dongyuhan@sz.tsinghua.edu.cn

Abstract. This paper presents a novel approach to camera-based 3D object detection, a critical task in autonomous driving systems. We propose a method that leverages historical information and introduces a plug-and-play characteristic during training. Our approach builds upon existing methods by extending the concept of historical feature augmentation and fully exploiting historical information, significantly enhancing detection performance. We also introduce an auxiliary loss operating at the Bird's Eye View (BEV) level, which meticulously cultivates the model's environmental cognition. To address the temporal dimension's inherent lack in the BEV framework, we incorporate a temporal embedding module into the BEV feature amalgamation. Our method elevates the detection paradigm by harnessing historical and temporal information and integrating a BEV-level supervisory framework. We validate our approach through extensive experiments, demonstrating its superiority in real-world scenarios and potential for applications in autonomous driving, video surveillance, and intelligent transportation systems.

Keywords: Object detection · Bird's Eye View · Autonomous driving systems

1 Introduction

In this paper, we propose a novel camera-based 3D object detection approach that incorporates temporal cues to enhance detection accuracy in autonomous driving systems. Our approach is based on insights gained from analyzing temporal data from spatiotemporal detectors [15] and T-CNN [5], which inform our methodology. We utilize these insights in video object detection through two primary strategies: prediction optimization and feature reutilization. Prediction optimization is facilitated through Faster R-CNN, which uses inter-frame motion to improve accuracy, while feature reutilization is demonstrated by MemDPC [2] and FGFA [21], which apply advanced techniques such as attention mechanisms and optical flow to enhance the understanding of object dynamics.

C. Wallraven et al. (Eds.): ICPRAI 2024, LNCS 14892, pp. 142–156, 2025.
https://doi.org/10.1007/978-981-97-8702-9_10

Expanding on the HoP approach [22], our strategy involves sharing the object decoder across training and inference phases, fully exploiting historical data for enhanced learning and performance. Additionally, we introduce an auxiliary loss at the Bird's Eye View (BEV) level to supervise occupancy, classification, and speed, enhancing environmental cognition and positional accuracy.

To address the temporal limitations of BEV, we integrate a temporal embedding module that cyclically updates with the BEV features, improving the integration of spatial and temporal data.

Overall, our approach not only advances the state-of-the-art in camera-based 3D object detection by integrating a plug-and-play feature during training but also demonstrates superior real-world efficacy, as validated by extensive experiments. This positions our method as highly effective for applications in autonomous driving, video surveillance, and intelligent transportation systems.

2   Related Work

2.1   Object Detection in Video

In video-based object detection, initial methods primarily utilized single-frame predictions to identify object bounding boxes in images. Yet, incorporating temporal information across consecutive frames has been shown to substantially improve detection accuracy. Spatiotemporal Detectors [15] and T-CNN [5] are notable for integrating temporal and spatial cues, utilizing motion patterns between frames to enhance predictions.

Temporal modeling in this domain is categorized into two main strategies: prediction refinement and feature reuse. Prediction refinement techniques, such as Faster R-CNN [12], enhance detection by tracking object movement across frames. Alternatively, models like MemDPC [2] and FGFA [21] use advanced architectures, including attention mechanisms and optical flow, to exploit intermediate features from previous frames, improving the detection's accuracy and robustness by better understanding object dynamics.

2.2   Temporal Modeling Based on Intermediate Features for Camera-Based 3D Object Detection

BEVFormer [7] introduced the novel direction of temporal fusion in Camera-Based 3D Object Detection. Leveraging BEV feature domain fusion for spatiotemporal alignment captures object motion within the BEV space, enhancing object detection. Solofusion [11] extends this concept by employing stereo methodology for 3D object detection, utilizing image features as intermediate fusion points. Sparse4D [9] employs 4D keypoint fusion across consecutive frames, enhancing intermediate features for temporal fusion. BEVDet4D-Depth [6] , an extension of BEVDet4D [4] , incorporates depth information from LiDAR sensors to enrich temporal fusion, improving the model's grasp of object motion and spatial relationships.

2.3   Temporal Modeling Based on Prediction Results for Camera-Based 3D Object Detection

In advancing camera-based 3D object detection, several strategies utilize historical object prediction data effectively. Techniques like MonoDIS [14] and Stream-PETR [16] apply RoIAlign to convert 2D bounding box features into 3D outputs, while SimMOD [20] and BEVFormerV2 [18] integrate single-view and DETR3D detection heads to enhance detection accuracy, albeit with significant inference overhead.

The HoP method [22] innovates with a temporally-augmented training paradigm, utilizing time decoders to create pseudo-BEV features from historical data, thereby bypassing the need for corresponding real-time camera images. This enhances the accuracy of object predictions through historical BEV feature augmentation, though it does not proportionally improve the training of object decoders.

Addressing this, we propose a shared object decoder approach for both training and inference, which not only improves inference efficiency but also significantly enhances decoder training, offering a robust solution to temporal training augmentation challenges in 3D object detection.

2.4   Auxiliary Loss in Camera 3D Object Detection

In contemporary research, auxiliary loss design primarily addresses two core objectives: enriching information accuracy and facilitating multitask learning to boost performance. BEVDepth leverages LiDAR supervision to refine depth network capabilities, enhancing 3D object detection by producing more precise Bird's Eye View (BEV) features [6]. MV-FCOS3D++ introduces a perspective-supervised auxiliary loss for pretraining image backbones, improving their handling of perspective details, which is crucial even when the primary detection utilizes BEV 3D [17]. BEVFormerV2 employs detection loss in camera views for auxiliary supervision, leveraging image data to enhance scene comprehension and multitask learning efficacy [18].

Our method innovates by applying an auxiliary loss at the BEV level, using the BEV grid as a base unit with varied supervisions—occupancy, category, and average velocity—within each grid cell. This approach not only refines object category predictions within each cell but also enhances the model's predictions of object movements and trajectories. By integrating these diverse supervisory elements, our methodology aims to significantly improve the performance of object detection or tracking systems.

3   Methodology

3.1   Overall Architecture

Our model embodies an innovative fusion of Historical Object Prediction, Bird's Eye View Auxiliary Loss, and Temporal Embedding Module. This synergistic approach results in a robust framework that not only capitalizes on historical context and explicit temporal cues but also effectively addresses challenges in object detection, making it a promising solution for advancing video-based vision tasks (Fig. 1).

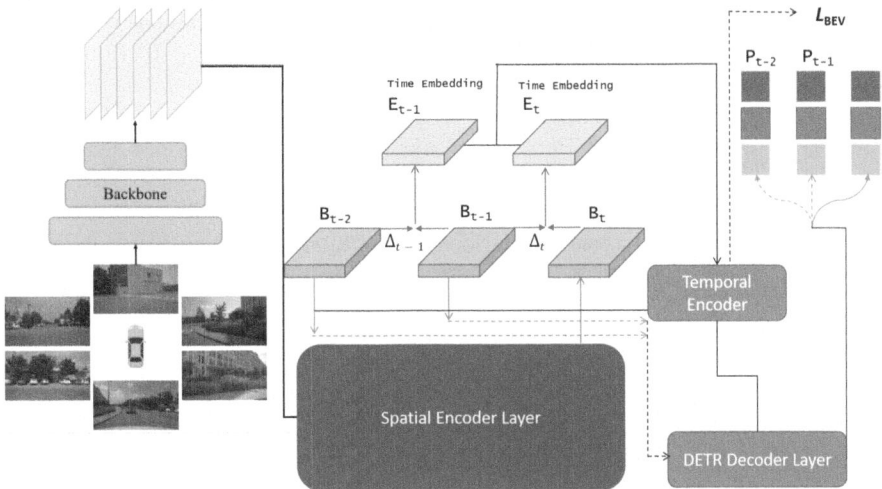

Fig. 1. To maximize the utilization of historical information, the original target decoder is employed to decode the BEV features, denoted as B_{t-i}, for each frame. The Bird's Eye View Auxiliary Loss, denoted as L_{BEV}, is applied to the BEV features generated by the Temporal Encoder, enhancing the model's capacity to leverage depth information for more accurate object detection.The dashed lines in the diagram illustrate that this sharing mechanism, along with the auxiliary task, is exclusively applied during the training phase. In the inference phase, only the solid lines are executed, and the predicted results for each frame, denoted as P_{t-i}, are supplemented with additional pseudo-labels for loss computation.

3.2   Historical Object Prediction

In our innovative scheme, we introduce a new strategy to enhance object detection performance, especially in the context between different frames in a time series. Different from traditional methods, our innovative method aims to enhance the Object Decoder's estimation of the object position in the current frame by making full use of historical information.

In this innovation, we propose a novel approach aimed at maximizing the use of historical information to enhance the performance of object detection in time series. Different from previous HoP [22] methods, we do not introduce an additional object decoder for training, but share the original object decoder for decoding fused BEV features. Such a design enhances the object position estimation ability of the object decoder in the current frame. At the same time, our innovation is not only to introduce the object detection result at the time stamp t_k for supervision, but also to make full use of the information of all historical frames.

Specifically, at time t, each BEV feature in the sequence $\{B_t, B_{t-1}, \ldots, B_{t-N}\}$ is individually fed into the decoder for object detection. For any B_j (where $t \geq j > t - N$), the object detection results are constrained by the consistency of the pseudo-labels generated from either the object detection results or the historical ground truth frames at the previous time step $j - 1$.

In our approach, we address two scenarios regarding labeling information availability in video object detection tasks. Firstly, when it's not feasible to obtain the historical ground truth G_{t-j} (recorded as P).Secondly, when the historical ground truth $G_{t-j}$is accessible (recorded as G). We have devised specific solutions tailored to each scenario to accommodate diverse data conditions (Fig. 2, 3).

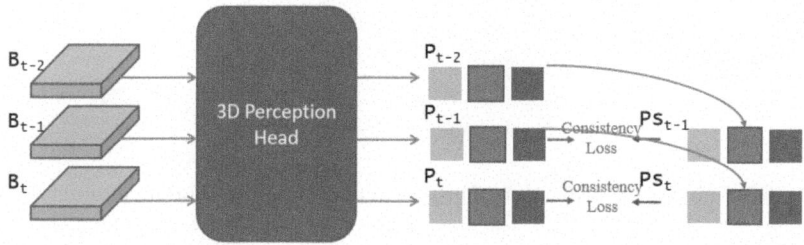

Fig. 2. In the absence of historical ground truth, for any given time t, each frame participating in the fusion process utilizes the prediction results from the previous frame P_{t-j-1}, along with the v_x and v_y velocity components and the time interval Δt, to generate the pseudo-labels for the current frame PS_{t-j}.

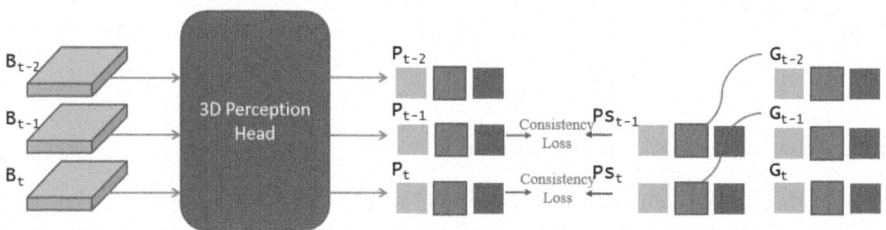

Fig. 3. In scenarios where historical ground truth are available, for any given time t, each frame participating in the fusion process utilizes the ground truth information from the previous frame G_{t-j-1}, along with the v_x and v_y velocity components and the time interval Δt, to generate the pseudo-labels for the current frame PS_{t-j}.

Given a prediction result from the previous frame P_{t-j-1}, the pseudo-label PS_{t-j} is generated based on either historical ground truth frames G_{t-j} or historical prediction results. The pseudo-label generation function g is defined as follows:

$$PS_{t-j} = g(P_{t-j-1}/G_{t-j-1}, \Delta t) \tag{1}$$

where Δt represents the time interval.

The consistency loss $L_{\text{consistency-sum}}$ is calculated using the pseudo-labels PS_{t-j} as follows:

$$L_{\text{consistency-sum}} = \sum_{j=1}^{N} L_{\text{consistency}}(P_{t-j}, PS_{t-j}) \tag{2}$$

where P_{t-j} is the prediction result at time $t-j$, and N is the number of historical frames.

Through this differentiated processing method, we can better deal with different data situations, so as to achieve better results in actual video object detection tasks. This strategy not only demonstrates the flexibility and adaptability of our innovative scheme, but also highlights its effectiveness under various uncertain situations.

The generated additional pseudo-ground truth is used to compute the consistency loss, which significantly enhances the object detection model's ability to predict object locations. This is also the core of our innovation. Through this way of making full use of historical frame information, the performance of target detection is further improved. This method not only efficiently utilizes historical information, but also enhances the accuracy and stability of object detection in time series, bringing important advantages to practical vision task applications.

3.3   Bird's Eye View Auxiliary Loss

Different from other look-around 3D detection methods, our scheme introduces a unique auxiliary loss to improve the performance of position prediction. To more fully leverage the explicit 3D spatial representation, we introduce an auxiliary loss at the Bird's Eye View (BEV) level. We explore supervisory signals for occupancy, category, and average speed in BEVs.

We Construct Ground Truth for Occupancy, Category and Average Speed Information in BEV. The input includes **gt_bboxes_3d** and **gt_labels_3d**, which represent the 3D coordinates and class labels of the target boxes, respectively. For each 3D object box, we extract key attributes including center, size and velocity based on the class label and velocity information. We calculated the coordinates of the four vertices of the target box and stored all points covered by these vertices in the **points_location** list . At the same time, we processed the velocity information, adding it to the **points_velocity** list. We map the information of the target box from the 3D coordinates to the indices in the 2D BEV grid, and then store these indices in the **indices_occ**, **indices_cls**, and **indices_velocity** lists along with the target's occupancy, category, velocity.

Algorithm 1. Generating BEV Labels

1: **Inputs:** Attributes of bounding boxes (`bboxes`)
2: **Outputs:** Ground truth represented at the BEV grid level (`GT`)
3: **for** *bbox, label* **in** *zip(gt_bboxes_3d, gt_labels_3d)* **do**
4:     1. Calculate four vertices of the bounding boxes
5:     2. Extract velocity components and labels
6:     3. Store location/velocity information into `points_location/velocity_list`
7: COMPUTE_INTERVALS(*grid_size*)
8: Initialize `class_indices`, `velocity_indices`
9: **for** *point* **in** `points_location_list` **do**
10:     1. Map 3D point to 2D grid indices
11:     2. Add category/velocity info to respective lists
12: Initialize `processed_cls`, `processed_velocity`, and `processed_cls` grids
13: **for** *index* **in** `grid_indices` **do**
14:     1. Calculate average velocity for grouped indices
15:     2. Assign occupancy, average velocity, and special class label (99) to processed grids

---

When dealing with possible duplicate points, in addition to calculating the average speed of these duplicate points and filling the corresponding positions, we also performed special processing on the category information of these duplicate points. For the category information contained in the duplicate points, we introduce a special category identifier, so that the existence of these duplicate points can be clearly indicated in the subsequent processing. Finally, we store the processed information in **gt_bevocc**, **gt_bevcls** and **gt_bevelo**.

The goal of this process is to map object information from 3D space to 2D BEV grid for subsequent object detection tasks. Given that BEV Grid supervision is not a core task, we employ the Lovasz Softmax loss function when performing explicit BEV Grid supervision. This function is very suitable for dealing with unbalanced data and fuzzy classification boundaries, especially suitable for solving class imbalance problems. We further optimize the supervised training of BEV Grid here using the Lovasz Softmax loss function.

3.4 Temporal Embedding Module

While the BEVFormer framework unifies the representation of 3D information within the Bird's Eye View space, temporal cues are implicitly integrated through the fusion of BEV features. However, the precise utilization of temporal information can be enhanced through an explicit approach.

Therefore, in addition to the BEV feature fusion, we introduce a temporal embedding module to explicitly integrate the time intervals between multiple frames, facilitating stable 3D perception. The temporal embedding module is designed in a recurrent manner.

The core concept is to encode time information using a historical frame sequence, considering the influence of multiple past time steps. We aggregate the temporal embeddings of historical frames to obtain the temporal embedding for the current frame (Fig. 4).

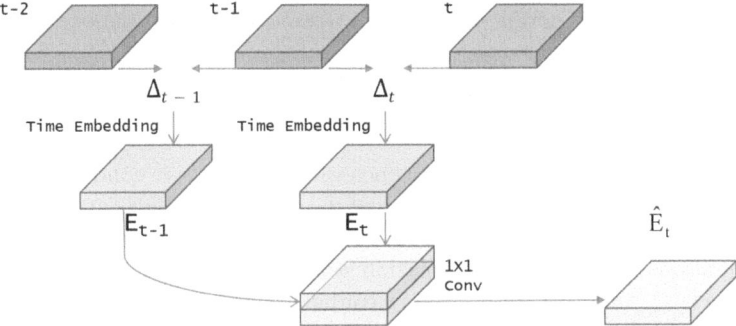

Fig. 4. For each frame, its temporal interval Δt_i with the preceding frame is transformed into a temporal feature. This feature undergoes iterative fusion, continually updated to provide the most up-to-date temporal representation for the current frame.

4   Experiments

4.1   Dataset and Metrics

The nuScenes dataset [1] is a pivotal resource for autonomous driving research, featuring a multi-sensor array including six cameras, one LiDAR, and five millimeter-wave radars, spanning 1000 real-world scenes across various environments. The dataset is divided into training, validation, and test sets to evaluate algorithm generalization. Detailed annotations provide essential data on objects' positions, bounding boxes, velocities, and orientations. For 3D detection tasks, nuScenes introduces several evaluation metrics: nuScenes Detection Score (NDS), mean Average Precision (mAP), and five True Positive (TP) metrics, including mean Average Translation Error (mATE), Scale Error (mASE), Orientation Error (mAOE), Velocity Error (mAVE), and Attribute Error (mAAE).

4.2   Experimental Settings

In our research, we utilize the ResNet [3] architecture with initializations from COCO dataset [8] checkpoints for our backbone in 2D detection tasks. Modifications to the BEVFormer V2's BEVFormerHead enhance the baseline configuration. Our experiments extensively employ historical and temporal information, along with an auxiliary loss at the BEV level, to optimize performance as demonstrated in Tables 1, 2, and 3.

Further, we explore the impact of depth information integration through explicit depth supervision. This exploration is extended into the Transformer's cross-attention module, where we test two novel positional encoding strategies based on depth information to evaluate their effectiveness in improving BEV object detection.

For optimization, the AdamW optimizer [10] is used with a starting learning rate of 4e-4, enabling a detailed analysis of the model's performance under varied conditions.

4.3 Ablation Study

In our investigation utilizing the nuScenes validation set, we conduct a thorough examination of the utilization of historical data, temporal cues, and depth information. Across all models, we maintain a consistent employment of ResNet-50 as the foundational network. In our ablation study pertaining to historical data and temporal cues, we maintain a training configuration involving a triad of image frames as input. In contrast, for the ablation study related to depth information, our training regimen incorporates a pair of image frames as input. Notably, the training duration is held constant at 24 epochs throughout all experimentation.

Leveraging Historical Information. In the experiments, we adopted different pseudo-label generation strategies. Specifically, these two strategies involve applying either the previous frame's predictions or ground truth labels to generate pseudo-labels.

Table 1. Ablation study of pseudo-labels on the nuScenes val set. We employed the two distinct strategies described in the text, represented by the identifiers P, G.

P	G	NDS	mAP	mATE	mASE	mAOE	mAVE	mAAE
		0.5073	0.3976	0.6780	**0.2807**	0.3829	0.3771	0.1963
✓		**0.5112**	**0.4000**	**0.6661**	0.2848	0.3812	0.3750	**0.1808**
	✓	0.5100	0.4001	0.6791	0.2864	**0.3801**	**0.3710**	0.1843

As demonstrated in Table 1, our baseline model achieves a commendable NDS of 50.7%. The integration of pseudo-labels yields marked enhancements across both mAP and mATE metrics. Specifically, leveraging the predictions from the antecedent frame as a basis for pseudo-label generation yields an elevated NDS of 51.1%. Similarly, when utilizing ground truth labels from the preceding frame for pseudo-label generation, a notable increase to 51.0% NDS is achieved, accompanied by an appreciable elevation of mAP by almost 1.4% and a notable reduction of mATE by 1.2% . This outcome consistently aligns with our analytical conjecture, affirming the efficacy of leveraging historical cues in augmenting object detection prowess.

It is noteworthy that the generation and utilization of pseudo-labels, devoid of any discernible inference-time burden, accentuates the forward-looking nature of this method.

Choice of Auxiliary Losses. In the conducted experiments, we investigate the impact of individual and combined auxiliary losses, namely occ (occlusion estimation), cls (class prediction) and velo (velocity prediction), under both non-consistency and consistency contexts on object detection performance.

Table 2. Ablation study of auxiliary losses on the nuScenes validation set. In our experimental evaluations, we investigated the impact of three distinct auxiliary losses: occ, cls, and velo, within both non-consistency and consistency contexts, on object detection performance.

occ	cls	velo	consistency	NDS	mAP	mATE	mASE	mAOE	mAVE	mAAE
				0.5073	0.3976	0.6780	**0.2807**	0.3829	0.3771	0.1963
✓				0.5097	0.4016	0.6527	0.2850	0.3976	0.3749	0.2007
	✓			0.5109	0.3996	0.6565	0.2858	**0.3821**	0.3778	0.1868
		✓		0.5089	0.4008	**0.6489**	0.2820	0.4162	0.3792	0.1883
✓			P	0.5061	0.3955	0.6724	0.2849	0.4051	0.3683	0.1859
	✓		P	0.5048	0.3953	0.6724	0.2862	0.3924	0.3844	0.1930
		✓	P	0.5045	0.4002	0.6749	0.2857	0.4024	0.3959	0.1970
✓	✓		P	**0.5144**	**0.4028**	0.6603	0.2813	0.3835	0.3648	**0.1800**
✓	✓		G	0.5118	0.4024	0.6600	0.2870	0.3894	0.3762	0.1812
✓	✓	✓	✓(P)	0.5106	0.4016	0.6571	0.2851	0.4108	**0.3600**	0.1890

Enhancement Through Individual Auxiliary Losses: In our analysis, when each auxiliary loss (cls, occ, velo) is separately integrated into the model, we observe a improvement in performance. This observation suggests that each auxiliary task independently contributes positively to object detection performance.

Synergistic Boost via Consistency and occ-cls Combinations: Notably, when amalgamating cls and occ auxiliary losses upon the foundation of consistency-driven training, substantial improvements are evident, particularly in terms of mAVE, mAAE, and mATE. Encouragingly, even though we adopt pseudo-labels derived from predictions of previous frames for maintaining consistency in our comparative experiments, NDS registers a commendable increase of nearly 0.7% when juxtaposed against the original baseline.

This finding indicates a synergistic effect between cls and occ losses, which complements and reinforces the model's learning process. As a result, the model becomes more adept at leveraging both the consistency loss and auxiliary tasks to further refine its object detection capabilities.

Analyzing the Combination of Consistency and Simultaneous occ-cls-velo Activation: Interestingly, in the context of incorporating consistency-driven training along with the simultaneous activation of occ, cls, and velo auxiliary losses, we observe that performance does not experience a significant increment beyond the established consistency gain.

This phenomenon may stem from the introduction of multiple auxiliary tasks, leading to information redundancy and intricate task interdependencies. Consequently, the potential performance gains from individual auxiliary losses are offset by the complexity introduced through their simultaneous activation.

Leveraging Temporal Information. In the experimental utilization of temporal information, our approach was implemented alongside the original baseline and a method integrating historical frame prediction for pseudo-label generation, complemented by auxiliary tasks of occ and cls. This comparative analysis aimed to evaluate the efficacy of our time embedding strategy.

Table 3. Ablation study of leveraging temporal information on the nuScenes val set. The strategy of simultaneously utilizing historical frame prediction information to generate pseudo-labels, along with the auxiliary tasks of occ and cls, is denoted as Con&Aux. Additionally, T indicates the explicit incorporation of time information.

Con&Aux	T	NDS	mAP	mATE	mASE	mAOE	mAVE	mAAE
		0.5073	0.3976	0.6780	**0.2807**	0.3829	0.3771	0.1963
✓		**0.5144**	0.4028	**0.6603**	0.2813	0.3835	0.3648	0.1800
	✓	0.5140	0.4013	0.6727	0.2861	**0.3719**	0.3512	0.1852
✓	✓	0.5135	**0.4045**	0.6813	0.2857	0.4067	**0.3406**	**0.1730**

As demonstrated in Table 3, it can be seen that our time embedding strategy does indeed have significant effectiveness; however, the performance improvement in the process of combining it with other strategies is not as ideal as desired.

Leveraging Depth Information. While our attempts to utilize depth information did not yield the desired results, we share the comparative experiments to foster constructive discussions and insights. We hope our efforts will contribute to further advancements in this field, as summarized in Algorithm 2 (Table 4).

Upsampling Module: Utilizes a 1×1 convolutional layer to perform feature mapping, followed by 32 groups of Group Normalization for linear transformation and normalization of features.

Depth Estimation Head: Comprises two 3×3 convolutional layers, each followed by 32 groups of Group Normalization and ReLU activation function to enhance the model's spatial information extraction capability and non-linear expression.

Depth Classification Layer: Maps the extracted feature maps to depth categories (depth_num_bins $+ 1$) using a 1×1 convolutional layer, enabling pixel-level depth estimation.

Algorithm 2. Depth Prediction Forward Pass

1: **Inputs:** Input features
2: **Outputs:** Depth logits , Bin depths , Weighted depths
3: Initialize Proj (Base convolution and normalization layer)
4: **if** multi_ scale is True **then**
5:     Initialize Upsample (Upsampling layers)
6: **if** complex_ model is True **then**
7:     Initialize Depth Head (Depth head: multiple convolutions and normalizations)
8:     Initialize Depth Classifier (Depth classifier: convolution layer)
9: **else**
10:     Initialize Depth MLP (Multilayer perceptron: linear layers and ReLU)
11: **for** each scale in input features **do**
12:     **if** multi_scale is True **then**
13:         Upsample features to the same spatial resolution and merge
14:     **else**
15:         Process only the smallest scale features
16:     **if** complex_model is True **then**
17:         Pass merged features through Depth Head
18:         Obtain depth logits using Depth Classifier
19:     **else**
20:         Obtain depth logits using Depth MLP
21:     Compute depth probability distribution (softmax)
22:     Compute bin depths and weighted depths
23:     **return** Depth logits , Bin depths , Weighted depths

Table 4. On the nuScenes validation dataset, we conducted a comprehensive analysis of the explicit depth supervision approach. All models employed the ResNet-50 backbone network and were trained with a 2-frame image input, maintaining a fixed epoch count of 24. In terms of depth processing, we explored three distinct architectural configurations: a 3-layer multi-layer perceptron (3-Layer MLP), a 6-layer multi-layer perceptron (6-Layer MLP), and a Depth Predictor. Furthermore, the term Multi-Scale signifies the consideration of employing multi-scale image features during the depth prediction process.

Method	Multi-Scale	NDS	mAP	mATE	mASE	mAOE	mAVE	mAAE
Baseline		0.4932	0.3872	**0.6753**	**0.2819**	0.4161	0.4378	0.1927
3-Layer MLP	✓	0.4826	0.3782	0.6988	0.2858	0.4408	0.4425	0.1966
3-Layer MLP		0.4880	0.3798	0.7040	0.2883	**0.3844**	0.4459	0.1958
6-Layer MLP	✓	0.4834	0.3828	0.6951	0.2878	0.4414	0.4536	0.2025
6-Layer MLP		0.4843	0.3793	0.6976	0.2836	0.4319	0.4437	0.1973
Depth Predictor	✓	0.4897	0.3882	0.6899	0.2838	0.4269	0.4514	0.1917
Depth Predictor		**0.4948**	**0.3927**	0.6893	0.2847	0.4207	**0.4336**	**0.1876**

Impact of Multi-scale Strategy: After examining the experimental results, an unexpected pattern emerges regarding the effectiveness of the multi-scale strategy. Surprisingly, experiments conducted without this approach outperformed their multi-scale counterparts. This unexpected outcome prompts a closer examination of the practical implications of the multi-scale strategy.

Influence of Depth Model Architecture and Complexity: Our investigation into depth model architectures reveals that although the Depth Predictor outperforms certain configurations of the multi-layer perceptron on the NDS metric, these improvements are subtle and sometimes fall below the baseline. This highlights the contextual advantages of the Depth Predictor model. However, it is crucial to note that relying solely on explicit depth supervision may not be sufficient for significant performance enhancements.

Impact of Depth Position Encoding: A critical facet of our investigation delves into the realm of depth position encoding. We specifically focus on the implementation and comparative analysis of two distinct encoding strategies: UV-Depth (UVD) encoding [19], and 3D Point Positional Encoding (3DPP) [13].

To clarify the operational principles of our encoding module, We represent the predicted depth within the system as d, 3D reference point as (x, y, z). *Ego2cam* represents the transformation from the ego-vehicle coordinate system to a camera coordinate system, and *SinePE* is the sine positional encoding function. the positional query, denoted as Q_p. The formula for Q_p is given by:

$$u, v, d = \text{Ego2cam}(x, y, z) \tag{3}$$
$$Q_p = \text{SinePE}(u, v, d) \tag{4}$$

For a given pixel located at the coordinates (u_c, v_c), the determination of the positional key, denoted as V_p. The V_p is formulated as follows:

$$Vp = SinePE(F(u_c, v_c, d[uc, vc])) \tag{5}$$

In the context of UVD encoding, the term $F(u_c, v_c, d[u_c, v_c]) = (u_c, v_c, d[u_c, v_c])$, where $d[u_c, v_c]$ denotes the value of d at the coordinate (u_c, v_c). Conversely, within the framework of 3DPP encoding, this necessitates a procedural transition through the coordinate transformation from 2D to 3D. The formulation of this transformation is presented as follows:

$$\begin{bmatrix} P_i^{3D}[0, u_c, v_c] \\ P_i^{3D}[1, u_c, v_c] \\ P_i^{3D}[2, u_c, v_c] \end{bmatrix} = \mathbf{R}_i \mathbf{K}_i^{-1} \mathbf{d}_i[u_c, v_c] \begin{bmatrix} u_c \\ v_c \\ 1 \end{bmatrix} + \mathbf{T}_i \tag{6}$$

In the 3DPP encoding framework, the function $F(u_c, v_c, d[u_c, v_c])$ is computed as described, where $d_i[u_c, v_c]$ represents the predicted depth at the pixel coordinates (u_c, v_c). The coordinates $P_{3D,i}[0, u_c, v_c]$, $P_{3D,i}[1, u_c, v_c]$, and $P_{3D,i}[2, u_c, v_c]$ denote the x, y, and z axes positions, respectively, of the 3D point associated with the pixel (u_c, v_c) in the i-th camera system. The intrinsic matrix of the i-th camera is $K_i \in \mathbb{R}^{3\times3}$, and the transformation matrices, rotation $R_i \in \mathbb{R}^{3\times3}$ and translation $T_i \in \mathbb{R}^{3\times1}$, facilitate coordinate transformation from the camera to the LiDAR system. The inclusion of the variable i accommodates the variation in intrinsic and extrinsic parameters across different camera views (Table 5).

Table 5. In the context of nuScenes validation, we conducted an extensive analysis of depth encoding strategies. Leveraging the optimal configuration of Explicit Depth Supervision, models were initialized with pre-trained weights and depth supervision loss was minimized (0.02) for enhanced depth encoding utilization. For query-pos, reference points were mapped to the image plane, generating positional encodings with depth processing inversion, followed by positional embedding. For value-pos, we explored uvd and 3DPP encoding techniques. Furthermore, the efficacy of freezing pre-trained depth models was examined, offering insights into its impact on overall performance.

Method	freeze	uvd	3dpp	NDS	mAP	mATE	mASE	mAOE	mAVE	mAAE
Baseline				0.4932	0.3872	**0.6753**	**0.2819**	0.4161	0.4378	0.1927
Depth Predictor	✓	✓		**0.4943**	0.3905	0.6877	0.2843	0.4109	0.4350	0.1915
Depth Predictor		✓		0.4926	0.3872	0.7008	0.2837	**0.4088**	**0.4288**	0.1878
Depth Predictor	✓		✓	0.4910	**0.3906**	0.6920	0.2824	0.4141	0.4622	0.1923
Depth Predictor			✓	0.4907	0.3864	0.6908	0.2839	0.4337	0.4311	**0.1852**

Our results indicate that using UVD encoding with a frozen pre-trained depth model slightly outperformed the baseline on the NDS metric, though the inherent trade-offs and incremental gains warrant further exploration to evaluate their wider applicability.

References

1. Caesar, H., Bankiti, V., Lang, A.H., et al.: Nuscenes: a multimodal dataset for autonomous driving. In: Proceedings of the IEEE/CVF Conference on Computer Vision and Pattern Recognition, pp. 11621–11631 (2020)
2. Han, T., Xie, W., Zisserman, A.: Memory-augmented dense predictive coding for video representation learning. In: European Conference on Computer Vision, pp. 312–329. Springer International Publishing (2020)
3. He, K., Zhang, X., Ren, S., Sun, J., et al.: Deep residual learning for image recognition. In: Proceedings of the IEEE Conference on Computer Vision and Pattern Recognition (CVPR), pp. 770–778 (2016)
4. Huang, J., Huang, G.: Bevdet4d: exploit temporal cues in multi-camera 3d object detection. arXiv preprint arXiv:2203.17054 (2022)
5. Kang, K., Li, H., Yan, J., et al.: T-CNN: tubelets with convolutional neural networks for object detection from videos. IEEE Trans. Circuits Syst. Video Technol. **28**(10), 2896–2907 (2017)

6. Li, Y., Ge, Z., Yu, G., et al.: Bevdepth: acquisition of reliable depth for multi-view 3d object detection. In: Proceedings of the AAAI Conference on Artificial Intelligence, vol. 37 (2023)
7. Li, Z., Wang, W., Li, H., et al.: Bevformer: learning bird's-eye-view representation from multi-camera images via spatiotemporal transformers. In: European Conference on Computer Vision, pp. 1–18. Springer Nature Switzerland (2022)
8. Lin, T.Y., Maire, M., Belongie, S., et al.: Microsoft coco: common objects in context. In: European Conference on Computer Vision (ECCV), pp. 740–755. Springer (2014)
9. Lin, X., Lin, T., Pei, Z., et al.: Sparse4d: multi-view 3d object detection with sparse spatial-temporal fusion. arXiv preprint arXiv:2211.10581 (2022)
10. Loshchilov, I., Hutter, F.: Decoupled weight decay regularization. In: International Conference on Learning Representations (ICLR) (2019)
11. Park, J., Xu, C., Yang, S., et al.: Time will tell: new outlooks and a baseline for temporal multi-view 3d object detection. In: The Eleventh International Conference on Learning Representations (September 2022)
12. Ren, S., He, K., Girshick, R., et al.: Faster r-cnn: towards real-time object detection with region proposal networks. Adv. Neural Inf. Process. Syst. **28** (2015)
13. Shu, C., Deng, J., Yu, F., Liu, Y.: 3DPPE: 3d point positional encoding for multi-camera 3d object detection transformers. In: Proceedings of the IEEE/CVF International Conference on Computer Vision (ICCV) (2023)
14. Simonelli, A., Bulo, S.R., Porzi, L., et al.: Disentangling monocular 3d object detection. In: Proceedings of the IEEE/CVF International Conference on Computer Vision (ICCV), pp. 1991–1999 (2019)
15. Singh, G., Choutas, V., Saha, S., et al.: Spatio-temporal action detection under large motion. In: Proceedings of the IEEE/CVF Winter Conference on Applications of Computer Vision, pp. 6009–6018 (2023)
16. Wang, S., Liu, Y., Wang, T., et al.: Exploring object-centric temporal modeling for efficient multi-view 3d object detection. In: Proceedings of the IEEE/CVF International Conference on Computer Vision, pp. 3621–3631 (2023)
17. Wang, T., Lian, Q., Zhu, C., et al.: MV-FCOS3D++: multi-view camera-only 4d object detection with pretrained monocular backbones. arXiv preprint arXiv:2207.12716 (2022)
18. Yang, C., Chen, Y., Tian, H., et al.: Bevformer v2: adapting modern image backbones to bird's-eye-view recognition via perspective supervision. In: Proceedings of the IEEE/CVF Conference on Computer Vision and Pattern Recognition, pp. 17830–17839 (2023)
19. Zhang, H., Li, H., Zeng, A., et al.: Introducing depth into transformer-based 3d object detection. arXiv preprint arXiv:2302.13002 (2023)
20. Zhang, Y., Zheng, W., Zhu, Z., et al.: A simple baseline for multi-camera 3d object detection. arXiv preprint arXiv:2208.10035 (2022)
21. Zhu, X., Wang, Y., Dai, J., et al.: Flow-guided feature aggregation for video object detection. In: Proceedings of the IEEE International Conference on Computer Vision, pp. 408–417 (2017)
22. Zong, Z., Jiang, D., Song, G., et al.: Temporal enhanced training of multi-view 3d object detector via historical object prediction. In: Proceedings of the IEEE/CVF International Conference on Computer Vision, pp. 3781–3790 (2023)

Adjustable Visual Appearance
for Generalizable Novel View Synthesis

Josef Bengtson[1(✉)], David Nilsson[1], Che-Tsung Lin[1], Marcel Büsching[2],
and Fredrik Kahl[1]

[1] Computer Vision Group, Chalmers University of Technology, Gothenburg, Sweden
{bjosef,david.nilsson,chetsung,fredrik.kahl}@chalmers.com
[2] KTH Royal Institute of Technology, Stockholm, Sweden
busching@kth.se

Abstract. We present a generalizable novel view synthesis method
which enables modifying the visual appearance of an observed scene so
rendered views match a target weather or lighting condition, without
any scene specific training or access to reference views at the target condition. Our method is based on a pretrained generalizable transformer
architecture and is fine-tuned on synthetically generated scenes under
different appearance conditions. This allows for rendering novel views in
a consistent manner for 3D scenes that were not included in the training
set, along with the ability to (i) modify their appearance to match the
target condition and (ii) smoothly interpolate between different conditions. Experiments on real and synthetic scenes show that our method is
able to generate 3D consistent renderings while making realistic appearance changes, including qualitative and quantitative comparisons. Please
refer to our project page for video results: https://ava-nvs.github.io.

Keywords: 3D Style Transfer · Generalizable Novel View Synthesis ·
NeRFs

1 Introduction

The field of novel view synthesis has seen rapid progress in the last few years
after the success of Neural Radiance Fields (NeRFs) [26] and follow-up works
[1,25,27,36,53]. A desired quality for these types of 3D scene representations is
to be able to disentangle different scene properties from each other, for instance,
being able to change the visual appearance without changing the content of
the scene. Existing works in this direction [25,40] are limited to interpolating
between *observed* visual appearances of the 3D scene, thus requiring images of
the scene with the desired visual appearance. In contrast, we develop a method
that is able to generalize to 3D scenes unseen during training, and that thus can
adjust the appearance of a scene without having access to any images of that
scene at the target visual appearance, see Fig. 1.

Supplementary Information The online version contains supplementary material
available at https://doi.org/10.1007/978-981-97-8702-9_11.

C. Wallraven et al. (Eds.): ICPRAI 2024, LNCS 14892, pp. 157–171, 2025.
https://doi.org/10.1007/978-981-97-8702-9_11

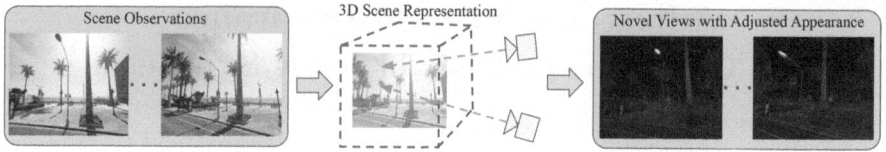

Fig. 1. Given multiple views of a scene in one weather and lighting condition, we want to generate novel views of the given scene with adjusted visual appearance corresponding to a target condition without scene specific optimization.

For traditional NeRF-based methods, the properties of the 3D scene are encoded in the weights of a multilayer perceptron (MLP), so each trained model is exclusive to that particular scene. A main challenge is thus that a separate optimization process has to be performed for each individual scene. One approach to handle this is to find ways to improve the efficiency of the training process [22, 27]. A different approach is to avoid per-scene training and instead train cross-scene generalizable methods [5, 24, 39, 48, 51], which are able to synthesize novel views of a scene given just images and corresponding camera poses, and do not require expensive scene-specific optimization. We present a generalizable novel view synthesis method that allows for changing the visual appearance of a scene while ensuring multi-view consistency. For this we build upon Generalizable NeRF Transformer (GNT) [39], a transformer-based [43] novel view synthesis method. Specifically, we introduce a latent appearance variable to enable the control of the visual appearance of rendered views. By using a generalizable NeRF model and the introduced latent appearance variable, we are able to render novel views and change the appearance of scenes that are not seen when training our model without the need for observations of the scene at the target appearance.

In summary, our main contributions are:

- We introduce a method that allows for changing the appearance of a novel scene, while ensuring multi-view consistency, by using a latent appearance variable conditioned on a target visual appearance.
- We propose a novel loss function which is designed to align the views rendered with a target appearance to the scene observed in that target condition, which enables jointly learning novel view synthesis and appearance change.
- We create a synthetic dataset containing urban scenes, with each scene available at four different diverse weather and lighting conditions. The dataset is used for training our model for visual appearance change and enables quantitative evaluation. The dataset, code, and pretrained models are available[1].

2   Related Work

Here we will review progress on NeRFs, focusing on generalizable methods. We will then review 2D style transfer methods and stylized NeRFs methods.

---

[1] https://github.com/josefbengtson/avanvs.

Neural Radiance Fields. NeRFs [26] synthesize consistent and photo-realistic novel views of a scene, by representing each scene as a continuous 5D radiance field parameterized by an MLP mapping 3D positions and 2D viewing directions to volume densities and view-dependent emitted radiances. Views are synthesized by querying points along camera rays and utilizing differentiable volumetric rendering to aggregate the output colors and densities into RGB values. There have been several works improving NeRFs further, e.g. to improve the efficiency [22, 27, 47] and handling few input views [21, 28, 51].

Generalizable Novel View Synthesis. The original NeRF methodology is constrained to training a neural network for representing a single scene, optimizing from scratch for each new scene, without leveraging any prior knowledge. Methods for generalizable neural rendering address this limitation by training on multiple scenes, enabling the learning of a general understanding of how to utilize source observations to synthesize novel views. Earlier methods such as [5, 51] use a multilayer perceptron (MLP) conditioned on feature vectors extracted from the source images to predict color and radiance values which are aggregated with volumetric rendering. To enhance generalization capabilities and rendering quality, recent approaches have incorporated transformer-based architectures [9, 43] for feature aggregation from the source images [24, 46], computing densities along the camera ray [48], and even for the entire rendering pipeline [11, 31, 35, 37–39]. While these methods have demonstrated impressive rendering quality, they are currently incapable of modifying the appearance of the rendered views.

2D Style Transfer. The success of Generative Adversarial Networks (GANs) [13] has largely driven advances in 2D style transfer. Methods such as Pix2Pix [20], Pix2Pix-HD [49], and BicycleGAN [56] utilize paired training data, which consists of corresponding images in the source and target conditions. CycleGAN [55] and CyEDA [2] employ cycle-consistency constraints to learn from unpaired data. NICE-GAN [6] reuses the discriminator for encoding the images of the target domain. In addition to GANs, the style-attentional network (SANet) [29] can synthesize a content image with the style of another image. Diffusion models [8, 17] have recently achieved superior results in image generation. Palette [34] introduced the first diffusion-based paired image-translation model, and DiffuseIT [23] recently presented a diffusion-based unsupervised image translation method. Instruct-Pix2Pix [3] re-trains a latent diffusion model [32] using paired images generated by prompt-to-prompt [16] and massive instructions generated by GPT-3 [4] to facilitate instruction-based style transfer. While the images translated by these 2D style transfer methods can individually appear realistic, they do not ensure temporal consistency. In contrast, our method inherently ensures 3D consistency. We experimentally compare our results with 2D style transfer methods applied frame by frame on rendered views.

Visual Appearance Change for NeRF Models. Prior works to enable changing the visual appearance of a NeRF model [25, 40] typically assign an appearance embedding vector to each image which affects the appearance but not geometry, and is optimized alongside the NeRF model parameters. In NeRF-W [25], low dimensional embeddings allow for smooth interpolation between lighting conditions. One limitation of this approach is that it requires access to images of the scene at both lighting conditions as input. In contrast, our method is a generalizable method that does not require images at both lighting conditions as input when rendering novel views with changed visual appearance. Another line of research is to edit the style of a NeRF model based on a given style prompt [14, 18, 19, 52] typically given as a reference image. More recent works [44, 45] use the joint language-image embedding space of CLIP [30] to enable specifying the desired style using a text prompt. These methods focus on artistic style changes and have thus not been specifically trained and evaluated on realistic appearance changes such as differences in weather or lighting, in contrast to our method. The recent method Instruct-NeRF2NeRF [15] enables editing a NeRF model based on a text-prompt, by iteratively updating dataset images using a pretrained 2D editing model [3]. This method allows for a variety of appearance changes since they utilize pre-trained diffusion models to perform the editing, but they require training per-scene NeRF models and additional per-scene optimization, in contrast to our method that does not require per-scene training.

3   Method

We now give an overview of Generalizable NeRF Transformer (GNT) [39] and present our method for adjusting the visual appearance of synthesized views.

3.1   Basics of GNT

GNT utilizes a two-stage transformer-based architecture that allows for novel view synthesis from source views. The first stage is a *view transformer* that aggregates information from neighboring views using epipolar geometry. The second stage is a *ray transformer* that performs rendering.

View Transformer. The *view transformer* computes a coordinate aligned feature field $\mathcal{F} : (\mathbf{x}, \theta) \rightarrow \mathbf{f} \in \mathbb{R}^d$ that maps a 3D position $\mathbf{x}$ and viewing direction θ to a feature vector $\mathbf{f}$. Firstly each source view is encoded to a feature map using a U-Net [33] Image Encoder $\mathbf{F}_i = \text{U-Net}(\mathbf{I}_i)$. The feature representation of a 3D point $\mathbf{x}$ is obtained by projecting it to every source image via the projections $\Pi_i(\mathbf{x})$ and fetching the corresponding value of $\mathbf{F}_i$. The *view transformer* (VT) is then used to combine all these feature vectors through attention as

$$\mathcal{F}(\mathbf{x}, \theta) = \text{VT}(\mathbf{F}_1(\Pi_1(\mathbf{x}), \theta), \ldots, \mathbf{F}_N(\Pi_N(\mathbf{x}), \theta)). \tag{1}$$

Ray Transformer. The *ray transformer* aggregates information along a given camera ray by performing attention between feature values $\mathbf{f}_i = \mathcal{F}(\mathbf{x}_i, \theta)$ on the ray. The GNT pipeline consists of stacking several view and ray transformers, which iteratively refines the feature field. The final *ray transformer* computes

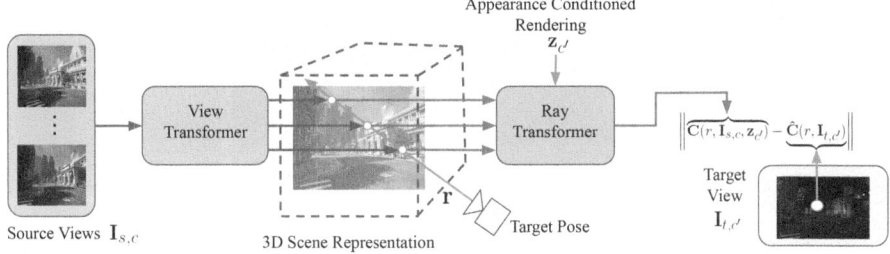

Fig. 2. Overview of our method for changing visual appearance of synthesized novel views. A target view direction is chosen and camera rays **r** are cast and the corresponding source views $\mathbf{I}_{s,c}$ are used to generate a scene representation. A latent appearance variable $\mathbf{z}_{c'}$ is included with the goal of adapting the appearance of the rendered image to match the target view. If the target view is at a different weather or daylight conditions ($c \neq c'$) then this means adapting the visual appearance to match that found in the target view $\mathbf{I}_{t,c'}$ instead of the visual appearance of the source views $\mathbf{I}_{s,c}$.

the RGB value $\mathbf{C}(\mathbf{r})$ corresponding to a camera ray **r** by feeding the sequence of feature vectors along the ray $\{\mathbf{f}_1, \cdots, \mathbf{f}_M\}$ into the *ray transformer*, performing mean pooling followed by an MLP as

$$\mathbf{C}(\mathbf{r}) = \text{MLP} \circ \text{Mean} \circ \text{RT}(\mathbf{f}_1, \ldots, \mathbf{f}_M). \tag{2}$$

This enables training the method using the standard color prediction loss term commonly used by NeRFs. The attention values from the ray transformer correspond to the importance of each feature vector $\mathbf{f}_i$ along the ray, filling a similar role as the opacity in a traditional NeRF method.

3.2 Adjusting Visual Appearance

To change the visual appearance of rendered views to match a target appearance, we propose to introduce a latent appearance variable $\mathbf{z}_{c'}$ as an additional input to the *ray transformer*, to condition the rendering on the target appearance. The proposed architecture can be seen in Fig. 2.

The latent variable should correspond to a predefined appearance condition and the value for each condition is jointly optimized with the rest of the network. Since our goal is to change the visual appearance, we include $\mathbf{z}_{c'}$ so that the geometry is kept unchanged. To ensure this, it is used to update the value-tokens in the *ray transformer* while keeping the attention values unchanged, i.e., $V_{c'} = f_z([V; \mathbf{z}_{c'}])$ where f_z is a single layer MLP that takes in the original value tokens V concatenated with the latent appearance variable $\mathbf{z}_{c'}$ and generates new value tokens $V_{c'}$. This enables computing a visual appearance change loss,

$$\mathcal{L}_{appearance} = \left\| \mathbf{C}(r, \mathbf{I}_{s,c}, \mathbf{z}_{c'}) - \hat{\mathbf{C}}(r, \mathbf{I}_{t,c'}) \right\|_2^2. \tag{3}$$

Fig. 3. Appearance change from the day condition into three other conditions. We observe that our method is able to take images at one condition and generate new views of that scene at the three other conditions by changing the overall visual appearance of the images to match the desired condition and by making local changes such as turning on street lamps.

This loss enforces that when inputting source views $\mathbf{I}_{s,c}$ from the condition c together with the latent appearance variable $\mathbf{z}_{c'}$ of the condition c', then the predicted color $\mathbf{C}(r, \mathbf{I}_{s,c}, \mathbf{z}_{c'})$ should match the ground truth color $\hat{\mathbf{C}}(r, \mathbf{I}_{t,c'})$ for the corresponding target images $\mathbf{I}_{t,c'}$, making it possible for the method to learn to adapt the appearance to match a target condition. If the condition for the target image $\mathbf{I}_{t,c}$ corresponds to that of the source images $\mathbf{I}_{s,c}$, then this becomes a traditional reconstruction loss $\mathcal{L}_{rec}$, and our full loss is $\mathcal{L} = \mathcal{L}_{rec} + \mathcal{L}_{appearance}$. Rendering images with changed visual appearance is done by computing the rendered color $\mathbf{C}(r, I_{s,c}, \mathbf{z}_{c'})$ for all pixels in an image, giving as input source views from one condition and a latent variable $\mathbf{z}_{c'}$ corresponding to the desired target condition.

4 Experiments

Qualitative and quantitative experiments are performed to test our method's ability to adapt the visual appearance of real and synthetic scenes that have not been seen during training.

Dataset. The used dataset is generated using the autonomous driving simulator CARLA [10], which enables the generation of synthetic images within a simulated city environment along with their ground truth camera poses. Additionally, weather and lighting conditions can easily be changed, allowing control of sun position, rain amount and cloudiness.

For our experiments, four conditions were defined, corresponding to *night, day, rain* and *evening*. A scene was defined as a sequence of 10 observations taken along a road. With four different conditions, this led to a total of 40 images per scene. All generated images are 800×600 pixels. The CARLA map was split into two regions, one to generate 145 training scenes, and the other to generate 38 evaluation scenes, ensuring separation between training and evaluation scenes. We also show qualitative examples evaluating our trained model on scenes from the Spaces dataset [12] to show that our method can generalize to real images.

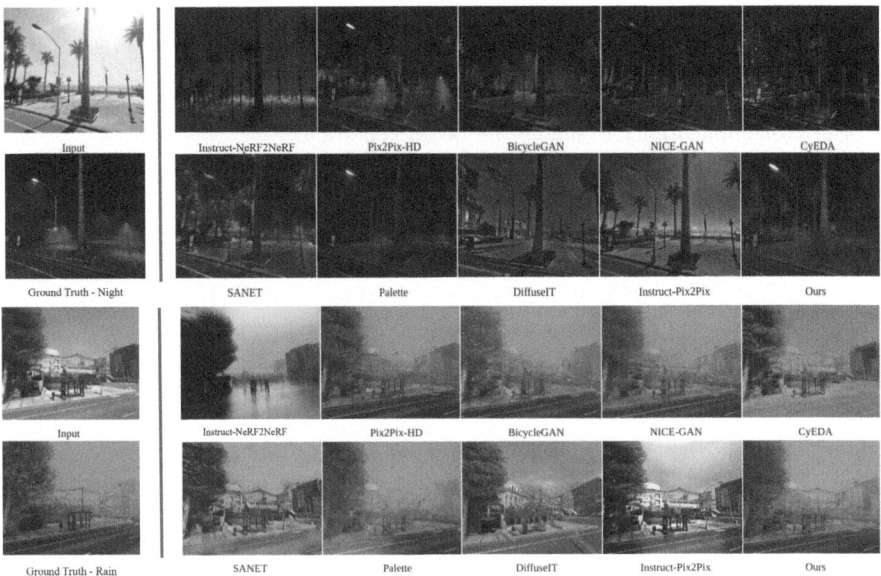

Fig. 4. Comparing our method with Instruct-NeRF2NeRF [15] as well as applying different 2D style transfer methods on rendered images. We note that Instruct-Pix2Pix [3] effectively generates realistic 2D edits; however, it exhibits significant inconsistencies that Instruct-NeRF2NeRF fails to consolidate in 3D, leading to an unrealistic appearance. Only our method, Pix2Pix-HD [49] and Palette [34] learn to turn on the street lamps. SANet [29] and CyEDA [2] achieve better structure preservation with some noticeable artifacts. The diffusion model-based DiffuseIT [23] and Instruct-Pix2Pix [3] can provide visually plausible results for individual images, but there are hallucinations that do not exist in the original images, leading to multi-view inconsistencies. Palette provides more realistic images, but it is however lacking in temporal consistency. Comparisons for additional conditions can be found in the supplementary material.

Implementation. The model was initialized with weights from a GNT network pretrained on a combination of synthetic and real data [39]. The model was trained to perform visual appearance change using the 145 training scenes from the introduced CARLA dataset, including the proposed appearance change loss term (3). The training was performed on a single A100 GPU, taking approximately 8 h, and the method was then able to generalize to scenes not seen during training. Note that the model was trained for all training scenes at the same time, and there is no scene-specific training for the test scenes. When we test the model, we only use images of the test scene in the source condition $I_{s,c}$ and not any images of the test scene in the target condition $c' \neq c$.

Baselines. The GAN-based methods, such as Pix2Pix-HD [49], BicycleGAN [56], NICE-GAN [6], and CyEDA [2], along with the diffusion model-based method Palette [34], have been retrained using our synthetic dataset. The reference-based

Table 1. Comparison of similarity of rendered views for our method with ground truth images for all combinations of weather and lighting conditions (**PSNR | SSIM | LPIPS**). The values along the diagonal correspond to novel view synthesis without appearance change. The off-diagonal values correspond to evaluating novel views with changed visual appearance to match the target condition.

	From Day	From Night	From Evening	From Rain
Into Day	23.9│0.77│0.60	15.3│0.56│0.62	16.7│0.64│0.61	15.7│0.59│0.60
Into Night	21.0│0.56│0.55	27.4│0.68│0.57	20.7│0.54│0.55	21.2│0.57│0.55
Into Evening	24.1│0.75│0.58	20.0│0.62│0.57	25.4│0.76│0.58	21.4│0.69│0.57
Into Rain	23.4│0.71│0.58	21.7│0.66│0.57	21.3│0.69│0.56	26.8│0.78│0.58

Table 2. Quantitative comparison of rendering quality against 2D style transfer methods (**PSNR | SSIM | LPIPS**). We observe that our method outperforms all 2D style transfer methods on these metrics, with significant increases in performance on PSNR and SSIM for most scenarios.

Type	Method	Scenarios					
		Day to Night	Day to Evening	Day to Rain	Night to Day	Evening to Day	Rain to Day
Non-diffusion	Pix2Pix-HD [49]	19.7│0.36│0.565	18.4│0.35│0.603	19.7│0.53│0.582	13.8│0.40│0.629	15.3│0.46│0.619	13.9│0.43│0.629
	BicycleGAN [56]	19.0│0.38│0.556	18.8│0.41│0.587	22.7│0.66│0.578	14.2│0.47│0.630	15.9│0.56│0.627	15.0│0.54│0.630
	NICE-GAN [6]	18.3│0.29│0.553	18.8│0.39│0.589	20.8│0.56│0.583	12.9│0.29│0.626	14.6│0.45│0.618	14.3│0.47│0.624
	CyEDA [2]	17.9│0.32│0.556	18.8│0.40│0.597	20.0│0.67│0.579	11.7│0.47│0.625	14.0│0.59│0.633	12.3│0.53│0.634
	SANet [29]	18.9│0.50│0.571	20.2│0.64│0.606	20.1│0.66│0.581	14.5│0.52│0.629	15.5│0.59│0.618	12.6│0.45│0.616
Diffusion Models	Palette [34]	19.4│0.42│0.577	20.6│0.54│0.618	22.6│0.66│0.601	12.1│0.41│0.689	9.8│0.38│0.688	9.8│0.38│0.695
	DiffuseIT [23]	17.1│0.32│0.594	17.2│0.44│0.627	16.0│0.43│0.613	11.2│0.35│0.626	12.3│0.38│0.618	11.8│0.35│0.625
	Instruct-Pix2Pix [3]*	15.9│0.34│0.579	14.3│0.53│0.653	14.1│0.53│0.638	11.5│0.46│0.647	8.7│0.34│0.674	13.4│0.52│0.640
	Ours	**21.0│0.56│0.549**	**24.1│0.75│0.585**	**23.4│0.71│0.577**	**15.3│0.56│0.624**	**16.7│0.64│0.615**	**15.7│0.59│0.602**

* Instruct-Pix2Pix is pre-trained on editing images based on text prompts and was therefore not retrained on our synthetic dataset.

methods, DiffuseIT [23] and SANet [29], are capable of performing image translation using a reference image at the target condition from the synthetic dataset. Instruct-Pix2Pix [3] is pre-trained on editing images based on text prompts and was not retrained on our synthetic dataset.

Furthermore, we compared our method with the Instruct-NeRF2NeRF [15] model, utilizing the official implementation that employs the Nerfstudio [41] Nerfacto NeRF model. Due to the unsatisfactory quality of the Nerfacto models when using 10 images, we increased the number of images in the sequence to 25 images. More details can be found in the supplementary material.

Qualitative Results. Our model is evaluated on the 38 evaluation scenes not seen during training. The method is capable of synthesizing novel views using only a set of images with corresponding camera poses. Furthermore, it is able to adapt the visual appearance of the scene to specified weather and lighting conditions, without having access to observations of the scene under those target conditions. We show several qualitative examples of this. Figure 3 shows that our method is

Table 3. Quantitative comparison of the consistency of novel view rendering against 2D style transfer methods and instruct-NeRF2NeRF (**tOF** | **tLP** [7]). We can observe that our method significantly outperforms most of the 2D methods. Please see the supplementary material for a video illustrating the rendering consistency.

Type	Method	Scenarios			
		Day to Night	Day to Evening	Day to Rain	Night to Day
Non-diffusion	Pix2Pix-HD [49]	2.59|0.147	1.58|0.169	1.60|0.030	2.49|0.078
	BicycleGAN [56]	5.13|0.053	4.79|0.083	5.10|0.024	5.20|0.047
	NICE-GAN [6]	1.93|0.040	1.24|0.081	1.25|0.014	2.09|0.055
	CyEDA [2]	1.62|0.027	1.21|0.115	**0.96**|0.022	**1.25**|**0.032**
	SANet [29]	2.37|0.069	2.05|0.097	1.73|0.088	2.01|0.092
Diffusion Models	Palette [34]	10.12|0.115	7.21|0.109	8.41|0.057	18.77|0.050
	DiffuseIT [23]	24.62|0.236	29.23|0.242	27.43|0.166	29.75|0.188
	Instruct-Pix2Pix [3]	1.62|0.123	1.37|0.121	1.45|0.088	1.48|0.092
NeRF Editing	IN2N [15]	7.29|0.137	6.09|0.085	5.65|0.051	- | -*
Ours	Ours	**1.44**|**0.026**	**1.10**|**0.035**	0.97|**0.013**	**1.25**|**0.032**

* We could not get satisfactory renderings for this condition, more details can be found in the supplementary material.

able to change the visual appearance of images to match a target weather and lighting condition, and Fig. 4 shows a comparison with other methods.

It also becomes possible to interpolate between two latent variables corresponding to different conditions by defining $\mathbf{z}_\alpha = \alpha \mathbf{z_c} + (1-\alpha)\mathbf{z_{c'}}$ for $\alpha \in [0, 1]$. In Fig. 5, we observe that this enables getting realistic intermediate visual appearances that are not included in the original images. The model trained on appearance change of synthetic scenes can also be applied to change the appearance of real scenes [12], as seen in Fig. 6 where we can see realistic appearance changes even though the model is not trained on any scenes from that dataset.

Quantitative Results. We now show quantitative rendering quality results. We show PSNR, SSIM [50] and LPIPS [54], where the images with changed appearance are evaluated against the corresponding ground truth images for the target weather and lighting conditions. In Table 1, we show how our method performs on all possible combinations of source and target conditions. Using the same source and target conditions corresponds to novel view synthesis without appearance change, which, as expected, gives better metrics, but the gap is small for some combinations, e.g. comparing Day into Evening with Evening into Evening. In Table 2, we compare our method with several 2D style transfer methods. We see that our method outperforms the 2D methods on the performance metrics for all combinations. We observe that performance varies for the different conditions and that adapting images from another condition into day is the most challenging while transforming from day gives significantly higher performance for all methods. A comparison against Instruct-NeRF2NeRF [15] was also performed,

Fig. 5. Gradually changing visual appearance by interpolating between latent appearance variables corresponding to day and night. The first row corresponds to latent variables generated with a given structure, enforcing that the evening condition lies between day and night in the latent space, and the second row corresponds to a learned latent variable with no enforced structure. Given images at one appearance condition our method is able to smoothly transition the appearance to match a different weather and lighting condition, generating plausible intermediate visual appearances.

but results varied largely for different scenes and prompts. Further details are included in the supplementary material.

We show two consistency metrics [7] in Table 3. If $(x_1, \ldots, x_n)$ and $(y_1, \ldots, y_n)$ are two image sequences rendered from the same pose sequences, we define tOF $= \|\text{OF}(y_{t+1}, y_t) - \text{OF}(x_{t+1}, x_t)\|_1$, where OF is the optical flow computed via RAFT [42] and tLP $= \|\text{LPIPS}(y_{t+1}, y_t) - \text{LPIPS}(x_{t+1}, x_t)\|_1$. The metrics are low if the reference images and the rendered images yield similar optical flow and similar changes in LPIPS, which is assumed to correspond to a consistent rendering. We observe that our method significantly outperforms most of the 2D style transfer methods. Notably, Instruct-NeRF2NeRF exhibits poorer consistency results than anticipated, primarily stemming from two key factors. Firstly, the NeRF models generate low-quality novel views for some scenes. Secondly, there are inconsistent appearance changes in response to certain prompts, which results in unrealistic alterations that do not clearly preserve the scene content. CyEDA gives comparable consistency metrics for some scenarios but gives less realistic rendered views as seen in Fig. 4 and Table 2.

Ablation Study. We compare two different ways of learning latent appearance variables $\mathbf{z}_c \in \mathbb{R}^d$. One approach is to initialize a random d-dimensional vector with no enforced structure for each condition as a learnable parameter that is optimized jointly with the rest of the model. Another approach is to enforce structure by representing each condition as a fixed 2D-coordinate, placing them such that the evening condition is in between day and night, based on the assumption that one should pass through evening when going from day to night. These fixed 2D coordinates are then fed through a small learned fully-connected network to generate $\mathbf{z}_c$. Comparing the performance metrics for these

Day	Evening	Night

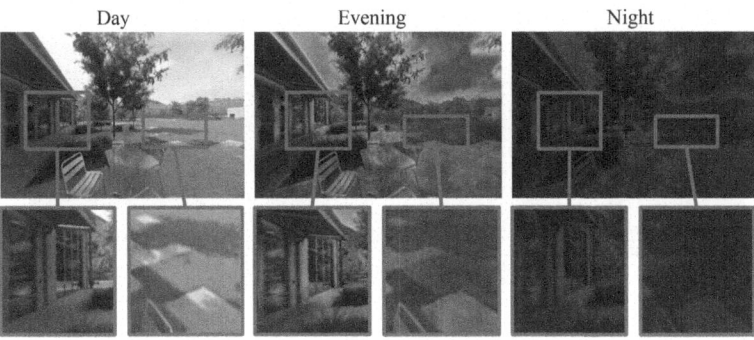

Fig. 6. Visual appearance change applied on a daytime scene from the Spaces dataset [12]. We observe that our method is able to make realistic appearance changes, such as adding sunlight on the background and light reflections in the windows for the evening condition and removing shadows for the night condition, without being trained on any scenes from this dataset.

Table 4. Ablation Study comparing two approaches for generating latent appearance variables, comparing the similarity of rendered views with ground truth images (**PSNR | SSIM | LPIPS**). We observe that both approaches give similar performance for changing appearance from one condition to another.

Latent Variables	Scenarios			
	Day to Night	Day to Evening	Day to Rain	Night to Day
Enforced structure	21.0|0.56|**0.55**	**24.1**|**0.75**|0.58	**23.4**|**0.71**|0.58	15.3|**0.56**|0.62
No enforced structure	**21.6**|**0.57**|**0.55**	23.2|0.71|**0.57**	22.8|0.70|**0.55**	**15.3**|**0.56**|**0.61**

two approaches, as can be seen in Table 4, shows that both approaches give similar performance. However, enforcing a structure on the latent space leads to more realistic lighting effects when interpolating, as can be seen in Fig. 5, giving the appearance of a sunset. Based on this, we decided to use the latent appearance variable with the enforced structure for our experiments. The choice of dimension $d = 136$, for the latent appearance variable, was made by observing that a higher dimension leads to a better ability to handle local appearance changes, such as turning on street lamps and removing shadows, as seen in Fig. 7. More details can be found in the supplementary material.

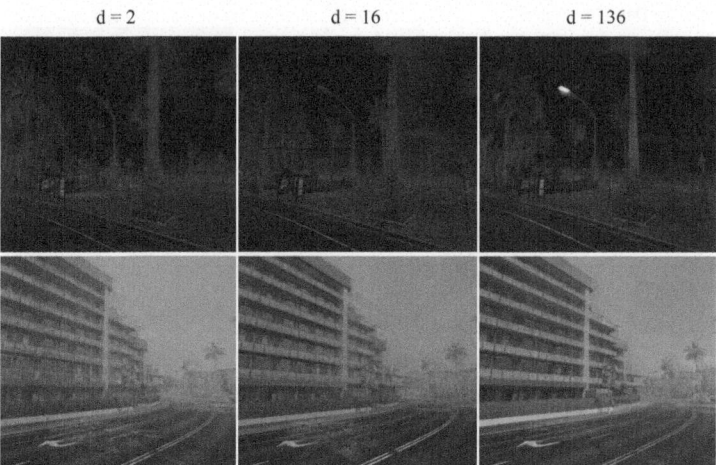

Fig. 7. Qualitative comparison of rendered views with changed appearance for different sizes d of the latent appearance variable $\mathbf{z_c}$. We observe that a higher value of d leads to better local appearance changes in rendered views, such as turning on street lamps and removing shadows.

5   Conclusions

We present a transformer-based generalizable novel view synthesis method that allows for changing the visual appearance without any scene-specific training. This is achieved by introducing a latent appearance variable that is used to change the visual appearance to match a given weather and lighting condition while keeping the scene structure unchanged. We also introduce a synthetic dataset based on CARLA for training and evaluating the methods and present experiments that show that this method is able to change the visual appearance of both synthetic and real scenes, to match a specified weather and lighting condition without any scene-specific training. The generated latent variables also make it possible to smoothly interpolate between different weather and lighting conditions. Compared to 2D style transfer, our method is view-consistent by design. We experimentally show that our method outperforms multiple 2D style transfer methods, both in terms of rendering quality and that the rendering of nearby views is more consistent. A comparison with Instruct-NeRF2NeRF shows that our method is more robust in providing desired appearance changes while ensuring multi-view consistency and preserving scene content. Our generalizable approach is also more flexible, not requiring training a NeRF model for each scene, and also allows using fewer input images.

Acknowledgments. This work received full support from the Wallenberg AI, Autonomous Systems, and Software Program (WASP) funded by the Knut and Alice Wallenberg Foundation. Computational resources were provided by the National Academic Infrastructure for Supercomputing in Sweden (NAISS) at Chalmers Centre for Computational Science and Engineering (C3SE), partially funded by the Swedish Research Council under grant agreement no. 2022-06725.

References

1. Barron, J.T., Mildenhall, B., Tancik, M., Hedman, P., Martin-Brualla, R., Srinivasan, P.P.: Mip-NeRF: a multiscale representation for anti-aliasing neural radiance fields. In: ICCV (2021)
2. Beh, J.C., et al.: CyEDA: cycle-object edge consistency domain adaptation. In: ICIP (2022)
3. Brooks, T., Holynski, A., Efros, A.A.: InstructPix2Pix: learning to follow image editing instructions. In: CVPR (2023)
4. Brown, T., et al.: Language models are few-shot learners. In: NeurIPS 33, pp. 1877–1901 (2020)
5. Chen, A., et al.: MVSNeRF: fast generalizable radiance field reconstruction from multi-view stereo. In: ICCV (2021)
6. Chen, R., Huang, W., Huang, B., Sun, F., Fang, B.: Reusing discriminators for encoding: towards unsupervised image-to-image translation. In: CVPR (2020)
7. Chu, M., Xie, Y., Mayer, J., Leal-Taixé, L., Thuerey, N.: Learning temporal coherence via self-supervision for GAN-based video generation. ACM Trans. Graph. (TOG) **39**(4), 75-1 (2020)
8. Dhariwal, P., Nichol, A.: Diffusion models beat GANs on image synthesis. In: NeurIPS (2021)
9. Dosovitskiy, A., et al.: An image is worth 16×16 words: transformers for image recognition at scale. In: ICLR (2022)
10. Dosovitskiy, A., Ros, G., Codevilla, F., Lopez, A., Koltun, V.: CARLA: an open urban driving simulator. In: Proceedings of the 1st Annual Conference on Robot Learning, pp. 1–16 (2017)
11. Du, Y., Smith, C., Tewari, A., Sitzmann, V.: Learning to render novel views from wide-baseline stereo pairs. In: CVPR (2023)
12. Flynn, J., et al.: DeepView: view synthesis with learned gradient descent. In: CVPR (2019)
13. Goodfellow, I., et al.: Generative adversarial networks. Commun. ACM **63**(11), 139–144 (2020)
14. Gu, J., Liu, L., Wang, P., Theobalt, C.: StyleneRF: a style-based 3D aware generator for high-resolution image synthesis. In: ICLR (2022)
15. Haque, A., Tancik, M., Efros, A., Holynski, A., Kanazawa, A.: InstructNeRF2NeRF: editing 3D scenes with instructions. In: ICCV (2023)
16. Hertz, A., Mokady, R., Tenenbaum, J., Aberman, K., Pritch, Y., Cohen-Or, D.: Prompt-to-prompt image editing with cross attention control. arXiv preprint arXiv:2208.01626 (2022)
17. Ho, J., Jain, A., Abbeel, P.: Denoising diffusion probabilistic models. In: NeurIPS (2020)
18. Huang, X., Belongie, S.: Arbitrary style transfer in real-time with adaptive instance normalization. In: ICCV (2017)
19. Huang, Y.H., He, Y., Yuan, Y.J., Lai, Y.K., Gao, L.: StylizedNeRF: consistent 3D scene stylization as stylized NeRF via 2D-3D mutual learning. In: CVPR (2022)
20. Isola, P., Zhu, J.Y., Zhou, T., Efros, A.A.: Image-to-image translation with conditional adversarial networks. In: CVPR (2017)

21. Jain, A., Tancik, M., Abbeel, P.: Putting NeRF on a Diet: semantically consistent few-shot view synthesis. In: ICCV (2021)
22. Kurz, A., Neff, T., Lv, Z., Zollhöfer, M., Steinberger, M.: AdaNeRF: adaptive sampling for real-time rendering of neural radiance fields. In: ECCV (2022)
23. Kwon, G., Ye, J.C.: Diffusion-based image translation using disentangled style and content representation. arXiv preprint arXiv:2209.15264 (2022)
24. Liu, Y., et al.: Neural rays for occlusion-aware image-based rendering. In: CVPR (2022)
25. Martin-Brualla, R., Radwan, N., Sajjadi, M.S.M., Barron, J.T., Dosovitskiy, A., Duckworth, D.: Nerf in the wild: Neural radiance fields for unconstrained photo collections. In: CVPR (2021)
26. Mildenhall, B., Srinivasan, P.P., Tancik, M., Barron, J.T., Ramamoorthi, R., Ng, R.: NeRF: representing scenes as neural radiance fields for view synthesis. In: ECCV (2020)
27. Müller, T., Evans, A., Schied, C., Keller, A.: Instant neural graphics primitives with a multiresolution hash encoding. ACM Trans. Graph. **41**(4), 102:1–102:15 (2022)
28. Niemeyer, M., Barron, J.T., Mildenhall, B., Sajjadi, M.S.M., Geiger, A., Radwan, N.: RegNeRF: regularizing neural radiance fields for view synthesis from sparse inputs. In: CVPR (2022)
29. Park, D.Y., Lee, K.H.: Arbitrary style transfer with style-attentional networks. In: CVPR (2019)
30. Radford, A., et al.: Learning transferable visual models from natural language supervision. In: ICML (2021)
31. Reizenstein, J., Shapovalov, R., Henzler, P., Sbordone, L., Labatut, P., Novotny, D.: Common objects in 3D: large-scale learning and evaluation of real-life 3D category reconstruction. In: ICCV (2021)
32. Rombach, R., Blattmann, A., Lorenz, D., Esser, P., Ommer, B.: High-resolution image synthesis with latent diffusion models. In: CVPR (2022)
33. Ronneberger, O., Fischer, P., Brox, T.: U-Net: convolutional networks for biomedical image segmentation. In: Medical Image Computing and Computer-Assisted Intervention (MICCAI). LNCS, vol. 9351, pp. 234–241. Springer (2015)
34. Saharia, C., et al.: Palette: image-to-image diffusion models. In: ACM SIGGRAPH (2022)
35. Sajjadi, M.S., et al.: Scene representation transformer: geometry-free novel view synthesis through set-latent scene representations. In: CVPR (2022)
36. Srinivasan, P.P., Deng, B., Zhang, X., Tancik, M., Mildenhall, B., Barron, J.T.: NeRV: neural reflectance and visibility fields for relighting and view synthesis. In: CVPR (2021)
37. Suhail, M., Esteves, C., Sigal, L., Makadia, A.: Generalizable patch-based neural rendering. In: ECCV (2022)
38. Suhail, M., Esteves, C., Sigal, L., Makadia, A.: Light field neural rendering. In: CVPR (2022)
39. Mukund Varma, T., Wang, P., Chen, X., Chen, T., Venugopalan, S., Wang, Z.: Is attention all that NeRF needs? In: ICLR (2023)
40. Tancik, M., et al.: Block-NeRF: scalable large scene neural view synthesis. In: CVPR (2022)
41. Tancik, M., et al.: Nerfstudio: a modular framework for neural radiance field development. In: ACM SIGGRAPH 2023. Association for Computing Machinery, New York (2023)

42. Teed, Z., Deng, J.: RAFT: recurrent all-pairs field transforms for optical flow. In: ECCV (2020)
43. Vaswani, A., et al.: Attention is all you need. In: NIPS (2017)
44. Wang, C., Chai, M., He, M., Chen, D., Liao, J.: CLIP-NeRF: text-and-image driven manipulation of neural radiance fields. In: CVPR (2022)
45. Wang, C., Jiang, R., Chai, M., He, M., Chen, D., Liao, J.: NeRF-Art: text-driven neural radiance fields stylization. IEEE Trans. Vis. Comput. Graph. 1–15 (2023)
46. Wang, D., Cui, X., Salcudean, S., Wang, Z.J.: Generalizable neural radiance fields for novel view synthesis with transformer (2022)
47. Wang, H., et al.: R2L: distilling neural radiance field to neural light field for efficient novel view synthesis. In: ECCV (2022)
48. Wang, Q., et al.: IBRNet: learning multi-view image-based rendering. In: CVPR (2021)
49. Wang, T.C., Liu, M.Y., Zhu, J.Y., Tao, A., Kautz, J., Catanzaro, B.: High-resolution image synthesis and semantic manipulation with conditional GANs. In: CVPR (2018)
50. Wang, Z., Bovik, A., Sheikh, H., Simoncelli, E.: Image quality assessment: from error visibility to structural similarity. IEEE Trans. Image Process. **13**(4), 600–612 (2004)
51. Yu, A., Ye, V., Tancik, M., Kanazawa, A.: pixelNeRF: neural radiance fields from one or few images. In: CVPR (2021)
52. Zhang, K., et al.: ARF: artistic radiance fields (2022)
53. Zhang, K., Riegler, G., Snavely, N., Koltun, V.: NeRF++: analyzing and improving neural radiance fields. arXiv preprint arXiv:2010.07492 (2020)
54. Zhang, R., Isola, P., Efros, A.A., Shechtman, E., Wang, O.: The unreasonable effectiveness of deep features as a perceptual metric. In: CVPR (2018)
55. Zhu, J.Y., Park, T., Isola, P., Efros, A.A.: Unpaired image-to-image translation using cycle-consistent adversarial networks. In: ICCV (2017)
56. Zhu, J.Y., et al.: Toward multimodal image-to-image translation. In: NIPS (2017)

Flexible Video Matting With Temporally Coherent Trimaps Generation

Chenhui Xue, Shugong Xu$^{(\boxtimes)}$, Shiyi Mu, and Yilin Gao

Shanghai University, Shanghai, China
shugong@shu.edu.cn

Abstract. Traditional video matting networks depend on user-annotated trimaps to estimate alpha mattes for the foreground in videos. However, creating trimaps is labor-intensive and rigid. Recent advancements in video matting aim to eliminate the need for trimaps, but these methods struggle to estimate alpha mattes for specific individuals in scenes featuring multiple instances. In this study, we propose the Flexible Video Matting (FVM) model, a novel video matting network capable of generating alpha mattes for any specified instance in a video using simple prompts such as text, bounding boxes, and points, without relying on user-annotated trimaps. FVM combines the Segment Anything Model (SAM) and a video object segmentation network to obtain semantic masks for the target instance. Additionally, we have designed a Mask-to-Trimap (MTT) module for FVM, based on a recurrent architecture. This module utilizes semantic masks and temporal information in the video to predict temporally consistent trimaps, which are subsequently fed into the matting module to generate temporally consistent alpha mattes. Experimental results on the video matting benchmark demonstrate that our model achieves state-of-the-art matting quality and exhibits superior temporal coherence compared with methods that directly apply image matting techniques to video matting tasks.

Keywords: Video Matting · Segment Anything · Mask-to-Trimap · Temporal Coherence

1 Introduction

Video matting plays an important role in video conferencing, scene switching, digital human generation, etc. The purpose of the matting task is to predict an alpha matte α for the input RGB frame I. Figure 1 provides an example of an RGB image and its corresponding alpha matte. Assume that F represents the foreground of the frame, and that B is the background. Then, the frame I can be expressed as:

$$I = \alpha F + (1 - \alpha)B. \tag{1}$$

The foreground is derived by multiplying the alpha matte with the input RGB frame.

C. Wallraven et al. (Eds.): ICPRAI 2024, LNCS 14892, pp. 172–185, 2025.
https://doi.org/10.1007/978-981-97-8702-9_12

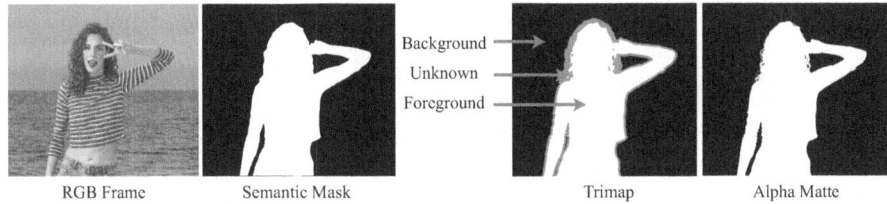

RGB Frame   Semantic Mask   Trimap   Alpha Matte

Fig. 1. An example of RGB image and its corresponding trimap and alpha matte.

Unlike image matting [5,8,13,15,21,26,33], which only involves extracting the foreground in a single image, video matting [1,4,25] requires extracting the foreground from each frame of a video. The challenge lies not only in ensuring the quality of predicted alpha mattes but also in maintaining their temporal coherence. Some existing methods [7,10,17] handle video matting frame by frame, treating each frame as an independent image. However, these approaches neglect the temporal information in the video, resulting in alpha mattes with poor temporal coherence and noticeable flickering issues. These factors contribute to a decline in the performance of video matting models. Therefore, incorporating and leveraging temporal information become crucial for effective video matting.

The trimap functions as a guide map, outlining the foreground, background, and uncertain regions within a given image, as depicted in Fig. 1. This assists trimap-based video matting methods in achieving precise matting, but the annotation process for trimaps is labor-intensive. To mitigate the challenges associated with trimaps, [17,23] proposed a trimap-free alternative, which needs to take an additional background picture without the target foreground. While the setup is less time-consuming than creating trimaps, the manual prior required by these methods limits their use in some real-time applications. Although other auxiliary-free methods [10,12,16,18] have been proposed, they can only generate alpha mattes for all instances in a video that belong to a certain category, and face challenges in estimating alpha mattes for a specified instance based on user prompts for interactive use. Therefore, it is crucial to develop a model that can achieve accurate and temporally coherent alpha mattes estimation without depending on user-annotated trimaps, while also being capable of handling simple user prompts in a flexible and efficient manner for interactive use.

Building upon the limitations of existing video matting methods, we propose the Flexible Video Matting (FVM) model. It allows users to generate alpha mattes for any specified instance by providing a straightforward prompt. The FVM model leverages interactive segmentation capabilities and excellent performance of Segment Anything Model (SAM) to acquire the semantic mask of an instance that the user intends to extract in the first frame, and then obtains the masks of the same instance in all frames through the space-time memory (STM) video object segmentation network [20]. The Mask-to-Trimap (MTT) module, a key component of our FVM model, directly generates trimaps based on these masks. To harness temporal information effectively, the MTT module adopts a recurrent architecture, enhancing the temporal coherence of the resultant trimaps. This enhancement contributes to an overall improvement in the temporal coherence of the alpha mattes. Our main contributions are as follows:

- Our proposed FVM model is the first video matting method to incorporate SAM. It allows users to select any specified instance for matting using points, text, or bounding boxes, eliminating the need for annotating trimaps. This capability enables our method to be applied in real-time scenarios.
- We develop a recurrent MTT module tailored for the video matting task. This module effectively utilizes semantic masks and temporal information to predict temporally coherent trimaps.
- We assess the performance of our FVM using a common video matting benchmark. The results indicate that our approach attains the highest matting accuracy, and the temporal consistency achieved by our method significantly exceeds that of directly applying image matting networks to video matting tasks.

2   Related Work

2.1   Trimap-Based Matting

Trimap-based deep matting networks [7,29–31] necessitate the input of an RGB image along with a trimap, which serves to delineate the foreground, background, and uncertain regions within the image. These networks are well-suited for interactive applications, as users can specify the target object by providing the corresponding trimap. However, in the realm of trimap-based video matting methods, [9,27,28] demand densely manually annotated trimaps, rendering them labor-intensive. In the case of [34], users are required to annotate trimaps at select keyframes. Subsequently, an independent trimap propagation network is used to extrapolate trimaps for all frames. [24] introduced a one-trimap video matting network, where users annotate the trimap for the initial frame, and the network simultaneously predicts the trimap and alpha matte for each subsequent video frame. Although these methods alleviate the burden on users to draw trimaps continuously, they still present practical inconveniences during application.

2.2   Background-Based Matting

Background-based matting methods [17,23] employ a background image devoid of a foreground as guidance information, eschewing the need for a trimap. However, in real-world usage scenarios, the diversity of video sources makes it nearly impossible to pre-define a suitable background image. Consequently, the practical utility of this approach is severely constrained.

2.3 Auxiliary-Free Matting

In recent years, substantial effort has been directed toward exploring methods for implementing video matting without the need for auxiliary input. MODNet [10], initially designed for image matting, treats video frames as independent images. It introduces a technique to mitigate flicker by conducting comparisons between adjacent frames. RVM [18] stands out as the pioneering work to incorporate a recurrent structure into the video matting network, resulting in a significant enhancement in the temporal consistency of output results. AdaM [16], on the other hand, leverages a data-driven approach to estimate foreground masks, guiding the network to adaptively discern between foregrounds and backgrounds. However, these methods exhibit performance instability owing to the absence of auxiliary information. Furthermore, they lack user interaction capabilities, prohibiting users from selecting the specific target instance they wish to extract.

2.4 Semantic Segmentation

The objective of semantic segmentation is to predict a binary mask for an RGB image, indicating whether each pixel belongs to a specific class of objects. Given that the pixel values in the segmentation mask are confined to 0 or 1, making it suitable primarily for a rough localization of a target within the image. SAM [11] is a powerful image segmentation network capable of segmenting various objects in an image. Through flexible prompting mechanism and extensive training data, it not only supports interactive segmentation methods but also demonstrates exceptional zero-shot performance across a diverse array of segmentation tasks. STM [20] is a video object segmentation network, it utilizes the mask from the first frame as auxiliary input to provide guidance for identifying target objects, subsequently predicting masks for the subsequent frames.

3   Methodology

This section provides an overview of the entire processing procedure of the FVM model, delineated into three key stages, namely the segmentation stage, the trimap prediction stage, and the matting stage. Figure 2 illustrates the comprehensive architecture of our FVM model. Subsequent subsections will delve into a detailed exposition of each of these stages.

3.1 Segmentation Stage

The segmentation stage focuses on extracting a mask for the target instance in each frame of the provided video $V \in \mathbb{R}^{T \times 3 \times H \times W}$. SAM and STM are the primary contributors to this stage. Initially, the first RGB frame $I \in \mathbb{R}^{3 \times H \times W}$ of the video and the user-provided prompt are input into SAM to generate the first mask. SAM's robust image encoder will extract the features of all instances within the input image, while its prompt encoder transforms the user-provided

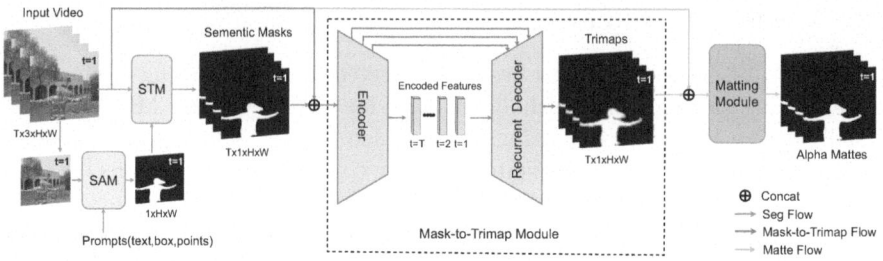

Fig. 2. Overview of the FVM model. The execution process of FVM comprises three stages. During the segmentation stage, masks of the target instance are primarily acquired through user prompts. Subsequently, in the trimap prediction stage, the MTT module anticipates trimaps based on the masks obtained in the segmentation stage. Finally, the input video and trimaps are forwarded to the trimap-based matting network to derive the alpha mattes.

prompt into the feature space. Subsequently, SAM decodes the instance features that correspond with the prompt features, ultimately deriving the mask for the targeted instance, denoted as $m_1 \in \mathbb{R}^{1 \times H \times W}$.

Following this, STM utilizes m_1 and V as inputs to consistently track the same target and derive a sequence of masks denoted as $M = \{m_1, m_2, ..., m_T\}$. STM operates by considering past frames with the masks as memory frames and current frames lacking masks as query frames. Both memory and query frames undergo encoding into pairs of key and value maps. Dense matching occurs across the spatio-temporal space of the video for every pixel on the key feature maps of the query and memory frames. The matching scores aid in addressing the value feature map of the memory frame, enabling the combination of corresponding values. Finally, the decoder generates the mask of the query frame based on the combined results.

3.2   Trimap Prediction Stage

The task of the trimap prediction stage is to generate temporally coherent trimaps, denoted as $T = \{T_1, T_2, ..., T_T\}$ for the target video instance, based on the predicted masks. Figure 3 illustrates the overall architecture of the MTT module. The MTT module is built upon the foundational framework of U-Net. It operates by processing a sequence of successive video frames along with their respective masks. Within its architecture, the encoder extracts features from the designated regions within each video frame, guided by the mask specific to that frame. Meanwhile, the decoder gradually decodes these extracted features, and generates the trimap that corresponds to each video frame. Different from traditional U-Net, we enhance the decoder part with several recurrent blocks to enhance the temporal coherence of the predicted trimaps. This refinement contributes to an overall improvement in the temporal coherence of the final output alpha mattes.

Feature Extraction. The encoder of MTT module comprises several repeated encoder blocks. Each encoder block is constructed with two 3×3 convolution layers, each succeeded by an ReLU and a BatchNorm layer, with a 2×2 max-pooling operation concluding the encoder block. We first concatenate V and M along the channel dimension to yield a 4-channel tensor $X \in \mathbb{R}^{T \times 4 \times H \times W}$. Then, X undergoes encoding to extract features across different scales.

It's important to note that the encoding process of the MTT module does not account for temporal information. Although X comprises multiple $x_t \in \mathbb{R}^{4 \times H \times W}$ from distinct moments, each x_t is individually processed through each encoder block to extract features. There is no interaction among different x_t during this feature extraction process. $f_i \in \mathbb{R}^{T \times \frac{256}{2^i} \times \frac{H}{2^{3-i}} \times \frac{W}{2^{3-i}}}$ represents the output feature map of the i th encoder block.

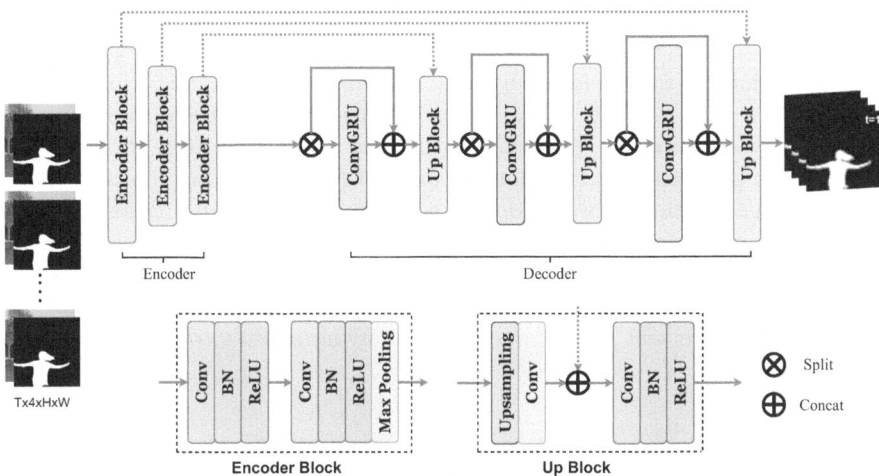

Fig. 3. The overall structure of the MTT module. We use U-Net as the core architecture, complemented by the introduction of ConvGRU to fuse temporal features throughout the decoding process.

Recurrent Feature Decoding. The decoder segment comprises three upsampling blocks and three recurrent blocks. Each upsampling block is composed of a bilinear upsampling layer paired with a 2×2 convolutional layer. Additionally, it involves concatenation from the corresponding feature map on the encoder side and a 3×3 convolution layer, which succeeded by an ReLU activation.

To preserve the temporal coherence of the output results, a recurrent block is incorporated before each upsampling block. ConvGRU (Convlutional Gated Recurrent Unit) [2] is selected as the recurrent block, with x_t representing the input and h_t denoting the output. The ConvGRU can be defined as follows:

$$z_t = \sigma(w_{zx} * x_t + w_{zh} * h_{t-1} + b_z)$$
$$r_t = \sigma(w_{rx} * x_t + w_{rh} * h_{t-1} + b_r)$$
$$o_t = tanh(w_{ox}(x_t + w_{oh}((r_t \odot h_{t-1}) + b_o)$$
$$h_t = z_t \odot h_{t-1} + (1 - z_t) \odot o_t$$

$$(2)$$

where w represent the parameters of the convolution layer, and b represent the biases of the convolution layer. The operators $*$ and $\odot$ represent convolution and element-wise product respectively. $tanh$ and σ represent hyperbolic tangent and sigmoid function. Before upsampling the feature map of a particular scale, ConvGRU is applied to fuse temporal features. To mitigate computational complexity, we split the channels of the feature map before each ConvGRU, perform feature fusion on only half of the channels, and then concatenate them back together.

3.3   Matting Stage

After obtaining the trimap for each frame, we employ a pretrained trimap-based matting network to generate alpha mattes. To demonstrate that our MTT module indirectly enhances the temporal consistency of alpha mattes, we utilize an image matting network as the matting module for FVM. This choice is made because image matting networks do not consider temporal information. Specifically, we select the state-of-the-art image matting network, ViTMatte.

In the matting stage, we sequentially concatenate each RGB frame $I \in \mathbb{R}^{3 \times H \times W}$ of input video and its trimap $\mathbb{R}^{T \times 1 \times H \times W}$ along the channel dimension, and these pairs are sent one by one to the matting module to obtain the final alpha mattes.

3.4   Loss Functions

Our FVM model predicts an alpha matte for each frame of the video, where α_t^{pre} represents the predicted alpha matte of the t th frame, and α_t^{gt} is the ground truth alpha matte. To ensure the quality of each alpha matte, we utilize accuracy loss L_{ac} calculated through the L1 loss L_1 and pyramid Laplacian loss L_{lap} between α_t^{pre} and α_t^{gt}:

$$L_{ac} = \sum_{t=1}^{T} L_1(\alpha_t^{pre}, \alpha_t^{gt}) + \sum_{t=1}^{T} L_{lap}(\alpha_t^{pre}, \alpha_t^{gt})$$

$$(3)$$

We incorporate a temporal coherence loss L_{tc} to enhance the temporal consistency of alpha mattes. We first calculate D^{pre} (the difference between the first $T-1$ and last $T-1$ predicted alpha mattes) and D^{gt} (the difference between the first $T-1$ and last $T-1$ ground truth alpha mattes). Subsequently, we calculate their Mean Squared Error (MSE) loss L_{mse}. The definitions of D^{pre}, D^{gt} and L_{tc} are as follows:

$$D^{pre} = (\alpha_2^{pre}, ..., \alpha_T^{pre}) - (\alpha_1^{pre}, ..., \alpha_{T-1}^{pre})$$

$$(4)$$

$$D^{gt} = (\alpha_2^{gt}, ..., \alpha_T^{gt}) - (\alpha_1^{gt}, ..., \alpha_{T-1}^{gt}) \tag{5}$$

$$L_{tc} = L_{mse}(D^{pre} - D^{gt}) \tag{6}$$

After obtaining L_{ac} and L_{tc}, we compute the total matting loss as:

$$L_{total} = \lambda_1 L_{ac} + \lambda_2 L_{tc} \tag{7}$$

Since L_{tc} is significantly smaller than L_{ac}, we set λ_1 to 1 and λ_2 to 10 to prevent the total loss being completely dominated by L_{ac}.

4 Experiments

4.1 Datasets

Our training dataset encompasses a diverse array of widely used matting datasets, including AIM [29], AM2K [14], Distinctions-646 [32], and Video-Matte240k [17]. VideoMatte240k, specifically designed for video matting, provides 484 video clips. Following RVM [18], we split VideoMatte240K into 475/4/5 video clips for training, validating, and testing, and we partition each training video clip into multiple sub-clips, where each sub-clip encompasses a sequence of consecutive T frames. AIM, AM2K, and Distinctions-646 are image matting datasets. The samples in each dataset consist solely of foreground RGB images and ground-truth alpha mattes. To train our model effectively, we generate composite RGB images and semantic masks for each sample. Background images $B \in \mathbb{R}^{3 \times H \times W}$ are randomly selected from the COCO [19] dataset. Composite images are obtained using Eq. (1).

To acquire semantic masks, we binarize the ground truth alpha mattes. All pixel values in the alpha mattes that are not part of the background are changed to 1. Following random erosion or dilation, these modified alpha mattes are employed as semantic masks.

4.2 Evaluation Metrics

Similar to the previous methods, we use the Mean of Absolute Difference (MAD), Mean Squared Error (MSE), Spatial Gradient (Grad) [22] and Connectivity (Conn) [22] errors as the evaluation metrics for video matting accuracy. Additionally, we assess the temporal consistency of alpha mattes using dtSSD [6].

4.3 Training Details

The parameters of SAM and STM are pre-trained. As the segmentation stage operates independently without interfering with other stages, they do not participate in the training process. We connect the MTT module and the matting module for end-to-end training. The parameters of the matting module are also pre-trained. We fix them and only update the parameters of the MTT module during the training process.

Image Training. Since temporal feature fusion is exclusively executed within the decoder section of the MTT module, the encoder's singular focus lies in precisely extracting foreground features without factoring in temporal information. Therefore, we adopt the strategy of employing the image matting network training methodology to pre-train the MTT module, consequently elevating the overall performance of the MTT encoder. Before using the video dataset, we initially train our MTT on multiple image matting datasets. During this phase, the MTT module employs the basic U-Net structure without incorporating ConvGRU. We train it for 15 epochs with an input resolution of 512×512. The batch size and learning rate are set to 16 and 1×10^{-3} respectively, and we use the Adam optimizer. The model is trained on Nvidia 2080 GPUs.

Video Training. Following image training, we proceed with video training on VideoMatte240K dataset. During this step, we retain the parameters trained in the image training phase and introduce ConvGRU in the decoder part. The trained parameters are not locked, and video clips are fed into the MTT module, with each video clip consisting of 4 frames ($T = 4$). The batch size is changed to 4, learning rate to 1×10^{-4}, and epochs to 40. The remaining settings remain consistent with image training.

Table 1. Comparison with state-of-the-art methods on the test split of Video-Matte240K dataset. The best result is in bold.

Method	Temporal Information	MAD↓	MSE↓	Grad↓	Conn↓	dtSSD↓
DeepLabV3 [3]	–	14.47	9.67	8.55	1.69	5.18
FBA [7]	–	8.36	3.37	2.09	0.75	2.09
BGMv2 [17]	–	25.19	19.63	2.28	3.26	2.74
MODNet [10]	–	9.41	4.30	1.89	0.81	2.23
RVM [18]	√	6.08	1.47	0.88	0.41	1.36
VMFormer [12]	√	6.02	1.00	0.75	0.37	–
AdaM [16]	√	5.30	0.78	0.72	0.30	**1.33**
FVM (Ours)	√	**5.29**	**0.59**	**0.61**	**0.26**	1.48

4.4   State-of-the-Art Comparison

We evaluate the performance of our FVM on the VideoMatte240K dataset, comparing it with prominent video matting baselines, including DeepLabV3 [3], trimap-based method (FBA [7]), background-based method (BGMv2 [17]), auxiliary-free methods (MODNet [10], RVM [18], AdaM [16]), etc. Among these, DeepLabV3, FBA, BGMv2, and MODNet are matting networks that do not utilize temporal information. The test results are presented in Table 1. It is evident from the results that our model surpasses all previous state-of-the-art works in terms of matting accuracy. Furthermore, our FVM exhibits comparable temporal consistency to existing best results and notably outperforms methods that directly apply image matting networks to video matting tasks.

4.5   Qualitative Analysis on Real Videos

Given that MODNet and RVM stand out as the most representative open-source video matting networks, we conduct a qualitative comparison with the FVM model on the test clip of VideoMatte240K. Figure 4 illustrates the qualitative results, indicating that the alpha mattes predicted by the FVM model are more accurate and exhibit less flickering compared with those predicted by RVM and MODNet.

In addition, we also compare the matting performance of our method with MODNet and RVM on real videos. Figure 5 shows the comparison results. It can be seen that due to the lack of trimap guidance, the matting results of RVM and MODNet on real videos will lose part of the foreground or over-matte part of the background, while our method is less effective on matting on real videos. The accuracy is higher than them.

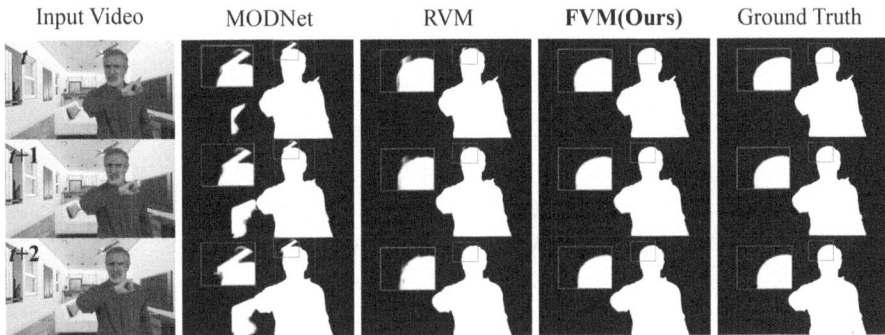

Fig. 4. Qualitative comparison results on test clip of VideoMatte240k.

4.6   Ablation Study

Ablation Study on The FVM Setup. Table 2 shows the results after removing different modules in FVM. Specifically, the initial and second rows of Table 2 represent the results derived by employing the segmentation network's output directly as the matting result. The third row portrays the results obtained without the utilization of the MTT module. Here, we directly corrode and expand the mask to obtain the rough trimaps. The fourth row denotes the results of the complete FVM network. The findings underscore that the alpha mattes predicted by our FVM exhibit greater precision compared to the masks, and the MTT module we designed can effectively improve the accuracy and temporal consistency of alpha mattes.

| MODNet | RVM | FVM(Ours) |

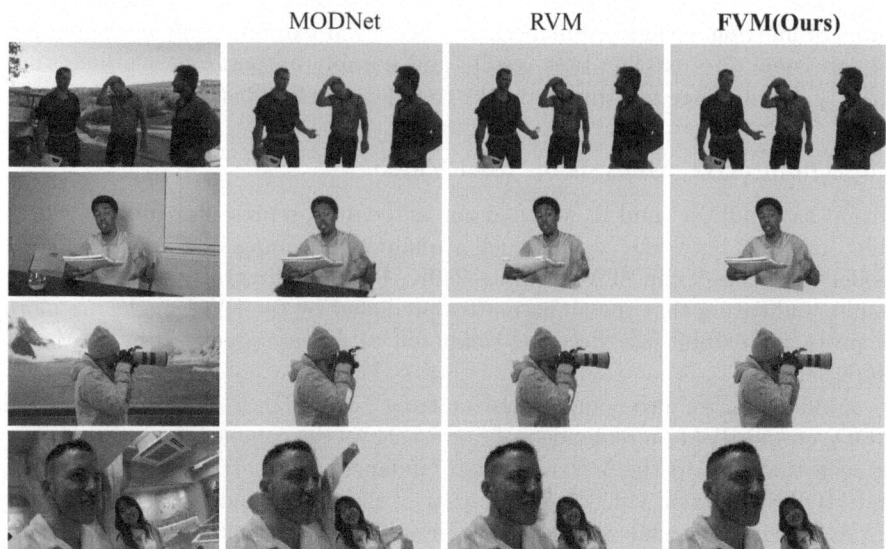

Fig. 5. Qualitative comparison results on real-world videos.

Table 2. Ablation study on the FVM setup. The best result is in bold.

Method	MAD↓	MSE↓	Grad↓	dtSSD↓
SAM	7.59	3.48	3.71	4.82
SAM+STM	6.43	2.32	1.73	4.36
SAM+STM+ViTMatte	5.81	1.02	0.90	1.79
SAM+STM+MTT+ViTMatte	**5.29**	**0.59**	**0.61**	**1.48**

Ablation Study on Temporal Information. To assess the significance of temporal information, we remove the recurrent blocks from the MTT module and examine whether the temporal consistency of the output alpha mattes is affected. The results in Table 3 indicate a reduction in the temporal consistency measures of alpha mattes predicted by the model without recurrent blocks, underscoring the role of recurrent blocks in enhancing temporal consistency.

Table 3. Ablation study on temporal information. The best result is in bold.

ConvGRU	MAD↓	MSE↓	Grad↓	dtSSD↓
–	5.66	0.90	0.72	1.60
√	**5.29**	**0.59**	**0.61**	**1.48**

Ablation Study on Number of Encoder and Decoder Blocks. In Table 4, we systematically varied the quantity of encoder and decoder blocks within the MTT module to investigate if a deeper architecture improves performance. Each decoder block consists of an up block and a ConvGRU. It is noteworthy that the number of encoder and decoder blocks remained consistent. Our findings reveal that the MTT module, when extended to a 3-layer depth, showcases superior performance compared to the 2-layer configuration. This outcome suggests that augmenting the depth of the MTT module yields favorable results.

Table 4. Ablation study on number of encoder and decoder blocks, where N indicates the number of encoder and decoder blocks. The best result is in bold.

N	MAD↓	MSE↓	Grad↓	dtSSD↓
1	71.29	43.70	5.39	4.43
2	5.32	0.65	0.68	1.56
3	**5.29**	**0.59**	**0.61**	**1.48**

5   Conclusion

We have introduced a novel video matting network, FVM, and devised a MTT module based on a recurrent architecture. This module utilizes masks to effectively obtain trimaps with high temporal consistency for input videos without the need for manual annotation, thereby significantly reducing labeling costs. The FVM model addresses the limitations of existing video matting approaches, particularly in terms of supporting flexible user interaction. Users can efficiently complete matting tasks through simple prompts such as text, points, and boxes.

We conduct a comparative evaluation of FVM against the existing video matting methods using the same benchmark. The experimental results reveal that FVM consistently outperforms all existing methods in matting quality for each frame of the video, with temporal consistency closely approaching the highest results. Notably, the convenience and flexibility of FVM enable its applicability to a wide range of scenarios, setting it apart from the existing approaches.

Acknowledgments. This study was supported by the National Natural Science Foundation of China (NSFC) under Grants 61871262, 61901251, and 62071284, the Innovation Program of Shanghai Municipal Science and Technology Commission under Grants 21ZR1422400, 20JC1416400 and 20511106603, Pudong New Area Science & Technology Development Fund, Key-Area Research and Development Program of Guangdong Province under Grant 2020B0101130012, and Foshan Science and Technology Innovation Team Project under Grant FS0AA-KJ919-4402-0060.

Disclosure of Interests. The authors have no competing interests to declare that are relevant to the content of this article.

References

1. Bai, X., Wang, J., Simons, D.: Towards temporally-coherent video matting. In: International Conference on Computer Vision/Computer Graphics Collaboration Techniques and Applications, pp. 63–74. Springer (2011)
2. Ballas, N., Yao, L., Pal, C., Courville, A.: Delving deeper into convolutional networks for learning video representations. arXiv preprint arXiv:1511.06432 (2015)
3. Chen, L.C., Papandreou, G., Schroff, F., Adam, H.: Rethinking atrous convolution for semantic image segmentation. arXiv preprint arXiv:1706.05587 (2017)
4. Choi, I., Lee, M., Tai, Y.W.: Video matting using multi-frame nonlocal matting Laplacian. In: Computer Vision–ECCV 2012: 12th European Conference on Computer Vision, Florence, Italy, 7–13 October 2012, Proceedings, Part VI 12, pp. 540–553. Springer (2012)
5. Dai, Y., Price, B., Zhang, H., Shen, C.: Boosting robustness of image matting with context assembling and strong data augmentation. In: Proceedings of the IEEE/CVF Conference on Computer Vision and Pattern Recognition, pp. 11707–11716 (2022)
6. Erofeev, M., Gitman, Y., Vatolin, D.S., Fedorov, A., Wang, J.: Perceptually motivated benchmark for video matting. In: BMVC, p. 99-1 (2015)
7. Forte, M., Pitié, F.: f, b, alpha matting. arXiv preprint arXiv:2003.07711 (2020)
8. Hou, Q., Liu, F.: Context-aware image matting for simultaneous foreground and alpha estimation. In: Proceedings of the IEEE/CVF International Conference on Computer Vision, pp. 4130–4139 (2019)
9. Huang, W.L., Lee, M.S.: End-to-end video matting with trimap propagation. In: Proceedings of the IEEE/CVF Conference on Computer Vision and Pattern Recognition, pp. 14337–14347 (2023)
10. Ke, Z., Sun, J., Li, K., Yan, Q., Lau, R.W.: MODNet: real-time trimap-free portrait matting via objective decomposition. In: Proceedings of the AAAI Conference on Artificial Intelligence, vol. 36, pp. 1140–1147 (2022)
11. Kirillov, A., et al.: Segment anything. arXiv preprint arXiv:2304.02643 (2023)
12. Li, J., Goel, V., Ohanyan, M., Navasardyan, S., Wei, Y., Shi, H.: VMFormer: end-to-end video matting with transformer. arXiv preprint arXiv:2208.12801 (2022)
13. Li, J., Jain, J., Shi, H.: Matting anything. arXiv preprint arXiv:2306.05399 (2023)
14. Li, J., Zhang, J., Maybank, S.J., Tao, D.: Bridging composite and real: towards end-to-end deep image matting. Int. J. Comput. Vis. **130**(2), 246–266 (2022)
15. Li, Y., Lu, H.: Natural image matting via guided contextual attention. In: Proceedings of the AAAI Conference on Artificial Intelligence, vol. 34, pp. 11450–11457 (2020)
16. Lin, C.C., et al.: Adaptive human matting for dynamic videos. In: Proceedings of the IEEE/CVF Conference on Computer Vision and Pattern Recognition, pp. 10229–10238 (2023)
17. Lin, S., Ryabtsev, A., Sengupta, S., Curless, B.L., Seitz, S.M., Kemelmacher-Shlizerman, I.: Real-time high-resolution background matting. In: Proceedings of the IEEE/CVF Conference on Computer Vision and Pattern Recognition, pp. 8762–8771 (2021)
18. Lin, S., Yang, L., Saleemi, I., Sengupta, S.: Robust high-resolution video matting with temporal guidance. In: Proceedings of the IEEE/CVF Winter Conference on Applications of Computer Vision, pp. 238–247 (2022)
19. Lin, T.Y., et al.: Microsoft COCO: common objects in context. In: Computer Vision–ECCV 2014: 13th European Conference, Zurich, Switzerland, 6–12 September 2014, Proceedings, Part V 13, pp. 740–755. Springer (2014)

20. Oh, S.W., Lee, J.Y., Xu, N., Kim, S.J.: Video object segmentation using space-time memory networks. In: Proceedings of the IEEE/CVF International Conference on Computer Vision, pp. 9226–9235 (2019)
21. Qiao, Y., et al.: Attention-guided hierarchical structure aggregation for image matting. In: Proceedings of the IEEE/CVF Conference on Computer Vision and Pattern Recognition, pp. 13676–13685 (2020)
22. Rhemann, C., Rother, C., Wang, J., Gelautz, M., Kohli, P., Rott, P.: A perceptually motivated online benchmark for image matting. In: 2009 IEEE Conference on Computer Vision and Pattern Recognition, pp. 1826–1833. IEEE (2009)
23. Sengupta, S., Jayaram, V., Curless, B., Seitz, S.M., Kemelmacher-Shlizerman, I.: Background matting: the world is your green screen. In: Proceedings of the IEEE/CVF Conference on Computer Vision and Pattern Recognition, pp. 2291–2300 (2020)
24. Seong, H., Oh, S.W., Price, B., Kim, E., Lee, J.Y.: One-trimap video matting. In: European Conference on Computer Vision, pp. 430–448. Springer (2022)
25. Sun, J., Ke, Z., Zhang, L., Lu, H., Lau, R.W.: MODNet-V: improving portrait video matting via background restoration. arXiv preprint arXiv:2109.11818 (2021)
26. Sun, Y., Tang, C.K., Tai, Y.W.: Semantic image matting. In: Proceedings of the IEEE/CVF Conference on Computer Vision and Pattern Recognition, pp. 11120–11129 (2021)
27. Sun, Y., Wang, G., Gu, Q., Tang, C.K., Tai, Y.W.: Deep video matting via spatio-temporal alignment and aggregation. In: Proceedings of the IEEE/CVF Conference on Computer Vision and Pattern Recognition, pp. 6975–6984 (2021)
28. Wang, T., Liu, S., Tian, Y., Li, K., Yang, M.H.: Video matting via consistency-regularized graph neural networks. In: Proceedings of the IEEE/CVF International Conference on Computer Vision, pp. 4902–4911 (2021)
29. Xu, N., Price, B., Cohen, S., Huang, T.: Deep image matting. In: Proceedings of the IEEE Conference on Computer Vision and Pattern Recognition, pp. 2970–2979 (2017)
30. Yao, J., Wang, X., Yang, S., Wang, B.: ViTMatte: boosting image matting with pretrained plain vision transformers. arXiv preprint arXiv:2305.15272 (2023)
31. Yao, J., Wang, X., Ye, L., Liu, W.: Matte anything: interactive natural image matting with segment anything models. arXiv preprint arXiv:2306.04121 (2023)
32. Yu, H., Xu, N., Huang, Z., Zhou, Y., Shi, H.: High-resolution deep image matting. In: Proceedings of the AAAI Conference on Artificial Intelligence, vol. 35, pp. 3217–3224 (2021)
33. Yu, Q., et al.: Mask guided matting via progressive refinement network. In: Proceedings of the IEEE/CVF Conference on Computer Vision and Pattern Recognition, pp. 1154–1163 (2021)
34. Zhang, Y., et al.: Attention-guided temporally coherent video object matting. In: Proceedings of the 29th ACM International Conference on Multimedia, pp. 5128–5137 (2021)

Adversarial Augmentation Training Makes Action Recognition Models More Robust to Realistic Video Distribution Shifts

Kiyoon Kim$^{(\boxtimes)}$, Shreyank N. Gowda , Panagiotis Eustratiadis ,
Antreas Antoniou , and Robert B. Fisher

University of Edinburgh, Edinburgh, UK
yoonkr33@gmail.com

Abstract. Despite recent advances in video action recognition achieving strong performance on existing benchmarks, these models often lack robustness when faced with natural distribution shifts between training and test data. We propose two novel evaluation methods to assess model resilience to such distribution disparity. One method uses two different datasets collected from different sources and uses one for training and validation, and the other for testing. More precisely, we created dataset splits of HMDB-51 or UCF-101 for training, and Kinetics-400 for testing, using the subset of the classes that are overlapping in both train and test datasets. The other proposed method extracts the feature mean of each class from the target evaluation dataset's training data (*i.e.* class prototype), and estimates test video prediction as a cosine similarity score between each sample to the class prototypes of each target class. This procedure does not alter model weights using the target dataset and it does not require aligning overlapping classes of two different datasets, thus it is a very efficient method to test the model robustness to distribution shifts, without prior knowledge of the target distribution. We address the robustness problem by adversarial augmentation training – generating augmented views of videos that are "hard" for the classification model by applying gradient ascent on the augmentation parameters – as well as "curriculum" scheduling the strength of the video augmentations. We experimentally demonstrate the superior performance of the proposed adversarial augmentation approach over baselines across three state-of-the-art action recognition models - TSM, Video Swin Transformer, and Uniformer. Our curated datasets and source code are publicly available (https://github.com/kiyoon/video-adversarial-augmentation). The presented work provides critical insight into model robustness to distribution shifts and presents effective techniques to enhance video action recognition performance in a real-world deployment.

Keywords: Action recognition · Distribution shifts · Adversarial training · Data augmentation

---

Supplementary Information The online version contains supplementary material available at https://doi.org/10.1007/978-981-97-8702-9_13.

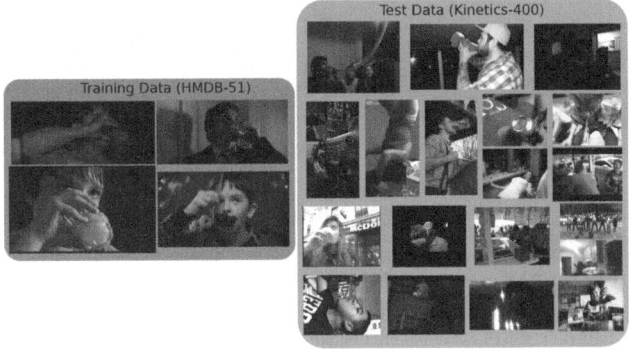

Fig. 1. A common scenario with biased training data and testing with real-life data, with an example class of "drink". The training data is from the HMDB-51 dataset whose video samples are usually taken from movies, and the test data is from the Kinetics-400 dataset which is from YouTube videos. There are many reasons why the test data looks so different: poor camera quality, wrong orientation, extreme camera shake, inconsistent frame rate, frame rate conversion artifacts (interlacing), poor lighting, lack of professional post-processing (*e.g.* color grading), different ways of performing the action, poor framing, inconsistent aspect ratios, editing artifacts, various actions happening at the same time. Thus, it is common for the performance to drop significantly when the trained model is applied in more general applications.

1 Introduction

Video action recognition is a vital computer vision task with applications in surveillance, robotics, and more. Video data exhibits greater diversity than image data, and therefore action recognition architectures are not as robust to distribution shifts [38, 42, 56]. In addition to image-level effects like viewpoint and appearance changes, video introduces effects such as camera motion, focus shifts, and background object movements. Moreover, an action class incorporates substantial intra-class variation as illustrated in Fig. 1. For example, the class "playing basketball" may involve dribbling, running, or shooting in different contexts. Furthermore, depending on the data source, there are biased video processing artifacts. For example, videos collected from YouTube have standardized YouTube processing (VP9 compression), making the dark areas have extremely low quality. Often, the videos go through a frame rate conversion algorithm, which can create frame interlacing artifacts. As a result, the slight distribution shift in video data can dramatically reduce the action recognition performance.

Data augmentation is one potential solution to account for this fragility. It is a popular method to create synthetic variations of the existing training data that will enable classification models to generalize better to previously unseen test data. However, it is not yet clear what kind of augmentation is necessary to generalize to test data with different distribution shifts. There has been much work on automatically selecting augmentation policies given training and validation data [8, 22, 24, 34, 35]. However, such approaches optimize augmentation of the training data, and it is not clear how well the resulting generalization applies to test data with much distribution shift.

To address the video domain shift problem, we propose an adversarial augmentation scheme that generates "hard" video examples for the action recognition networks. The pipeline is simple to implement, and results in a meaningful improvement in performance on the proposed datasets with realistic distribution shifts compared to no augmentation and random augmentation baselines. The benefits are demonstrated using three popular action recognition architectures. The training and validation datasets are subsets of HMDB-51 or UCF-101, and the test data are a subset from equivalent Kinetics-400 classes, to realistically evaluate distribution shifts over the same action classes.

This approach and evaluation requires multiple datasets with common aligned action classes. The paper also presents another simple method to evaluate robustness using a target dataset with different classes using cosine similarity of features as logits. The method requires no training (*i.e.* fine-tuning) on the target dataset, and thus it correctly measures the transferability of the trained classifier on the target dataset.

To summarize, our contributions are:

1. Experiments reveal substantial performance degradation on our cross-dataset benchmarks, quantitatively demonstrating the challenge posed by real-world distribution shift.
2. We propose two novel evaluation protocols to assess model resilience to distribution disparity using naturally sourced datasets, as opposed to solely artificially corrupted data:
   2*a*) We construct new cross-dataset benchmarks by identifying overlapping classes between HMDB-51, UCF-101, and Kinetics-400. Models are trained on either HMDB or UCF, and evaluated on Kinetics data.
   2*b*) We further introduce a similarity-based evaluation approach that estimates predictions using cosine similarity between embedded training and test features, without requiring class alignment.
3. Through extensive experiments across multiple state-of-the-art architectures, we empirically demonstrate that the proposed adversarial augmentation and curriculum adversarial training frameworks enhance robustness to realistic distribution shifts between the training and test datasets.
4. We publicly release the constructed subsets of HMDB-51, UCF-101, and Kinetics-400 to enable further research on this important problem.

2   Related Work

Action Recognition. Action recognition is the task of categorizing video sequences into predefined action classes. Architectures based on 3D convolutional neural networks were previously dominant for spatiotemporal feature learning. These include approaches such as inflating 2D models [7], incorporating relational reasoning with non-local operations [53], and dual-stream designs [14,46].

More recently, transformer networks have become prominent, demonstrating strong performance [12,33,39] despite their exponential computational complexity [29]. For efficient video recognition, 2D backbone models remain popular, using techniques like temporal feature aggregation [51], relational modeling [61], temporal shift modules [36], frame selection [20,31,55], channel-wise convolutions (*i.e.* height-width, height-time, width-time) [54] or analyzing short-term and long-term temporal difference [50].

Data Augmentation. [44] summarizes image data augmentation techniques for deep learning. AutoAugment [8] is an augmentation policy search algorithm that finds the best augmentation on a target dataset, based on the highest validation accuracy. Due to AutoAugment's expensive policy search, Population-Based Augmentation [24], FastAutoAugment [35], and FasterAutoAugment [22] proposed more efficient searching algorithms, by learning a schedule policy over a fixed-policy, using density matching, and using differential augmentation with a generative adversarial network (GAN) [18] architecture that involves a policy generator and a discriminator, respectively. Differentiable Automatic Data Augmentation [34] proposed a data augmentation policy searching algorithm (using the Relaxed Bernoulli distribution [26]) which is differentiable, similar to FasterAutoaugment, and further introduced an unbiased gradient estimator that enables joint optimization of the augmentation policies and network parameters, instead of using a GAN. RandAugment [9] showed that simple random augmentations with randomly sampled transformations achieve similar performance more efficiently.

However, the policies in most works are optimized on the training set, and we focus on the scenario where test data can have severe distribution disparities which are unknown during the training time.

Adversarial Training. Adversarial training (AT) is framed as a min-max problem whereby the trained model uses observed training samples to minimize its prediction error, while an adversary attempts to generate training samples that maximize it. It is well-established that AT is the most effective way to achieve adversarial robustness [2]. It has further been shown to yield other types of robustness, *e.g.* against natural corruptions [10], domain shift [30,43,62], and others. Note that even though the classical definition of AT uses adversarial input noise [6,19], more adversarial image augmentations have been studied, *e.g.* rotations [52,60], contrast, jitter, etc. [3]. AT should be approached with care, as generating adversarial training examples that are too challenging for the trained model may actually harm downstream performance [5].

In this paper, we employ two measures to control the trade-off between augmentation strength and performance: (i) We create maximally informative adversarial examples (confusing to the model, but near the classification boundaries) via maximum-entropy regularization, as per the work of [11,27,57]. (ii) We train with curriculum AT as per the work of [5,58], which means training with harder adversarial examples over time.

Domain Adaptation. Domain adaptation is a transfer learning task where the source and target datasets have a significant distribution shift while sharing the same task. [13] explains types of domain adaptation tasks and approaches.

There are discrepancy-based techniques that learn transferable features from a source domain to a target domain [40,59], reconstruction-based methods that utilize autoencoders, which aim to extract useful features for the target domain [16,17], and adversarial domain adaptation approaches involving a source/target discriminator that distinguishes where the data come from and a feature extractor that aims to confuse the discriminator by trying to produce generic features regardless of the domain [1,4,15,25,41,45,48,49]. More recently, analyzing frequency components of deep feature maps using attention to filter domain-general components [37] is proposed.

Domain adaptation for video action recognition was first proposed by using a feature alignment approach on online test videos [38]. This work was evaluated using computationally simulated corrupted videos, while we propose to use real examples that involve more diverse types of discrepancy between the domains.

It is important to note that most domain adaptation techniques require examples from the target dataset to be present, while our work focuses on evaluating using a completely unknown dataset.

Corruption Robustness Analysis. [23] provided benchmarks for measuring a neural network's robustness to corruptions and perturbations, by evaluating with 15 algorithmically-generated corruptions (*e.g.* noise, blur, pixelate, compression artifacts). [56] extended this to video classification tasks and video corruptions (*e.g.* video compression artifacts, frame rate conversion, bit error, packet loss). [42] reported a large-scale robustness analysis of deep action recognition models again using pre-defined perturbations.

These approaches were evaluated using simulated data, while we propose to use real data for testing. Evaluating robustness with augmented data prohibits the same augmentations to be used for training. This paper focuses on a more realistic scenario where a known set of data augmentation strategies is used for training and evaluation is done with unprocessed real data.

3   Problem and Methodology

Action recognition predicts an action category label given a video sequence. This paper explores how well different variations of action recognition models, training, and loss functions generalize by evaluating on a different data domain.

The main difference with transfer learning is that our approach does not tune model parameters using the target evaluation dataset, whereas transfer learning usually involves fine-tuning the model with the target dataset's training set.

To improve generalizability, the training data is augmented. Hard-to-classify adversarial examples are generated by applying gradient ascent on the augmentation parameters which are fully differentiable. We then train the classifier using the AT (Adversarial Training) loss, calculated using both clean and adversarial examples.

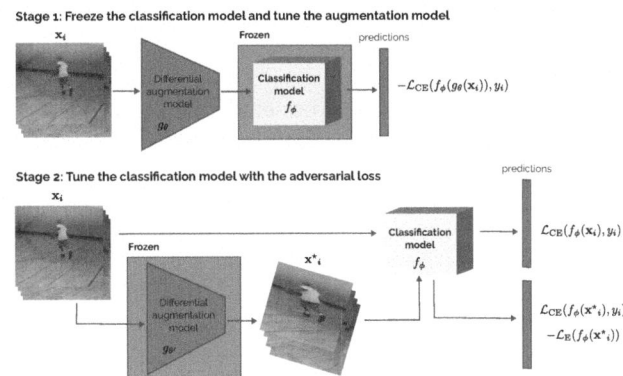

Fig. 2. The proposed adversarial augmentation training has two separate stages. Firstly, the classification model is frozen while the differential augmentation model is trained using the negative cross-entropy loss. This is equivalent to performing gradient ascent to maximize normal cross-entropy loss. As a result, the augmentation model will generate hard augmentations for the classification model. The second stage trains the classification model using both clean and adversarial examples. The maximum entropy regularization loss is integrated by subtracting the entropy of the adversarial examples, encouraging the predictions to be evenly balanced.

3.1   Adversarial Augmentation Training

Adversarial augmentation training uses a two stage training loop. See Fig. 2.

Stage 1: Generate Adversarial Examples. "Hard" adversarial examples are found by tuning the augmentation parameters using gradient ascent.

Let $g_\theta(\mathbf{x})$ be an augmentation model with fully differentiable parameters θ, and $f_\phi(\mathbf{x})$ be a video classification model with parameters ϕ, that outputs class predictions given an input video $\mathbf{x}$. The goal of stage 1 is to find the augmentation parameters θ' that maximize categorical cross-entropy loss. Note that by *maximizing* the loss, we aim to find the augmentation strategy that is challenging for the classifier, and in Fig. 2, this is described as *minimizing* the negative cross-entropy loss.

At each training step, the augmentation parameters θ are randomly initialized. Gradient ascent is then done only on θ, freezing the classification parameters ϕ to learn adversarial augmentations, with the cross-entropy loss $\mathcal{L}_{\mathrm{CE}}(f_\phi(g_\theta(\mathbf{x}_i)), y_i)$. This optimizes augmentation parameters θ' for generating adversarial examples.

Stage 2: Optimize the Classification Model. Next, the classification parameters ϕ are optimized while freezing the augmentation parameters θ. For simplicity, $\mathbf{x}_i^\star = g_{\theta'}(\mathbf{x}_i)$ denotes the generated adversarial example of $\mathbf{x}_i$. The vanilla AT loss is defined as:

$$\mathcal{L}_{\mathrm{AT}}(f_\phi(\mathbf{x}_i), f_\phi(\mathbf{x}_i^\star), y_i) = \alpha \mathcal{L}_{\mathrm{CE}}(f_\phi(\mathbf{x}_i), y_i) + (1-\alpha)\mathcal{L}_{\mathrm{CE}}(f_\phi(\mathbf{x}^\star_i), y_i) \quad (1)$$

which is a weighted average of the cross-entropy loss using the clean sample and the augmented sample.

Max-Entropy Regularization. The cross-entropy loss encourages predictions to be over-confident by pushing the examples further from the classification boundaries. However, adversarial examples are supposed to be confusing. We regularize the cross-entropy-based adversarial loss in Eq. (1) by maximizing the entropy, encouraging the overall predictions to be evenly balanced for adversarial examples.

$$\mathcal{L}_{\text{AT-ME}}(f_\phi(\mathbf{x}_i), f_\phi(\mathbf{x}_i^\star), y_i) = \alpha \mathcal{L}_{\text{CE}}(f_\phi(\mathbf{x}_i), y_i) \\ + (1 - \alpha)\mathcal{L}_{\text{CE}}(f_\phi(\mathbf{x}^\star{}_i), y_i) - \gamma \mathcal{L}_{\text{E}}(f_\phi(\mathbf{x}^\star{}_i)) \tag{2}$$

where entropy loss $\mathcal{L}_{\text{E}}$ is defined as

$$\mathcal{L}_{\text{E}}(f_\phi(\mathbf{x}_i^\star)) = -\frac{1}{C} \sum_{c=1}^{C} f_\phi^{(c)}(\mathbf{x}_i^\star) \log(f_\phi^{(c)}(\mathbf{x}_i^\star)) \tag{3}$$

C is the number of classes, and $f_\phi^{(c)}(\mathbf{x}_i^\star)$ is the prediction score of class c for the adversarial example $\mathbf{x}_i^\star$.

Curriculum Adversarial Training. Applying curriculum training by starting from training with "easy" samples and gradually generating "harder" samples makes the model more robust [5]. Here, the classification models are trained initially from clean data without augmentation, and gradually harder adversarial examples are added by scheduling the learning rate of the augmentation model.

3.2   Cross-Dataset Evaluation

We train on one dataset and test on another dataset, where there are distribution shifts between the train and the test data. We propose two different evaluation approaches.

Matched Class Evaluation (Expt. 1). The first approach creates two datasets that share the same classes, but have a significant disparity in the train and test data distribution. Classes that are common to the two initial datasets are identified following the procedure described in TruZe [21]. We describe the procedure and curated datasets in Supplementary Material. This is the most realistic method to evaluate on a distribution shift, but it requires some manual procedures as well as finding datasets that share largely similar classes.

Cosine Similarity Evaluation (Expt. 2). The second method applies the feature extractor trained on the source dataset to the videos in the target dataset, which are split into a training subset and a test subset. This is a simpler method that does not require manual class matching. A more descriptive procedure can be found in the Supplementary Material.

Formally, the class prototype $\mathbf{c}_k \in \mathbb{R}^M$ for each class k is the M-dimensional mean vector of the embedded features belonging to that class in the training subset. Let S_k be the set of videos in the training subset of the target dataset from class k. $\mathbf{c}_k$ is computed by the following, where $y_i = k$ for all $(\mathbf{x}_i, y_i) \in S_k$:

$$\mathbf{c}_k = \frac{1}{|S_k|} \sum_{(\mathbf{x}_i, y_i) \in S_k} h_\omega(\mathbf{x}_i) \tag{4}$$

$h_\omega()$ is the embedded feature extraction function computed by training on the source dataset.

For a given test video from the test subset of the target dataset $\mathbf{x}_i \in S_k^{test}$, the probability of a given class label k is estimated using the cosine similarity of the embedding to the target dataset's class prototype $\mathbf{c}_k$, followed by softmax. Given the cosine similarity function $d(\mathbf{x}, \mathbf{c}) = \frac{\mathbf{x} \cdot \mathbf{c}}{\|\mathbf{x}\|\|\mathbf{c}\|}$ we get:

$$P(y = k | \mathbf{x}_i \in S_k^{test}) = \frac{\exp(-d(h_\omega(\mathbf{x}_i), \mathbf{c}_k))}{\sum_{k'} \exp(-d(h_\omega(\mathbf{x}_i), \mathbf{c}_{k'}))} \tag{5}$$

where y denotes the class label. If the largest estimated $P(\cdot)$ is for the same class as the ground truth, then this is a successful classification. Accuracy is computed over all samples in the test subset of the target dataset.

The parameter ω is not tuned during this operation. That is, the target dataset does not contribute to fine-tuning the model. The motivation of this approach is to measure the transferability of the model from a source dataset to a target dataset without actually tuning the model parameters, showing the robustness of the model to sample distribution shift.

4   Experiments

HMDB/Kinetics and UCF/Kinetics Datasets (Expt. 1). HMDB-51 [32] is a popular human action recognition dataset that is composed of around 7,000 video clips divided into 51 categories, collected from mainly movies as well as YouTube. The UCF-101 [47] dataset consists of 13,320 videos in 101 action classes collected from YouTube. Kinetics-400 [28] is a large-scale action dataset in which each video clip is around 10 s long, and there are over 300,000 videos in 400 classes.

Training datasets are created from subsets of HMDB-51 or UCF-101 and the subset of the Kinetics-400 test set is used for testing. The subsets share the same classes between the training and test sets. The motivation for this approach to creating the datasets is to simulate a real-world environment where the test data comes from many unknown sources, with many variations in actions, capture conditions, aspect ratio, and so on. The Kinetics-400 dataset has many more samples in the fine-grained classes, so it was used for testing.

TruZe [21] is used to identify shared classes from the HMDB-51 and Kinetics-400, and UCF-101 and Kinetics-400 datasets, based on the visual and semantic similarity. More details on this procedure can be found in the Supplementary Material. The final datasets are named HMDB-28/Kinetics-28 and UCF-65/Kinetics-65, where the training sets are subsets of the HMDB and UCF data, respectively, and test subsets come from Kinetics. The 28 and 65 refer to the number of shared classes. The three official published splits of HMDB-51 and UCF-101 are used, but only the shared classes are selected. The results in Table 1 are the average performance over the three splits. The HMDB-28/Kinetics-28 dataset consists of 3445 HMDB and 43406 Kinetics videos, and the UCF-65/Kinetics-65 dataset consists of 8935 UCF and 78583 Kinetics videos.

HMDB ↔ UCF Evaluation (Expt. 2). For the experiments using the cosine similarity function, the HMDB-28 trained models are tested on UCF-101, and the UCF-65 trained models are tested on HMDB-51, using the cosine similarity measure with class prototypes as predictions. The feature extractor trained using the training data is then used on the target dataset. It is used to create class prototype vectors (for each target class) from one part of the target dataset, and evaluation is based on the classification accuracy of the other part of the dataset. This assesses the quality of the feature extractor on another dataset with distribution shifts. The results in Table 1 are the average performance over the nine splits, three runs from the source dataset and each run evaluates with three splits from the target dataset.

See the Supplementary Material for the resulting matching datasets in Table 1, and a summary table of all experimental datasets (Expt. 1 and Expt. 2), in Table 3.

Augmentation Methods. Results are compared for four different training approaches: training without augmentation, with random augmentation, with adversarial augmentation, and with curriculum AT [5] as described in Sect. 3.1. Experiments used the popular efficient 2D TSM model [36] with a ResNet50 backbone, Video Swin Transformer [39] Tiny, and Uniformer-S [33] model. ImageNet pre-trained models were used instead of Kinetics pre-trained, so that the models never get to see the Kinetics data distribution.

Augmentation used translation to a maximum of 28 pixels, 10° rotation, shear transform of 0.1, and scale from 0.9 to 1.5. For curriculum training, no augmentation was used for 20 epochs, then AT with a zero learning rate of the augmentation model was used for 20 more epochs. Then, AT with a triangular learning rate scheduling from 0.1 to 1.0 on the augmentation model was used for the rest of the training, except for the Uniformer model. For Uniformer, the above was done for only 20 epochs, and then trained with random augmentation for 20 more epochs and fine-tuning with no augmentation for the rest to mitigate under-fitting issues.

See the Supplementary Material for implementation details.

5   Results

5.1   Shared Class Experiments 1a, 1b

When the adversarial training approaches presented in Sect. 3.1 are applied, target dataset performance improves. Table 1 summarizes the main cross-dataset evaluation results for the four augmentation strategies presented in Sect. 3.1.

Table 1. Results from three models (TSM ResNet50, Video Swin Transformer Tiny, and Uniformer-S), two training datasets (UCF-65 and HMDB-28), four augmentation strategies (no augmentation, random, adversarial, and curriculum), and two test datasets (Kinetics, and HMDB/UCF). In all cases, adversarial augmentation or curriculum adversarial augmentation training outperformed all baselines. The columns labeled Test Accuracy show the performance on the target test set. The values in brackets in the Train Dataset columns show the "no augmentation" accuracy on the test set of the same dataset to demonstrate the performance drop when evaluating to the Kinetics dataset.

Model	Train Dataset	Augmentation	Test Accuracy	
			Kinetics-65	HMDB-51
			Matched Expt 1a	Cosine Expt 2a
TSM	UCF-65 [77.50]	None	39.13 ± 0.56	37.61 ± 1.88
		Random	40.90 ± 0.32	38.19 ± 1.39
		Adversarial	42.42 ± 0.63	38.99 ± 1.26
		Curriculum	**42.51 ± 0.62**	**39.14 ± 1.21**
Swin	UCF-65 [81.15]	None	37.08 ± 1.43	38.91 ± 1.63
		Random	40.80 ± 1.90	40.61 ± 1.40
		Adversarial	**42.27 ± 0.24**	41.48 ± 1.58
		Curriculum	41.20 ± 0.72	**41.58 ± 1.63**
Uniformer	UCF-65 [52.05]	None	18.78 ± 0.22	21.39 ± 1.32
		Random	22.42 ± 0.98	24.92 ± 1.66
		Adversarial	22.95 ± 0.68	**26.16 ± 2.10**
		Curriculum	**23.61 ± 0.27**	24.93 ± 1.60

Model	Train Dataset	Augmentation	Test Accuracy	
			Kinetics-28	UCF-101
			Matched Expt 1b	Cosine Expt 2b
TSM	HMDB-28 [55.45]	None	29.75 ± 1.08	60.51 ± 0.79
		Random	30.13 ± 0.42	61.21 ± 0.57
		Adversarial	32.44 ± 0.48	62.60 ± 0.59
		Curriculum	**32.82 ± 1.41**	**63.18 ± 0.71**
Swin	HMDB-28 [54.67]	None	25.26 ± 0.80	59.88 ± 0.55
		Random	26.63 ± 0.97	60.99 ± 1.30
		Adversarial	27.31 ± 0.57	62.57 ± 0.72
		Curriculum	**27.60 ± 0.62**	**62.95 ± 0.82**
Uniformer	HMDB-28 [29.43]	None	14.53 ± 0.51	28.23 ± 0.94
		Random	14.33 ± 1.03	28.67 ± 1.36
		Adversarial	15.13 ± 0.79	29.88 ± 2.62
		Curriculum	**15.25 ± 0.75**	**30.83 ± 1.04**

The different adversarial augmentation strategies gave improved accuracy for the target datasets (see Kinetics-28 and 65 results columns).

Also, unlike what is reported in [42], the convolutional architecture performed better with the distribution shift compared to transformer models in most of the cases except for the Swin Transformer trained on UCF-65 and tested on HMDB-51. We hypothesize that this is because the Kinetics test dataset shows natural and realistic distribution shifts. In addition, we did not use the Kinetics pre-trained models, and the transformer architectures require large-scale data to reach the maximum potential.

In all cases, the adversarial augmentation or curriculum methods outperform all baselines, given a fixed network architecture, for all training and test datasets. Although the "random augmentation" and "adversarial augmentation" allow an identical range of transforms, generating adversarial examples through gradient ascent produces "harder than random" augmentation which improves the overall performance. Furthermore, adding the simple curriculum mostly improved over the adversarial benchmark.

See the Supplementary Material for confusion matrices that show per-class performance drop with distribution shifts and improvements using the proposed adversarial augmentation.

5.2   Cosine Similarity Evaluation 2a, 2b

The cosine-similarity-based accuracy results on HMDB-51 and UCF-101 are shown in the Cosine Expt columns of Table 1. The results follow a very similar trend to the "realistic" Kinetics Expt 1. The advantage of using this accuracy measure as compared to testing on Kinetics with overlapping classes is that it requires no thorough analysis of the source and target datasets to find overlapping classes, making it simple to set up the cross-dataset experiments even using new datasets.

6   Conclusion

This paper addressed the problem of model generalization to realistic test distribution shifts. Two new datasets that are comprised of three existing datasets were created that shared the same subset of label classes. Although the same classes were used, the variety of videos in the original dataset sources meant that there was a huge distribution shift from the source to the target datasets. When using the target datasets, action recognition performance dropped significantly. This led to trying adversarial augmentation, with and without curriculum scheduling, as an approach to generating hard adversarially augmented videos. This approach gave a small but meaningful improvement in performance, even with the large distribution shift in the test data. The second cross-dataset evaluation approach, using the cosine similarity as logits, also showed a similar trend as the matching dataset experiments, providing a simpler alternative method without having to curate datasets with matching classes.

References

1. Ajakan, H., Germain, P., Larochelle, H., Laviolette, F., Marchand, M.: Domain-adversarial neural networks. arXiv preprint arXiv:1412.4446 (2014)
2. Bai, T., Luo, J., Zhao, J., Wen, B., Wang, Q.: Recent advances in adversarial training for adversarial robustness. In: International Joint Conference on Artificial Intelligence (IJCAI) (2021)
3. Blaas, A., Suau, X., Ramapuram, J., Apostoloff, N., Zappella, L.: Challenges of adversarial image augmentations. In: I (Still) Can't Believe It's Not Better! Workshop at NeurIPS 2021 (2021)
4. Bousmalis, K., Silberman, N., Dohan, D., Erhan, D., Krishnan, D.: Unsupervised pixel-level domain adaptation with generative adversarial networks. In: Proceedings of the IEEE Conference on Computer Vision and Pattern Recognition, pp. 3722–3731 (2017)
5. Cai, Q.Z., Du, M., Liu, C., Song, D.: Curriculum adversarial training. arXiv preprint arXiv:1805.04807 (2018)
6. Carlini, N., Wagner, D.A.: Towards evaluating the robustness of neural networks. In: Symposium on Security and Privacy (2017)
7. Carreira, J., Zisserman, A.: Quo vadis, action recognition? A new model and the kinetics dataset. In: Proceedings of the IEEE Conference on Computer Vision and Pattern Recognition, pp. 6299–6308 (2017)
8. Cubuk, E.D., Zoph, B., Mane, D., Vasudevan, V., Le, Q.V.: AutoAugment: learning augmentation strategies from data. In: Proceedings of the IEEE/CVF Conference on Computer Vision and Pattern Recognition (CVPR) (2019)

9. Cubuk, E.D., Zoph, B., Shlens, J., Le, Q.V.: RandAugment: practical automated data augmentation with a reduced search space. In: Proceedings of the IEEE/CVF Conference on Computer Vision and Pattern Recognition Workshops, pp. 702–703 (2020)

10. Dong, J., Moosavi-Dezfooli, S.M., Lai, J., Xie, X.: The enemy of my enemy is my friend: exploring inverse adversaries for improving adversarial training. In: Proceedings of the IEEE/CVF Conference on Computer Vision and Pattern Recognition (CVPR), pp. 24678–24687 (2023)

11. Eustratiadis, P., Gouk, H., Li, D., Hospedales, T.M.: Weight-covariance alignment for adversarially robust neural networks. In: International Conference on Machine Learning (ICML) (2021)

12. Fan, H., et al.: Multiscale vision transformers. In: Proceedings of the IEEE/CVF International Conference on Computer Vision, pp. 6824–6835 (2021)

13. Farahani, A., Voghoei, S., Rasheed, K., Arabnia, H.R.: A brief review of domain adaptation. Advances in data science and information engineering. In: Proceedings from ICDATA 2020 and IKE 2020, pp. 877–894 (2021)

14. Feichtenhofer, C., Fan, H., Malik, J., He, K.: Slowfast networks for video recognition. In: Proceedings of the IEEE/CVF International Conference on Computer Vision, pp. 6202–6211 (2019)

15. Ganin, Y., Lempitsky, V.: Unsupervised domain adaptation by backpropagation. In: International Conference on Machine Learning, pp. 1180–1189. PMLR (2015)

16. Ghifary, M., Kleijn, W.B., Zhang, M., Balduzzi, D., Li, W.: Deep reconstruction-classification networks for unsupervised domain adaptation. In: Computer Vision–ECCV 2016: 14th European Conference, Amsterdam, The Netherlands, 11–14 October 2016, Proceedings, Part IV 14, pp. 597–613. Springer (2016)

17. Glorot, X., Bordes, A., Bengio, Y.: Domain adaptation for large-scale sentiment classification: a deep learning approach. In: Proceedings of the 28th International Conference on Machine Learning (ICML-11), pp. 513–520 (2011)

18. Goodfellow, I., et al.: Generative adversarial networks. Commun. ACM **63**(11), 139–144 (2020)

19. Goodfellow, I.J., Shlens, J., Szegedy, C.: Explaining and harnessing adversarial examples. In: International Conference on Learning Representations (ICLR) (2015)

20. Gowda, S.N., Rohrbach, M., Sevilla-Lara, L.: Smart frame selection for action recognition. In: Proceedings of the AAAI Conference on Artificial Intelligence, vol. 35, pp. 1451–1459 (2021)

21. Gowda, S.N., Sevilla-Lara, L., Kim, K., Keller, F., Rohrbach, M.: A new split for evaluating true zero-shot action recognition. In: DAGM German Conference on Pattern Recognition, pp. 191–205. Springer (2021)

22. Hataya, R., Zdenek, J., Yoshizoe, K., Nakayama, H.: Faster autoaugment: learning augmentation strategies using backpropagation. In: Computer Vision–ECCV 2020: 16th European Conference, Glasgow, UK, 23–28 August 2020, Proceedings, Part XXV 16, pp. 1–16. Springer (2020)

23. Hendrycks, D., Dietterich, T.: Benchmarking neural network robustness to common corruptions and perturbations. In: Proceedings of the International Conference on Learning Representations (2019)

24. Ho, D., Liang, E., Chen, X., Stoica, I., Abbeel, P.: Population based augmentation: efficient learning of augmentation policy schedules. In: International Conference on Machine Learning, pp. 2731–2741. PMLR (2019)

25. Hoffman, J., et al.: CyCADA: cycle-consistent adversarial domain adaptation. In: International Conference on Machine Learning, pp. 1989–1998. PMLR (2018)
26. Jang, E., Gu, S., Poole, B.: Categorical reparameterization with Gumbel-Softmax. In: International Conference on Learning Representations (2017)
27. Jeddi, A., Shafiee, M.J., Karg, M., Scharfenberger, C., Wong, A.: Learn2Perturb: an end-to-end feature perturbation learning to improve adversarial robustness. In: Conference on Computer Vision and Pattern Recognition (CVPR) (2020)
28. Kay, W., et al.: The kinetics human action video dataset. arXiv preprint arXiv:1705.06950 (2017)
29. Kim, K., Gowda, S.N., Aodha, O.M., Sevilla-Lara, L.: Capturing temporal information in a single frame: channel sampling strategies for action recognition. In: 33rd British Machine Vision Conference 2022, BMVC 2022, London, UK, 21–24 November 2022. BMVA Press (2022). https://bmvc2022.mpi-inf.mpg.de/0355.pdf
30. Kim, M., Li, D., Hospedales, T.M.: Domain generalisation via domain adaptation: an adversarial Fourier amplitude approach. In: International Conference on Learning Representations (ICLR) (2023)
31. Korbar, B., Tran, D., Torresani, L.: SCSampler: sampling salient clips from video for efficient action recognition. In: Proceedings of the IEEE/CVF International Conference on Computer Vision, pp. 6232–6242 (2019)
32. Kuehne, H., Jhuang, H., Garrote, E., Poggio, T., Serre, T.: HMDB: a large video database for human motion recognition. In: Proceedings of the International Conference on Computer Vision (ICCV) (2011)
33. Li, K., et al.: UniFormer: unified transformer for efficient spatial-temporal representation learning. In: International Conference on Learning Representations (2022)
34. Li, Y., Hu, G., Wang, Y., Hospedales, T., Robertson, N.M., Yang, Y.: Differentiable automatic data augmentation. In: Computer Vision–ECCV 2020: 16th European Conference, Glasgow, UK, 23–28 August 2020, Proceedings, Part XXII 16, pp. 580–595. Springer (2020)
35. Lim, S., Kim, I., Kim, T., Kim, C., Kim, S.: Fast autoaugment. In: Advances in Neural Information Processing Systems 32 (2019)
36. Lin, J., Gan, C., Han, S.: TSM: temporal shift module for efficient video understanding. In: Proceedings of the IEEE/CVF International Conference on Computer Vision, pp. 7083–7093 (2019)
37. Lin, S., et al.: Deep frequency filtering for domain generalization. In: Proceedings of the IEEE/CVF Conference on Computer Vision and Pattern Recognition (CVPR), pp. 11797–11807 (2023)
38. Lin, W., Mirza, M.J., Kozinski, M., Possegger, H., Kuehne, H., Bischof, H.: Video test-time adaptation for action recognition. In: Proceedings of the IEEE/CVF Conference on Computer Vision and Pattern Recognition (CVPR), pp. 22952–22961 (2023)
39. Liu, Z., et al.: Video swin transformer. In: Proceedings of the IEEE/CVF Conference on Computer Vision and Pattern Recognition, pp. 3202–3211 (2022)
40. Long, M., Cao, Y., Wang, J., Jordan, M.: Learning transferable features with deep adaptation networks. In: International Conference on Machine Learning, pp. 97–105. PMLR (2015)
41. Pei, Z., Cao, Z., Long, M., Wang, J.: Multi-adversarial domain adaptation. In: Proceedings of the AAAI Conference on Artificial Intelligence, vol. 32 (2018)
42. Schiappa, M.C., et al.: A large-scale robustness analysis of video action recognition models. In: Proceedings of the IEEE/CVF Conference on Computer Vision and Pattern Recognition (CVPR), pp. 14698–14708 (2023)

43. Shankar, S., Piratla, V., Chakrabarti, S., Chaudhuri, S., Jyothi, P., Sarawagi, S.: Generalizing across domains via cross-gradient training. In: International Conference on Learning Representations (ICLR) (2018)

44. Shorten, C., Khoshgoftaar, T.M.: A survey on image data augmentation for deep learning. J. Big Data **6**(1), 1–48 (2019)

45. Shrivastava, A., Pfister, T., Tuzel, O., Susskind, J., Wang, W., Webb, R.: Learning from simulated and unsupervised images through adversarial training. In: Proceedings of the IEEE Conference on Computer Vision and Pattern Recognition, pp. 2107–2116 (2017)

46. Simonyan, K., Zisserman, A.: Two-stream convolutional networks for action recognition in videos. In: Advances in Neural Information Processing Systems, pp. 568–576 (2014)

47. Soomro, K., Zamir, A.R., Shah, M.: UCF101: a dataset of 101 human actions classes from videos in the wild. arXiv preprint arXiv:1212.0402 (2012)

48. Taigman, Y., Polyak, A., Wolf, L.: Unsupervised cross-domain image generation. arXiv preprint arXiv:1611.02200 (2016)

49. Tzeng, E., Hoffman, J., Darrell, T., Saenko, K.: Simultaneous deep transfer across domains and tasks. In: Proceedings of the IEEE International Conference on Computer Vision, pp. 4068–4076 (2015)

50. Wang, L., Tong, Z., Ji, B., Wu, G.: TDN: temporal difference networks for efficient action recognition. In: Proceedings of the IEEE/CVF Conference on Computer Vision and Pattern Recognition, pp. 1895–1904 (2021)

51. Wang, L., et al.: Temporal segment networks for action recognition in videos. IEEE Trans. Pattern Anal. Mach. Intell. **41**(11), 2740–2755 (2018)

52. Wang, R., Yang, Y., Tao, D.: Art-point: improving rotation robustness of point cloud classifiers via adversarial rotation. In: Conference on Computer Vision and Pattern Recognition (CVPR) (2022)

53. Wang, X., Girshick, R., Gupta, A., He, K.: Non-local neural networks. In: Proceedings of the IEEE Conference on Computer Vision and Pattern Recognition, pp. 7794–7803 (2018)

54. Wu, W., He, D., Lin, T., Li, F., Gan, C., Ding, E.: MVFNet: multi-view fusion network for efficient video recognition. In: Proceedings of the AAAI Conference on Artificial Intelligence, vol. 35, pp. 2943–2951 (2021)

55. Wu, Z., Xiong, C., Ma, C.Y., Socher, R., Davis, L.S.: AdaFrame: adaptive frame selection for fast video recognition. In: Proceedings of the IEEE/CVF Conference on Computer Vision and Pattern Recognition, pp. 1278–1287 (2019)

56. Yi, C., Yang, S., Li, H., Peng Tan, Y., Kot, A.: Benchmarking the robustness of spatial-temporal models against corruptions. In: Thirty-Fifth Conference on Neural Information Processing Systems Datasets and Benchmarks Track (Round 2) (2021)

57. Yu, T., Yang, Y., Li, D., Hospedales, T.M., Xiang, T.: Simple and effective stochastic neural networks. In: Conference on Artificial Intelligence (AAAI) (2021)

58. Zhang, J., et al.: Attacks which do not kill training make adversarial learning stronger. In: International Conference on Machine Learning, pp. 11278–11287. PMLR (2020)

59. Zhang, X., Yu, F.X., Chang, S.F., Wang, S.: Deep transfer network: unsupervised domain adaptation. arXiv preprint arXiv:1503.00591 (2015)

60. Zhao, Y., Wu, Y., Chen, C., Lim, A.: On isometry robustness of deep 3D point cloud models under adversarial attacks. In: Conference on Computer Vision and Pattern Recognition (CVPR) (2020)

61. Zhou, B., Andonian, A., Oliva, A., Torralba, A.: Temporal relational reasoning in videos. In: Proceedings of the European Conference on Computer Vision (ECCV), pp. 803–818 (2018)
62. Zhou, K., Yang, Y., Hospedales, T.M., Xiang, T.: Deep domain-adversarial image generation for domain generalisation. In: Conference on Artificial Intelligence (AAAI) (2020)

Egocentric View Hand Action Recognition by Leveraging Hand Surface and Hand Grasp Type

DongYoon Seo[1] , Hyunggun Chi[2] , Sunghee Hong[3] , Byoung Soo Koh[4] ,
Karthik Ramani[2] , and Sangpil Kim[1]([✉])

[1] Korea University, 145 Anam-ro, Seoul, South Korea
{dyseo,spk7}@korea.ac.kr
[2] Purdue University, West Laffayette, IN, USA
{hgchi,ramani}@purdue.edu
[3] Korea Electric Technology Institute, Seongnam-si, Gyeonggi-do 13509, South Korea
shhong@keti.re.kr
[4] DigiCAP Inc., Gangseo-gu, Seoul, Korea

Abstract. We introduce a multi-stage framework that uses local geometry changes on a hand surface and focuses on learning interaction between a primary and assistive hand/object for hand action recognition in videos from a egocentric view RGB camera. Our method does not require 3D information of objects such as the 6D object pose which is difficult to annotate or the depth of the image requires additional a depth sensor for learning an objects' behavior while it interacts with hands. Instead, the proposed method learns the changes within the surface of the hand, the hand type which is positively correlated with the hand action and the location of objects and hands in the 2D image space. The framework synthesizes the mean curvature of the primary hand mesh model to encode the hand surface geometry. Also, we introduce a feature pooling layer to handle diverse scenarios: having one hand, two hands, one hand with one object, and two hands with two objects. Our method outperforms the state-of-the-art hand action recognition methods that use 6D object poses of objects or a depth sensor.

Keyword: Machine perception, hand action recognition, deep learning, surface modality

1 Introduction

People have been using hands in their daily activities to interact with the world and communicate with others. Therefore, a significant amount of research has focused on hand action recognition [9,11,14,19]. Unlike hand gestures, hand actions involve objects, and therefore, understanding the behavior of both the objects and the hands are essential. Also, people use both hands to perform an action in many cases, for example, holding a tool with a primary hand and

C. Wallraven et al. (Eds.): ICPRAI 2024, LNCS 14892, pp. 201–215, 2025.
https://doi.org/10.1007/978-981-97-8702-9_14

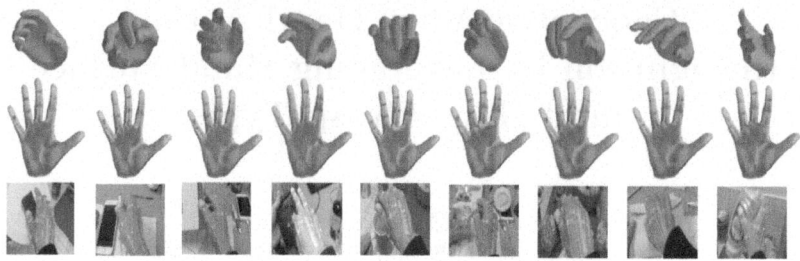

Fig. 1. The first row shows fitted hand mesh models given the primary hand image from the third row. Mean curvature distribution on hand mesh is shown in the second row. The values are color-coded from low value as blue to high value as red. The images on the last row are primary hands from nine different hand action videos. (Color figure online)

a target object with the assistive hand. This brings us to learn object-object relation and their interaction with hands for hand action recognition.

The advancement of low-cost wearable sensors and augmented reality/virtual reality technologies, motivates the computer vision community to tackle egocentric view hand action recognition. However, egocentric view hand action recognition is extremely challenging because the perception model needs to be robust on diverse topology of both rigid and non-rigid objects. Additionally, in cluttered real-world scenes, hand dorsum and objects create a large occlusion region of hands, and the fast movement of a camera view makes the prediction of hand actions challenging [20]. Fingertips in particular, which are the major functional parts of the hands, are occluded in the egocentric view in many cases. To address these problems, the computer vision community incorporates depth sensors [14,31] and multiple cameras with different views to handle occluded hand regions [37]. Also, many works [28,32] have shown that considering hand and object interactions increases the accuracy of prediction of hand actions and 3D hand poses.

However, these works contain limitations as following: First, the works which use 6D pose of objects for learning hand-object interactions do not consider the complexity of object space and the cost of annotating 6D pose of objects. Second, depth sensors are not robust under high luminance nature lights, and are more expensive than an RGB cameras. Third, there are no methods that focus on the relation of the right hand object and the left hand object. Lastly, multi-camera setting is also not efficient since it requires camera calibration and synchronising frames from multiple cameras is extremely difficult.

The proposed method tackles these problems without using 6D pose of objects to learn hand-object interactions. Instead, we use the semantic meaning between object-object relations and their encoded 2D image features from the deep neural networks. In biomechanics, the hand action with objects is positively related to the grasp or pre-grasp types, the geometry, and weights of objects. However, we find that the grasp type is too general for identifying hand actions and hand surface is more descriptive (see Fig. 1). With this biomechanical evidence, our approach utilizes primary hand surface curvatures and relative locations of the primary hand and the object for learning hand-object interactions for hand action recognition. With this encoded information, the low-level features of the hand surface further transform into high-level concept of hand action in the framework. We find that the hand surface and the interactions between the primary and the assistive hand/object are important factors for modeling hand-object interactions for the hand action recognition.

Our contributions are listed as follows:

- We present a temporal framework to merge the distribution of synthesized curvatures of the hand, which imposes detailed kinematic information and invariant from the global location of the hand, while interacting with a object.
- We introduce the object-hand interaction learning from their relative locations and hand types with a deep neural encoder, which does not require 6D object pose labels for the hand action recognition task in egocentric-view videos.
- We propose a feature pooling layer for hand action estimation that handles four cases: one hand, two hands, two hands with one object, and two hands with two objects.

Each of the above contributions improves overall hand action recognition performance, and we show the improvement quantitatively in Sect. 4.2. Our method outperforms the state-of-the-art methods that use complex annotations such as 6D object pose and depth information for training, with a sophisticated hand action dataset.

2   Related Work

Hand Action Recognition. The 3D hand pose is widely used as a feature input for hand action recognition [14, 32]. This is because the hand pose implies the object geometry and the grasp type, which is positively correlated with the hand action. Another popular approach is using a depth sensor [14] since a depth image is texture-invariant and imposes 3D information, which is critical for estimating 3D hand poses. Therefore, knowing depth enhances the accuracy of 3D hand pose estimation. Hand action involves object manipulation and using a tool for doing an action. Therefore, Tekin [32] used the hand and object interaction for the hand action recognition. People look at their hands while using their hands. Therefore, eye gazing is a signal that can be used for improving the accuracy of hand action recognition in case of the egocentr ic view. Li [19] used eye gazing as a region of interest and extracted meaningful features in the area for solving hand action recognition. Optical flow and motion vector are used to encode temporal information, and many works use these properties for action recognition [25, 30, 36]. Hand action recognition utilizes the sequence of the frames, and knowing the temporal relation between frames is critical for the perception of the action in the video. Aksoy [1] used the semantic meaning

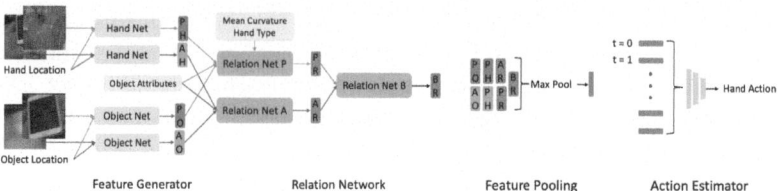

Fig. 2. The pipeline of the framework. The feature generator extracts features from the primary and assistive objects/hands images. These features are further fed into a relation network that learns the object-hand interaction and relation between the primary and assistive instances. The feature pooling layer picks the most predominant features from the relation network and the feature generator for action estimator that is a temporal model for hand action estimation.

between action and object relation for hand action recognition. To the best of our knowledge, no work in literature has identified the primary and the assistive hand for learning two hands interaction as well as object-object relation for hand action estimation, which are core semantic information that describes the hand action in the videos.

Curvature for Non-rigid Object. Non-rigid objects have specific properties different from rigid objects. For example, the diffusion of geometry-based descriptors constructs invariant metrics on rigid objects but these metrics are variant on non-rigid objects [33]. Therefore, surface information is used for shape features for the shape analysis of a non-rigid object. Limberger [21] proposed a shape descriptor based on a Lagrangian formulation of dynamics on the surface of the object for the retrieval task. The descriptor is a curvature-based scheme that identifies joints of the non-rigid object. Laskov [18] proposed algorithms that use the relationship between Gaussian curvatures and geometric properties of a deformable non-rigid object for motion correspondence estimation accuracy. Deboeverie [10] segmented a human body based on the curvature of the human body given gray scales images, which showed that human body parts could be approximated by nearly cylindrical surfaces. Chen [7] introduced the statistic index of curvatures from the curve in pixel space for estimating the human action recognition task. This work showed the effectiveness of the curvature representation as a spatiotemporal feature for high-level concept estimation. Chang [5] proposed a feature descriptor in curvature scale space with translation, scale, and rotation invariant properties for recognition of hand pose for hand pose estimation. As shown in the works above, curvature is a robust feature for a non-rigid object, such as a hand in our case. In our work, we use the mean curvature of the primary hand for estimating hand actions.

Grasp Type for Hand Action. The grasp type is symbolic representation of human intention while performing hand related tasks. Therefore, many works established the taxonomy of the grasp type for the manipulation applications in robotics and cognitive recognition in computer vision. Feix [13] established the taxonomy of grasp type for one hand which is static and stable grasps. The taxonomy consists of 33 grasp types based on the opposition type, the virtual finger, the position of thumb, and the power adjustment of grasp based on the object shape. Cutkosky [8] developed analytical models to describe grasps in a manufacturing environment and established a taxonomy of manufacturing grasps which are used in designing of robot hands. Yang [34] used grasp types as symbolic representation for reasoning human actions and used them as cognitive features for human intention prediction by applying the grasp types into the action segmentation task. Cai [4] incorporated grasp type directly into hand action recognition task by learning the relation between grasp types and object attributes. Underline assumption is that the grasp types and holding objects contain complementary information for recognizing the hand action. We notice that these works only consider the grasp type but not the pre-grasp type: flat hand. We propose the concept of the pre-grasp type which is frequently appearing in hand action videos.

3   Methods

3.1   Overview

The purpose of our work is to develop a robust framework that estimates the hand action given a video from a egocentric view RGB camera. In this work, hand action covers *verb+object* such as "drink mug" and *verb* only "high five". The framework predicts a hand action from a sequence of frames $\mathbf{I}^t \in R^{W \times H}$ where $\{0 \leq t \leq N\}$. Here, we denote the cropped image from input frame with a bounding box (BBox) of the primary hand, the primary object, the assistive hand, and the assistive object as h_p, o_p, h_a, o_a, respectively, and the object name as an attribute of the assistive and primary object as o_a^a and o_p^a. The framework first estimates $\{h_p, o_p, h_a, o_a\} = D(\mathbf{I}^t)$,where D is the detector (see Fig. 3). Then $\{o_p, o_a\}$ are fed in to the object classification network f_c to estimate $\{o_p^a, o_a^a\}$. With the h_p, the hand type estimator f_t estimates hand type $t_h = f_t(h_p)$ and successively synthesize the mean curvature H_p of the primary hand with the mapping function given t_h and the image feature from f_t (see Fig. 4). After that, $\{h_p, o_p, h_a, o_a\}$ are encoded with convolutional networks as $\{ph, ah, po, ao\}$ for learning hand-object interaction with three relation networks for the primary, assistive, and both hand/object interactions. These three relation networks are denoted as R_p, R_a, and R_b. With these relation networks, the frame work encodes three relation features: $PR = R_p(H_p, t_h, o_p^a, ph, po)$, $AR = R_a(o_a^a, ah, ao)$, and $BR = R_b(pr, ar)$ (see Fig. 2). However, in many cases, these features are not valid. For example, in the case of action "light candle", it contains two hands with two objects. To handle these dynamics, we propose the feature pooling layer

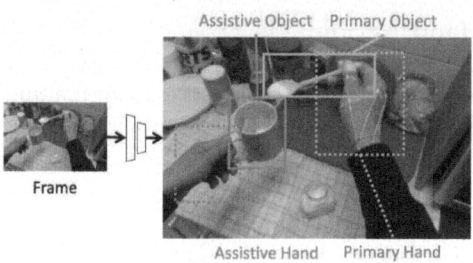

Fig. 3. The detector network identifies the primary and assistive objects and hands along with categories of objects.The relation of the assistive and primary instances is learned in relation to the network for hand action recognition.

P_m which picks the most predominant feature named "key feature" and denotes as $k^t = P_m(\mathbf{S}^t)$, where $\mathbf{S}^t$ is a set of valid features in $\mathbf{I}^t$. Finally, every k^t in a sequence are batched and fed into the temporal model for the final hand action recognition prediction.

3.2   Primary-Assistive Hand/Object Selection

The framework identifies the pair of the primary hand/object, which is the main hand/object that is used in an action and the assistive hand/object that is helping the primary hand/object conduct the task. We use an object detection network for estimating the primary hand/object and the assistive hand/object. To do so, we label the primary and the assistive object to train the detector (see Fig. 3). Defining the primary and the assistive objects does not require extra labeling effort since the action name itself contains the object name in most cases, for example: pouring the orange juice. Even though there is no object name in an action, picking one frame in the video is sufficient to identify the primary and the assistive object. Also, it is much easier to annotate with a BBox than 6D object pose. A primary hand is determined among predicted hands by their Euclidean distance: the primary object is located closer to the primary hand. If only one hand is presented in the image, that hand is considered the primary hand.

After defining the BBoxes of the primary/assistive objects/hands, center locations of these BBoxes are fed into the R_p and R_a for learning the interaction of the hand and the object. The relation between the primary and the assistive pairs of objects/hands are implicitly encoded as a latent vector by mapping corresponding hand actions given primary hand grasp types with deep neural networks. Therefore, a hidden vector representing the relation of primary-assistive object/hand can be implicitly trained and used as features for the hand action estimation.

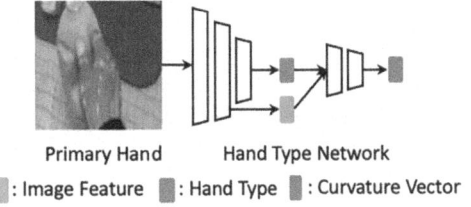

Primary Hand   Hand Type Network

▨ : Image Feature   ▨ : Hand Type   ▮ : Curvature Vector

Fig. 4. The hand type network estimates the hand type and the mean curvature vector from the primary hand image.

3.3 Hand Type and Surface Curvature

Hand Type Estimation. One challenging part of hand action recognition is occlusion of fingers when holding an object. To resolve this problem, we use the hand type, which is a high-level concept for all people. For the hand type estimation, we first establish the hand type taxonomy (see Fig. 6). We use the taxonomy of grasp types from Feix [13] as our base taxonomy and added "flattened palm" hand type on the taxonomy. The hand actions of "high-five" and "receive coin" do not require grasping. Hence, we add "flattened palm" on the taxonomy. With this hand type taxonomy, we sparsely label the hand type in the video by marking the transition frames that show significant hand type changes. Then we train the hand type estimator shown in Fig. 4 to estimate the hand type given a cropped image of the primary hand.

Hand Surface Estimation. The hand type is too general to take care of the detailed changes of hands. We find that one action can have multiple hand types as shown in the scatter plot in Fig. 7. Therefore, we introduce hand surface modality, which is invariant from the global position of the hand and fingers. To describe the hand surface, we use the mean curvature as the surface representation (see Fig. 5). First, we fit MANO [27] hand mesh model, which consists of 778 vertices and 1538 faces, onto the primary hand image with gradient-based optimization [2]. Then, with this fitted hand mesh model, we compute the mean curvature of each vertex from 1-ring neighborhood of the vertex. For the model training, the model takes the primary hand cropped image as inputs and jointly learns the curvature vector and the hand type as shown in Fig. 4. After training, the hand type network simultaneously estimates hand type and mean curvature. If the primary hand is the left hand, then the network uses the symmetric property of hands and flips the image to be oriented as a right hand.

3.4 Feature Pooling and Temporal Model

Feature Generator and Relation Networks. The feature generator consists of two networks: hand net and object net. This network takes a cropped image of a hand or object and their image location for encoding feature vectors. For

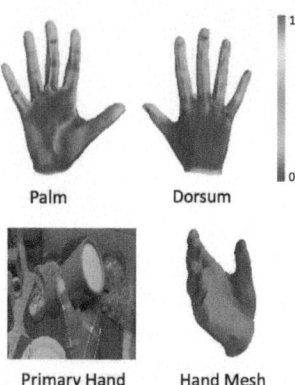

Palm   Dorsum

Primary Hand   Hand Mesh

Fig. 5. The first row figures show the mean curvature distribution on the fitted hand mesh model that is shown in the right figure in the second row. The left image in the second row, named primary hand, is the input image.

the notation, the features from the primary hand and object cropped images are notated as PH and PO. In the same convention, the features from the assistive hand and the object cropped images are notated as AH and AO. These feature vectors are fed into the relation nets R_p,R_a and R_b. The primary object and hands are fed into R_p and output PR. The assistive object and hand are fed into R_a and outputs AR. Finally, PR and AR are fed into R_b, which fuses these two features into a feature vector named BR.

To make the framework efficient, we conditionally process the cropped images. In the egocentric view of hand manipulation, there are four possible view cases: one hand, two hands, one hand with one object, and two hands with two objects. To make it computationally efficient, the framework extract features when it is necessary. The feature generator and the relation network generate the feature set $\{PH\}$, $\{PH, AH\}$, $\{PH, PO, PR\}$, and $\{PH, AH, PO, AO, PR, AR, BR\}$, for one hand, two hands, one hand with one object, and two hands with two objects cases, respectively. The hand and object net in the feature generator share the same parameters for processing the primary and assistive object/hand in the framework, but the hand net and object net does not share the parameters.

Feature Pooling Layer. To deal with diverse cases of hand actions, a feature pooling layer selects the predominate feature from the feature set, which is inspired by the view-pooling layer [29]. This selected feature is used for final action estimation. Using the feature pooling layer is effective, because estimating the hand type and synthesizing curvatures is not accurate when the primary hand is heavily occluded by the object. In this case, relying on the primary hand feature is not a good choice.

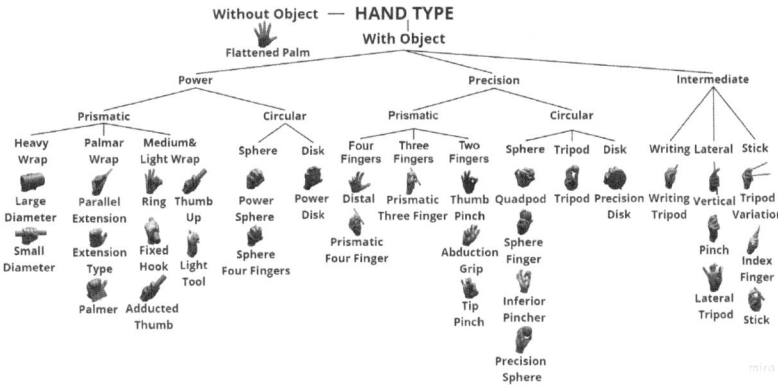

Fig. 6. Taxonomy of hand types for hand action recognition. Hand images are from MANO [27].

Temporal Model for Action Recognition. The hand action is not a static representation but a sequence of frames which contains spatiotemporal information. Therefore, encoding the temporal information is essential for accurate hand action estimation. In our framework, we accumulate the features from the feature pooling layer in each frame and use LSTM layers along with a non-linear activation function to encapsulate temporal information for the final hand action estimation.

3.5   Loss Function

We train the main framework that predicts the hand action by minimizing objective function $\mathcal{L}_{action}$ 1. p^a, p^h, p^o are a probability of action, hand type, and object attribute. C^a, C^h, C^o are a number of action classes, hand type class, and object attribute class, respectively. $\mathbf{v} \in R^{778}$ is a vector that represents mean curvatures of the hand mesh model. We train the main framework that predicts the hand

$$\mathcal{L}_{action} = \sum_i^{C^a} y_i^a log(p_i^a) + \alpha \sum_i^{C^o} y_i^o log(p_i^o) \qquad (1)$$

$$\mathcal{L}_{hand} = \sum_i^{C^h} y_i log(p_i^h) + \beta ||\hat{\mathbf{v}} - \mathbf{v}||_2^2 \qquad (2)$$

, where $\alpha{=}1$ and $\beta{=}0.1$. As shown on Fig. 4, hand type is an intermediate result of the hand type network. For training the hand type network, we jointly regress the mean curvature of the primary hand mesh and minimizes cross entropy of hand type: $\mathcal{L}_{hand}$ 2. The detector is trained with YOLOv4 [3]. After the hand type network and detector are trained, we freeze these networks' parameters and jointly train the feature generator, the relation network, and the action estimator by following other works [6,35].

4 Experiment

In this section, we first elaborate on the dataset for the framework. Then, we illustrate an ablation study of the methods and compare it with other state-of-the-art methods. For the experiment, we use Xavier [15] initialization method and python-based deep learning framework PyTorch [24] to develop.

4.1 Dataset

We use the First-Person Hand Action (FPHA) dataset [14] for our experiment. This is the only public dataset for 3D hand-object action recognition that contains 3D hand pose, which is used to fit MANO hand model on the image with a gradient-based optimization [2]. FPHA consists of 1175 videos performed by 6 subjects, 24 different objects, and 45 different hand action categories. The total number of frames is 105,459 with accurate 3D hand poses and 6D pose object annotations. The data has a subset split named TinyFPHA that has 3D object mesh models which belong to 10 actions. Additionally, we annotate hand types in the videos by indexing the frame number if there are hand type transitions based on the hand type taxonomy with 36 different hand types (see Fig. 6).

4.2 Experimental Results

All the experiments in this paper use the dataset provided by FPHA [14]. The dataset is divided into train and test set based on the split schema from the author.

Primary and Assistive H/O Detection. For our hand/object detector, we utilize the large YOLOv4 [3] network that uses mish activation (YOLOv4-L) to identify the four classes which are the primary hand, the assistive hand, the primary Object, and the assistive Object. The network was trained on images with size 480×270 and a batch size of 8 for 20 epochs. For the evaluation, we use the Generalized Intersection over Union (gIoU) with a 0.05 gIoU loss gain and the mean average precision (mAP) at both confidence thresholds 0.5 and 0.5 to 0.95 as our performance metrics. The mAP of the YOLOv4-L is 78.12% at a confidence threshold of 0.5 and 46.15% at a confidence threshold between 0.5 to 0.95. Table 1 describes the mAP values and the gIoU for the other versions of YOLOv4 with the same training conditions mentioned previously. For identifying object attributes, we use ResNet18 [16] pre-trained on ImageNet as the backbone following by a 36-way fully connected layer. We use 0.0001 as the learning rate and a batch size of 32. The network is fully trained within 15 epochs. Using more recently detectors makes bounding box areas accurate, which can lead to performance imporvements.

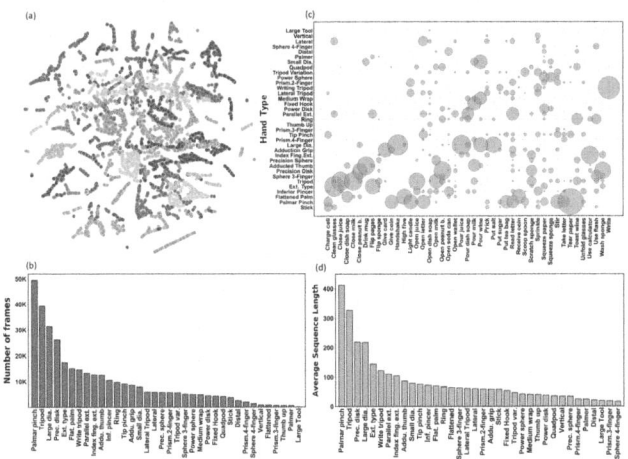

Fig. 7. (a) t-SNE visualization of action class embedding over dataset (b) Number of frames per hand type.(c) Scatter plot that shows the distribution of the hand type per hand action in the dataset. The y axis shows the hand type and the x axis represents the action type. The size of the circles represents the frequency of occurrence of a hand type per action class. (d) Average number of frames in each video per hand type.

Table 1. Performance of three different variations of YOLOv4 for tthe primary/assistive object and hand detection.

Model	Size (M)	mAP@0.5 (%)	mAP@0.5:0.95 (%)	gIoU
YOLOv4-S	9.124	76.87	42.88	0.037
YOLOv4-M	24.369	77.22	45.00	0.036
YOLOv4-L	96.433	78.12	46.15	0.035

Hand Type and Curvature Estimation. The hand type network takes cropped image of primary hand image of size 224 × 224. The network first encodes the image into feature vector with pre-trained ResNet50 as a feature extractor. This feature vector from ResNet50 is used to predict the hand type with fully connected (FC) layer to solve classification problem. The logit of the hand type is concatenated with the feature vector from ResNet50 for estimating the hand curvature with series of FC layers. We use 0.0001 as the running rate and 128 as the batch size. The network is fully trained with 100 epochs. L_2 loss of test set of the mean curvature is 4.119 and hand accuracy is 82.02%.

Hand Action Recognition. We perform ablation studies and comparison of other state-of-the-art works with two datasets: TinyFHPA and FHPA. Our method performs at a 97.14% accuracy on TinyFPHA dataset and 83.69% on the full FPHA dataset. We observe that adding the mean curvature creates a performance leap on both datasets. The relation network, the hand type, and the mean curvature of the primary hand mesh all contribute significantly to the performance of both datasets, and our method outperforms other state-of-the-art methods by a large margin (see Table 2 and 3). The framework uses YOLOv4-L for detecting the primary and assistive hand/object. We use ResNet18 which is pre-trained on ImageNet for "Object Net" on Fig. 2. The hand net and object net

Table 2. The performance evaluation on TinyFPHA of the hand action recognition. HP, OP, HO, RN, HT, and MC stands for hand pose, object pose, 2D hand and object bounding box, relation network, hand type, and a mean curvature vector, respectively. Our method outperformed other methods in a large margin.

Method	Model	Accuracy (%)
FPHA [14]	OP	87.45
	3D HP	74.45
	HP + OP	91.97
H+O [32]	Image	85.56
	HP	89.47
	OP	85.71
	HP + OP	94.73
	HP + OP + Interaction	96.99
Ours	Image	84.21
	RN	93.35
	RN + HT	95.12
	RN + HT + MC	**97.14**

Table 3. The performance evaluation on FPHA of the hand action recognition. Abbreviation is the same as Table 2. Our method outperforms other methods by a large margin.

Method	Input modality	Accuracy (%)
FPHA [14]	Depth	72.06
HOG [22]	Depth	59.83
JOULE [17]	Depth	60.17
NON4D [23]	Depth	70.61
Novel View [26]	Depth	69.21
H+O [32]	Color	82.43
JOULE [17]	Color	66.78
Two stream - all [12]	Color	75.30
Two stream - color [12]	Color	61.56
Two stream - flow [12]	Color	69.91
Ours - RN	Color	79.14
Ours - RN + HT	Color	81.41
Ours - RN + HT + MC	Color	**83.69**

take image size of 224 × 224 and output a vector size 256. For temporal model, we use a 2-layer LSTM with a hidden state size of 512. To prevent overfitting, we augment data by randomly changing the saturation, hue, and exposure of the images by a maximum factor of 50% and randomly translate and rotate them by a maximum 10% offset. For optimizing the network, we use a stochastic gradient descent optimization method with 0.001 learning rate and decay by 10 on every 80 epochs. The action estimator is trained with a batch size of 32 for 250 epochs.

5   Conclusion and Future Work

In this work, we tackle a hand action recognition problem with a egocentric view video from a RGB camera. We propose a method that does not require 6D object pose nor a depth sensor for learning hand-object interaction. Instead, we use 2D bounding boxes that represent the primary and assistive object/hand which are used for learning hand-object interaction and propose feature pooling layer that processes multiple cases: one hand, two hands, one hand with one object, and two hands with two objects. Additionally, the framework estimates the hand type and the mean curvature of the primary hand surface as priors. These priors improve the hand action recognition accuracy. The proposed method outperforms state-of-the-art methods. As future works, the proposed methods can be applied to more general cases that involve multi-person in the view. Also, the work can apply into 3D hand pose estimation while interacting with objects.

Acknowledgements. This work was supported by Electronics and Telecommunications Research Institute(ETRI) grant funded by the Korean government (24ZC1200, Research on hyper-realistic interaction technology for five senses and emotional experience, 80%), the Ministry of Education and National Research Foundation of Korea(Project Name: "Leaders in Industry-university Cooperation 3.0", 1%), Culture, Sports, and Tourism R&D Program through the Korea Creative Content Agency grant funded by the Ministry of Culture, Sports and Tourism in 2024 ((Project Name: Research on neural watermark technology for copyright protection of generative AI 3D content, 14%),(International Collaborative Research and Global Talent Development for the Development of Copyright Management and Protection Technologies for Generative AI, 5%)), and Ministry of Science and ICT and National IT Industry Promotion Agency(Project name: SW High Growth Club).

References

1. Aksoy, E.E., Abramov, A., Wörgötter, F., Dellen, B.: Categorizing object-action relations from semantic scene graphs. In: 2010 IEEE International Conference on Robotics and Automation, pp. 398–405. IEEE (2010)
2. Baek, S., Kim, K.I., Kim, T.K.: Pushing the envelope for rgb-based dense 3d hand pose estimation via neural rendering. In: Proceedings of the IEEE Conference on Computer Vision and Pattern Recognition, pp. 1067–1076 (2019)
3. Bochkovskiy, A., Wang, C.Y., Liao, H.Y.M.: Yolov4: optimal speed and accuracy of object detection. arXiv preprint arXiv:2004.10934 (2020)

4. Cai, M., Kitani, K.M., Sato, Y.: Understanding hand-object manipulation with grasp types and object attributes. In: Robotics: Science and Systems, vol. 3. Ann Arbor, Michigan (2016)
5. Chang, C.C., Chen, I.Y., Huang, Y.S.: Hand pose recognition using curvature scale space. In: Object Recognition Supported by User Interaction for Service Robots, vol. 2, pp. 386–389. IEEE (2002)
6. Chapelle, O., Wu, M.: Gradient descent optimization of smoothed information retrieval metrics. Inf. Retrieval **13**(3), 216–235 (2010)
7. Chen, H., Chirikjian, G.S.: Curvature: a signature for action recognition in video sequences. In: Proceedings of the IEEE/CVF Conference on Computer Vision and Pattern Recognition Workshops, pp. 858–859 (2020)
8. Cutkosky, M.R., et al.: On grasp choice, grasp models, and the design of hands for manufacturing tasks. IEEE Trans. Robot. Autom. **5**(3), 269–279 (1989)
9. Damen, D., et al.: Scaling egocentric vision: the epic-kitchens dataset. In: Proceedings of the European Conference on Computer Vision (ECCV), pp. 720–736 (2018)
10. Deboeverie, F., De Geest, R., Tuytelaars, T., Veelaert, P., Philips, W.: Curvature-based human body parts segmentation in physiotherapy. Proc. VISAPP **2015**(1), 630–637 (2015)
11. Fathi, A., Ren, X., Rehg, J.M.: Learning to recognize objects in egocentric activities. In: CVPR 2011, pp. 3281–3288. IEEE (2011)
12. Feichtenhofer, C., Pinz, A., Zisserman, A.: Convolutional two-stream network fusion for video action recognition. In: Proceedings of the IEEE Conference on Computer Vision and Pattern Recognition, pp. 1933–1941 (2016)
13. Feix, T., Romero, J., Schmiedmayer, H.B., Dollar, A.M., Kragic, D.: The grasp taxonomy of human grasp types. IEEE Trans. Hum.-Mach. Syst. **46**(1), 66–77 (2015)
14. Garcia-Hernando, G., Yuan, S., Baek, S., Kim, T.K.: First-person hand action benchmark with rgb-d videos and 3d hand pose annotations. In: Proceedings of the IEEE Conference on Computer Vision and Pattern Recognition, pp. 409–419 (2018)
15. Glorot, X., Bengio, Y.: Understanding the difficulty of training deep feedforward neural networks. In: Proceedings of the Thirteenth International Conference on Artificial Intelligence and Statistics, pp. 249–256 (2010)
16. He, K., Zhang, X., Ren, S., Sun, J.: Deep residual learning for image recognition. In: Proceedings of the IEEE Conference on Computer Vision and Pattern Recognition, pp. 770–778 (2016)
17. Hu, J.F., Zheng, W.S., Lai, J., Zhang, J.: Jointly learning heterogeneous features for rgb-d activity recognition. In: Proceedings of the IEEE Conference on Computer Vision and Pattern Recognition, pp. 5344–5352 (2015)
18. Laskov, P., Kambhamettu, C.: Curvature-based algorithms for nonrigid motion and correspondence estimation. IEEE Trans. Pattern Anal. Mach. Intell. **25**(10), 1349–1354 (2003)
19. Li, Y., Liu, M., Rehg, J.M.: In the eye of beholder: joint learning of gaze and actions in first person video. In: Proceedings of the European Conference on Computer Vision (ECCV), pp. 619–635 (2018)
20. Li, Y., Ye, Z., Rehg, J.M.: Delving into egocentric actions. In: Proceedings of the IEEE Conference on Computer Vision and Pattern Recognition, pp. 287–295 (2015)
21. Limberger, F.A., Wilson, R.C.: Curvature-based spectral signatures for non-rigid shape retrieval. Comput. Vis. Image Underst. **172**, 1–11 (2018)

22. Ohn-Bar, E., Trivedi, M.M.: Hand gesture recognition in real time for automotive interfaces: a multimodal vision-based approach and evaluations. IEEE Trans. Intell. Transp. Syst. **15**(6), 2368–2377 (2014)
23. Oreifej, O., Liu, Z.: Hon4d: histogram of oriented 4d normals for activity recognition from depth sequences. In: Proceedings of the IEEE Conference on Computer Vision and Pattern Recognition, pp. 716–723 (2013)
24. Paszke, A., et al.: Automatic differentiation in pytorch (2017)
25. Piergiovanni, A., Ryoo, M.S.: Representation flow for action recognition. In: Proceedings of the IEEE Conference on Computer Vision and Pattern Recognition, pp. 9945–9953 (2019)
26. Rahmani, H., Mian, A.: 3d action recognition from novel viewpoints. In: Proceedings of the IEEE Conference on Computer Vision and Pattern Recognition, pp. 1506–1515 (2016)
27. Romero, J., Tzionas, D., Black, M.J.: Embodied hands: modeling and capturing hands and bodies together. ACM Trans. Graph. (ToG) **36**(6), 245 (2017)
28. Sridhar, S., Mueller, F., Zollhöfer, M., Casas, D., Oulasvirta, A., Theobalt, C.: Real-time joint tracking of a hand manipulating an object from rgb-d input. In: European Conference on Computer Vision, pp. 294–310. Springer (2016)
29. Su, H., Maji, S., Kalogerakis, E., Learned-Miller, E.: Multi-view convolutional neural networks for 3d shape recognition. In: Proceedings of the IEEE International Conference on Computer Vision, pp. 945–953 (2015)
30. Sun, S., Kuang, Z., Sheng, L., Ouyang, W., Zhang, W.: Optical flow guided feature: a fast and robust motion representation for video action recognition. In: Proceedings of the IEEE Conference on Computer Vision and Pattern Recognition, pp. 1390–1399 (2018)
31. Tang, Y., Tian, Y., Lu, J., Feng, J., Zhou, J.: Action recognition in rgb-d egocentric videos. In: 2017 IEEE International Conference on Image Processing (ICIP). pp. 3410–3414. IEEE (2017)
32. Tekin, B., Bogo, F., Pollefeys, M.: H+ o: Unified egocentric recognition of 3d hand-object poses and interactions. In: Proceedings of the IEEE Conference on Computer Vision and Pattern Recognition, pp. 4511–4520 (2019)
33. Wang, X., Bennamoun, M., Sohel, F., Lei, H.: Diffusion geometry derived keypoints and local descriptors for 3d deformable shape analysis. J. Circ. Syst. Comput. 2150016 (2020)
34. Yang, Y., Fermuller, C., Li, Y., Aloimonos, Y.: Grasp type revisited: a modern perspective on a classical feature for vision. In: Proceedings of the IEEE Conference on Computer Vision and Pattern Recognition, pp. 400–408 (2015)
35. Yi, K.M., Trulls, E., Lepetit, V., Fua, P.: Lift: learned invariant feature transform. In: European Conference on Computer Vision, pp. 467–483. Springer (2016)
36. Zhang, B., Wang, L., Wang, Z., Qiao, Y., Wang, H.: Real-time action recognition with enhanced motion vector cnns. In: Proceedings of the IEEE Conference on Computer Vision and Pattern Recognition, pp. 2718–2726 (2016)
37. Zimmermann, C., Ceylan, D., Yang, J., Russell, B., Argus, M., Brox, T.: Freihand: a dataset for markerless capture of hand pose and shape from single rgb images. In: Proceedings of the IEEE International Conference on Computer Vision, pp. 813–822 (2019)

Oral Session: Knowledge Representation

Visual Concept Networks: A Graph-Based Approach to Detecting Anomalous Data in Deep Neural Networks

Debargha Ganguly[1(✉)], Debayan Gupta[2], and Vipin Chaudhary[1]

[1] Case Western Reserve University, Cleveland, USA
{debargha.ganguly,vipin}@case.edu
[2] Ashoka University, Tirupati, Sonipat, India
debayan.gupta@ashoka.edu.in

Abstract. Deep neural networks (DNNs), while increasingly deployed in many applications, struggle with robustness against anomalous and out-of-distribution (OOD) data. Current OOD benchmarks often oversimplify, focusing on single-object tasks and not fully representing complex real-world anomalies. This paper introduces a new, straightforward method employing graph structures and topological features to effectively detect both far-OOD and near-OOD data. We convert images into networks of interconnected human understandable features or visual concepts. Through extensive testing on two novel tasks, including ablation studies with large vocabularies and diverse tasks, we demonstrate the method's effectiveness. This approach enhances DNN resilience to OOD data and promises improved performance in various applications.

Keywords: Out-of-Distribution Detection · Deep Neural Networks Robustness · Graph-Based Anomaly Detection

1 Introduction

Trustworthy machine learning (ML) systems need to refer low-confidence decisions to human experts. They often rely on the closed-world assumption, expecting test data to mirror the training data's distribution [20]. However, real-world scenarios frequently encounter deviations from this ideal, particularly in open-world settings where test samples might be out-of-distribution (OOD) [7]. These OOD samples arise from either semantic shifts (different classes) [16] or covariate shifts (different domains) [2], necessitating specialized handling. Related areas such as outlier, anomaly, novelty detection, and open set recognition [28,30,37,48] share techniques for managing such data variances.

Issues: The literature often overlooks significant challenges in validating OOD detection methods. A key issue is the unrealistic perfection suggested by

This research was supported in part by NSF awards #2104377, #2112606 and #2117439.

many studies, where the area under the receiver operating characteristic curve (AUROC) scores near or reach 100 [4]. This raises a critical question: do these tasks accurately represent the complexities of OOD detection, or are they overly simplistic? The gap between academic datasets and real-world applications highlights the complexity of the issue. Using simpler datasets like CIFAR-10 versus CIFAR-100, or comparing MNIST to SVHN, oversimplifies the OOD detection challenge. These 'toy tasks' don't fully represent the range and intricacy of data encountered in actual production environments [15]. To solve this the Open OOD benchmark was introduced, with more difficult and nuanced tasks [51]. However, performance on these benchmarks are also saturated at near perfect levels [32].

Benchmark Contributions. To address existing gaps, we introduce two new OOD detection tasks using the LSUN and ImageNet datasets for more accurate in-distribution representation. These machine-annotated datasets, with their diverse and extensive distribution, aim to overcome the limitations of current OOD benchmarks. This enables researchers and practitioners to engage with a new benchmark that is both realistic and challenging, enhancing OOD detection methods. Additionally, because of the multi-object complex scenes, the OOD detection method must also have some level of explainability for "why" certain data points are classified as OOD, building upon tasks such as the anomaly segmentation task in [15].

Algorithmic Intuition. Our approach is rooted in the idea that graphs, with their ability to capture complex relationships, are ideal for analyzing entities and interactions in intricate domains. We hypothesize that using graph-based representations of visual features, which are interpretable by humans, will more effectively encode domain knowledge and identify OOD scenarios. This is because it allows the AI system to utilize the intricate relationships among visual concepts and infer latent semantics, while maintaining explanations that are understandable to humans.

2 Background and Related Work

Detecting out-of-distribution (OOD) points in lower-dimensional spaces, as discussed in Pimentel et al.'s review [33], typically relies on techniques such as density estimation, nearest neighbor algorithms, and clustering, which predict OOD points by assessing their density or distance from cluster [45].

Techniques: Research in OOD data is concentrated on network adjustments and the development of specialized scoring functions. Methods like network truncation, including techniques such as ODIN [25], ReAct [42], and DICE [43], modify a network's signals or weights to differentiate regular data from OOD data, but they require a complementary scoring function for effective OOD detection. These scoring functions can generally be surrogate classifier-based, like MSP [16] and the energy function [27], which rely on the network's classification layer, or distance-based, such as the Mahalanobis detector [24] and KNN [44], which assess the dissimilarity of input from regular data based on features. Apart from these, post-hoc methods like temperature scaling, gradient input modifications, and statistical measurements have been introduced, offering the advantage of being easily integrated into various model architectures without requiring major alterations to the network itself.

Additionally, there's a focus on enhancing OOD detection through training-time regularization techniques that aim to refine model training. This includes incorporating confidence estimation branches [25], altering loss functions [16], or utilizing contrast learning objectives [50] to develop stronger models with more precise uncertainty estimates, albeit at the cost of increased computational resources. Some strategies also involve the integration of external OOD samples during the training phase to sharpen the model's ability to discern between in-distribution and OOD data [17]. These methods range from promoting varied predictions on OOD samples [19] to employing clustering techniques to sift out in-distribution samples. Although leveraging external data is a prevalent practice, particularly in the industry, it presents challenges such as selecting suitable data sets and preventing the model from overfitting to specific OOD samples.

Recent advancements in out-of-distribution (OOD) detection primarily utilize deep neural networks (DNNs). Techniques like convolutional neural networks (CNNs) for anomaly detection [38], and methods combining transfer and representation learning [1,8], are prevalent. In critical areas like healthcare, generative adversarial networks (GANs) are used for unsupervised tasks [40]. However, these approaches, involving additional neural layers or alterations, face a notable risk: DNNs can be overly confident in incorrect decisions in OOD contexts [13, 16, 22].

Before the advent of deep learning, image analysis techniques like Visual Bag-of-Words (BoW) treated image regions as 'words' to create a visual vocabulary and represent images as histograms, whereas Probabilistic Latent Semantic Analysis (pLSA) interpreted images as compositions of latent visual topics, considering each 'visual word' as a manifestation of these topics. CSKGs are emerging as valuable sources of domain-specific knowledge, aiding in tasks like question answering and planning [12, 18]. In our study, we leverage these graphs, combined with the latest in geometric learning, to enhance OOD data detection.

3   Problem Setup

This paper addresses the challenge of distinguishing in-distribution (ID) and out-of-distribution (OOD) images using a pre-trained neural network. We define two distributions within the feature space $\mathcal{X}$: D_{in} for ID and D_{out} for OOD. The ID dataset $\mathcal{D}^{in}$ is composed of pairs $\left(\mathbf{x}^{in}, y^{in}\right)$, where $\mathbf{x}$ is the input feature and y^{in} belongs to the set of class labels $\mathcal{Y}^{in} := 1, \ldots, K$. The OOD dataset $\mathcal{D}^{out}$ includes pairs $(\mathbf{x}^{out}, y^{out})$, with y^{out} in $\mathcal{Y}^{out} := K + 1, \ldots, K + O$, ensuring $\mathcal{Y}^{out} \cap \mathcal{Y}^{in} = \emptyset$.

Our technique involves representing each input image X as a network of visual features, with a high-dimensional embedding in latent space Z, obtained from a mixture distribution P_{X*Z}. The latent representation Z is then analyzed to determine whether X originates from the in-distribution $\mathcal{D}in$ or not. We explore two formulations, one with access to OOD samples during the training phase, similar to [17] testing performance against a held-out set, and a the other being zero-shot with no access to OOD outputs (Fig. 1).

Types of Shift: Model performance is subject to different distribution shifts: *covariate shift* impacts the input space $\mathcal{X}$, while *semantic shift* affects the label space $\mathcal{Y}$. With a joint distribution $P(X, Y)$ over $\mathcal{X} \times \mathcal{Y}$, shifts can alter either the marginal $P(X)$ or both $P(X)$ and $P(Y)$. Notably, changes in $P(Y)$ inherently influence $P(X)$.

Covariate shifts, seen in cases like adversarial attacks [11], domain changes [34], and style variations [10], mainly impact $P(X)$, testing models' generalization while keeping Y constant. Semantic shifts, however, involve changes in the label space Y between in-distribution (ID) and out-of-distribution (OOD) data, crucial in many detection tasks. Models must be cautious in making predictions here. OOD detection's effectiveness largely depends on the semantic similarity between outliers and inliers. Near OOD tasks, like shifts from SVHN to MNIST, pose greater challenges, with current methods achieving about 93% AUROC [8]. Far OOD tasks, with clearer semantic differences, generally see AUROCs near 99% [8].

Table 1. OOD detection tasks based on [52]

Far-OOD Tasks	Near-OOD Tasks
Bridge vs (Classroom, Conf. Room, Dining, Kitchen, Living Room, Restaurant, Bedroom)	Bedroom vs (Classroom, Conf. Room, Dining, Kitchen, Living Room, Restaurant);
	Living Room vs Restaurant
Church Outdoor vs (Classroom, Conf. Room, **Dining**, Kitchen, Living Room, Restaurant, Bedroom)	Church Outdoor vs (Tower, Bridge), Bridge vs Tower;
	Classroom vs (Conf. Room, Dining, Kitchen, Living Room, Restaurant);
	Kitchen vs (Living Room, Restaurant)
Tower vs (Classroom, Conf. Room, Dining, Kitchen, Living Room, Restaurant, Bedroom)	Conf. Room vs (Dining, Kitchen, Living Room, Restaurant);
	Dining vs (Kitchen, Restaurant, **Living Room**)

3.1   Benchmarking Tasks

Our benchmarking innovation uses the Large-scale Scene Understanding (LSUN) dataset [52] to enrich out-of-distribution (OOD) detection benchmarks. LSUN's diverse range of real-world images, from 120k to 3 million across ten categories like bedrooms and living rooms, forms the basis of our benchmarks. We classify these categories into discrete domains and create pairwise combinations, distinguishing them as far-OOD or near-OOD based on semantic closeness. This setup allows for a more nuanced and rigorous evaluation of OOD detection capabilities.

Further, we incorporate the ImageNet dataset, structured on the WordNet lexical hierarchy, to introduce a complex task. We focus on its broad top-tier classes like 'entities' and 'natural objects', each encompassing varied subclasses. This approach tests models' ability to classify images and identify their broader distributions, simulating real-world applications where understanding both specific details and overarching contexts is crucial.

Our benchmarks mark a significant step forward in OOD detection research. Unlike foundational datasets like CIFAR-10 and CIFAR-100, which focus on single-object images, our approach reflects the complexity and diversity of real-world visual data, often featuring multiple objects across classes. This design ensures models are tested against realistic, multifaceted scenarios, elevating the standard for OOD detection task evaluations.

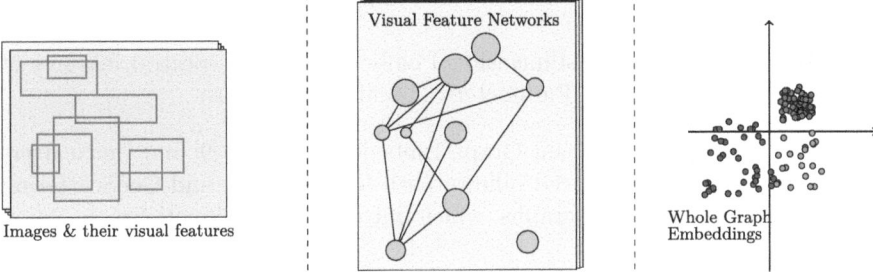

Images & their visual features

Visual Feature Networks

Whole Graph Embeddings

Fig. 1. An illustrative representation of the image-to-graph transformation process for out-of-distribution detection. The diagram commences with input images and their associated visual features, demarcated by bounding boxes. This visual information is then channeled into a graph structure, with nodes demonstrating unique visual elements and edges establishing interconnections. The concluding stage showcases the embedding of the entire graph into a 2D space, where similar visual patterns manifest as proximal clusters.

3.2   Graph Embedding Algorithms

In our approach, each unique concept from the visual vocabulary is represented as a node in the graph. Edges are constructed only between nodes present in the image. Given multiple object pairs, multiple edges are drawn. The weight of each edge is determined based on both the Intersection over Union (IoU) score, denoted by the Jaccard Index J, and the euclidean distance between the centroids of the bounding boxes. Formally, for a graph $G(x) = (V, E)$ where $G(x) \in G$, the weight of the edge between objects obj_1 and obj_2 is defined as:

$$E_{\text{weight}}^{\text{obj}_1,\text{obj}_2} = \begin{cases} 1 + \|\text{obj}_1, \text{obj}_2\| \times J(\text{obj}_1, \text{obj}_2) & \text{if weighted} \\ 1 & \text{if unweighted} \end{cases}$$

1. **Graph2Vec** [31] uses Weisfeiler-Lehman tree features to generate a 128-dimensional embedding with feature co-occurrence matrices. Parameters: 2 Weisfeiler-Lehman iterations, 10 epochs, learning rate of 0.025.
2. **Wavelet Characteristic** [49] employs wavelet function weights and node features to produce a 1000-dimensional embedding. Parameters: $\tau = 1.0$, $\theta_{max} = 2.5$, 5 function evaluations.
3. **LDP** [3] calculates degree profile histograms to form a 160-dimensional graph representation. Parameters: 32 histogram bins.
4. **Feather Graph** [36] uses random walk weights for node features to create a 500-dimensional embedding. Parameters: $\theta_{max} = 2.5$, 25 evaluation points.
5. **GL2Vec** [5] leverages line graphs and edge features, similar to Graph2Vec, to form a 128-dimensional embedding.
6. **NetLSD** [46] uses the heat kernel trace for a 250-dimensional embedding. Parameters: 200 eigenvalue approximations, 250-time scale steps.
7. **SF** [23] derives a 128-dimensional embedding from the lowest eigenvalues of the normalised laplacian.
8. **FGSD** [47] creates a 200-dimensional embedding using spectral features of the normalized laplacian. Parameters: 200 histogram bins.

Despite considering Invariant Graph Embeddings (IGE) [9] and GeoScattering, challenges arose. IGE faced infinite path length issues, and GeoScattering necessitated fully connected graphs, which our dataset didn't satisfy.

3.3   Evaluation Metrics

To assess our system's effectiveness in distinguishing in-distribution and out-of-distribution samples, consistent with OOD detection literature [8,25], we use several metrics, presenting weighted averages for comprehensive understanding. The Area Under the Receiver Operating Characteristic curve (AUROC) [6], a threshold-independent metric, measures the trade-off between true positive rate (TPR) and false positive rate (FPR), indicating a perfect detector at 100%. The Area Under the Precision-Recall curve (AUPR) [29,39], also threshold-independent, evaluates the precision-recall graph, especially useful in scenarios with infrequent anomalies. It reports the average precision (AP) score, summarizing the precision-recall curve. Lastly, the F1 Score, the harmonic mean of precision and recall, is crucial in OOD detection for balancing false positives and negatives, providing a single metric to gauge this balance. For multi-class classification in identifying originating distributions, we use the One-vs-Rest (OVR) approach for AUROC.

3.4   Results and Discussion

In this section, we first demonstrate our method's effectiveness in detecting OOD datapoints on the LSUN-based benchmark (in Table 1). We employ the DETIC model [53], an advanced open vocabulary object detection system developed by Meta, as our primary tool for feature extraction. Renowned for its comprehensive coverage and versatility, DETIC can discern and categorize a wide array of object classes, making it particularly apt for our assessment needs on diverse benchmarks.

Due to computational constraints, we test 100,000 images in each in-distribution and out-of-distribution classes on each near-OOD and far-OOD benchmark. In addition, 20% of the data is held out for unseen testing. The task for each category was randomly chosen from Table 1. In Table 2, we describe the AUROC and average precision scores computed for Far-OOD detection between "Church (Outdoor)" and "Dining room" classes. Table 3 describes the AUROC and average precision scores computed for Near-OOD detection between "Living Room" and "Dining room" classes. For both these tasks, logistic regression and gradient boosting were used as the downstream model.

In the foundational implementation, the whole graph embedding model [35] is designed to assimilate visual concepts and features by integrating data from both in-distribution and out-of-distribution sources. The model learns to represent various characteristics by exploiting the relationships and similarities between different classes and domains. In a subsequent variation, the focus shifted towards exploring the model's zero-shot performance. In this experiment, the graph embedding model is trained exclusively on in-distribution data. After the training phase, the model's adaptability to out-of-distribution samples is assessed. This is executed by employing a one-class Support Vector Machine (SVM) with a Radial Basis Function (RBF) kernel. The one-class SVM can be formally represented as: minimize $\frac{1}{2}\|\mathbf{w}\|^2 - \rho$ subject to $\langle \mathbf{w}, \Phi(x_i) \rangle - \rho \leq \varepsilon$ for $i = 1, \ldots, n$ and $\rho \leq 0$. Here, $\mathbf{w}$ denotes the normal vector to the hyperplane, while $\Phi(x_i)$ represents the mapping of data points using the RBF kernel. The variable ρ is associated with the margin, and ε acts as a slack variable that permits certain misclassifications. This adaptation allows for an exploration of the model's potential to generalize across unseen datasets, shedding light on its capacities for zero-shot learning.

[24] proposed using the Mahalanobis distance for OOD detection by fitting a Gaussian distribution to the class-conditional embeddings. Conventionally, they let $f(x)$ denote the embedding of an input x (e.g., the penultimate layer before computing the logits). We, instead, fit a Gaussian distribution to the whole graph embeddings, computing the per-class mean $\mu_c = \frac{1}{N_c} \sum_{i:y_i=c} f(x_i)$ and a shared covariance matrix: $\Sigma = \frac{1}{N} \sum_{c=1}^{K} \sum_{i:y_i=c} (f(x_i) - \mu_c)(f(x_i) - \mu_c)^T$. The Mahalanobis score (negative of the distance) is then computed as $\text{score}_{\text{Maha}}(x) = -\min_c \frac{1}{2}(f(x) - \mu_c)^T \Sigma^{-1}(f(x) - \mu_c)$. The performance of a downstream model is computed and presented.

A note on Explainability : In our methodology, we represent images as visual concept networks where nodes are objects and edges depict their relationships. These graphs, uniform in node count (linked to the vocabulary) are distinct in topology, capture each image's unique configuration. Our analysis begins by encoding an image into a visual concept network, then projecting it onto a latent space Z, preserving key features. We then identify the nearest in-distribution graph to our target image's graph within this latent space. The crux of our explainability lies in the analysis of the topological differences between the target image's graph and its nearest in-distribution counterpart. By examining the disparities in node connections, we can uncover "why" an image is out of distribution.

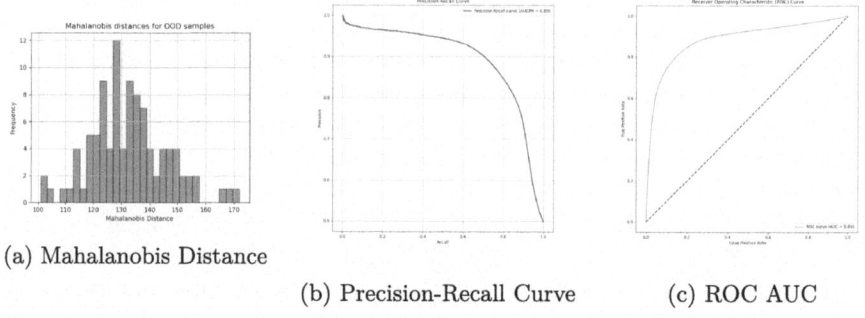

(a) Mahalanobis Distance

(b) Precision-Recall Curve   (c) ROC AUC

Fig. 2. Far OOD evaluation metrics while using class conditioned mahalanobis score. (a) Mahalanobis distance. (b) Precision-Recall Curve. (c) ROC AUC.

Task Characteristics: Our findings show that Far OOD tasks are easier than Near OOD tasks due to the distinct visual differences between the categories. For example, an outdoor scene varies greatly from a living room, simplifying the Far OOD detection.

Benchmarking Graph Embedding Techniques: In benchmarking various graph embedding methods, we observed similar performances among some techniques and their associated models. This suggests these methods may extract similar graph features, leading to comparable decision-making patterns. Graph2Vec, GL2Vec, and FGSD stood out for their ability to capture structural graph details, particularly in Far OOD tasks. While some variations in performance were noted, the choice of downstream model was key to achieving the best results.

Classifier Performance. The Gradient Boosting classifier consistently outperformed Logistic Regression in training and testing across most graph embeddings, notably in the AUROC metric. The close alignment between training and testing scores suggests minimal overfitting, highlighting the embeddings' effectiveness in both standard and OOD scenarios. This consistent performance across different embedders and classifiers reinforces the reliability of our graph representation methods for OOD detection.

Table 2. Comparative evaluation of different graph embedding methods on the Far OOD task, using the COCO Vocabulary as a primary reference. Metrics include AUROC, AUPR, and F1-Score for both training and testing sets. Results are shown for Logistic Regression and Gradient Boosting classifiers. Additional results are provided for ablation studies using different vocabularies: Objects365, LVIS, and OpenImages.

	AUROC				AUPR				F1-Score			
	Logistic Reg		Grad Boost		Logistic Reg		Grad Boost		Logistic Reg		Grad Boost	
	Train	Test	Train	Test	Train	Test	Train	Test	Train	Test	Train	Test
Graph2Vec	89.91	88.84	90.74	88.65	85.59	85.8	86.5	86.1	89.98	88.47	90.85	88.07
GL2Vec	89.54	88.88	90.04	87.06	85.12	83.33	85.7	80.25	89.61	89.48	90.13	88.29
FGSD	90.15	86.02	**91.50**	**91.46**	86.02	86.36	89.29	89.37	86.35	89.29	91.17	91.16
SF	90.15	90.27	90.15	90.27	86.02	86.35	86.02	86.35	90.18	90.35	90.18	90.35
NetLSD	90.15	90.27	90.15	90.27	86.02	86.35	86.02	86.35	90.18	90.35	90.18	90.35
FeatherGraph	90.15	90.27	90.15	90.27	86.02	86.35	86.02	86.35	90.18	90.35	90.18	90.35
LDP	90.15	90.27	90.15	90.27	86.02	86.35	86.02	86.35	90.18	90.35	90.18	90.35
Wavelet Char	90.15	90.27	90.15	90.27	86.02	86.35	86.02	86.35	90.18	90.35	90.18	90.35
COCO (vocab)	89.91	88.84	90.74	88.65	85.59	85.80	86.50	86.10	89.98	88.47	90.85	88.07
Objects365 (vocab)	86.35	84.30	90.23	89.62	81.35	81.96	85.77	85.43	86.32	82.6	90.37	89.75
LVIS (vocab)	85.64	86.17	88.08	88.42	79.89	80.94	82.76	83.47	85.97	86.45	88.38	88.76
OpenImages (vocab)	85.61	83.9	88.58	88.39	79.88	79.96	83.16	83.11	85.92	83.05	88.95	88.86

Table 3. Comparative evaluation of different graph embedding methods on the Near OOD task, using the COCO Vocabulary as a primary reference. Additional results are provided for ablation studies using different vocabularies: Objects365, LVIS, and OpenImages.

	AUROC				AUPR				F1-Score			
	Logistic Reg		Grad Boost		Logistic Reg		Grad Boost		Logistic Reg		Grad Boost	
Method	Train	Test	Train	Test	Train	Test	Train	Test	Train	Test	Train	Test
Graph2Vec	54.59	55.40	56.55	55.58	52.67	53.22	52.52	53.31	55.54	60.75	62.55	62.21
GL2Vec	55.23	53.56	56.64	54.35	52.79	52.14	53.58	52.60	57.50	65.44	62.60	61.45
FGSD	54.51	54.35	**70.85**	**70.21**	52.35	52.61	64.86	64.56	59.69	59.76	70.35	69.90
SF	56.07	55.86	56.07	55.86	53.23	53.47	52.23	52.47	62.73	62.75	62.73	62.75
NetLSD	54.95	52.90	56.08	55.86	52.68	52.90	53.23	53.47	51.85	51.82	62.74	62.75
FeatherGraph	56.07	55.86	56.07	55.86	53.23	53.47	53.23	53.47	62.73	62.75	62.73	62.75
LDP	54.95	54.72	56.07	55.86	52.68	52.90	53.23	53.47	51.85	51.82	62.73	62.75
Wavelet Characteristic	56.07	55.86	56.07	55.86	53.23	53.47	53.23	53.47	62.73	62.75	62.73	62.75
COCO (vocab)	54.59	55.40	56.55	55.58	52.67	53.22	52.52	53.31	55.54	60.75	62.55	62.21
Objects365 (vocab)	58.53	58.44	59.28	58.93	54.98	55.18	55.56	55.69	56.71	59.7	56.45	55.67
LVIS (vocab)	60.32	59.75	60.54	60.09	56.3	56.07	56.49	56.49	57.78	60.62	57.58	57.59
OpenImages (vocab)	58.97	59.19	59.92	59.63	55.35	55.95	56.08	56.23	55.98	54.39	56.05	55.76

Ablation Studies with Richer Vocabularies : Our ablation study explored the impact of using extensive vocabularies, like COCO [26] with 80 concepts, Objects365 [41] with 365, OpenImages [21] with 500, and LVIS [14] with over 1200. While a broader vocabulary increases the model's expressive power, it also leads to larger, less interconnected visual concept networks, posing challenges in creating meaningful embeddings. Nonetheless, our results showed consistent performance across these vocabularies, demonstrating the robustness of our graph embedding techniques (Table 4).

Table 4. Comparison of different embedders on zero-shot Far-OOD and Near OOD tasks, using one-class SVM.

Embedder	AUROC	AUPR
Far-OOD		
FGSD	0.5372	0.5372
SF	0.3851	0.3851
NetLSD	0.4920	0.4920
FeatherGraph	**0.8526**	**0.8526**
LDP	0.4841	0.4841
WaveletCharacteristic	0.8526	0.8526
Near OOD		
FGSD	0.5132	0.5132
SF	0.5192	0.5192
NetLSD	0.5391	0.5391
FeatherGraph	0.4847	0.4847
LDP	0.5154	0.5154
WaveletCharacteristic	0.4847	0.4847

Zero-shot Performance: Using a one-class SVM, graph embedders showed varying efficacy in zero-shot Far-OOD and Near OOD tasks. For Far-OOD, *FeatherGraph* and *WaveletCharacteristic* excelled in identifying vastly different visual concepts, contrasting with the struggles of *SF* and average results from *FGSD*, *NetLSD*, and *LDP*. However, in Near OOD tasks, all models' performances converged, nearly resembling random guesses, highlighting the challenge of differentiating similar visual categories. Notably, *NetLSD* showed a slight advantage, but former Far-OOD leaders like *FeatherGraph* and *WaveletCharacteristic* matched the performance of *LDP* and *SF*. This shift emphasizes the complex nature of Near OOD tasks and the need for graph embeddings specifically tailored to capture these subtle distinctions (Table 5).

ImageNet Performance: Our ImageNet study, leveraging the WordNet hierarchy, aimed at evaluating category recognition. Limited by computational resources, we used the Graph2Vec embedder with RandomForest (RF) and GradientBoosting (GB) classifiers. RF, while showing perfect training scores (accuracy, AUC, AUPR, F1-Score all at 1.0), suggested overfitting due to its lower test performance. GB displayed more balanced training and testing results, indicating a better-generalized model. Overall, GB proved slightly more effective than RF in broader ImageNet category detection.

Table 5. Performance of RandomForest (RF) and GradientBoosting (GB) classifiers using the Graph2Vec embedder on the ImageNet dataset (multiclass) distribution detection. Metrics are weighted averages

Classifier (Set)	Accuracy	AUC	AUPR	F1-Score
RF (Train)	1.0	**1.0**	1.0	1.0
RF (Test)	0.6045	0.6612	0.5554	0.5807
GB (Train)	0.6239	**0.7135**	0.6284	0.6054
GB (Test)	0.6089	0.6672	0.5638	0.5865

Mahalanobis Score Based Performance : Using Lee et al.'s (2018) approach, Gaussian distributions were fitted to graph embeddings. The Mahalanobis distances for OOD samples showed a clear Gaussian pattern (Fig. 2), validating its use for OOD detection in our study. The model's high accuracy is evidenced by an AUCPR of 0.89 and a matching ROC curve AUC.

Constraints: Our approach hinges on an open vocabulary object detector to pinpoint key features within a specified dataset and domain. Ideally, this detector should also recognize features likely in out-of-distribution data. Given a complete feature list, graphs in $\mathbb{G}$ would have nodes for each feature, with edges formed based on observed pairwise relationships. This method of utilizing auxiliary models for verifying decisions mirrors the essence of boosting, fitting successive models to prior residuals. Such a structure could potentially lower the chances of operational failures.

4   Conclusion

Our paper introduces the use of graph-based representations of visual semantics for more effective out-of-distribution (OOD) detection across two novel tasks. By transforming outputs from pre-trained object-detection networks into semantic graphs, we enhance the AI's ability to discern and rationalize OOD instances. This method not only boosts OOD detection accuracy but also offers clear explanations for AI decisions, crucial for building trust in AI applications.

We thoroughly compare different graph embedding algorithms within our framework, illustrating the strengths of graph representations in OOD detection and guiding the selection of the most suitable embedding techniques. Our findings highlight the potential of graph methods for improving both interpretability and efficacy in OOD detection. This paper charts a new course in OOD detection research, spotlighting the value of semantic graphs and graph-based learning, and is poised to influence future explorations in OOD detection and AI.

References

1. Andrews, J., Tanay, T., Morton, E.J., Griffin, L.D.: Transfer representation-learning for anomaly detection. In: JMLR (2016)
2. Ben-David, S., Blitzer, J., Crammer, K., Kulesza, A., Pereira, F., Vaughan, J.W.: A theory of learning from different domains. Mach. Learn. **79**, 151–175 (2010)
3. Cai, C., Wang, Y.: A simple yet effective baseline for non-attributed graph classification. arXiv preprint arXiv:1811.03508 (2018)
4. Cao, S., Zhang, Z.: Deep hybrid models for out-of-distribution detection. In: Proceedings of the IEEE/CVF Conference on Computer Vision and Pattern Recognition, pp. 4733–4743 (2022)
5. Chen, H., Koga, H.: Gl2vec: Graph embedding enriched by line graphs with edge features. In: International Conference on Neural Information Processing, pp. 3–14. Springer (2019)
6. Davis, J., Goadrich, M.: The relationship between precision-recall and roc curves. In: Proceedings of the 23rd international conference on Machine learning. pp. 233–240 (2006)
7. Drummond, N., Shearer, R.: The open world assumption. In: eSI Workshop: the Closed World of Databases meets the Open World of the Semantic Web, vol. 15, p. 1 (2006)
8. Fort, S., Ren, J., Lakshminarayanan, B.: Exploring the limits of out-of-distribution detection. Adv. Neural. Inf. Process. Syst. **34**, 7068–7081 (2021)
9. Galland, A., Lelarge, M.: Invariant embedding for graph classification. In: ICML 2019 Workshop on Learning and Reasoning with Graph-Structured Data (2019)
10. Gatys, L.A., Ecker, A.S., Bethge, M.: Image style transfer using convolutional neural networks. In: Proceedings of the IEEE Conference on Computer Vision and Pattern Recognition, pp. 2414–2423 (2016)
11. Goodfellow, I.J., Shlens, J., Szegedy, C.: Explaining and harnessing adversarial examples. arXiv preprint arXiv:1412.6572 (2014)
12. Guan, N., Song, D., Liao, L.: Knowledge graph embedding with concepts. Knowl-Based Syst. **164**, 38–44 (2019)
13. Guo, C., Pleiss, G., Sun, Y., Weinberger, K.Q.: On calibration of modern neural networks. In: International Conference on Machine Learning, pp. 1321–1330. PMLR (2017)
14. Gupta, A., Dollar, P., Girshick, R.: Lvis: A dataset for large vocabulary instance segmentation. In: Proceedings of the IEEE/CVF Conference on Computer Vision and Pattern Recognition, pp. 5356–5364 (2019)
15. Hendrycks, D., et al.: Scaling out-of-distribution detection for real-world settings. arXiv preprint arXiv:1911.11132 (2019)
16. Hendrycks, D., Gimpel, K.: A baseline for detecting misclassified and out-of-distribution examples in neural networks. arXiv preprint arXiv:1610.02136 (2016)
17. Hendrycks, D., Mazeika, M., Dietterich, T.: Deep anomaly detection with outlier exposure. arXiv preprint arXiv:1812.04606 (2018)
18. Ilievski, F., Szekely, P., Zhang, B.: Cskg: the commonsense knowledge graph. In: European Semantic Web Conference, pp. 680–696. Springer (2021)
19. Jeong, T., Kim, H.: Ood-maml: meta-learning for few-shot out-of-distribution detection and classification. Adv. Neural. Inf. Process. Syst. **33**, 3907–3916 (2020)
20. Krizhevsky, A., Sutskever, I., Hinton, G.E.: Imagenet classification with deep convolutional neural networks. In: Advances in Neural Information Processing Systems, vol. 25 (2012)

21. Kuznetsova, A., et al.: The open images dataset v4: unified image classification, object detection, and visual relationship detection at scale. Int. J. Comput. Vision **128**(7), 1956–1981 (2020)

22. Lakshminarayanan, B., Pritzel, A., Blundell, C.: Simple and scalable predictive uncertainty estimation using deep ensembles. In: Advances in Neural Information Processing Systems, vol. 30 (2017)

23. de Lara, N., Pineau, E.: A simple baseline algorithm for graph classification. arXiv preprint arXiv:1810.09155 (2018)

24. Lee, K., Lee, K., Lee, H., Shin, J.: A simple unified framework for detecting out-of-distribution samples and adversarial attacks. In: Advances in Neural Information Processing Systems, vol. 31 (2018)

25. Liang, S., Li, Y., Srikant, R.: Enhancing the reliability of out-of-distribution image detection in neural networks. arXiv preprint arXiv:1706.02690 (2017)

26. Lin, T.-Y., et al.: Microsoft COCO: common objects in context. In: Fleet, D., Pajdla, T., Schiele, B., Tuytelaars, T. (eds.) ECCV 2014. LNCS, vol. 8693, pp. 740–755. Springer, Cham (2014). https://doi.org/10.1007/978-3-319-10602-1_48

27. Liu, W., Wang, X., Owens, J., Li, Y.: Energy-based out-of-distribution detection. Adv. Neural. Inf. Process. Syst. **33**, 21464–21475 (2020)

28. Mahdavi, A., Carvalho, M.: A survey on open set recognition. In: 2021 IEEE Fourth International Conference on Artificial Intelligence and Knowledge Engineering (AIKE), pp. 37–44. IEEE (2021)

29. Manning, C., Schutze, H.: Foundations of statistical natural language processing. MIT Press (1999)

30. Miljković, D.: Review of novelty detection methods. In: The 33rd International Convention MIPRO, pp. 593–598. IEEE (2010)

31. Narayanan, A., Chandramohan, M., Venkatesan, R., Chen, L., Liu, Y., Jaiswal, S.: graph2vec: learning distributed representations of graphs. arXiv preprint arXiv:1707.05005 (2017)

32. Park, J., Jung, Y.G., Teoh, A.B.J.: Nearest neighbor guidance for out-of-distribution detection. In: Proceedings of the IEEE/CVF International Conference on Computer Vision, pp. 1686–1695 (2023)

33. Pimentel, M.A., Clifton, D.A., Clifton, L., Tarassenko, L.: A review of novelty detection. Sig. Process. **99**, 215–249 (2014)

34. Quinonero-Candela, J., Sugiyama, M., Schwaighofer, A., Lawrence, N.D.: Dataset shift in machine learning. Mit Press (2008)

35. Rozemberczki, B., Kiss, O., Sarkar, R.: Karate club: an API oriented open-source python framework for unsupervised learning on graphs. In: Proceedings of the 29th ACM International Conference on Information & Knowledge Management, pp. 3125–3132 (2020)

36. Rozemberczki, B., Sarkar, R.: Characteristic functions on graphs: birds of a feather, from statistical descriptors to parametric models. In: Proceedings of the 29th ACM International Conference on Information & Knowledge Management, pp. 1325–1334 (2020)

37. Ruff, L., et al.: A unifying review of deep and shallow anomaly detection. Proc. IEEE **109**(5), 756–795 (2021)

38. Sabokrou, M., Fayyaz, M., Fathy, M., Moayed, Z., Klette, R.: Deep-anomaly: fully convolutional neural network for fast anomaly detection in crowded scenes. Comput. Vis. Image Underst. **172**, 88–97 (2018)

39. Saito, T., Rehmsmeier, M.: The precision-recall plot is more informative than the roc plot when evaluating binary classifiers on imbalanced datasets. PLoS ONE **10**(3), e0118432 (2015)

40. Schlegl, T., Seeböck, P., Waldstein, S.M., Schmidt-Erfurth, U., Langs, G.: Unsupervised anomaly detection with generative adversarial networks to guide marker discovery. In: International Conference on Information Processing in Medical Imaging, pp. 146–157. Springer (2017)
41. Shao, S., et al.: Objects365: a large-scale, high-quality dataset for object detection. In: Proceedings of the IEEE/CVF International Conference on Computer Vision, pp. 8430–8439 (2019)
42. Sun, Y., Guo, C., Li, Y.: React: Out-of-distribution detection with rectified activations. Adv. Neural. Inf. Process. Syst. **34**, 144–157 (2021)
43. Sun, Y., Li, Y.: Dice: leveraging sparsification for out-of-distribution detection. In: European Conference on Computer Vision, pp. 691–708. Springer (2022)
44. Sun, Y., Ming, Y., Zhu, X., Li, Y.: Out-of-distribution detection with deep nearest neighbors. In: International Conference on Machine Learning, pp. 20827–20840. PMLR (2022)
45. Theis, L., Oord, A.v.d., Bethge, M.: A note on the evaluation of generative models. arXiv preprint arXiv:1511.01844 (2015)
46. Tsitsulin, A., Mottin, D., Karras, P., Bronstein, A., Müller, E.: Netlsd: hearing the shape of a graph. In: Proceedings of the 24th ACM SIGKDD International Conference on Knowledge Discovery & Data Mining, pp. 2347–2356 (2018)
47. Verma, S., Zhang, Z.L.: Hunt for the unique, stable, sparse and fast feature learning on graphs. In: Advances in Neural Information Processing Systems, vol. 30 (2017)
48. Wang, H., Bah, M.J., Hammad, M.: Progress in outlier detection techniques: a survey. IEEE Access **7**, 107964–108000 (2019)
49. Wang, L., Huang, C., Ma, W., Cao, X., Vosoughi, S.: Graph embedding via diffusion-wavelets-based node feature distribution characterization. In: Proceedings of the 30th ACM International Conference on Information & Knowledge Management, pp. 3478–3482 (2021)
50. Wang, T., Isola, P.: Understanding contrastive representation learning through alignment and uniformity on the hypersphere. In: International Conference on Machine Learning, pp. 9929–9939. PMLR (2020)
51. Yang, J., et al.: Openood: benchmarking generalized out-of-distribution detection. Adv. Neural. Inf. Process. Syst. **35**, 32598–32611 (2022)
52. Yu, F., Zhang, Y., Song, S., Seff, A., Xiao, J.: Lsun: construction of a large-scale image dataset using deep learning with humans in the loop. arXiv preprint arXiv:1506.03365 (2015)
53. Zhou, X., Girdhar, R., Joulin, A., Krähenbühl, P., Misra, I.: Detecting twenty-thousand classes using image-level supervision. In: European Conference on Computer Vision, pp. 350–368. Springer (2022)

Contrastive Language-Entity Pre-training for Richer Knowledge Graph Embedding

Andrea Papaluca[1(✉)], Daniel Krefl[2], Artem Lensky[3,4],
and Hanna Suominen[1,5,6]

[1] School of Computing, The Australian National University, Canberra, Australia
andrea.papaluca@anu.edu.au
[2] Canberra, Australia
[3] School of Engineering and Technology, The University of New South Wales,
Kensington, Australia
[4] School of Biomedical Engineering, The University of Sydney, Sydney, Australia
[5] School of Medicine and Psychology, The Australian National University,
Canberra, Australia
[6] Department of Computing, University of Turku, Turku, Finland

Abstract. In this work we propose a pretraining procedure that aligns a
graph encoder and a text encoder to learn a common multi-modal graph-
text embedding space. The alignment is obtained by training a model
to predict the correct associations between Knowledge Graph nodes and
their corresponding descriptions. We test the procedure with two popular
Knowledge Bases: Wikidata (formerly Freebase) and YAGO. Our results
indicate that such a pretraining method allows for link prediction without the need for additional fine-tuning. Furthermore, we demonstrate
that a graph encoder pretrained on the description matching task allows
for improved link prediction performance after fine-tuning, without the
need for providing node descriptions as additional inputs. We make available the code used in the experiments on GitHub(https://github.com/
BrunoLiegiBastonLiegi/CLEP) under the MIT license to encourage further work.

Keywords: Knowledge Graphs · Multi-modal Learning

1 Introduction

In recent years, significant progress has been achieved in developing models capable of learning a joint representation of text and image modalities, and interest
in such models has been growing steadily in the machine learning community
([6,9,11]). One of the reasons being that such models, which are able to connect
representations of textual and image data modalities, have proven very powerful
in image caption and generation tasks. A notable example is the *Contrastive
Language-Image Pretraining* (CLIP) procedure ([9]) that lies at the core of two
popular models, CLIP-cap ([6]) and latent diffusion ([11]). The former model

---

Independent—D. Krefl.

yielded substantial improvement in performance on the image captioning task, while the latter on the image generation task.

This success behooves us to ask if there are other data modalities that are suitable for learning a joint representation in a similar fashion. In this work, we will explore the replacement of the image modality with a graph modality. In particular, Knowledge Graphs (KG), also known as Knowledge Bases (KB), seem suitable for such joint learning for the following reason: In this kind of graphs, the nodes represent entities and the links describe the relations between them. Many KG can be viewed as a graphical representation or summarization of a textual corpus, with the entities being the common entities occurring in the corpus and the relations the factual relations described in the text. Hence, most KG are natural descendants from natural language corpora, yielding a very distilled representation of the information contained therein.

This also explains why KG play a fundamental role in several language-related tasks. In particular, the mutual inclusion of graph and textual information has been proven to be beneficial for both text and knowledge representation learning. Language models utilizing KG as additional sources of information have demonstrated stronger performance in language-related tasks, such as relation extraction ([1,7,8,15]), question answering ([24]) and entity linking ([19,21]). At the same time, the inclusion of textual information (*e.g.*, entity descriptions) has been proven to be helpful in Knowledge Representation Learning tasks, such as Link Prediction ([13,18,20,23]).

Therefore, we investigate in this work whether a graph encoder pre-trained to learn such a multi-modal graph-text representation, similarly manifests enriched node embedding capabilities. This would represent an effective way to inject textual information into graph embeddings without the need of explicitly providing it to the graph model in downstream tasks. Furthermore, such a model, capable of interchangeably using graph and text as inputs, might serve as a foundation model for natural language and graph-related tasks, similar to what CLIP ([9]) represents for text and images. Therefore, opening the way to new research directions that build on it, as happened for CLIP-cap ([6]) and stable diffusion ([11]). In order to achieve such a joint representation of text and graph modalities, we propose to train a model to predict the correct association between Knowledge Base nodes, *i.e.*, entities, and their descriptions found in the KB.

The outline is as follows. First, in the next Section a summary of the relevant literature is provided. After introducing our model for caption prediction, we demonstrate that alignment of the resulting KG entities and textual descriptions embedding is achievable for two popular Knowledge Bases: Wikidata, and YAGO. Furthermore, we observe that a model trained in this entity-description matching task is capable of performing also link prediction using hybrid triples, composed of head entities (*graph*) and tail descriptions (*text*). The model is competitive with baseline models under common link prediction metrics without the need for additional finetuning. Finally, we provide experimental evidence to indicate that the pre-training procedure allows the graph encoder to learn richer node representations. Namely, the performance in the link prediction task increases further under additional fine-tuning, without the need to explicitly provide descriptions as additional input. We conclude this study by providing a summary of the main outcomes and outlining a possible future line of research based on the methods introduced here.

2   Related Work

The starting point of our work has been the CLIP procedure by [9]. The authors of this previous work proposed to leverage natural language supervision to learn a multi-modal image-text embedding space. Here, natural language supervision refers to letting the model learn the correct associations between images and corresponding captions. It turned out that such a pre-training procedure enabled zero-shot transfer in a plethora of tasks involving image representation learning, such as geo-localization, optical character recognition (OCR), facial emotion recognition and activity recognition in videos ([9]). Furthermore, this aligned image-text representation has served as a foundation for other tasks involving language and image processing. Two examples being image captioning ([6]) and generation ([11]). Our work is based on a similar pre-training pipeline, but with images replaced by KG entities.

The aim of finding a multi-modal embedding space to increase the ability and performance of models is not unique to tasks involving image modalities. Other attempts to find a joint embedding of data modalities, which are related to our work, can be found in approaches to incorporate KG embeddings into word representations. In particular, the models introduced in [1, 7, 8, 15, 19, 21, 24] are of relevance to us. The authors of [24] have proposed a pipeline capable of fusing the language and graph representations of a text and its corresponding extracted subgraph, to achieve *state-of-the-art* performance in several commonsense reasoning benchmarks. [19, 21] focused on the task of linking entity mentions in text with their counterpart in a KB, *i.e.* entity linking. The first work developed a toolkit to build representations of Wikipedia entities based on the textual content of their page and of other linked entities. The latter work proposed a contrastive learning pipeline to align entity mentions in text with their descriptions found in the knowledge base. The methods introduced by [1, 7, 8, 15] led to improved performance under the Relation Extraction task in Natural Language Processing. In particular, ranging from the dynamic inclusion of the relevant information contained in the KG ([7]), to the more simple static augmentation of word encodings with pretrained KG node embeddings ([8]).

Similarly, augmentation of graph embeddings with KG entity descriptions has been considered in [13, 18, 20, 23], and tested in Knowledge Representation Learning tasks. In detail, [20] proposed to simultaneously minimize a *structure-based* and a *description-based* energy to learn coupled graph-description embeddings optimal for link prediction. The other works are instead based on varying approaches to finetune a pre-trained BERT model ([4]) in the link prediction task. In detail, the models are fed with entity and relation descriptions in the form of *head-relation-tail* triples, and their truthfulness is predicted.

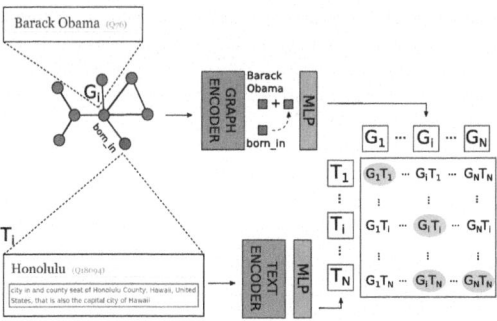

Fig. 1. Entity-description matching pre-training procedure. The graph and text encoders provide the embeddings for the node-description pairs, which are then projected to the joint multi-modal latent space by the two mapping networks. The complete model is trained to maximize the cosine similarity of the correct pairs (highlighted elements of the matrix shown) while minimizing that of the incorrect ones.

All these previous works, however, considered the case of both textual and graph information being provided to the model at inference time in downstream tasks. In this work, we rather aim at achieving a deep alignment of the two underlying representations to obtain a truly multi-modal graph-text latent space. This space will integrate features coming from both the modalities, possibly mitigating the need of providing them at inference time. Similarly to [13,18, 20,23], we test this hypothesis by exploring how this joint training impacts the graph representation for link prediction.

3   The CLEP Model

Inspired by the language-image pre-training procedure by [9], we propose here a similar pipeline to train a model to predict the correct association between Knowledge Graph entities and corresponding textual descriptions. The goal of the procedure is to learn coupled graph and description embeddings such that the positions in the respective embedding spaces are close, thereby encoding features coming, both, from the topological structure of the graph and the textual meaning of the entities.

For a KB triple (e^{head}, r, e^{tail}), composed of the head and tail entities and the relation between them, we match the translation of head entities e^{head} through relations r in the graph space with the corresponding tail descriptions d^{tail}. Therefore, given the set of triples

$$\left\{ \left(e_1^{head}, r_1, d_1^{tail}\right), \ldots, \left(e_n^{head}, r_n, d_n^{tail}\right) \right\},\tag{1}$$

we first encode the head entity $(h_i^{(g)})$ and the relation $(\rho_i^{(g)})$

$$\left(h_i^{(g)}, \rho_i^{(g)}\right) = \text{GraphEncoder}\left(e_i^{head}, r_i\right),\tag{2}$$

and, then, combine them via the proper composition mechanism we want to enforce. For instance, in our case we consider translation ([2]):

$$x_i^{(g)} = h_i^{(g)} + \rho_i^{(g)} \ . \tag{3}$$

Therefore, Eq. (3) represents the predicted tail representation in the graph space and can be aligned with the corresponding description of the tail in the text space. Note that the combination via translation can be replaced with any other composition operation compatible with the *graph encoder*, e.g., multiplication ([22]).

The encoding of the description of the tail is provided by the *text encoder* instead

$$x_i^{(t)} = \text{TextEncoder}\big(d_i^{tail}\big) \ . \tag{4}$$

Mapping networks are stacked on top of both encoders to provide a mapping from the text, respectively graph, latent space to a common multi-modal embedding space:

$$\tilde{x}_i^{(g)} = \text{MLP}_g\big(x_i^{(g)}\big) , \tag{5}$$

$$\tilde{x}_i^{(t)} = \text{MLP}_t\big(x_i^{(t)}\big) , \tag{6}$$

where we indicated with MLP a standard multi-layer feed-forward network with identical architecture for MLP_g and MLP_t, but with independent weights.

The two encoders and mapping networks are trained to maximize the cosine similarity of the correct node-description associations, while minimizing the cosine similarity of the incorrect ones. This is achieved by considering a matrix M with elements $m_{i,j}$ given by

$$m_{i,j} = \frac{\tilde{x}_i^{(g)} \cdot \tilde{x}_j^{(t)}}{\|\tilde{x}_i^{(g)}\|\|\tilde{x}_j^{(t)}\|} \cdot e^\tau \ .$$

with τ, temperature parameter initialised as $e^\tau = 0.07$ and learnt during training. We define the row-wise cross-entropy of M as

$$\text{CE}\big(M\big) = -\frac{1}{n} \sum_{i=1}^{n} \log \frac{e^{m_{i,i}}}{\sum_{j=1}^{n} e^{m_{i,j}}}, \tag{7}$$

and take as loss function

$$\mathcal{L} = \frac{1}{2}\Big(\text{CE}\big(M\big) + \text{CE}\big(M^\top\big) \Big). \tag{8}$$

Note that we included the transpose of M in the loss function in order to enforce the minimization simultaneously in rows and columns.

Table 1. Statistics of the datasets.

	Entities	Relations	Train Triples	Test Triples
FB15k-237	14,296	235	256,862	19,062
YAGO3-10	110,250	32	774,091	3,547

4   Experiments

4.1   Datasets and Methodology

In our experiments we considered two popular link prediction datasets: FB15k-237 ([14]) and YAGO3-10 ([5]). The descriptions of entities were provided by corresponding Knowledge Bases, as detailed below. Unfortunately, not for all entities a description was available. We tested the use of a "caption not available" description for those entities, but, as will be discussed in more detail in the next Section, such a sharing of entities descriptions hinders the alignment. Therefore, to better evaluate the effect of the added descriptions with the least possible contamination, we decided to discard those entities that were missing captions. As a result, we worked with slightly cut-off versions of the original datasets, as reported in Table 1. In particular, this means that we can not directly compare with other results reported in the literature. Note, however, that the comparison of the performance obtained by our CompGCN [16]) on the cut-off datasets and on the original ones (*c.f.* Table 3), indicates that the complexity of tasks did not decrease under usage of the reduced datasets.

In order to obtain the descriptions for the FB15k-237 ([14]) dataset we mapped the entities to the Wikidata KB ([17]). 245 entities were missing, which we cut according to the previous discussion. The YAGO KB ([5]) provided the majority of entity descriptions needed for the YAGO3-10 ([5]) dataset. For the missing cases we again fell back to the Wikidata KB, but we had to discard roughly 10% of the entities (12933), as no description could be found there as well.

In order to train the model for the CLEP procedure we used the original train-validation-test split of the triples provided by the dataset itself. Note that we always provided the graph encoder with a graph built only out of the training triples. No test or validation triple has been fed to the model at this stage.

In the experiments detailed below, we tested a CompGCN ([16]) graph encoder composed by two layers with an encoding dimension equal to 200. For the entity descriptions, we used GPT2 ([10]) taking the last token encodings as a representation of the descriptions. The language model is pre-trained and we allow only the last 4 layers to adapt during training in order to keep intact the text representation it originally learnt. Finally, for the MLP part, Eq. (5)–(6), we decided to use a simple linear feed-forward layer, because it preserves most of the structure of the original graph and language spaces. For example, if the graph encoder allowed for the composition of entities and relations via translation, we would like to preserve this even after the mapping.

4.2   The Multi-modal Graph-Language Space

In order to verify that the graph and language latent spaces are indeed aligned after training, we performed two tests of alignment.

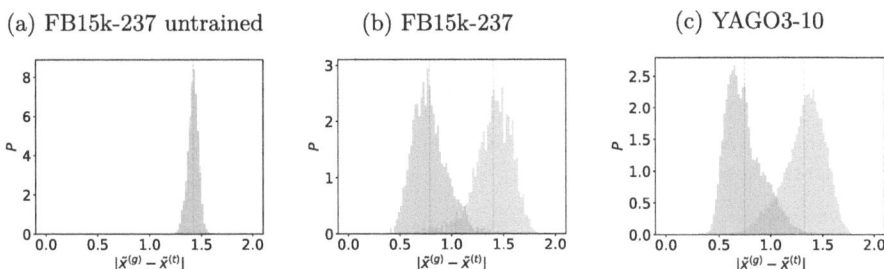

(a) FB15k-237 untrained   (b) FB15k-237   (c) YAGO3-10

Fig. 2. Distribution of the Euclidean distances of the correct (9) and incorrect (10) entity-description associations represented in green and red, respectively. Each embedding vector was normalized before calculating the Euclidean distance. The mean of each distribution is marked by a vertical dashed line. For reference, we also include, in Figure (a), the results obtained by an untrained model. (Color figure online)

In the first case we consider as a measure of alignment the Euclidean distance between the embedding of the entities (5) and descriptions (6) after normalization. We compare the empirical distance distributions P of

– Correct entity-description associations:

$$P\left(\|\tilde{x}_i^{(g)} - \tilde{x}_i^{(t)}\|\right). \tag{9}$$

– Incorrect entity-description associations:

$$P\left(\|\tilde{x}_i^{(g)} - \tilde{x}_j^{(t)}\|_{i \neq j}\right). \tag{10}$$

For alignment of the two latent spaces one would expect a clear separation between the two distributions (9) and (10), with the first (correct associations) shifted more to the left, *i.e.*, closer to zero, than the second (incorrect associations). In Fig. 2 empirical histograms are plotted for the distributions (9) and (10) for the two datasets considered. They were all obtained by training a CompGCN encoder alongside the GPT2 language model with the CLEP procedure of Fig. 1. As expected, there is a clear separation between the correct and incorrect entity-description associations visible. In particular, the mean of the incorrect association distribution is for all datasets almost twice as far away. However, it is interesting to note that a certain degree of overlapping between the distributions (9) and (10) is observable for both the tested datasets. As a consequence, sporadically some of the incorrect associations are located closer than the correct ones. A possible explanation of this may be found in the fact that a similar overlap exists between entity descriptions too. In particular, short descriptions such as "Music genre" or "American actress" are often shared over a wider range of different entities.

Table 2. Link prediction performance obtained by a CompGCN ([16]) trained with the CLEP procedure (*c.f.* Fig. 1) and using the scoring function (11) on the FB15k-237 dataset. For comparison, we also include the results obtained by a RGCN ([12]) baseline. The RGCN has access to the complete graph information (both head and tail nodes are provided), while the CompGCN relies on head nodes and tail descriptions, as illustrated in text.

	MR	MRR	hits@1	hits@10
CompGCN$_{CLEP}$	**198**	0.222	0.137	0.396
RGCN+Distmult	315	**0.237**	**0.156**	**0.407**

As another test of alignment, we tested whether the CLEP procedure allows for link prediction. Being able to predict links between head entities and corresponding tail descriptions, *i.e.*, across the graph and text embedding space, would mean that we can substitute graph information with textual information in our representation and, as a consequence, provide strong evidence that an alignment between the embedding spaces exists.

In general, for link prediction evaluation, each test edge $\epsilon = (h, r, t)$ is corrupted by substituting the tail t with every other possible node in the graph. The corrupted edges are then scored against the original edge to obtain the ranking.

In our case, however, instead of the tail node t, its description d^{tail} is considered. We define the score function f to be the cosine similarity

$$f(h, r, t) = \frac{\mathrm{MLP}_g\big(x_{head}^{(g)}\big) \cdot \mathrm{MLP}_t\big(x_{tail}^{(t)}\big)}{\|\mathrm{MLP}_g\big(x_{head}^{(g)}\big)\| \, \|\mathrm{MLP}_t\big(x_{tail}^{(t)}\big)\|} , \tag{11}$$

with $x_{head}^{(g)}$ and $x_{tail}^{(t)}$ obtained as in (3) and (4), representing the graph embedding of the head translated by the relation and the text encoding of the tail's description. Rankings are obtained by calculating the similarity score (11) for each description d_i in the dataset and comparing it with the score obtained using the correct tail description d^{tail}.

In Table 2 several common link prediction metrics are reported: *Mean Rank* (MR), *Mean Reciprocal Rank* (MRR), *hits@1* and *hits@10*, obtained by a CompGCN ([16]) trained with the CLEP procedure. In the FB15k-237 dataset ([14]), the model was able to be competitive with a RGCN ([12]) baseline trained on the standard link prediction task (i.e. making use of both head and tail entities coming from the graph) and significantly outperformed it for the *Mean Rank* metric. Note that due to GPU memory limitations of our available hardware, we were not able to perform the above link prediction test on the YAGO3-10 dataset ([5]).

(a) FB15k-237

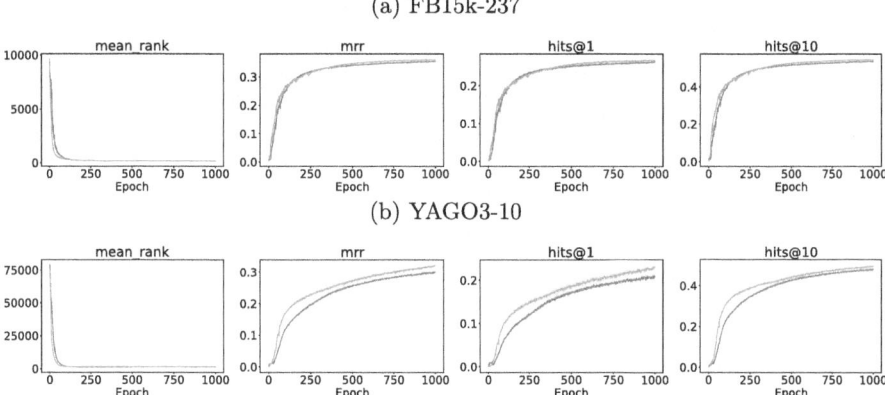

(b) YAGO3-10

Fig. 3. Comparison of several link prediction metrics for the FB15k-237 (a) and the YAGO3-10 (b) datasets, between the baseline model (blue) and the one that was pretrained on the caption prediction task (orange). An CompGCN ([16]) encoder (*batchsize* = 1024) combined with a ConvE ([3]) head was used. The relative metric calculated on the validation set is reported for each epoch of the training. Note that we plot the mean over the performed repetitive runs. The standard deviation is indicated by the shaded regions. (Color figure online)

4.3 Link Prediction Finetuning

In the previous section, we found evidence that the pre-training procedure is able to yield an alignment of the graph and text spaces, making it possible to use to some extent graph and language information interchangeably. Moreover, as the graph and text encoders are unfrozen and free to change during the alignment process, information can flow from one to the other. As a result, we expect that the graph encoder might feature richer node representations, which would allow for improved performance on downstream tasks. In particular, without the need to explicitly provide entity descriptions as additional inputs, as for instance proposed in ([13, 18, 20, 23]).

In order to verify that this is indeed the case, we compare the link prediction performance of a baseline graph encoder and an identical model that has been pretrained with the CLEP procedure. In both cases, we stack on top of the encoder a ConvE ([3]) head to perform link prediction as proposed in ([12,16]). If our hypothesis is correct, the pretrained model should be able to finetune for the task by making use of the additional information learned during pretraining, resulting in a stronger performance. Note that this differs from what is presented in the previous Section as we consider here the standard link prediction scheme in the graph embedding space, i.e. both head and tail entities come from the graph and no entity description is used at this stage.

In Fig. 3 we report the results obtained for the two datasets considered: FB15k-237 ([14]) and YAGO3-10 ([5]). The baseline model (shown in blue) and the one that has undergone the description matching pretraining (in orange) are compared under the commonly used link prediction metrics: *MR, MRR, hits@1* and *hits@10*. All the metrics are calculated on the validation set and plotted for each training epoch. The average metric value across three different runs with randomly initialized weights is represented as a solid line and the standard deviation as a shaded area around the mean.

For the FB15k-237 dataset, we trained the CompGCN encoder for 1000 epochs with a batch size of 1024. The model that has gone through the CLEP pretraining outperforms the vanilla model by a small $1 - 2\%$ margin in most of the metrics. Still, the separation in performance between the two models is visible in Fig. 3a, as the deviation is larger than the standard deviation obtained across the different runs.

For the YAGO3-10 ([5]) dataset, again, the CompGCN ([16]) encoder with the ConvE head ([3]) was trained for 1000 epochs with 1024 batch size. However, the three curves for the different metrics *MRR, hits@1* and *hits@10*, suggest that convergence has not been reached and that both models probably would have benefited from longer training. Unfortunately, since training for 1000 epochs has been already quite time intensive for this dataset, we could not afford to train further due to computational cost. Nonetheless, since the separation between the two models remains consistent over the first 1000 epochs, we expect that longer training would keep the relative performance between the two models intact, but yield larger absolute values for the metrics. In this case we saw an improvement

Table 3. Link prediction performance of a CompGCN ([16]) graph encoder with a ConvE head ([3]) after finetuning, under the four metrics MR, MRR, hits@1 and hits@10. The models for which the entity-description matching pretraining has been performed are marked with a *CLEP* subscript. For reference, we also include the original results reported in ([12,16]) for RGCN and CompGCN, as well as several other *state-of-the-art* models that make use of descriptions: KG-BERT ([23]), LaSS ([13]) and SimKGC ([18]). We indicate with a * all the results that we only report, but that we did not reproduce. In particular, as we have been using a slightly cut-off version of the FB15k-237 dataset, direct comparison with those models is not possible.

		MR	MRR	hits@1	hits@10
FB15k-237	RGCN *	–	0.249	0.151	0.41
	RGCN+Distmult	315	0.237	0.156	0.407
	CompGCN *	199	0.352	0.264	0.530
	CompGCN+ConvE	151	0.354	0.262	0.534
	CompGCN$_{CLEP}$+ConvE	168	**0.359**	**0.266**	**0.544**
	KG-BERT *	153	–	–	0.42
	KG-BERT	137	–	–	0.427
	LaSS *	**108**	–	–	0.533
	SimKGC *	-	0.336	0.249	0.511
YAGO3-10	CompGCN+ConvE	1299	0.302	0.211	0.480
	CompGCN$_{CLEP}$+ConvE	1369	**0.323**	**0.233**	**0.498**

for the CLEP based model in the *MRR*, *hits@1* and *hits@10* metrics ranging in the $\sim 6 - 9\%$ interval.

In Table 3 we report the summary of the performance obtained in our experiments with and without the entity-description matching pretraining. For reference, we also include the results obtained by several other models found in the literature. Note, however, that direct comparison on the FB15k-237 dataset is not possible as we have been using a slightly cut off dataset. Nonetheless, the results reported in ([16]) for the CompGCN on the full dataset are in line with our CompGCN baselines, indicating that the complexity of the task did not decrease. No one of the aforementioned models was tested on the YAGO3-10 dataset in the original works.

5   Conclusion and Future Work

In summary, in this work we proposed an architecture to learn a multi-modal joint graph-text embedding by training a graph encoder and a language model to generate aligned representations of KB entities and their descriptions. We were able to verify successful alignment for two popular Knowledge Bases (Wikidata and YAGO) by measuring the Euclidean distance between embeddings generated for matching entity and description pairs. We also demonstrated that a model trained on the entity-description matching task is able to perform link prediction across the graph and text spaces, providing additional strong evidence of successful alignment.

Furthermore, our experiments on the link prediction task showed that a graph encoder pre-trained with our proposed scheme achieves better performance compared to a randomly initialized encoder in the majority of cases. This indicates that the entity-description matching allows the encoder to learn richer node representations. We suspect that this is due to some of the information contained in the descriptions being able to flow from the language model to the graph encoder during pre-training. Therefore, the graph encoder gained additional textual information, which becomes available for downstream tasks without the need of explicitly providing it. This warrants further research to verify that, firstly, the graph encoder manifests the same improvements in other graph-related tasks, such as node classification, and vice versa, that the language model similarly benefits from the joint pre-training. Moreover, it will be interesting to test whether the combined use of the two aligned encoders enables zero-shot classification capabilities as demonstrated by CLIP ([9]). Zero-Shot Entity Linking, for instance, appears to be a perfect candidate for future experiments.

We believe that the multi-modal graph-text embedding presented in this work might form a foundation for the joint processing of tasks involving graphical and textual information, similar to what CLIP ([9]) achieved for text and images. In particular, one example of such a task may be found in graph generation from textual inputs. This is similar in spirit to the popular stable diffusion model for image generation ([11]), which is based on the multi-modal image-text embedding provided by CLIP ([9]). The envisaged mechanism of generating a graph from textual inputs could be viewed as an alternative way to perform information extraction from unstructured text and will be an interesting avenue for future research.

References

1. Bastos, A., Nadgeri, A., Singh, K., Mulang, I.O., Shekarpour, S., Hoffart, J., Kaul, M.: Recon: Relation extraction using knowledge graph context in a graph neural network. In: Proceedings of the Web Conference 2021. p. 1673-1685. WWW '21, Association for Computing Machinery, New York, NY, USA (2021). https://doi.org/10.1145/3442381.3449917, https://doi.org/10.1145/3442381.3449917
2. Bordes, A., Usunier, N., Garcia-Duran, A., Weston, J., Yakhnenko, O.: Translating embeddings for modeling multi-relational data. In: Burges, C., Bottou, L., Welling, M., Ghahramani, Z., Weinberger, K. (eds.) Advances in Neural Information Processing Systems. vol. 26. Curran Associates, Inc. (2013), https://proceedings.neurips.cc/paper/2013/file/1cecc7a77928ca8133fa24680a88d2f9-Paper.pdf
3. Dettmers, T., Minervini, P., Stenetorp, P., Riedel, S.: Convolutional 2d knowledge graph embeddings (2017https://doi.org/10.48550/ARXIV.1707.01476, https://arxiv.org/abs/1707.01476
4. Devlin, J., Chang, M.W., Lee, K., Toutanova, K.: Bert: Pre-training of deep bidirectional transformers for language understanding (2018).https://doi.org/10.48550/ARXIV.1810.04805, https://arxiv.org/abs/1810.04805
5. Mahdisoltani, F., Biega, J.A., Suchanek, F.M.: Yago3: A knowledge base from multilingual wikipedias. In: Conference on Innovative Data Systems Research (2015)
6. Mokady, R., Hertz, A., Bermano, A.H.: Clipcap: Clip prefix for image captioning (2021https://doi.org/10.48550/ARXIV.2111.09734, https://arxiv.org/abs/2111.09734
7. Nadgeri, A., Bastos, A., Singh, K., Mulang', I.O., Hoffart, J., Shekarpour, S., Saraswat, V.: KGPool: Dynamic knowledge graph context selection for relation extraction. In: Findings of the Association for Computational Linguistics: ACL-IJCNLP 2021. pp. 535–548. Association for Computational Linguistics, Online (Aug 2021https://doi.org/10.18653/v1/2021.findings-acl.48, https://aclanthology.org/2021.findings-acl.48
8. Papaluca, A., Krefl, D., Suominen, H., Lenskiy, A.: Pretrained knowledge base embeddings for improved sentential relation extraction. In: Proceedings of the 60th Annual Meeting of the Association for Computational Linguistics: Student Research Workshop. pp. 373–382. Association for Computational Linguistics, Dublin, Ireland (May 2022https://doi.org/10.18653/v1/2022.acl-srw.29, https://aclanthology.org/2022.acl-srw.29
9. Radford, A., Kim, J.W., Hallacy, C., Ramesh, A., Goh, G., Agarwal, S., Sastry, G., Askell, A., Mishkin, P., Clark, J., Krueger, G., Sutskever, I.: Learning transferable visual models from natural language supervision. CoRR **abs/2103.00020** (2021), https://arxiv.org/abs/2103.00020
10. Radford, A., Wu, J., Child, R., Luan, D., Amodei, D., Sutskever, I.: Language models are unsupervised multitask learners. In: nill (2019)
11. Rombach, R., Blattmann, A., Lorenz, D., Esser, P., Ommer, B.: High-resolution image synthesis with latent diffusion models (2021).https://doi.org/10.48550/ARXIV.2112.10752, https://arxiv.org/abs/2112.10752

12. Schlichtkrull, M., Kipf, T.N., Bloem, P., Berg, R.v.d., Titov, I., Welling, M.: Modeling relational data with graph convolutional networks (2017).https://doi.org/10.48550/ARXIV.1703.06103, https://arxiv.org/abs/1703.06103

13. Shen, J., Wang, C., Gong, L., Song, D.: Joint language semantic and structure embedding for knowledge graph completion. In: Proceedings of the 29th International Conference on Computational Linguistics. pp. 1965–1978. International Committee on Computational Linguistics, Gyeongju, Republic of Korea (Oct 2022), https://aclanthology.org/2022.coling-1.171

14. Toutanova, K., Chen, D.: Observed versus latent features for knowledge base and text inference. In: Proceedings of the 3rd Workshop on Continuous Vector Space Models and their Compositionality. pp. 57–66. Association for Computational Linguistics, Beijing, China (Jul 2015).https://doi.org/10.18653/v1/W15-4007, https://aclanthology.org/W15-4007

15. Vashishth, S., Joshi, R., Prayaga, S.S., Bhattacharyya, C., Talukdar, P.: RESIDE: Improving distantly-supervised neural relation extraction using side information. In: Proceedings of the 2018 Conference on Empirical Methods in Natural Language Processing. pp. 1257–1266. Association for Computational Linguistics, Brussels, Belgium (Oct-Nov 2018https://doi.org/10.18653/v1/D18-1157, https://aclanthology.org/D18-1157

16. Vashishth, S., Sanyal, S., Nitin, V., Talukdar, P.: Composition-based multi-relational graph convolutional networks (2019).https://doi.org/10.48550/ARXIV.1911.03082, https://arxiv.org/abs/1911.03082

17. Vrandečić, D.: Wikidata: A new platform for collaborative data collection. In: Proceedings of the 21st International Conference on World Wide Web. p. 1063-1064. WWW '12 Companion, Association for Computing Machinery, New York, NY, USA (2012https://doi.org/10.1145/2187980.2188242, https://doi.org/10.1145/2187980.2188242

18. Wang, L., Zhao, W., Wei, Z., Liu, J.: SimKGC: Simple contrastive knowledge graph completion with pre-trained language models. In: Proceedings of the 60th Annual Meeting of the Association for Computational Linguistics (Volume 1: Long Papers). pp. 4281–4294. Association for Computational Linguistics, Dublin, Ireland (May 2022https://doi.org/10.18653/v1/2022.acl-long.295, https://aclanthology.org/2022.acl-long.295

19. Wu, L., Petroni, F., Josifoski, M., Riedel, S., Zettlemoyer, L.: Scalable zero-shot entity linking with dense entity retrieval. In: Proceedings of the 2020 Conference on Empirical Methods in Natural Language Processing (EMNLP). pp. 6397–6407. Association for Computational Linguistics, Online (Nov 2020).https://doi.org/10.18653/v1/2020.emnlp-main.519, https://aclanthology.org/2020.emnlp-main.519

20. Xie, R., Liu, Z., Jia, J., Luan, H., Sun, M.: Representation learning of knowledge graphs with entity descriptions. Proceedings of the AAAI Conference on Artificial Intelligence **30**(1) (Mar 2016).https://doi.org/10.1609/aaai.v30i1.10329, https://ojs.aaai.org/index.php/AAAI/article/view/10329

21. Yamada, I., Asai, A., Sakuma, J., Shindo, H., Takeda, H., Takefuji, Y., Matsumoto, Y.: Wikipedia2Vec: An efficient toolkit for learning and visualizing the embeddings of words and entities from Wikipedia. In: Proceedings of the 2020 Conference on Empirical Methods in Natural Language Processing: System Demonstrations. pp. 23–30. Association for Computational Linguistics, Online (Oct 2020https://doi.org/10.18653/v1/2020.emnlp-demos.4, https://aclanthology.org/2020.emnlp-demos.4

22. Yang, B., Yih, W.t., He, X., Gao, J., Deng, L.: Embedding entities and relations for learning and inference in knowledge bases (2014).https://doi.org/10.48550/ARXIV.1412.6575, https://arxiv.org/abs/1412.6575

23. Yao, L., Mao, C., Luo, Y.: Kg-bert: Bert for knowledge graph completion (2019).https://doi.org/10.48550/ARXIV.1909.03193, https://arxiv.org/abs/1909.03193

24. Yasunaga, M., Bosselut, A., Ren, H., Zhang, X., Manning, C.D., Liang, P., Leskovec, J.: Deep bidirectional language-knowledge graph pretraining (2022).https://doi.org/10.48550/ARXIV.2210.09338, https://arxiv.org/abs/2210.09338

Fine-Tuning Pre-trained Model with Prototype Learning for OOD Detection

Jia-Yi Liu$^{(\boxtimes)}$ and Zhi-Dong Deng

Department of Computer Science and Technology, Tsinghua University,
Beijing, China
liujiayi20@mails.tsinghua.edu.cn, michael@tsinghua.edu.c

Abstract. Out-of-distribution (OOD) detection primarily learns the in-distribution (ID) representation to distinguish OOD samples from ID classes. Recent methods often fine-tune a pre-trained model with classification objective (cross-entropy, CE) to learn ID representation, disregarding the discrimination between ID and unknown OOD. In this work, we propose to fine-tune pre-trained models in the framework of open-set recognition, which trains a multi-class classifier with ID samples while considering OOD rejection according to distances to ID classes. We adopt prototype learning, which aims to discriminate the ID classes while guiding compact distributions for ID classes in the feature space. The compact ID distributions favor classification and OOD detection using distances, including Euclidean distance and Mahalanobis distance. We evaluated the method on various backbone architectures including ResNet, ViTs and BEiT, and the results show that the prototype learning method on pre-trained models outperforms classification-based method and produces state-of-the-art performance in OOD detection.

Keywords: Out-of-distribution Detection (OOD) · Pre-trained models (PTM) · Open-set recognition · Prototype learning

1 Introduction

Anomaly detection (AD) [1], which is also called out-of-distribution(OOD) detection, is the task of determining if a sample deviates from the distribution of known classes (in-distribution (ID) classes). OOD detection is useful and required in many application fields, where the recognition model inevitably encounters inputs that are beyond the classes that the model has learned. A reliable visual recognition system not only provides correct predictions on ID data but also detects unknown OOD samples and rejects them to human intervention for safety purposes. It is often found in many safety-critical areas such as healthcare [2], fraud detection [3], and autonomous driving [4].

Many previous OOD detection many rely on outlier exposure (OE) [5] to achieve decent performance of OOD detection, which basically transform OOD

C. Wallraven et al. (Eds.): ICPRAI 2024, LNCS 14892, pp. 247–201, 2025.
https://doi.org/10.1007/978-981-97-8702-9_17

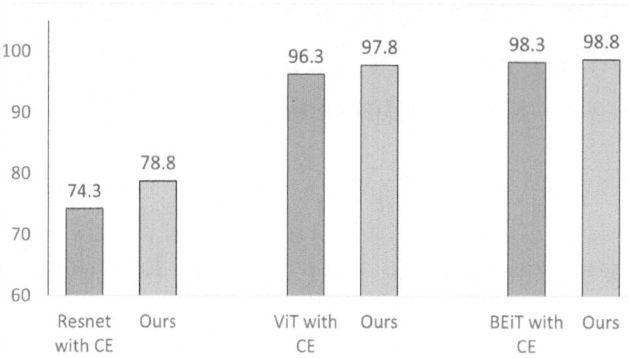

Fig. 1. OOD detection performance (AUROC) using different pre-trained backbone architectures, adopting CIFAR-100 as ID and CIFAR-10 as OOD.

detection into a binary classification problem, requiring outlier samples in training. These methods tend to perform very poorly when outlier samples are not available. Since outlier/anomaly samples are usually hard to collect in practical applications, recent works tend to design OOD detection models without training with outlier samples. These methods learn the ID representation from ID samples only to discover the boundary of ID distributions, in the spirit of one-class classification [6], so as to identify OOD samples according to the deviation from ID distribution or distance from ID class centers.

In the framework of OOD detection using neural network models, the performance of OOD detection largely depends on the representation ability of the backbone network and the classification and rejection rule, Existing methods mostly focused on the learning of backbone architecture. Self-supervised learning algorithms, such as contrasive learning [7] have been found very effective for pre-training representation model from a large dataset [8]. The pre-trained model, after fine-tuned on labeled data of downstream tasks, can achieve high performance. For OOD detection, previous methods usually fine-tuned pre-trained models under the generic classification objective, e.g., cross-entropy of softmax probabilities. This indeed can adapt the feature representation to facilitate OOD detection as ID classification because of the discrimination ability of representation. However, classification-oriented training or fine-tuning is likely to suffer from overfitting, i.e., adapting the feature presentation to fit the ID data of closed set, and resulting lower-dimensional representation that is unfavorable for open world classification. Previous research on backdoor attack [9] also shows that when learning through a closed-world assumed classification task, networks tend to take a shortcut to classify known-class samples. Also, classification-oriented fine-tuning ignores the separation boundary between ID and OOD data, so the learned representation maybe unfavorable to OOD detection.

Similarly, there have been many methods proposed to open-set recognition (OSR) [10], which can be viewed as an extended task of OOD detection, in the sense that both OOD detection and ID classification are performed. Some

OSR methods based on generative models assume that the ID classes undergo compact local distributions in the feature space, so that classification and OOD detection can be decided according to the distances to ID class centers or probability densities. This framework can be applied to OOD model design by learning local distributions for known classes from ID data only. Inspired by the open-set recognition method convolutional prototype network [11], we propose to fine-tune pre-trained models with prototype learning for OOD detection. Owing to the compact ID distributions learned by prototype learning, OOD detection can be performed using distances, including Euclidean distance and Mahalanobis distance. We evaluated the method on various backbone pre-trained models (PTMs) including ResNet and ViTs, and the results show that the prototype learning method on pre-trained models outperforms classification-based method. And when using advanced vision transformer as backbone, state-of-the-art performance in OOD detection can be achieved. Figure 1 shows the OOD detection results (AUROC) on three backbone architectures (ResNet, ViT and BEiT). It is shown that fine-tuning using prototype learning objective can improve the OOD detection performance evidently.

The contributions of this paper is summarized as follows:

– We propose a fine-tuning method based on open-set recognition framework using prototype learning, which trains a multi-class classifier with ID samples while guiding compact local distributions for the known classes, so that OOD samples can be rejected according to distances to known classes.
– We implement the fine-tuning method with various backbone architectures as pre-trained models, and the results show that fine-tuning with prototype learning improves the OOD detection performance significantly, and with strong transformer backbone, the proposed method yields state-of-the-art performance.

2 Related Work

2.1 Out-of-Distribution Detection

Out-of-distribution (OOD) detection usually assume that outlier samples are distant from the high-density region of in-distribution (ID) samples. Therefore, the majority of existing OOD detection approaches estimates the ID density and reject test samples that deviate from the estimated density [12–14]. Alternative methods include reconstruction-based methods [15,16], decision boundary learning [17–19], distance computing between training and test features [20–22]. These methods assume that the ID samples distributed in a subspace from which outlier samples deviate.

The proposed method in this paper falls in distance-based methods, which underlie the assumption that OOD samples are distant from the center of the ID data [23] in the feature space. The detection performance largely relies on the design of the distance metric and the feature space. Well known baseline methods in this line of approaches include the maximum softmax probability

(MSP) [24] which learns feature space by minimizing the cross-entropy (CE) loss on the output softmax probabilities, and uses the MSP as the decision rule for OOD detection. Improved performance has been achieved when using the Mahalanobis distance [25] as decision rule, which assumes Gaussian distribution to each ID class or the union of ID classes. The Mahalanobis distance performs better than MSP and the Euclidean distance because it takes advantage of the Gaussian distribution. Alternative distance-based methods include k-nearest neighbors (k-NN) [22], prototype-based methods [26], energy score [27], and virtual-logit matching (ViM) [28].

2.2 Vision Transformer

Deep neural networks have been popularly used for feature representation learning for various computer vision and pattern recognition tasks including OOD detection. In the past, the convolutional neural network (CNN) was popularly used to computer vision tasks. And recently, the vision transformer (ViT), which is based on self-attention mechanism, is showing superior performance in representation learning. The transformer architecture [29] was initially proposed for natural language processing (NLP) tasks, and later extended to process images. Transformer networks have achieved outstanding performance in computer vision (such as the BEiT [30]) and NLP (such as the BERT [31]). Since transformer networks have large number of weight parameters than CNN and need much more data for training, they are often pre-trained on unlabeled data by unsupervised or self-supervised learning, and when applied to specific downstream tasks, a small labeled dataset is used to fine-tune the network for achieved high performance. Vision transformer networks are usually pre-trained on the ImageNet-21k dataset [32]. This strategy has been applied to OOD detection [33] using vision transformer (ViT) [34]. A latest work in this line is the masked image modeling (MIM) for OOD detection (MOOD) [35]. Due to the powerful representation learning ability, ViT models can achieve high OOD detection performance even when fine-tuning without outlier data and using simple metrics such as MSP, remarkably outperforming CNN. Adding a few outlier samples in fine-tuning (called as Outlier Exposure [36]) can further improve the performance. However, in practical applications, outlier samples are hard to collect, OOD detection models are usually trained without outlier data, which makes the OOD detection problem more challenging.

2.3 Open-Set Recognition

Open-set recognition (OSR) can be viewed as an extended task of OOD detection in that it performs ID classification in additional to OOD detection: when the input sample is accepted as ID, it is classified into an ID class. The model is a multi-class classifier which outputs probability/distance/similarity/logit scores to each ID class. OOD detection/rejection is usually decided according to the maximum probability/logit of minimum distance of ID classes. The performance of OSR (ID classification accuracy and OOD rejection AUROC) also relies on the feature representation and the classification rule. It is usually desired that the ID classes are separated well and the OOD samples are distant from the local density regions of ID classes. Many methods have been proposed for OSR [10], including traditional methods based on hand-crafted features and deep neural networks which learns feature representation. Traditional methods include statistics based methods [37–39], distance based methods [40], reconstruction based methods [41–43], domain based methods [44,45], and information theory based methods. Statistics or density based methods and distance based methods assume each ID class distributed in a local region in feature space. Reconstruction based methods assume that ID samples can be projected into a low-dimensional subspace with low error while OOD samples have high reconstruction error when projecting onto the ID subspace.

As to neural network based methods, Augusteijn and Folkert [46] proposed using threshold based multi-layer perception (MLP) for novelty detection. Hawkins et al. [47] and Williams et al. [48] proposed to train an auto-encoder on known samples and use the reconstruction error to distinguish between ID and OOD data. In recent years, deep neural networks (such as CNN and auto-encoder) are more popularly in OSR. The methods can be categorized into discriminative models and generative models [10]. Some methods re-calibrate (post-process) the output scores while training the network using closed-set classification objective (such as CE on softmax probabilities) and some latest methods consider OOD boundary during network training, such as the convolutional prototype network [11]. The CPN performs classification and OOD rejection according to distances to known (ID) classes. While in training, in addition to the classification objective (distance-based CE loss), a prototype loss (PL) is used to guide feature space learning to produce compact distribution for each known class. In our OOD detection method, we take the inspiration of prototype learning, and use pre-trained transformer network instead of CNN to achieve superior performance.

3   The Proposed Method

Our proposed out-of-distribution (OOD) detection method is based on the framework that a pre-trained network is fine-tuned on the in-distribution (ID) dataset with the objective of both classification and OOD bounding. Unlike that most previous methods performed fine-tuning using ID classification objective (such as cross-entropy on softmax probabilities) only, we further consider the boundary between ID and OOD data even though OOD samples are not available in training. Inspired by the open-set recognition method convolutional prototype network (CPN) [11], we assume each ID class has a compact density in feature space and learn a prototype for each class (prototype learning), so that OOD samples can be differentiated according to the distances from ID class prototypes. Based on prototype learning, using Mahalanobis distance instead of Euclidean distance can give even higher OOD detection performance.

For a given ID dataset X_{ID}, the goal of OOD detection is to identify whether an input image belongs to ID ($x \in X_{ID}$) or OOD ($x \notin X_{ID}$). Generally, an OOD score function $s(x)$ is defined to indicate $x \notin X_{ID}$ when $s(x)$ is greater than a threshold. For performance evaluation, multiple thresholds are used to give the receiver operating characteristic curve (ROC) measuring the trade-off between the true positive (correct identification of OOD) and false positive (accepting ID as OOD) rates. The area under ROC curve (AUROC) is taken as the overall performance metric of OOD detection. In the case of multi-class ID learning, the closed-set classification accuracy (Acc) is also reported.

3.1   Pre-trained Models and OOD Detection Performance

Both the network architecture and the score function are important to the OOD detection performance. To choose the effective pre-trained model (PTM) as the backbone for our method, we compared the performance of several PTMs, including Big Transfer (BiT) [31], MLP-Mixer and ViT's performance on OOD detection as conducted in [33]. In addition, we evaluate the state-of-the-art network BEiT [30] as used in the recent MIM based OOD (MOOD) detection method [35], where the BEiT model was pre-trained with Masked Image Modeling (MIM) pretext on a large dataset and fine-tuned on the ID dataset. In comparing these networks, the ID and OOD datasets are CIFAR-100 and CIFAR-10 [49], respectively. This is considered a hard near-OOD task since the two sets are very close in semantics and construction.

Table 1. Various PTMs versus AUROC (%) of OOD detection. The bold items indicate the best results. The ID and OOD datasets are CIFAR-100 and CIFAR-10, respectively.

PTM	Fine-tuning Acc (%)	AUROC (%)
BiT R50 [33]	87.01	81.71
BiT R101 [33]	91.55	90.10
MLP-Mixer [33]	90.40	95.31
ViT-B_16 [33]	90.95	95.53
R50 + ViT_16 [33]	91.71	96.23
ViT-L_16	92.50	96.30
BEiT	**94.28**	**98.30**

The results in Table 1 show that the backbone vision transformers (ViTs) significantly outperform other PTMs as they are utilized to generate the AUROC score of any OOD detection tasks. Although the method R50 + ViT [34] produced state-of-the-art results on near-distribution OOD detection [33], where the CNN architecture ResNet50 was used for visual feature extraction, the simple transformer architecture ViT-Large-16 with more parameters yields better performance in both fine-tuning accuracy and OOD detection AUROC. The advanced transformer architecture BEiT performs best among these PTMs. We will evaluate some representative CNN and transformer architectures as PTM in our framework of fune-tuning with prototype learning.

3.2   Fine-Tuning PTM with Prototype Learning

Following previous methods [33], we use a vision transformer (ViT) pre-trained on the large image dataset ImageNet-21k [32] as the backbone of OOD detection model, then fine-tune the full network on the downstream OOD detection task using multi-class ID data.

Unlike many previous methods that fine-tuned the OOD detection model using the ordinary classification objective (cross-entropy (CE) loss), which considers the boundary between ID classes but not the boundary between ID and OOD data. Without OOD data in training, we assume that each ID class distributes in a compact local region in the feature space, so that OOD samples can be detected according to the distances to ID class prototypes. Inspired by the open-set recognition framework convolutional prototype network (CPN) (CPN) [11], we adopt the distance-based cross entropy (DCE) loss and the prototype loss into the fine-tuning of pre-trained transformer networks for OOD detection.

In prototype-based classification, the class posterior probabilities are calculated by distance-based softmax. Assume each ID class i has K prototypes $m_{ij} \in R^d$ (d is the dimensionality of feature space). For a training samples (x, y) (x denoting sample image and y denoting class label), the probability of ground-truth class y is

$$p(y|x) = \sum_{j=1}^{K} p(x \in m_{ij}|x),\tag{1}$$

where

$$p(x \in m_{ij}|x) = \frac{e^{-\gamma d(f(x), m_{ij})}}{\sum_{k=1}^{C} \sum_{l=1}^{K} e^{-\gamma d(f(x), m_{lk})}},\tag{2}$$

where $f(x)$ denotes the feature vector extracted by the backbone network, and $d(f(x), m_{ij})$ represents the square Euclidean distance between the feature vector and the prototype m_{ij}. The prototypes m_{ij} are learnable parameters together with the connecting weights of the backbone network. Using a deep neural network as backbone, using only one prototype ($K = 1$) per class performs sufficiently well, as shown in previous works [11].

Based on the class conditional probability $p(y|x)$, the distance-based cross-entropy (DCE) loss is calculated as

$$loss_{DCE}((x, y), \theta) = -\log p(y|x),\tag{3}$$

where θ denotes the set of model parameters (including the prototypes).

The minimization of DCE loss yields similar effect of ID classification to the ordinary CE loss on softmax probabilities. This objective does not consider the boundary between ID and OOD data, however. To improve the OOD detection performance, we can thus combine the prototype loss (PL) [11]:

$$loss_{PL}((x, y), \theta) = d(f(x), m_{ij}),\tag{4}$$

which was derived from the maximum likelihood criterion under the assumption of hyper-spherical Gaussian density per class. The total loss in training (fine-tuning) is thus

$$loss = loss_{DCE} + \lambda * loss_{PL} \tag{5}$$

Intuitively, we can observe that the minimization of the DCE and PL losses results in the decrease of the distances of ID sample from the prototype of true class and the increase of the ones to all prototypes of incorrect classes. The incorporation of PL loss results in the decrease of mutual distance between ID samples of the same class, so that the samples of one class distribute in a compact local subspace. This is helpful to overcome the overfitting of ordinary CE learning which aims to maximize the between-class discrimination without regarding the compactness of within-class distribution. The compactness of within-class distribution is intuitively helpful to OOD detection because the distance of ID samples to ID class prototype is kept small while OOD samples are more distant from ID class prototypes.

3.3   OOD Detection Score

Commonly-used OOD detection scores include the maximum softmax probability (MSP) [24], Entropy [50], Energy [27], GradNorm [51] and Mahalanobis distance [25]. Euclidean distance is usually used for prototype-based classification and detection. Mahalanobis distance may yield higher performance than Euclidean distance because the actual ID class distribution is not guaranteed to be spherically Gaussian though withi-class compactness is assumed by the prototype loss (PL). Even when training networks under softmax based CE, Mahalanobis distance has also shown high performance in OOD detection [33]. In our experiments of OOD detection, we thus use Mahalanobis distance and Euclidean distance for prototype-based OOD detection. Mahalanobis distance is also used for the ordinary CE-based model (baseline) for its higher performance than MSP.

4   Experiments

We evaluate our prototype learning based fine-tuning method on some representative backbone architectures (including CNN and ViTs), compared with the baseline method of fine-tuning with multi-class classification CE loss.

4.1   Experimental Setup

Following previous works [33], we evaluate the OOD detection performance by means of the commonly used Area Under the ROC Curve (AUROC) as a threshold-free metric. We perform experiments on the CIFAR-10 dataset [49], which consists of 50,000 training image samples and 10,000 test ones in 10 classes, and the CIFAR-100 dataset [49], which contains 50,000 training image samples and 10,000 test ones in 100 classes. We alternately employ the above two datasets as ID and OOD samples, respectively.

In terms of the backbone architecture, we evaluate the representative transformer models ViT-Base_16, ViT-Large_16, and BEiT pre-trained on ImageNet-21k [32], as well as the CNN model ResNet18 pre-trained on ImageNet-21k. We fine-tune the whole model with three loss functions: classification CE (baseline), DCE and DCE+PL, in an end-to-end manner for 200 epochs. We set the DCE hyper-parameter $\gamma = 0.1$ and $\lambda = 0.01$.

4.2   One-Class OOD Detection

Following prior work [33], we also evaluate the OOD detection performance in one-class setting: the multiple ID classes are unified into one positive class, though multi-class objective is taken in model training (fine-tuning). In this case, Mahalanobis distance to the ID distribution center can still yield promising OOD detection performance. We conduct our experiments on two datasets, CIFAR-10 and CIFAR-100, which are adopted as ID and OOD datasets alternately. The results are shown in Table 2 and Table 3.

Table 2. One-class OOD detection. AUROC (%) comparison of different fine-tuning methods, with CIFAR-10 as ID and CIFAR-100 as OOD.

PTM Architecture	Baseline AUROC (%)	DCE AUROC (%)	DCE+PL AUROC (%)
ResNet18	88.32	89.36↑	91.50↑
ViT-B_16	97.30	97.23	97.50↑
ViT-L_16	97.60	97.73↑	98.05↑
BEiT	98.50	98.84↑	**99.00**↑

Table 3. One-class OOD detection. AUROC (%) comparison of different fine-tuning methods, with CIFAR- 100 as ID and CIFAR-10 as OOD.

PTM Architecture	Baseline AUROC (%)	DCE AUROC (%)	DCE+PL AUROC (%)
ResNet18	72.18	76.45↑	78.36↑
ViT-B_16	95.53	95.10	96.51↑
ViT-L_16	96.30	95.38	97.30↑
BEiT	97.50	98.16↑	**98.30**↑

The results in Tables 2 and 3 show that compared to the baseline fune-tuning method, the proposed DCE-based prototype learning method performs comparably or slightly better, while the DCE+PL method outperforms the baseline method significantly in all the cases. This implies that combining the prototype loss is critical to enhance the advantage of prototype learning in one-class OOD detection task.

Table 4. Multi-class OOD detection. AUROC (%) comparison of different funetuning methods, with CIFAR-10 as ID and CIFAR-100 as OOD.

PTM Architecture	Metric	Baseline AUROC (%)	DCE AUROC (%)	DCE+PL AUROC (%)
ResNet18	Mahalanobis	90.61	90.70↑	91.88↑
	Euclidean	–	92.90↑	93.85↑
ViT-B_16	Mahalanobis	97.50	97.85↑	98.10↑
	Euclidean	–	96.90	97.78↑
ViT-L_16	Mahalanobis	98.00	98.27↑	98.50↑
	Euclidean	–	97.80	98.10↑
BEiT	Mahalanobis	99.40	99.16	**99.50↑**
	Euclidean	–	98.50	98.86

Table 5. Multi-class OOD detection. AUROC (%) comparison of different fine-tuning methods, wtih CIFAR-100 as ID and CIFAR-10 as OOD.

PTM Architecture	Metric	Baseline AUROC (%)	DCE AUROC (%)	DCE+PL AUROC (%)
ResNet18	Mahalanobis	74.36	77.68↑	78.85↑
	Euclidean	–	78.80↑	79.04↑
ViT-B_16	Mahalanobis	95.81	96.01↑	97.54↑
	Euclidean	–	95.90↑	97.48↑
ViT-L_16	Mahalanobis	96.13	96.70↑	97.81↑
	Euclidean	–	96.30↑	97.19↑
BEiT	Mahalanobis	98.30	98.51↑	**98.80↑**
	Euclidean	–	98.21	98.75↑

4.3   Multi-class OOD Detection

In the multi-class OOD detection setting, the fine-tuned model is used as a multi-class classifier. Besides ID classification, OOD is identified according to the maximum posterior probability or minimum distance to ID class prototypes. We conduct experiments on datasets CIFAR-10 and CIFAR-100, which are used as ID and OOD alternately. Mahalanobis distances to class centers and Euclidean distances to learned prototypes are used as decision metrics for OOD detection. The results are shown in Table 5.

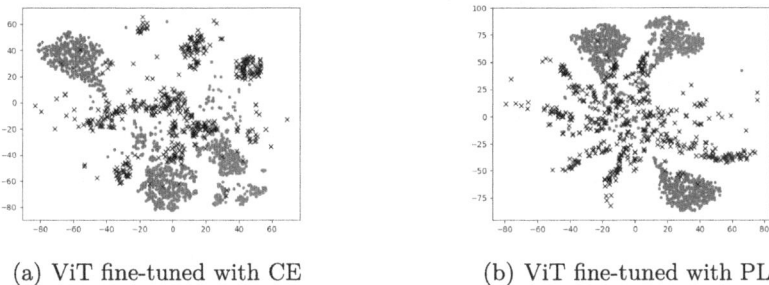

(a) ViT fine-tuned with CE   (b) ViT fine-tuned with PL

Fig. 2. 2D projection by t-SNE of the embedding vectors for (a) $ViT-L\_16$ fine-tuned with cross-entropy (CE) and (b) $ViT-L\_16$ fine-tuned with prototype learning (DCE+PL), with examples of 3 ID classes from CIFAR-10 and OOD samples from CIFAR-100. The colored points are projections of three ID classes "plane" (blue plus dots), "car" (green dots) and "bird" (red dots), while the black crosses are the OOD samples. (Color figure online)

The results in Tables 4 and 5 show that when using Mahalanobis distance for OOD detection, the DCE based fine-tuning method outperforms the baseline CE method slightly on all the backbone architectures, and the DCE+PL further improves the performance. This demonstrate the advantage of prototype learning in fine-tuning pre-trained models. Particularly, the use of prototype loss (PL) in training is effective based on its effect of generating compact ID class distributions. Using Euclidean distance to learned prototypes, the OOD detection performance is also promising, while the PL loss leads to remarkable improvement. Comparing the backbone architectures, the advanced transformer model BEiT produced the best performance via fine-tuning with prototype learning method.

To show the effects on sample distribution by prototype learning, we plot the 2D projections of three ID classes (from CIFAR-10) and OOD samples from CIFAR-100 using the t-SNE algorithm, as shown in Fig. 2. It shown that the ViT fine-tuned with the baseline CE method is able to discriminate ID classes from each other, but does not guarantee compact distribution for each class (for some classes, the samples are dispersed), and so, OOD samples many overlap with ID distributions in the feature space. On the other hand, the ViT fine-tuned with PL leads to compact distributions of ID classes, and the overlapping of OOD samples with ID distributions is mitigated. Compact distributions of ID classes also facilitate distance-based classification and OOD detection.

5   Conclusion

In this paper, to improve the performance of OOD detection using pre-trained models, we cast fine-tuning in the framework of open-set recognition using prototype learning, which trains a multi-class classifier with ID samples while considering the rejection of unknown OOD according to distance to ID class prototypes. We apply prototype learning to vision transformer (ViT) architectures for achieving high performance. In experiments on various backbone architectures including ResNet, ViTs and BEiT, the prototype learning method is demonstrated effective in improving the OOD detection performance on various architectures. Particularly, the fine-tuned BEiT yields state-of-the-art performance on benchmark datasets. In the future, the prototype learning based fine-tuning method can be applied to more advanced backbone architectures and evaluated on more datasets in different application scenarios.

References

1. Chandola, V., Banerjee, A., Kumar, V.: Anomaly detection: a survey. ACM Comput. Surv. **41**(3), 1–58 (2009)
2. Roy A.G., Ren J., Azizi S.,et al.: Does your dermatology classifier know what it doesn't know? Detecting the long-tail of unseen conditions. arXiv preprint arXiv:2104.03829,2021
3. Phua C., Lee V., Smith K., Gayler R.: A comprehensive survey of data mining based fraud detection research. arXiv preprint arXiv:1009.6119, 2010
4. Feng R., Chen J., Fernandes E., et al.: Robust physical hard-label attacks on deep learning visual classification. In: Proceedings of the IEEE Conference on Computer Vision and Pattern Recognition, pp. 1625–1634 (2018)
5. Sehwag V., Chiang M., Mittal P.: SSD: a unified framework for self-supervised outlier detection. arXiv preprint arXiv:2103.12051, 2021
6. Ruff L., Vandermeulen R., Goernitz N., et al.: Deep one-class classification. In: International Conference on Machine Learning. PMLR, pp. 4393–4402 (2018)
7. Krishnan, R., Rajpurkar, P., Topol, E.J.: Self-supervised learning in medicine and healthcare. Nat. Biomed. Eng. **6**(12), 1346–1352 (2022)
8. Fort S., Ren J., Lakshminarayanan B.: Exploring the limits of out-of-distribution detection. In: Advances in Neural Information Processing Systems 34 (NeurIPS 2021) (2021)
9. Saha A., Subramanya A., Pirsiavash H.: Hidden trigger backdoor attacks. In: Proceedings of the AAAI Conference on Artificial Intelligence, vol. 34, no. 07, pp. 11957–11965 (2020)
10. Geng, C., Huang, S.-J., Chen, S.: Recent advances in open set recognition: a survey. IEEE Trans. Pattern Anal. Mach. Intell. **43**(10), 3614–3631 (2021)
11. Yang, H.M., Zhang, X.Y., Yin, F., et al.: Convolutional prototype network for open set recognition. IEEE Trans. Pattern Anal. Mach. Intell. **44**(5), 2358–2370 (2022)
12. Danuser, G., Stricker, M.: Parametric model fitting: from inlier characterization to outlier detection. IEEE Trans. Pattern Anal. Mach. Intell. **20**(3), 263–280 (1998)
13. Wang H., Wu X., Huang Z.,et al.: High-frequency component helps explain the generalization of convolutional neural networks. In: Proceedings of the IEEE/CVF Conference on Computer Vision and Pattern Recognition, pp. 8684–8694 (2020)

14. Zhai S., Cheng Y., Lu W., et al.: Deep structured energy based models for anomaly detection. In: International Conference on Machine Learning, pp. 1100–1109. PMLR (2016)
15. Adler, A., Elad, M., Hel-Or, Y., et al.: Sparse coding with anomaly detection. J. Sig. Process. Syst. **79**(2), 179–188 (2015)
16. Gong D., Liu L., Le V., et al.: Memorizing normality to detect anomaly: memory-augmented deep autoencoder for unsupervised anomaly detection. In: Proceedings of the IEEE/CVF International Conference on Computer Vision, pp. 1705–1714 (2019)
17. Hanson S.J., Brunswick S.N., Kulikowski C.: Concept-learning in the absence of counter-examples: an autoassociation-based approach to classification. Dissertation, New Brunswick Rutgers, The State University of New Jersey (1999)
18. Liu F.T., Ting K.M., Zhou Z.H.: Isolation forest. In: Proceedings of the 18th IEEE International Conference on Data Mining, pp. 413–422. IEEE (2008)
19. Zhang B., Zuo W.: Learning from positive and unlabeled examples: a survey. In: 2008 International Symposiums on Information Processing, pp. 650–654. IEEE (2008)
20. Makhzani, A., Shlens, J., Jaitly, N., et al.: Adversarial autoencoders. arXiv preprint arXiv:1511.05644 (2015)
21. Tack J., Mo S., Jeong J., et al.: CSI: Novelty detection via contrastive learning on distributionally shifted instances. In: Advances in Neural Information Processing Systems, vol. 33, pp. 11839–11852 (2020)
22. Tian J., Azarian M.H., Pecht M.: Anomaly detection using self-organizing maps-based k-nearest neighbor algorithm. In: PHM Society European Conference, vol. 2 (2014)
23. Yang J., Zhou K., Li Y.,et al.: Generalized out-of-distribution detection: a survey. arXiv preprint arXiv:2110.11334 (2021)
24. Hendrycks, D., Gimpel, K.: A baseline for detecting misclassified and out-of-distribution examples in neural networks. In: International Conference on Learning Representations (2017)
25. Lee K., Lee K., Lee H., et al.: A simple unified framework for detecting out-of-distribution samples and adversarial attacks. In: Advances in Neural Information Processing Systems (NeurIPS) (2018)
26. Syarif I., Prugel-Bennett A., Wills G.B.: Unsupervised clustering approach for network anomaly detection. In: International Conference on Networked Digital Technologies, pp. 135–145. Springer (2012)
27. Liu, W., Wang, X., Owens, J.D., et al.: Energy-based out-of-distribution detection. In: Advances in Neural Information Processing Systems, vol. 33, pp. 21464–21475 (2020)
28. Wang, H., Li, Z., Feng, L., et al.: ViM: out-of-distribution with virtual-logit matching. In: Proceedings of the IEEE/CVF Conference on Computer Vision and Pattern Recognition, pp. 4921–4930 (2022)
29. Vaswani, A., Shazeer, N., Parmar, N., et al.: Attention is all you need. In: Advances in Neural Information Processing Systems, pp. 6000–6010 (2017)
30. Bao, H., Dong, L., Wei, F.: BEiT: BERT pre-training of image transformers. arXiv preprint arXiv:2106.08254 (2021)

31. Devlin, J., Chang, M.W., Lee, K., et al.: BERT: pre-training of deep bidirectional transformers for language understanding. arXiv preprint arXiv:1810.04805 (2018)
32. Deng, J., Dong, W., Socher, R., et al.: ImageNet: a large-scale hierarchical image database. In: Proceedings of the IEEE Conference on Computer Vision And Pattern Recognition, pp. 248–255 (2009)
33. Fort, S., Ren, J., Lakshminarayanan, B.: Exploring the limits of out-of-distribution detection. In: Advances in Neural Information Processing Systems, vol. 34, pp. 7068–7081 (2021)
34. Dosovitskiy, A., Beyer, L., Kolesnikov, A., et al.: An image is worth 16x16 words: transformers for image recognition at scale. arXiv preprint arXiv:2010.11929 (2020)
35. Li, J., Chen, P., He, Z., et al.: Rethinking out-of-distribution (OOD) detection: masked image modeling is all you need. In: Proceedings of the IEEE/CVF Conference on Computer Vision and Pattern Recognition, pp. 11578–11589 (2023)
36. Sehwag V., Chiang M., Mittal P.: SSD: a unified framework for self-supervised outlier detection. arXiv preprint arXiv:2103.12051 (2021)
37. Clifton, D.A., Hugueny, S., Tarassenko, L.: Novelty detection with multivariate extreme value statistics. Signal Process. Syst. **65**(3), 371–389 (2011)
38. Yamanishi, K., Takeuchi, J., Williams, G.J., et al.: On-line unsupervised outlier detection using finite mixtures with discounting learning algorithms. Data Mining Knowl. Discov. **8**(3), 275–300 (2004)
39. Ntalampiras S., Potamitis I., Fakotakis N.: Probabilistic novelty detection for acoustic surveillance under real-world conditions. arXiv preprint arXiv:1410.8516 (2014)
40. Ghoting, A., Parthasarathy, S., Otey, M.E.: Fast mining of distance-based outliers in high-dimensional datasets. In: Proceedings of the 6th SIAM International Conference on Data Mining, April 20–22 (2006)
41. Albertini, M.K., de Mello, R.F.: A self-organizing neural network for detecting novelties. In: Proceedings of the 2007 ACM Symposium on Applied Computing, pp. 462–466 (2007)
42. Hoffmann, H.: Kernel PCA for novelty detection. Pattern Recogn. **40**(3), 863–874 (2007)
43. Kassab, R., Alexandre, F.: Incremental data-driven learning of a novelty detection model for one-class classification with application to high-dimensional noisy data. Mach. Learn. **74**, 191–234 (2009)
44. Wu, M., Ye, J.: A small sphere and large margin approach for novelty detection using training data with outliers. IEEE Trans. Pattern Anal. Mach. Intell. **31**(11), 2088–2092 (2009)
45. Gardner, A.B., Krieger, A.M., Vachtsevanos, G., et al.: One-class novelty detection for seizure analysis from intracranial EEG. J. Mach. Learn. Res. **7**, 1025–1044 (2006)
46. Augusteijn, M.F., Folkert, B.A.: Neural network classification and novelty detection. Int. J. Remote Sens. **23**(14), 2891–2902 (2002)
47. Hawkins S., He H., Williams G., et al.: Outlier detection using replicator neural networks. In: International Conference on Data Warehousing and Knowledge Discovery, pp. 170–180 (2002)
48. Williams G., Baxter R., He H., et al.: A comparative study of RNN for outlier detection in data mining. In: Proceedings of the IEEE International Conference on Data Mining, pp. 709–712 (2002)

49. Krizhevsky A., Hinton G.: Learning multiple layers of features from tiny images. Handbook of Systemic Autoimmune Diseases, vol. 1, no. 4 (2009)
50. Hendrycks, D., Gimpel, K.: A baseline for detecting misclassified and out-of-distribution examples in neural networks. arXiv preprint arXiv:1610.02136 (2016)
51. Huang, R., Geng, A., Li, Y.: On the importance of gradients for detecting distributional shifts in the wild. In: Advances in Neural Information Processing Systems, vol. 34, pp. 677–689 (2021)

Prototype-Guided Contrastive Knowledge Graph Representation Learning for Diagnosis Prediction

Wooyeol Park[1] , Ahmad Wisnu Mulyadi[2] , Eunsong Kang[2] ,
and Heung-Il Suk[1,2(✉)]

[1] Department of Artificial Intelligence, Korea University, Seoul, Republic of Korea
{wooyual,hisuk}@korea.ac.kr
[2] Department of Brain and Cognitive Engineering, Korea University,
Seoul, Republic of Korea
{wisnumulyadi,eunsong1210}@korea.ac.kr

Abstract. The medical knowledge graph (KG) constructed from electronic health records (EHR) offers a comprehensive understanding of patients as it facilitates interconnections among medical codes. While KG has been proven to improve diagnostic accuracy, it inevitably contains noisy and incomplete attributes that could compromise the verdicts. Hence, direct utilization of medical KG for downstream clinical tasks may entail inadequacy, even by resorting to proper machine learning methods. Several prior studies have initiated noise filtering methods upon medical KG to relieve such issues by masking its task-irrelevant nodes and relations. However, they focused solely on a patient-wise perspective that feasibly overlooked essential shared traits from a (sub-)population viewpoint. This study proposes a novel prototype-guided predictive model called ProtoCare to predict diagnoses in EHR by unifying prototype and contrastive learning. ProtoCare leverages a set of prototypes to discover latent shared characteristics among groups of patients, while contrastive learning plays the role of noise filtering and KG refinement accounting for both learned patient and selected prototype features. Experimental results on the real-world EHR cohort exhibited that our proposed ProtoCare outperformed several baselines on the diagnosis prediction task.

Keywords: Medical Knowledge Graph · Graph Representation Learning · Prototype Learning · Contrastive Learning · Diagnosis Prediction

1 Introduction

Electronic Health Records (EHR) encompass a broad range of patient healthcare information, including vital measurements, diagnoses, procedures, prescriptions, and clinical notes collected throughout their longitudinal admissions. The EHR cohort can be further exploited for various beneficial downstream analyses, such as mortality prediction [21,26], medication recommendations [22,27], and diagnosis prediction [1,6,19]. However, performing adequate analysis tasks over EHR

C. Wallraven et al. (Eds.): ICPRAI 2024, LNCS 14892, pp. 262–275, 2025.
https://doi.org/10.1007/978-981-97-8702-9_18

data is non-trivial due to its intricate attributes, including high-dimensionality, sparsity, temporality, irregularity, and bias [3]. In practice, such diverse yet sparse medical codes across admissions are commonly registered in an EHR system in a standalone manner without a clear relationship between such codes. To provide a comprehensive understanding of a patient's medical conditions, several efforts in modeling and analyzing the EHR cohort were carried out by incorporating external informative relations among medical entities, resulting in the formation of a medical knowledge graph [2].

Harnessing knowledge graphs (KGs) shall be approached carefully, as they often come with inevitable drawbacks, including noise and incomplete information [23]. In pursuing accurate predictive healthcare, it may be inadequate to employ unrefined medical KGs directly, even when resorting to machine or deep learning approaches. Therefore, several studies utilizing medical KGs have stretched their attempts to adeptly filter out noisy medical nodes and relations by proposing patient-wise noise filtering models [7,25]. While this method can be considered as a personalized approach, we argue that there exist shared yet latent characteristics among groups of patients that may collectively play a significant role in representing specific diseases [12]. We refer to this perspective as a (sub-)population viewpoint. By complementing both personalized (*i.e.*, local) and population-based (*i.e.*, global) perspectives, we refine medical KGs to extract more insightful representations specific to individual patients as well as groups of patients with similar medical conditions. This effective refinement process can, in turn, facilitate more accurate predictions for medical diagnoses.

In this study, we introduce a novel framework called ProtoCare, designed specifically to predict diagnoses of patients in an EHR cohort by effectively filtering noise within medical KGs via a seamless integration of prototype and contrastive learning. In particular, we extract meaningful patient features through bidirectional sequence learning enhanced by attention mechanisms. Subsequently, we establish a set of prototypes to characterize groups of patients, which is achieved by clustering patient features and imposing them closer to prototypes while also introducing a penalty for the proximity of each prototype. Both patient representations and prototypes provide individual and group perspectives, which can be leveraged to assist us in refining medical KGs through contrastive learning in our multi-view graph representation learning (GRL) module. For enhanced diagnosis predictions, we devise a multi-view attention block followed by a final classifier that considers graph-level features from both patient and prototype perspectives.

In summary, the main contributions of our study are as follows:

- We propose a novel ProtoCare framework that unifies prototype and contrastive learning aiming to filter task-irrelevant nodes and relations and refine medical KGs with both local and global perspectives for diagnosis prediction.
- We validate our ProtoCare on the MIMIC-III cohort by comparing its predictive performances against several existing baselines in the literature, where it consistently achieves the highest diagnostic prediction performances.

2   Related Works

Graph-Free Approach. Prior works have tackled predictive analytics in healthcare by solely relying on sequence models without forming auxiliary graphs. For instance, T-LSTM [1] extended long short-term memory (LSTM) [9] to further consider the irregular time gap by devising a component that forgets the prior cell states according to the observed time gap. RETAIN [6] exploited a two-level attention mechanism by means of visit-wise and code-wise attention scores. Dipole [18] extracted patient features using three attention-based mechanisms and bidirectional RNNs. Meanwhile, LSAN [29] and HiTANet [17] exploited a Transformer architecture that uses self-attentions to consider the relationships between visits and determine the significance of different visits.

Graph-Aware Approach. There exists a research direction on the organization and utilization of medical KGs (or co-occurrence graphs, at the least) as a piece of additional domain knowledge to enhance predictive healthcare upon EHR data. In particular, GRAM [5], KAME [19], and CGL [16] employed ontology-based medical graphs to capture the hierarchical relations between observed disease codes. GRAM and KAME learned the code embedding by aggregating the representation of their corresponding ancestor and child nodes via attention-based mechanisms. Meanwhile, CGL identified common ancestor nodes shared by two distinct disease codes within a medical ontology graph by formulating the distance between them. Moreover, MedPath [28] elevated the predictive performances and interpretability as a diagnosis prediction model by incorporating KG augmented with a set of semantic relations. In contrast to relying on external-sourced medical graphs, CGL and Chet [15] exploited co-occurrence graphs to capture the associations among medical codes. Those prior studies have proven the benefits of being a graph-aware approach in predictive healthcare by leveraging additional domain knowledge. Nonetheless, several recent studies [7,25] have argued that the data extracted from patients' EHR data (including medical KGs) could potentially introduce task-irrelevant noise and shall be effectively filtered through a noise filtering approach.

Graph Noise Filtering. The authors of MedSkim [7] argued that when predicting specific target diseases, particular medical code data or specific patient visit data might not substantially contribute to the predictive tasks. These elements could act as noise, potentially interfering with the model's learning process. Hence, they proposed a model that utilizes Gumbel-Softmax [10] to adeptly filter out the noise associated with medical codes and visits from a patient's diagnostic history while also taking into account both the patient's characteristics and the target disease. Likewise, SeqCare [25] exploited a graph-aware approach to mask out the irrelevant nodes and interconnected edges using analogous Gumbel-Softmax. However, their approach remains solely on the individual patient's perspective, overlooking a perspective from a group of patients. In this study, we propose a novel approach that alleviates noise within medical KGs by taking into account both individual and population perspectives.

3   Problem Formulation

Electronic Health Records. An EHR cohort is comprised of N number of patients' records denoted as $\{(\mathbf{X}^n, \mathbf{y}^n)\}_{n=1}^N$ indicating their longitudinal records coupled with a disease risk label, correspondingly. Each n-th patient holds a series of visit sequences $\mathbf{X}^n = [\mathbf{x}_1^n, \ldots, \mathbf{x}_t^n, \ldots, \mathbf{x}_{T^n}^n]^\top$ with T^n denotes the total admissions of a given patient. For every admission, a set of medical codes (*i.e.*, diagnosis and procedure codes) $\mathbf{c} = \{c_1, c_2, \ldots, c_{|\mathcal{C}|}\} \in \mathbb{R}^{|\mathcal{C}|}$ is observed with $\mathcal{C}$ indicates the medical code set and $|\cdot|$ refer to its cardinality. Thus, at the t-th visit of a given patient can be represented as a multi-hot vector $\mathbf{x}_t^n \in \{0,1\}^{|\mathcal{C}|}$. Meanwhile, the respective multi-hot label $\mathbf{y}^n \in \{0,1\}^{|\mathcal{D}|}$ with $\mathcal{D} \subset \mathcal{C}$ constitutes a set of forthcoming observed diagnosis from a particular patient. For decluttering, we exclude the superscript n in the remaining sections when unambiguous.

Medical Knowledge Graph. Medical KG is a graph comprising heterogeneous medical entities interconnected by various relations. It can be denoted as $\mathcal{G} = \{\Gamma = (u, r, v) | u, v \in \mathcal{E}, r \in \mathcal{R}\}$, which represents a set of triples (*i.e.*, head entity, relation, tail entity) with $\mathcal{E}$ and $\mathcal{R}$ indicates a set of entities and relations, respectively. We construct $\mathcal{G}$ for each patient by compiling all observed records across their admissions, such that $\mathcal{E} = \{\mathbb{1}(\mathbf{x}_1) \cup \mathbb{1}(\mathbf{x}_2) \ldots \cup \mathbb{1}(\mathbf{x}_T)\}$, where $\mathbb{1}(\cdot)$ denotes a function that returns only the observed codes. Meanwhile, relation set $\mathcal{R}$ (*e.g.*, ontology, semantics) is extracted from diverse external knowledge [8,13] to facilitate linkages between such entities. As we integrate the ontology in structuring $\mathcal{G}$, we additionally incorporate the respective ancestor codes for each observed medical entity in $\mathcal{E}$ according to the designated ontology (*i.e.*, ICD-9).

Diagnosis Prediction Task. Our final objective in this study is to tackle the task of diagnosis prediction in an EHR cohort, which can be regarded as a multi-label prediction task. Given the visit sequence $\mathbf{X}$ and medical KG $\mathcal{G}$ of a patient, we devise ProtoCare that adeptly refines medical KG $\mathcal{G}$ and forecasts the diagnosis label $\mathbf{y}$ by deriving the probability of diagnosis risk as $p(\hat{\mathbf{y}}|\mathbf{X}; \mathcal{G})$.

4   Proposed Method

The overall architecture of the proposed ProtoCare is depicted in Fig. 1. It consists of four main modules, namely (i) patient feature extraction, (ii) prototype learning, (iii) multi-view GRL, and (iv) diagnosis prediction. In particular, (i) aims to extract patient embedding via bidirectional sequence models to account for both directions of the visit sequence. With extracted patient features at hand, (ii) further learns prototypes and selects the most similar unit for each patient to be incorporated in (iii) for filtering the task-irrelevant node and edges while simultaneously extracting features from the original and pruned KGs. All of these modules act as patient encoders for extracting meaningful features via pre-training before jointly fine-tuning the downstream module (iv) that predicts the forthcoming diagnosis label using aggregated predictive features from patient-wise and prototype features to be fed into the final classifier.

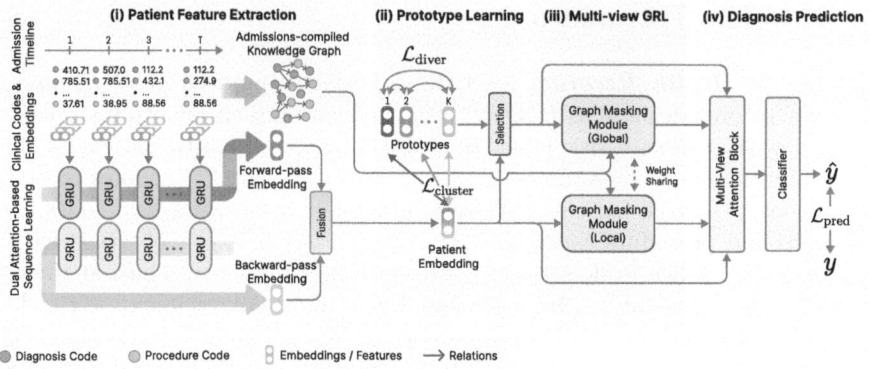

Fig. 1. Overview of our ProtoCare in engaging diagnosis prediction task.

Patient Feature Extraction. Effective extraction of patient features from their visit sequence $\mathbf{X}$ holds great significance as we require it in refining the medical KG simultaneously with inferring prototypes. We transform each observed code in patient records $\mathbf{x}_t[i]$ to $\mathbf{e}_i \in \mathbb{R}^{d_e}$ and further aggregate them to obtain the visit embedding $\mathbf{v}_t$ as an input for gated recurrent units (GRUs) [4] as

$$\mathbf{e}_i = \mathbf{E}\mathbf{x}_t[i], \tag{1}$$

$$\mathbf{v}_t = \sum_i^{|\mathcal{C}|} \mathbf{e}_i, \tag{2}$$

where $\mathbf{E} \in \mathbb{R}^{d_e \times |\mathbf{C}|}$ and d_e denotes a learnable embedding matrix and the dimension of code embeddings, respectively. We fed such features $\mathbf{v}_{1:T}$ to bidirectional sequence learning that captures temporal features of forward-pass via $\overrightarrow{\mathrm{GRU}}$ and backward-pass via $\overleftarrow{\mathrm{GRU}}$, independently. Each GRU calculates attention scores across visits and infers a patient embedding via

$$\overrightarrow{\mathbf{h}_1}, \overrightarrow{\mathbf{h}_2}, \cdots \overrightarrow{\mathbf{h}_T} = \overrightarrow{\mathrm{GRU}}(\mathbf{v}_1, \mathbf{v}_2, \cdots, \mathbf{v}_T), \tag{3}$$

$$a_t = \mathbf{w}_a \overrightarrow{\mathbf{h}_t} + b_a, \tag{4}$$

$$\alpha_1, \alpha_2, \dots \alpha_T = \mathrm{Softmax}(a_1, a_2, \dots, a_T), \tag{5}$$

$$\overrightarrow{\mathbf{p}} = \sum_{t=1}^T \alpha_i \overrightarrow{\mathbf{h}_t}, \tag{6}$$

where $\overrightarrow{\mathbf{h}_t} \in \mathbb{R}^{d_h}$, $\mathbf{w}_a \in \mathbb{R}^{1 \times d_h}$, $b_a \in \mathbb{R}$, and d_h is the dimension of GRU output. Likewise, the patient embedding $\overleftarrow{\mathbf{p}}$ can be calculated in a similar fashion using $\overleftarrow{\mathrm{GRU}}$ with a reversed order of the visit features $\mathbf{v}_{T:1}$ as the input. Finally, we obtain the unified patient embedding $\mathbf{p}$ by fusing $\overrightarrow{\mathbf{p}}$ and $\overleftarrow{\mathbf{p}}$ formulated as

$$\beta_1, \beta_2 = \mathrm{Softmax}(\mathbf{W}_\beta[\overrightarrow{\mathbf{p}}; \overleftarrow{\mathbf{p}}] + \mathbf{b}_\beta), \tag{7}$$

$$\mathbf{p} = \beta_1 \overrightarrow{\mathbf{p}} + \beta_2 \overleftarrow{\mathbf{p}}, \tag{8}$$

where $\mathbf{W}_\beta \in \mathbb{R}^{2 \times d_h}$, $\mathbf{b}_\beta \in \mathbb{R}^2$, and operator $[;]$ concatenates the given features.

Prototype Learning. Having extracted the patient embedding **p**, we employ a set of prototypes $\mathcal{P} = \{\boldsymbol{\rho}_1, \boldsymbol{\rho}_2, \cdots, \boldsymbol{\rho}_{|\mathcal{P}|}\}$ and select the most resembled prototypes $\boldsymbol{\rho}$ in representing the population features. We employ two objective functions for prototype learning, namely clustering loss $\mathcal{L}_{\text{cluster}}$ and diversity loss $\mathcal{L}_{\text{diver}}$ in Eq. (9) and Eq. (10), correspondingly. Specifically, clustering loss is calculated using cosine similarity between patient embedding and each prototype. A complementary diversity loss inspired by [24] is employed to control the proximity of prototypes from severely overlapping with each other in an embedding space. Overall prototype learning loss $\mathcal{L}_{\text{proto}}$ is measured via Eq. (11).

$$\mathcal{L}_{\text{cluster}} = \sum_{k=1}^{|\mathcal{P}|} \text{sim}(\mathbf{p}, \boldsymbol{\rho}_k) \tag{9}$$

$$\mathcal{L}_{\text{diver}} = \sum_{k=1}^{|\mathcal{P}|} \sum_{l=1, l \neq k}^{|\mathcal{P}|} \max(0, \text{sim}(\boldsymbol{\rho}_k, \boldsymbol{\rho}_l) - \delta) \tag{10}$$

$$\mathcal{L}_{\text{proto}} = \mathcal{L}_{\text{cluster}} + \mathcal{L}_{\text{diver}} \tag{11}$$

Here, the $\text{sim}(\cdot)$ denotes the cosine similarity function, while δ is a given margin. We expect that each prototype unit discovers particular latent characteristics representing a large group of patients as auxiliary population perspective.

Multi-view GRL. To refine medical KG $\mathcal{G}$, we devise a Graph Masking module equipped with the Gumbel-Softmax [10] as depicted in Fig. 2 in adeptly masking nodes and edges. Foremost, we employ L graph convolutional networks (GCN) [14] layers to enrich and extract its embeddings. We obtain the enriched node embedding $\mathbf{n}_u \in \mathbb{R}^{d_g}$ of node u. We select the nodes to be masked by accounting for patient and prototype features concatenated with $\mathbf{n}_u$ via

$$\mathbf{m}_u^{\mathbf{P}} = \text{Gumbel-Softmax}(\mathbf{W}_{\text{node}}[\mathbf{p}; \mathbf{n}_u]) \tag{12}$$

$$\mathbf{m}_u^{\boldsymbol{\rho}} = \text{Gumbel-Softmax}(\mathbf{W}_{\text{node}}[\boldsymbol{\rho}; \mathbf{n}_u]) \tag{13}$$

where $\mathbf{W}_{\text{node}} \in \mathbb{R}^{(d_h + d_g) \times 2}$ and $\mathbf{m}_u^{\{\mathbf{P}, \boldsymbol{\rho}\}} \in \{0, 1\}^2$ denotes one-hot vectors preserving a node u if the first element is 1, discarding otherwise. Subsequently, we employ a pruning process over the edges $r \in \mathcal{R}$ that connect the head node $\mathbf{n}_u$ and tail node $\mathbf{n}_v$ as

$$\mathbf{m}_r^{\mathbf{P}} = \text{Gumbel-Softmax}(\mathbf{W}_{\text{edge}}[\mathbf{p}; \mathbf{n}_u; \mathbf{n}_v]) \tag{14}$$

$$\mathbf{m}_r^{\boldsymbol{\rho}} = \text{Gumbel-Softmax}(\mathbf{W}_{\text{edge}}[\boldsymbol{\rho}; \mathbf{n}_u; \mathbf{n}_v]) \tag{15}$$

where $\mathbf{W}_{\text{edge}} \in \mathbb{R}^{(d_h + 2 \times d_g) \times 2}$ and $\mathbf{m}_r^{\{\mathbf{P}, \boldsymbol{\rho}\}} \in \{0, 1\}^2$ to determine whether to preserve or mask an edge r in a similar way to node masking.

To this end, we acquire two pruned subgraphs $\widetilde{\mathcal{G}}_{\mathbf{p}}$ and $\widetilde{\mathcal{G}}_{\boldsymbol{\rho}}$ accounted for the featurs of patient **p** and prototype $\boldsymbol{\rho}$, respectively. We denote subgraphs $\widetilde{\mathcal{G}}_{\mathbf{p}} = \{\Gamma = (u, r, v) | u, v \in \widetilde{\mathcal{E}}_{\mathbf{p}}, r \in \widetilde{\mathcal{R}}_{\mathbf{p}}\}$ with $\widetilde{\mathcal{E}}_{\mathbf{p}} = \{u | u \in \mathcal{E}, \mathbf{m}_u^{\mathbf{P}}[0] = 1\}$, $\widetilde{\mathcal{R}}_{\mathbf{p}} = \{r | r \in \mathcal{R}, \mathbf{m}_r^{\mathbf{P}}[0] = 1\}$, and $\widetilde{\mathcal{G}}_{\boldsymbol{\rho}}$ can be inferred in similar fashion. We extract graph-level features $\mathbf{g}_{\mathbf{p}}$ and $\mathbf{g}_{\boldsymbol{\rho}}$ by employing the category-aware graph attention mechanism [25]. It maps the head and tail node embeddings $\mathbf{n}_{\{u, v\}}$ to edge embedding space and calculates the attention weights of each relation as

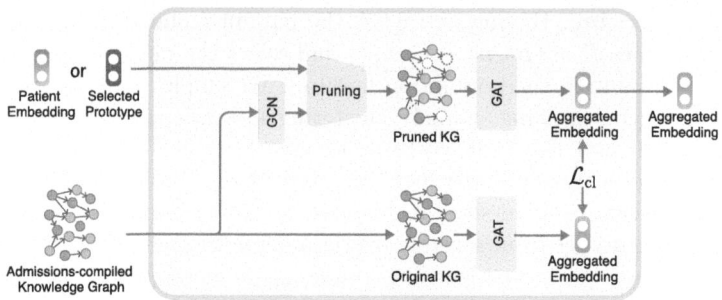

Fig. 2. Overview of the Graph Masking module

$$s_\Gamma = \mathbf{W}_{\text{attn}} \tanh\left(\mathbf{W}_r \mathbf{n}_u + \mathbf{W}_r \mathbf{n}_v + \mathbf{r}\right), \tag{16}$$

$$\gamma_\Gamma = \frac{\exp(s_\Gamma)}{\sum_{v' \in \mathcal{N}_u} \exp\left(s_{\Gamma'}\right)}, \tag{17}$$

where $\mathbf{W}_{\text{attn}} \in \mathbb{R}^{d_r}$, $\mathbf{W}_r \in \mathbb{R}^{d_r \times d_g}$, and $\mathbf{r} \in \mathbb{R}^{d_r}$ denotes the edge embedding, d_g and d_r are the dimensions of the nodes and edges, respectively. We then utilize γ_Γ to aggregate and update the node embeddings at the l-th layer as

$$\mathbf{n}_{aggr}^{(l)} = \sum_{v \in \mathcal{N}_u} \gamma_\Gamma \mathbf{n}_v^{(l)}, \tag{18}$$

$$\mathbf{n}_u^{(l+1)} = \text{LeakyReLU}\left(\mathbf{W}_{aggr}\left(\mathbf{n}_u^{(l)} + \mathbf{n}_{aggr}^{(l)}\right)\right), \tag{19}$$

where $\mathbf{W}_{aggr} \in \mathbb{R}^{d_g \times d_g}$. Across L_k layers of operation, we obtain a final node embedding $\bar{\mathbf{n}}_u$ by concatenating entire embeddings in $\{\mathbf{n}_u^{(1)}, \cdots, \mathbf{n}_u^{(l)}, \cdots, \mathbf{n}_u^{(L)}\}$. Finally, to extract graph-level embeddings from patient-view graphs ($\mathcal{G}_\mathbf{p}, \widetilde{\mathcal{G}}_\mathbf{p}$) and prototype-view graphs ($\mathcal{G}_\rho, \widetilde{\mathcal{G}}_\rho$), we subsequently fed the learned node embedding to the read-out function and feed-forward network (FFN) as

$$\mathbf{g}_\mathbf{p} = \text{FFN}(\text{Readout}(\mathcal{G}_\mathbf{p})), \tag{20}$$

$$\widetilde{\mathbf{g}}_\mathbf{p} = \text{FFN}(\text{Readout}(\widetilde{\mathcal{G}}_\mathbf{p})), \tag{21}$$

where we employ a global pooling layer as the readout function. Likewise, the prototype-view graph-level features $\mathbf{g}_\rho$ and $\widetilde{\mathbf{g}}_\rho$ can be obtained with similar operation comparable to Eq. (20–21).

To adequately learn this module, we employ graph contrastive learning that imposes the similar patient's (or prototype's) features closer while pushing other dissimilar features farther away. Specifically, we calculate a contrastive loss $\mathcal{L}_\mathbf{p}$ for patient features when batch size is B expressed as

$$\ell_{\mathbf{p}}(\mathbf{g}_{\mathbf{p}}^n, \widetilde{\mathbf{g}}_{\mathbf{p}}^n) = -\log \frac{\exp(\mathrm{sim}(\mathbf{g}_{\mathbf{p}}^n, \widetilde{\mathbf{g}}_{\mathbf{p}}^n)/\tau)}{\sum_{i=1, i \neq n}^{B} \exp(\mathrm{sim}(\mathbf{g}_{\mathbf{p}}^n, \widetilde{\mathbf{g}}_{\mathbf{p}}^i)/\tau)}, \tag{22}$$

$$\mathcal{L}_{\mathbf{p}} = \frac{1}{2B} \sum_{n=1}^{B} [\ell_{\mathbf{p}}(\mathbf{g}_{\mathbf{p}}^n, \widetilde{\mathbf{g}}_{\mathbf{p}}^n) + \ell_{\mathbf{p}}(\widetilde{\mathbf{g}}_{\mathbf{p}}^n, \mathbf{g}_{\mathbf{p}}^n)], \tag{23}$$

where both $\mathbf{g}_{\mathbf{p}}^n$ and $\widetilde{\mathbf{g}}_{\mathbf{p}}^n$ represent the patient-wise features for n-th patient and τ is a temperature. In addition, an additional contrastive learning loss $\mathcal{L}_{\rho}$ is dedicated to the graph-level features of $(\mathbf{g}_{\rho}, \widetilde{\mathbf{g}}_{\rho})$ accounted for the closest prototype relative to patient features similarly measured as to Eq. (22–23). Finally, an integrated contrastive loss $\mathcal{L}_{\mathrm{cl}}$ is calculated as

$$\mathcal{L}_{\mathrm{cl}} = \mathcal{L}_{\mathbf{p}} + \mathcal{L}_{\rho}. \tag{24}$$

Note that we consider all of the prior modules up to this point to be optimized with a devoted loss during the pre-training stage, calculated as

$$\mathcal{L}_{\mathrm{pre\text{-}train}} = \mathcal{L}_{\mathrm{cl}} + \mathcal{L}_{\mathrm{proto}} \tag{25}$$

Diagnosis Prediction. Having pre-training the prior aforementioned modules, we employ a tuple of extracted features (*i.e.*, the patient embedding $\mathbf{p}$, selected prototype ρ, and refined graph-level features $\widetilde{\mathbf{g}}_{\mathbf{p}}$, $\widetilde{\mathbf{g}}_{\rho}$) to eventually obtain a final patient predictive embedding $\mathbf{o}$. Here, the patient embedding $\mathbf{p}$ and its corresponding graph-level features $\widetilde{\mathbf{g}}_{\mathbf{p}}$ contains important information from a given patient perspective. In addition, such features are complemented with a piece of crucial information from the population viewpoint using prototype ρ and features $\widetilde{\mathbf{g}}_{\rho}$. We take a further step to merge the patient and prototype features to infer the final features $\mathbf{o}$ using an attention mechanism expressed as

$$\mathbf{o}_{\mathbf{p}} = [\mathbf{p}; \widetilde{\mathbf{g}}_{\mathbf{p}}], \tag{26}$$

$$\mathbf{o}_{\rho} = [\rho; \widetilde{\mathbf{g}}_{\rho}], \tag{27}$$

$$\lambda_1, \lambda_2 = \mathrm{Softmax}(\mathbf{W}_{\lambda}[\mathbf{o}_{\mathbf{p}}; \mathbf{o}_{\rho}] + \mathbf{b}_{\lambda}), \tag{28}$$

$$\mathbf{o} = \lambda_1 \mathbf{o}_{\mathbf{p}} + \lambda_2 \mathbf{o}_{\rho}, \tag{29}$$

where $\mathbf{W}_{\lambda} \in \mathbb{R}^{2 \times (d_h + d_g)}$ and $\mathbf{b}_{\lambda} \in \mathbb{R}^2$. Eventually, we fed it to a cosine classifier [25] denoted as $\mathcal{F}_{\cos}(\cdot)$ in Eq. (30) to predict the diagnosis on the forthcoming risk of disease label $\hat{\mathbf{y}}$. The prediction loss $\mathcal{L}_{\mathrm{pred}}$ and fine-tune loss $\mathcal{L}_{\mathrm{fine\text{-}tune}}$ for the prediction step are optimized via Eq. (31) and Eq. (32), respectively.

$$\hat{\mathbf{y}}^n = \mathcal{F}_{\cos}(\mathbf{o}^n) \tag{30}$$

$$\mathcal{L}_{\mathrm{pred}} = \frac{1}{N} \sum_{n=1}^{N} (\mathbf{y}^n \log \hat{\mathbf{y}}^n + (1 - \mathbf{y}^n) \log(1 - \hat{\mathbf{y}}^n)) \tag{31}$$

$$\mathcal{L}_{\mathrm{fine\text{-}tune}} = \mathcal{L}_{\mathrm{proto}} + \mathcal{L}_{\mathrm{pred}} \tag{32}$$

Table 1. Pre-processed MIMIC-III cohort summary.

Items	Size
Patients	7,499
Visits	19,911
Diagnoses	4,880
Procedures	1,522
Mean/Max of # Visits	2.66/42
Mean/Max of # Diagnoses	13.1/39
Mean/Max of # Procedures	3.86/33

5   Experiment

5.1   Experimental Settings

Dataset. We validated the effectiveness of our ProtoCare framework on the MIMIC-III [11] as a publicly available real-world EHR dataset. We extracted all observed medical codes out of DIAGNOSES and PROCEDURES tables from the database. We excluded patients who had only a single visit since the last admission records were treated as ground truth labels of diagnosis. To make such diagnosis category labels, we grouped the diagnosis codes using the second hierarchy according to ICD-9 ontology. For instance, the category label of "250.1: Diabetes with ketoacidosis" is "249–259: Diseases of other endocrine glands". We presented the cohort statistic summary in Table 1. As for medical KG construction, we structured the graph across admissions for each patient by imposing ICD-9 ontology (*i.e.*, PARENTS_OF) and further augmenting it with directed relations extracted from SemMed [13]. By following [28], we utilized 9 relations contained in SemMed, namely AFFECTS, AUGMENTS, CAUSES, DIAGNOSES, INTERACTS_WITH, PART_OF, PRECEDES, PREDISPOSES, and PRODUCES.

Baselines. We compared our ProtoCare against closely related baselines in the literature. In particular, we designated: T-LSTM [1] that modeled the irregular time gap between visits; RETAIN [6] that employed the attention to capturing the importance of each visit as well as visit; HiTANet [17] as a Transformer-based model accounted for time-awareness; Chet [15] that divided co-occurrence relationships among disease codes to account for disease developments; and finally SeqCare [25] that exploited a graph contrastive learning model to mask the task-irrelevant noise from the medical KG.

Evaluation Metrics. We reported a set of evaluation metrics commonly reported in a diagnosis prediction task, namely the area under the receiver operating characteristic (AUROC) (Macro & Micro), the area under the Precision-Recall curve (PRAUC) (Macro & Micro), and the weighted F1 score (w-F1). Such a w-F1 score refers to a weighted sum of F1 scores for every label. Since we utilized 5-fold cross-validation, we selected the best model based on the validation sets and further reported the prediction performances over the test sets.

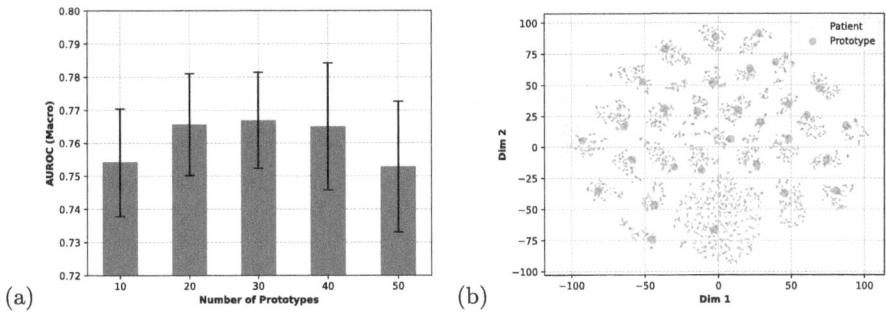

Fig. 3. Visualization of (a) AUROC (Macro) performance for different numbers of prototypes and (b) t-SNE of the learned patient embeddings and prototypes.

Implementation Details. All reported experiments were carried out on a machine with RTX Titan 2080 Ti GPU and PyTorch 1.12.1. To ensure a fair comparison, we utilized the hyperparameter settings reported in the respective papers of baselines when available. We fixed a set of hyperparameters for our ProtoCare framework as follows: $d_e = 64, d_h = 128, d_g = 64, d_r = 96, \delta = 0.3, \tau = 0.5, B = 64, L = 1, L_k = 2$. We applied a dropout layer in the final prediction step with a rate of 0.5. We assigned the number of iterations for pre-training and fine-tuning stages to 100 and 150, respectively. Finally, we optimized the proposed modules in our framework using Adam optimizer with a learning rate of $1e - 3$.

5.2   Experimental Results

Ablation Studies. We conducted a preliminary ablation study to investigate the effect of the number of prototypes upon the prediction performances of our ProtoCare model, as illustrated in Fig. 3a. Based on these experimental results, we discovered that 30 was the optimal number of prototypes that achieved the highest AUROC (Macro) among other scenarios. The performance degraded when the number of prototypes was either too large or too small. We visualized the learned embedding space of patient features (blue-colored dots) in the training set and such 30 units of prototypes (red-colored dots) by using t-SNE [20], as shown in Fig. 3b. Overall, we observed that the prototype learning effectively clustered patient embeddings around prototypes with restrained proximity, discovering a group of patients who shared similar latent attributes.

In addition, we evaluated a set of ProtoCare variants, namely ProtoCare$_{\rho-}$ that dismissed the utilization of prototypes, ProtoCare$_{\overrightarrow{\text{GRU}}}$ and ProtoCare$_{\overleftarrow{\text{GRU}}}$ that solely utilized the forward-pass and backward-pass GRU, respectively. As shown in Table 2, ProtoCare$_{\rho-}$ exhibited overall degraded performances implying a significant role of prototypes in drawing more accurate prediction verdicts. Among ProtoCare$_{\overrightarrow{\text{GRU}}}$ and ProtoCare$_{\overleftarrow{\text{GRU}}}$ variants, we observed roughly compa-

Table 2. Performances of ProtoCare variants against baselines in diagnosis prediction task on MIMIC-III cohort. $*$: p-value < 0.05

Model	AUROC		PRAUC		w-F1
	Macro	Micro	Macro	Micro	
T-LSTM [1]	$0.5656 \pm 0.019^*$	$0.8952 \pm 0.014^*$	$0.2005 \pm 0.008^*$	$0.4722 \pm 0.009^*$	$0.3920 \pm 0.016^*$
RETAIN [6]	$0.5608 \pm 0.020^*$	$0.9218 \pm 0.003^*$	$0.2187 \pm 0.003^*$	$0.5359 \pm 0.018^*$	$0.3511 \pm 0.017^*$
HiTANet [17]	$0.5685 \pm 0.011^*$	$0.9024 \pm 0.008^*$	$0.2091 \pm 0.003^*$	$0.4772 \pm 0.014^*$	$0.3989 \pm 0.020^*$
Chet [15]	$0.5559 \pm 0.027^*$	$0.9150 \pm 0.004^*$	$0.2032 \pm 0.003^*$	$0.5067 \pm 0.020^*$	$0.3561 \pm 0.013^*$
SeqCare [25]	$0.7179 \pm 0.029^*$	$0.9614 \pm 0.006^*$	$0.3199 \pm 0.015^*$	$0.6762 \pm 0.016^*$	$0.4441 \pm 0.033^*$
SeqCare$_+$ [25]	$\underline{0.7595 \pm 0.016}$	$0.9564 \pm 0.007^*$	$0.3837 \pm 0.013^*$	$0.6623 \pm 0.012^*$	$0.4754 \pm 0.006^*$
ProtoCare$_{\rho-}$	$0.7440 \pm 0.019^*$	$0.9446 \pm 0.002^*$	$0.3639 \pm 0.007^*$	$0.6287 \pm 0.016^*$	$\underline{0.5484 \pm 0.013}$
ProtoCare$_{\overline{GRU}}$	$0.7544 \pm 0.022^*$	$\underline{0.9707 \pm 0.003^*}$	$\underline{0.4051 \pm 0.016^*}$	$\underline{0.7389 \pm 0.011}$	$0.4819 \pm 0.032^*$
ProtoCare$_{\overleftarrow{GRU}}$	$0.7509 \pm 0.019^*$	$0.9679 \pm 0.002^*$	$0.3892 \pm 0.016^*$	$0.7242 \pm 0.011^*$	$0.4499 \pm 0.035^*$
ProtoCare	$\mathbf{0.7649 \pm 0.018}$	$\mathbf{0.9731 \pm 0.003}$	$\mathbf{0.4160 \pm 0.020}$	$\mathbf{0.7471 \pm 0.008}$	$\mathbf{0.5538 \pm 0.025}$

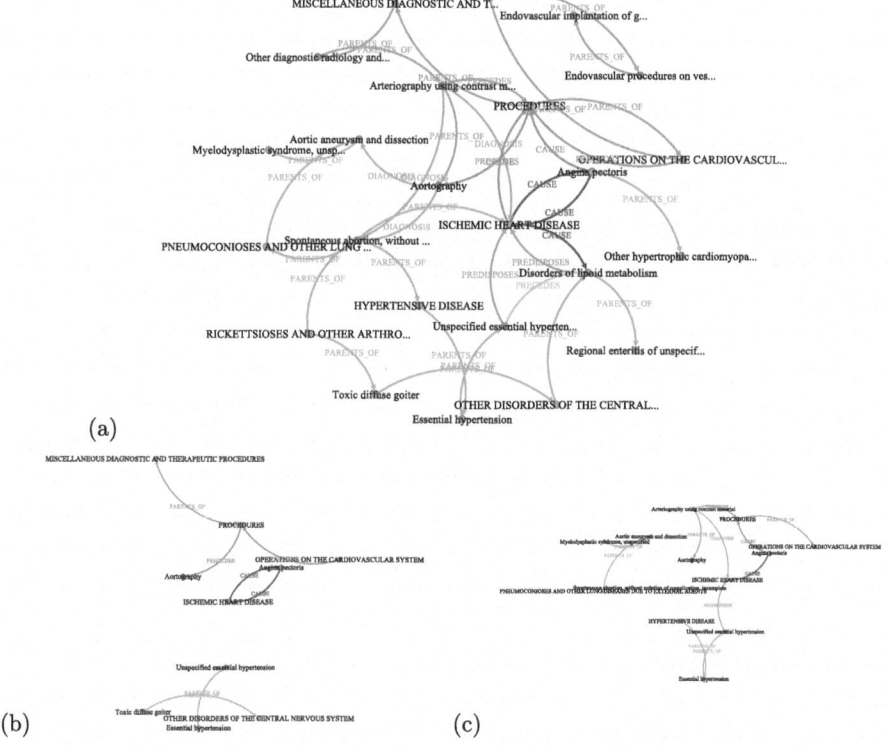

Fig. 4. Comparison of the graph masked by local and global view (a) is an original knowledge graph of a patient, (b) and (c) is the knowledge graph masked by patient and prototype viewpoints, respectively.

rable performances with slightly favorable outcomes on the forward-pass setting. Bidirectional variant greatly enhanced prediction results as shown in ProtoCare.

Experimental Results. We reported the performance comparison of our ProtoCare against baselines in predicting diagnoses in Table 2. Among graph-free sequence models, we observed that RETAIN achieved higher overall performances than T-LSTM and HiTANet, except for its w-F1 score. One possible reason for their struggle might be due to the shorter average sequence length of patients' admissions in the MIMIC-III cohort. Their modeling capability was also repressed by lacking auxiliary domain knowledge in the form of medical KGs. This case was clearly demonstrated by SeqCare, which took into account the medical KGs equipped with its contrastive learning to refine the graphs, which outperformed other baselines, including Chet. By purposefully replacing SeqCare's patient extractor with our proposed bidirectional sequence learning, the SeqCare$_+$ variant could achieve even higher outcomes in terms of AUROC (Macro), PRAUC (Macro) and w-F1 score, emphasizing the benefits of our proposed patient extractor. Surpassing all baselines, our ProtoCare exhibited significantly greater overall performances in addressing the task of diagnosis prediction.

Refined Graph Analysis. We further devoted an analysis by simply depicting the refined KGs according to the patient and its closest prototype perspectives, as shown in Fig. 4b and Fig. 4c, correspondingly. Note that these graphs were acquired from a patient's admission records with the least observed medical codes to ease the visualization purpose. Although both refined medical KGs originated from one initial graph in Fig. 4a, we observed distinctive filtered medical entities and relations. These findings showcased that paired patient and prototype perspectives distinguished what would be essential aspects of the KGs and further complemented each other to facilitate more accurate predictions.

6   Conclusion

In this study, we proposed a novel ProtoCare predictive model equipped with prototype and contrastive learning for tackling the diagnosis prediction task that offers not only patient-level but also (sub-)population-level in refining medical KGs. To achieve this, we devised attention-based bidirectional sequence learning to extract patient features and learned prototypes representing groups of patients with shared traits. Contrastive learning allows us to focus on essential elements from local and global perspectives for filtering task-irrelevant nodes and relations on medical KGs. Eventually, graph-level features from the refined medical KGs based on those perspectives were further dispatched into our multi-view attention block prior to a final classifier to acquire and improve the diagnosis prediction outcomes. We conducted exhaustive experiments on the MIMIC-III EHR cohort to validate the effectiveness of our ProtoCare against several baselines in the literature, outperforming such baselines in the diagnosis prediction task.

Acknowledgments. This work was supported by National Research Foundation of Korea (NRF) grant funded by the Korea government (MSIT) No. 2022R1A2C2006865 (Development of deep learning techniques for data-driven medical knowledge graph generation and interpretable multi-modal electronic health records analysis) and Institute of Information & communications Technology Planning & Evaluation (IITP) grant funded by the Korea government (MSIT) (No. RS-2019-II190079, Artificial Intelligence Graduate School Program(Korea University)).

References

1. Baytas, I.M., Xiao, C., Zhang, X., Wang, F., Jain, A.K., Zhou, J.: Patient subtyping via time-aware LSTM networks. In: Proceedings of the 23rd ACM SIGKDD International Conference on Knowledge Discovery and Data Mining, pp. 65–74 (2017)
2. Chandak, P., Huang, K., Zitnik, M.: Building a knowledge graph to enable precision medicine. Sci. Data **10**(1), 67 (2023)
3. Cheng, Y., Wang, F., Zhang, P., Hu, J.: Risk prediction with electronic health records: a deep learning approach. In: Proceedings of the 2016 SIAM International Conference on Data Mining, pp. 432–440. SIAM (2016)
4. Cho, K., et al.: Learning phrase representations using rnn encoder-decoder for statistical machine translation. In: Proceedings of the 2014 Conference on Empirical Methods in Natural Language Processing, pp. 1724–1734 (2014)
5. Choi, E., Bahadori, M.T., Song, L., Stewart, W.F., Sun, J.: GRAM: graph-based attention model for healthcare representation learning. In: Proceedings of the 23rd ACM SIGKDD International Conference on Knowledge Discovery and Data Mining, pp. 787–795 (2017)
6. Choi, E., Bahadori, M.T., Sun, J., Kulas, J., Schuetz, A., Stewart, W.: RETAIN: an interpretable predictive model for healthcare using reverse time attention mechanism. In: Advances in Neural Information Processing Systems, vol. 29 (2016)
7. Cui, S., Luo, J., Ye, M., Wang, J., Wang, T., Ma, F.: MedSkim: denoised health risk prediction via skimming medical claims data. In: 2022 IEEE International Conference on Data Mining (ICDM), pp. 81–90. IEEE (2022)
8. Donnelly, K., et al.: SNOMED-CT: The advanced terminology and coding system for eHealth. Stud. Health Technol. Inform. **121**, 279 (2006)
9. Hochreiter, S., Schmidhuber, J.: Long short-term memory. Neural Comput. 1735–1780 (1997)
10. Jang, E., Gu, S., Poole, B.: Categorical reparameterization with Gumbel-Softmax. arXiv preprint arXiv:1611.01144 (2016)
11. Johnson, A.E., et al.: MIMIC-III, a freely accessible critical care database. Sci. Data **3**(1), 1–9 (2016)
12. Kent, D.M., Steyerberg, E., van Klaveren, D.: Personalized evidence based medicine: predictive approaches to heterogeneous treatment effects. BMJ **363** (2018)
13. Kilicoglu, H., Fiszman, M., Rodriguez, A., Shin, D., Ripple, A., Rindflesch, T.C.: Semantic MEDLINE: a web application for managing the results of PubMed searches. In: Proceedings of the Third International Symposium for Semantic Mining in Biomedicine, vol. 2008, pp. 69–76. Citeseer (2008)
14. Kipf, T.N., Welling, M.: Semi-supervised classification with graph convolutional networks. arXiv preprint arXiv:1609.02907 (2016)
15. Lu, C., Han, T., Ning, Y.: Context-aware health event prediction via transition functions on dynamic disease graphs. In: Proceedings of the AAAI Conference on Artificial Intelligence, vol. 36, pp. 4567–4574 (2022)

16. Lu, C., Reddy, C.K., Chakraborty, P., Kleinberg, S., Ning, Y.: Collaborative graph learning with auxiliary text for temporal event prediction in healthcare. arXiv preprint arXiv:2105.07542 (2021)
17. Luo, J., Ye, M., Xiao, C., Ma, F.: HitaNet: hierarchical time-aware attention networks for risk prediction on electronic health records. In: Proceedings of the 26th ACM SIGKDD International Conference on Knowledge Discovery & Data Mining, pp. 647–656 (2020)
18. Ma, F., Chitta, R., Zhou, J., You, Q., Sun, T., Gao, J.: Dipole: diagnosis prediction in healthcare via attention-based bidirectional recurrent neural networks. In: Proceedings of the 23rd ACM SIGKDD International Conference on Knowledge Discovery and Data Mining, pp. 1903–1911 (2017)
19. Ma, F., You, Q., Xiao, H., Chitta, R., Zhou, J., Gao, J.: KAME: knowledge-based attention model for diagnosis prediction in healthcare. In: Proceedings of the 27th ACM International Conference on Information and Knowledge Management, pp. 743–752 (2018)
20. van der Maaten, L., Hinton, G.: Visualizing data using t-SNE. J. Mach. Learn. Res. 9(86), 2579–2605 (2008)
21. Mulyadi, A.W., Jun, E., Suk, H.I.: Uncertainty-aware variational-recurrent imputation network for clinical time series. IEEE Trans. Cybern. 52(9), 9684–9694 (2021)
22. Mulyadi, A.W., Suk, H.I.: KindMed: knowledge-induced medicine prescribing network for medication recommendation. arXiv preprint arXiv:2310.14552 (2023)
23. Shi, B., Weninger, T.: Open-world knowledge graph completion. In: Proceedings of the AAAI Conference on Artificial Intelligence, vol. 32 (2018)
24. Trinh, L., Tsang, M., Rambhatla, S., Liu, Y.: Interpretable and trustworthy deepfake detection via dynamic prototypes. In: Proceedings of the IEEE/CVF Winter Conference on Applications of Computer Vision, pp. 1973–1983 (2021)
25. Xu, Y., et al.: SeqCare: sequential training with external medical knowledge graph for diagnosis prediction in healthcare data. In: Proceedings of the ACM Web Conference 2023, pp. 2819–2830 (2023)
26. Yan, L., et al.: An interpretable mortality prediction model for COVID-19 patients. Nat. Mach. Intell. 2(5), 283–288 (2020)
27. Yang, C., Xiao, C., Ma, F., Glass, L., Sun, J.: SafeDrug: dual molecular graph encoders for recommending effective and safe drug combinations. arXiv preprint arXiv:2105.02711 (2021)
28. Ye, M., Cui, S., Wang, Y., Luo, J., Xiao, C., Ma, F.: MedPath: augmenting health risk prediction via medical knowledge paths. In: Proceedings of the Web Conference 2021, pp. 1397–1409 (2021)
29. Ye, M., Luo, J., Xiao, C., Ma, F.: LSAN: modeling long-term dependencies and short-term correlations with hierarchical attention for risk prediction. In: Proceedings of the 29th ACM International Conference on Information & Knowledge Management, pp. 1753–1762 (2020)

Oral Session: Explainability and Uncertainty

Stop Overkilling Simple Tasks with Black-Box Models, Use More Transparent Models Instead

Matteo Rizzo[✉][iD], Matteo Marcuzzo[iD], Alessandro Zangari[iD], Michele Schiavinato[iD], Andrea Albarelli[iD], and Andrea Gasparetto[iD]

Department of Environmental Sciences, Informatics, and Statistics, Ca' Foscari University of Venice, 30172 Mestre, VE, Italy
{matteo.rizzo,matteo.marcuzzo,alessandro.zangari,michele.schiavinato, albarelli,andrea.gasparetto}@unive.it

Abstract. The ability of deep learning-based approaches to extract features autonomously from raw data while outperforming traditional methods has led to several breakthroughs in artificial intelligence. However, these models suffer from intrinsic opacity, making it difficult to explain their predictions. This is problematic not only because it hinders debugging but, most importantly, because it negatively affects the perceived trustworthiness of the systems. What is often overlooked is that many relatively simple tasks can be solved efficiently and effectively with data processing strategies paired with traditional models that are inherently more transparent. This work highlights the frequently neglected perspective of using knowledge-based and explainability-driven problem-solving in ML. We introduce a set of guidelines to design explainable models and apply them to the task of classifying the ripeness of banana crates. This is done by planning explainability and model design together. We showcase how the task can be solved using opaque deep learning models and more transparent strategies. Notably, there is a minimal loss of accuracy but a significant gain in explainability, which is truthful to the model's inner workings. Finally, we perform a user study to evaluate the perception of explainability by the end users and discuss our findings.

Keywords: Explainable AI · Fruit Ripeness Classification · Deep Learning · Interpretability

1 Introduction

Over the past decade, Machine Learning (ML) research has significantly advanced with deep models based on Artificial Neural Networks (ANNs), improving accuracy in various cognitive tasks. However, these developments present challenges, notably in explainability - making model decisions comprehensible to

---

M. Rizzo, M. Marcuzzo, A. Zangari—Authors contributed equally.

humans [20]. This is particularly complex for deep models due to their opaque, intricate architectures. Explainability in DL is vital for confirming attributes like fairness and trustworthiness, especially in critical decision-making scenarios. With AI's expanding role, there is a push for regulatory measures such as the European AI Act, advocating for users' rights to explanations [7,25]. This regulatory trend contrasts with the intuitive, trial-and-error-based design process of DL models. The theoretical framework by Rizzo et al. provides clarity on key terms in Explainable Artificial Intelligence (XAI) [20]. An explanation involves interpreting evidence to answer "why" questions in this context. This concept divides into understanding the extent of *evidence* (*i.e.*, factual information used for the explanation) in model computations and how this evidence is transformed, and thus should be associated with an *interpretation* (*i.e.*, semantic for the evidence), within the model. Testing interpretations for faithfulness and plausibility is crucial, and presenting these explanations through an eXplanation User Interface (XUI) is essential for effective knowledge transfer [20]. Recent methods in ML focus on minor accuracy enhancements, often overlooking the need for explainability strategies. While techniques like SHAP (SHapley Additive exPlanations) offer explanations based on game theory, they have limitations and have been critiqued for questionable accuracy ([3,12,13]). This paper proposes a solution-oriented approach in ML, leveraging simpler models for a comprehensive design and analysis of model explainability, illustrated through a practical industry-relevant example.

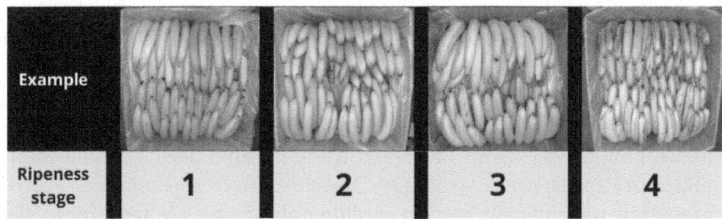

Fig. 1. Ripeness stages for crates of bananas from least ripe (1) to ripest (4).

1.1   Task and Approach

To showcase our design strategy, we analyze a straightforward real-world scenario and how the concepts mentioned above of accuracy and explainability affect it. Our target task is the classification of the ripeness of banana crates on a scale from 1 (least ripe) to 4 (ripest) (see Fig. 1 for an example).

In our approach, we design for competitive accuracy and explainability simultaneously. To tackle the classification task, we select a pool of three DL methods: (i) a simple Convolutional Neural Network (CNN) model with three convolutional blocks, (ii) a pre-trained convolutional model based on the MobileNetV2 framework [23], and (iii) a pre-trained Vision Transformer (ViT) [6]. As we will show, the latter allows for almost perfect results and is the best neural model across our proposed methods; however, none of the XAI methods we have tried seem capable of explaining its prediction accurately. On the other hand, we show that our approach, based on simple color features and a fine-tuned Decision Tree (DT), can provide competitive accuracy while exposing the information needed (i.e., the *evidence*) for producing adequate and global explanations.

1.2   Contributions

Our experiments reveal that three neural models achieve high accuracy quickly, questioning the necessity of complex, opaque methods for seemingly simple tasks. This finding points to the viability of simpler, more explainable models without sacrificing accuracy. Key contributions of our work include:

- Establishing design principles for ML problems prioritizing explainability;
- Analyzing DL methods for an explicative classification task, focusing on accuracy and explainability with a selection of models providing a broad view of the task;
- Demonstrating the effectiveness of a simpler, more transparent DT model with minimal feature engineering in solving the same task;
- Conducting a user study to verify explanations align with stakeholders' needs;
- Releasing our code and self-collected dataset[1] to support reproducibility and extension of our research.

2   Related Work

Our research intersects two significant areas: (i) enhancing explainability in AI and (ii) optimizing fruit ripeness grading.

Explainable AI. DL models are often criticized for their opacity, which makes explaining their predictions challenging. Efforts to derive explanations have used various techniques, including gradient information [26], attention scores [4], and model-agnostic methods like LIME and SHAP [13,18]. However, these explanations have faced reliability challenges in several contexts. Alvarez-Melis et al. [3] report that SHAP and other model-agnostic saliency-based methods are susceptible to instability, leading to significant saliency differences in the face of minor input modifications that do not alter the overall prediction. Adebayo et al. [2] demonstrate that some gradient-based methods tend to act like edge-detectors, generating dangerously misleading visual maps, and reveal that these can be manipulated in unexpected ways. Other authors have highlighted the unreliability of several gradient-based methods, as the dependence on reference points to determine saliency makes the heatmaps highly sensitive to minor input transformations [11]. Additionally, substantial shifts in important features can result in

---

[1] https://gitlab.com/distration/dsi-nlp-publib/-/tree/main/stop-overkilling-24.

zero gradient due to the models' non-linearity [17]. The authors of [9, 27] criticize the use of attention weights to determine importance, discovering that multiple attention distributions yield identical results. They also find a weak correlation between attention weights and other saliency measures, thereby questioning the reliability of this approach. Despite these issues, which may impact these XAI methods to varying degrees depending on the specific problem, we believe the primary limitation of these techniques is their inability to provide a semantic explanation of the model's decision that effectively conveys an unambiguous meaning to the human stakeholder. Referring to the nomenclature introduced by Rizzo et al. [20], they could be considered as *evidence* extractors, but more research and effort are needed to fill the gap between these and faithful interpretations, ultimately needed to deliver true explanations. Despite all these issues, SHAP remains a leading approach in saliency-based explainability, offering local and global model explanations. Because of this, in this study, we compare the usage of SHAP for explaining DL models with our more transparent approach.

Rudin et al. [22] emphasize the importance of using transparent models for high-stakes tasks. Aligning with this, our research advocates for simpler, transparent models that still achieve satisfactory performance and a strategy for faithful explanation.

Fruit Ripeness Recognition. Grading fruit ripeness has been addressed using statistical methods [15], traditional ML [16], and DL approaches [24]. DL methods, known for high accuracy and minimal feature engineering, are currently top-performing. Rizzo et al. [19] provide a comprehensive survey on fruit ripeness grading. Recent trends focus on minor accuracy improvements, often overlooking explainability [14].

3 Designing for Explainability

Our proposed guidelines aim to find the problem features that are most intuitive for the stakeholders and process them as little as possible through the simplest ML method adequate for the task. "Simplicity", in this case, relates to the number of parameters regulating the model (the lower, the better) and its reliance on human-understandable processing of the features (the more, the better).

In particular, we want to produce a pipeline from raw data to prediction, where each step is as transparent as possible. The proposed design process follows these high-level steps: (i) understand the task to be solved by the ML method, the available data, and the stakeholders of the final product; (ii) for each stakeholder, discuss which attributes they consider relevant in solving the task and define which features can be considered part of an explanation; (iii) find an ML model that is powerful enough to process the features but also offers the possibility to extract interesting evidence with a reasonable effort. The evidence must suggest an interpretation that is faithful by design to how the model works and possibly aligns with human intuition for plausibility [20]; (iv) test model performance and effectiveness of the generated explanations: the model should provide competitive accuracy with the state-of-the-art, while also satisfying the expectations of the stakeholders with the produced explanations. We find that a user study is an effective way to get qualitative evidence of the efficacy of the proposed XUI.

Step (ii) is perhaps the most challenging point, especially when very little problem-specific knowledge is available to the stakeholders. In this scenario, a preliminary analysis of the performance of top black-box models can indicate how hard the task is. If the specific task exposes intuitive features that can be leveraged to solve it, a model that tends towards transparency is worth trying. Intuitiveness is critical to optimizing the design and reaching a final explanation faithful to the model behavior and plausible to the human stakeholder. On the other hand, we acknowledge that finding meaningful features or even just effective data representation can be challenging for some tasks. In Natural Language Processing, for example, handcrafting general context-sensitive and human-understandable features is often very difficult or impractical, partly due to the inherent complexity of languages. That is why we advocate reasoning about an ML problem and try a broader explainability-driven approach, especially when the task is simple. For some tasks, simple or explainable solutions may not be there yet. The following sections showcase how we applied such guidelines to our example task.

3.1 Task Definition, Stakeholders, and Data

From a practical perspective, this work deals with a multiclass image classification task. Our stakeholders are workers at the wholesale fruit market of Treviso, Italy, who are interested in automating the ripeness grading of banana bunches. Currently, operators manually label bunches on an increasing ripeness value (1 to 4, least to most ripe, see Fig. 1). All the bananas within a crate are assumed to be in the same ripeness stage. The ML classifier resulting from this work would aid operators in labeling large numbers of incoming crates. Moreover, this is the first step in digitalizing the fruit processing pipeline, from inspection and assessment of fruit quality to online sales. Given the impact of the assessment step on fruit pricing, our stakeholders stressed the importance of maintaining transparency in the grading process to allow human supervision.

We collected an *ad-hoc* dataset comprising 927 images to develop the ML solution with a reasonable balance between the four ripeness classes. The dataset was manually labeled by the operators that perform the quality assessment of incoming products. To understand human performance on this classification task, we also asked three operators to re-label a subset of images from the dataset. More technical details on the data are provided in Sect. 4.1, while human performance is reported in Sect. 5.

3.2 Feature Selection

After consultation with the stakeholders, we determined that color is the most reliable and intuitive factor in determining the ripeness of banana bunches. Images are encoded using the RGB color space, a well-known color model backed up by solid theory based on the human perception of colors. Since color is the most important feature of our dataset, we process images to extract valuable color information and train our classifier to recognize the ripeness stage by considering such color. Section 4.1 details how this information is extracted and used in the proposed solution.

3.3   On the Choice of Models

We select state-of-the-art DL-based methods and simpler, more transparent classifiers for this task. Testing DL models gives us an idea of the best performance that can be achieved, as well as the problem's difficulty. As stated, our objective is to choose the model of the lowest complexity that achieves adequate performance to preserve as much transparency as possible. We selected a DT, a Support Vector Machine (SVM) with different kernels, and a multinomial Naive Bayes (NB) classifier as baseline models for comparison, eventually choosing the DT as the best model of the three.

We point out that the DT learns discriminative rules that partition the feature space into sub-spaces corresponding to each target class (*i.e.*, the ripeness stage). By extracting color information in the RGB space and limiting the number of extracted features, we can obtain a *global* explanation mapping each ripeness stage to specific areas of the color space. We highlight that this explanation is *faithful*, in the sense that it describes the DT "reasoning" process and *plausible*, meaning that it is aligned with the human understanding of the problem. These characteristics make this strategy effective concerning the point (iii) in our guidelines.

3.4   Testing for Accuracy and Explainability

We compare the performance of the baseline models (DT, SVM, NB) and select the DT to be the best compromise between the complexity and intuitiveness of the explanation that can be derived from it, as discussed in the previous section. The NB classifier achieves lower performance than the DT. Conversely, the SVM with a high-degree polynomial kernel achieved slightly better results (less than 0.5% accuracy and F1-score improvement). However, given the minimal difference in results and considering that the decision boundaries of the SVM are more difficult to understand because of their complexity, the DT appears to be a better choice. The complete results of these tests are reported in the supplementary material. Additionally, we compare the DT with some state-of-the-art DL models that would be the obvious off-the-shelf DL solutions for this task, in line with recent Computer Vision (CV) trends. Results are reported in Sect. 5, showcasing that the DT achieves competitive performance and is well above human classification performance. Finally, we want to assess the efficacy of the generated explanations for our stakeholders. To do this, we conducted a user study to investigate the users' preferences about the generated explanations. More details on the results are provided in Sect. 5.3 while the complete questionnaire is reported in the supplementary materials.

4   Methods and Explanations

4.1   Data Processing

Our dataset consists of 927 RGB images of banana crates captured at 4160×3120 pixels using a CZUR Shine Ultra scanner under consistent lighting. The images are balanced across classes, with details in the supplementary material. Images were resized to 224×224 pixels for compatibility with pre-trained models and to facilitate reasonable inference times. The dataset underwent augmentation with random transformations such as rotation, affine and elastic morphology transformations, cropping, gaussian blur, and perspective changes to mimic real-world scenarios like smartphone photography. About half of the dataset was augmented and incorporated into the training set, with further details in the supplementary material. The dataset's visual inspection indicated noise, especially around crate boundaries. To address this, we applied semantic segmentation using the SLIC algorithm [1], which improved results for all methods. Our report focuses on the outcomes with segmented images. For the selected DL models, feature extraction is automated from the raw RGB input. However, we employed minimal feature engineering for the DT, focusing on color features. Each image was represented by its average color's normalized R, G, and B channel values. We also adjusted luminance by converting images to YUV space, normalizing the Y channel, and reverting to RGB. This process is important since RGB embeds luminance within its channels, unlike spaces like YUV with a separate luminance channel.

4.2   Deep Learning Approach

In addressing the task of banana ripeness classification, we run and compare three neural approaches. The first architecture consists of a simple CNN using three convolutional blocks, each characterized by two bi-dimensional convolutions and max pooling interleaved by ReLU activation functions. The convolutional layers extract features fed to a three-layer feed-forward ANN, which outputs the final prediction. Before being processed by the CNN, the data is normalized to mean and standard deviation. The second architecture we consider is the pre-trained MobileNetV2 network [23]. Still convolutional by nature, the strategy at the core of this method is based on depth-wise convolutions and inverted residual connections. The designers aimed to build a powerful, pre-trainable model for low-tier devices. The third architecture we examine is the Vision Transformer (ViT) [6]. Transformers [28] are neural architectures based on multi-head attention [4], widely studied and employed by the NLP community [8,31]. This architecture has seen recent applications to CV tasks with various strategies (see [10] for a survey). Briefly, ViT splits images into fixed-size patches and linearly embeds them. Positional embeddings are then added to retain position information before feeding the resulting sequence of vectors to a standard Transformer encoder. Classification is achieved by adding a learnable "classification token" to the sequence. In our experiments, we use the `vit-base-patch16` model [29], which was pre-trained on ImageNet.

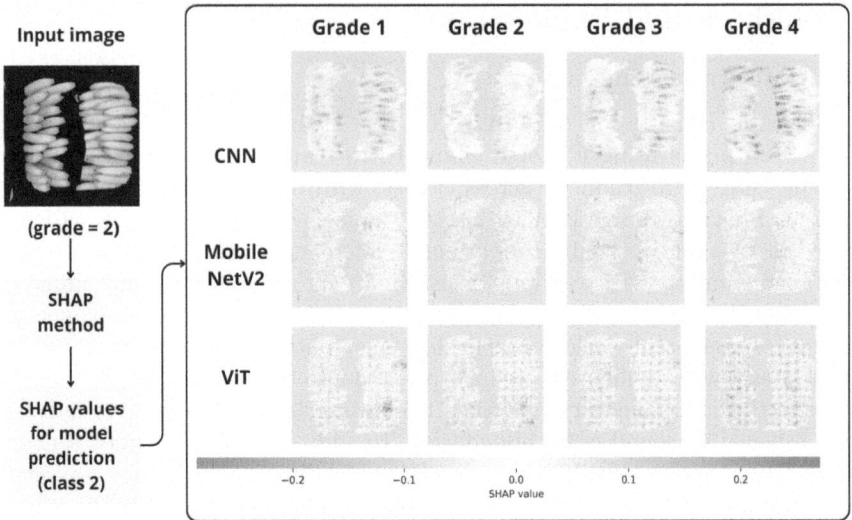

Fig. 2. Examples of explanations for DL models generated using SHAP.

Deep Learning Explainability Strategy. As previously mentioned, we used SHAP [13] to explain the predictions of the DL models. When dealing with images, SHAP allows generating heat maps (which constitute the XUI) to deliver the explanation to the user. These are supposed to describe the importance of each pixel in the image toward the model's prediction. Intuitively, warm colors indicate the regions of the image that contributed the most to the prediction. In contrast, colder colors indicate areas that contributed negatively to the prediction of the same class. Example explanations generated with SHAP are presented in Fig. 2. As mentioned in Sect. 2, feature importance heatmaps commonly produced with saliency methods lend themselves to potentially different (and deceiving) interpretations by the final users that may not reflect the actual decision-making process of the model. This is an alarming condition where the explanations convey to the user "a convincing lie" about how the model behaves. The next sections show how our design addresses faithfulness and plausibility.

4.3   Decision Tree

In contrast to the examined DL methods' inner complexity, we propose tackling the same task using a simple, more transparent model based on a DT classifier. In particular, we adopt the implementation offered by scikit-learn, based on the CART algorithm [5].

Explainability Strategy. One may argue that a DT is an intrinsically explainable model. We argue that there is no such thing as intrinsic explainability: a transparent model still needs to provide some explanation that is somewhat understandable to the users and answers their "why" questions. As stated by Rizzo et al. [20], models provide evidence, and generating a good explanation requires giving the evidence a semantic meaning, a process named *interpretation*. Moreover, different end-users are likely to have different requirements for explainability. An *explanation interface* must then convey the interpreted information to the users. For example, ML experts may be satisfied with understanding the range of feature values mapped to each target class (in our case, the RGB values). Non-expert users may need these rules to be further processed to be represented more clearly. Serving explainability is intuitively much easier with specific models, such as those regulated by a few parameters, though this is yet to be formalized in the literature. Admittedly, a DT has a very intuitive and faithful interpretation: for every non-leaf node, the DT learns a threshold value for one of its given features, thus producing two children (above and below the threshold). In our case, each instance is classified by following a path to a leaf labeled with a specific ripeness value. Conveniently, the set of rules given by the traversed path defines an area within the RGB color space that is part of our explanation. Binding the explanation to the intuitive process of discriminating banana crates based on color (as our stakeholders do) sets the premises for it to be plausible. Albeit simple for relatively shallow trees, the decision paths can grow exponentially for features with complex interactions. As anticipated, such numerical features split within the DT can still appear opaque to the average user. Thus, we take our explanation further by devising an XUI that aims to be human-understandable and tested accordingly. More specifically, we use the rules extracted from the decision path as constraints on the RGB gamut to identify portions of such a space representing the four ripeness classes. Hence, it is easy to describe each unknown input data point as its average color in the 3D RGB color space and determine which region it belongs to. This plot is our proposed explanation for the DT's behavior. Figure 3 is an example visualization of the whole process (more examples are reported in the supplementary material). It is worth stressing that the area of the color space extracted from the decision rules learned by the DT is, by definition, a *global* explanation. As such, our strategy allows us to understand which colors are associated with each label class unequivocally. One of the benefits of such an interpretable explanation is the ability to validate the classifier's behavior. Unexpected colors would appear in the proposed XUI, pointing out a negative bias in the model.

5   Experiments

In this section, we compare the performance achieved by our employed methods. First, we analyze the classification metrics achieved by the three DL-based models and the DT. Then, we study the explanations generated according to the strategies proposed in Sect. 4.2 and Sect. 4.3 and compare them through a user study involving the stakeholders for the task of banana ripeness classification in a real fruit market.

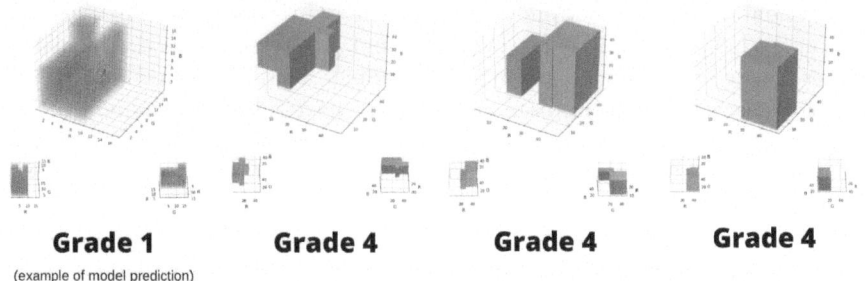

Grade 1   **Grade 4**   **Grade 4**   **Grade 4**

(example of model prediction)

Fig. 3. Explanation generated from the constraints imposed by the DT on the RGB color gamut. The four grades identify different areas within the gamut.

Table 1. Macro-averaged performance metrics for the models averaged over ten random seeds (standard deviation in brackets).

	Accuracy	Precision	Recall	F_1
Decision Tree	0.9716 (± .0104)	0.9723 (± .0106)	0.9678 (± .0119)	0.9697 (± .0110)
CNN	0.9349 (± .0115)	0.9298 (± .0131)	0.9308 (± .0123)	0.9377 (± .0123)
MobileNet V2	0.9743 (± .0046)	0.9726 (± .0046)	0.9717 (± .0054)	0.9718 (± .0049)
ViT	0.9967 (± .0015)	0.9960 (± .0020)	0.9966 (± .0017)	0.9962 (± .0018)
Human Performance	0.7500 (± .0589)	0.7588 (± .0453)	0.7500 (± .0589)	0.7519 (± .0524)

5.1   Performance

To measure the ability of our selected models to produce correct predictions, we resort to commonly used classification metrics: accuracy, macro-averaged precision, macro-averaged recall, and macro-averaged F1 score. All methods are tested using 5-fold cross-validation, repeated ten times with different random seeds to strengthen the results. Table 1 showcases the results achieved with both deep-learning methods and the DT. We additionally report the human performance, which is the average of the scores obtained by three stakeholders on the classification of a balanced dataset of 300 randomly sampled images from the original non-augmented dataset ($\sim$ 20%). It is easy to see that all methods achieve excellent results, with all metrics surpassing the 90 s percentile scores and improving on a human baseline. It is worth remembering that these results are achieved on the datasets augmented with images that have gone through various augmentations, which makes them more robust at the cost of small decreases in performance.

Further detailed in the supplementary material, error analysis reveals that mistakes always occur because the classifiers select an adjacent class (*e.g.*, class 2 instead of 1). The ViT model achieves a near-perfect score among the selected methods for all metrics. The DT also obtained outstanding results, though this required comparatively more effort (including the standardization of the luminance and the extensive grid search). Nevertheless, this process allows the DT to have results comparable to those of MobileNetV2.

5.2 Explainability

We compare the SHAP explanations for the DL models with the handcrafted explanations based on RGB color designed for the DT. Figure 2 and 3 compare the two types of explanations for the same input. It is easy to see that the masks produced by SHAP do not highlight meaningful features of the image. Indeed, we can observe that the regions highlighted seem random. Not only that, in our case, SHAP's visualization for the CNN always presented the same result for all classes, seemingly valuing features for grade 4 highly (even when the CNN correctly classified other ripeness stages). The situation does not change when we visually examine the explanations generated by the methods throughout the whole dataset. This does not necessarily mean that the explanations generated by SHAP are not faithful to the model's inner workings. Rather, our intuitive interpretation of the highlighted regions is misaligned with how the model uses those features internally. As such, we can only conclude that, despite their plausibility, these visualizations are inadequate as significant explanations. However, this may not always be the case. Assuming that the visualization correctly reflects the model's inner workings, the position of the important pixels would be much more meaningful in coarse-grained classification tasks. For instance, in a detection task on ImageNet, if the important pixels are located on an animal's muzzle, the intuitive interpretation is that the muzzle is the crucial part of the image. Nevertheless, even in this scenario, the interpretation of the heatmap comes from the user, not from the model. In slightly more challenging cases, different users might arrive at different interpretations. This exemplifies why we believe saliency-based methods do not fully solve the explanation problem on their own but rather support the process of generating an explanation. On our specific dataset, however, the position of these highlighted regions does not convey intelligible information. Conversely, our explanation for the DT is faithful to the model's inner workings by design. This strategy provides the user with a much more informative explanation that is intuitively understandable, plausible, and faithful to how the model works. An *ad hoc* user study confirms such results.

5.3 User Study

We designed a user study to investigate the users' preferences about the generated explanations for the model predictions. The users involved in the study are stakeholders in the grading of banana ripeness, consisting of 20 people with different backgrounds and expertise with AI tools. We submitted an online questionnaire to each user. The complete questionnaire is reported in the supplementary material. The questionnaire introduces the task and asks the users to compare two types of explanations for the same input and prediction: (i) the mask generated by SHAP and (ii) the representation of the input color in the RGB gamut. Explanations (i) pertain to the ViT model (the best-performing one), while explanation (ii) is generated from the DT. The object of the comparison is how much the proposed explanation allows you to answer why the model made that prediction. When asked about the importance of explaining the model's behavior, all participants believed that an associated explanation is somewhat necessary, with most thinking it to be essential. As for the preferred explanation method, ten out of twenty respondents considered the RGB gamut area produced by the DT to be the most effective, and eight voted for the SHAP heatmap explanation. Three declared that no explanation was helpful to them[2]. This result is certainly interesting; though SHAP's visualizations do not provide an unambiguous explanation, their visual nature was enough to make half of the participants deem them trustworthy in conveying why the prediction was made. Finally, 80% respondents declared that the chosen explanation would improve their trust in the model, and 70% are ready to trade about 5% of the classifier accuracy for a more transparent and human-explainable decision process. Considering that the accuracy loss between the DT and the most accurate model is only around 2.5% for our classification task and well above human performance, there appears to be little reason to prefer the latter to the more explainable one. We report the detailed results of our user study as supplementary material.

6   Future Work

Using simple classifiers on a few manually extracted features can be much more problematic on more complex tasks, as this could severely limit the performance of the models. Indeed, we do not make the point that more transparent models should *always* be used; many cognitive tasks would be nearly impossible without the progress obtained through DL. For this specific task, we selected a simple strategy to provide an intuitive explanation to non-ML-expert users based on the average color of the whole image. This can be refined iteratively to incorporate more complex features while accounting for explainability. We plan to explore strategies to serve explanations using higher numbers of features, for example, considering the pixel color distribution and sampling to obtain a more accurate color representation.

Moreover, in line with the *explainability by design* principle, we plan to research the usage of regularization strategies to improve the explainability of complex DL models. This topic has already been explored [30], mostly tackling the problem of robustness, which has indeed been linked to the issue of explainability [21]. It would be interesting to explore whether and how adding constraints on the features extracted by NNs could help produce more understandable explanations by the end-users.

7   Conclusions

This paper discusses the explainability of ML models by providing high-level guidelines to tackle ML problems. For example, we compare three DL models

---

[2] One participant selected both the RGB explanation and the "neither" option.

to a DT for classifying bananas into four ripeness stages. While the DT leads to slightly lower accuracy scores, it produces more explainable results. This task showcases how *model design* can devise an intuitive explanation strategy rather than with a *post-hoc* approach. We argue that working with a more transparent model and stakeholder-understandable features, where possible, can allow for satisfactory explanations with minimal loss in accuracy. To validate our claim, we conducted a pilot user study on 20 users, comparing the explanations produced by SHAP, a popular model-agnostic XAI method for DL models, against those produced by combining color features and DT rule interpretations. The study results indicate users' tendency to accept minor accuracy losses, favoring a more understandable model. However, they also showcase how non-expert users prefer more straightforward explanations, regardless of whether they are well-founded.

Acknowledgments. This study was funded by the European Union - NextGenerationEU, in the framework of the iNEST - Interconnected Nord-Est Innovation Ecosystem (iNEST ECS_00000043 - CUP H43C22000540006). The views and opinions expressed are solely those of the authors and do not necessarily reflect those of the European Union, nor can the European Union be held responsible for them. This paper was funded by Veneto Agricoltura within the scope of the project "Guaranteeing the continuity of the agrifood chain: the digitization of wholesale markets".

Disclosure of Interests. The authors have no competing interests to declare relevant to this article's content.

References

1. Achanta, R., Shaji, A., Smith, K., Lucchi, A., Fua, P., Süsstrunk, S.: Slic superpixels compared to state-of-the-art superpixel methods. IEEE Trans. Pattern Anal. Mach. Intell. **34**(11), 2274–2282 (2012). https://doi.org/10.1109/TPAMI.2012.120
2. Adebayo, J., Gilmer, J., Muelly, M., Goodfellow, I., Hardt, M., Kim, B.: Sanity checks for saliency maps. In: Proceedings of 32nd International Conference on Neural Information Processing Systems, pp. 9525–9536, December 2018
3. Alvarez-Melis, D., Jaakkola, T.S.: On the robustness of interpretability methods. In: ICML Workshop on Human Interpretability in Machine Learning (WHI 2018) (2018). https://doi.org/10.48550/arXiv.1806.08049
4. Bahdanau, D., Cho, K., Bengio, Y.: Neural machine translation by jointly learning to align and translate. In: 3rd International Conference on Learning Representations, ICLR 2015, San Diego, CA, USA, 7-9 May 2015, Conference Track Proceedings (2015). http://arxiv.org/abs/1409.0473
5. Breiman, L.: Classification and Regression Trees. Routledge, New York (1984).https://doi.org/10.1201/9781315139470
6. Dosovitskiy, A., et al.: An image is worth 16×16 words: transformers for image recognition at scale. In: International Conference on Learning Representations (2021). https://openreview.net/forum?id=YicbFdNTTy
7. EC: Laying down harmonised rules on artificial intelligence (artificial intelligence act) and amending certain union legislative acts (2021). https://eur-lex.europa.eu/legal-content/EN/TXT/?uri=CELEX:52021PC0206

8. Gasparetto, A., Zangari, A., Marcuzzo, M., Albarelli, A.: A survey on text classification: practical perspectives on the Italian language. PLOS ONE **17**(7) (2022). https://doi.org/10.1371/journal.pone.0270904

9. Jain, S., Wallace, B.C.: Attention is not explanation. In: Proceedings of the 2019 Conference of the North American Chapter of the ACL: Human Language Technologies, vol. 1, pp. 3543–3556. Assoc. Comput. Linguist., Minneapolis, Minnesota, June 2019. https://doi.org/10.18653/v1/N19-1357

10. Khan, S., Naseer, M., Hayat, M., Zamir, S.W., Khan, F.S., Shah, M.: Transformers in vision: a survey. ACM Comput. Surv. **54**(10s) (2022). https://doi.org/10.1145/3505244

11. Kindermans, P.-J., et al.: The (Un)reliability of saliency methods. In: Samek, W., Montavon, G., Vedaldi, A., Hansen, L.K., Müller, K.-R. (eds.) Explainable AI: Interpreting, Explaining and Visualizing Deep Learning. LNCS (LNAI), vol. 11700, pp. 267–280. Springer, Cham (2019). https://doi.org/10.1007/978-3-030-28954-6_14

12. Kumar, I.E., Venkatasubramanian, S., Scheidegger, C., Friedler, S.: Problems with shapley-value-based explanations as feature importance measures. In: Proceedings of the 37th International Conference on Machine Learning. Proceedings of Machine Learning Research, vol. 119, pp. 5491–5500. PMLR, 13–18 July 2020. https://proceedings.mlr.press/v119/kumar20e.html

13. Lundberg, S.M., Lee, S.I.: A unified approach to interpreting model predictions. In: Proceedings of the 31st International Conference on Neural Information Processing Systems, p. 47684777. NIPS'17, Curran Associates Inc., Red Hook, NY, USA (2017). https://doi.org/10.48550/arXiv.1705.07874

14. Marcuzzo, M., Zangari, A., Albarelli, A., Gasparetto, A.: Recommendation systems: an insight into current development and future research challenges. IEEE Access **10**, 86578–86623 (2022). https://doi.org/10.1109/ACCESS.2022.3194536

15. Mendoza, F., Aguilera, J.: Application of image analysis for classification of ripening bananas. J. Food Sci. **69**(9), E471–E477 (2006). https://doi.org/10.1111/j.1365-2621.2004.tb09932.x

16. Ni, X., Li, C., Jiang, H., Takeda, F.: Deep learning image segmentation and extraction of blueberry fruit traits associated with harvestability and yield. Hortic. Res. **7**(1), 110 (2020). https://doi.org/10.1038/s41438-020-0323-3

17. Nielsen, I.E., Dera, D., Rasool, G., Ramachandran, R.P., Bouaynaya, N.C.: Robust explainability: a tutorial on gradient-based attribution methods for deep neural networks. IEEE Signal Process. Mag. **39**(4), 73–84 (2022). https://doi.org/10.1109/MSP.2022.3142719

18. Ribeiro, M.T., Singh, S., Guestrin, C.: Why should i trust you?: explaining the predictions of any classifier. In: Proceedings of the 22nd ACM SIGKDD International Conference on Knowledge Discovery and Data Mining, KDD 2016, pp. 1135–1144. Association for Computing Machinery, New York, NY, USA (2016). https://doi.org/10.1145/2939672.2939778

19. Rizzo, M., Marcuzzo, M., Zangari, A., Gasparetto, A., Albarelli, A.: Fruit ripeness classification: a survey. Artif. Intell. Agric. **7**, 44–57 (2023). https://doi.org/10.1016/j.aiia.2023.02.004

20. Rizzo, M., Veneri, A., Albarelli, A., Lucchese, C., Nobile, M., Conati, C.: A theoretical framework for AI models explainability with application in biomedicine (2023). https://doi.org/10.1109/CIBCB56990.2023.10264877

21. Ross, A., Doshi-Velez, F.: Improving the adversarial robustness and interpretability of deep neural networks by regularizing their input gradients. In: Proceedings of

the AAAI Conference on Artificial Intelligence, vol. 32, no. 1, April 2018. https://doi.org/10.1609/aaai.v32i1.11504

22. Rudin, C.: Stop explaining black box machine learning models for high stakes decisions and use interpretable models instead. Nat. Mach. Intell. **1**(5), 206–215 (2019). https://doi.org/10.1038/s42256-019-0048-x

23. Sandler, M., Howard, A., Zhu, M., Zhmoginov, A., Chen, L.C.: Mobilenetv2: inverted residuals and linear bottlenecks. In: 2018 IEEE/CVF Conference on Computer Vision and Pattern Recognition, pp. 4510–4520 (2018). https://doi.org/10.1109/CVPR.2018.00474

24. Saranya, N., Srinivasan, K., Kumar, S.K.P.: Banana ripeness stage identification: a deep learning approach. J. Ambient. Intell. Humaniz. Comput. **13**(8), 4033–4039 (2022). https://doi.org/10.1007/s12652-021-03267-w

25. Selbst, A.D., Powles, J.: Meaningful information and the right to explanation. Int. Data Priv. Law **7**(4), 233–242 (2017). https://doi.org/10.1093/idpl/ipx022

26. Selvaraju, R.R., Cogswell, M., Das, A., Vedantam, R., Parikh, D., Batra, D.: Gradcam: Visual explanations from deep networks via gradient-based localization. In: 2017 IEEE International Conference on Computer Vision (ICCV), pp. 618–626 (2017). https://doi.org/10.1109/ICCV.2017.74

27. Serrano, S., Smith, N.A.: Is attention interpretable? In: Proceedings of the 57th Annual Meeting of the ACL, pp. 2931–2951. Association for Computational Linguistics, Florence, Italy, July 2019. https://doi.org/10.18653/v1/P19-1282

28. Vaswani, A., et al.: Attention is all you need. In: Advances in Neural Information Processing Systems, vol. 30, p. 60006010. Curran Associates, Inc. (2017). https://doi.org/10.48550/arXiv.1706.03762

29. Wu, B., et al.: Visual transformers: token-based image representation and processing for computer vision (2020). https://doi.org/10.48550/arXiv.2006.03677

30. Wu, C., Gales, M.J.F., Ragni, A., Karanasou, P., Sim, K.C.: Improving interpretability and regularization in deep learning. IEEE/ACM Trans. Audio Speech Lang. Process. **26**(2), 256–265 (2018). https://doi.org/10.1109/TASLP.2017.2774919

31. Zangari, A., Marcuzzo, M., Rizzo, M., Giudice, L., Albarelli, A., Gasparetto, A.: Hierarchical text classification and its foundations: a review of current research. Electronics **13**(7) (2024). https://doi.org/10.3390/electronics13071199

Feature-Based Explainable Reinforcement Learning in Environments with Multiple Sources of Risk

Omid Davoodi$^{(\boxtimes)}$ and Majid Komeili(iD)

Carleton University, Ottawa, ON, Canada
omiddavoudi@cmail.carleton.ca

Abstract. Explainable Reinforcement Learning is key in bringing the current neural network-based state-of-the-art reinforcement learning methods to real-world environments. In particular, explaining the risks of the agent's decision-making process is critical to deploying such models in safety-critical tasks. The previous feature-based methods for characterizing risk in reinforcement learning settings were not well suited for handling situations when there are multiple sources of risk. This work attempts to address this shortcoming by providing a post-hoc method that can explain multiple sources of risk. Our experiments show that the proposed method can provide more insights into the workings of the agent while avoiding the issues faced by the previous work in multi-risk environments.

Keywords: Explainable AI · XAI · Reinforcement Learning · Explainable RL

1 Introduction

Interpretable and explainable artificial intelligence (XAI) is a very important prerequisite for the deployment of AI models in areas where trust, transparency, responsibility, and regulatory compliance are needed. This has been catalysis for a varied body of research into many aspects and methods of interpretability and explainability [4,11,13,16]. The goal of these is to offer humans insights into the decision-making process of an AI model.

Reinforcement Learning (RL) agents, same as other important machine learning methods, can have interpretability and explainability requirements before their real-world deployment. Many inherently interpretable RL methods have been proposed in the past [8,9,12,18]. These use interpretable base models to construct their policy function in the hopes of ensuring interpretability for the entire RL agent. However, such methods do not scale well to more complex tasks. Even if the method itself can scale, the resulting model will usually be too large to be human-understandable [11].

It is also important to note that the current state-of-the-art RL methods almost exclusively use black-box neural networks as their policy function estimator [1,10,17]. In such cases, explanations can be generated to demystify the black-box model using explainable AI approaches. An important category of such methods is referred to as post-hoc explanation methods. First offered by Ribeiro et al. [16] for post-hoc explainability of general machine-learning models, they generate local explanations for the decisions of the model long after the model itself is trained. Due to not putting any meaningful constraints on the base AI model itself, these methods have become an important tool for offering explainability while being able to enjoy the power of the state-of-the-art neural network models. Such post-hoc approaches have also been proposed in the area of reinforcement learning [3].

Interpretability and explainability are usually needed when there is some notion of consequence for the mistakes of the AI. In a supervised learning setting, the consequences of a mistake in predicting criminal recidivism are much larger than the consequences of a mistake in detecting a spam email. In reinforcement learning, the notion of consequence is usually in the form of risk [6]. An agent operating in environments where risky states and actions are possible requires far more scrutiny than one that operates in a safe environment. For this reason, risk is a very important factor when designing interpretable and explainable RL methods.

To this end, Davoodi et al. [3] offered a post-hoc risk explanation framework that is independent of the agent running on the environment. Instead, their method only depends on the environment the agent operates in. It first creates a state-transition model, a directed state-transition graph in particular, from a log of agent interactions with the environment. It also requires a risk function for which they used a binary risky/not-risky classification. Risky states were defined as states which are either fatal/terminal, or states that, once an agent reaches them, will always lead to a fatal state. The latter category is called a supercritical state. The method offered by Davoodi et al. [3] offered two types of risk-based explanations for agent behavior: The local direction of risk in relation to the current state of the agent s and the distance of the agent to the closest risky state in terms of the number of actions. To calculate these, S^*, a set of states reachable from s by at most n actions, were created using the state-transition graph. The distance to the nearest risky state was then found using a breadth-first search from the current state of the agent. The local direction of risk g is a concept borrowed from the explanations of LIME [16]. g which is a vector of the size of the state dimensions, is the direction of changes each feature of s needs to reach a risky state. It can be seen as a rough approximation of the gradient of the risk function at s. It is calculated by training a linear classifier on the states in S^*. The goal of the classification will be to separate the risky and non-risky states and the final coefficients vector of the trained classifier will be g. Figure X shows a schema of the method and Fig. 4 shows examples of its explanations for a task.

The method proposed by Davoodi et al. has a main drawback: it cannot distinguish between different sources of risk. In environments where there is only one source of risk, this will not be an issue. However, many real-world RL problems have complex and varied risk sources that can cause the method to generate misleading explanations for the agent. In some cases, one source of risk might dominate g while smaller sources could be closer to the agent itself. In other cases, the agent might be surrounded by sources of risk and a single g might not be enough to show the true dangers of the environment.

In this work, we offer a method for generating explanations for multiple sources of risk in the environment. This helps prevent issues such as g being dominated by a farther, larger source of risk, or misleading information that can arise when the agent is surrounded by different risk sources. Finally, by explaining the multiple sources of risk, more insight can be offered to humans about the characteristics of the environment itself, helping them create more effective agents overall.

2 Proposed Method

Our proposed method is based on the work done by Davoodi et al. [3]. We first create a state-transition graph from a list of prior agent interactions with the environment. We merge graph nodes that have a distance of less than ϵ by using the representative state of one of the nodes while we are in the process of generating the graph. We also define a binary risk function which will recognize a state as risky when it is either a terminal state or one in which all possible resulting states from that state are risky themselves. This definition of risk, usually referred to as supercritical states, was first defined by Pecka et al. [14]. What is different in the new method is the differentiation between different sources of risk in the environment.

We take a hierarchical graph clustering approach for finding these different sources of risk. By separating risky states into similar clusters, we can use the direction of the change of state space towards those risky clusters as our multiple directions of risk. First, we form the initial risk clusters from all supercritical states that have any direct links between themselves in the transition graph. Then, for each pair of nodes in the directional state transition graph belonging to two separate risk clusters, if those two nodes are both reachable by at most d_m moves from any graph node, we merge the clusters they belong to.

To perform this task efficiently, we define the concept of risk neighborhoods. Risk neighborhoods are clusters of risky and non-risky nodes within the graph. At first, we initialize the risk neighborhoods the same as the risk clusters. We then grow these neighborhoods by adding any node within the graph that has a directional link going to at least one of the nodes within a neighborhood to that neighborhood. If a node starts to belong to more than one risk neighborhood, the corresponding risk neighborhoods *and* the risk clusters will be merged. After performing this action d_m times, our final merged risk clusters will be created.

Once the risk clusters are created, we can create explanations for the actions of any agent operating within the environment. Noticeably, this can be any type of agent including humans, RL-based or non-RL-based agents. For an agent in some state s in the environment, we first use the state-transition graph to get S^*, the set of reachable states by at most n actions from the state s. Breadth-first-search (BFS) on the state-transition graph starting from s with a depth limit of n can give us S^*. We then find all risky states in S^* and separate them into the sets $S_{r_1}, S_{r_2}, ..., S_{r_k}$ based on their membership in the k risk clusters present in S^*.

We can then use these to find $g_1, g_2, ..., g_k$, the multiple directions of risk from state s. For each g_i, we train a linear logistic regression classifier on the set of non-risky states from S^* combined with S_{r_i}. We give risky states the class label of 1 and the non-risky ones the label of 0. g_i is the coefficient vector of the trained classifier. Figure 1 shows an example of g_i obtained this way and its meaning in a simplified environment.

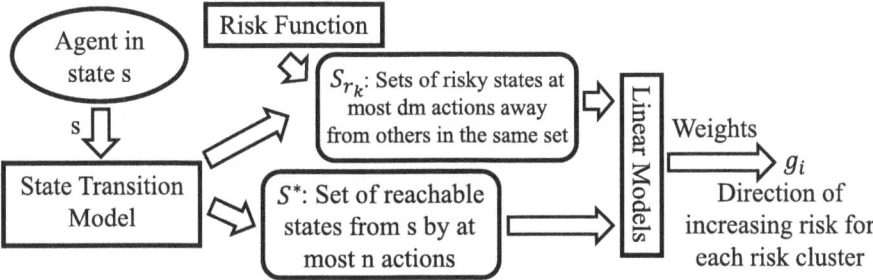

Fig. 1. A schema of our method

Another explanation given by our method is how many graph nodes away the agent is from each risk cluster. This can be seen as the current distance of the agent to each risk source. In many real-world environments, the uncertainty about the result of an agent's actions and the potential for other dynamic sources of change means that agents should try to stay within a reasonable distance of risky states. Otherwise, the stochastic nature of the environment might push the agent towards risk. Knowing the distance to the different risk sources within an environment during an agent's run can give humans important insights into its workings.

The choice of hyperparameters ϵ and d_m depends on the knowledge of the environment and the task. Higher ϵ leads to improved speed, memory usage, and generalization at the expense of granularity and precision of the state-transition graph. d_m should be chosen based on the knowledge of the nature of risk in the environment and the choice of n. It is good to monitor the number of remaining clusters as we increase d_m and pick a value that is at the beginning of a plateau in the number of remaining clusters. It is also important to note the ramifications of high d_m. If d_m is higher than the depth limit n, all risky states in S^* will always belong to the same cluster.

3   Experiments

We performed a number of experiments to assess the capabilities of our method. The experiments included complex robotics environments with risky states, small handcrafted gridworld environments to show the capabilities of our method more clearly, and also a real-world medical dataset used for designing RL agents with the goal of treating sepsis.

3.1   Lunar Lander

The first experiment was done on the Lunar Lander environment from OpenAI's gym [2]. In this environment, the agent is a falling spacecraft that has to use its thrusters to safely land on the surface of a planet. The environment is interesting because the direction of risk depends on the current orientation of the lander and there can be sudden changes in the direction of risk if the angle of descent changes enough. A screenshot of the environment can be seen in Fig. 2.

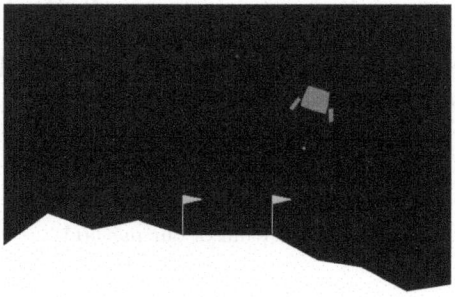

Fig. 2. An example of the Lunar-Lander environment.

We trained a TD3 [5] agent on this environment until it managed to solve the task. We then created the state transition graph of our method using the interactions of the agent and the environment during the training process. The state transition graph contained 39 critical and 54 supercritical states. Those supercritical states were divided into 33 initial risk clusters. We tested a variety of different merging distance values and decided to pick $d_m = 2$ as it was far enough from our value of $n = 10$ and going higher would only have increased our computation time without any change in the risk cluster status. This resulted in 19 risk clusters in total. The number of remaining risk clusters after merging with different d_m can be found in Fig. 3.

We then used these risk clusters to generate explanations for our TD3 agent. We also plotted the different directions of risk during one of the agent's runs. As our method differentiates between the different sources of risk, it gives a better picture of the situation compared to the previous method that calculated a single

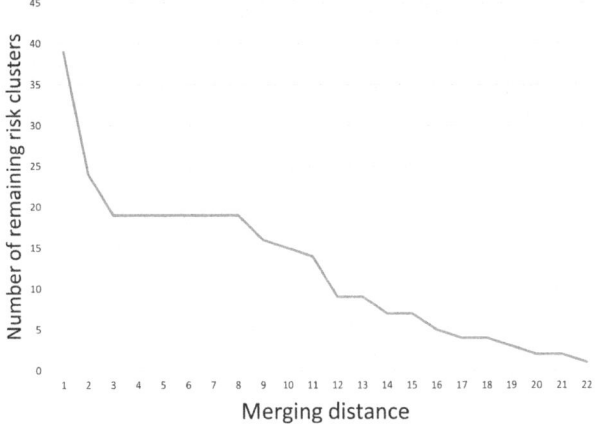

Fig. 3. The effect of merging distance on the final number of clusters in the Lunar Lander environment.

direction for risk. The explanations of our method for a single run can be seen in Fig. 4.

The figure shows the distance of the agent to each risk cluster during the entirety of its run. It also includes the direction of risk vectors g_i in the form of a heatmap. An example is provided to show how to interpret the heatmap. In this case, it shows a strong correlation between increasing risk and the decrease of both horizontal and vertical velocity, as well as the increase of the angular velocity. The first 2 are obvious as the lander will stop when it crashes, but the correlation between the increase in angular velocity and risk shows the danger of further tilting the lander in a clockwise direction. Note that by looking at Fig. 4-C, it can be noted that a decrease in the angular velocity will also lead to increasing risk. In other words, the agent should not change its angular velocity in general if it wants to avoid risk. But looking at Fig. 4-F, it can be seen that by not separating the sources of risk, source #2 is overpowering source #1 in the direction vector and wrongly implying that by increasing the angular velocity, risk can be avoided. This is an example of the advantage of the new method over the old one.

3.2   Bipedal Walker

Our second experiments were done in the gym's Bipedal Walker environment. This environment contains a bipedal robot trying to reach the end of the environment by walking and running without falling to the ground. The actuators are the joint motors in the hips and the knees of the robot. This environment is interesting because it is much easier for the agent to fail and it can happen at any time during the run. This creates a large number of risk clusters in the state transition graph. At the same time, the environment is a case where at any given point in the run, there is usually only a single source of risk in the immediate future. In other words, many of these risk clusters are quite far apart. This is an instance where our method rarely offers a better explanation than the single risk source approach.

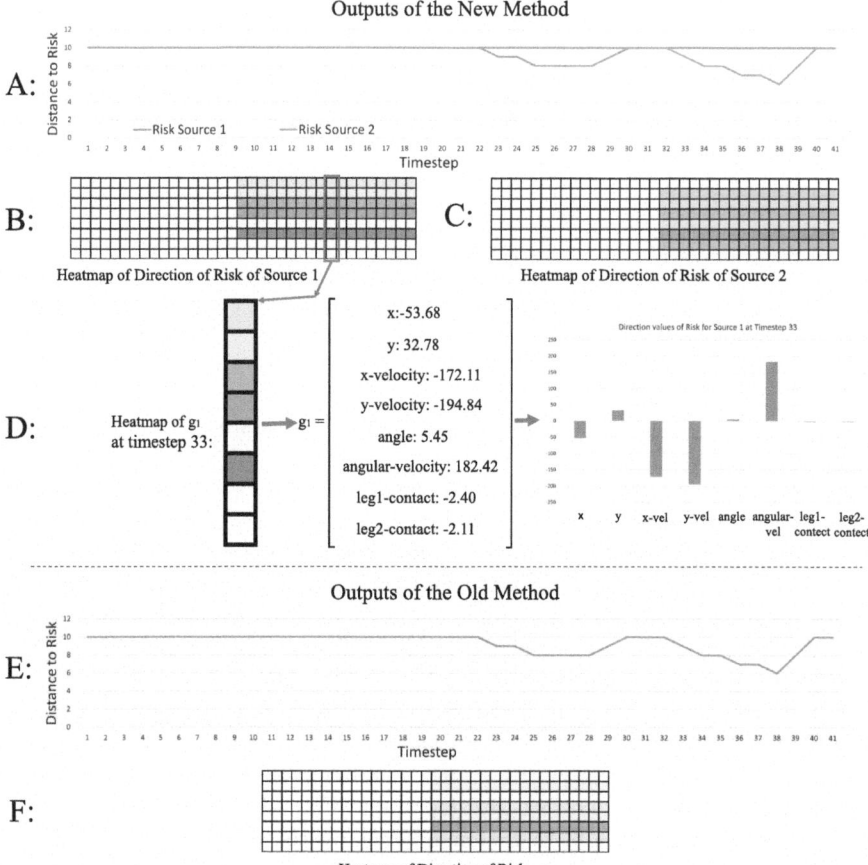

Fig. 4. Comparison of our method (subfigures A-D) and the previous method [3] (subfigures E and F) on the Lunar-Lander experiment. Both runs are for the same successful run. A shows the distance of the agent to each risk source for the duration of the run clamped to the value of 10. As can be seen, there are two different sources of risk in this particular run. B and C show the heatmaps of the directions of risk. Each column j is a normalized representation of g_i on timestep j of the run. Brighter blue colors show a positive correlation between risk and that particular feature. Brighter red colors show a negative correlation between risk and that feature. White shows very little correlation between risk and that feature. D shows g_1 for timestep $j = 33$. The heatmap is derived from the vector and each element shows the direction of risk with respect to the risk source #1 in terms of the features of the state space. E shows the distance of the agent to *any* risk source and F shows the heatmap for the general direction of risk from the previous method [3].

Like Lunar Lander, we trained a TD3 agent on this environment and then generated our state transition graph using the agent's interactions with the environment. The state transition graph contained 163 critical and 369 supercritical states. It also had 135 risk clusters before merging. We tested different values of d_m to find the number of remaining risk clusters. The results of those tests can be found in Fig. 5. As can be seen, not only does this environment have a large number of initial risk clusters, but those clusters also require large values of d_m to effectively merge together, suggesting they are quite far from each other in the state transition graph. As $n = 10$ in this experiment, we chose $d_m = 6$ so that it would be easier to find the rare instances where there are multiple directions of risk in the near future.

Same as before, we used these risk clusters to generate explanations for one of the agent's runs. This particular run was during the early phases of training of the agent where it had still not been able to reliably stand on its feet and could fall either backwards or facedown. Figure 6 shows the distance to risk clusters for this run and also the explanations of the old method for the same run. From the new method, it can be seen that the agent tried to avoid the first risk source, but over-corrected and moved towards other types of risky states. As the old method does not distinguish between these two different sources of risk, it is unable to offer a comprehensive explanation of the agent's failure.

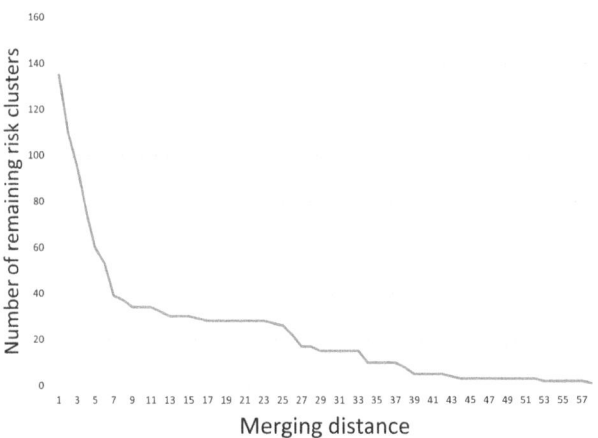

Fig. 5. The effect of merging distance on the final number of clusters in the Bipedal-Walker environment.

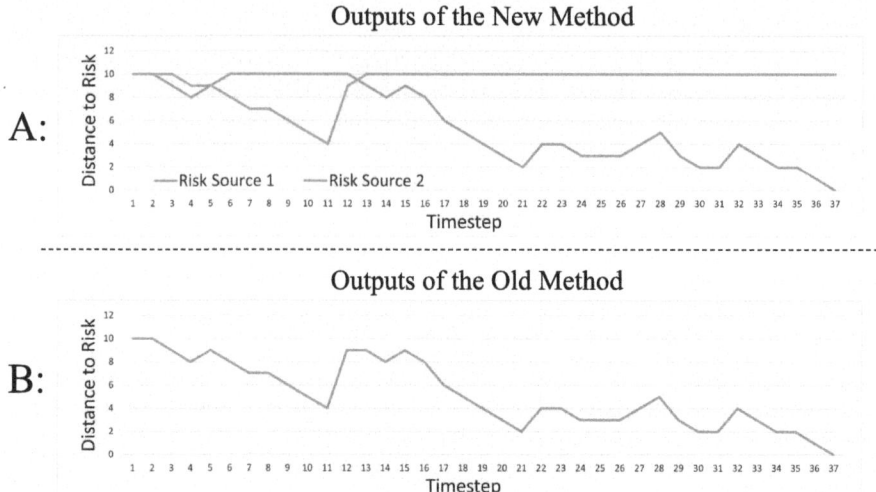

Fig. 6. Comparison of our method (subfigure A) and the previous method [3] (subfigure B) on the Bipedal-Walker experiment. Both runs are for the same unsuccessful run.

3.3 Grid-World Experiment

Our third experiment was done in a custom grid-world environment. This environment consists of an agent in a simple grid with the task of reaching a position at the top right of the environment. The agent can move forward or change directions as its action. There are obstacles in the environment that block movement and lava tiles which will terminate the run if the agent moves into them. There is a 10% chance that the agent will move to an adjacent tile of the current position, either left or right based on the current direction the agent is facing, instead of forward when it takes the move forward action. There is a line of lava tiles to the left of the beginning area and a long line of blocked tiles to the right. In the middle of the block tiles, there is also a lava tile. Figure 7 shows the environment and the agent at the starting position.

This Environment is interesting because it shows one of the failures of the previous single direction of risk method of [3]. As there is a chance for moving sideways when trying to move forward, a well-trained agent will try to move in the middle of the corridor towards the top in order to prevent itself from accidentally falling into either of the lava pits. The problem is that in a single direction of risk scheme, the number of lava pits to the left outweighs the single lava pit to the right and will cause the direction to always point towards the larger lava pool. This will happen even when the agent is adjacent to the small lava pool. This causes a discrepancy between the direction of risk and the distance to risk given by the previous method where going away from risk will paradoxically decrease our distance to it. The new approach solves this issue by separating these two sources of risk. A comparison between the explanations given by the previous method and the new one for this environment can be found in Fig. 8.

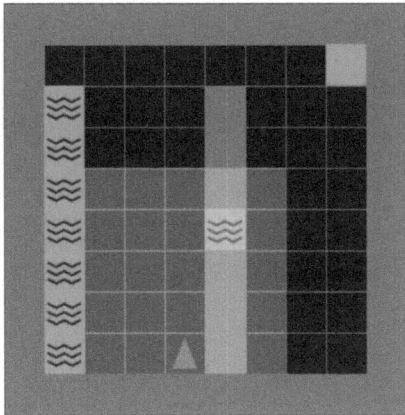

avoid the lava and get to the green goal square

Fig. 7. The custom gridworld environment used in our experiments with the agent at the starting position. The highlighted 5×5 square is the agent's perception range.

From the perspective of the previous method, the initial move to the left is going directly towards risk because $g = (x : -0.89, y : 0.13)$ and a move to the left is $(x : -1, y : 0)$. But the new separate understanding of risk sources in the new method shows that there is another source of risk that needs to be avoided by moving to the middle of the corridor. Similarly in the unsafe run, the old method witnesses a sudden drop in the distance to risk even though the agent is not moving in the supposed direction of risk. The new method shows that the risk source to the right is the culprit for this sudden drop.

3.4   Real-World Medical Dataset Experiment

Our final experiment was to gauge the results of our new method in a real-world scenario. For this, we chose the MIMIC-III medical dataset [7]. MIMIC-III is a medical dataset consisting of the information of over 40,000 patients in a critical-care section of the Beth Israel Deaconess Medical Center. It is of special interest to us because there are many attempts at training reinforcement learning agents to devise strategies for the treatment of sepsis using this dataset. In the sensitive field of healthcare, mistakes in treatment—whether done by a person or an AI agent—can have catastrophic consequences. Therefore, our risk-focused method is a good fit for such environments.

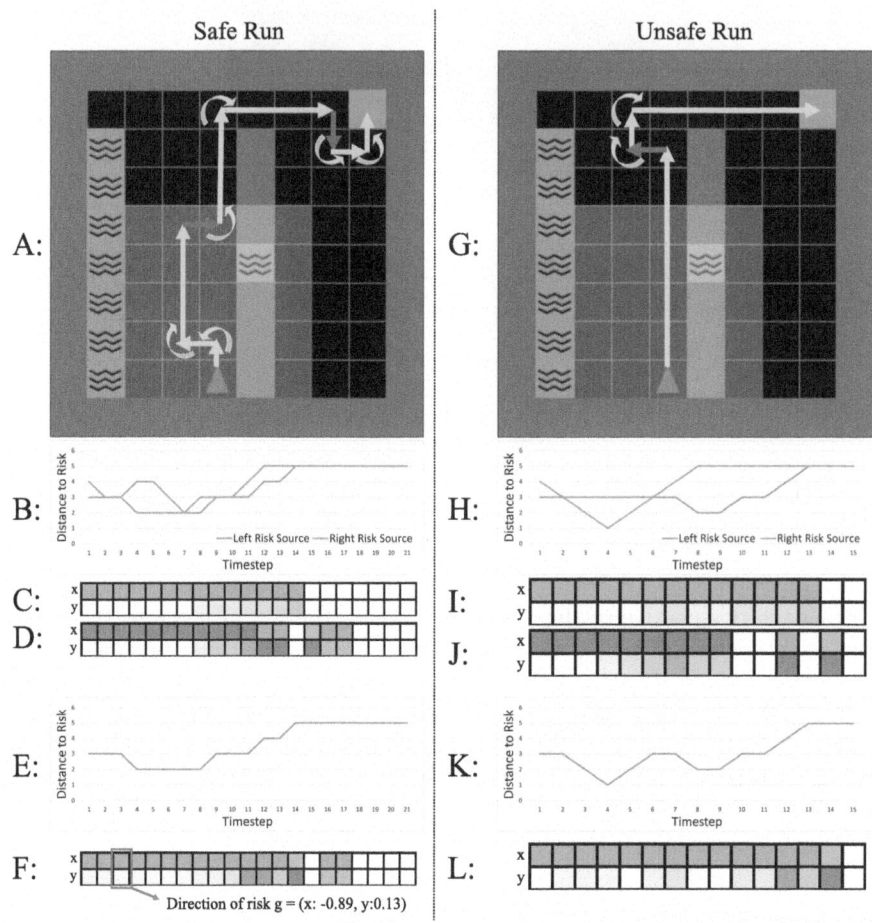

Fig. 8. Comparison of our method (subfigures B, C, D, H, I, and J) and the previous method [3] (subfigures E, F, K, and L) on two different runs (subfigures A and G) in the gridworld experiment. A shows an agent that tries to be as far as it can from both of the risk sources (safe run). G shows an agent that is making the risky decision of getting close to one of the risk sources (unsafe run). Yellow arrows show the agent's wilful decisions. Red arrows are the unintended random sideways moves that are coded into the environment. B and H plot the distance between the agent and each risk source in the vicinity. C and D show the heatmap of the direction of each risk source for the first agent (C shows the left source and D shows the right source). In the same manner, I and J show the heatmap of the directions of each type of risk for the second agent (I for the left source and J for the right source). E, F, K, and L illustrate the outputs of the old method of [3] for these agents.

We used the feature generation and data preparation process used by Raghu et al. [15] for this task. In total 47 different health features from the patients were extracted from the dataset for every 4 h of their stay in the critical care unit.

When the data for a particular health feature was not available for a timestamp, interpolation between other known values at other times was used. Overall, this created about 270,000 unique states in the dataset which were condensed into around 170,000 graph nodes by merging states that have less distance than $\epsilon = 0.2$. We differed from Davoodi et al. [3] in our choice of the risk function for this environment. They used a continuous risk function definition that required iterative updating. We, on the other hand, used the same terminal-supercritical risk dichotomy that is used in our other experiments. This led to a total of 1182 critical and 3875 supercritical states in the graph. After merging the risk clusters with $d_m = 8$, 533 final risk clusters were left in the model. Interestingly, increasing d_m beyond 23 did not change the number of risk clusters at all which suggests that the generated state-transition graph is disjoint. The effect of d_m on the number of final clusters can be seen in Fig. 9. The differences for the distance to risk between a patient who survived and one that passed away can be seen in Fig. 10.

The old method is unable to show the different types of risk present in these situations. In the successful treatment, it is unable to explain that the first two increases in risk were different from the third one. The new method, however, explains that the last increase in risk was of a different nature to that of the first two. A similar situation can be seen in the case of the unsuccessful treatment where different sources of risk were at some periods of time, more prominent for the patient. The new method offers a more granular insight into the complex environment of this dataset.

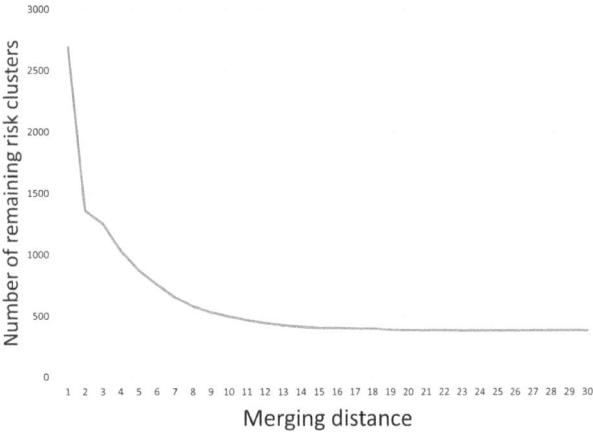

Fig. 9. The effect of merging distance on the final number of clusters in the Mimic III environment.

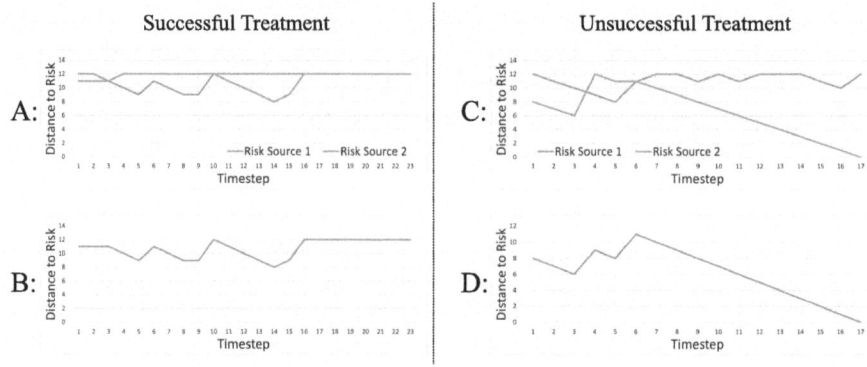

Fig. 10. Comparison of our method (subfigures A and C) and the previous method [3] (subfigures B and D) on the MIMIC-III experiment. A and C are for the same successfully recovered patient and B and D are for the same unsuccessful treatment.

4   Discussion

In this work, we have proposed a method for creating post-hoc explanations for risk in reinforcement learning environments. Our approach takes multiple sources of risk into account, which allows it to generate more detailed and insightful explanations of agent behavior. This is very important for two main reasons: First, it offers better interpretability by offering more information about the environment and the local neighborhood of the current state, and second, it does not offer misleading information about risk when one source of risk overwhelms another in the current locality. Our experiments show the validity and interpretability of our new method compared to the previous literature on a variety of environments, including a real-world medical environment.

Acknowledgement. This research was enabled in part by support provided by the Digital Research Alliance of Canada (alliancecan.ca) and the Natural Sciences and Engineering Research Council of Canada (NSERC).

Disclosure of Interests. The authors have no competing interests to declare that are relevant to the content of this article.

References

1. Arulkumaran, K., Deisenroth, M.P., Brundage, M., Bharath, A.A.: Deep reinforcement learning: a brief survey. IEEE Signal Process. Mag. **34**(6), 26–38 (2017)
2. Brockman, G., et al.: OpenAI gym. arXiv preprint arXiv:1606.01540 (2016)
3. Davoodi, O., Komeili, M.: Feature-based interpretable reinforcement learning based on state-transition models. In: 2021 IEEE International Conference on Systems, Man, and Cybernetics (SMC), pp. 301–308. IEEE (2021)
4. Du, M., Liu, N., Hu, X.: Techniques for interpretable machine learning. Commun. ACM **63**(1), 68–77 (2019)

5. Fujimoto, S., Hoof, H., Meger, D.: Addressing function approximation error in actor-critic methods. In: International Conference on Machine Learning, pp. 1587–1596. PMLR (2018)
6. Heger, M.: Consideration of risk in reinforcement learning. In: Machine Learning Proceedings 1994, pp. 105–111. Elsevier (1994)
7. Johnson, A.E., et al.: MIMIC-III, a freely accessible critical care database. Sci. Data **3**(1), 1–9 (2016)
8. Li, X., Serlin, Z., Yang, G., Belta, C.: A formal methods approach to interpretable reinforcement learning for robotic planning. Sci. Robot. **4**(37), eaay6276 (2019)
9. Liu, G., Schulte, O., Zhu, W., Li, Q.: Toward interpretable deep reinforcement learning with linear model U-trees. In: Machine Learning and Knowledge Discovery in Databases: European Conference, ECML PKDD 2018, Dublin, Ireland, 10–14 September 2018, Part II, pp. 414–429. Springer (2019)
10. Mnih, V., et al.: Human-level control through deep reinforcement learning. Nature **518**(7540), 529–533 (2015)
11. Molnar, C.: Interpretable Machine Learning (2020). Lulu.com
12. Mott, A., Zoran, D., Chrzanowski, M., Wierstra, D., Jimenez Rezende, D.: Towards interpretable reinforcement learning using attention augmented agents. In: Advances in Neural Information Processing Systems, vol. 32 (2019)
13. Murdoch, W.J., Singh, C., Kumbier, K., Abbasi-Asl, R., Yu, B.: Definitions, methods, and applications in interpretable machine learning. Proc. Natl. Acad. Sci. **116**(44), 22071–22080 (2019)
14. Pecka, M., Svoboda, T.: Safe exploration techniques for reinforcement learning–an overview. In: Modelling and Simulation for Autonomous Systems: First International Workshop, MESAS 2014, Rome, Italy, 5–6 May 2014, Revised Selected Papers 1, pp. 357–375. Springer (2014)
15. Raghu, A., Komorowski, M., Celi, L.A., Szolovits, P., Ghassemi, M.: Continuous state-space models for optimal sepsis treatment: a deep reinforcement learning approach. In: Machine Learning for Healthcare Conference, pp. 147–163. PMLR (2017)
16. Ribeiro, M.T., Singh, S., Guestrin, C.: "Why should i trust you?" Explaining the predictions of any classifier. In: Proceedings of the 22nd ACM SIGKDD International Conference on Knowledge Discovery and Data Mining, pp. 1135–1144 (2016)
17. Sewak, M.: Deep Reinforcement Learning. Springer (2019)
18. Verma, A., Murali, V., Singh, R., Kohli, P., Chaudhuri, S.: Programmatically interpretable reinforcement learning. In: International Conference on Machine Learning, pp. 5045–5054. PMLR (2018)

Probing Network Decisions: Capturing Uncertainties and Unveiling Vulnerabilities Without Label Information

Youngju Joung[1] , Sehyun Lee[1] , and Jaesik Choi[1,2]( )

[1] Korea Advanced Institute of Science and Technology, Daejeon, Korea
{ojoo_o,sehyun.lee,jaesik.choi}@kaist.ac.kr
[2] INEEJI, Seongnam-si, Gyeonggi, Korea

Abstract. To improve trust and transparency, it is crucial to be able to interpret the decisions of Deep Neural classifiers (DNNs). Instance-level examinations, such as attribution techniques, are commonly employed to interpret the model decisions. However, when interpreting misclassified decisions, human intervention may be required. Analyzing the attributions across each class within one instance can be particularly labor-intensive and influenced by the bias of the human interpreter. In this paper, we present a novel framework to uncover the weakness of the classifier via counterfactual examples. A prober is introduced to learn the correctness of the classifier's decision in terms of binary code - *hit* or *miss*. It enables the creation of the counterfactual example concerning the prober's decision. We test the performance of our prober's misclassification detection and verify its effectiveness on the image classification benchmark datasets. Furthermore, by generating counterfactuals that penetrate the prober, we demonstrate that our framework effectively identifies vulnerabilities in the target classifier without relying on label information on the MNIST dataset.

Keywords: Image classification · Prober · Interpretable machine learning

1 Introduction

Interpretable machine learning is crucial for explaining the decisions of Deep Neural classifiers (DNNs). In particular, mission-critical systems in the real world, such as autonomous driving or AI-assisted medical diagnosis programs, should provide suitable reasons why the classifier makes such decisions. However, it is challenging to comprehend the decisions due to the complexity of these models.

Y. Joung and S. Lee—These authors contributed equally to this work.

For instance-level explanation, the attribution techniques are commonly employed to highlight the influence of input features on the model decisions. By observing the gradient or activations of the classifiers, the decisions can be interpreted by calculating the saliency of input features. However, it requires human intervention to interpret the salient features since the techniques produce multiple attributions across the classes. Moreover, some cases are reported where the input attribution techniques show disagreement within the same classifier by issuing the robustness of explanations [14,20]

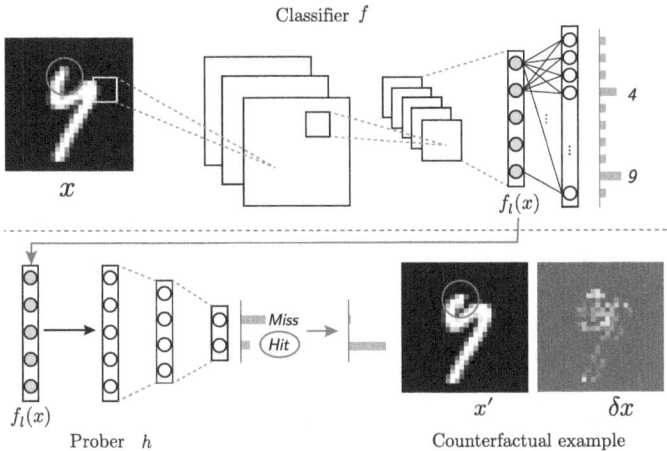

Fig. 1. Overview of the proposed framework to investigate the misclassified samples. In this example, the sample is classified as 9 while the true label is 4. Given the hidden representation of the layer of the instance, the prober predicts whether the classifier is *hit* or *miss*. Then, the counterfactual example is generated through the classifier and the prober. In this process, *obstructive* features are modified, contributing to the reduction of uncertainty in the classifier's confidence.

Our goal is to reduce human interference and produce more objective explanations in interpreting the classifier. The main idea involves introducing a prober to encode the classifier's decision into binary code (*hit* and *miss*) so that it simplifies the number of target classes. In detail, *hit* represents cases where the classifier correctly predicts the answer, while *miss* indicates cases where the classifier fails to predict the correct answer. This binary encoding approach reduces the effort required for users to compare interpretations across various classes.

In this paper, we propose a simple yet novel framework to discover vulnerabilities in the classifier at the instance-level. Our contributions are as follows. First, by introducing a shallow Feed Forward Network (FFN) called a prober, we conduct detection for misclassified samples. Additionally, we construct a *Hit-Miss* Dataset for the experiment and explore the evidence behind how the prober operates effectively. Second, through analyzing the prober, we indirectly investigate the classifier to identify *obstructive* features that confuse the classifier. Since our method employs a binary encoding approach, it is enable to access potential labels even in opaque scenarios where the true label is unknown. Moreover, the advantage of our framework demonstrates the possibility of facilitating auto-correction capabilities for the classifier.

2   Related Work

Prober. Probers are widely applied for testing specific properties of the internal representations within a neural classifier. Exploring the internal workings of a neural classifier is typically challenging, so employing a relatively simple prober for indirect analysis is preferred. [1,3,21]. In the case of Natural Language Processing (NLP), probing techniques are extensively utilized to evaluate knowledge of Language Models (LM). For example, detecting true-false relationships can be employed to validate the model's ability to handle hallucinations [2]. Predicting verb tense is used to assess the model's understanding of sentence structure [24]. To prevent additional biases and ensure the simplicity of the prober, a simple feedforward classifier is typically employed to measure probing accuracy.

Misclassification Detection. Misclassification detection aims to identify the misclassified samples from the given classifier to enhance the reliability of confidence estimation. It is closely related to out-of-distribution (OOD) detection, but misclassification is not constrained to whether the sample comes from in-distribution or out-of-distribution explicitly. A baseline of misclassification detection is using the maximum softmax probability [10]. OpenMix [26] proposed utilizing the outlier exposure method [11] for more reliable misclassification detection. However, extra actions are still required to interpret the misclassified samples.

Counterfactual Explanations. The counterfactual-based explanation [16,23] method aims to explain the causal relationship between input and the model's final decision. In the classification task, to understand why the input could not be classified into another class, a situation opposite to what is actually observed is assumed. As counterfactual examples aim to provide semantically different examples compared to adversarial examples, a generative model is employed to generate more semantically meaningful counterfactual examples [8]. Specifically, they propose the Approximated Diffeomorphic Counterfactuals (ADC) approach, utilizing normalizing flow to find optimal values in the latent space of the generator along the data manifold. We embrace the ADC method for discovering and analyzing vulnerabilities in the classifier.

3   Methodology

In this section, we first suggest the proposed framework to provide an explanation through counterfactual examples representing a likely *hit* decision from the perspective of the classifier as illustrated in Fig. 1. Then, we present the following three core elements comprising this framework including a *Hit-Miss* datasets, a prober, and a counterfactual generator.

3.1   Probing Framework

In this subsection, we present an overview of the probing framework along with relevant notations. The framework is designed to work with a classifier f of interest, initially trained for a specific task $x \mapsto \hat{y}$, where x represents the input and $\hat{y}$ is the prediction. The primary focus of this paper is on the image classification task, but it should be noted that the framework is versatile and adaptable to diverse domains and tasks.

The classifier evaluates an annotated dataset $\mathcal{D} = \{x^{(i)}, y^{(i)}\}$ and generates the intermediate representation of x at the layer l, denoted as $f_l(x)$. To encode the classifier's decision into binary code, a probing label o is scored to indicate whether the classifier predicts the class correctly or incorrectly. Following this, a prober $h : f_l(x) \mapsto \hat{o}$ is trained on the *Hit-Miss* dataset $\mathcal{D}_P = \{f_l(x)^{(i)}, o^{(i)}\}$, which consists of representations and the corresponding probing label. The prober allows for the indirect analysis of the *obstructive* feature that straightforwardly hindered the prediction of the classifier.

3.2   The *Hit-Miss* Dataset

In the context of our work, we leverage a *Hit-Miss* dataset $\mathcal{D}_P = \{f_l(x)^{(i)}, o^{(i)}\}$ encoded in binary form $o = \{0, 1\}$, enabling us to frame the problem as binary classification. A positive class represents the prediction of the classifier is the same as the true class - *hit*. In contrast, a negative class indicates the prediction is different - *miss*.

We assume the decisions of the classifier are reliable, believing that the classifier correctly captures the meaningful features. However, this assumption introduces an imbalance in the *Hit-Miss* dataset concerning probing labels. A substantial difference in counts between *hit* and *miss* instances is observed in Table 1. This imbalance poses a challenge for the prober, as it may be prone to consistently indicating that the classifier is always *hit*. Strategies to address this issue will be discussed in the following subsection.

3.3   Prober

To capture the hidden features of the target classifier without becoming overly complex and without introducing additional biases, a simple Feed Forward Network (FFN) is chosen. This involves using three fully connected layers with ReLU activations. The prober takes the hidden representations of a specific layer in the target classifier as input and produces an output indicating whether the classifier classifies the given sample correctly or not. Due to the significant imbalance ratio between the *hit* and *miss* labels, two strategies are employed for mitigation: adjustment of loss weight and application of label-smoothing regularization [18]. The cross-entropy objective is expressed as:

$$q(k) = o_k(1 - \alpha) + \frac{\alpha}{K} \tag{1}$$

$$\mathcal{L} = -\sum_{k=1} q(k) \log p(k) + w(1 - q(k)) \log (1 - p(k)) \tag{2}$$

where K represents the number of classes and $q(k)$ is the likelihood the model assigned to the k-th class. Here, $K = 2$, because the prober predicts whether it is *hit* or *miss*. In the case of *hit* label that is represented as one hot vector, it is transformed from $[0, 1]$ to $[\frac{\alpha}{2}, 1 - \frac{\alpha}{2}]$ given a label smoothing parameter α. To mitigate the imbalance of labels, the weight w is assigned to the *miss* class. These adjustments help alleviate the risk of overfitting, promote generalization, and prevent excessive model confidence [22]. It is empirically demonstrated how the prober shows the misclassification performance on the *Hit-Miss* dataset in Sect. 4.3.

3.4 Counterfactual Generator

The prober evaluates the likelihood of misclassification by manipulating the internal information of the classifier. Consequently, interpreting the prober facilitates an indirect examination of the classifier's behavior. Traditional Explainable Artificial Intelligence (XAI) methods predominantly analyze models under the assumption of knowing the target label. However, an explanation is often required for unlabeled data in the real world. Hence, we specifically consider scenarios where the true label remains unknown.

We then aim to generate Approximated Diffeomorphic Counterfactuals [8] for the prober's *hit* score (ADC_{hit}) to analyze the conditions under which the classifier approaches the actual answer. Given the original image x, we perform gradient ascent on the *hit* logit of the prober and the optimal value z^* is explored in the latent space of the generator g. The optimization process for finding the optimal value z^* and generating ADC_{hit} is as follows.

$$z = g^{-1}(x) \tag{3}$$

$$z^{(i+1)} = z^{(i)} + \lambda \frac{\partial ((h \circ f_l) \circ g)_{hit}}{\partial z}(z^{(i)}) \tag{4}$$

$$ADC_{hit}(x) = g(z^*) \tag{5}$$

where f, g, h, λ and l denote the classifier, generative model, prober, step size, and the target layer to extract a hidden representation of the classifier, respectively. In addition, pre-trained RealNVP [7,8] is employed as a generative model. In this study, our focus is on comprehending the limitations of the classifier rather than emphasizing correctly predicted samples. Therefore, the primary analysis set comprises samples predicted as *miss* by the prober. (The results can be found in Sect. 4.4).

4 Experiments

4.1 Experimental Setup

Datasets. We employ four different benchmark datasets that encompass image classification task. MNIST [17] is a dataset of hand-written digits, consisting of grayscale images with 10 classes and a total of 60k images, characterized by low resolution. Fashion-MNIST (F-MNIST) [25] is similar to MNIST, but the images contain 10 different types of clothing, making it slightly more complex than MNIST. CIFAR-10 [15] consists of 60k color images distributed across 10 classes. ImageNette [12] is a subset of the ImageNet [6] dataset comprising 10 easily classified classes, representing almost 10% of the original dataset. This allows testing performance on the high-resolution image (we use 128px).

Table 1. Comparison of image classification accuracy of image classification benchmark datasets: MNIST, F-MNIST, CIFAR10, and ImageNette.

Dataset	Classifier	Train		Test	
		Top-1	Top-5	Top-1	Top-5
MNIST	CNN	98.60	99.99	98.50	99.97
F-MNIST	CNN	98.03	99.99	92.86	99.87
CIFAR10	ResNet18	91.07	99.83	79.63	98.75
ImageNette	XResNet50	86.63	99.00	83.92	98.29

Model Architecture. The model architectures for each dataset were selected based on established precedents. For MNIST and F-MNIST, we use a CNN with four blocks, each comprising batch normalization, non-linear ReLU activation, max-pooling, and dropout, following the architecture outlined in [8]. For CIFAR-10, we adapt a ResNet18 architecture by adjusting the kernel size of the first convolutional layer to 3 and replacing max-pooling to be an identity function in accordance with [4]. In the case of ImageNette, we use XResNet-50 [13] architecture. Hidden representations are extracted just before the final fully-connected layer, resulting in dimensions of 256, 256, 256, and 2048 for the respective datasets. The prober utilizes a simple feedforward classifier with three fully connected layers and non-linear ReLU activation in all models.

Table 2. Comparison of misclassification detection performance on benchmark datasets - MNIST, FMNIST, CIFAR10, and ImageNette. The performance are reported with **AUPR** ($\uparrow$), **AUROC** ($\uparrow$), **FPR95** ($\downarrow$) and **Accuracy** ($\uparrow$). AUPR is calculated by treating the *miss* class as positive. All metrics are presented as percentages. Imbalance ratio (IR) indicates the proportion of the instances in the *hit* class to the number of instances in the *miss* class based on Top-1 accuracy. The larger the value of IR, the greater the extent of imbalance.

Dataset	IR_{train}/IR_{test}	Prober	AUPR	AUROC	FPR95	ACC
MNIST	70.8/51.3	256-128-64	39.98	98.37	3.57	98.60
F-MNIST	37.8/13.0	256-256-64	48.29	86.39	45.45	92.30
CIFAR10	8.54/3.74	256-256-64	46.66	84.17	69.18	84.10
ImageNette	6.03/6.54	2048-512-64	51.44	84.24	59.50	84.59

Training Details. During the training of classifiers, we adhered to the conventional train/test dataset split with standard cross-entropy loss. When a classifier is capable of capturing the proper features, it is valuable to utilize the counterfactuals because it exhibits sufficient discriminative power. Under this assumption, the classifiers achieve high classification accuracy, resulting in an imbalance between the number of *hit* and *miss* classifications in the dataset, as detailed in Table 1. To ensure the prober does not express excessive confidence in *hit* predictions, we applied label smoothing regularization with a coefficient of 0.2 and assigned a weight of 2 to the *miss* label empirically.

4.2   Results of the Misclassification Detection

We initiate the evaluation of the prober's performance by assessing its ability to accurately classify misclassified samples across diverse benchmark datasets, including MNIST, F-MNIST, CIFAR10, and ImageNette. The evaluation employs essential metrics, including Area Under the Precision-Recall curve (AUPR), Area under the Receiver Operating Characteristic curve (AUROC), False Positive Rate at 95% True Positive Rate (FPR95), and Test Accuracy (ACC) [5,9,26].

AUPR quantifies the model's performance across various levels of precision and recall, which is especially useful for an imbalanced dataset. AUROC represents the relationship between True Positive Rate (TPR) and False Positive Rate (FPR), offering the classifier's discriminatory ability. FPR95, the False Positive Rate at 95% TPR, indicates the probability of misclassified examples being predicted as *hit* when the TPR reaches 95%. Test Accuracy (ACC) serves as a fundamental metric to assess overall classifier performance. Collectively, these metrics facilitate a comprehensive evaluation of the prober's achievement in identifying misclassified samples across diverse datasets.

Table 2 presents the performance of the prober, empirically demonstrating the ability to predict the correctness of classifier predictions based on hidden representation. Overall, the prober achieved high accuracy and AUROC across all datasets. The significance lies in its competent success, even on high-resolution image dataset such as ImageNette. Notably, for MNIST, the prober shows exceptional performance, particularly in terms of AURC and FPR95. Due to the high imbalance, it was challenging to learn the proper relationship between hidden representation and *Hit-Miss* label. With a small number of *miss* instances in the test dataset, since the prober has high confidence in *hit*, it causes a poor FPR95. Relatively, AURC captures the precision-recall trade-off over the thresholds, showing a different aspect than FPR95. There is much room for accurately improving the prober to learn the *Hit-Miss* dataset. Throughout the remainder of the study, we analyze the MNIST dataset and use the prober that shows the best performance among datasets.

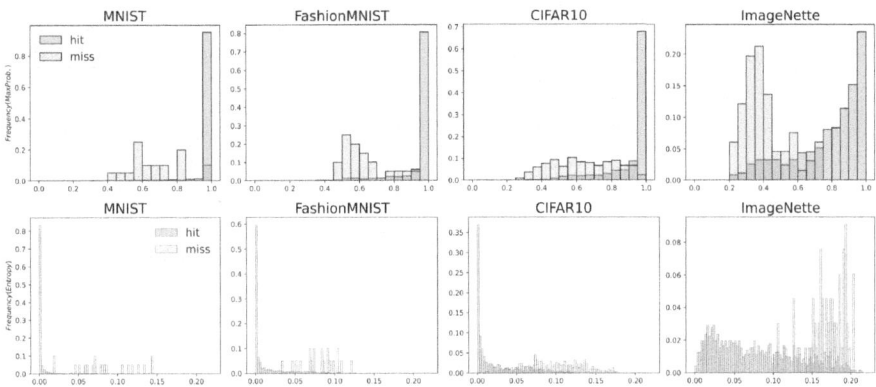

Fig. 2. Maximum probability (first row) and entropy of probability (second row) of the classifier.

4.3 How the Prober Works

As mentioned above, despite employing a compact FFN model as the prober, It adeptly anticipates the actions of the classifier for a variety of datasets. Then, how does the prober possess the foresight to discern whether the classifier is lying or not? In addressing this question, we hypothesize that the prober captures information about *uncertainty* within the hidden representation of the classifier.

To validate the hypothesis, we partition the data samples into two groups based on the prober's predictions (*hit* and *miss*). Subsequently, we observe the classifier's behavior when classifying these samples. Figure 2 illustrates the frequency of (1) the probability of the classifier's final prediction and (2) the entropy of probability for instances categorized into the *hit* and *miss* groups, respectively. It is evident that the *hit* group exhibits a higher maximum probability and lower probability entropy compared to the *miss* group. More closely, we conduct a statistical test to determine whether there is a significant difference in the medians between the two groups. The hypothesis for testing is formulated as follows where m_A^{prob}, m_A^{ent} represents the medians of the maximum probability and probability entropy of group A respectively.

$$\begin{cases} H_0^{prob} : m_{hit}^{prob} \leq m_{miss}^{prob} \\ H_1^{prob} : m_{hit}^{prob} > m_{miss}^{prob} \end{cases} , \quad \begin{cases} H_0^{ent} : m_{hit}^{ent} \geq m_{miss}^{ent} \\ H_1^{ent} : m_{hit}^{ent} < m_{miss}^{ent} \end{cases} \tag{6}$$

In most cases, since the normality assumption is not satisfied, we follow the non-parametric approach known as the Mann-Whitney U-test [19]. As indicated in Table 3, the null hypotheses are rejected at the 5% significance level, so that the alternative hypotheses are adopted. It suggests that samples within the *hit* group exhibit significantly higher maximum probability and lower probability entropy on the classifier compared to the *miss* group. This supports our conjecture that the prober would detect *uncertainty* from the hidden representation of the classifier. Indeed, upon visualizing the classifier's hidden space, the prober tends to output *hit* for samples where the classifier is confident and *miss* where the classifier lacks confidence (See Fig. 3).

Table 3. Results of the Mann-Whitney U-test. Non-parametric approach is employed to assess significant differences between the two groups. The hypothesis is formulated as in Eq. (6). The alternative hypotheses are adopted under the 5% significance level across all cases. In other words, it can be confirmed that the classifier exhibits low uncertainty for samples within the *hit* group and high uncertainty for samples within the *miss* group. The experiment was conducted on both the train and test sets of the prober. (* $p < 0.05$)

Dataset	Value	Train		Test	
		U	p-value	U	p-value
MNIST	Max-Prob	24878068.5*	3.52e−253	57.5*	4.31e−14
	Entropy	620721.0*	3.52e−253	665.0*	5.64e−9
F-MNIST	Max-Prob	20804015.0*	4.56e−213	37998.0*	7.12e−13
	Entropy	523957.5*	1.33e−211	1742.0*	1.05e−12
CIFAR10	Max-Prob	215370525.5*	0.0	464464.0*	1.84e−113
	Entropy	917.51*	0.0	39471.0*	1.49e−121
ImageNette	Max-Prob	17172817.0*	0.0	43285.0*	6.76e−29
	Entropy	2031060.0*	0.0	3970.0*	1.90e−29

4.4 Uncovering Weaknesses via Counterfactual-Based Analysis

Figure 4 and 5 illustrate the counterfactual examples of performing gradient ascent in the latent space for the *hit*-logit of the prober, called ADC_{hit}, on the MNIST dataset. The analysis is conducted only on samples that the prober classifies as *miss* in the test set. Among them, we categorize cases where the classifier accurately predicts the true label as *True Miss* and cases where the classifier fails to predict the true label as *False Miss*. As mentioned earlier, we assume an opaque situation regarding the labels. Therefore, to generalize over all *miss* instances independent of the classifier's behavior, we divide the analysis into two cases. As depicted in Fig. 4, for the *True Miss* samples, ADC_{hit} provides examples that closely align with the potential label as viewed from the prober's perspective based on the original image x. It is noteworthy that the prober operates without any knowledge of the true labels. Despite this lack of information, the prober can manipulate instances by emphasizing or removing certain regions δx that might confuse the classifier. In the case of *False Miss* where the classifier has already correctly predicted the answer, as presented in Fig. 5, it can be inferred that counterfactual examples are generated in a direction that reduces the uncertainty of the classifier.

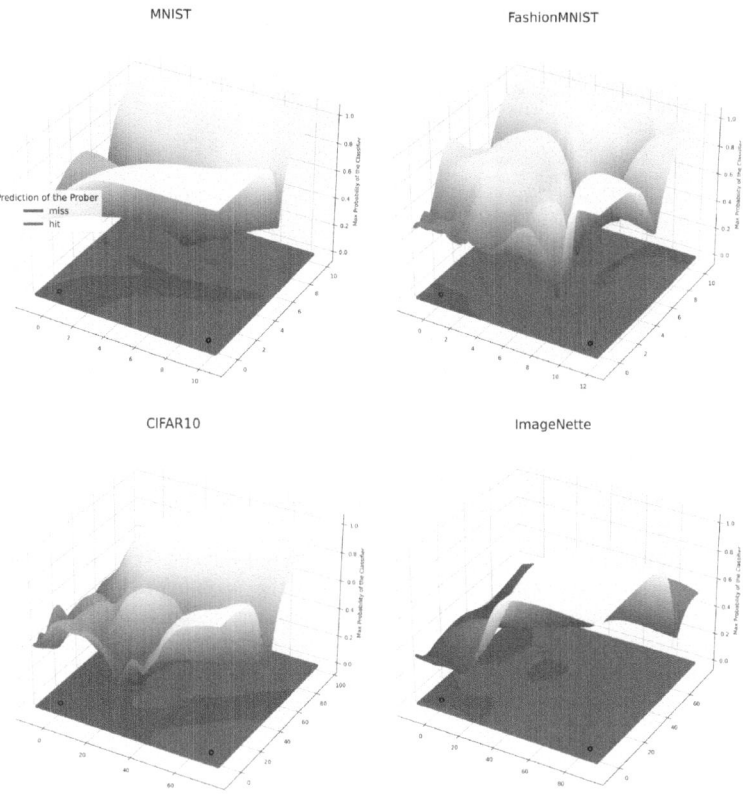

Fig. 3. The action of the prober according to the maximum probability of the classifier. The xy-plane displays a 2D plane formed by three selected points from the dataset. At the bottom, for samples lying on the plane, the predicted action of the classifier (*miss* or *hit*) by the prober is denoted in red or blue. The z-axis represents the probability of the prediction when the sample is fed into the classifier. It implies that the prober tends to output *hit* for samples where the classifier is confident and *miss* when the classifier lacks confidence.

To clarify, we experiment to re-classify using the newly generated ADC_{hit} examples. Table 4 reports the changes in classifier accuracy for true labels and the maximum probability for the final prediction when replacing original images with ADC_{hit} samples. The results indicate that, for the *True Miss* samples, ADC_{hit} leads to an approximately 86.67% improvement in classifier accuracy. Regarding *False Miss* cases, where the original answers were correctly predicted, it's essential to note that the starting accuracy is 100%. However, with an increase of around 33.40% in the maximum probability for the final decision, it is concluded that ADC_{hit} can be an example that complements the classifier's weaknesses. As a result, the introduction of the prober holds significance in that it allows for the identification of vulnerabilities in the classifier at the instance-level. Indeed, it is

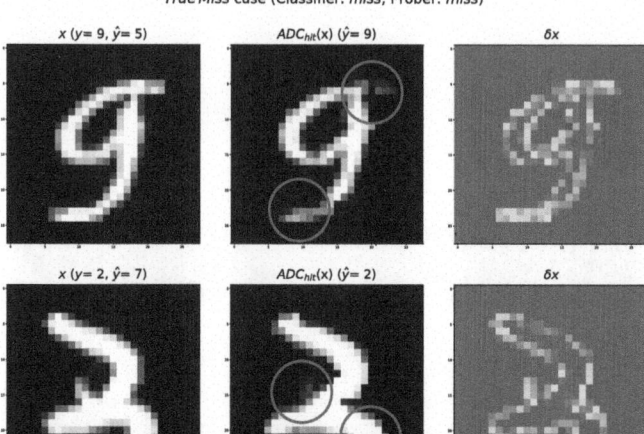

Fig. 4. Counterfactual examples $ADC_{hit}(x)$ generated for the *True Miss* cases where both the classifier fails to classify accurately, and the prober predicts as *miss*. y and $\hat{y}$ denote the label and the prediction of the classifier, respectively. Despite lacking information about the true label, the prober identifies vulnerabilities in the classifier for each sample x. With this framework, we obtain examples close to the correct answer by modifying the regions indicated in red, corresponding to δx. (Color figure online)

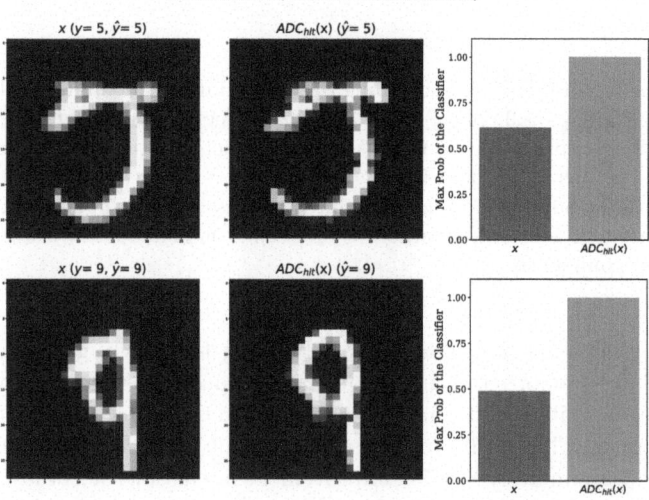

Fig. 5. Counterfactual examples $ADC_{hit}(x)$ generated for the *False Miss* cases where the classifier correctly classifies, but the prober predicts as *miss*. y and $\hat{y}$ denote the label and the prediction of the classifier, respectively. Even though the original image x is already correctly classified, $ADC_{hit}(x)$ is generated in a direction aimed at reducing uncertainty from the perspective of the classifier.

Table 4. Re-classification experiments for ADC_{hit} of MNIST: changes in the classifier's accuracy and maximum probability. The accuracy is calculated for the true label, and the variation of the maximum probability is averaged across all target samples. The classifier demonstrates high accuracy and confidence for ADC_{hit} generated in an unsupervised manner. This implies that the prober adeptly captures the weakness of the classifier, without relying on label information and regardless of whether the classifier correctly predicts the actual label or not.

	Prediction of the Prober		
	Miss	*True Miss*	*False Miss*
Accuracy (%)	$25 \rightarrow 90$	$0 \rightarrow 86.67$	$100 \rightarrow 100$
Δ Max Probability (%)	+29.21	+29.21	+33.40

advantageous in providing interpretations in all cases, even without information about the true label and regardless of the predictions made by the classifier.

5 Conclusion

In this paper, we presented a framework for addressing the weakness of the classifier by providing counterfactual examples. The prober was trained to predict whether the classifier's decision is correct (*hit*) or incorrect (*miss*) based on the hidden representation of the classifier. The underlying hypothesis is that the prober can capture the confidence of the classifier's predictions by inferring decision probabilities. We have successfully validated that the prober captures the uncertainty in the classifier's decision by investigating the maximum and entropy of probability. Moreover, we generated semantically meaningful counterfactual examples to demonstrate how the input should appear if the prober expects the classifier to output the correct answer. It edited the indiscriminative features that obstruct the classifier's decision without access to the true label. Future developments can include the improvement of the performance of the prober and the counterfactual explanations in more complicated datasets. Another possible future direction is expanding to auto-correction and utilizing our framework to address model-level interpretation.

Acknowledgement. This work was conducted by Center for Applied Research in Artificial Intelligence (CARAI) grant funded by DAPA and ADD (UD230017TD) and partly supported by Institute of Information & Communications Technology Planning & Evaluation (IITP) grant funded by the Korea government (MSIT) (No. 2022-0-00984, Development of Artificial Intelligence Technology for Personalized Plug-and-Play Explanation and Verification of Explanation; No. 2019-0-00075, Artificial Intelligence Graduate School Program (KAIST)).

References

1. Adi, Y., Kermany, E., Belinkov, Y., Lavi, O., Goldberg, Y.: Fine-grained analysis of sentence embeddings using auxiliary prediction tasks. In: 5th International Conference on Learning Representations, ICLR 2017, Conference Track Proceedings (2017)
2. Azaria, A., Mitchell, T.: The internal state of an LLM knows when it's lying. In: The 2023 Conference on Empirical Methods in Natural Language Processing (2023)
3. Conneau, A., Kruszewski, G., Lample, G., Barrault, L., Baroni, M.: What you can cram into a single $&!#* vector: probing sentence embeddings for linguistic properties. In: Proceedings of the 56th Annual Meeting of the Association for Computational Linguistics, ACL 2018 (2018)
4. Dadalto, E.: Detectors: a python library for generalized out-of-distribution detection (2023). https://doi.org/10.5281/zenodo.7883596, https://github.com/edadaltocg/detectors
5. Davis, J., Goadrich, M.: The relationship between precision-recall and ROC curves. In: Machine Learning, Proceedings of the Twenty-Third International Conference (ICML 2006) (2006)
6. Deng, J., Dong, W., Socher, R., Li, L.J., Li, K., Fei-Fei, L.: ImageNet: a large-scale hierarchical image database. In: 2009 IEEE Conference on Computer Vision and Pattern Recognition. pp. 248–255 (2009). https://doi.org/10.1109/CVPR.2009.5206848
7. Dinh, L., Sohl-Dickstein, J., Bengio, S.: Density estimation using real NVP (2017)
8. Dombrowski, A.K., Gerken, J.E., Müller, K.R., Kessel, P.: Diffeomorphic counterfactuals with generative models. IEEE Trans. Pattern Anal. Machi. Intell. (2023)
9. Geifman, Y., El-Yaniv, R.: Selective classification for deep neural networks. In: Advances in Neural Information Processing Systems 30: Annual Conference on Neural Information Processing Systems 2017 (2017)
10. Hendrycks, D., Gimpel, K.: A baseline for detecting misclassified and out-of-distribution examples in neural networks. CoRR abs/1610.02136 (2016). http://arxiv.org/abs/1610.02136
11. Hendrycks, D., Mazeika, M., Dietterich, T.G.: Deep anomaly detection with outlier exposure. In: 7th International Conference on Learning Representations, ICLR 2019 (2019)
12. Howard, J., Gugger, S.: Fastai: a layered API for deep learning. CoRR abs/2002.04688 (2020). https://arxiv.org/abs/2002.04688
13. Howard, J., Gugger, S.: Fastai: a layered API for deep learning. Information **11**(2), 108 (2020)
14. Jeon, G., Jeong, H., Choi, J.: Distilled gradient aggregation: Purify features for input attribution in the deep neural network. In: Advances in Neural Information Processing Systems 35: Annual Conference on Neural Information Processing Systems 2022, NeurIPS 2022 (2022)
15. Krizhevsky, A.: Learning multiple layers of features from tiny images (2009). https://api.semanticscholar.org/CorpusID:18268744
16. Kusner, M.J., Loftus, J.R., Russell, C., Silva, R.: Counterfactual fairness (2018)
17. LeCun, Y., Bottou, L., Bengio, Y., Haffner, P.: Gradient-based learning applied to document recognition. Proc. IEEE **86**(11), 2278–2324 (1998)
18. Müller, R., Kornblith, S., Hinton, G.E.: When does label smoothing help? In: Advances in Neural Information Processing Systems 32: Annual Conference on Neural Information Processing Systems 2019, NeurIPS 2019 (2019)

19. Nachar, N.: The mann-whitney U: a test for assessing whether two independent samples come from the same distribution. Tutor. Quant. Methods Psychol. **4** (2008)
20. Nam, W., Gur, S., Choi, J., Wolf, L., Lee, S.: Relative attributing propagation: interpreting the comparative contributions of individual units in deep neural networks. In: The Thirty-Fourth AAAI Conference on Artificial Intelligence, AAAI 2020 (2020)
21. Ravichander, A., Belinkov, Y., Hovy, E.H.: Probing the probing paradigm: does probing accuracy entail task relevance? In: Proceedings of the 16th Conference of the European Chapter of the Association for Computational Linguistics: Main Volume, EACL 2021 (2021)
22. Szegedy, C., Vanhoucke, V., Ioffe, S., Shlens, J., Wojna, Z.: Rethinking the inception architecture for computer vision. In: 2016 IEEE Conference on Computer Vision and Pattern Recognition, CVPR 2016 (2016)
23. Verma, S., Dickerson, J.P., Hines, K.: Counterfactual explanations for machine learning: a review. CoRR abs/2010.10596 (2020)
24. Williams, A., Nangia, N., Bowman, S.R.: A broad-coverage challenge corpus for sentence understanding through inference. In: Proceedings of the 2018 Conference of the North American Chapter of the Association for Computational Linguistics: Human Language Technologies, NAACL-HLT 2018 (2018)
25. Xiao, H., Rasul, K., Vollgraf, R.: Fashion-MNIST: a novel image dataset for benchmarking machine learning algorithms. CoRR abs/1708.07747 (2017)
26. Zhu, F., Cheng, Z., Zhang, X.Y., Liu, C.L.: OpenMix: exploring outlier samples for misclassification detection. In: 2023 IEEE/CVF Conference on Computer Vision and Pattern Recognition (CVPR) (2023)

Enhancing Robustness
of Over-Parameterized Models
via Feature Reweighting Using
Logit-Wise Mixup

Woo-Seok Jo, Yeong-Joon Ju, and Seong-Whan Lee[✉]

Department of Artificial Intelligence, Korea University, Seoul, Republic of Korea
{ws_jo,yj_ju,sw.lee}@korea.ac.kr

Abstract. Over-parameterization in machine learning often leads to models heavily relying on 'spurious' features, which lack causal relationships with the true labels. This reliance can significantly impair the model's performance, especially concerning minority subgroups. Alleviating this issue is particularly challenging in the absence of subgroup labels. To improve the generalizability of the model without the subgroup annotations, we propose LogitMixup Feature Reweighting (LFR), a novel two-stage method to enhance the robustness of the model. Initially, we train an auxiliary model deliberately tuned to amplify spurious correlations. We subsequently divide the dataset into two pseudo-groups based on the output logits of the auxiliary model: one group aligns with the bias, while the other conflicts with the bias. We then apply mixup augmentation on pairs from these two groups within the same class, organizing a reweighting dataset. In the following stage, we freeze the feature extractor and retrain only the decision layer of the model originally trained via empirical risk minimization. LFR enhances the robustness of the model without requiring additional supervision, such as annotation or labels of spurious attributes. Furthermore, LFR retrains only the decision layer of the model with only a few epochs, which does not require supervision at model selection time. Our experiments on benchmark datasets demonstrate that LFR improves the model's group robustness. LFR not only outperforms the existing methods that do not use group labels but also competes closely with 'oracle' methods that utilize subgroup annotations.

Keywords: Spurious correlations · Robustness · Domain generalization

1 Introduction

Deep learning models have demonstrated unparalleled performance in a wide variety of applications, transforming industries and everyday life. However, these

C. Wallraven et al. (Eds.): ICPRAI 2024, LNCS 14892, pp. 322–336, 2025.
https://doi.org/10.1007/978-981-97-8702-9_22

models are often riddled with a critical problem: the dependence on spurious correlations [2,7,9,25]. A spurious correlation refers to a relationship that appears to exist between two variables, which in reality is a coincidence or can be attributed to the influence of a third variable [23]. In the context of deep learning, models may inadvertently learn these spurious correlations in the data during the training process, leading to overfitting and poor generalization performance [14]. Despite the widespread recognition of this issue, devising methods to effectively mitigate the reliance of deep learning models on spurious correlations remains an open challenge. Therefore, our primary task is to find ways to enhance robustness against spurious correlations in the data and to minimize the worst-group error.

Existing studies commonly assume that deep learning models trained via Empirical Risk Minimization (ERM) with datasets exhibiting spurious correlations fail to learn the core features. To address this issue, one of the best approaches uses a supervised loss function known as Group Distributionally Robust Optimization (Group DRO) [25] to directly minimize the loss of minority subgroups during the training process. However, it requires the knowledge of group information during training, which is not always feasible or practical, especially in large datasets. Numerous studies have attempted to overcome this obstacle. They propose methods that estimate minority groups, thus eliminating the need for supervision of spurious group annotations. For example, both Nam *et al.* [18] and Liu *et al.* [16] employ an ERM model as an auxiliary model to identify minority samples and train a robust model with emphasis on identified minority samples. However, these methods present their own set of problems [29]. To achieve optimal performance, a labeled validation set with subgroup information is used for supervision during model selection stages like early stopping, which limits their practicality in real-world applications. Contrary to the aforementioned assumption that the models fail to learn the core features from spurious datasets [8,27], Kirichenko *et al.* [12] recently provided empirical evidence that the ERM feature extractor continues to learn the essential core features, even without relying on these features during the prediction process. Therefore, simply retraining the last layer of the model with a group-balanced dataset can improve the group robustness, which is known as Deep Feature Reweighting (DFR). This challenges the traditional understanding and opens up new perspectives on the learning capabilities of such models [13,22,32]. However, the DFR method heavily relies on the availability of a labeled, group-balanced validation set for retraining. Without a sufficient number of group-balanced samples, performance can drastically decrease [31]. Furthermore, similar to prior methods that train models from scratch, DFR is also sensitive to hyperparameters and thus requires supervision at model selection using a validation set with group labels. These drawbacks give rise to the following question: *Can we effectively eliminate the model's reliance on the spurious features without using group information during the entire training procedure?*

In this paper, we introduce a simple yet highly effective algorithm known as LogitMixup Feature Reweighting (LFR). Following the insights from Kirichenko *et al.* [12], we 'freeze' the feature extractor, which continues to learn the core feature, and focus our efforts on retraining the decision layer of the model. Unlike DFR, rather than using a group-balanced dataset to retrain the last layer, we employ a 'mixup' dataset drawn directly from the training distribution. LFR trains two neural networks: a deliberately biased auxiliary model for identifying bias-aligned and bias-conflicted distributions, and the other model focused on debiasing. The former emphasizes data points that generate output logits with small differences among the logits corresponding to each class. These bias-conflicted samples identified by the biased models are used for a logit-wise mixup within the same class with bias-aligned samples, thus reducing the impact of spurious features. Subsequently, using the reweighting dataset, LFR re-weights the decision layer of the model which was initially trained with ERM. Our evaluation on both synthetic and real-world benchmark datasets confirms the effectiveness of LFR. LFR outperforms the worst group accuracy and minority group accuracy of baseline methods that do not use group labels. LFR also competes closely with 'oracle' baseline methods that utilize group labels. Furthermore, We show the qualitative evaluation of LFR by comparing Grad-CAM visualization of the prediction of the LFR model with the baseline ERM model [20]. Finally, we run additional ablation experiments that demonstrate the superiority of our approach by comparing the auxiliary model type and class-wise grouping type.

2   Related Works

2.1   Spurious Correlations

Neural networks tend to rely on the easy-to-learn features. This phenomenon exists even if the easy-to-learn features are less predictive of the class label than the complex features in the dataset [27]. For instance, ERM models resort to spurious correlations including background [25,30], texture of object [6], logographic watermarks [3] and co-existing secondary objects [15,24,28] in making decisions. Recent studies empirically show that neural networks trained on datasets containing spurious correlations not only rely on easy-to-learn spurious features but also ignore the core features [10,17,21,27]. This tendency leads to failure for minority subgroups against spurious correlations, which hurts the robustness of the model.

2.2   Improving Robustness Against Spurious Correlations

Current strategies aimed at enhancing robustness to spurious correlations can be divided into two distinct research streams, each distinguished by the use or non-use of group annotations. The former approach focuses on strategies that employ group annotations to mitigate the impact of spurious correlations. With access to group information, Sagawa *et al.* [25] enhance the group robustness by minimizing the worst group loss. However, obtaining group annotation labels in reality is challenging and cost-expensive. Therefore, methods have been proposed for the efficient use of these spurious annotations.

Nam *et al.* [19] train an auxiliary model for predicting spurious labels with a small portion of the sample with group labels, then perform distributionally robust optimization with pseudo group labels. Kirichenko *et al.* [12] retrain the last layer of the pre-trained ERM model with a group-balanced validation set. Deng *et al.* [5] initially train the model with a small group balanced warm-up subset and progressively expand the warm-up training distribution to learn the core features. However, due to the often unknown or hard-to-annotate nature of groups, methods that do not use group annotations have sparked significant interest. The latter research stream, which aligns more closely with the issues this paper aims to address, focuses on the strategies for improving the group robustness without resorting to group annotations [4]. Several efforts have been made to reduce the subgroup-level supervision. Such methods usually train two networks. The primary model identifies the minority examples, which then aids in formulating a weighted loss for the subsequent model. Liu *et al.* [16] and Nam *et al.* [18] train the robust model by upweighting the identified minority samples. Zhang *et al.* [34] train the robust model with contrastive learning to learn similar representations within the same class. We note that all of the methods described above use a validation set with a high representation of minority groups to tune the hyperparameters and optimize worst-group performance.

3   Preliminaries

3.1   Problem Setting

Our main focus is on the group robustness setting within classification models. Specifically, we consider a dataset D where each input x belongs to a specific group g, defined by a combination of the class label y and a spurious attribute a, which lack a causal relationship with the class label. We consider a scenario where these groups are heavily imbalanced rather than equally distributed within the dataset. Due to this significant imbalance, in standard training of deep learning models with these datasets, the target attribute a becomes a spurious feature as it correlates with y but lacks a genuine causal relationship. For instance, in the Waterbirds dataset, approximately 95% of each class is correlated with a similar background, which we denote as bias-aligned groups (i.e., Waterbirds with water backgrounds, Landbirds with land backgrounds). Consequently, models trained on this dataset tend to rely on the background feature rather than the core foreground features, leading to underperformance in minority groups, which we denote as bias-conflicted groups (Waterbirds on land backgrounds, Landbirds on water backgrounds). Therefore, we evaluate the robustness of our debiased model using the accuracy of the bias-conflicted groups.

Most of the previous methods have achieved optimal performance by utilizing the validation set with explicit spurious labels for supervision at model selection, which is impractical for real-world applications. Contrary to previous methods, we tackle a more challenging scenario where supervision for group attributes is unavailable in both training and validation sets. We aim to enhance the robustness of the model without requiring the supervision of subgroup annotations during training and model selection (Fig. 1).

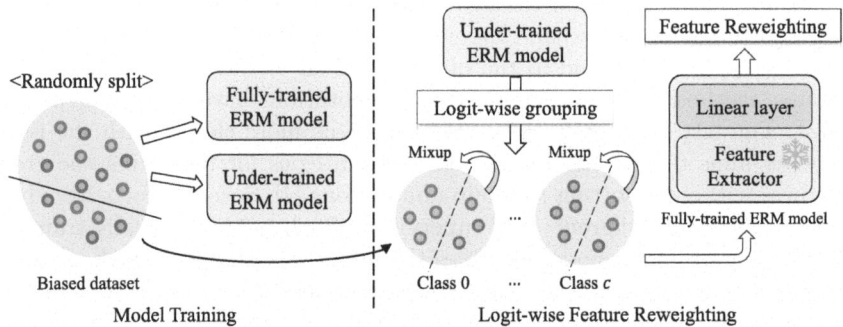

Fig. 1. Overall process of our proposed method. LFR is a two-stage framework for group robustness of the deep learning model.

In this paper, we follow the assumption proposed by Nam *et al.* [18], which assumes that a biased dataset does not necessarily cause the model to learn the unintended decision rule. Due to the easy-to-learn nature of spurious features, models tend to rely on spurious correlations during the learning process, leading to potential pitfalls. Furthermore, deep learning models typically start by learning simpler features in the initial stages of the training process and progressively incorporate more complex features. This pattern further underscores the tendency for models to initially latch onto spurious features. Therefore, we tackle the problem by focusing on the group robustness setting under the assumption that a hierarchy between these core and spurious features exists.

4   LogitMixup Feature Reweighting

In this section, we introduce LogitMixup Feature Reweighting (LFR), our novel two-stage training algorithm to enhance group robustness against spurious correlations without the need for supervising spurious attributes. LFR is based on the insight that despite the presence of spurious correlations, the pre-trained ERM model still successfully learns the essential core features. Building upon this foundation, we reweight the weights of the pre-trained feature extractor using a curated reweighting dataset. We partition the training dataset into two portions, D_a and D_b. D_a is utilized for training two distinct models, while D_b is employed for creating the mixed-up reweighting dataset D_{re}.

4.1   Organizing Reweighting Dataset

In this phase, our objective is to develop a reweighting dataset that mitigates the influence of spurious correlations and ensures a balanced representation of features. To achieve this, we employ a two-pronged approach: Identification for logit-wise grouping and logit-wise mixup augmentation.

Identification for Logit-Wise Grouping. In organizing the reweighing dataset, the process of dividing D_b into bias-aligned and bias-conflicted groups can significantly influence the performance of the proposed method. Therefore, training an appropriately under-trained ERM model becomes a critical aspect. As we discussed in the preliminary section, spurious features tend to be more 'easy-to-learn' compared to core features. This characteristic leads to these spurious features being primarily learned in the earlier stages of the training process, while core features are gradually learned over time. Consequently, we observe a tendency that the loss of the majority group samples decreases faster than that of the minority group samples in the early stage of training.

To leverage this property, we intentionally under-train our first-stage model with the D_a dataset, which is a subset of the original training dataset. We utilize the generalized cross entropy loss [35] to under-train the ERM model.

$$\mathcal{L}_{\mathbf{GCE}} = \frac{1 - p(x)^q}{q}, \tag{1}$$

where $p(x)$ represents the probability outputs of the ERM model, and q is a hyperparameter. Compared to traditional cross-entropy loss, the gradient of the GCE loss gives priority to examples with samples with high confidence. This intentional bias allows the model to output higher logits on majority (bias-aligned) samples, while it may output lower logits on minority (bias-conflicted) samples. Consequently, we can effectively identify distributions with higher output logits (generally samples from bias-conflicted groups) and distributions with lower output logits (usually samples from bias-aligned groups). The effectiveness of this under-training approach is dependent on the precise selection of training epochs. Following the methodologies of Nam *et al.* [18] that employ the GCE loss, we propose a training duration of approximately 20 epochs. This strategic selection is designed to maintain a balance to satisfy the trade-off between learning spurious and core features. As a result, the under-trained ERM model is deliberately biased towards emphasizing the easy-to-learn spurious features. Therefore, samples from majority subgroups (bias-aligned groups) exhibit high confidence logits, while those from minority subgroups (bias-conflicted groups) display low confidence logits regardless of the correctness of each sample's inference. To prepare for the logit-wise grouping process, we use the D_b dataset, which is another distinct subset of the original training dataset, as input for the deliberately under-trained biased model. This step generates the necessary logits for the subsequent grouping process. The grouping based on these logits allows us to categorize samples effectively into bias-aligned and bias-conflicted groups, setting the stage for further augmentation processes.

To refine our logit-wise grouping strategy, we introduce a logit threshold, τ, which serves as a discriminant for intra-class group assignments. Specifically, we examine the absolute difference between the logits corresponding to each class.

If the absolute difference exceeds the threshold τ, the sample is assigned to a bias-aligned group within its class. Conversely, if the difference falls short of the threshold, the sample is assigned to a bias-conflicted group. This distinction is crucial as it permits more nuanced segregation within each class, enabling targeted mix-up augmentations. When the logit threshold τ is set excessively high, most of the samples are classified into bias-conflicted groups. In contrast, setting τ too low results in most of the samples falling into bias-aligned groups. Therefore, choosing an appropriate logit threshold τ is a crucial step in our process. To ensure the robustness of our model, we have established the threshold τ in such a way that the bias-aligned samples and bias-conflicted samples are distributed proportionally to the original dataset. This decision is grounded in the understanding that maintaining the inherent distribution of the original dataset within our confidence-based subsets provides a more generalizable model. To ensure that the grouping based on the logit threshold τ preserves the original group distribution, we employ a greedy search algorithm. This technique systematically adjusts the threshold value to find the optimal τ that results in a distribution of majority and minority groups mirroring the inherent distribution patterns found in the original dataset.

Logit-Wise Mixup Augmentation. Upon the establishment of the appropriate logit threshold τ, the D_b dataset undergoes a logit-wise grouping. The grouped D_b dataset then becomes the cornerstone for the mixup augmentation process. Building on the idea of Mixup [33], we randomly select a sample from the bias-conflicted distribution. Then, we apply a mixup augmentation with another sample which is randomly selected from the bias-aligned distribution with the same label.

$$(x_e, y_e) = (\lambda x_i + (1 - \lambda)x_j, \lambda y_i + (1 - \lambda)y_j), \qquad (2)$$

where each sample (x_i, y_i), (x_j, y_j) is randomly chosen from each distribution respectively. This procedure allows us to alleviate the influence of spurious features through the linear combination of these two examples. By systematically pairing samples from contrasting groups—bias-aligned with bias-conflicted—we create a new reweighting dataset D_{re} that embodies the characteristics of both ends of the spectrum. Through the mixup process within the same class, the spurious features present in bias-aligned samples are augmented with opposing features. Therefore, this methodology enables us to introduce a level of diversity and robustness into the training process. It is crucial to note that this process is carried out based on the D_b dataset, which has been previously inferred from the biasedly trained model. We set the value of λ in a way that the mixed samples lean more towards the minority groups. This measure is aimed at alleviating the extreme imbalance between the minority and majority groups and also ensuring the diversity of the minority groups.

4.2 Retraining the Decision Layer

In this stage, we retrain the last layer of the fully-trained ERM model with the reweighting dataset D_{re}.

Unlike other methods that require training from scratch, LFR focuses on training only the decision layers and does so with no more than three epochs. This simple process not only reduces the computational burden but also removes the necessity of the model selection for optimal performance.

Most of the baseline methods involve hundreds of epochs of training, relying heavily on a group-labeled validation set to determine the best hyperparameters or to decide when to implement early stopping for optimal worst group accuracy. However, the dependence on a validation set can introduce its own biases, especially when the validation distribution is similar to the test distribution. LFR, on the other hand, achieves robust performance without the need for a group-labeled validation set. This is a significant advantage, particularly in scenarios where a group-balanced validation set is unavailable or impractical to obtain.

Algorithm 1. LogitMixup Feature Reweighting (LFR)

Require: Two subsets of the original training dataset, D_a, D_b, Number of iterations T_0 for undertraining, Number of iterations T_1 for full training, model f_{under}, model f_{fully}, logit threshold τ, hyperparameter s

1: **Stage 1: Organizing reweighting dataset**
2: Train model f_{under} for T_0 iterations using the loss L^{GCE} on D_a
3: Train model f_{fully} for T_1 iterations using the loss L^{CE} until convergence on D_a
4: Infer f_{under} on D_b and divide into two pseudo-groups based on logit threshold τ:
5: **for** each sample (x_i, y_i) in D_b **do**
6:     Compute logits $Z = f_{under}(x_i)$
7:     Compute absolute difference $\Delta = |Z_{class1} - Z_{class2}|$
8:     **if** $\Delta > \tau$ **then**
9:         Assign x_i to $Group_1$
10:    **else**
11:        Assign x_i to $Group_2$
12:    **end if**
13: **end for**
14: Create reweighting dataset D_{re}
15: **for** each class c **do**
16:    **for** each sample x_i, x_k in class c **do**
17:        Select x_i, x_k from $Group_1$ and $Group_2$ of class c uniformly at random
18:        $x_{new} \leftarrow (1 - s)x_i + sx_k$
19:        Add x_{new} to D_{re}
20:    **end for**
21: **end for**
22: **Stage 2: Debiasing via retraining the decision layer**
23: Freeze the feature extractor of a fully-trained ERM model.
24: Retrain the final layer of the model using D_{re}.

Table 1. Comparison with baseline methods on Waterbirds and bFFHQ. The number in bold indicates the best performance metrics in methods without using group annotations.

Method	Group Info.	Val. Info.	Early-stopping	Training type	Waterbirds		bFFHQ	
					Worst	Mean	Minority	Mean
Group DRO [25]	Yes	Yes	Yes	FS	89.9	93.0	-	-
DFR [12]	Yes	Yes*	Yes	LLR	90.2	94.2	62.3	95.1
DFR†	Yes	Yes*	Yes	LLR	82.5	86.8	54.2	90.2
ERM	No	Yes	Yes	FS	72.9	95.2	49.3	98.6
LFF [18]	No	Yes	Yes	FS	78.0	85.1	54.3	59.8
JTT [16]	No	Yes	Yes	FS	85.6	88.0	55.8	94.2
Masktune [1]	No	No	No	FT	86.0	93.0	53.7	89.9
Ours	No	No	No	LLR	**86.7**	94.2	**59.4**	97.2

Table 2. Comparison with baseline methods when early stopping is not done using validation group labels on Waterbirds.

Method	Group Info.	Val. Info.	Early-stopping	Training type	Waterbirds	
					Worst	Mean
Group DRO [25]	Yes	No	No	FS	81.4	94.2
DFR [12]	Yes	Yes*	No	LLR	79.9	93.0
ERM	No	No	No	FS	45.9	94.9
LFF [18]	No	No	No	FS	57.0	85.5
JTT [16]	No	No	No	FS	71.6	89.0
Ours	No	No	No	LLR	**86.7**	94.2

5   Experiments

In this section, we evaluate our method LFR with popular group robustness benchmarks. To evaluate the model's robustness against reliance on spurious correlations, we evaluate our method with worst group accuracy which is the minimum accuracy across all the subgroups and minority group accuracy which is the accuracy of all the bias-conflicted samples. Also, for a qualitative evaluation of the models trained with ERM and LFR, we have conducted visualizations using Grad-CAM [26].

5.1   Datasets

We consider several image classification problems with synthetic and real-world datasets.

Waterbirds Dataset. The Waterbirds dataset is a synthetic image classification dataset. In this paper, the objective is to train the model to distinguish between Waterbirds and Landbirds based on the images provided. The foreground images of the birds are synthetically added to their natural backgrounds. Given that 95% of Waterbirds are typically found in aquatic settings such as rivers or lakes, and 95% of Landbirds are found in terrestrial environments like woods, mountains, or forests, the background serves as a spurious feature. Therefore, Waterbirds with terrestrial backgrounds and Landbirds with aquatic backgrounds are considered minority groups.

bFFHQ Dataset. The bFFHQ dataset is a real-world image classification dataset. In this paper, we aim to train the model to classify whether the individual in the image is male or female. Considering that 99.5% of male individuals are old and 99.5% of female individuals are young, age serves as a spurious feature. Therefore, young males and old females comprise the minority group.

5.2   Baselines

Our selection of baseline models was done with consideration of several factors. These included the use of early stopping, the type of training implemented, utilization of group annotations in the training set and validation set. We consider 6 baseline methods that work under different assumptions on the information available at the training time.

Empirical Risk Minimization (ERM) represents a conventional training strategy where the model is trained to minimize the average loss on the training data, which does not have any procedures for enhancing worst-group accuracies. Learning From Failure (LFF) and Just Train Twice (JTT) are the methods that train the robust model with detected minority group examples on train data with auxiliary model, only using a validation set with group annotations to tune hyperparameters [16,18]. Group DRO is a so-called 'oracle' method, which uses group information and minimizes the losses of minority subgroups during training [25]. Deep Feature Reweighing (DFR) is a method that retrains only the last layer of the pre-trained model with a group-balanced validation set, which uses fewer group labels compared to conventional methods using group annotations [12]. Masktune is a method that finetunes model only one epoch with the dataset where input mask is applied to the most activated part of the image based on the gradient of pre-trained ERM model [1].

5.3   Implementation Details

For the experiments on Waterbirds, we use the standard Waterbirds dataset following the experimental setting of group DRO [25]. We use the ResNet-50 architecture pre-trained on ImageNet. We use random crops and horizontal flips as data augmentation. We train all models with SGD with a momentum decay of 0.9 and a constant learning rate. On Waterbirds, we train the models for 200 epochs with weight decay 1×10^{-4}, learning rate 1×10^{-3} and batch size 32. For the experiments on bFFHQ, we follow the experimental setting of Kim *et al.* [11]. We use the ResNet-18 architecture pre-trained on ImageNet. We train the models for 200 epochs with a learning rate $1 \times 10{-4}$ and batch size 64.

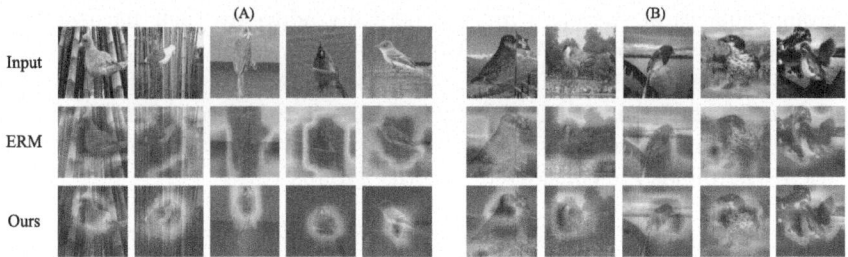

Fig. 2. Activation visualization of ERM and LFR on Waterbirds samples.
(A) represents the minority samples correctly predicted by our method but not by
ERM, while (B) includes the majority samples correctly predicted by both ERM and
our method.

To ensure a fair comparison, we further conduct an experiment with the DFR
method, utilizing the same number of bias-conflicted samples as used in LFR.
In both experiments on the Waterbirds and bFFHQ datasets, LFR does not
use early stopping and splits the training dataset in a 70%-30% proportion to
construct D_a for training and D_b for reweighting. Moreover, for LFR, we set the
hyperparameter q to 0.7 for the GCE loss and retrain the last layer for 3 epochs.

5.4   Results

Main Results. In Table 1, we demonstrate the worst group accuracy and minority group accuracy for baselines evaluated on Waterbirds and bFFHQ datasets.
We report the average results of three independent runs with different seeds for
each baseline method. 'Group Info.' and 'Val. Info' column shows if the methods utilize the group label in training and model selection respectively. Symbol
* shows that DFR utilizes group-labeled validation data for both training and
model selection. 'Training type' represents whether the baseline method trains
from scratch (FS), finetunes one epoch (FT), or applies last-layer retraining
(LLR). For DFR, experiments are carried out with different sizes of group-labeled
validation datasets. Symbol † represents the experiment of DFR when utilizing
the same number of bias-conflict samples as LFR utilizes. The primary metric
for comparison was the worst group accuracy for the Waterbirds dataset and the
minority group accuracy for the bFFHQ dataset.

Remarkably, compared to other methods that do not use group annotations,
LFR consistently demonstrated the highest worst group accuracy and minority
group accuracy. Additionally, LFR enhanced worst group accuracy while maintaining overall accuracy compared to baselines. LFR conducted a limited number of epochs for the last layer retraining, as opposed to hundreds of epochs for
training from scratch with supervision at model selection. Furthermore, when
compared with methods that do utilize group annotations such as DFR and
group DRO, LFR maintained a similar level of performance. Note that when
DFR utilizes the same number of bias-conflicted samples as LFR, LFR out-

performs DFR. LFR consistently enhances the robustness of the model even in situations where bias-conflicted samples are limited. This highlights the efficacy of LFR in achieving high levels of accuracy without the need for supervision at model selection or the use of group annotations during training.

Table 2 illustrates the comparison with other baseline methods when early stopping is not done using subgroup annotations of the validation set on the Waterbirds dataset. Unlike LFR, other baseline methods consider scenarios when subgroup annotations of the validation set are available. Therefore, when model selection under human supervision is not available, the performance drops drastically. In those scenarios, LFR outperforms existing baseline methods in a huge gap.

Activation Visualization. We visualized the decision-making patterns of our debiased model using Grad-CAM [26]. Figure 2 illustrates two cases: on the left, it shows where ERM fails but LFR succeeds in prediction, and on the right, it displays where both ERM and LFR are successful in prediction. The left side depicts samples from the minority group for which ERM incorrectly predicted the outcome, while LFR made a correct prediction. ERM made an incorrect prediction due to the reliance on spurious correlations in the background. On the other hand, LFR, focusing on the core foreground features, made the correct prediction. The right side is the case of samples from the majority group which are correctly predicted by both ERM and LFR. ERM often shows activations in the background which represents the spurious features. In contrast, LFR consistently shows activation in the foreground core features. This underscores the robustness of LFR in making accurate predictions by focusing on the primary attributes of the sample, rather than being induced by spurious correlations.

Table 3. Ablation study for auxiliary model

Auxiliary model type	Training epochs	Worst
ERM + random initialize	0	43.7
ERM + CE loss	200	77.6
ERM + GCE loss (ours)	20	86.7

Table 4. Ablation study for grouping method

Grouping type	Group info.	Worst
Random	No	63.2
w/ labels	Yes	87.5
Ours	No	86.7

Ablation Study. We conduct ablation experiments on the Waterbirds dataset to verify the effectiveness of using an undertrained auxiliary model, as well as the efficiency of logit-wise grouping. As shown in Table 3, we compared three cases: random initialize, trained ERM model until convergence, and ours. We verify the need for biasedly training the auxiliary model for the identification of pseudo-groups. Table 4 presents the results of our ablation study for grouping types for mixup augmentation. We compared our logit-wise grouping approaches with two cases: random grouping, and grouping with explicit group annotations. Compared to grouping with group labels, our pseudo-grouping approaches achieve competitive worst group accuracy, which is significantly higher than random grouping.

6   Conclusion

In this research, we have introduced a debiasing training algorithm, termed Log-itMixup Feature Reweighing (LFR), for the training of neural networks in the presence of spurious correlations in the dataset. By effectively managing the learning of core and spurious features, our method ensures the robust performance of the model. LFR leverages a reweighting dataset with an emphasis on minority groups through mixup augmentation for retraining the last layer. This technique boosts model performance without the need for group annotations or supervision at model selection, enhancing efficiency and cost-effectiveness. Additionally, we validated LFR with standard group robustness benchmark datasets, offering valuable insights for advancing the practical mitigation of spurious correlations, laying the groundwork for trustworthy and responsible AI.

Acknowledgment. This work was supported by the Institute of Information & communications Technology Planning & Evaluation (IITP) grant funded by the Korea government (MSIT) (No. 2019-0-00079, Artificial Intelligence Graduate School Program (Korea University) and No. 2022-0-00984, Development of Artificial Intelligence Technology for Personalized Plug-and-Play Explanation and Verification of Explanation).

References

1. Asgari, S., et al.: Masktune: mitigating spurious correlations by forcing to explore. In: Advances in Neural Information Processing Systems (NeurIPS), pp. 23284–23296 (2022)
2. Beery, S., et al.: Recognition in terra incognita. In: Proceedings of the European Conference on Computer Vision (ECCV), pp. 456–473 (2018)
3. Bykov, K., Müller, K.-R., Höhne, M.-M.-C.: Mark my words: dangers of water-marked images in ImageNet. In: Proceedings of the European Conference on Artificial Intelligence (ECAI), pp. 426–434 (2023)
4. Cho, N.-G., Yuille, A., Lee, S.-W.: A novel linelet-based representation for line segment detection. IEEE Trans. Pattern Anal. Mach. Intell. **40**, 1195–1208 (2017)

5. Deng, Y., Yang, Y., Mirzasoleiman, B., Gu, Q.: Robust learning with progressive data expansion against spurious correlation. In: Advances in Neural Information Processing Systems (NeurIPS), pp. 1390–1402 (2024)
6. Geirhos, R., et al.: ImageNet-trained CNNs are biased towards texture; increasing shape bias improves accuracy and robustness. In: International Conference on Learning Representations (ICLR), pp. 1–12 (2018)
7. Geirhos, R., et al.: Shortcut learning in deep neural networks. Nat. Mach. Intell. **2**, 665–673 (2020)
8. Hermann, K., Lampinen, A.: What shapes feature representations? Exploring datasets, architectures, and training. In: Advances in Neural Information Processing Systems (NeurIPS), pp. 9995–10006 (2020)
9. Izmailov, P., Kirichenko, P., Gruver, N., Wilson, A.-G.: On feature learning in the presence of spurious correlations. In: Advances in Neural Information Processing Systems (NeurIPS), pp. 38516–38532 (2022)
10. Ju, Y.-J., Park, J.-H., Lee, S.-W.: NeuroInspect: interpretable neuron-based debugging framework through class-conditional visualizations. arXiv preprint arXiv:2310.07184 (2023)
11. Kim, E., Lee, J., Choo, J.: Biaswap: removing dataset bias with bias-tailored swapping augmentation. In: Proceedings of the IEEE/CVF International Conference on Computer Vision (ICCV), pp. 14992–15001 (2021)
12. Kirichenko, P., Izmailov, P., Wilson, A.-G.: Last layer re-training is sufficient for robustness to spurious correlations. In: International Conference on Learning Representations (ICLR), pp. 1–17 (2022)
13. LaBonte, T., Muthukumar, V., Kumar, A.: Towards last-layer retraining for group robustness with fewer annotations. In: Advances in Neural Information Processing Systems (NeurIPS), pp. 11552–11579 (2024)
14. Lee, S.-W., Song, H.-H.: A new recurrent neural-network architecture for visual pattern recognition. IEEE Trans. Neural Netw. **8**, 331–340 (1997)
15. Li, Z., et al.: A whac-a-mole dilemma: shortcuts come in multiples where mitigating one amplifies others. In: Proceedings of the IEEE/CVF Conference on Computer Vision and Pattern Recognition (CVPR), pp. 20071–20082 (2023)
16. Liu, E.-Z., et al.: Just train twice: improving group robustness without training group information. In: International Conference on Machine Learning (ICML), pp. 6781–6792 (2021)
17. Nagarajan, V., Andreassen, A., Neyshabur, B.: Understanding the failure modes of out-of-distribution generalization. In: International Conference on Learning Representations (ICLR), pp. 1–12 (2020)
18. Nam, J., Cha, H., Ahn, S., Lee, J., Shin, J.: Learning from failure: de-biasing classifier from biased classifier. In: Advances in Neural Information Processing Systems (NeurIPS), pp. 20673–20684 (2020)
19. Nam, J., Kim, J., Lee, J., Shin, J.: Spread spurious attribute: improving worst-group accuracy with spurious attribute estimation. In: International Conference on Learning Representations (ICLR), pp. 1–12 (2021)
20. Nam, W.-J., Gur, S., Choi, J., Wolf, L., Lee, S.-W.: Relative attributing propagation: interpreting the comparative contributions of individual units in deep neural networks. In: Proceedings of the AAAI Conference on Artificial Intelligence (AAAI), pp. 2501–2508 (2020)
21. Pezeshki, M., et al.: Gradient starvation: a learning proclivity in neural networks. In: Advances in Neural Information Processing Systems (NeurIPS), pp. 1256–1272 (2021)

22. Qiu, S., Potapczynski, A., Izmailov, P., Wilson, A.-G.: Simple and fast group robustness by automatic feature reweighting. In: International Conference on Machine Learning (ICML), pp. 28448–28467 (2023)
23. Roh, M.-C., Kim, T.-Y., Park, J., Lee, S.-W.: Accurate object contour tracking based on boundary edge selection. Pattern Recogn. **40**, 931–943 (2007)
24. Rosenfeld, A., Zemel, R., Tsotsos, J.-K.: The elephant in the room. arXiv preprint arXiv:1808.03305 (2018)
25. Sagawa, S., Koh, P.-W., Hashimoto, T.-B., Liang, P.: Distributionally robust neural networks for group shifts: on the importance of regularization for worst-case generalization. In: International Conference on Learning Representations (ICLR), pp. 1–14 (2019)
26. Selvaraju, R.-R., et al.: Grad-CAM: visual explanations from deep networks via gradient-based localization. In: Proceedings of the IEEE International Conference on Computer Vision (ICCV), pp. 618–626 (2017)
27. Shah, H., Tamuly, K., Raghunathan, A., Jain, P., Netrapalli, P.: The pitfalls of simplicity bias in neural networks. In: Advances in Neural Information Processing Systems (NeurIPS), pp. 9573–9585 (2020)
28. Singla, S., Feizi, S.: Salient ImageNet: how to discover spurious features in deep learning? In: International Conference on Learning Representations (ICLR), pp. 1–13 (2021)
29. Thung, K.-H., et al.: Conversion and time-to-conversion predictions of mild cognitive impairment using low-rank affinity pursuit denoising and matrix completion. Med. Image Anal. **45**, 68–82 (2018)
30. Xiao, K.-Y., Engstrom, L., Ilyas, A., Madry, A.: Noise or signal: the role of image backgrounds in object recognition. In: International Conference on Learning Representations (ICLR), pp. 1–10 (2020)
31. Xue, Y., Payani, A., Yang, Y., Mirzasoleiman, B.: Eliminating spurious correlations from pre-trained models via data mixing. arXiv preprint arXiv:2305.14521 (2023)
32. Ye, H., Zou, J., Zhang, L.: Freeze then train: towards provable representation learning under spurious correlations and feature noise. In: International Conference on Artificial Intelligence and Statistics (AISTATS), pp. 8968–8990 (2023)
33. Zhang, H., Cisse, M., Dauphin, Y.-N., Lopez-Paz, D.: Mixup: beyond empirical risk minimization. In: International Conference on Learning Representations (ICLR), pp. 1–13 (2018)
34. Zhang, M., Sohoni, N.-S., Zhang, H.-R., Finn, C., Re, C.: Correct-N-Contrast: a contrastive approach for improving robustness to spurious correlations. In: International Conference on Machine Learning (ICML), pp. 26484–26516 (2022)
35. Zhang, Z., Sabuncu, M.: Generalized cross entropy loss for training deep neural networks with noisy labels. In: Advances in Neural Information Processing Systems (NeurIPS), pp. 1–13 (2018)

Oral Session: Applications

Language-Aware Non-autoregressive Khmer Textline Recognition

Rina Buoy[1]($\boxtimes$), Masakazu Iwamura[1], Sovila Srun[2], and Koichi Kise[1]

[1] Osaka Metropolitan University, Osaka 599-8531, Japan
sp22676n@st.omu.ac.jp
[2] Royal University of Phnom Penh, Phnom Penh 12156, Cambodia

Abstract. Unlike the Latin script, Khmer does not use spaces between words, leading to text recognition typically being done at the textline level. This results in high latency for a language-aware autoregressive (AR) decoder that decodes one character at a time by conditioning on previously-decoded characters. On the other hand, a non-autoregressive (NAR) decoder decodes characters in parallel by assuming no character dependencies; hence, it is not language-aware. For the same feature extractor, an AR decoder not only achieves higher recognition accuracy but also incurs higher latency compared to an NAR decoder. In this paper, we introduce an efficient Khmer textline recognition method based on an NAR decoder, ensuring low decoding latency while maintaining character dependencies and, consequently, linguistic awareness. This is achieved by utilizing a Khmer-specific subword modeling approach that captures the syntactic, morphological, and orthographic aspects of the Khmer script. Instead of character-level recognition, the proposed method recognizes Khmer subwords (i.e., character clusters) in parallel and, thus, character dependencies are implicitly captured. The experimental results demonstrate that the proposed method outperforms the character-level baseline NAR model in terms of recognition accuracy while maintaining the same low latency. When compared with the character-level baseline AR model, the proposed method achieves comparable or improved recognition accuracy while also achieving significantly lower latency. When compared with the recent state-of-the-art (SOTA) NAR and AR Khmer textline recognition methods, our proposed method achieves superior recognition performance.

Keywords: Textline recognition · Khmer · character cluster · subword · low-resource

1 Introduction

The Khmer script is regarded as one of the most complex writing systems due to its possession of the largest alphabet, as officially recorded in the Guinness World

---

Supplementary Information The online version contains supplementary material available at https://doi.org/10.1007/978-981-97-8702-9_23.

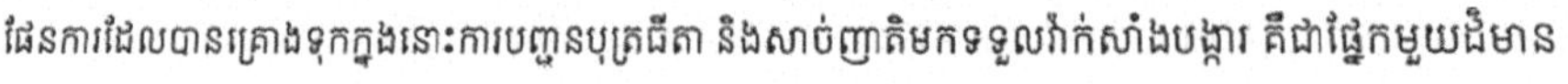

ផែនការដែលបានគ្រោងទុកក្នុងនេះ៖ការបញ្ចូលបុគ្រជីគ និងសាច់ញាតិមកទទួលវិកសាំងបង្ការ គឺជាផ្នែកមួយដ៏មាន

(a) 99 characters

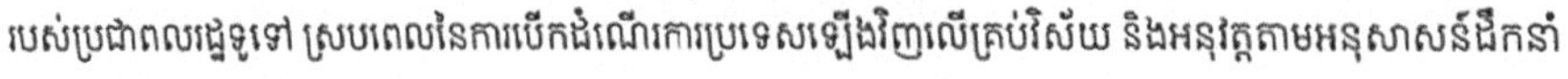

របស់ប្រជាពលរដ្ឋទូទៅ ស្របពេលនៃការបើកដំណើរការប្រទេសឡើងវិញលើគ្រប់វិស័យ និងអនុវត្តតាមអនុសាសន៍ដ៏កន្ទៅ

(b) 95 characters

អ្នកគ្រប់គ្រងមណ្ឌលថែទាំកុមារ ព្រមទាំងសាធារណជនទាំងអស់ឱ្យបានជ្រាបថា កន្លងមកយុទ្ធនាការចាក់វ៉ាក់សាំង

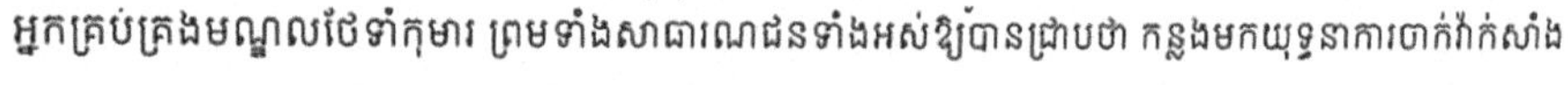

(c) 98 characterss

Fig. 1. A few samples of real Khmer textline images, all containing over 90 characters. These samples are extracted from real PDF documents, which have a low resolution because of compression or double scanning.

Records [1]. In contrast to the Latin script, Khmer lacks spaces between words, leading to a vague concept of word boundaries [2]. As a result, text recognition is often performed at the textline level, which has an arbitrarily large number of characters [3]. Figure 1 displays a few examples of Khmer textline images, all containing over 90 characters. In contrast, the average text length of the publicly available Latin scene text benchmark datasets is approximately five characters [4].

Since an autoregressive (AR) decoder decodes one character at a time during decoding by conditioning on previously-decoded characters, the resulting decoding complexity is $O(n)$ for n characters. Because of conditional decoding, an AR decoder is language-aware but it also has a significantly high decoding latency for Khmer textline recognition, which deals with an arbitrarily large number of characters. In contrast, a non-autoregressive (NAR) decoder decodes all characters in parallel (i.e., $O(1)$). Because of parallel decoding, an NAR decoder is not language-aware. Due to the absence of linguistic information during decoding, an NAR decoder exhibits lower recognition accuracy compared to an AR decoder [5,6].

In this paper, we present an efficient Khmer textline recognition method that is language-aware, yet non-autoregressive. This seemingly contradictory achievement that allows parallel decoding while maintaining language-awareness is made possible through the utilization of a Khmer-specific subword modeling approach based on Khmer character clusters (KCCs). A KCC (or a subword) is an orthographic syllable formed by combining atomic Khmer characters by utilizing the fact that certain Khmer characters (i.e., dependent vowels, diacritics, and subscripts) must be attached to a base consonant [7]. A KCC is larger than or equal to an atomic Khmer character but smaller than or equal to a Khmer word. Figure 2 demonstrates that the underlying atomic characters (a) of a textline can be grouped into KCCs or subwords (b). Instead of conventional character-level recognition [3,8], our proposed method recognizes KCCs or subwords in parallel. Since a KCC can function as either a subword or a word, linguistic information is implicitly learnt during training and incorporated during decoding. Although the number of KCCs is greater than that of atomic characters,

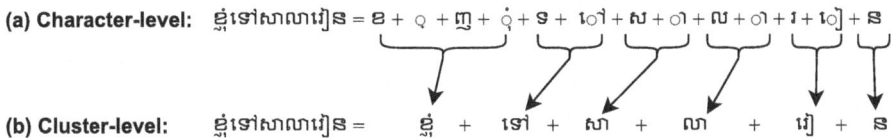

Fig. 2. Character vs. KCC representations. The underlying characters (a) of the textline (translation: *I go to school.*) can be grouped into KCCs or subwords (b).

employing a KCC-based approach can restrict a recognition result to an orthographically valid text.

To validate the proposed method, we conducted experiments with a Khmer textline recognition model at the KCC level. This model utilizes an encoder consisting of a ResNet [9]-based visual extractor and Transformer encoder units [10], alongside an NAR decoder based on a connectionist temporal classification (CTC) decoder [11]. We compared the recognition accuracy of the proposed model with the character-level baseline and state-of-the-art (SOTA) models employing both NAR and AR decoders. The models were trained on synthetically generated data and evaluated on two real evaluation datasets.

Our contributions can be summarized as follows:

1. We introduce an efficient language-aware NAR method for Khmer textline recognition. The proposed method relies on a Khmer-specific subword modeling approach based on Khmer character clusters that capture the syntactic, morphological, and orthographic aspects of the Khmer script. To the best of our knowledge, this marks the first endeavor to employ a subword modeling approach in Khmer textline recognition.
2. Compared with the character-level baseline NAR model, our proposed method achieves superior recognition accuracy while maintaining the same low decoding latency. When compared with the character-level baseline AR model, our proposed method demonstrates comparable or improved recognition accuracy. In terms of decoding complexity, the latter has a constant complexity of $O(1)$, as opposed to $O(n)$ complexity required by the former for n characters.
3. Compared with the SOTA NAR and AR Khmer textline recognition methods, our proposed method achieves the SOTA performance.

2   The Khmer Script

The Kingdom of Cambodia designates the Khmer language as its official tongue, with its script tracing its origins back to the Brahmi script. Since the 6th century, this script has undergone numerous transformations. In the contemporary era, it holds the status of being the official writing system for the Khmer language as well as several ethnic languages.

According to the Guinness World Records, the Khmer writing system holds the record for having the largest alphabet [1] and is regarded as one of the

most complex writing systems [1,12]. The Khmer script comprises 33 conso-
nants, 40 independent and dependent vowels, 13 diacritics, and numerous other
symbols [7]. Depending on its role, a consonant can take two forms: base and
subscript (or sub-consonant) forms. A comprehensive list of the Khmer alphabet,
including their Unicode points, is provided in [3].

Khmer text is a sequence of either character clusters or atomic characters.
Generally, each KCC is made of a base consonant or an independent vowel, along
with up to two consonant subscripts, a dependent vowel, and a diacritic [1,7].
Although Khmer text is typically written from left to right, the arrangement of
atomic characters within a KCC is not strictly linear. Within a KCC, vowels
and subscripts can be positioned to the left, right, above, below, or even around
the base consonant. Similar to the Arabic script, a diacritic within a KCC can
undergo a complete shape change because of a vowel. Likewise, akin to the
Hindi script, a ligature forms within a KCC when a vowel is attached to the
base consonant.

3   Related Work

Latin Text Recognition (LTR): Depending on whether characters are generated in parallel or one at a time, LTR methods can be categorized as NAR and
AR. The NAR methods generate all characters in parallel [5]. Several CTC-based
methods [13–16] map a sequence of features to a sequence of characters in one
generation step. This is because of the strong conditional independence assumption made by a CTC decoder. Instead of employing a CTC decoder, other NAR
methods [17–19] utilize a position-based attention module to predict all characters in parallel. While the parallel decoding scheme offers a substantial speedup,
which is desirable for textline recognition, the recognition accuracy of the NAR
methods is constrained because of the neglect of character dependencies [5].
On the other hand, the AR methods [20–28] consider character dependencies
by utilizing an attention-based decoder to generate characters one at a time,
typically following a left-to-right order. Although the AR methods deliver satisfactory recognition accuracy, their decoding complexity scales with $O(n)$ for
n characters [5], which can pose an efficiency bottleneck for textline recognition. This efficiency challenge is particularly pronounced when dealing with the
Khmer script since textline images can contain an arbitrarily large number of
characters, as illustrated in Fig. 1.

Khmer Text Recognition (KTR): In comparison to LTR, KTR is still in its
infancy, primarily due to the script's inherent complexity and its low-resource
low-attention nature. Previous KTR methods [29–31] mainly emphasized standalone character recognition rather than textline or word recognition. A complete
KTR system proposed by Sok and Taing [32] consists of three stages: character
segmentation, character classification, and rule-based character assembly to form
character clusters. However, the system is susceptible to segmentation noises. In
contrast, Valy et al. [1,33] introduced various attention-based two-dimensional

(2D) methods for recognizing short ancient Khmer words in the historical palm leaf manuscripts.

Tesseract-OCR [34] is an open-source multilingual optical character recognition (OCR) project that includes support for the Khmer script. It is considered as one of the earliest deep-learning-based end-to-end KTR systems and still serves as a robust baseline. Recently, Buoy et al. [3,8] introduced attention-based sequence-to-sequence (seq2seq) and Transformer-based methods for recognizing Khmer printed textline images. In comparison to Tesseract-OCR and other baseline methods, the systems demonstrated enhanced recognition accuracy on multiple real benchmark datasets. However, because of AR decoding of the attention-based and Transformer-based decoders, the proposed methods experience a decoding efficiency bottleneck for long textlines.

4 Proposed Method

Khmer Character Clusters (KCCs): Khmer text can be represented as a sequence of KCCs or subwords, formed from atomic characters. The concept of KCCs is based on the fact that certain Khmer characters (i.e., dependent vowels, diacritics, and subscripts) cannot be written alone by themselves and must be attached to a base consonant [7]. Generally, each KCC is an inseparable subword unit and is made of a base consonant or an independent vowel, along with up to two consonant subscripts, a dependent vowel, and a diacritic [1,7]. A KCC can be as small as a character and as large as a word. However, many KCCs are subwords, which are larger than a character but smaller than a word. The formation of a KCC is based on Khmer syntactic and morphological rules. The simplified formulation of a KCC is as follows

$$\text{KCC} = C_b + \{C_s\} + [V_d] + [D], \tag{1}$$

where C_b represents the base consonant and C_s represents the consonant subscript. V_d and D are the dependent vowel and diacritic, respectively. { } indicates up to two occurrences while [ ] indicates up to one occurrence. + indicates character joining.

Using Eq. (1), we can convert a Khmer text into a sequence of KCCs by following the procedure outlined in Algorithm 1. Given a valid Khmer text (Fig. 2(a)), Algorithm 1 identifies a base character to which other characters are attached. This process is iterated until the last character of the text, returning a collection of KCCs (Fig. 2(b)). As illustrated in Fig. 2, utilizing cluster-level representations results in a shorter sequence (i.e., six clusters) for the given textline, compared with the character-level representations (i.e., 13 characters). In addition, the cluster-level representations implicitly capture character dependencies. Unlike the statistical BPE encoding [35], which iteratively forms character n-grams by merging the most frequent pairs, the KCC-based subword modeling approach captures various aspects of the Khmer script, including its syntax, morphology, and orthography. While the maximum number of merging operations in BPE is a hyperparameter, a KCC has a maximum character limit determined by the orthographic rule defined in Eq. (1).

Thus, the KCC approach can be considered as an optimal Khmer-specific subword modeling approach that captures the syntactic, morphological, and orthographic aspects of the Khmer script. In this study, we propose a KCC-level method for Khmer textline recognition.

Algorithm 1. Get a sequence of KCCs for an input Khmer text.

1: **procedure** GETKCC(TEXT)   ▷ TEXT from Figure 2(a).
2:      tmp = ∅
3:      kccs = [ ]
4:      $i = 0$ ▷ i is an index variable.
5:      $c = ∅$ ▷ c is a character.
6:      **for** each (i, c) in TEXT **do**
7:          tmp = tmp + c ▷ tmp and c are concatenated.
8:          nextc = TEXT$[i + 1]$ ▷ nextc is the next character after c=TEXT[i].
9:          **if** nextc is a base consonant **then**   ▷ checking if grouping finishes.
10:             kccs.append(tmp) ▷ collecting a final KCC and adding it to a collection.
11:             tmp = ∅   ▷ resetting for a new KCC.
12:         **end if**
13:     **end for**
14:     return kccs   ▷ a collection of valid KCCs.
15: **end procedure**

Our Proposed Khmer Textline Recognition: Because of the absence of spaces between words, Khmer text recognition is commonly executed at the textline level, which can involve an arbitrarily large number of characters. Achieving high recognition accuracy with a language-aware AR decoder introduces a latency bottleneck because of the one-at-a-time decoding process. In contrast, a non-language-aware NAR decoder mitigates the latency issue but at the expense of accuracy.

In this section, we introduce an efficient Khmer textline recognition method that is language-aware, yet non-autoregressive. It is efficient because of its utilization of a CTC decoder, which generates character clusters in parallel. Thus, the proposed system can handle an arbitrarily long textline without an increase in latency (i.e., $O(1)$). Moreover, it is language-aware as it operates at the KCC or subword level rather than the character level, implicitly capturing character dependencies. Thus, the proposed method does not sacrifice recognition accuracy. The overall architecture of our proposed method is depicted in Fig. 3.

We employ a pretrained convolutional neural network (CNN) feature extractor [17], which was trained on Latin scene text datasets, to extract 2D visual features. Essentially, any pretrained CNN architectures found in publications can serve as a feature extractor, and increasing the complexity of the backbone

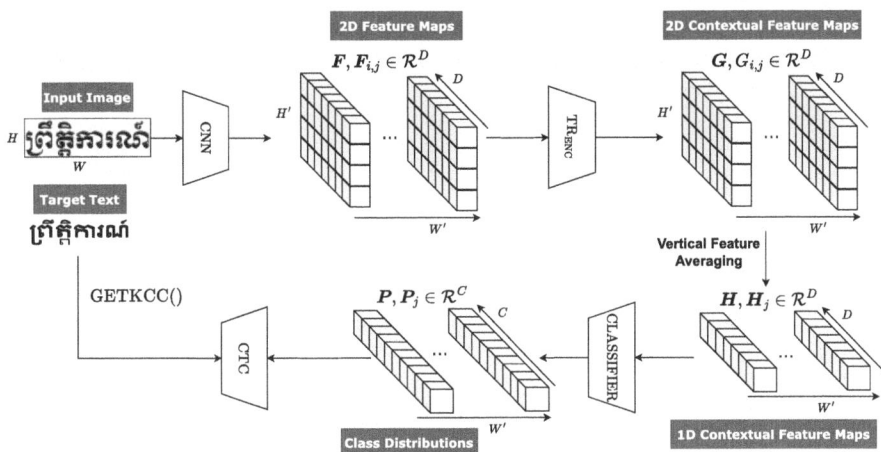

Fig. 3. The proposed Khmer textline recognition method at the KCC level. The 2D CNN feature maps, $F = (F_{1,1}, ..., F_{H',W'})$, are input to a stack of Transformer encoder units to produce the contextual feature maps, $G = (G_{1,1}, ..., G_{H',W'})$. G is averaged vertically to produce $H = (H_1, ..., H_{W'})$, from which a class distribution sequence, $P = (P_1, ..., P_{W'})$, is predicted. Finally, a CTC loss is computed between the P and the KCC sequence of the target Khmer text. H' and W' are the height and width of the feature maps.

usually leads to a modest improvement in recognition [37]. The visual features are then processed through a stack of Transformer encoder units [10] to capture visual feature dependencies. The resulting 2D contextual feature maps are condensed along the height dimension and input to the KCC classifier, which generates a sequence of class distributions over KCCs. Subsequently, we compute a CTC loss between the sequence of class distributions and the KCCs of the target Khmer text.

Mathematically, the CNN module takes an input image, I, and returns 2D visual feature maps, $F = (F_{1,1}, ..., F_{H',W'})$, $F_{i,j} \in \mathcal{R}^D$, where D is the model dimension. F is expressed as

$$F = \text{CNN}(I), \tag{2}$$

where CNN refers to the pretrained CNN module [17], which generates 2D visual feature maps with H' for the height and W' for the width. To capture the dependencies among visual features, F is fed to a stack of Transformer encoder units. The resulting contextual features, $G = (G_{1,1}, ..., G_{H',W'})$, $G_{i,j} \in \mathcal{R}^D$, are expressed as

$$G = \text{TR}_{ENC}(F), \tag{3}$$

where TR_{ENC} is a stack of Transformer encoder units. G is condensed along the height dimension to create 1D contextual feature maps, $H = (H_1, ..., H_{W'})$, $H_j \in \mathcal{R}^D$. H_j is expressed as

$$H_j = \frac{1}{H'} \sum_{i=1}^{H'} G_{i,j}. \tag{4}$$

H is then passed to the KCC classifier to generate 1D class distributions over KCCs, $P = (P_1, ..., P_{W'})$, $P_j \in \mathbb{R}^C$, where C represents the size of the KCC vocabulary including a no-label token (ϵ) that is required by a CTC decoder. P is expressed as

$$P = \mathrm{CLASSIFIER}(H), \tag{5}$$

where CLASSIFIER refers to a simple feedforward neural network, followed by a softmax normalization layer.

During inference, text can be decoded greedily by selecting the most likely KCC in each frame, j. During training, we compute a CTC loss between the sequence of class distributions and the KCCs of the target text. A CTC loss can be expressed as

$$\mathrm{Loss} = \mathrm{CTC}(P, \mathrm{GETKCC}(Y)), \tag{6}$$

where GETKCC(), defined in Algorithm 1, is the procedure for converting the target Khmer text, Y, into a KCC sequence.

5   Experiment

Synthetic Training Datasets: We used the same synthetic training datasets provided by Buoy et al. [3]. The datasets comprise 2.8 million samples, including both scene text and document OCR images. Training samples are provided in Fig. 4.

<table>
<tr><td>(a) Document OCR samples</td><td>(b) Scene text samples</td></tr>
</table>

Fig. 4. Training samples

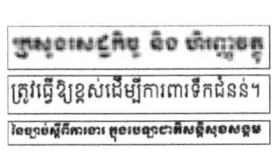

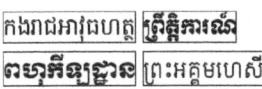

(a) KHOB textline samples

(b) A sample annotated page from the Khmer word spotting dataset

(c) Cropped word samples from the Khmer word spotting dataset

Fig. 5. Evaluation samples. (a) Samples from the KHOB dataset. (b) A sample annotated page from the Khmer word spotting dataset. (c) Cropped word samples from the Khmer word spotting dataset.

(a) 1.0   (b) 1.5   (c) 2.0   (d) 2.5

Fig. 6. Samples at different downsampling factors.

Real Evaluation Datasets: To evaluate and compare recognition accuracy, we relied on two manually-labeled textline datasets, namely, the KHOB[1] and the Khmer word spotting[2] [36] datasets.

The KHOB dataset was extracted from PDF documents, and annotations were manually created at the textline level. While the textline images have relatively clean backgrounds, they suffer from poor resolution because of image compression and double scanning, as shown in Fig. 5(a). After excluding the textlines containing non-Khmer characters, the processed KHOB dataset has approximately 1,300 images. The average text length is 77 characters, with a standard deviation of 26 characters.

On the other hand, the Khmer word spotting dataset consists of manually annotated word-level text images, originally intended for a word spotting task rather than recognition, as shown in Fig. 5(b). After filtering out images with short texts and non-Khmer characters, the processed dataset contains approximately 6,000 images. In contrast to the KHOB dataset, the word spotting dataset has a significantly higher resolution, as shown in Fig. 5(c). With high-resolution inputs, the role of linguistic context is not obvious as most characters can be decoded correctly by relying only on visual features. To make this dataset more interesting for a language-aware decoder, we also created three realizations of this dataset with different difficulty levels by downsizing it by factors of 1.5, 2.0, and 2.5. As the downsizing factor increases, the input images become more blurry and the role of linguistic context becomes more prudent in resolving ambiguities and accurately predicting characters. The average text length is 12 characters, with

---

[1] https://github.com/EKYCSolutions/khmer-ocr-benchmark-dataset.

[2] https://www.kaggle.com/datasets/keatchakravuth/khmer-annotation.

a standard deviation of two characters. The downsampled samples are shown in Fig. 6.

Experiment Setup: We utilized the pretrained CNN module [17]. The Transformer encoder module (TR_{ENC}) comprises three Transformer encoder units. Both the CNN and Transformer encoder modules share the model dimension of 512. For an input image of $H \times W$ pixels, the feature maps of both the CNN and Transformer encoder modules are $\frac{H}{8} \times \frac{W}{8}$. The total number of individual Khmer characters is 131, including special tokens such as no-label (ϵ for a CTC decoder), SOS (start-of-sentence), and EOS (end-of-sentence). In terms of Khmer character clusters, we processed the entire training corpus, resulting in a total of 4,782 unique KCCs, including the special tokens. The average KCC length is approximately four characters, with a standard deviation of one character. The training images were resized to a common height of 32 pixels, preserving aspect ratios (i.e., arbitrarily long width). We applied the same data augmentation pipeline as that in [3]. Instead of resizing or padding to a common maximum width, we applied the image chunking and merging technique [3,37].

Evaluation Metric: While a word error rate (WER) is a standard evaluation metric for the Latin script, a character error rate (CER) is used for non-Latin scripts without explicit word boundaries, such as the Khmer script. However, since word-level annotations are available for the Khmer word spotting dataset, it is possible to compute both CER and WER. In contrast, only a CER is computed for the KHOB dataset because it has textline-level annotations only. While it is technically possible to perform word segmentation to compute a WER, segmentation errors can inevitably distort the resulting WER.

6   Results and Discussion

Recognition Accuracy Comparison with the Character-Level Baseline Models on the Khmer Word Spotting Dataset: To validate our proposed model (CTC-KCC) that predicts at the KCC level in parallel, we established two character-level baseline models using both CTC and Transformer-based decoders (denoted as CTC-CHAR and TR.DEC.-CHAR, respectively). The Transformer-based decoder employs three units of the Transformer decoder [10], generating one character at a time in a left-to-right order. Each unit has a model dimension of 512, a feed-forward dimension of 2048, eight attention heads, and a dropout probability of 10%. Thus, the TR.DEC.-CHAR model is language-aware. The recognition accuracies of these baseline models should theoretically set the minimum and maximum bounds for our proposed CTC-KCC model, with the CTC-CHAR model being fully non-autoregressive and the TR.DEC.-CHAR model being fully autoregressive.

As shown in Table 1, Tesseract-OCR for the Khmer script obtained the highest CERs and WERs across all the downsampling factors. Compared with the

Table 1. Character and word error rates (%) comparison with the character-level baseline models on the Khmer word spotting dataset. Bold: lowest. Italic: second lowest.

Model	Downsampling Factor							
	1.0		1.5		2.0		2.5	
	CER	WER	CER	WER	CER	WER	CER	WER
Tesseract-OCR (Baseline)	6.30	35.32	8.79	42.65	16.72	60.19	29.68	80.00
CTC-CHAR (Baseline)	0.57	5.55	0.92	8.76	2.45	18.94	8.51	42.60
TR.DEC.-CHAR (Baseline)	**0.32**	*3.38*	*0.49*	*4.43*	**1.06**	**7.46**	**4.41**	**20.89**
CTC-KCC (Ours)	*0.34*	**3.13**	**0.42**	**3.99**	*1.20*	*8.53*	*5.01*	*23.74*

baseline CTC-CHAR and TR.DEC.-CHAR models, our proposed CTC-KCC model achieved comparable recognition accuracy with the TR.DEC.-CHAR model and significantly outperformed the CTC-CHAR model, especially at higher downsampling factors. This suggests that by using the KCC subword modeling approach, it is possible to incorporate language model capacity into our proposed non-autoregressive model, which is, otherwise, not language-aware at the character level.

The increasing CER and WER discrepancies between the non-language-aware model (i.e., CTC-CHAR) and the language-aware models (i.e., CTC-KCC and TR.DEC.-CHAR) at high downsampling factors highlight the importance of considering language information when images are visually distorted and visual features are less informative.

Recognition Accuracy Comparison with the Character-Level SOTA and Baseline Methods on the KHOB Dataset: In this section, we compare the recognition accuracy of our proposed CTC-KCC model with the SOTA methods as well as the baseline methods. As shown in Table 2, CRNN [13] and TRBC [38] are CTC-based models while TRBA [38] is an attention-based model. The SOTA models by Buoy et al. [3] are based on Transformer networks. CRNN [13], TRBC [38], and TRBA [38] are based on the implementations by Buoy et al. [3].

Compared with the CTC-based and attention-based SOTA methods, our proposed CTC-KCC model achieved superior recognition performance, as depicted in Table 2. Specifically, the proposed model obtained a CER more than two times lower than CRNN [13], TRBC [38], and TRBA [38]. In addition, compared with the recent Transformer-based SOTA models by Buoy et al. [3], our proposed CTC-KCC model also achieved superior recognition performance. Specifically, our proposed CTC-KCC model achieved a CER of 2.33% compared to 2.55% by the best-performing 1D-ResNet model. However, it is noteworthy that the proposed CTC-KCC model generates text in parallel at the KCC level, whereas the Transformer-based SOTA models generate text one character at a time.

Compared with the baseline NAR and AR methods, our proposed CTC-KCC model also achieved superior recognition performance. On the KHOB dataset that is characterized by long and low-resolution textline images, our proposed

Table 2. Character error rate (%) comparison with the character-level SOTA and baseline models on the KHOB dataset. Bold: lowest. Italic: second lowest. Att.: attention-based decoder. Tr.: Transformer decoder.

Model	Decoder	CER
CRNN [13]	CTC	6.17
TRBC [38]	CTC	5.42
TRBA [38]	Att.	7.77
1D-VGG [3]	Tr.	3.32
1D-ResNet [3]	Tr.	*2.55*
2D-VGG [3]	Tr.	3.03
2D-ResNet [3]	Tr.	3.41
Tesseract-OCR (Baseline)	CTC	9.19
CTC-CHAR (Baseline)	CTC	2.72
TR.DEC.-CHAR (Baseline)	Tr.	3.23
CTC-KCC (Ours)	CTC	**2.33**

CTC-KCC model obtained a CER of 2.33% compared to 2.72% and 3.23% by the baseline CTC-CHAR and TR.DEC.-CHAR models, respectively. This highlights that the performance of the Transformer decoder of the TR.DEC.-CHAR model is more sensitive to textline length (i.e., character count) and resolution than our proposed CTC-KCC model and the baseline CTC-CHAR model.

Efficiency Comparison: In terms of inference speed, both our proposed CTC-KCC and the CTC-CHAR models had approximately constant decoding times, regardless of the number of decoded characters. On average, these models achieved an inference speed of approximately 18 ms per image. In contrast, the inference speed of the TR.DEC.-CHAR model scaled linearly with the number of decoded characters, with a rate of 5.5 ms per character. This means that it takes approximately 577 ms to decode a textline image containing 100 characters (Fig. 7).

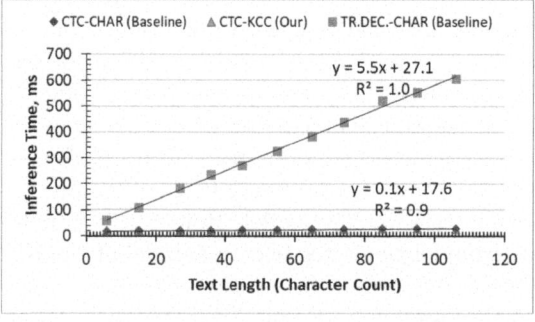

Fig. 7. Inference speed on an RTX 2060 GPU.

7   Conclusion

In this article, we introduced an efficient approach for recognizing Khmer textlines that integrates language-awareness with a non-autoregressive decoder. This achievement is facilitated by employing a Khmer-specific subword modeling technique based on Khmer character clusters. The experimental results demonstrate that our proposed model consistently outperformed the character-level baseline NAR model in terms of recognition accuracy on the Khmer word spotting dataset, irrespective of the downsampling factor. In comparison to the character-level baseline AR model, our proposed model achieved comparable recognition accuracy on the same dataset.

On the KHOB dataset, characterized by low resolution and long textlines, our proposed model significantly outperformed the character-level baseline models using NAR and AR decoders in terms of recognition accuracy. Additionally, our proposed model exhibited a substantial efficiency advantage over the baseline AR model. Compared with the SOTA Khmer textline recognition methods, our proposed method achieved the SOTA recognition accuracy.

Acknowledgment. This work was supported by JSPS Kakenhi Grant Number 22H00540 and RUPP-OMU/HEIP.

References

1. Valy, D., Verleysen, M., Chhun, S.: Text recognition on Khmer historical documents using glyph class map generation with encoder-decoder model. In: Proceedings of the 8th International Conference on Pattern Recognition Applications and Methods (2019)
2. Kaing, H., et al.: Towards tokenization and part-of-speech tagging for Khmer: data and discussion. ACM Trans. Asian Low-Resource Lang. Inf. Process. **20**, 1–16 (2021)
3. Buoy, R., Iwamura, M., Srun, S., Kise, K.: Toward a low-resource non-latin-complete baseline: an exploration of Khmer optical character recognition. IEEE Access **11**, 128044–128060 (2023)
4. Bautista, D., Atienza, R.: Scene text recognition with permuted autoregressive sequence models. Lecture Notes in Computer Science, pp. 178–196 (2022)
5. Qiao, Z., et al.: PIMNet: a parallel, iterative and mimicking network for scene text recognition. In: Proceedings of the 29th ACM International Conference on Multimedia (2021)
6. Saharia, C., Hinton, G., Norouzi, M., Jaitly, N., Chan, W.: Imputer: sequence modelling via imputation and dynamic programming. In: ICML (2020)
7. Kaing, H., Parsing, C.: Towards Morphological and Syntactic Analyses for the Khmer Language. Nara Institute of Science (2022)
8. Buoy, R., Taing, N., Chenda, S., Kor, S.: Khmer printed character recognition using attention-based Seq2Seq Network. Ho Chi Minh City Open Univ. J. Sci. Eng. Technol. **12**, 3–16 (2022)
9. He, K., Zhang, X., Ren, S., Sun, J.: Deep residual learning for image recognition. In: Proceedings of the IEEE Conference on Computer Vision and Pattern Recognition, pp. 770–778 (2016)

10. Vaswani, A., et al.: Attention is all you need. In: Advances in Neural Information Processing Systems, vol. 30 (2017)

11. Graves, A., Fernández, S., Gomez, F., Schmidhuber, J.: Connectionist temporal classification. In: Proceedings of the 23rd International Conference on Machine Learning, ICML 2006 (2006)

12. Horton, J., Sok, M., Durdin, M., Ty, R.: Spoof-vulnerable rendering in Khmer Unicode implementations. In: Proceedings of ACIS, pp. 177–180 (2017)

13. Shi, B., Bai, X., Yao, C.: An end-to-end trainable neural network for image-based sequence recognition and its application to scene text recognition. IEEE Trans. Pattern Anal. Mach. Intell. **39**, 2298–2304 (2017)

14. Wang, J., Hu, X.: Gated recurrent convolution neural network for OCR. In: Proceedings of the 31st International Conference on Neural Information Processing Systems, pp. 334–343 (2017)

15. Liu, W., Chen, C., Wong, K., Su, Z., Han, J.: Star-net: a spatial attention residue network for scene text recognition. In: Proceedings of the British Machine Vision Conference 2016 (2016)

16. Borisyuk, F., Gordo, A., Sivakumar, V.: Rosetta. In: Proceedings of the 24th ACM SIGKDD International Conference on Knowledge Discovery and Data Mining (2018)

17. Fang, S., Xie, H., Wang, Y., Mao, Z., Zhang, Y.: Read like humans: autonomous, bidirectional and iterative language modeling for scene text recognition. In: 2021 IEEE/CVF Conference on Computer Vision and Pattern Recognition (CVPR) (2021)

18. Wang, Y., Xie, H., Fang, S., Wang, J., Zhu, S., Zhang, Y.: From two to one: a new scene text recognizer with visual language modeling network. In: 2021 IEEE/CVF International Conference on Computer Vision, ICCV 2021, Montreal, QC, Canada, 10–17 October 2021, pp. 14174–14183 (2021). https://doi.org/10.1109/ICCV48922.2021.01393

19. Yu, D., et al.: Towards accurate scene text recognition with semantic reasoning networks. In: 2020 IEEE/CVF Conference on Computer Vision and Pattern Recognition (CVPR) (2020)

20. Shi, B., Wang, X., Lyu, P., Yao, C., Bai, X.: Robust scene text recognition with automatic rectification. In: 2016 IEEE Conference on Computer Vision and Pattern Recognition (CVPR) (2016)

21. Shi, B., Yang, M., Wang, X., Lyu, P., Yao, C., Bai, X.: Aster: an attentional scene text recognizer with flexible rectification. IEEE Trans. Pattern Anal. Mach. Intell. **41**, 2035–2048 (2019)

22. Lee, C., Osindero, S.: Recursive recurrent nets with attention modeling for OCR in the wild. In: 2016 IEEE Conference on Computer Vision and Pattern Recognition (CVPR) (2016)

23. Cheng, Z., Bai, F., Xu, Y., Zheng, G., Pu, S., Zhou, S.: Focusing attention: towards accurate text recognition in natural images. In: 2017 IEEE International Conference on Computer Vision (ICCV) (2017)

24. Sheng, F., Chen, Z., Xu, B.: NRTR: a no-recurrence sequence-to-sequence model for scene text recognition. In: 2019 International Conference on Document Analysis and Recognition (ICDAR) (2019)

25. Li, H., Wang, P., Shen, C., Zhang, G.: Show, attend and read: a simple and strong baseline for irregular text recognition. In: Proceedings of the AAAI Conference on Artificial Intelligence, vol. 33, pp. 8610–8617 (2019)

26. Wang, T., et al.: Decoupled attention network for text recognition. In: The Thirty-Fourth AAAI Conference on Artificial Intelligence, AAAI 2020, The Thirty-Second Innovative Applications of Artificial Intelligence Conference, IAAI 2020, The Tenth AAAI Symposium on Educational Advances in Artificial Intelligence, EAAI 2020, New York, NY, USA, 7–12 February 2020, pp. 12216–12224 (2020). https://ojs.aaai.org/index.php/AAAI/article/view/6903

27. Cui, M., Wang, W., Zhang, J., Wang, L.: Representation and correlation enhanced encoder-decoder framework for scene text recognition. In: Lladós, J., Lopresti, D., Uchida, S. (eds.) ICDAR 2021. LNCS, vol. 12824, pp. 156–170. Springer, Cham (2021). https://doi.org/10.1007/978-3-030-86337-1_11

28. Xie, X., Fu, L., Zhang, Z., Wang, Z., Bai, X.: Toward understanding wordart: corner-guided Transformer for scene text recognition. Lecture Notes in Computer Science, pp. 303–321 (2022)

29. Chey, C., Kumhom, P., Chamnongthai, K.: Khmer printed character recognition by using wavelet descriptors. Int. J. Uncertainty Fuzziness Knowl.-Based Syst. **14**, 337–350 (2006)

30. Annanurov, B., Noor, N.: A compact deep learning model for Khmer handwritten text recognition. IAES Int. J. Artif. Intell. (IJ-AI) **10**, 584 (2021)

31. Meng, H., Morariu, D.: Khmer character recognition using artificial neural network. In: 2014 Asia-Pacific Signal and Information Processing Association Annual Summit and Conference (APSIPA) (2014)

32. Sok, P., Taing, N.: Support Vector Machine (SVM) based classifier for Khmer printed character-set recognition. In: 2014 Asia-Pacific Signal and Information Processing Association Annual Summit and Conference (APSIPA) (2014)

33. Valy, D., Verleysen, M., Chhun, S.: Data augmentation and text recognition on Khmer Historical Manuscripts. In: 2020 17th International Conference on Frontiers in Handwriting Recognition (ICFHR) (2020)

34. Tesseract-OCR: Tesseract-OCR/tesseract: Tesseract open source OCR engine (main repository). https://github.com/tesseract-ocr/tesseract

35. Sennrich, R., Haddow, B., Birch, A.: Neural machine translation of rare words with subword units. arXiv Preprint arXiv:1508.07909 (2015)

36. Keat, C.: Unlocking Insights: Annotated Khmer Dataset for Word Spotting. Institute of Technology of Cambodia (2023)

37. Diaz, D., Qin, S., Ingle, R., Fujii, Y., Bissacco, A.: Rethinking text line recognition models. arXiv Preprint arXiv:1040.7787 (2021)

38. Baek, J., et al.: What is wrong with scene text recognition model comparisons? Dataset and model analysis. In: 2019 IEEE/CVF International Conference on Computer Vision (ICCV) (2019)

ATA: Attentive Text Augmentation for Typo-Robust Language Models

Jihye Han[1] and Sang Keun Lee[1,2(✉)]

[1] Department of Computer Science and Engineering, Korea University, Seoul,
Republic of Korea
{hjhsophia1,yalphy}@korea.ac.kr
[2] Department of Artificial Intelligence, Korea University, Seoul, Republic of Korea

Abstract. Text data generated by humans in real-world scenarios
often contains a substantial amount of noise, including misspellings,
typographical errors, and abbreviations. Pre-trained language models
(PLMs) often struggle to make accurate predictions when encountering such noise. To handle this issue, we introduce the **A**ttentive **T**ext
Augmentation for Typo-Robust Language Models (ATA), leveraging
attention weights to compute each word's contribution to the model prediction. We train PLM with a dataset augmented by ATA and evaluate
its performance on datasets containing textual noise. Our experimental
results on four text classification datasets demonstrate that the proposed
method effectively enhances the model's robustness against textual noise.

Keywords: Data Augmentation · Textual Noise · Out-of-Vocabulary

1 Introduction

Transformer-based pre-trained language models (PLMs) like BERT [6] and GPT-
2 [18] have demonstrated remarkable performance in various Natural Language
Understanding (NLU) and Natural Language Generation (NLG) tasks. These
pre-trained language models are usually trained and evaluated on clean corpora that have limited textual noise [9]. However, in real-world scenarios, texts
generated by human users contain substantial levels of textual noise, including
typographical errors, misspelled words, or abbreviations [22].

Despite employing sub-word tokenizers such as WordPiece [25] that are
specifically designed to handle out-of-vocabulary (OOV) words, PLMs generally suffer a decline in performance when encountering textual noise [1,7,8,13].
In order to demonstrate how vulnerable language models are to typos, [13] developed a method for adding perturbations to input texts. They have shown that
even a minor level of noise might result in a substantial decline in performance
on downstream tasks.

In order to address this challenge, recent studies have employed data augmentation techniques to train PLMs on textual noise [9,20,27]. These studies
inserted character- or word-level textual noise into the training data, thereby

C. Wallraven et al. (Eds.): ICPRAI 2024, LNCS 14892, pp. 354–365, 2025.
https://doi.org/10.1007/978-981-97-8702-9_24

generating augmented datasets. Following this approach, the produced datasets are incorporated to train the models, improving their ability to handle textual errors or noise.

Inspired by previous works, we aim to develop a standard data augmentation strategy to produce a dataset that can be used for training the typo-robust model. Previous studies augmented sentences by randomly selecting words and adding textual noise to them. However, the importance of words can vary depending on the task at hand. Additionally, the impact of typos on model predictions will vary depending on the importance of the words. As a result, typos in words that carry significance in sentiment analysis tasks (e.g., good, awesome) could lead to a more significant drop in model performance compared to less significant words (e.g., that, the). Motivated by this idea, we propose **A**ttentive **T**ext **A**ugmentation for Typo-Robust Language Models (ATA), which utilizes attention weights and considers the contribution of each word to the model prediction. When incorporating the augmented data using our proposed method into the training process, the model learns typo variants of important words, thereby effectively enhancing its robustness to typographical errors.

To validate the effectiveness of our augmentation method, we conducted experiments on four sentiment classification tasks. The experimental results demonstrate that models trained with our proposed method show significant performance improvements over the baselines on test sets containing typos. Additionally, through qualitative evaluations, we confirm that word importance is appropriately scored by ATA. The contributions of this work can be summarized as follows:

- We propose a novel text augmentation strategy, ATA, which utilizes word significance scores calculated by attention weights.
- Experimental results indicate that the text augmented by our proposed method effectively enhances the performance of the BERT model against noisy data.
- Our qualitative analysis demonstrates that the attention weights contain sufficient information about word contributions, and ATA utilized them to select important words to perturb.

2   Related Work

In this section, we explore how previous research has addressed textual noise, dividing our review into two parts. The prevailing trend was to focus on generating high quality word embeddings. Hence, in Sect. 2.1, we introduce studies focused on generating or enhancing embeddings for out-of-vocabulary (OOV) words. Next, in Sect. 2.2, we summarize earlier studies that attempted to develop models robust to typos during the training process.

2.1   Out-of-Vocabulary Word Embeddings

Word embeddings are vectors that encode the syntactic and semantic features of words [12,15]. They play a crucial role in neural networks within the field of Natural Language Processing (NLP). However, these approaches usually utilize a vocabulary of fixed size, restricting the model to knowing only words that have been previously seen during the training step. Efforts have been made to address the issue of performance degradation when models encounter out-of-vocabulary (OOV) words, from the perspective of word embeddings. Previous studies have focused on enhancing the quality of static embeddings by learning the semantic and syntactic features of words from a large corpus [3,24,26]. However, these studies are time-consuming and expensive because they require training from scratch. Therefore, recent works take advantage of pre-trained static [3] or contextual [6] embeddings and attempt to improve them with additional training steps [4,10,16,19]. Yet, in order to improve or generate embeddings for OOV words, this approach involves additional training time and resources [10]. Therefore, our research aims to tackle the issue of text noise without improving the quality of word embeddings to reduce training costs.

2.2   Dealing with Noise in Training Perspective

In order to train models that are robust to textual noise, several studies have utilized data augmentation techniques that involve perturbing the characters or words within the data. The study conducted by [9] revealed that training a transformer-based model with a moderate level of random textual noise not only results in strong performance on noisy data but also preserves its performance on the original data. Furthermore, [20,27] have addressed the problems that arise from misspelled queries in dense retrieval. They inserted typos in the original queries to augment them, and they incorporated the augmented queries to train the model to be robust against misspelled queries. These works augmented data by perturbing random letters of the original data. This is different from our research in that previous works randomly selected words and characters for augmentation, ignoring the priority of words or tokens per instance in the dataset. We aim to train a model robust to textual noise by augmenting data while considering the contribution of words per instance to the model prediction.

3   Method

This section describes ATA, a text augmentation technique that we propose. At first, we illustrate how ATA identifies the words that carry significance and augments the input data. We next introduce the training objective using the augmented datasets.

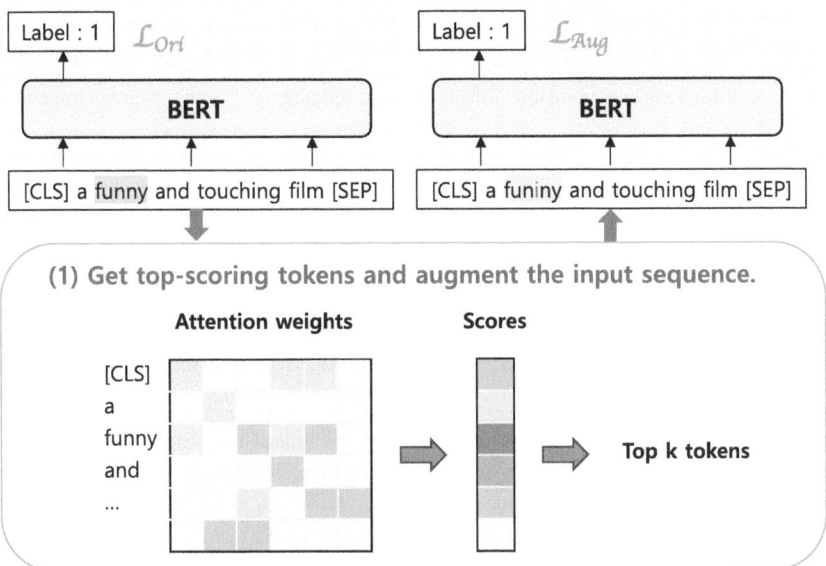

Fig. 1. Overview of our method. (1) First, we identify the highest-scoring words by utilizing attention weights and then add perturbation to augment the input text. (2) Afterward, we train the BERT model using both the original and augmented input texts. Two BERT models in the figure indicate the same model.

3.1 ATA: Attentive Text Augmentation for Typo-Robust Language Models

Attentive Text Augmentation for Typo-Robust Language Models, ATA, is applied to each instance in every training batch. First, it identifies the important words in a given input text—those that significantly influence the model's prediction. Next, selected words are corrupted to augment the input text, which is then used to train the model.

Selecting Target Words to Corrupt. Our approach differs from earlier studies [9,20,27] in that we choose words for augmentation selectively rather than randomly. The self-attention mechanism in Transformer-based language models computes attention weights, which represent the relative significance between each pair of tokens [23]. This approach is commonly used for explaining the output of a Transformer-based model by demonstrating how these weights allocate significance among the input tokens [5,17]. Building upon this inspiration, we employ the attention weights obtained from the last layer of the BERT model to calculate the individual impact of each token on the model prediction. This is accomplished by summing the attention scores as illustrated in Fig. 1. Based

Table 1. Description and examples of different word-corrupting strategies.

Method	Description	Example
Delete	Delete a random character	awesome → awsome
Insert	In a random position, add a random character	awesome → awesoeme
Swap	Two random characters next to each other change positions	awesome → awseome
Keyboard	Change random character with a close character on the keyboard	awesome → awqsome

on the highest-scoring tokens, we then choose the top k words from the input texts and corrupt them to generate the augmented input text data.

Data Augmentation. Following the step of selecting important words, we corrupt these words to generate augmented input text. Through the utilization of the *nlpaug* library, we applied four different methods of corruption that were used in earlier studies [1,4,27]: Delete, Insert, Swap, and Keyboard.[1] Table 1 provides a detailed explanation of each corrupting technique, along with examples of its application. One of the four word corruption strategies is chosen at random for each selected word. We generate one augmented input text per instance in the batch by corrupting the selected words.

3.2 Training

Here, we describe the training process incorporating data augmented by ATA. Figure 1 illustrates the entire training process. For each original input x_i and its label y_i, we generate an augmented input x_i' and y_i through the proposed augmentation strategy. Then, each input is fed into the model for training. We minimize the following loss function with a hyperparameter λ:

$$L_{Total} = L_{Ori} + \lambda L_{Aug} \tag{1}$$

where cross-entropy loss is used for both L_{Ori} and L_{Aug}. By minimizing L_{Ori}, the model learns the task from the original data, while minimizing L_{Aug} allows it to learn to be robust against textual noise. Ultimately, we expect the model to become robust with both the original and noise-included data after the training.

4 Experiments

4.1 Experimental Setup

Datasets. For our experimental evaluation, we used four sentiment classification datasets. These include SST-2 [21], MR [14], and IMDB [11], all of which

---

[1] https://github.com/makcedward/nlpaug.

are movie review datasets. Additionally, we incorporate the Emotion dataset from TweetEval [2], which is derived from social media contents. To evaluate the robustness of our model against textual noises like typos, we conducted experiments using a corrupted test set created by adding noise to the original test set. For generating the corrupted test set, we utilized the OCR engine from the *nlpaug* library and added OCR errors to random words in the dataset.

Baselines. To demonstrate the efficacy of our approach, we conducted a comparative analysis between our methodology and the baseline methods listed below.

- BERT: Standard BERT-base model.
- BERT + LOVE [4]: BERT-base model with word embeddings generated by a trained encoder. Here, the encoder is designed to generate high-quality embeddings for out-of-vocabulary words, which includes textual noise such as typos.
- BERT + Random Aug: BERT-base model trained additionally with augmented data. Here, corrupted words are selected randomly.

Implementation Details. In all our experiments, we utilized a pre-trained BERT-base model. For evaluation metrics, we used accuracy across all tasks. Each task was trained for 3, 4, or 5 epochs with a learning rate of 2e−5. The models were optimized using an AdamW optimizer. For SST2, MR, and Emotions, we trained with a batch size of 32 and 16 for IMDB. All experiments were conducted on a single NVIDIA RTX 2080Ti GPU.[2]

Table 2. Comparison of our method against baselines across four datasets. The 'Original' column shows performance on the original test set, while the 'Corrupted' column reflects performances on the test set with textual noise. We did not report the BERT+LOVE results of the IMDB dataset due to the limitation of computing resources. Instead of using token embeddings in the BERT model, method of LOVE [4] uses generated embeddings for all words in dataset, leading to increase in vocabulary size.

	SST2		MR		IMDB		Emotion	
	Original	Corrupted	Original	Corrupted	Original	Corrupted	Original	Corrupted
BERT	91.28	75.26	85.26	68.69	**93.81**	81.02	80.44	63.31
BERT + LOVE	91.50	77.08	85.08	70.47	–	–	80.09	59.68
BERT + Random Aug	**91.72**	79.7	**85.64**	74.34	93.02	82.38	80.98	66.96
BERT + ATA (Ours)	91.53	**80.31**	85.01	**74.93**	92.7	**84.02**	**81.07**	**68.52**

---

[2] Our code is available at: https://github.com/jihye-h/ATA.

4.2   Main Results

Table 2 displays our main results. The 'Corrupted' column shows the performance of our model on the corrupted test sets. Following the approach of [4], we corrupted 10%, 30%, 50%, 70%, and 90% of the words from the original test set to create five different corrupted test sets. The reported results are the average performance across these five corrupted sets. Our model showed the best performance on all tasks for the corrupted test sets. Additionally, for the original tasks, our model showed similar or better performance compared to the baselines of all tasks. The methods applying data augmentation (BERT+Random Aug and BERT+ATA) showed notable performance improvements on the corrupted test sets compared to the other two baselines (BERT and BERT+LOVE). This shows the effectiveness of data augmentation strategies for training models robust to noisy data, which aligns with previous findings. Our proposed method, ATA, outperformed random augmentation on all tasks with corrupted sets, highlighting the effectiveness of a selective word augmentation strategy.

4.3   Analysis

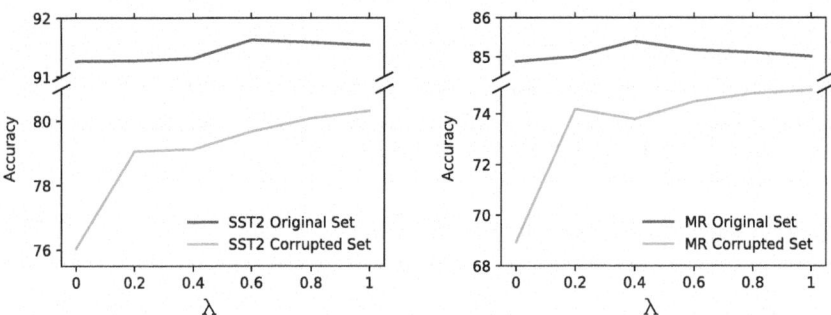

Fig. 2. Impact of hyperparameter λ in loss function of Sect. 3.2. Two graph illustrate the accuracy of SST2 and MR datasets, respectively. (Color figure online)

Impact of Hyperparameter λ. In order to measure the influence of data augmented using our proposed approach, we conducted evaluations with different λ values. λ serves as a hyper-parameter in the loss function, as described in Sect. 3.2. Figure 2 illustrates the performance of the BERT model across different lambda values. Observing the results of corrupted sets (yellow line) in both graphs, we can find that as λ increases, the model performance improves. This suggests that by incorporating data augmented by ATA we can train the model to become robust against textual noise. Looking at the results of original set (blue line), we noticed that the performance is higher at λ values between 0.4 and 0.6 compared to when λ is 0. This indicates that training with an appropriate amount of corrupted data can also enhance performance on the original dataset.

Qualitative Analysis. We analyzed whether our proposed method, ATA effectively identifies important words. As mentioned in Sect. 3.1, we selected words with the highest summed attention weights as having significant influence on model predictions. To verify this assumption, we analyzed the words selected during the training process. Table 3 shows the top 50 most chosen words in the SST2 [21] and Emotion [2] tasks. Since both datasets are for sentiment classification, both results include sentiment words like 'love' or 'bad'. Specifically, for the SST2 task, which is a movie review dataset, words that are directly related to movie reviews, such as 'film' and 'entertaining', were chosen. Similarly, the results of the Emotion dataset show words like 'angry','shocking', and 'happy'. This experiment proves that ATA effectively selects important words that align with human intuition. Using attention weights, we can simply identify words contributing significantly to model predictions. Figure 3 illustrates the actual examples of augmentation. For example, in the SST2 dataset, words like 'funny' and 'bad' were chosen, and the figure depicts how these important words are corrupted to create augmented data. These analyses demonstrate that our method accurately calculates the importance of each word in the input text and effectively generates augmented data.

Table 3. Top 50 words selected by ATA utilizing attention weights for the SST2 [21] and Emotion [2] tasks. Selected words represents the most significant words of the instance in each dataset for model prediction.

Task	Top 50 Words
SST2	film, movie, like, one, rrb, makes, bad, good, funny, never, well, enough, best, feels, better, seems, comedy, us, make, still, also, little, see, much, made, something, manages, watching, works, way, entertaining, yet, offers, drama, love, great, without, work, watch, nothing, gives, really, even, comes, would, gets, look, worth, compelling, ultimately
Emotion	user, sad, angry, depression, sadness, love, awful, anxiety, fucking, rage, lost, horrible, shocking, anger, terrible, like, fuming, fear, depressing, You, The, nightmare, outrage, bully, amazing, hilarious, terrorism, This, blues, bitter, happy, get, life, feel, hate, still, offended, unhappy, nervous, horror, My, sadly, never, fuck, furious, bad, revenge, smile, panic, raging

Task	Type	Examples
SST2	Original	a funny and touching film that is gorgeously acted
	Augmented	a funiny and touching film that is gorgeousy acted
	Original	too bad none of it is funny
	Augmented	too bab non4 of it is funny
MR	Original	perhaps the best sports movie i ' ve ever seen
	Augmented	perhaps the bset sports mlvie i ' ve eve4 seen
	Original	i loved the look of this film
	Augmented	i lved the look of this film

Fig. 3. Examples of the data augmentation of our proposed method, ATA, in SST2 [21] and MR [14] datasets.

5 Conclusion

In this study, we have introduced a new text augmentation strategy, ATA, that helps reinforce the model's robustness against text noise. The suggested approach utilizes attention weights to determine the importance of individual words in impacting the model's prediction. It then selectively chooses words to perturb and builds augmented data that the model incorporates in the training process to improve robustness against textual noise. Through experiments on four sentiment classification tasks, we have confirmed that by incorporating data augmented by ATA into the training process, the model effectively learns to handle textual noise. Our qualitative experiments have revealed that the word importance scores, calculated simply using attention weights, are reliable. Our research demonstrates that a simple and effective data augmentation approach can help train models to be robust against textual noise such as typos and misspellings without additional pre-training processes. For future work, we aim to cover various methods for calculating the significance of words in data.

References

1. Almagro, M., Almazán, E.J., Ortego, D., Jiménez, D.: LEA: improving sentence similarity robustness to typos using lexical attention bias. In: Proceedings of the 29th ACM SIGKDD Conference on Knowledge Discovery and Data Mining, KDD 2023, Long Beach, CA, USA, 6–10 August 2023, pp. 36–46. ACM (2023). https://doi.org/10.1145/3580305.3599402
2. Barbieri, F., Camacho-Collados, J., Anke, L.E., Neves, L.: TweetEval: unified benchmark and comparative evaluation for tweet classification. In: Findings of the Association for Computational Linguistics: EMNLP 2020, Online Event, 16–20 November 2020, Findings of ACL, vol. EMNLP 2020, pp. 1644–1650. Association for Computational Linguistics (2020). https://doi.org/10.18653/V1/2020.FINDINGS-EMNLP.148

3. Bojanowski, P., Grave, E., Joulin, A., Mikolov, T.: Enriching word vectors with subword information. Trans. Assoc. Comput. Linguistics **5**, 135–146 (2017). https://doi.org/10.1162/TACL_A_00051

4. Chen, L., Varoquaux, G., Suchanek, F.M.: Imputing out-of-vocabulary embeddings with LOVE makes language models robust with little cost. In: Proceedings of the 60th Annual Meeting of the Association for Computational Linguistics (Volume 1: Long Papers), ACL 2022, Dublin, Ireland, 22–27 May 2022, pp. 3488–3504. Association for Computational Linguistics (2022). https://doi.org/10.18653/V1/2022.ACL-LONG.245

5. Clark, K., Khandelwal, U., Levy, O., Manning, C.D.: What does BERT look at? An analysis of BERT's attention. In: Proceedings of the 2019 ACL Workshop BlackboxNLP: Analyzing and Interpreting Neural Networks for NLP, BlackboxNLP@ACL 2019, Florence, Italy, 1 August 2019, pp. 276–286. Association for Computational Linguistics (2019). https://doi.org/10.18653/V1/W19-4828

6. Devlin, J., Chang, M., Lee, K., Toutanova, K.: BERT: pre-training of deep bidirectional transformers for language understanding. In: Proceedings of the 2019 Conference of the North American Chapter of the Association for Computational Linguistics: Human Language Technologies, NAACL-HLT 2019, Minneapolis, MN, USA, 2–7 June 2019, Volume 1 (Long and Short Papers), pp. 4171–4186. Association for Computational Linguistics (2019). https://doi.org/10.18653/V1/N19-1423

7. Edizel, B., Piktus, A., Bojanowski, P., Ferreira, R., Grave, E., Silvestri, F.: Misspelling oblivious word embeddings. In: Proceedings of the 2019 Conference of the North American Chapter of the Association for Computational Linguistics: Human Language Technologies, NAACL-HLT 2019, Minneapolis, MN, USA, 2–7 June 2019, Volume 1 (Long and Short Papers), pp. 3226–3234. Association for Computational Linguistics (2019). https://doi.org/10.18653/V1/N19-1326

8. Jin, D., Jin, Z., Zhou, J.T., Szolovits, P.: Is BERT really robust? A strong baseline for natural language attack on text classification and entailment. In: Proceedings of the AAAI Conference on Artificial Intelligence, vol. 34, pp. 8018–8025 (2020). https://doi.org/10.1609/AAAI.V34I05.6311

9. Karpukhin, V., Levy, O., Eisenstein, J., Ghazvininejad, M.: Training on synthetic noise improves robustness to natural noise in machine translation. In: Proceedings of the 5th Workshop on Noisy User-generated Text, W-NUT@EMNLP 2019, Hong Kong, China, 4 November 2019, pp. 42–47. Association for Computational Linguistics (2019). https://doi.org/10.18653/V1/D19-5506

10. Liang, Z., Lu, Y., Chen, H., Rao, Y.: Graph-based relation mining for context-free out-of-vocabulary word embedding learning. In: Proceedings of the 61st Annual Meeting of the Association for Computational Linguistics (Volume 1: Long Papers), ACL 2023, Toronto, Canada, 9–14 July 2023, pp. 14133–14149. Association for Computational Linguistics (2023). https://doi.org/10.18653/V1/2023.ACL-LONG.790

11. Maas, A.L., Daly, R.E., Pham, P.T., Huang, D., Ng, A.Y., Potts, C.: Learning word vectors for sentiment analysis. In: The 49th Annual Meeting of the Association for Computational Linguistics: Human Language Technologies, Proceedings of the Conference, 19–24 June, 2011, Portland, Oregon, USA, pp. 142–150. The Association for Computer Linguistics (2011). https://aclanthology.org/P11-1015/

12. Mikolov, T., Chen, K., Corrado, G., Dean, J.: Efficient estimation of word representations in vector space. In: 1st International Conference on Learning Representations, ICLR 2013, Scottsdale, Arizona, USA, 2–4 May 2013, Workshop Track Proceedings (2013). http://arxiv.org/abs/1301.3781

13. Moradi, M., Samwald, M.: Evaluating the robustness of neural language models to input perturbations. In: Proceedings of the 2021 Conference on Empirical Methods in Natural Language Processing, EMNLP 2021, Virtual Event/Punta Cana, Dominican Republic, 7–11 November 2021, pp. 1558–1570. Association for Computational Linguistics (2021). https://doi.org/10.18653/V1/2021.EMNLP-MAIN.117

14. Pang, B., Lee, L.: Seeing stars: exploiting class relationships for sentiment categorization with respect to rating scales. In: ACL 2005, 43rd Annual Meeting of the Association for Computational Linguistics, Proceedings of the Conference, 25–30 June 2005, University of Michigan, USA, pp. 115–124. The Association for Computer Linguistics (2005). https://doi.org/10.3115/1219840.1219855, https://aclanthology.org/P05-1015/

15. Pennington, J., Socher, R., Manning, C.D.: Glove: global vectors for word representation. In: Proceedings of the 2014 Conference on Empirical Methods in Natural Language Processing, EMNLP 2014, 25–29 October 2014, Doha, Qatar, A meeting of SIGDAT, a Special Interest Group of the ACL, pp. 1532–1543. ACL (2014). https://doi.org/10.3115/V1/D14-1162

16. Pinter, Y., Guthrie, R., Eisenstein, J.: Mimicking word embeddings using subword RNNs. In: Proceedings of the 2017 Conference on Empirical Methods in Natural Language Processing, EMNLP 2017, Copenhagen, Denmark, 9–11 September 2017, pp. 102–112. Association for Computational Linguistics (2017). https://doi.org/10.18653/V1/D17-1010

17. Qiang, Y., Pan, D., Li, C., Li, X., Jang, R., Zhu, D.: AttCAT: explaining transformers via attentive class activation tokens. In: Advances in Neural Information Processing Systems 35: Annual Conference on Neural Information Processing Systems 2022, NeurIPS 2022, New Orleans, LA, USA, 28 November–9 December 2022 (2022). http://papers.nips.cc/paper_files/paper/2022/hash/20e45668fefa793bd9f2edf19be12c4b-Abstract-Conference.html

18. Radford, A., Wu, J., Child, R., Luan, D., Amodei, D., Sutskever, I.: Language models are unsupervised multitask learners (2019). https://api.semanticscholar.org/CorpusID:160025533

19. Sasaki, S., Suzuki, J., Inui, K.: Subword-based compact reconstruction of word embeddings. In: Proceedings of the 2019 Conference of the North American Chapter of the Association for Computational Linguistics: Human Language Technologies, NAACL-HLT 2019, Minneapolis, MN, USA, 2–7 June 2019, Volume 1 (Long and Short Papers), pp. 3498–3508. Association for Computational Linguistics (2019). https://doi.org/10.18653/V1/N19-1353

20. Sidiropoulos, G., Kanoulas, E.: Analysing the robustness of dual encoders for dense retrieval against misspellings. In: SIGIR 2022: The 45th International ACM SIGIR Conference on Research and Development in Information Retrieval, Madrid, Spain, 11–15 July 2022, pp. 2132–2136. ACM (2022). https://doi.org/10.1145/3477495.3531818

21. Socher, R., et al.: Recursive deep models for semantic compositionality over a sentiment treebank. In: Proceedings of the 2013 Conference on Empirical Methods in Natural Language Processing, EMNLP 2013, 18–21 October 2013, Grand Hyatt Seattle, Seattle, Washington, USA, A meeting of SIGDAT, a Special Interest Group of the ACL, pp. 1631–1642. ACL (2013). https://aclanthology.org/D13-1170/

22. Sun, L., et al.: Adv-BERT: BERT is not robust on misspellings! generating nature adversarial samples on BERT. CoRR abs/2003.04985 (2020). https://arxiv.org/abs/2003.04985

23. Vaswani, A., et al.: Attention is all you need. In: Advances in Neural Information Processing Systems 30: Annual Conference on Neural Information Processing Systems 2017, 4–9 December 2017, Long Beach, CA, USA, pp. 5998–6008 (2017). https://proceedings.neurips.cc/paper/2017/hash/3f5ee243547dee91fbd053c1c4a845aa-Abstract.html

24. Wieting, J., Bansal, M., Gimpel, K., Livescu, K.: Charagram: embedding words and sentences via character n-grams. In: Proceedings of the 2016 Conference on Empirical Methods in Natural Language Processing, EMNLP 2016, Austin, Texas, USA, 1–4 November 2016, pp. 1504–1515. The Association for Computational Linguistics (2016). https://doi.org/10.18653/V1/D16-1157

25. Wu, Y., et al.: Google's neural machine translation system: bridging the gap between human and machine translation. CoRR abs/1609.08144 (2016). http://arxiv.org/abs/1609.08144

26. Zhang, Y., Chen, Q., Yang, Z., Lin, H., Lu, Z.: Biowordvec, improving biomedical word embeddings with subword information and mesh. Sci. Data **6**(1), 52 (2019)

27. Zhuang, S., Zuccon, G.: Dealing with typos for BERT-based passage retrieval and ranking. In: Proceedings of the 2021 Conference on Empirical Methods in Natural Language Processing, EMNLP 2021, Virtual Event/Punta Cana, Dominican Republic, 7–11 November 2021, pp. 2836–2842. Association for Computational Linguistics (2021). https://doi.org/10.18653/V1/2021.EMNLP-MAIN.225

A Linguistic Comparison Between Human and ChatGPT-Generated Conversations

Morgan Sandler[1]($\boxtimes$), Hyesun Choung[1], Arun Ross[1], and Prabu David[2]

[1] Michigan State University, East Lansing, USA
{sandle20,choungh,rossarun}@msu.edu
[2] Rochester Institute of Technology, Rochester, USA
pxdpro@rit.edu

Abstract. This study explores linguistic differences between human and LLM-generated dialogues, using 19.5K dialogues generated by ChatGPT-3.5 as a companion to the EmpathicDialogues dataset. The research employs Linguistic Inquiry and Word Count (LIWC) analysis, comparing ChatGPT-generated conversations with human conversations across 118 linguistic categories. Results show greater variability and authenticity in human dialogues, but ChatGPT excels in categories such as social processes, analytical style, cognition, attentional focus, and positive emotional tone, reinforcing recent findings of LLMs being "more human than human." However, no significant difference was found in positive or negative affect between ChatGPT and human dialogues. Classifier analysis of dialogue embeddings indicates implicit coding of the valence of affect despite no explicit mention of affect in the conversations. The research also contributes a novel, companion ChatGPT-generated dataset of conversations between two independent chatbots, which were designed to replicate a corpus of human conversations available for open access and used widely in AI research on language modeling. Our findings enhance understanding of ChatGPT's linguistic capabilities and inform ongoing efforts to distinguish between human and LLM-generated text, which is critical in detecting AI-generated fakes, misinformation, and disinformation.

Keywords: Social Computing · Computational Linguistics · Large Language Models (LLMs) · Empathic Communication

1 Introduction

Words are the building blocks of human language, and the richness of human language enables expressions of intricate thoughts and feelings. From the early days of computing, endowing machines with such human language capability has captured the imagination of technologists [1].

Until recently, those efforts to build chatbots with language proficiency have come up short. But with the rapid advances in generative large language models (LLMs), AI applications such as OpenAI's ChatGPT, Meta's LLaMA, Google's Gemini, Anthropic's Claude, and others are demonstrating proficiencies, albeit

C. Wallraven et al. (Eds.): ICPRAI 2024, LNCS 14892, pp. 366–380, 2025.
https://doi.org/10.1007/978-981-97-8702-9_25

in specific settings and domains [2] signaling the dawn of new possibilities and challenges in natural language processing (NLP) and artificial intelligence.

The success of LLMs at mimicking human language capabilities has been achieved through machine learning algorithms that have ingested a vast amount of human language data. Given the human origin of the training data, similarities in language use can be expected between LLMs and humans, which heightens concerns related to deepfakes, disinformation, misinformation, plagiarism, and algorithmic bias [9]. Recent studies have examined various linguistic features [10, 21] and cognitive attributes [30] of LLM-generated content.

To further contribute to this research, we examine potential differences in linguistic features between human- and LLM-generated conversations using computational linguistic analysis [4], a popular technique used in psychology, communication, and related areas [17, 31].

The analysis is built on computerized analysis of words and groupings of words, which have been used successfully to characterize personality [6], deception [22], authenticity [12], social status [13], and self-presentation [16]. Researchers have found that analysis of words used in writing and conversation can reveal underlying thoughts and emotions of the communicator [4, 22].

In a typical conversation, we focus more on content words that convey meaning, emotions, and actions and less on grammatical or function words, such as pronouns, conjunctions, and articles. However, these function words also are associated with important communication and psychological dynamics [5]. Researchers believe that both content and function words play complementary roles, with content words conveying what we say and function words conveying how we say it [24].

A widely used tool for language analysis is the Linguistic Inquiry and Word Count (LIWC) [29]. This tool includes dictionaries that categorize words into various classes such as pronouns, prepositions, conjunctions, articles, and words conveying positive and negative emotions, or relating to friends and family. These words are further grouped into higher-level categories like personal pronouns, impersonal pronouns, affect, cognition, and social processes, among others. They are utilized in formulas to compute summary variables such as *clout, authenticity, analytical thinking,* and *emotional tone* [4]. The linguistic categories generated by LIWC provide a detailed profile of language use, offering insights into the thoughts and emotions of the speaker or writer. When combined with machine learning methods, LIWC has proven effective in identifying mental health disorders [3], assessing cognitive engagement [15], and predicting the emotional intelligence of individuals [8]. Given its ability to reliably detect thoughts and emotions of individuals, we chose to employ LIWC for the linguistic analysis in this study.

Using LIWC, we compared conversations between two individuals and corresponding conversations between two ChatGPT-3.5 chatbots. The corpus of human conversations was obtained from EmpathicDialogues, a dataset with 25K dialogues associated with 32 emotions, which is available to the public [25]. These dialogues were generated by conversations among 810 crowd-workers on Amazon Mechanical Turk (MTurk). Similar dialogues between two ChatGPT chatbots were simulated by passing scenarios and emotions from the EmpathicDialogues dataset through prompt engineering. Differences between human conversations and ChatGPT conversations were examined for 118 linguistic features generated by LIWC.

Among other linguistic categories, emotion is a compelling feature of language and communication. To understand the encoding of emotion in ChatGPT, in addition to the analysis of the linguistic features of affect, we examined the implicit coding of affect valence in LLM embeddings using an emotion classifier. The key contributions and findings of this study are summarized below:

1. A dataset consisting of 19.5K dialogues generated by two ChatGPT chatbots that serve as a companion to the EmpathicDialogues dataset. This dataset, named 2GPTEmpathicDialogues, is a resource for communities interested in NLP and language modeling.
2. Comparisons of human conversations with ChatGPT conversations on 118 linguistic categories offered by LIWC.
3. Findings suggest more variability and authenticity in human dialogues compared to ChatGPT dialogues.
4. On the other key linguistic categories, such as *social processes and behaviors, analytical style, cognition, attentional focus*, and *positive emotional tone*, ChatGPT scored higher than humans, reinforcing recent findings [11], that LLMs are "more human than human" in their language use.
5. Linguistic features associated with positive and negative affect were not different between ChatGPT and human conversations.
6. Embeddings of ChatGPT and human conversations analyzed using a classifier revealed implicit coding of positive and negative affect valence in the embeddings even though there was no explicit mention of affect in the dialogues.

In summary, we contribute a novel, ChatGPT-generated dataset and findings that can be used to advance research in NLP and language modeling. Further, our study offers a rigorous comparison of linguistic differences between human dialogues and dialogues simulated between two independent ChatGPT-3.5 chatbots. Findings from this study contribute to the ongoing efforts to detect differences between human and LLM-generated dialogues.

2   Generating Conversational Data

2.1   Human Conversations: EmpathicDialogues

Samples of human conversations used in this study were obtained from an open-domain dataset offered by Rashkin et al. [25], which was developed to serve as a resource for conversational models. The dataset consists of 25K distinct, dyadic dialogues based on situations associated with 32 emotions and generated by 810 individuals on Amazon Mechanical Turk (MTurk).

From the total corpus of 25K conversations, the training dataset of 19,533 dialogues was chosen for this study because of its accessibility and its roughly even distribution across emotion categories [25]. An even distribution of emotion categories enables comparisons across a diverse range of emotional contexts. Each dialogue in the dataset was generated by two conversational partners. The initiating speaker in the dialogue chose from one of 32 emotions (e.g., afraid) and wrote a scenario (e.g., hearing noises around the house at night) associated with the emotion before sharing it with the other speaker in the conversation. The speaker receiving the scenario was instructed to respond to the scenario but was unaware of the emotion chosen by the initiating speaker. The speakers were asked not to exceed six conversational turns after the initial exchange. On average, each conversation lasted approximately four conversational turns ($M = 4.31$).

2.2 ChatGPT Conversations: 2GPTEmpathicDialogues

To compare ChatGPT conversations with human conversations, we developed a dyadic conversational system that replicated the human conversations represented in the EmpathicDialogues dataset. The system consisted of two independent instances of ChatGPT that communicated through a Coordinator Program (see Fig. 1). The coordinator program, developed in Python, establishes dyadic communication between two ChatGPT-3.5-Turbo instances using OpenAI's public-use API. It manages two separate API sessions, processing and relaying messages between the instances, and handles API calls efficiently. The program incorporates error handling and asynchronous programming to ensure smooth and consistent communication. This setup enables seamless exchange of information and overcomes challenges arising from network issues. The initiating ChatGPT was prompted to begin the conversation with a scenario associated with an emotion. To liken the design to the human conversations, the instance of ChatGPT receiving the scenario was not made aware of the emotion associated with the scenario.

A sample human conversation and an equivalent ChatGPT conversation are shown side by side in Table 1. Using seed prompts (see Fig. 1), the two instances of ChatGPT communicated by passing messages via a Coordinator Program. Each dialogue lasted approximately three to four turns, and the dialogue was captured in a CSV file for further analysis. We observed instances of role confusion during some conversation turns, where the receiving speaker responded as though they were the initiating speaker, and vice versa. To address this issue, we modified the prompts to include the instruction, "Do not generate responses for the listener/speaker". However, this adjustment was not entirely effective due to the stochastic nature of LLMs, a point that is further discussed in the limitations section. Further, the temperature parameter was set at 0.5 and a maximum token limit was set at 250 to limit verbosity. Despite this setting, the word count for ChatGPT dialogues ($M = 300$, $SD = 25.6$) was significantly ($p < .001$) longer in comparison to the human dialogues ($M = 58$, $SD = 120.5$), which is addressed in the section on limitations. ChatGPT dialogues were generated using ChatGPT-3.5-Turbo API and it took about 48 h to generate the 19.5K conversations.

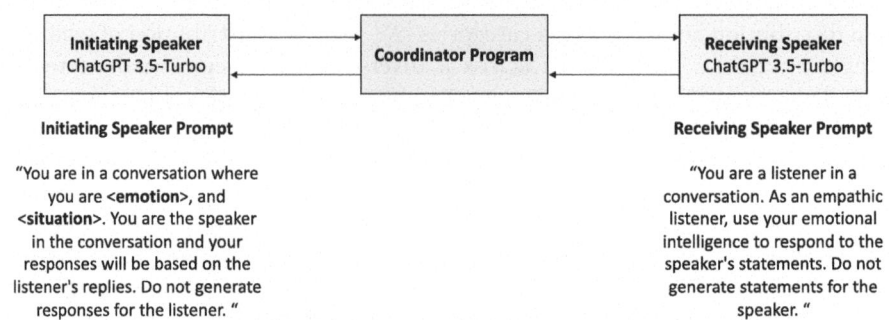

Fig. 1. Framework for generating the 2GPTEmpathicDialogues dataset, along with the prompts used. In this setup, two instances of the ChatGPT-3.5-Turbo API engage in conversation via a coordinating program. We observed instances of role confusion during some conversation turns, where the receiving speaker responded as though they were the initiating speaker, and vice versa. To address this issue, we modified the prompts to include the instruction, "Do not generate responses for the listener/speaker". However, this adjustment was not entirely effective due to the stochastic nature of LLMs, a point that is further discussed in the limitations section.

3   Analysis and Results

Analysis was conducted in three steps: (1) analyzing and coding the linguistic features in the conversations, (2) statistical comparisons of the linguistic features extracted by LIWC, (3) additional valence classification analysis using the LLM embeddings that represent human- and ChatGPT-generated dialogues.

LIWC Analysis. Dialogues from humans and ChatGPT were analyzed with LIWC-22 [4], which codes and summarizes the linguistic features of dialogues into 118 categories. Each category is a dictionary of curated words chosen through research for their correlation to psychological constructs. The category counts were converted into a percentage based on the total number of words analyzed. The linguistic dimension scores for each ChatGPT conversation were matched with the scores for the equivalent human conversation, and the differences between the two conditions were examined. Summary statistics and statistical significance tests for all 118 linguistic categories are presented in the Appendix available on our Github link provided in Sect. 4. From the 118 categories, in this paper, we focus only on a few higher-level categories associated with social process, cognition, and emotion.

Comparison Between Human and ChatGPT Dialogues. Differences in mean and variance for each linguistic feature were examined using an independent sample t-test and Levene's test for equality of variance. To adjust for the number of significance tests, which can lead to higher likelihood of type I error and false positives, a Bonferroni correction was applied and statistical significance was set at $p < .001$.

Table 1. Excerpt of human-generated vs. ChatGPT-generated empathic dialogues.

Initiating Scenario	Emotion	Empathic Dialogue	ChatGPT Empathic Dialogue
I was furious when I found out a classmate was being cruel to my daughter	Furious	Speaker1: I was extremely upset when I found out a classmate was being cruel to my daughter Speaker2: Oh that is terrible! Kids can be so mean! What did you do? Speaker1: I spoke with the school counselor and told her about my daughter's concerns that it might get worse Speaker2: I hope that it only gets better	ChatGPT1: I cannot believe what I just found out! I am absolutely furious right now! ChatGPT2: What happened? Why are you so angry? ChatGPT1: I just found out that my best friend has been spreading rumors about me behind my back. It's so hurtful and infuriating to think that someone I trusted would do that to me. I feel so betrayed ChatGPT2: I can understand why you're feeling furious and hurt right now. Discovering that someone you considered a close friend has been spreading rumors about you is a significant breach of trust. It's natural to feel betrayed in this situation. Is there anything I can do to support you?

Out of the 118 categories, 110 were significant at $p < .001$. The absence of statistical significance was observed for a few linguistic features, such as *space* within the perception category and *health* within the physical category. Null effects were also observed for positive and negative emotions which are examined in detail later in the paper. From among the categories that were significantly different, we examined only those associated with social processes, cognition, and emotion.

Along with mean differences, we also examined differences in variance for each of the 118 categories using Levene's test. As expected, the variance between human- and ChatGPT-generated conversations was different at $p < .001$ for all 118 linguistic categories. The lower variance in ChatGPT conversations can be attributed to the temperature setting of 0.5 used in this study and to the characteristics of the LLM that is trained to yield predictions that appeal to a broad range of users.

Social Behaviors. Given the efforts to make chatbots social and the critical role of language in conveying social information, we used the LIWC's social behavior category to examine ChatGPT's linguistic features signifying social behaviors, which is a composite measure of prosocial behaviors (e.g., *caring, helping*), politeness (e.g., *please, thank you*), interpersonal conflict (e.g., *fight, argue*), moralization (e.g., *good, bad*) and communication (e.g., *talk, explain*).

While humans have real experience in such social behavior categories, Chat-GPT's statistical models are tuned to predict these social behaviors based only on context.

Linguistic features that characterize social behaviors were more prevalent in ChatGPT conversations than human conversations (see Table 2 for summary statistics). ChatGPT conversations scored higher on all subcategories, including social behavior, prosocial behavior, politeness, and communication. ChatGPT also scored less on interpersonal conflict. Effect size (.26 to .69) was small to medium for all differences. In brief, ChatGPT conversations were slightly more socially sensitive than human conversations.

Attentional Focus. According to best practices in communication, a good conversational partner is an active listener interested in what others have to say. This attentional focus directed toward others is captured by the clout index in LIWC, which is derived from an analysis of personal pronouns. Over a series of studies, it has been observed that people who focus on others use the first-person singular pronoun (I) sparingly in comparison to the first-person plural pronoun (we) and the second-person pronoun (you) [13].

Our findings show that ChatGPT ($M = 64.79$, $SD = 23.91$) conversations were better ($\delta = 1.25$, large effect) in attentional focus than human conversations ($M = 34.89$, $SD = 31.35$) with more frequent use of you and we pronouns and less frequent use of the I pronoun. ChatGPT demonstrated empathy and interest in others through the strategic use of pronouns, which is a useful insight considering its wide deployment as a help agent in various contexts.

Authenticity. Authenticity is a direct and simple mode of communication that leads to positive outcomes like likability, trust, and support. An authentic communication style connects with the general public and is well-suited for contemporary media, such as TV and social. Researchers have observed that over the years political communication has become more authentic and less nuanced [12]. Psychologists [27] and communication researchers [18] have used the authenticity index in LIWC, and details about the components of the formula can be found in a paper by Markowitz et al. [18]. Although the origin of this category can be traced to research on deception [22], it is distinct from deception. For example, one can lie and still be authentic, which is not uncommon among politicians [12]. Our analysis revealed that authenticity is the only category in which humans ($M = 63.99$, $SD = 33.53$) outperformed ChatGPT ($M = 52.49$, $SD = 27.66$, $\delta = .42$). The effect was small to medium, highlighting a weakness in ChatGPT's ability.

Analytical Thinking. While authenticity captures the linguistic features of simple and direct communication, analytical thinking in LIWC captures the use of "formal, logical, and hierarchical thinking" [23]. Analytical thinking is associated with reasoning and is detected by aggregating small function words that receive little attention. While the use of articles and prepositions are indicative of higher analytical thinking, pronouns, conjunctions, negation, and adverbs are associated with lower analytical thinking that is more "narrative and personal"

[23]. On the linguistic dimension of analytical thinking, scores for ChatGPT (M = 20.19, SD = 16.30) dialogues were higher than human dialogues (M = 17.04, SD = 18.64), δ = .19 (small effect).

Cognition. Cognition is closely related to analytical thinking and is a key psychological construct that includes sub-categories such as dichotomous thinking, cognitive processes, and memory words (e.g., *remember, forget*). Other components of cognition include insight, and cause and effect. For cognition, ChatGPT-generated dialogues (M = 17.68, SD = 4.39) scored higher than human dialogues (M = 13.01, SD = 5.77), δ = 1.06 (large effect).

Emotion. Human language is equipped to capture and convey the range of emotions that make up the human experience. LIWC has a number of metrics to examine the emotions expressed via language, including positive and negative affect. In this study, we focus on two higher-level LIWC dimensions, namely emotional tone and affect. Emotional Tone is operationalized as a psycholinguistic variable that includes affect (e.g., *joy, sorrow*) as well as words associated with affect (e.g., *birth, death*). Affect, on the other hand, is limited only to emotions. The emotional dimensions from LIWC have been used to examine sentiments in personal diaries following 9–11 [7], and on social media during Covid [20].

The emotional tone of ChatGPT dialogues was more positive (M = 65.66, SD = 37.75) than human dialogues (M = 54.37, SD = 40.10), δ = .30 (small effect). The positive emotions scores for ChatGPT (M = 2.40, SD = 2.00) and humans (M = 2.36, SD = 2.59) were not significantly different. Similarly, for negative emotions, the difference between ChatGPT (M = 1.45, SD = 1.60) and humans (M = 1.49, SD = 2.05) was not significantly different.

Table 2. Comparison of linguistic features between human and ChatGPT conversations.

Category	Human Conversation		ChatGPT Conversation		Statistics
	Mean	SD	Mean	SD	
Social Behaviors (e.g., said, love, care)	2.76	2.83	4.42	2.39	t = 62.6, p < .001, δ = .69
Prosocial Behaviors (e.g., care, help)	0.72	1.38	1.75	1.45	t = 71.9, p < .001, δ = .71
Politeness (e.g., thank, please)	0.22	0.78	0.49	0.05	t = 38.3, p < .001, δ = .46
Interpersonal conflict (e.g., fight, attack)	0.20	0.75	0.11	0.35	t = 15.5, p < .001, δ = .26
Communication (e.g., sad, tell, thank)	0.87	1.65	1.28	1.09	t = 29.2, p < .001, δ = .38
Attentional Focus	34.89	31.15	64.79	23.91	t = 105.4, p < .001, δ = 1.25
Authenticity	63.99	33.54	52.49	27.66	t = 37.0, p < .001, δ = .42
Analytical thinking	17.04	18.64	20.19	16.30	t = 17.8, p < .001, δ = .19
Cognition	13.01	5.77	17.68	4.39	t = 89.9, p < .001, δ = 1.06
Emotional Tone	54.37	40.10	65.66	37.75	t = 28.65, p < .001, δ = .30
Emotion Positive	2.36	2.59	2.40	2.00	t = 1.73, ns, δ = .02
Emotion Negative	1.49	2.05	1.45	1.60	t = 2.00, ns, δ = .02

Note: *df* for the unequal variance t-tests varied from row to row and ranged between 27–39K. δ = Glass' Delta, used to compute power (0.2 or lower = small effect, 0.5 = medium effect, 0.8 or higher = large).

Valence Classification of ChatGPT Embeddings. Next, we analyzed Chat-GPT embeddings to determine if emotion cues are latently present in them. To explore ChatGPT embeddings, we conducted two types of analysis: (a) a binary-class valence classification experiment involving the training and testing of three different classifiers, and a (b) Uniform Manifold Approximation and Projection (UMAP) [19] scheme for the visualization of each dataset in three dimensions. The valence classification experiment assesses a classifier's ability to distinguish between positive and negative valence emotion cues present within the ChatGPT embeddings. The UMAP experiment explores the spatial distribution of embeddings with respect to their valence categories, providing insight into how the different underlying emotion categories are clustered in high-dimensional space. To organize the dialogues for the binary valence classification problem, we grouped the underlying emotions into positive or negative valence (see Table 3).

Then, we extracted embeddings for each conversation in the Human and ChatGPT datasets and examined them using three classifiers: Random Forest classifier, Support Vector Machine (SVM), and Multi-Layer Perceptron (MLP). We used OpenAI's publicly available text-embedding-ada-002 model for extracting all dialogues embeddings from both human and ChatGPT-generated datasets. Then we employed a stratified 5-fold cross-validation to ensure a balanced representation of valence categories across the folds, and a grid search to determine the hyperparameters for each classifier model. Given that each dataset comprises 19,533 samples we allocated 15,626 samples for training and 3,907 for testing in each fold of our stratified cross-validation process, and ensured an approximately equal representation of each underlying emotion category between train and test sets. For the Random Forest classifier, we evaluated using 50, 100, and 200 trees per forest. In the case of SVM, we examined values of 'C' at 0.1, 1, and 10, and γ at 0.001, 0.01, and 0.1. For the MLP model, we tested a single-layer (100 nodes), triple-layer (300, 200, 100 nodes), and dual-layer (150, 150 nodes) configurations, with maximum iterations set at either 300 or 500. Table 4 shows the average weighted F1-score across all folds for each classifier. We observed that the SVM exhibited the best performance for both datasets, achieving an average weighted F1-score of 90.0% on the human-generated dataset and 95.3% on the ChatGPT-generated dataset. Interestingly, the higher F1-score from the ChatGPT-generated dataset classifier suggests that the language patterns used by ChatGPT may be more consistent or distinct in expressing different valences compared to human-generated text. This could be due to the structured nature of LLM-generated language, which might adhere more closely to identifiable patterns of sentiment expression.

Table 3. Binary valence classification of emotions: 16 positive and 16 negative valence emotions.

Positive Valence	Negative Valence
anticipating, caring, confident, content, excited, faithful, grateful, hopeful, impressed, joyful, nostalgic, prepared, proud, sentimental, surprised, trusting	afraid, angry, annoyed, anxious, apprehensive, ashamed, devastated, disappointed, disgusted, embarrassed, furious, guilty, jealous, lonely, sad, terrified

Using the best-performing SVM model for each dataset, we analyzed the top-10 misclassified dialogues. Our findings, as presented in Table 5, reveal that certain emotions are consistently misclassified across both the human-generated and ChatGPT-generated datasets. Notably, emotions such as *anxious, surprised, trusting, jealous, apprehensive, sentimental, caring, hopeful, faithful,* and *sad* featured among the top-10 misclassified sentiments in each dataset. This pattern underscores specific challenges in the binary valence classification of certain emotion categories.

The consistent misclassification of certain emotions in our experiments suggests inherent complexities in valence classification. We hypothesize that this challenge is partly due to the ambiguity and overlap in emotional expressions. For instance, emotions like *sentimental, surprise,* or *hopeful* often exhibit characteristics of both positive and negative sentiments, making them difficult to categorize in a binary system. Additionally, the context-dependent nature of emotions can lead to potential valence misclassifications. Moreover, the complexity of human emotions such as *jealousy* or *caring,* underscores the limitations of a binary valence framework in capturing the full range of human emotions. These factors highlight the need for more nuanced classification approaches. Our classification only uses emotional valence. Future research may use additional dimensions, such as arousal [32], to analyze embeddings.

Table 4. Average weighted F1-scores for valence classification across 5-folds.

Classifier	Human-Generated Dialogues		ChatGPT-Generated Dialogues	
	Avg. Weighted F1	SD	Avg. Weighted F1	SD
Random Forest	0.8778	0.0034	0.9324	0.0032
SVM	0.9000	0.0023	0.9527	0.0036
MLP	0.8953	0.0045	0.9579	0.0037

In addition to classification experiments, we utilized UMAP to visualize the embeddings from both human-generated and ChatGPT-generated dialogues datasets. UMAP, a dimensionality reduction technique effective at preserving global and local spatial information [19], was used to project these high-dimensional embeddings into a three-dimensional space. This approach facilitates visual exploration of the distribution of embeddings with respect to the valence categories. The resulting UMAP visualizations are shown in Fig. 2a for the human-generated dataset and Fig. 2b for the ChatGPT-generated dataset. In these figures, data points (representing each dialogue) are color-coded based on the corresponding valence—positive or negative—as designated by the aforementioned mapping function from the 32 original emotion categories. These visualizations offer an empirical view of the valence clustering within the embeddings, thereby providing a supplementary perspective to our analysis in understanding the valence classification capabilities of the embeddings.

The UMAP projections of both the human-generated and ChatGPT-generated dialogues reveal notable differences in cluster separation. Specifically, the

ChatGPT model demonstrates a more distinct separation of clusters, as indicated by a higher Dunn Index value of 0.222, compared to 0.153 for the human-generated dialogues. This metric, which quantifies cluster separation based on the minimization of intra-cluster distances and maximization of inter-cluster distances, suggests that the ChatGPT-generated dialogues exhibit a clearer delineation between valence categories.

In the UMAP projection of the human-generated dialogues, we observed an outlier blue cluster. This cluster represents a specific subset of emotions or dialogue characteristics that are distinctly separate from the main clusters. Within this outlier cluster, emotions such as *prepared, caring, trusting, proud,* and *impressed* coexist alongside negative valence emotions like *afraid, terrified, lonely, and devastated.* This phenomenon may occur in human dialogues and not in ChatGPT dialogues because human emotional expression often encompasses a complex and nuanced blend of sentiments, reflecting the intricate nature of human psychology and social interactions. In contrast, ChatGPT, while advanced, might not capture the same depth and subtlety in emotional expression due to its algorithmic foundations and training data constraints. Consequently, human dialogues exhibit a richer, more varied emotional landscape where seemingly contradictory emotions can coexist within the same context, leading to such unique clustering. This complexity is less pronounced in ChatGPT-generated dialogues, which tend to follow more predictable and uniform patterns of emotional expression. The presence of this unique grouping within the human-generated dialogues, and its relative absence in the ChatGPT-generated dialogues, further underscores the differences in how valence categories are represented and separated in embeddings from the two datasets. The interactive UMAP visualization code is available via the GitHub link provided in Sect. 4 for further detailed analysis.

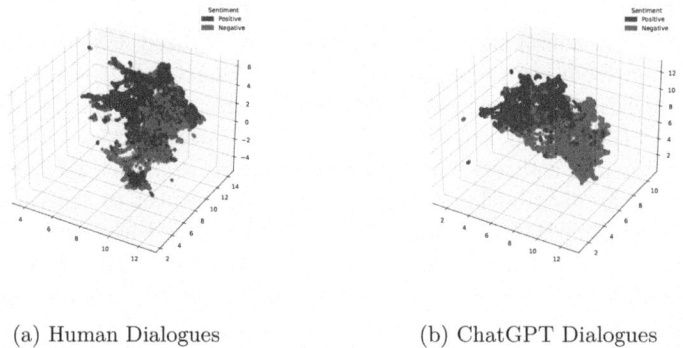

(a) Human Dialogues   (b) ChatGPT Dialogues

Fig. 2. 3-D UMAP visualizations of human- and ChatGPT-generated dialogues. The dialogues are color-coded by positive or negative valence values, determined by each dialogue's underlying emotion category.

Table 5. Comparison of the top-10 misclassification frequencies in the valence analysis: human-generated dialogues (2,180 out of 19,533) vs. ChatGPT-generated dialogues (1,132 out of 19,533). There are certain emotions, such as 'anxious', that more frequently result in valence (positive or negative) misclassifications in both datasets.

Human-Generated Dialogues				ChatGPT-Generated Dialogues			
Emotion	Misclassified	Emotion	Misclassified	Emotion	Misclassified	Emotion	Misclassified
anxious	224	sentimental	119	trusting	137	anticipating	72
surprised	211	caring	119	caring	133	apprehensive	65
trusting	170	hopeful	101	surprised	132	anxious	61
jealous	168	faithful	90	sentimental	78	hopeful	52
apprehensive	127	sad	71	jealous	74	faithful	52

4   Summary and Discussion

This study explores linguistic differences between human and LLM-generated dialogues, specifically focusing on ChatGPT-3.5 in comparison to the Empathic-Dialogues dataset. Using LIWC analysis across 118 linguistic categories, we analyzed 19.5K dialogues. Our findings show that while human dialogues exhibit greater variability and authenticity, ChatGPT demonstrates superior proficiency in areas like *social processes, analytical style, cognition, attentional focus*, and *positive emotional tone*, echoing the narrative that LLMs can be "more human than human" in many aspects of language use [11]. A key contribution of this research is the development of the 2GPTEmpathicDialogues dataset, a novel collection of ChatGPT-generated dialogues, which serves as a valuable resource for exploring AI language modeling. Additionally, the study reveals implicit coding of affect in dialogue embeddings, despite no direct mentions of affect, highlighting the emotional intelligence of AI. This research not only contributes to our understanding of the linguistic capabilities of ChatGPT but also plays a crucial role in informing the ongoing efforts to distinguish between human and AI-generated text [28].

As AI becomes proficient in human language and enters the realm of social interactions, we face a future where distinguishing between conversations with humans and AI may become increasingly challenging. Our findings demonstrate that ChatGPT's linguistic proficiency, in many aspects, surpasses human capabilities. Language proficiency is one of the markers of human excellence, and language is a distinguishing feature of our humanity and identity as social beings. Our analysis shows that on cognitive features like *analytical thinking, cognition*, and *attentional focus*, ChatGPT scores higher than humans. Given that computers are not vulnerable to human variability, such as individual differences and fatigue, this consistency offers significant advantages in contexts demanding constant cognitive engagement and analytical precision.

However, this consistency could also be perceived as a weakness in situations where human-like variability and adaptability are valued. The essence of human communication often lies in the subtleties—the unstructured, the unpredictable, and the emotional nuances—that are not purely cognitive prowess but involve a complex interplay of factors, including empathy, cultural context, and personal experiences. While ChatGPT demonstrates impressive capabilities in mimicking these aspects to a certain extent, the question remains whether it can fully replicate the depth and richness of human interactions [26].

In the social realm, where generative AI is increasingly deployed, from customer service to medical service, the implications of our findings are significant. ChatGPT's advanced linguistic abilities could enhance user experiences by providing more coherent, contextually relevant, and emotionally attuned interactions. Nevertheless, it also raises ethical considerations about AI's role in human interactions, particularly concerning authenticity and the potential replacement of human roles in certain areas.

Limitations. The findings from this study must be viewed along with some limitations. Firstly, our analysis is specific to ChatGPT-3.5-Turbo, and may not apply to newer models like GPT-4, Claude, and Gemini, which could show different linguistic features. Future studies should expand the comparison across different LLMs and enhance the companion dataset.

Secondly, the use of ChatGPT's default word limits resulted in conversations averaging 300 words—far exceeding the 60-word average in human dialogues. Although future studies could adjust this setting to minimize such discrepancies, our use of LIWC metrics, which normalize word counts into percentages, ensures the validity of our findings. Additionally, efforts to reduce role confusion through prompt engineering were not entirely successful. While this does not significantly impact the conversation-level LIWC analysis, it does highlight the need for further methodological refinements in future studies.

In our valence analysis of the embeddings, we employed a method that relied on a dichotomous classification of the 32 emotions into positive or negative valence. This approach may be overly simplistic, as indicated by the results of the UMAP visualizations and classification experiment metrics. Emotions are inherently complex, and according to the co-activation theory of emotions [14], it is possible to experience both positive and negative emotions simultaneously. Consequently, further research is necessary to develop a more nuanced classification system that includes additional emotional dimensions, such as the arousal dimension.

Overall, our findings contribute to the emerging literature on LLMs through a rigorous comparison of linguistic features of human conversations and ChatGPT conversations. As AI evolves, the line between human-generated and AI-generated content will continue to blur. The findings from our study show that this has already occurred to a large extent. How we respond to this dissolving identity is a larger philosophical question that extends beyond language and will likely shape our future.

Data and Software Availability. Software and data resources utilized in the studies presented in this paper can be accessed via the following link: https://github.com/morganlee123/2GPTEmpathicDialogues. LIWC is a proprietary software and must be obtained separately.

References

1. Adamopoulou, E., Moussiades, L.: An overview of chatbot technology. In: IFIP International Conference on Artificial Intelligence Applications and Innovations, pp. 373–383. Springer (2020)
2. Ayers, J.W., et al.: Comparing physician and artificial intelligence chatbot responses to patient questions posted to a public social media forum. JAMA Intern. Med. (2023)
3. Bartal, A., Jagodnik, K.M., Chan, S.J., Babu, M.S., Dekel, S.: Identifying women with postdelivery posttraumatic stress disorder using natural language processing of personal childbirth narratives. Am. J. Obstetr. Gynecol. MFM **5**, 3 (2023)
4. Boyd, R.L., Ashokkumar, A., Seraj, S., Pennebaker, J.W.: The development and psychometric properties of LIWC-22. University of Texas at Austin (2022)
5. Chung, C., Pennebaker, J.: The psychological functions of function words. In: Social Communication, pp. 343–359. Psychology Press (2011)
6. Chung, C.K., Pennebaker, J.W.: Revealing dimensions of thinking in open-ended self-descriptions: An automated meaning extraction method for natural language. J. Res. Pers. **42**(1), 96–132 (2008)
7. Cohn, M.A., Mehl, M.R., Pennebaker, J.W.: Linguistic markers of psychological change surrounding September 11, 2001. Psychol. Sci. **15**(10), 687–693 (2004)
8. Dover, Y., Amichai-Hamburger, Y.: Characteristics of online user-generated text predict the emotional intelligence of individuals. Sci. Rep. **13**, 1 (2023)
9. Ghosal, S.S., Chakraborty, S., Geiping, J., Huang, F., Manocha, D., Bedi, A.S.: Towards possibilities & impossibilities of AI-generated text detection: a survey. arXiv preprint arXiv:2310.15264 (2023)
10. Hasan, M.R., Hossain, M.Z., Gedeon, T., Rahman, S.: LLM-GEm: large language model-guided prediction of people's empathy levels towards newspaper article. In: Graham, Y., Purver, M. (eds.) Findings of the Association for Computational Linguistics: EACL 2024, St. Julian's, Malta, pp. 2215–2231. Association for Computational Linguistics (2024)
11. Jakesch, M., Hancock, J.T., Naaman, M.: Human heuristics for AI-generated language are flawed. Proc. Natl. Acad. Sci. **120**(11), e2208839120 (2023)
12. Jordan, K.N., Sterling, J., Pennebaker, J.W., Boyd, R.L.: Examining long-term trends in politics and culture through language of political leaders and cultural institutions. Proc. Natl. Acad. Sci. **116**(9), 3476–3481 (2019)
13. Kacewicz, E., Pennebaker, J.W., Davis, M., Jeon, M., Graesser, A.C.: Pronoun use reflects standings in social hierarchies. J. Lang. Soc. Psychol. **33**(2), 125–143 (2014)
14. Larsen, J.T., McGraw, A.P., Cacioppo, J.T.: Can people feel happy and sad at the same time? J. Pers. Soc. Psychol. **81**(4), 684 (2001)
15. Liu, Z., et al.: Dual-feature-embeddings-based semi-supervised learning for cognitive engagement classification in online course discussions. Knowl.-Based Syst. **259** (2023)
16. Markowitz, D.M.: Self-presentation in medicine: how language patterns reflect physician impression management goals and affect perceptions. Comput. Hum. Behav. **143**, 107684 (2023)
17. Markowitz, D.M., Hancock, J.T., Bailenson, J.N.: Linguistic markers of inherently false AI communication and intentionally false human communication: evidence from hotel reviews. J. Lang. Soc. Psychol. **43**(1), 63–82 (2024)

18. Markowitz, D.M., Kouchaki, M., Gino, F., Hancock, J.T., Boyd, R.L.: Authentic first impressions relate to interpersonal, social, and entrepreneurial success. Soc. Psychol. Pers. Sci. **14**(2), 107–116 (2023)
19. McInnes, L., Healy, J., Saul, N., Großberger, L.: UMAP: uniform manifold approximation and projection. J. Open Sour. Softw. **3**(29), 861 (2018)
20. Monzani, D., Vergani, L., Pizzoli, S.F.M., Marton, G., Pravettoni, G.: Emotional tone, analytical thinking, and somatosensory processes of a sample of Italian tweets during the first phases of the COVID-19 pandemic: observational study. J. Med. Internet Res. **23**(10), e29820 (2021)
21. Muñoz-Ortiz, A., Gómez-Rodríguez, C., Vilares, D.: Contrasting linguistic patterns in human and LLM-generated news text (2024)
22. Newman, M.L., Pennebaker, J.W., Berry, D.S., Richards, J.M.: Lying words: predicting deception from linguistic styles. Pers. Soc. Psychol. Bull. **29**(5), 665–675 (2003)
23. Pennebaker, J.W.: Mind mapping: using everyday language to explore social & psychological processes. Procedia Comput. Sci. **118**, 100–107 (2017)
24. Pennebaker, J.W., Boyd, R.L., Jordan, K., Blackburn, K.: The development and psychometric properties of LIWC2015. Technical report (2015)
25. Rashkin, H., Smith, E.M., Li, M., Boureau, Y.-L.: Towards empathetic open-domain conversation models: A new benchmark and dataset. In: Proceedings of the 57th Annual Meeting of the Association for Computational Linguistics, Florence, Italy, pp. 5370–5381. Association for Computational Linguistics (2019)
26. Reif, E., Kahng, M., Petridis, S.: Visualizing linguistic diversity of text datasets synthesized by large language models. In: IEEE Visualization and Visual Analytics (VIS), pp. 236–240 (2023)
27. Slabu, L., Lenton, A.P., Sedikides, C., Bruder, M.: Trait and state authenticity across cultures. J. Cross Cult. Psychol. **45**(9), 1347–1373 (2014)
28. Tang, R., Chuang, Y.-N., Hu, X.: The science of detecting LLM-generated text. Commun. ACM **67**(4), 50–59 (2024)
29. Tausczik, Y.R., Pennebaker, J.W.: The psychological meaning of words: LIWC and computerized text analysis methods. J. Lang. Soc. Psychol. **29**(1), 24–54 (2010)
30. Wang, B., Yue, X., Sun, H.: Can ChatGPT defend its belief in truth? evaluating LLM reasoning via debate. In: Bouamor, H., Pino, J., Bali, K. (eds.) Findings of the Association for Computational Linguistics: EMNLP 2023, Singapore, pp. 11865–11881. Association for Computational Linguistics (2023)
31. Yaden, D.B., et al.: Characterizing empathy and compassion using computational linguistic analysis. Emotion (2023)
32. Zhang, Y., Chen, W., Zhang, R., Zhang, X.: Representing affect information in word embeddings. Exp. Linguist. Mean. **2**, 310–321 (2023)

A Comparative Study: Enhancing Conditional Generative Adversarial Networks for Functional Connectivity Synthesis in Major Depressive Disorder

Ji-Hye Oh[ID], Eunjung Jo[ID], and Tae-Eui Kam[✉][ID]

Department of Artificial Intelligence, Korea University, Seoul, Republic of Korea
{meeeo_,jeju1993do,kamte}@korea.ac.kr

Abstract. Major Depressive Disorder (MDD) is a prevalent mental health condition, affecting a significant number of individuals globally and representing a critical health challenge. The use of functional connectivity (FC), obtained from resting-state functional Magnetic Resonance Imaging (rs-fMRI), is vital in identifying patterns linked to MDD, thereby aiding in its precise diagnosis. Nevertheless, the scarcity of FC poses a significant hurdle in the effective diagnosis of MDD. To overcome this issue, various studies have utilized Conditional Generative Adversarial Networks (cGAN) to create synthetic FC. This synthetic FC is then used as additional training data for MDD diagnosis. However, most previous research has primarily focused on using cGAN validated in fields such as natural image processing, which may not be sufficient for generating realistic synthetic FC given the limited quantity and complex patterns of FC. Therefore, we introduce the utilization of three existing techniques, i.e., class-wise scaling loss, pre-trained autoencoder, and label embedding projection, aimed at enhancing cGAN performance, enabling cGAN to generate synthetic FC with more accurate and improved representations. We assessed the methods on the rs-fMRI dataset available to the public and the results indicate that employing these methods with the cGAN provides significant assistance in synthetic FC generation.

Keywords: Conditional generative adversarial networks · major depressive disorder · resting-state functional Magnetic Resonance Imaging (rs-fMRI) · synthetic functional connectivity

1 Introduction

Major Depressive Disorder (MDD) is a prevalent psychiatric disorder, characterized by persistent and severe symptoms. These symptoms include a constant low mood, cognitive impairment, sleep disturbances, and a loss of pleasure or interest [1]. MDD has a significant impact on the global economy and society, and this burden has been further exacerbated by the recent COVID-19 pandemic, leading

© The Author(s), under exclusive license to Springer Nature Singapore Pte Ltd. 2025
C. Wallraven et al. (Eds.): ICPRAI 2024, LNCS 14892, pp. 381–393, 2025.
https://doi.org/10.1007/978-981-97-8702-9_26

to a marked increase in the prevalence of MDD [2]. Considering the persistent severity of MDD symptoms and the possibility of recurrence, there is a growing importance in promptly diagnosing and implementing effective treatment strategies [3].

In recent decades, resting-state functional Magnetic Resonance Imaging (rs-fMRI) has emerged as a crucial tool for diagnosing and understanding MDD [4]. This non-invasive neuroimaging technique allows for the examination of functional connectivity within different brain networks [5]. Through the analysis of subtle fluctuations in blood oxygen level-dependent (BOLD) signals, rs-fMRI uncovers changes in brain activity among individuals with MDD, shedding light on the neural mechanisms underlying the disorder [6]. Recent studies, especially in the context of understanding the intricate functional interplays among brain regions in MDD, are increasingly concentrating on functional connectivity (FC) [7]. FC is determined by assessing the correlation between averaged BOLD signals from pairs of regions of interest (ROIs) within the brain. By analyzing FC, researchers gain the ability to identify specific brain activity patterns linked to MDD [8]. This deepens our understanding of the disorder and plays a crucial role in enhancing early diagnostic and treatment methodologies.

With the rapid advancement of deep learning (DL), numerous researchers have employed DL-based techniques for FC analysis in the diagnosis of MDD [9, 10]. DL-based methods have demonstrated potential in the field, yet for reliable MDD diagnosis, the need for substantial data becomes evident. This is due to the intrinsic requirement of DL techniques for large datasets to achieve higher accuracy and more generalizable results. However, in the field of neuroimaging, collecting such extensive datasets faces challenges due to privacy concerns, high costs, and the time needed for data acquisition. Consequently, recent studies have explored using Generative Adversarial Networks (GAN) [11,12] to generate realistic synthetic FC, addressing the issue of limited data availability.

Previous studies have shown that utilizing synthetic FC generated from GAN can lead to improved diagnostic performance [12,13]. However, most studies predominantly focused on the utilization of Conditional GAN (cGAN) that has already been validated in areas such as natural image processing for generating synthetic FC. However, in the case of FC, the available data is scarce, and as demonstrated in Fig. 1, the patterns are diverse and complex. Therefore, relying solely on cGAN models may not be sufficient for creating realistic and high-quality synthetic FC [14]. Furthermore, most cGAN struggle to accurately learn the true data distribution due to their unstable training processes. This instability can be exacerbated when dealing with complex and limited data [15]. Consequently, designing cGAN architectures with a strong emphasis on achieving stability throughout the training process is crucial. Additionally, in previous studies, when conditioning the generator of cGAN, label information was often simply combined with Gaussian noise. However, recent research indicates that applying effective projection techniques to label embeddings can significantly improve cGAN performance [16,17]. As shown in Fig. 1, while there is a diversity of patterns within classes, the mean differences between MDD and normal control (NC) are not substantial. Thus, it is essential to adopt a conditioning approach that effectively incorporates label information.

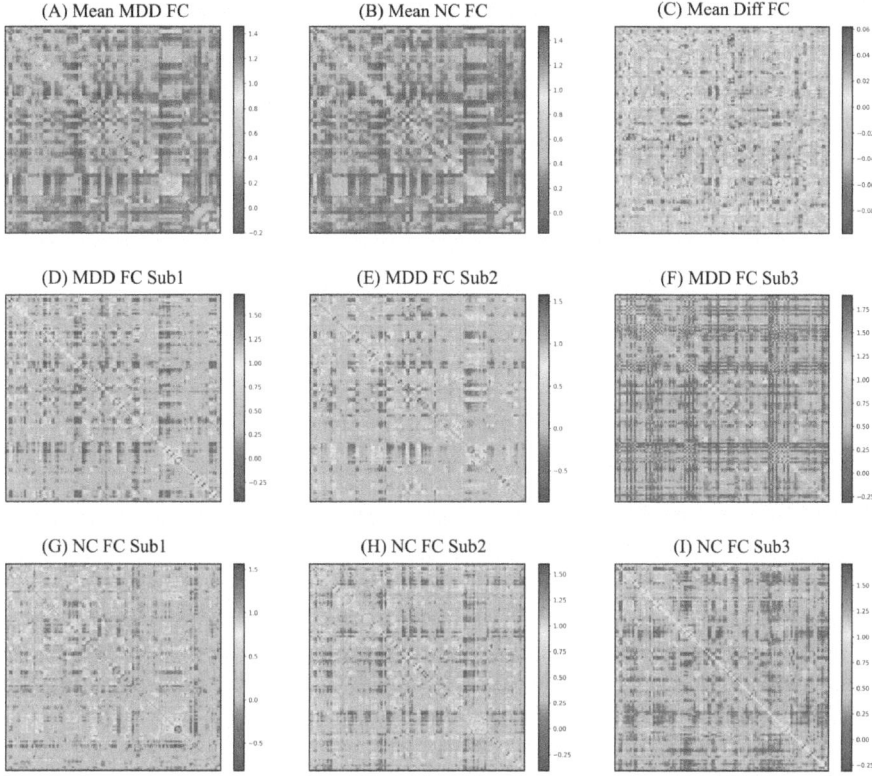

Fig. 1. The figure illustrates the mean FC for each class, the difference between the mean FCs of the classes, and the FCs belonging to the MDD and NC.

To improve the training stability and data representation of cGAN previously used for generating synthetic FC, and to ensure accurate reflection of given conditions, we utilize three effective methods previously suggested for cGAN, i.e., class-wise scaling loss [18], pre-trained autoencoder [15], and label embedding projection [16,17], in a unified framework. First, to generate synthetic FC that more closely resembles real FC, we introduce a class-wise scaling loss into the original generator loss function. This loss is a version modified to be class-specific, based on the loss previously proposed by Zhang et al. [18]. The loss guides the generator towards more stable and accurate synthetic FC generation. Second, to enhance stability and representation in cGAN, we employ the decoder of an autoencoder as a pre-trained model for the generator. This method prevents the discriminator from converging too quickly, avoiding training collapse, and enables the generator to use the enhanced representational learning from the autoencoder to produce high-fidelity synthetic FC [15]. Last, for the generation of precise and diverse synthetic FC within given classes, we implement label embedding projection in the generator [16,17]. We modified the existing method of label embedding projection and applied it to the generator. This method can be applied across various cGAN.

We demonstrate the effectiveness of utilizing the three methods on a publicly accessible rs-fMRI dataset for MDD diagnosis through detailed ablation studies involving various types of cGAN. In our experiments, the adoption of these methods led to a substantial improvement in the performance of cGAN models.

2   Methods for Enhanced Synthetic FC Generation

Figure 2 illustrates how the three methods are applied to the Auxiliary Classifier GAN (ACGAN) to assist the generator in achieving more stable training processes and more effective synthetic FC generation. These methods can be utilized independently of the discriminator, allowing for their application even with varying discriminator architectures in different cGAN models.

2.1   Class-Wise Scaling Loss

As shown in Fig. 1, FC has a very small range of values and the differences between classes are also minimal. These characteristics are critical when generating synthetic FC using cGAN, as it's essential to accurately capture these subtle distinctions. However, due to the limited amount of FC available, traditional cGAN might struggle to learn these subtle variations. Therefore, as shown in Fig. 2(A), we employ a class-wise scaling loss, which supports the generator in creating synthetic FC that closely resembles the real FC for each class. This loss is a class-specific adaptation of the loss originally proposed by Zhang et al. [18]. Such a method enables a more precise reflection of the subtle variations in FC, thereby enhancing the performance of cGAN.

The class-wise scaling loss is calculated based on the mean difference between the real FC and fake FC within each class. This loss can be used as an additional regulation for the generator in cGAN. The class-wise scaling loss is controlled by the hyperparameter α, which is initially set at 2 to encourage faster scaling of FC in the early training phases. As training progresses and the model learns effectively, the value of α is gradually decreased. This reduction prevents the loss from obstructing the learning of diverse patterns, allowing the model to initially adapt and learn essential features quickly and later focus on acquiring more complex and varied patterns. Mathematically, the class-wise scaling loss can be expressed as follows:

$$\mathcal{L}_{cs} = \alpha\left(\frac{1}{M}\sum_{i=1}^{M}(X_{\text{real\_i}} - X_{\text{fake\_i}})^2 + \frac{1}{N}\sum_{j=1}^{N}(X_{\text{real\_j}} - X_{\text{fake\_j}})^2\right) \qquad (1)$$

where M and N indicate the total number of MDD and NC subjects [18].

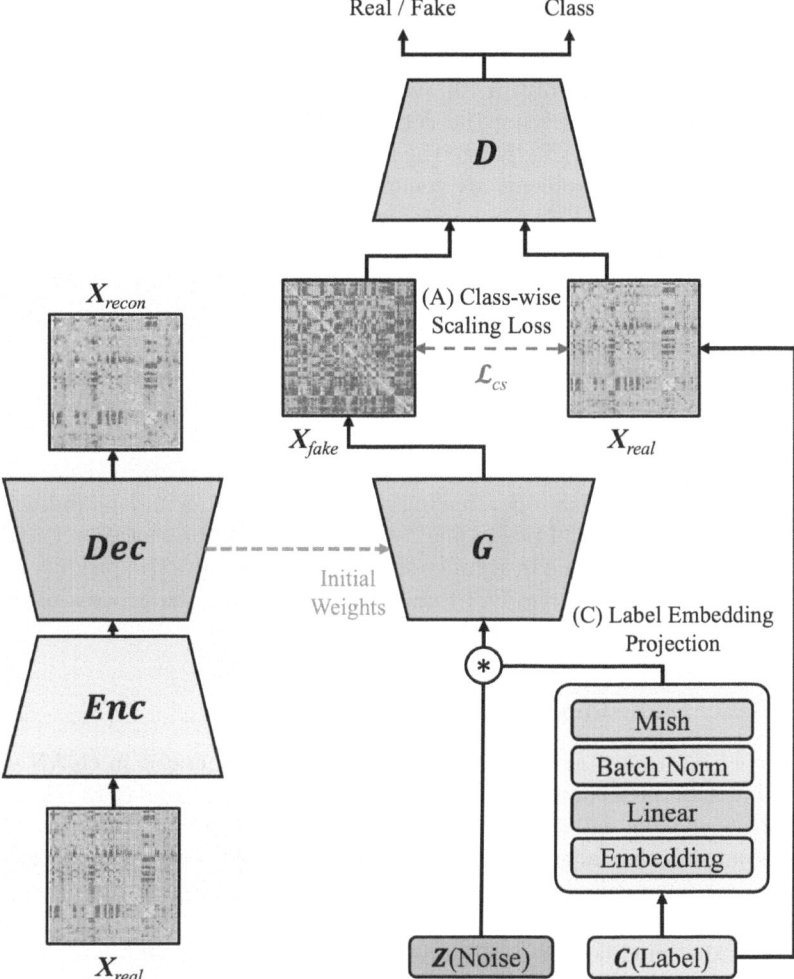

Fig. 2. The overall architecture where all three methods are applied to existing ACGAN. The architecture of the discriminator can vary depending on the specific GAN model being utilized.

The total generator loss for a cGAN can be expressed as follows, where the $\mathcal{L}_G$ is a generator loss corresponds to that used in a cGAN:

$$\mathcal{L}_{G_{total}} = \mathcal{L}_G + \mathcal{L}_{cs} \tag{2}$$

2.2   Pre-trained Autoencoder

cGAN training can be prone to collapse primarily due to two issues. The first is the vanishing gradient problem [19], which arises when the discriminator learns too quickly, thereby depriving the generator of valuable learning signals. The second is mode collapse [20], where the generator repeatedly produces similar or identical data. These problems are generally caused by the difference in learning speeds between the cGAN's generator and discriminator, leading to a highly unstable training process for cGAN.

To mitigate these issues, Ham et al. [15] suggest using the decoder of a pre-trained variational autoencoder as the initial weight for the generator in GAN. Drawing inspiration from this study, we opt to utilize the decoder of a pre-trained autoencoder instead of a variational autoencoder as the initial weight for cGAN's generator. This autoencoder has a symmetrical structure with its decoder, which mirrors the structure of the cGAN's generator architecture. The autoencoder was pre-trained with the training data that will be used in the cGAN. The pre-trained decoder, having already acquired an understanding of the real data distribution and possessing a degree of data representation capability, can mitigate early training instability and guide the generator in producing more precise and varied synthetic FC. Figure 2(B) illustrates the process of using a pre-trained decoder to set initial weights for the generator.

2.3   Label Embedding Projection

Effectively incorporating conditional labels into the generator in cGAN significantly impacts the training process and the quality of generated data [21]. Proper utilization of label embeddings is essential for cGAN to produce diverse and precise outputs that align with specific conditions or classes. Therefore, previous research has focused on improving label projection methods to enhance the performance of cGAN [16]. In our work, we propose a label embedding projection block that modifies the label projection methods from previous research [16]. This block consists of PyTorch's embedding function, linear layer, batch normalization, and the Mish [22] activation function. By incorporating batch normalization and an activation function into the traditional label projection method, nonlinearity is introduced, which helps in achieving clearer distinctions between classes while also enabling the generation of more diverse outputs. After the label information passes through this block, the resultant projected label embedding is used as the conditional input to the generator. Through the structure of the label embedding projection block, the generator can learn to effectively generate data that matches the given condition. Figure 2(C) illustrates the architecture of ACGAN utilizing the label embedding projection block. The label information processed through this block is multiplied with Gaussian noise and then fed into the generator as its input. This approach enables the generation of data that not only conforms to the given condition but also exhibits diversity and precision.

3   Experimental Results

3.1   Data Acquisition and Pre-processing

In this study, we utilized the REST-meta-MDD dataset[1] [23], which is publicly available and considered the most extensive rs-fMRI dataset for MDD diagnosis. This dataset is provided by the Depression Imaging REsearch ConsorTium (DIRECT) [24]. From this dataset, we specifically focused on data from Site 20, the largest site, comprising 249 subjects with MDD and 228 NC subjects, all of whom were part of studies approved by local Institutional Review Boards (IRB) [23,24]. The rs-fMRI data were collected using a Simens Tim Trio 3T scanner with specific parameters, including a TR/TE of 2,000/30 ms, 32 slices, 242 time points, a voxel size of $3.44 \times 3.44 \times 4.00$ mm^3, and a field of view (FOV) of 220×220 a flip angle of $90°$, a slice thickness of 3.0 mm, an interslice gap of 1.0 mm [23].

To pre-process the rs-fMRI data, the Data Processing Assistant for Resting-State fMRI (DPARSF) [25] is utilized. This involved discarding the first 10 time points and then performing various processing steps such as slice-timing correction, head motion correction, band-pass filtering, and removal of confounding factors [26]. After these steps, co-registration was performed between T1-weighted and mean functional images, and then the data was transformed from the individual's native space to the Montreal Neurological Institute (MNI) template space [26]. The processed data was segmented into 112 ROIs as defined by the Harvard Oxford atlas [27]. From these ROIs, the rs-fMRI BOLD signal time series were extracted and averaged. To construct a 112×112 FC matrix for each subject, we calculated Pearson's correlation coefficients between the ROIs, applying Fisher's z transformation for the correlation [28].

3.2   Experimental Setting

To evaluate the effectiveness of the three methods introduced earlier, we sequentially applied each method to three different cGAN models and conducted a comparative analysis of their performance. Specifically, we focused on ACGAN [12], as utilized in prior research, Twin Auxiliary Classifiers GAN(TACGAN) [29], and Conditional GANs with Auxiliary Discriminative Classifier (ADCGAN) [30] which improves the generative capabilities of ACGAN. ACGAN improves its discriminator by incorporating an auxiliary classifier. This classifier aids in differentiating real from generated samples and categorizes them using extra label information. TACGAN is a model proposed to mitigate the low intra-class problem in ACGAN. It utilizes two auxiliary classifiers in the discriminator to generate higher-quality data. ADCGAN is the most recent model designed to effectively address the low intra-class problem that can arise in ACGAN and TACGAN. The discriminator in this model simultaneously takes the input of label information for the desired data generation and information about whether it is real or fake, enhancing the discriminator's discrimination and generation capabilities.

---

[1] https://rfmri.org/REST-meta-MDD.

In this study, the classifier utilized a structure consisting of five fully connected layers, with batch normalization integrated at each stage and the Mish activation function used at all but the final layer. The generator employed a similar structure to the classifier, featuring five fully connected layers, batch normalization, and the Mish activation function. One distinction, however, is that the Tanh function was used after the last layer to limit the output range to between -1 and 1. For ACGAN and TACGAN, the discriminator was designed with five fully connected layers, and for the last two layers, batch normalization was included. For ADCGAN, the discriminator was designed with five fully connected layers, following a similar activation pattern.

Table 1. Learning rates for the generator (G) and discriminator (D) in each cGAN model.

cGAN Type	G learning rate	D learning rate
ACGAN	$1 \cdot e^{-04}$	$9 \cdot e^{-05}$
TACGAN	$1 \cdot e^{-04}$	$2 \cdot e^{-04}$
ADCGAN	$3 \cdot e^{-05}$	$1 \cdot e^{-05}$

The training regime for these cGAN models was standardized, with identical hyperparameters for both discriminator and generator, except for the learning rate. The learning rate for each cGAN model is shown in Table 1. A consistent weight decay of $5 \cdot e^{-03}$ and the Adam optimization algorithm [31] with specific parameters (0.5, 0.9) were used. An exponential scheduler with a decay factor of 0.998, a training duration of 200 epochs, and a batch size of 100 was applied. The classifier settings included a learning rate of $1 \cdot e^{-05}$ and a weight decay of $1 \cdot e^{-04}$, along with the Adam optimization algorithm and an exponential scheduler. The classifier training extended over 1,000 epochs with a batch size of 200.

We conducted our experiments using a 5-fold cross-validation approach, using 80% of the data for the training dataset and 20% for the test dataset. To ensure an unbiased and robust evaluation, we repeated the experiments five times using various random seeds and analyzed the results. The key metrics evaluated were classification accuracy (ACC), sensitivity (SEN), specificity (SPEC), and the F1 score (F1). Notably, in all experiments, the amount of synthetic FC matched that of the real training FC, achieving a 100% augmentation ratio by using it as additional training data. To objectively evaluate the performance improvements attributable to data augmentation, we kept all classifier hyperparameters consistent across experiments.

3.3   Results

We conducted a stepwise comparative study to observe the impact of the three methods, namely class-wise scaling loss, pre-trained autoencoder, and label

Table 2. The MDD classification results are obtained by applying three methods sequentially to various cGAN models, and using the synthetic FC generated by these models as additional training data for the classifier. Within each cGAN model, the best performance for each metric is highlighted in bold.

cGAN Type	CS Loss	Pre-trained AE	LEP	ACC (%)	SEN (%)	SPEC (%)	F1 (%)
–	–	–	–	63.61 ± 4.28	62.04 ± 9.95	65.35 ± 7.57	63.69 ± 6.00
ACGAN	–	–	–	64.35 ± 3.47	66.29 ± 8.40	62.25 ± 8.60	65.79 ± 4.50
	O	–	–	64.41 ± 3.29	65.74 ± 8.38	62.97 ± 7.56	65.63 ± 4.63
	O	O	–	64.70 ± 3.09	67.02 ± 7.91	62.17 ± 7.52	66.28 ± 4.02
	O	O	O	**65.58 ± 4.01**	**67.74 ± 7.60**	**63.20 ± 8.19**	**67.12 ± 4.49**
TACGAN	–	–	–	63.86 ± 4.30	66.06 ± 8.85	61.47 ± 7.85	65.38 ± 5.38
	O	–	–	64.00 ± 3.36	65.25 ± 8.31	62.63 ± 7.43	65.20 ± 4.54
	O	O	–	64.44 ± 3.54	**66.29 ± 7.34**	62.46 ± 5.92	65.90 ± 4.32
	O	O	O	**65.16 ± 2.94**	65.66 ± 8.39	**64.63 ± 7.78**	**66.07 ± 4.18**
ADCGAN	–	–	–	64.03 ± 4.50	64.86 ± 8.47	63.12 ± 6.43	65.11 ± 5.28
	O	–	–	64.19 ± 3.38	65.42 ± 7.11	62.87 ± 6.53	65.45 ± 4.05
	O	O	–	65.33 ± 3.64	**67.98 ± 7.06**	62.42 ± 7.47	**67.06 ± 4.07**
	O	O	O	**65.41 ± 3.85**	67.02 ± 7.30	**63.64 ± 7.22**	66.78 ± 4.32

embedding projection, on performance improvement. Table 2 presents the results of a comparative study on classifier performance without using synthetic FC generated from cGAN as additional training data, and when such methods are applied across various cGANs to use the synthetic data as additional training data for the classifier. In the Table 2, "CS Loss", "Pre-trained AE", and "LEP" stand for the class-wise scaling loss, pre-trained autoencoder, and label embedding projection, respectively.

When using "CS Loss", ACC improved in all cGAN while the results on other evaluation metrics are controversial. Specifically, the employment of "CS Loss" to ACGAN and TACGAN results in an improvement in SPEC compared to cGAN without "CS Loss", but there is a similar trend of SEN decreasing. This leads to an overall interpretation that "CS Loss" does not significantly impact on performance.

Further analysis with the addition of "Pre-trained AE" shows a significant improvement in ACC, SEN, and F1 across all cGAN models. Notably, in the case of ADCGAN, the application of "Pre-trained AE" results in an increase of 1.14% in ACC, 2.56% in SEN, and 1.61% in F1. The results imply that the use of "Pre-trained AE" enables the generator to produce data with improved accuracy and better quality.

Upon examining the final results with the implementation of the previous two methods and "LEP", it is observed that ACGAN showed performance improvement across all metrics, while TACGAN also exhibited improvements in all metrics except for SEN. For ADCGAN, there was a slight increase in ACC and a significant rise in SPEC. Although the use of "LEP" did not enhance performance in every metric for all cGANs, it was noted that ACC increased and SPEC significantly improved across all cGANs. These results suggest that "LEP" is effective in aiding the generation of NC, thereby contributing to better overall performance.

A comprehensive analysis of the Table 2 results clearly show that, compared to using a cGAN alone, the application of all three methods significantly improves performance in all evaluation metrics across all models. This demonstrates that the three methods introduced for enhancing cGAN's performance are effective in generating higher-quality FC, highlighting their practical utility.

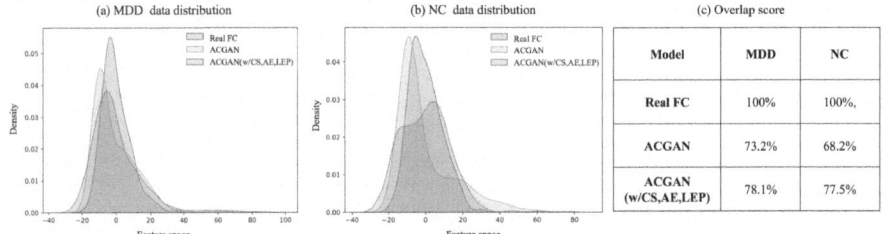

Fig. 3. The class-wise (MDD/NC) data distributions of the real FC (blue) and synthetic FC generated by the ACGAN with the application of class-wise scaling loss, pre-trained autoencoder, and label embedding projection (green) and original ACGAN (orange), with the overlap score (%) between the distributions of synthetic and real FC, respectively. (Color figure online)

4   Discussion

To verify the effectiveness of the application of three methods, i.e., class-wise scaling loss, pre-trained autoencoder, and label embedding projection, in generating synthetic FC that is both similar to real FC and diverse across classes, we analyzed the data distribution using Kernel Density Estimation (KDE) [32]. KDE, a non-parametric method of estimating density using kernel functions, is extensively utilized in GAN research to evaluate model distributions. As depicted in Fig. 3, we visualized the distribution of synthetic and real FC and measured the percentage of overlap between the two distributions. This measurement indicates how well each model generates realistic synthetic FC, with the overlap score reflecting the similarity of the generated data. According to our findings, the application of three methods to ACGAN achieved the highest overlap scores of 78.1% for MDD and 77.5% for NC. These results suggest that using the three methods results in the generation of more realistic synthetic FC compared to when they are not used.

5   Conclusion

In this study, we evaluate the effects of three methods, i.e., the class-wise scaling loss, pre-trained autoencoder, and label embedding projection, in improving the capability of cGAN to generate synthetic FC for MDD diagnosis. Our experiments, applying these three methods across various cGAN models, demonstrated that these approaches significantly contribute to enhancing the performance of existing cGANs in FC generation for MDD diagnosis.

In future studies, there are some exciting research directions for further enhancing the quality of synthetic FC by leveraging advanced techniques. One potential avenue is the adoption of a filtering process, which can be achieved through the integration of reinforcement learning mechanisms. This approach can refine the quality of generated synthetic FC by iteratively selecting the most accurate and representative FC patterns through a trial and error process.

Acknowledgements. This work was supported by Institute of Information & communications Technology Planning & Evaluation (IITP) grant (No. 2019-0-00079, Artificial Intelligence Graduate School Program(Korea University), No. 2022- 0-00871, Development of AI Autonomy and Knowledge Enhancement for AI Agent Collaboration), and the National Research Foundation of Korea (NRF) grant funded by the Korea government (MSIT) (No. RS202300212498)

References

1. Otte, C., et al.: Major depressive disorder. Nat. Rev. Dis. Primers **2** (2016)
2. Yoch, M., Sirull, R.: New global burden of disease analyses show depression and anxiety among the top causes of health loss worldwide, and a significant increase due to the COVID-19 pandemic. Inst. Health Metrics Eval. (2021)
3. Trivedi, M.H., Daly, E.J.: Treatment strategies to improve and sustain remission in major depressive disorder. Dialogues Clin. Neurosci. **10**(4), 377–384 (2008)
4. Brakowski, J., et al.: Resting state brain network function in major depression - depression symptomatology, antidepressant treatment effects, future research. J. Psychiatr. Res. **92**, 147–159 (2017)
5. Smith, S.M., et al.: Functional connectomics from resting-state fMRI. Trends Cogn. Sci. **17**(12), 666–682 (2013)
6. Van Den Heuvel, M.P., Hulshoff Pol, H.E.: Exploring the brain network: a review on resting-state fMRI functional connectivity. Eur. Neuropsychopharmacol. **20**(8), 519–534 (2010)
7. Albert, K.M., Potter, G.G., Boyd, B.D., Kang, H., Taylor, W.D.: Brain network functional connectivity and cognitive performance in major depressive disorder. J. Psychiatr. Res. **110**, 51–56 (2019)
8. Ye, M., Yang, T., Peng Qing, X., Lei, J.Q., Liu, G.: Changes of functional brain networks in major depressive disorder: a graph theoretical analysis of resting-state fMRI. PLoS One **10**(9), e0133775 (2015)
9. Liu, Z., et al.: Classification of major depressive disorder using machine learning on brain structure and functional connectivity. J. Affect. Disord. Rep. **10**, 100428 (2022)

10. Lee, D.-J., et al.: Spectral graph neural network-based multi-atlas brain network fusion for major depressive disorder diagnosis. IEEE J. Biomed. Health Inform. (2024)

11. Odena, A.: Semi-supervised learning with generative adversarial networks. arXiv preprint arXiv:1606.01583 (2016)

12. Odena, A., Olah, C., Shlens, J.: Conditional image synthesis with auxiliary classifier GANs. In: International Conference on Machine Learning, pp. 2642–2651. PMLR (2017)

13. Oh, J.-H., et al.: Graph-based conditional generative adversarial networks for major depressive disorder diagnosis with synthetic functional brain network generation. IEEE J. Biomed. Health Inform. (2023)

14. Karras, T., Aittala, M., Hellsten, J., Laine, S., Lehtinen, J., Aila, T.: Training generative adversarial networks with limited data. Adv. Neural. Inf. Process. Syst. **33**, 12104–12114 (2020)

15. Ham, H., Jun, T.J., Kim, D.: Unbalanced GANs: pre-training the generator of generative adversarial network using variational autoencoder. arXiv preprint arXiv:2002.02112 (2020)

16. Miyato, T., Koyama, M.: cGANs with projection discriminator. In: International Conference on Learning Representations (2018)

17. Han, L., et al.: Dual projection generative adversarial networks for conditional image generation. In: Proceedings of the IEEE/CVF International Conference on Computer Vision, pp. 14438–14447 (2021)

18. Zhang, L., Wang, L., Zhu, D., Alzheimer's Disease Neuroimaging Initiative, et al.: Predicting brain structural network using functional connectivity. Med. Image Anal. **79**, 102463 (2022)

19. Tan, H.H., Lim, K.H.: Vanishing gradient mitigation with deep learning neural network optimization. In: 2019 7th International Conference on Smart Computing & Communications (ICSCC), pp. 1–4. IEEE (2019)

20. Bau, D., et al.: Seeing what a GAN cannot generate. In: Proceedings of the IEEE/CVF International Conference on Computer Vision, pp. 4502–4511 (2019)

21. Gao, L., Chen, D., Zhao, Z., Shao, J., Shen, H.T.: Lightweight dynamic conditional GAN with pyramid attention for text-to-image synthesis. Pattern Recogn. **110**, 107384 (2021)

22. Misra, D.: Mish: a self regularized non-monotonic activation function. arXiv preprint arXiv:1908.08681 (2019)

23. Yan, C.G., et al.: Reduced default mode network functional connectivity in patients with recurrent major depressive disorder. Proc. Natl. Acad. Sci. U.S.A. **116**(18), 9078–9083 (2019)

24. Chen, X., Lu, B., Li, H.-X., Li, X.-Y., Wang, Y.W.: The DIRECT consortium and the REST-meta-MDD project: towards neuroimaging biomarkers of major depressive disorder. Psychoradiology **2**(1), 32–42 (2022)

25. Yan, C.-G., Zang, Y.-F.: DPARSF: a MATLAB toolbox for "pipeline" data analysis of resting-state fMRI. Front. Syst. Neurosci. **4**, 13 (2010)

26. Fang, Y., Wang, M., Potter, G.G., Liu, M.: Unsupervised cross-domain functional MRI adaptation for automated major depressive disorder identification. Med. Image Anal. **84**, 102707 (2023)

27. Kennedy, D.N., Lange, N., Makris, N., Bates, J., Meyer, J., Caviness Jr., V.S.: Gyri of the human neocortex: an MRI-based analysis of volume and variance. Cereb Cortex **8**(4), 372–84 (1998)

28. Bhuvaneshwari, B., Kavitha, A.: Assessment of brain connectivity patterns in progression of Alzheimer's disease. Age (Years) **72**, 1–2 (2016)

29. Gong, M., Xu, Y., Li, C., Zhang, K., Batmanghelich, K.: Twin auxilary classifiers GAN. In: Advances in Neural Information Processing Systems, vol. 32 (2019)
30. Hou, L., Cao, Q., Shen, H., Pan, S., Li, X., Cheng, X.: Conditional GANs with auxiliary discriminative classifier. In: International Conference on Machine Learning, pp. 8888–8902. PMLR (2022)
31. Kingma, D.P., Ba, J.L.: Adam: a method for stochastic optimization (2015)
32. Casanova, A., Careil, M., Verbeek, J., Drozdzal, M., Soriano, A.R.: Instance-conditioned GAN. In: Advances in Neural Information Processing Systems, vol. 34, pp. 27517–27529 (2021)

Iris-SAM: Iris Segmentation Using a Foundation Model

Parisa Farmanifard[(✉)] and Arun Ross[(✉)]

Michigan State University, East Lansing, MI 48824, USA
{farmanif,rossarun}@msu.edu

Abstract. Iris segmentation is a critical component of an iris biometric system and it involves extracting the annular iris region from an ocular image. In this work, we develop a pixel-level iris segmentation model from a foundation model, viz., Segment Anything Model (SAM), that has been successfully used for segmenting arbitrary objects. The primary contribution of this work lies in the integration of different loss functions during the fine-tuning of SAM on ocular images. In particular, the importance of Focal Loss is borne out in the fine-tuning process since it strategically addresses the class imbalance problem (i.e., iris versus non-iris pixels). Experiments on ND-IRIS-0405, CASIA-Iris-Interval-v3, and IIT-Delhi-Iris datasets convey the efficacy of the trained model for the task of iris segmentation. For instance, on the ND-IRIS-0405 dataset, an average segmentation accuracy of 99.58% was achieved, compared to the best baseline performance of 89.75%.

Keywords: Iris Segmentation · Biometrics · Segment Anything Model

1 Introduction

The human iris is a highly intricate structure whose distinctive patterns form the basis of one of the most secure forms of biometric recognition [7,13]. The structure of the iris includes the pupillary zone immediately surrounding the pupil, the ciliary zone comprising the rest of the iris, and the collarette forming a boundary between the two zones. The iris also features contraction furrows, which are circular folds created by the contraction of the pupillary muscles, and crypts, which are small openings or depressions in the iris tissue (Fig. 1) [14].

The process of accurately delineating the iris from the surrounding structures (sclera, pupil, eyelids, eyelashes) is termed iris segmentation [22]. A well-segmented iris results in more reliable feature extraction, which, in turn, enhances the accuracy of recognition systems. Several iris segmentation methods have been developed, ranging from the simple Integro-Differential Operator [8] to those based on complex convolutional neural networks [15]. However, iris segmentation has its own challenges. Variability in illumination, occlusions from eyelashes or eyelids, reflections, and low resolution in distant captures are among

C. Wallraven et al. (Eds.): ICPRAI 2024, LNCS 14892, pp. 394–409, 2025.
https://doi.org/10.1007/978-981-97-8702-9_27

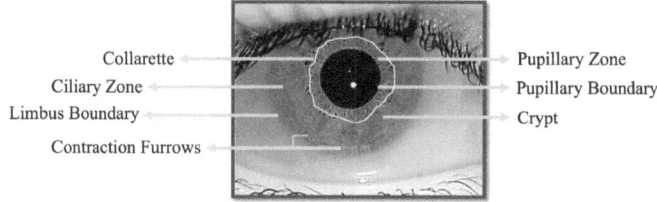

Fig. 1. Iris anatomy in the near-infrared spectrum.

the issues complicating the process [4] and can substantially affect the segmentation quality. Additionally, intrinsic challenges such as the dynamic nature of the iris, aging effects, and diseases can further complicate the segmentation task.

Traditional segmentation methods have evolved significantly with the integration of deep learning techniques. Fully Convolutional Network (FCN) [20] and U-Net [25] have laid the groundwork for advanced segmentation tasks. These models have been instrumental in achieving state-of-the-art performance in various segmentation challenges, demonstrating the power of deep learning in extracting meaningful patterns from complex visual data.

Further, the recent surge in the capabilities of foundation neural network models offers a promising path for advanced segmentation. The advent of foundation models has revolutionized various domains of research and application. These models, characterized by their vast size, extensive training data, and remarkable generalization abilities, have set new benchmarks in tasks ranging from natural language processing to image recognition [5,11].

Among the recent advancements in foundation segmentation models, the Segment Anything Model (SAM) by Meta stands out as a versatile and powerful tool. SAM's architecture, designed to handle a wide range of segmentation tasks, represents a significant leap in the field [17]. Its ability to segment diverse objects in complex scenes has shown great promise in extending the boundaries of what segmentation models can achieve. However, applying foundation models like SAM to specific domains, such as iris segmentation, presents unique challenges. As explained, the complexity of iris patterns, variations in lighting, occlusions due to eyelashes, varying pupil sizes, the pose of the iris with respect to the camera, the acquisition of the image in the near-infrared spectrum, etc., are significant hurdles in achieving high-precision segmentation [7]. The transfer of knowledge from general segmentation tasks to such a specialized domain requires careful fine-tuning and adaptation of the model. Approaches like transfer learning, where a model trained on a large dataset is fine-tuned on a smaller, domain-specific dataset, have proven effective [24].

The central inquiry of this study thus emerges: how effective are these foundation models, particularly the Segment Anything Model (SAM), when applied to the task of iris segmentation? By exploring this question, in this paper, we delve into the challenge of iris segmentation, a crucial component for iris recognition and other tasks such as eye tracking, gaze estimation and proximity detection in eye surgery, and investigate how foundation models can be fine-tuned and augmented with specific loss functions [19] to achieve enhanced performance.

2   Background

2.1   Foundation Models

One of the most popular foundation models, OpenAI's GPT-3, was trained on diverse internet text. This vast training allows it to write essays, answer questions, and even generate code with minimal task-specific prompts [5]. Google's BERT uses bi-directional training on vast text corpora to capture intricate language relationships, setting new performance benchmarks across numerous NLP tasks [9]. In the visual domain, Vision Transformers (ViT) tessellate images into fixed-size patches, linearly embed them, and process them through transformer layers [10].

While foundation models emerged with a strong emphasis on NLP tasks, their underlying architecture and learning mechanisms have found relevance in computer vision. The ability of these models to capture hierarchical features and understand contexts makes them suitable for visual tasks, where often, object representations and spatial relationships dictate the outcome. For instance, Vision Transformers (ViT) have demonstrated how techniques originally designed for sequence data (like text) can be repurposed for image data, leading to impressive results in image classification [10]. The success of such models suggests potential utility in more intricate tasks like segmentation, where both global and local contexts matter.

2.2   SAM

The Segment Anything Model (SAM) [17] exemplifies the adaptability of foundation models in complex computer vision tasks like segmentation. Its architecture includes an image encoder creating high-dimensional embeddings, a prompt encoder for interpreting user inputs (like bounding boxes) into features, and a mask decoder that merges these to predict segmentations. SAM's vision encoder, a key component, processes images to generate detailed feature maps, crucial for capturing contextual, localizing, and pattern-recognition information across large image areas. The mask decoder then translates these features into precise pixel-level decisions for segmentation, using up-sampling layers to refine the output. SAM's ability to acquire a broad knowledge base from varied training scenarios enables it to adapt to new segmentation tasks with minimal additional training, bridging foundation model capabilities with the specific needs of segmentation accuracy.

2.3   Iris Segmentation

Over the years, iris segmentation methods have evolved from traditional image processing techniques to sophisticated machine learning algorithms. The seminal work of Daugman utilized integro-differential operators to detect the iris' circular patterns by maximizing contour sharpness [7]. This approach, however, has its limitations with non-circular and partially occluded irides. Subsequent advances have introduced active contour models [1,26], which iteratively evolve a curve under constraints in order to fit non-circular and non-elliptical boundaries. These models, while more flexible than their predecessors, require careful initialization and can be computationally intensive. OSIRIS [23] is an open-source software for iris recognition, using Hough transform and Gabor filters for accurate iris segmentation. It serves as a benchmark in evaluating new iris segmentation techniques. SegNet [3] is another well-known segmentation method that emerged as a notable deep learning architecture. Originally developed for scene understanding, SegNet's efficient encoder-decoder structure makes it well-suited for iris segmentation tasks. It effectively captures contextual information and detailed spatial resolution, crucial for accurately delineating the iris from other ocular components. The U-Net architecture, a variant of CNNs, has gained traction for its efficacy in segmenting medical images, including the iris [18], by using a contracting path to capture context and a symmetrically expanding path that enables precise localization [25].

3   Proposed Method

In this work, the SAM technique, renowned for its adaptability in medical image segmentation [21], has been fine-tuned for the specific task of iris segmentation. In the context of iris segmentation, the bounding box prompt emerges as the most effective, providing clear demarcation of the Region of Interest (ROI) with minimal user input. This approach is not only intuitive but also aligns with standard ophthalmic measurement practices, ensuring both accuracy and efficiency [21]. In the context of iris segmentation using SAM, bounding boxes are crucial for directing the model's focus to the relevant region (the iris) in each image. These bounding boxes are derived from ground truth masks during training using a specialized function that calculates the minimum and maximum coordinates encompassing the iris, with random adjustments in perturbed bounding boxes that entail unpredictably altering their size and position. This randomness enhances a model's flexibility and generalization to new data. This approach ensures that the model consistently focuses on the iris region across different images. *(Note that the proposed method does not require bounding boxes as input during the inference stage.)*

In iris segmentation, one often encounters a significant class imbalance. That is, the number of pixels belonging to the target object (iris pixels) might be much smaller compared to the background (non-iris pixels). Traditional loss functions, such as Cross-Entropy or Mean Squared Error, when used in such scenarios, tend to get overwhelmed by the sheer number of negative samples (non-iris pixels), leading the model to produce trivial solutions that identify everything as the background (Fig. 5).

Focal Loss, introduced by Lin et al. [19], provides a refined approach to handle the prevalent issue of class imbalance. Rather than treating all misclassified samples uniformly, the Focal Loss assigns varying weights to samples based on their misclassification levels (gives more weight to samples that the model struggles to identify as either part of the iris or non-iris, and less weight to samples that the model finds easy to categorize as belonging to the iris or non-iris regions). This is done to focus the model's learning more on challenging cases. Focal Loss is derived from standard cross-entropy loss [6] that is inadequate to address this imbalance, predominantly focusing on the majority class and, thus, overlooking the minority class, i.e., the iris pixels in our case.

Below, we see the cross-entropy (CE) loss for binary classification. For a given probability p of the positive class (iris) and the ground truth label y, the CE loss is defined as [19]:

$$CE(p, y) = \begin{cases} -\log(p), & \text{if } y = 1 \\ -\log(1 - p), & \text{otherwise.} \end{cases} \quad (1)$$

For a pixel p_i, the cross-entropy loss is given by:

$$L_{CE}(p_i) = -y_i \log(\hat{y}_i) - (1 - y_i) \log(1 - \hat{y}_i), \quad (2)$$

where, y_i is the ground truth (1 for iris, 0 for background) and $\hat{y}_i$ is the predicted probability for the pixel being part of the iris. However, in such scenarios with a large class imbalance, the CE loss can be overwhelmed by a great number of easy-to-classify negative samples (non-iris pixels). As a result, we need to have balancing and focusing factors to solve the issue.

Focal Loss is introduced to down-weight the correctly classified pixels, thus forcing the model to focus on hard-to-classify pixels. To address the limitations of cross-entropy loss in the presence of class imbalance, Focal Loss, denoted as $FL(p_t)$, is introduced [19]. It is formulated as:

$$FL(p_t) = -(1 - p_t)^\gamma \log(p_t). \quad (3)$$

p_t is the model's estimated probability for the class with label $y = 1$. α is a weighting factor to balance the importance of positive vs. negative examples and γ is the focusing parameter, adjusting the rate at which easy examples are down-weighted. For our problem, we adapt it as follows:

If the ground truth label $y = 1$ (iris), then $p_t = \hat{y}_i$; otherwise $p_t = 1 - \hat{y}_i$. The modified Focal Loss for a pixel p_i becomes:

$$L_{\text{Focal}}(p_i) = -\alpha(1 - p_t)^\gamma y_i \log(p_t) - (1 - \alpha)p_t^\gamma (1 - y_i) \log(1 - p_t). \quad (4)$$

Focal Loss, with its modulating factor $(1 - p_t)^\gamma$ diminishes the contribution of well-classified (easy) pixels and amplifies the loss for misclassified ones, especially near the iris boundary. Here, α is a balancing factor, and γ is the focusing parameter that determines how much the weight of well-classified examples should be reduced. As γ increases, the effect of the modulating factor becomes more pronounced. The intuition behind Focal Loss can be visualized in the iris segmentation task. In an eye image, vast areas are not part of the iris (sclera, pupil, eyelids, etc.). When using standard cross-entropy, the model quickly learns to predict these easy, non-iris regions correctly, while struggling with the actual iris region due to class imbalance. The function comprises two parts:

- The first part, $-\alpha(1-p_t)^\gamma y_i \log(p_t)$, focuses on the positive class. The modulating factor $(1-p_t)^\gamma$ increases the loss for misclassified or uncertain positive examples.
- The second part, $-(1-\alpha)p_t^\gamma(1-y_i)\log(1-p_t)$, focuses on the negative class. The modulating factor p_t^γ increases the loss for misclassified or overconfident negative examples.

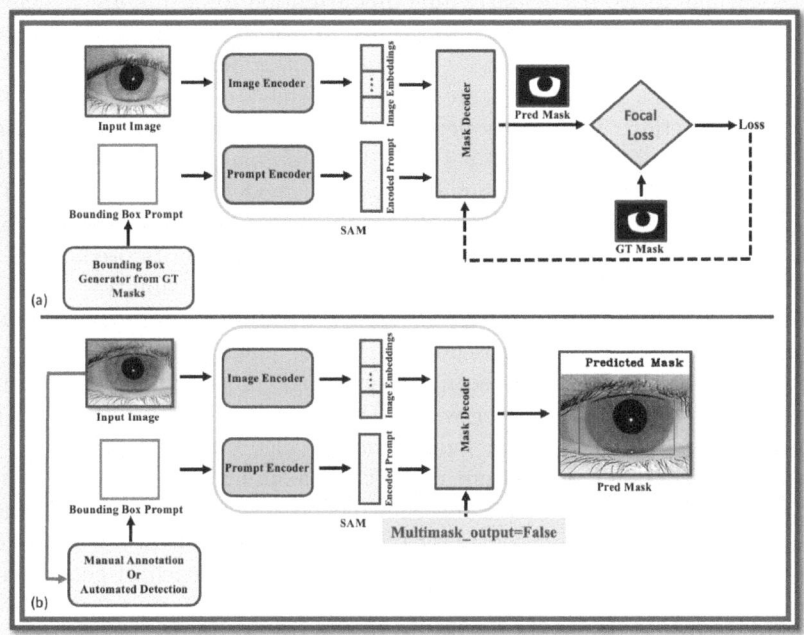

Fig. 2. Proposed network (Iris-SAM) using Segment Anything Model (SAM) [17]. (a) Training and (b) Inference/Testing. During training, prompts (bounding boxes) are generated from ground truth masks to guide the model. For inference/testing, the model automatically generates bounding boxes (visualized in green) from the input image, allowing it to predict the iris masks (depicted in blue) without needing explicit bounding box inputs.

By adjusting α and γ, Focal Loss can be fine-tuned for different datasets and imbalance problems, aiming to improve the performance on hard examples. During the training phase, we utilize a dataset consisting of iris images $I_1, I_2, \ldots, I_n$, each paired with a specific bounding box $B_1, B_2, \ldots, B_n$ and a corresponding ground truth mask $M_1, M_2, \ldots, M_n$. The model, when presented with an image I_j, produces a predicted mask O_j. A key objective is to enhance the agreement between O_j and the ground truth mask M_j, with the Intersection over Union (IoU) metric serving as the measure of this congruence. The IoU is defined as $\text{IoU}(O_j, M_j) = \frac{|O_j \cap M_j|}{|O_j \cup M_j|}$, indicating the extent of overlap between the predicted and actual iris regions (the standard deviation of IoU across all images is also computed, offering insight into the consistency of the model's performance). Crucially, the difference between the predicted mask O_j and the ground truth mask M_j plays a pivotal role in the training process. This disparity indicates how much the model's predictions deviate from the real iris area, forming a basis for calculating the weights used in the Focal Loss function. These weights, derived from the degree of misalignment between O_j and M_j, are employed to adjust the model's learning focus, particularly directing attention toward more challenging segmentation areas. In Focal Loss, the weights for each example are dynamically calculated using the formula $\alpha \times (1 - p_t)^\gamma$, where p_t is derived from the model's output. The model's output logits are first transformed into a probability p using the sigmoid function. Then, p_t is determined based on the ground truth label y: if $y = 1$, $p_t = p$; if $y = 0$, $p_t = 1 - p$. This approach ensures that the loss focuses more on challenging examples where the model is less confident. This adjustment is vital for refining the accuracy of the model's mask decoder, as it guides the model to learn more effectively from areas where its predictions are less accurate, thereby enhancing its overall segmentation capability.

SAM's versatile architecture allows for the generation of multiple masks corresponding to various objects or regions within an image. However, to tailor its capability to our specific need of segmenting a single object (the iris), we utilize the `multimask_output` parameter within the model's prediction method. The parameter is a boolean flag that guides the model's output behavior. As can be seen in Fig. 2, setting `multimask_output` to `False` instructs SAM to deviate from its default behavior of identifying multiple objects. Instead, it concentrates on generating a singular focused mask output. This output, in the context of our work, is the segmented iris region. This focused approach of generating a single mask output ensures that the model's computational resources and learning capacity are entirely devoted to the task of iris segmentation. It negates the diversion of attention to multiple regions, thereby enhancing the precision and accuracy of the segmentation process. This modification is pivotal for the specific requirements of iris biometric systems, where the delineation precision of the iris region directly impacts the system's reliability and performance.

The data split information for the experiments can be seen in Table 1. Datasets are captured using diverse camera systems and under varying environmental conditions, resulting in a wide range of image qualities, iris textures, and lighting variations. In our experiments, the SGD optimizer with a learning rate of 0.0001 and training for 100 epochs was optimal, achieving convergence without overfitting. This configuration not only optimized the learning curve but also stabilized the loss across epochs, as seen in the accompanying plots (Fig. 4).

4 Experimental Results

4.1 Dice, Triplet, and Focal Losses

In our iris segmentation experiments, Focal Loss outperformed Dice and Triplet losses, excelling in managing class imbalance by focusing on difficult examples, as shown in our training loss graph (Fig. 3a). This approach effectively emphasized critical iris details and boundaries, leading to more accurate segmentation. Focal Loss achieved lower, stable loss values rapidly, indicating efficient learning. Conversely, Dice Loss showed higher, fluctuating loss values, struggling with false positives and false negatives, while Triplet Loss, proved ineffective for segmentation, lacking in pixel-wise accuracy.

Table 1. Dataset information.

Dataset	Total (Images/Identities)	Train (Images/Identities)	Test (Images/Identities)
CASIA-Iris-Interval-v3	2655/249	2294/199	361/50
ND-Iris-0405	804/346	624/276	180/70
IIT-Delhi-Iris	2240/224	1790/179	450/45

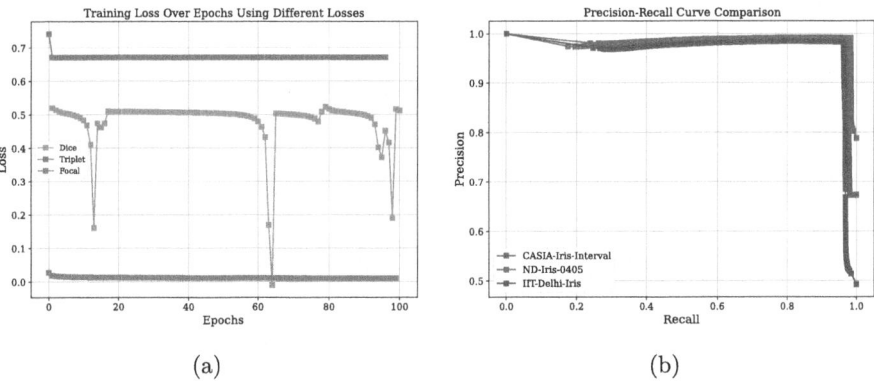

(a)   (b)

Fig. 3. (a) Training loss over 100 epochs for Dice, Triplet, and Focal Loss functions on the Casia-Iris-Interval-v3 dataset. Focal Loss converges rapidly to a lower value, indicating efficient learning, while Dice and Triplet losses exhibit higher variability and slower convergence. (b) Precision-Recall curve of our method on different test datasets when the Focal Loss was used during training.

4.2   Segmentation Results

Our experimentation spanned across various settings of the focusing parameter, γ, within the Focal Loss, examining its impact on the model's performance. We tested γ values of 1, 2, and 5 on the CASIA-Iris-Interval-v3 dataset (Fig. 4a), aiming to calibrate the loss function's sensitivity to misclassified instances. A γ value of 2 emerged as the optimal choice, striking a delicate balance between learning efficiency and robustness (Fig. 4b). While a higher γ of 5 initially seemed promising, it ultimately led to overfitting–a testament to the nuanced trade-offs in model training. The overfitting was evidenced by a good performance on the training set that did not generalize well to unseen data.

As can be seen in Table 2, a γ value of 2, achieved a high Average IoU of 96.94% on the CASIA-Iris-Interval-v3 and 99.58% on the ND-Iris-0405 dataset, demonstrating its effectiveness in iris segmentation. However, performance slightly dipped on the IIT-Delhi-Iris dataset with an Average IoU of 94.34%, indicating a nuanced variance in efficacy across different datasets. This marginal drop in performance can be attributed to the dataset's unique characteristics, particularly, the prevalence of dense eyelashes. The eyelashes present a complex segmentation challenge. Our model's nuanced attempt to delineate these eyelashes more accurately contributed to the slight reduction in the overall IoU score. It is a reflection of the model's sensitivity to fine-grained features, a trait that is both a strength and a point of careful consideration in dataset diversity.

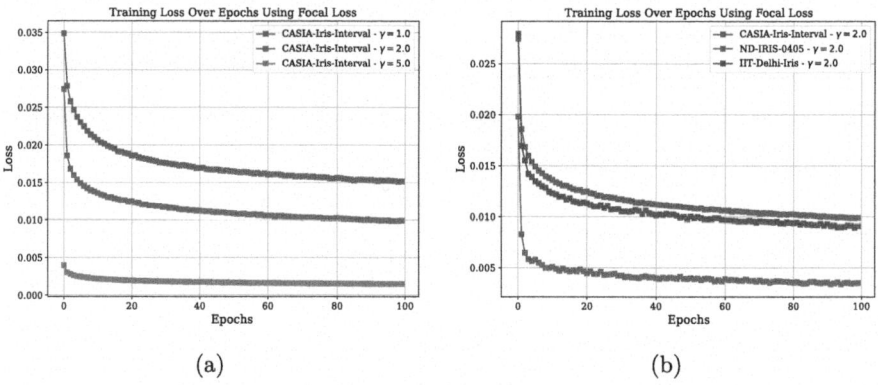

Fig. 4. (a) FineTuning + Focal Loss (Iris-SAM) using the default pre-trained model "ViT_h" with different γ values on CASIA-Iris-Interval-v3 dataset. (b) FineTuning + Focal Loss (Iris-SAM) using the default pre-trained model "ViT_h" on three different datasets.

The good performance of our model is further underscored by the standard deviation associated with the Average IoU scores, which is between 0.002 to 0.008 across the evaluated datasets. The limited variance in the IoU scores suggests a high level of consistency and reliability in the model's ability to segment iris regions, despite the inherent challenges presented by different images. Such consistency is particularly noteworthy when considering the complexity of iris textures and the potential for occlusions like eyelashes and reflections, which typically introduce variability in segmentation tasks.

The baseline section of Table 2 reports the performance of established iris segmentation models that are used as benchmarks. The OSIRIS model provides a baseline with an average IoU of 86.28% ($\pm$6.50), while the DRN and Context-100k models show improved performance and consistency, with IoUs around 89% and lower standard deviations. SegNet achieves an IoU of 89.75% but with slightly higher variability. The numerical performance of the baseline methods further conveys the efficacy of the proposed method which has significantly higher IoU scores and near-zero standard deviation underscoring its advanced segmentation accuracy and consistency across various datasets. In Figs. 6, 7 and 8 we demonstrate the effectiveness of incorporating Focal Loss into our fine-tuning process for the Segment Anything Model (SAM). The bounding box is denoted in green and the pixels classified as iris are marked in blue. Prior to the integration of Focal Loss, the SAM's performance, while adequate, fell short of achieving the high levels of accuracy needed for precise iris segmentation (Fig. 5). The initial fine-tuning phase was unable to consistently differentiate the intricate iris patterns from surrounding ocular structures. However, the adaptation of Focal Loss marked a significant turning point in our experiments and allowed the SAM to focus more on discerning the nuanced boundaries of the iris. The post-Focal Loss fine-tuning results, as showcased in the figures, reveal a substantial alignment with the ground-truth data. The contrast between the pre and post-Focal Loss output is a testament to the loss function's impact. Where the original fine-tuning failed to capture certain iris details, the model augmented with Focal Loss succeeded in delineating the iris with remarkable precision. These results not only validate the rationale behind using the Focal Loss but also underscore its potential in handling diversity of pixels in both the positive and negative classes.

As depicted in Fig. 10 and Fig. 11, our fine-tuned SAM model, with Focal Loss, exhibited the ability to not only match but sometimes surpass the ground-truth masks in accuracy. This was particularly evident when the model adeptly filled in missing iris segments and refrained from misclassifying eyelashes as iris tissue. To further validate our results, we plotted precision and recall curves for the three datasets (Fig. 3b), which reveal the model's strong segmentation capability, with ND-Iris-0405 showing near-perfect precision. Precision reflects the proportion of true positive pixels among the predicted positives, and recall represents the proportion of true positive pixels among the actual positives. While CASIA-Iris-Interval-v3 and IIT-Delhi-Iris experience minor precision declines at full recall, the consistently high performance indicates effective feature capture for iris segmentation (Fig. 9).

Table 2. Iris segmentation accuracy in terms of Average IoU% ± STD. Our method is observed to perform much better than the four baseline techniques. Further, it exhibits good generalization capability.

Our Method	Dataset	Accuracy
Iris-SAM	CASIA-Iris-Interval-v3	**96.94 ± 0.005**
Iris-SAM	ND-Iris-0405	**99.58 ± 0.003**
Iris-SAM	IIT-Delhi-Iris	**94.34 ± 0.008**
Our Method's Generalization		
Train	Test	Accuracy
ND-Iris-0405	IIT-Delhi-Iris	**93.75 ± 0.016**
ND-Iris-0405	CASIA-Iris-Interval-v3	**95.26 ± 0.009**
CASIA-Iris-Interval-v3	IIT-Delhi-Iris	**93.86 ± 0.010**
CASIA-Iris-Interval-v3	ND-Iris-0405	**98.86 ± 0.002**
IIT-Delhi-Iris	ND-Iris-0405	**98.92 ± 0.002**
IIT-Delhi-Iris	CASIA-Iris-Interval-v3	**95.49 ± 0.008**
Baselines [16]		
Method	Dataset	Accuracy
OSIRIS	ND-Iris-0405	86.28 ± 6.50
DRN	ND-Iris-0405	89.61 ± 5.08
Context-100k	ND-Iris-0405	89.45 ± 3.85
SegNet	ND-Iris-0405	89.75 ± 4.95

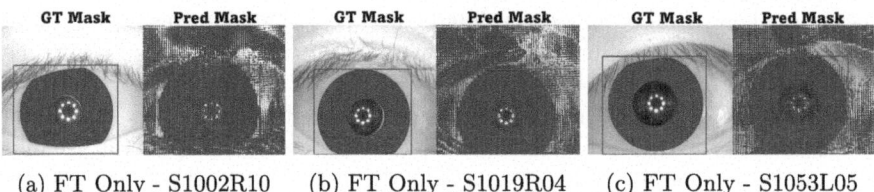

(a) FT Only - S1002R10   (b) FT Only - S1019R04   (c) FT Only - S1053L05

Fig. 5. FineTuning (FT) sample results (CASIA-Iris-Interval-v3).

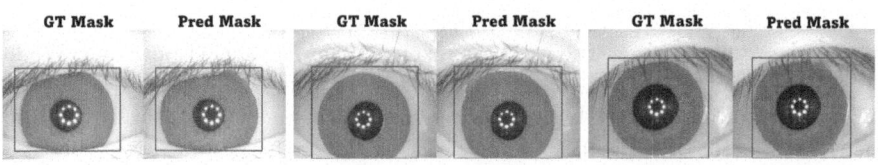

(a) FT+Focal - S1002R10   (b) FT+Focal - S1019R04   (c) FT+Focal - S1053L05

Fig. 6. FT + Focal Loss (Iris-SAM) sample results (CASIA-Iris-Interval-v3).

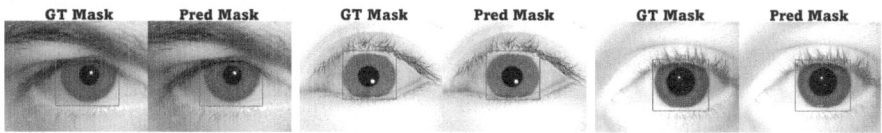

(a) FT+Focal - 04267d227   (b) FT+Focal - 04350d458   (c) FT+Focal - 04370d361

Fig. 7. FT + Focal Loss (Iris-SAM) sample results (ND-IRIS-0405).

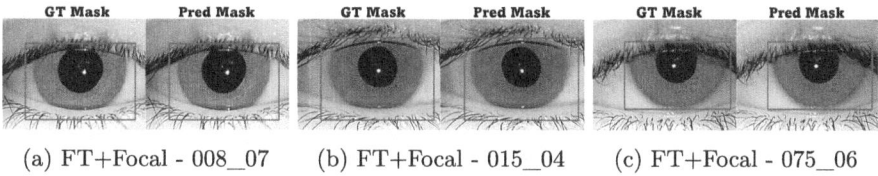

(a) FT+Focal - 008_07   (b) FT+Focal - 015_04   (c) FT+Focal - 075_06

Fig. 8. FT + Focal Loss (Iris-SAM) sample results (IIT-Delhi-Iris).

4.3   Cross-Dataset Model Generalization

The generalization capability of our method was further put to the test by training on ND-Iris-0405 and evaluating on the IIT-Delhi-Iris and CASIA-Iris-Interval-v3 datasets resulting in a very competitive accuracy of 93.75% and 95.26%, respectively. For training, we utilized our fine-tuned model already trained on each dataset. This cross-dataset validation underscores our model's adaptability and its potential for deployment in varied scenarios (more generalization results are shown in Table 2).

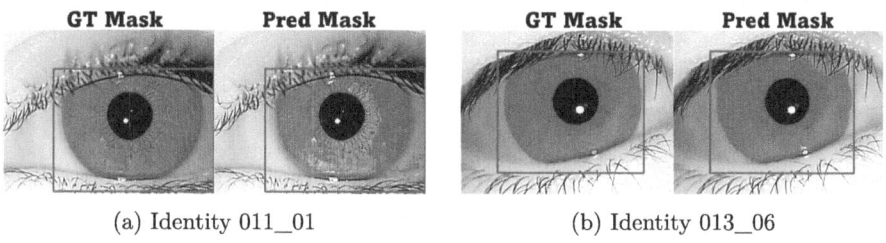

(a) Identity 011_01   (b) Identity 013_06

Fig. 9. Generalization results using ND-Iris-0405 (train) and IIT-Delhi-Iris (test). (a) A example of failure in segmentation. (b) An interesting observation of the model trying to segment the eyelashes on a previously unseen dataset.

5   Is Iris-SAM More Accurate Than Ground Truth?

A notable observation from our experiments, as illustrated in Fig. 10 and Fig. 11, is the occasional superiority of the model-predicted masks over the ground-truth (GT) masks.

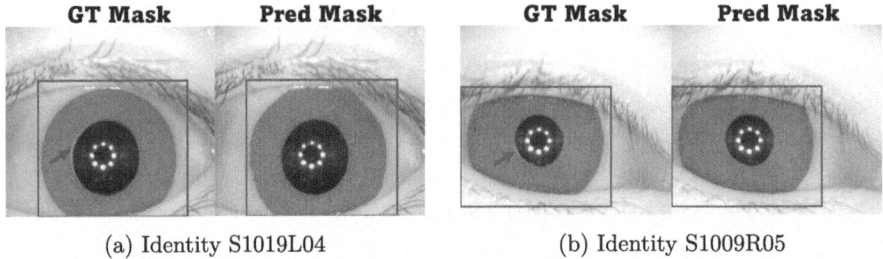

Fig. 10. Examples where the predicted mask appears to be more accurate than the ground truth mask in the CASIA-Iris-Interval-v3 dataset.

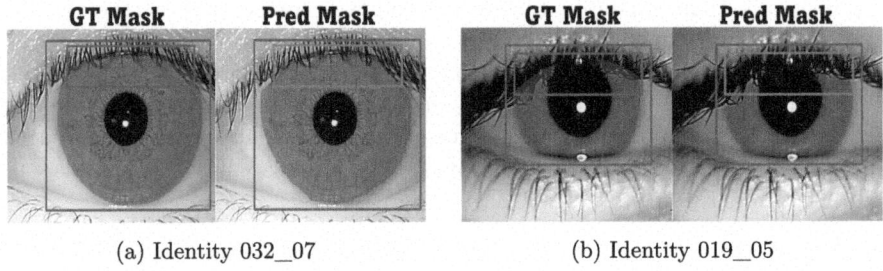

Fig. 11. Examples where the predicted mask appears to be more accurate than the ground truth mask in the IIT-Delhi-Iris dataset.

In Fig. 10, marked by a red arrow, we observe an instance where the ground-truth mask partially omits a segment of the iris. In contrast, the model's prediction captures this missing section, demonstrating a nuanced understanding of the iris structure. This instance is especially interesting considering the model achieved this higher accuracy with a relatively straightforward fine-tuning process. It suggests that the model, guided by the Focal Loss, has developed a nuanced perception of iris features, surpassing even the manually annotated ground truth in certain aspects. Figure 11 presents a scenario where the ground-truth mask inaccurately depicts eyelashes as part of the iris. However, the model's predicted mask displays an interesting discernment by correctly excluding the eyelashes from the iris segmentation. This precision highlights the model's capability to distinguish between closely situated but distinct features within the ocular region, a crucial requirement for reliable iris segmentation. Firstly, the model's refined handling of ground-truth annotations showcases its deep understanding of iris morphology. Secondly, its precise discrimination between the iris and adjacent elements underscores the model's accuracy, which is essential for the reliability of iris biometric systems (Fig. 13).

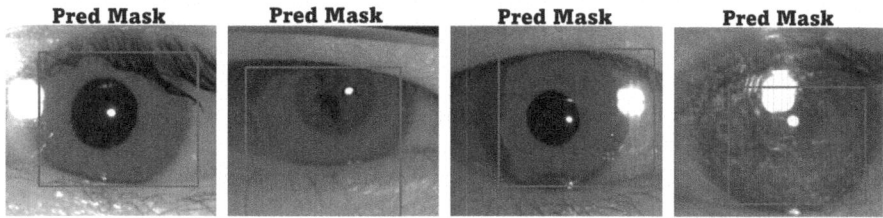

Fig. 12. Evaluation of our model on a challenging dataset (irides with glasses) without further tuning. As can be seen, the results vary, with some instances showing good outcomes and others less favorable.

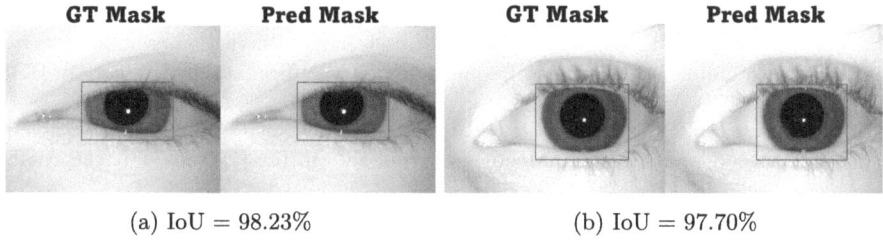

(a) IoU = 98.23%   (b) IoU = 97.70%

Fig. 13. Samples from the ND-Iris-0405 dataset illustrating segmentation results with low IoU scores.

To further examine our method and its robustness, we also tested it on a more challenging dataset. In the provided images depicting failure cases (Fig. 12), it is apparent that challenges arise primarily from occlusions and reflections, common in practical scenarios such as eyewear (glasses) and varied lighting conditions. The presence of eyewear introduces additional reflective surfaces and distortions that complicate the segmentation process. Similarly, difficult lighting conditions can produce glares or shadows on the iris, further complicating accurate segmentation. These factors can lead to inaccuracies where the predicted mask either overextends beyond the actual iris boundaries or fails to encompass the entire iris, as the model struggles to differentiate between the iris, the occlusions, and reflections.

6   Conclusion and Future Work

In our study, the enhanced SAM model with Focal Loss has significantly advanced iris segmentation, achieving Average IoU scores of 96.94% and 99.58%

on CASIA-Iris-Interval-v3 and ND-Iris-0405 datasets, respectively, and maintaining consistent performance with a very low standard deviation. Notably, the model handled complex scenarios, including dense eyelashes, as evidenced by its performance on the IIT-Delhi-Iris dataset, though it highlighted areas for future refinement. This work sets a new benchmark for iris segmentation and paves the way for the exploration of other challenges in iris segmentation, such as the processing of off-axis irides and images acquired in other spectral bands besides NIR.

Acknowledgement. We thank the University of Salzburg and Halmstad University for providing the ground truth datasets [2,12]. The code supporting the findings of this study is publicly available. (Repository: https://github.com/ParisaFarmanifard/Iris-SAM).

References

1. Abdullah, M.A., Dlay, S.S., Woo, W.L., Chambers, J.A.: Robust iris segmentation method based on a new active contour force with a noncircular normalization. IEEE Trans. Syst. Man, Cybern. Syst. **47**(12), 3128–3141 (2016)
2. Alonso-Fernandez, F., Bigun, J.: Near-infrared and visible-light periocular recognition with gabor features using frequency-adaptive automatic eye detection. IET Biometrics **4**(2), 74–89 (2015)
3. Badrinarayanan, V., Kendall, A., Cipolla, R.: SegNet: a deep convolutional encoder-decoder architecture for image segmentation. IEEE Trans. Pattern Anal. Mach. Intell. **39**(12), 2481–2495 (2017)
4. Bowyer, K.W., Hollingsworth, K., Flynn, P.J.: Image understanding for iris biometrics: a survey. Comput. Vis. Image Underst. **110**(2), 281–307 (2008)
5. Brown, T., et al.: Language models are few-shot learners. Adv. Neural. Inf. Process. Syst. **33**, 1877–1901 (2020)
6. Cover, T.M.: Elements of Information Theory. Wiley, Hoboken (1999)
7. Daugman, J.: How iris recognition works. In: The essential guide to image processing, pp. 715–739. Elsevier (2009)
8. Daugman, J.G.: High confidence visual recognition of persons by a test of statistical independence. IEEE Trans. Pattern Anal. Mach. Intell. **15**(11), 1148–1161 (1993)
9. Devlin, J., Chang, M.W., Lee, K., Toutanova, K.: Bert: Pre-training of deep bidirectional transformers for language understanding. arXiv preprint arXiv:1810.04805 (2018)
10. Dosovitskiy, A., et al.: An image is worth 16x16 words: transformers for image recognition at scale. arXiv preprint arXiv:2010.11929 (2020)
11. He, K., Zhang, X., Ren, S., Sun, J.: Deep residual learning for image recognition. In: Proceedings of the IEEE Conference on Computer Vision and Pattern Recognition, pp. 770–778 (2016)
12. Hofbauer, H., Alonso-Fernandez, F., Wild, P., Bigun, J., Uhl, A.: A ground truth for iris segmentation. In: 22nd International Conference on Pattern Recognition, pp. 527–532 (2014)
13. Jain, A.K., Nandakumar, K., Ross, A.: 50 years of biometric research: accomplishments, challenges, and opportunities. Pattern Recogn. Lett. **79**, 80–105 (2016)
14. Jain, A.K., Ross, A.A., Nandakumar, K.: Introduction to Biometrics. Springer Publishing Company, New York (2011)

15. Jalilian, E., Uhl, A.: Iris segmentation using fully convolutional encoder–decoder networks. In: Bhanu, B., Kumar, A. (eds.) Deep Learning for Biometrics. ACVPR, pp. 133–155. Springer, Cham (2017). https://doi.org/10.1007/978-3-319-61657-5_6

16. Kerrigan, D., Trokielewicz, M., Czajka, A., Bowyer, K.W.: Iris recognition with image segmentation employing retrained off-the-shelf deep neural networks. In: International Conference on Biometrics (ICB), pp. 1–7 (2019)

17. Kirillov, A., et al.: Segment anything. In: Proceedings of the IEEE/CVF International Conference on Computer Vision, pp. 4015–4026 (2023)

18. Lian, S., Luo, Z., Zhong, Z., Lin, X., Su, S., Li, S.: Attention guided u-net for accurate iris segmentation. J. Vis. Commun. Image Represent. **56**, 296–304 (2018)

19. Lin, T.Y., Goyal, P., Girshick, R., He, K., Dollár, P.: Focal loss for dense object detection. IEEE Trans. Pattern Anal. Mach. Intell. **42**(2), 318–327 (2020)

20. Long, J., Shelhamer, E., Darrell, T.: Fully convolutional networks for semantic segmentation. In: Proceedings of the IEEE Conference on Computer Vision and Pattern Recognition, pp. 3431–3440 (2015)

21. Ma, J., He, Y., Li, F., Han, L., You, C., Wang, B.: Segment anything in medical images. Nat. Commun. **15**(1), 654 (2024)

22. Nguyen, K., Fookes, C., Jillela, R., Sridharan, S., Ross, A.: Long range iris recognition: a survey. Pattern Recogn. **72**, 123–143 (2017)

23. Othman, N., Dorizzi, B., Garcia-Salicetti, S.: OSIRIS: an open source iris recognition software. Pattern Recogn. Lett. **82**, 124–131 (2016)

24. Pan, S.J., Yang, Q.: A survey on transfer learning. IEEE Trans. Knowl. Data Eng. **22**(10), 1345–1359 (2009)

25. Ronneberger, O., Fischer, P., Brox, T.: U-Net: convolutional networks for biomedical image segmentation. In: Navab, N., Hornegger, J., Wells, W.M., Frangi, A.F. (eds.) MICCAI 2015. LNCS, vol. 9351, pp. 234–241. Springer, Cham (2015). https://doi.org/10.1007/978-3-319-24574-4_28

26. Shah, S., Ross, A.: Iris segmentation using geodesic active contours. IEEE Trans. Inf. Forensics Secur. (TIFS) **4**(4), 824–836 (2009)

Test-Time Adaptation for EEG-Based Driver Drowsiness Classification

Geun-Deok Jang[1] , Dong-Kyun Han[2] , and Seong-Whan Lee[1]([⊠])

[1] Department of Artificial Intelligence, Korea University, Seoul, Republic of Korea
{gd_jang,sw.lee}@korea.ac.kr
[2] Department of Brain and Cognitive Engineering, Korea University,
Seoul, Republic of Korea
dk_han@korea.ac.kr

Abstract. Driver drowsiness significantly impacts global road safety, leading to numerous traffic accidents. While electroencephalogram (EEG) stands out for its direct assessment of cognitive states in drivers, the inherent variability of EEG signals poses substantial challenges to accurate decoding for driver state classification. To tackle this, we introduce a novel BCI framework for EEG-based driver drowsiness classification using test-time adaptation. To dynamically adjust to target distributions within online BCI framework, we utilizes a memory technique and optimizes batch normalization layers. We also introduce prototype learning for reliable predictions within distribution shift environments. Extensive experiments demonstrate that our framework effectively adapts to non-stationary EEG signals and varying subject states. Through our calibration-free framework, we address the critical challenge of online BCI framework for EEG-based driver drowsiness classification.

Keywords: Brain-computer interface · Driver drowsiness · Test-time adaptation

1 Introduction

Drowsy driving is a major road safety concern, significantly increasing the risk of traffic accidents. Detecting drowsiness accurately is crucial for car safety research. Recently, compared to other physiological indicators such as electrocardiogram and electrooculogram, electroencephalogram (EEG) has gained attention as an effective tool for this purpose [15]. Along with its portability and cost-effectiveness [16], EEG provides a direct assessment of human cognitive states, making it increasingly preferred in the development of driver drowsiness monitoring systems.

However, a major obstacle to the brain-computer interface (BCI) systems is the variability of the EEG signals between individuals and within the same individual across sessions. This variability is caused by many factors, including psychological state, electrode placement, and the variety of head shapes

C. Wallraven et al. (Eds.): ICPRAI 2024, LNCS 14892, pp. 410–424, 2025.
https://doi.org/10.1007/978-981-97-8702-9_28

and sizes. Such variability inherent in EEG data poses a challenge to achieving accurate decoding in BCI [11]. Recent studies [3,24] have developed subject-independent BCI systems to avoid laborious and uncomfortable calibration sessions. Furthermore, to address the variability between the individuals in the subject-independent BCI systems, researchers have studied domain adaptation (DA) and domain generalization (DG) methods for driver state classification.

DA aims to minimize the discrepancy between the source and target distributions during training [7]. However, in online BCI systems, it is often impractical to assume that all target data can be acquired during training. In contrast, DG does not require access to the target subject data, making it more suitable for real-world applications. DG methods aim to mitigate inter-subject variability using several techniques such as data augmentation [12] and domain-invariant representations [24]. However, a significant challenge for DG techniques is to generalize the model without any prior knowledge of the target data, which often results in diminished performance.

To address the challenges associated with DA and DG in computer vision tasks, many researchers have focused on test-time adaptation (TTA), which adapts the model to the target distribution during inference. To the best of our knowledge, no study has yet explored an EEG-based driver classification framework incorporating TTA methods. To implement TTA algorithms in an EEG-based driver drowsiness classification framework, we explore several challenges relevant to EEG-based online BCI systems. First, the framework should be adaptable to streaming EEG data from the target subject for online BCI systems, ensuring that the system remains responsive to the varying state of the driver. Second, due to the variability inherent in the non-stationary EEG signals, their distributions are temporally correlated, meaning that the distributions are not independent but are influenced by preceding data points. Such algorithms should be capable of adapting to the changing patterns of driver states in online BCI framework.

To handle these issues, we propose *test-time entropy minimization with prototype learning for EEG signals* (TEMPLE). More specifically, TEMPLE introduces a memory bank, which accumulates incoming target instances over time. We manage the memory bank with a sampling technique considering the energy score and the timeliness, discarding the most unreliable samples over time. Then, TEMPLE adjusts the learnable parameters of the batch normalization (BN) layers with entropy minimization while preserving the pre-trained normalization statistics. Furthermore, TEMPLE introduces prototype learning based on the data in the memory bank, encouraging robust predictions against the distribution shifts. Our proposed methods allow the system to accurately capture and respond to the fluctuating characteristics of the EEG signals over time.

2   Related Works

2.1   Subject-Independent Driver Drowsiness Classification

Recent studies have focused on investigating the architecture of neural networks to enhance the forecasting of driver states on a sustained-attention driving dataset [2]. Cui et al. [3] introduced a convolutional neural network (CNN) with separable convolutions [17] to identify patterns in driver mental states, while Lin et al. [20] converted EEG signals into multi-dimensional images for their 4-D CNN model. Li et al. [19] proposed a decomposition-based hybrid ensemble CNN to address individual differences. Further, Zhang et al. [33] built a two-layer recurrent neural network to extract the features in the temporal relation domain and fuse these features with the features in the spatial relation domain.

On the other hand, to address the inherent variability in BCI systems, other researchers have studied algorithms that mitigate domain shifts and improve generalization. Cui et al. [4] employed episodic training with power spectral density features. Hwang et al. [7] adopted domain adversarial training alongside a clustering algorithm that utilizes Wasserstein distance for enhanced subject-invariant learning. Kim et al. [12] introduced the MixStyle [34] to augment the data and class relationship alignment to generalize the model. Paulo et al. [24] examined spatio-temporal image encoding representations [22,28] by converting the features into recurrent plots and gramian angular fields to capture temporal recurrences and correlations.

2.2   Test-Time Adaptation

TTA primarily aims to optimize the model performance on target domain data by dynamically adjusting to unlabeled test samples during the inference phase. This approach allows enhanced adaptability and efficacy in practical applications, particularly in scenarios where labeled data are scarce or unavailable.

Several studies on TTA have examined the practical setups for real-world applications [6,23,30,32]. For example, Wang et al. [30] assumed that the target data are streamed from continually changing target domains and accordingly adapted the models. Yuan et al. [32] proposed a robust BN layer and a category-balanced sampling technique to cope with practical TTA settings where distribution changes and correlated sampling occur during inference.

TTA methods can be categorized into two groups: batch-based and batch-agnostic approaches. Batch-based approaches update the model parameters batch-by-batch [29,32]. Wang et al. [29] proposed to estimate the batch statistics and update the learnable parameters of the BN layers via entropy minimization on the incoming target mini-batches. However, since these batch-based approaches do not assume an online environment, they exhibit large performance degradation when adapting to the target distribution of the streaming data [23].

On the other hand, batch-agnostic approaches [6,23,30] have been proposed to effectively adapt the model to the streaming data from target domains. Gong et al. [6] proposed an instance-aware batch normalization layer and a prediction-balanced reservoir sampling to address the challenges of temporally correlated test streams. Niu et al. [23] investigated why TTA fails and then found that the normalization statistics of the BN layers are ruined when it adapts to the target instances. To solve this problem, they proposed sharpness-aware entropy minimization.

Moreover, several studies [1,9] have been proposed to use prototype learning (PL), taking advantage of capturing the underlying structure of the data. They have shown that PL is particularly useful for online TTA setup, where the framework needs to be improved for each target instance.

3 Method

To address the challenge of variability inherent in subject-independent BCI systems, we propose TEMPLE, a novel online BCI framework for an EEG-based driver drowsiness classification incorporating TTA. TEMPLE manages the memory bank with the sampling technique considering the energy score and the timeliness of the memory data over time. Only the learnable parameters of the BN layers are updated with the adjusted memory data via entropy minimization while preserving the pre-trained statistics. Subsequently, prototypes are adjusted and constructed based on the features of the memory data. Predictions are made by an inner product between the current input feature and the adjusted prototypes. This approach facilitates the development of an online BCI framework that does not require a calibration session. The overall framework of the proposed TTA methods are described in Fig. 1.

3.1 Memory-Based Online Entropy Minimization

BN [8] is a commonly used technique in neural network training because it promotes convergence and ensures a more stable training process. Let $\mathbf{z}_t$ denote as the input for a BN layer at time step t. Given the feature map and the statistics, the BN layer computes:

$$\mathrm{BN}(\mathbf{z}_t; \mu, \sigma) = \gamma \cdot \frac{\mathbf{z}_t - \mu}{\sqrt{\sigma^2 + \epsilon}} + \beta, \tag{1}$$

where μ and σ^2 are the normalization statistics (mean and variance), γ and β are learnable parameters (scale and shift), and ϵ is a small positive constant to prevent numerical instability.

Following recent works [6,29,32], we focus on tuning BN layers for performing TTA on a given feature extractor during inference, primarily involving two approaches. Several studies [6,32] update both the normalization statistics and the learnable parameters based on the input target data. Subsequently, they normalize and transform the input target data using the adjusted statistics and parameters for prediction. Conversely, other studies [29,30] utilize the current input batch statistics for normalization and update the learnable parameters.

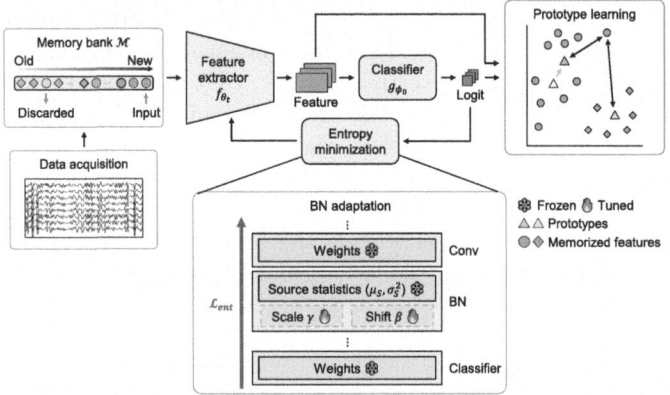

Fig. 1. The overall framework of the proposed methods. The framework inputs the streaming EEG signals from the target subject. A memory bank is dynamically managed through a sampling technique, considering the energy score and the timeliness. The transparency of the memory data visually denotes the level of sampling score. Within the feature extractor, only the learnable parameters of the BN layers are updated with the memory data. The prototypes are adjusted and constructed from the features in the memory bank.

They then normalize and transform the input target data using the current input batch statistics and the adjusted parameters for prediction.

Although both approaches update the learnable parameters in response to the input target data, they differ in their treatment of the statistics used for the normalization. The former approaches continuously update these statistics, while the latter approaches initialize the pre-trained normalization statistics and use the current input batch statistics for each time step. However, since statistics estimation tends to be biased towards the distributions of the predominant classes [23], both updating the normalization statistics and using the batch statistics based on the streaming EEG data lead to unstable statistics.

Since the model has been trained on multiple source subjects during the pre-training process, we assume that the BN layers in the model already store robust normalization statistics. Thus, unlike conventional TTA methods updating the BN layers, we fix the normalization statistics in the BN layers with the pre-trained ones while updating the learnable parameters with the input target data, as illustrated in Fig. 1. We normalize and transform the input target data using the fixed normalization statistics and the adjusted parameters for prediction:

$$\mathrm{BN}(\mathbf{z}_t; \mu_S, \sigma_S) = \gamma \cdot \frac{\mathbf{z}_t - \mu_S}{\sqrt{\sigma_S^2 + \epsilon}} + \beta, \tag{2}$$

where μ_S and σ_S^2 represent the fixed normalization statistics, which are pre-trained with source subjects.

BN layers estimate the channel-wise statistics of mini-batches, and the reliability of these statistics is closely tied to the batch size [23]. This means that it

---

Algorithm 1: Online TTA of the proposed methods

---

1 **Require:** Target sample $\mathbf{x}_t$, feature extractor f_{θ_t}, pre-trained classifier g_{ϕ_0}, prototypes $\mathcal{P}_t$, memory bank $\mathcal{M}$ of capacity $\mathcal{N}$, occupation $\mathcal{O}$ of $\mathcal{M}$, total number of classes C, smoothing factor α

2 **for** $t = 1$ **to** T **do**

3   **if** $t == 1$ **then**

        `// Memory initialization`

4   **while** $\mathcal{O} < \mathcal{N}$ **do**

5   Gaussian noise transformation w_i, permutation transformation h_i

6             $\mathbf{o}'_1 \leftarrow g_{\phi_0}(f_{\theta_1}(w_i(\mathbf{x}_1)))$

7             $\mathbf{o}''_1 \leftarrow g_{\phi_0}(f_{\theta_1}(h_i(\mathbf{x}_1)))$

8   Add $(w_i(\mathbf{x}_1), \mathbf{o}'_1), (h_i(\mathbf{x}_1), \mathbf{o}''_1)$ into $\mathcal{M}$

9   **end**

10   Initialize $\mathcal{P}_t$ with the weights from g_{ϕ_0}

11   **end**

12   **else**

13   Find the least reliable sample $\mathcal{M}[k]$ with (4)

14   Discard $\mathcal{M}[k]$ from $\mathcal{M}$ `// Memory management`

15         $\mathbf{z}_t \leftarrow f_{\theta_{t-1}}(\mathbf{x}_t)$

16         $\mathbf{o}_t \leftarrow \mathbf{z}_t \cdot \mathcal{P}_{t-1}$

17   Add $(\mathbf{x}_t, \mathbf{o}_t)$ into $\mathcal{M}$ `// Add current data`

18   **end**

19   Compute entropy loss $\mathcal{L}_{ent}$ as in (5)

20     $\theta_t \leftarrow \text{Optimize}(\theta_{t-1}, \mathcal{L}_{ent})$ `// Update BN layers`

21   Extract samples $\tilde{\mathbf{x}}$ from memory bank $\mathcal{M}$

22   Compute feature representations $\tilde{\mathbf{z}}$ using f_{θ_t}

23   **for** $i = 1$ **to** $\mathcal{N}$ **do**

24         $\hat{y}_i \leftarrow \arg\max_c P(y = c | \tilde{\mathbf{z}}_i; \phi_0)$ `// Compute pseudo-labels`

25   **end**

26   **for** $c = 1$ **to** C **do**

27         $\hat{\mathcal{P}}_{t,c} \leftarrow \frac{1}{\sum_{i=1}^{\mathcal{N}} \mathbf{1}_{\hat{y}_i=c}} \sum_{i=1}^{\mathcal{N}} \tilde{\mathbf{z}}_i \mathbf{1}_{\hat{y}_i=c}$

28         $\mathcal{P}_{t,c} \leftarrow \alpha \mathcal{P}_{t-1,c} + (1-\alpha)\hat{\mathcal{P}}_{t,c}$ `// Update prototypes`

29   **end**

30 **end**

---

can lead to instability during the adaptation process when batch statistics are estimated from single instances. Consequently, using smaller batch sizes may impede the network's ability to accurately learn the true distribution of data, which poses significant challenges for practical applications.

Following the existing TTA methods that introduce a memory bank [6,32], we present a memory bank using a novel sampling technique for an EEG-based BCI framework. To initialize the memory bank, when the first single instance is input, we augment it until the memory bank is full. As for the augmentation techniques, we use a permutation technique that randomly mixes segments of the input EEG signals and an additive white Gaussian noise [10]. After initialization, we compute the sampling score, which incorporates the energy score and the timeliness to assess the reliability of the samples in the memory bank. Specifically, we utilize the negative energy score [5,21], used for out-of-distribution detection, for every logit in the memory bank. Given a logit, we compute the negative energy score as follows:

$$E(\mathbf{o}) = \log \sum_{c=1}^{C} \exp(\mathbf{o}_c), \tag{3}$$

where C is the total number of classes and $\mathbf{o}$ represents a given logit, which is the output of the classifier.

Inspired by [32], we integrate the negative energy score with a timeliness-based regularization term:

$$S(\mathbf{o}) = \frac{1}{E(\mathbf{o})} + \lambda \mathrm{Sigmoid}(\mathcal{A}/\mathcal{N}), \tag{4}$$

where $\mathcal{N}$ is the memory capacity, λ is the balance weight for the timeliness, and $\mathcal{A}$ represents the duration that the logit remained in the memory bank.

As detailed in (4), our proposed sampling technique selectively eliminates the least reliable samples—typically, these are older samples with high confidence or newer samples with low confidence, filtering out the old overconfident samples and the out-of-distribution samples. This allows the memory to align with the current distribution of the streaming data.

Furthermore, as illustrated in Fig. 1, we update only the learnable parameters of the BN layers in a way that minimizes the entropy based on the data in the memory bank:

$$\mathcal{L}_{ent} = -\frac{1}{\mathcal{N}} \sum_{i=1}^{\mathcal{N}} \sum_{c=1}^{C} p_{i,c} \log p_{i,c}, \tag{5}$$

where $p_{i,c}$ represents the probability that the i-th memory instance belongs to class c, i.e., $p_{i,c} = P(y = c | \mathbf{x}_i; \theta_t, \phi_0)$.

3.2   Prototype Learning

PL is essentially consistent with the principle of few-shot learning [18,27], where a model is designed to learn information from a very limited amount of data. However, PL for the few-shot learning assumes that we have few labeled data, which is different in the TTA setup. In TTA, we only have unlabeled samples from the target domain over time. Since PL typically involves updating the representations of class centers, it can be performed relatively quickly, making it suitable for real-time adaptation. It is crucial for applications that need to respond immediately to changing conditions.

Our study utilizes PL in the context of TTA, building on the premise that PL is effectively combined with a memory bank for real-world scenarios. Our sampling technique is designed to retain the confident samples in the memory bank and efficiently capture the dynamics of the current target distributions. To leverage the embedded source knowledge, we initialize the prototypes with the weights of the pre-trained classifier. We then extract features from the instances in the memory bank and generate pseudo-labels using the adjusted feature extractor. Subsequently, prototypes are generated by averaging the features based on the pseudo-labels. The prototypes are then updated using an exponential moving average with both the newly generated prototypes and the previous ones, as denoted in Algorithm 1. Predictions are derived from the similarity between the adjusted prototypes and the current input features via an inner product. This approach enables us to deliver reliable predictions for current input instances, maintaining its efficacy even in the presence of class imbalances within the memory bank.

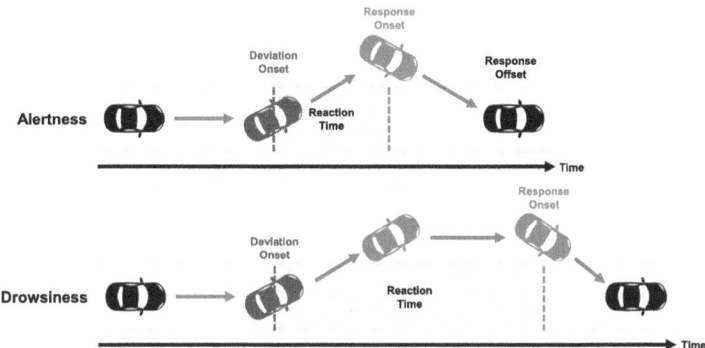

Fig. 2. Experimental paradigms of the sustained-attention driving dataset used in this study. Each trial was performed in the following order: response offset, deviation onset, and response onset. We focused primarily on the RTs between deviation onset and response onset. Drowsy drivers have longer RTs than alert drivers.

4 Experiments

4.1 Materials

We used the preprocessed version of the dataset available from a previous study [3]. The original dataset [2] consists of 62 sessions involving 27 healthy subjects who participated in a 90-minute driving task in a virtual reality simulator. Each subject was required to drive on a highway while keeping the vehicle in the center of the lane. During sessions, randomly induced lane departure events cause the car to drift to the left or right lane, as illustrated in Fig. 2. Subjects were instructed to respond by steering the vehicle back into the center lane as quickly as possible. The times of lane departure, steering, and return to the center lane are referred to as deviation onset, response onset, and response offset, respectively. Moreover, the EEG signals were processed with 1–50 Hz band-pass filtering and artifact rejection. This dataset was downsampled to 128 Hz, and a 3-second segment was extracted prior to each deviation onset.

Following previous studies [24,31], two metrics were calculated for each sample: the local reaction time (RT), defined as the time it takes to respond to a lane departure event, and the global RT, which represents the average of the RTs measured within a 90-s window immediately preceding the lane departure event. Samples in which both local RT and global RT were shorter than 1.5 times the alert RT were labeled as alertness, while those in which both were longer than 2.5 times the alert RT were labeled as drowsiness. To ensure the balance and validity of the data, sessions with less than 50 samples in either class were discarded. If multiple sessions were available for the same subject, sessions with the most balanced class distribution were used.

4.2   Baselines

We established three categories of baselines for comparison. For clarity and conciseness, "Source" was referred to as the pre-trained models directly on the target data without any TTA. Source evaluated the performance of conventional methods such as DeepConvNet [26], EEGNet8,2 [14], InterpretableCNN [3], and ResNet1D-8 [12].

Existing TTA baselines are categorized into batch-based approaches and batch-agnostic approaches. Batch-based approaches refer to methods that were originally designed for mini-batch unit adaptation. Wang et al. [29] proposed Tent, which estimates the batch statistics and updates the learnable parameters in the BN layers via entropy minimization on mini-batches of the current target data. Yuan et al. [32] introduced RoTTA, which uses a robust batch normalization layer and a memory bank with category-balanced sampling, considering timeliness and uncertainty.

Batch-agnostic approaches refer to methods that are not greatly affected by batch size. Wang et al. [30] presented CoTTA, which introduces a weight-averaged teacher model and augmentation-averaged prediction. Gong et al. [6] proposed NOTE, which introduces an instance-aware batch normalization layer and a novel memory scheme. Niu et al. [23] developed SAR, which partially filters out noisy test samples with sharp minima. Iwasawa et al. [9] proposed T3A, which uses online unlabeled data to adjust the prototypes based on pseudo-labels.

4.3   Experimental Settings

To investigate the efficacy of our proposed TTA methods within an online BCI framework, we established a rigorous experimental setup. Our experiments were evaluated by a leave-one-subject-out cross-validation [25], where one subject was set as the target subject and the others were set as the source subjects, repeated for every subject.

Table 1. Overall F1-score (%) comparison for driver drowsiness classification on a sustained-attention dataset

Categories	Methods	S1	S2	S3	S4	S5	S6	S7	S8	S9	S10	S11	Avg. (std.)
Source	DeepConvNet [26]	81.44	8.66	56.13	62.50	70.71	81.00	80.79	62.61	77.19	49.32	60.91	62.84 (21.06)
	EEGNet8,2 [14]	73.86	29.52	62.04	68.97	76.04	87.04	83.02	64.23	77.23	52.50	65.12	67.23 (15.96)
	InterpretableCNN [3]	67.47	19.33	64.23	66.67	80.00	73.85	**83.81**	65.59	80.79	54.55	75.76	66.55 (17.89)
	ResNet1D-8 [12]	81.97	33.46	50.98	66.02	52.63	73.91	80.57	67.12	77.66	60.98	75.76	65.55 (15.00)
Batch-based	Tent [29]	3.51	26.06	1.10	12.00	0.00	7.75	1.83	0.00	0.00	11.02	5.59	6.26 (7.88)
	RoTTA [32]	60.98	4.48	59.78	57.50	83.33	90.53	80.19	16.77	22.68	3.03	50.51	48.16 (31.67)
Batch-agnostic	CoTTA [30]	16.82	27.69	1.10	19.78	4.96	4.69	0.00	9.94	3.75	16.36	10.07	10.47 (8.75)
	NOTE [6]	43.48	24.36	43.37	52.56	38.64	82.93	67.78	69.29	15.69	35.21	27.38	45.52 (20.83)
	SAR [23]	39.05	6.11	56.15	65.85	77.25	88.29	31.01	66.14	75.72	51.95	48.42	55.09 (23.56)
	T3A [9]	75.98	**34.11**	67.13	69.70	79.40	87.11	82.63	70.50	81.90	51.22	70.27	70.00 (15.39)
	TEMPLE (ours)	**94.74**	28.76	**95.84**	**72.36**	**98.25**	**93.58**	83.33	**90.59**	**84.07**	**62.79**	**87.64**	**81.09 (20.37)**

In the pre-training process, we used the Adam [13] with a learning rate of 0.001. We trained an EEGNet8,2 [14] with a sustained-attention driving dataset [3]. We set the batch size and epochs as 32 and 100, respectively. After the pre-training process, we obtained a pre-trained model for each target subject.

A critical aspect of our experimental setup was how to handle the configuration of the BN layers after the pre-training process. As outlined in Sect. 3.1, we prevented the BN layers from changing the normalization statistics for the input target instance. Consequently, we focused on updating only the learnable parameters within the BN layers.

In the inference process, we also used the Adam with a learning rate of 0.001. We employed a test batch size of 1 to simulate the sequential arrival of EEG samples, which is essential for online BCI systems. Following recent studies [6, 29, 30], we set the adaptation step to 1. In addition, we set the balance weight λ to 2.0, as defined in (4), to ensure optimal balancing of the sampling score. We also set the smoothing factor α to 0.9, as outlined in Algorithm 1, to facilitate the update of the adaptive prototypes.

For the TTA baselines, we used the best hyperparameter values reported in their respective publications or provided in their official implementation code. For a fair comparison, we set the memory bank capacity as 8 for all TTA baselines that use the memory technique.

4.4 Results

In this study, we evaluated the effectiveness of TEMPLE compared to source baselines and various TTA baselines on a sustained-attention driving dataset [3]. All methods were evaluated with the F1-score metric, which is a harmonic mean of precision and recall. F1-score is particularly useful in situations where the label distribution is imbalanced. As shown in Table 1, the results showed significant increases in performance compared to the other baseline methods.

The source provided a baseline with an average F1-score ranging from 62.84% to 67.23%. In the context of batch-based TTA methods, Tent [29] exhibited a marked degradation in performance, registering at only 6.26%, due to normalization relying on the statistics of the input single instances. Though RoTTA [32] fared better with an average F1-score of 48.16%, it still struggled to match the performance of the sources. These performance drops were due to their underlying assumptions that the model depends on the batch unit adaptation. Within the batch-agnostic baselines, CoTTA [30] attained an inferior average F1-score of 10.47%, due to normalization using the input single instances. T3A [9] showed a modest enhancement in performance, achieving an average F1-score of 70%, attributed to its design for online TTA.

Notably, TEMPLE significantly outperformed all other baselines, achieving the highest average F1-score of 81.09%, which suggests a strong balance between precision and recall. TEMPLE illustrated an average improvement of 11.09% over the best performance of the baselines. These comprehensive results demonstrated the capacity of TEMPLE in adapting to the dynamic distributions of the EEG signals for driver drowsiness classification. This robustness of TEMPLE and its ability to handle non-stationary EEG signals make it suitable for real-world BCI applications.

Table 2. Contributions of components in TEMPLE

Method	F1-score	AUROC	Precision	Recall
EEGNet8,2 (source)	67.23	73.18	74.90	67.46
TEMPLE w/o BN updates	72.11	77.32	**80.63**	72.66
TEMPLE w/o memory and PL	73.41	76.18	70.95	80.50
TEMPLE w/o PL	74.26	77.41	73.16	82.81
TEMPLE	**81.09**	**83.92**	80.55	**88.88**

4.5   Ablation Study

We conducted an ablation study to understand the individual contributions of each component by removing them. The "EEGNet8,2 (source)" configuration serves as the baseline, in which EEGNet8,2 was trained only on the data from the multiple source subjects without any TTA process. The importance of each component in our TEMPLE is illustrated in Table 2.

When we did not update the BN layers, referred to as "TEMPLE w/o BN updates", we introduced the memory bank and PL for TTA. In this scenario, it showed a marked improvement in performance over the "EEGNet8,2 (source)" model. Compared to the performance of T3A [9], which used PL for TTA as present in Table 1, "TEMPLE w/o BN updates" exhibited a performance improvement. This suggests that introducing the memory bank plays a pivotal role in capturing the evolving distribution of the target domain and removing noisy samples over time.

When updating only the learnable parameters of the BN layers, "TEMPLE w/o memory and PL" resulted in significant increases in recall and the F1-score, indicating that updating the BN layers even with a single target instance successfully adapts to the target domain. This demonstrates that normalization with the fixed statistics is robust against a smaller batch size and the distribution shifts when updating the learnable parameters.

The variant "TEMPLE w/o PL" showed performance improvements across all metrics compared to "TEMPLE w/o memory and PL". This suggests that employing the memory bank to update the learnable parameters of the BN layers enhances stability, in contrast to updates based on individual instances.

TEMPLE showed significant improvements in performance across all metrics. Specifically, the increases in the F1-score of 81.09% and the area under receiver operating characteristic (AUROC) of 83.92% are particularly noteworthy, addressing a strong ability of the model to discriminate between the driver states under domain shift conditions.

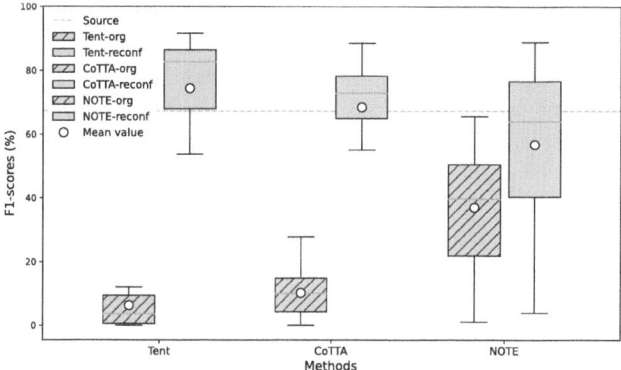

Fig. 3. Performance comparison for the configuration of the existing TTA baselines on a sustained-attention driving dataset. The gray horizontal line represents the average F1-score of the pre-trained EEGNet8,2 model without TTA. "org" (hatch pattern) and "reconf" (plain pattern) of every method indicate their proposed setup and manipulated setup with our proposed configuration, respectively. The overall performances of the existing TTA baselines significantly increase after the manipulation of the BN layers.

4.6   Configuration of the BN Layers for the Existing TTA Baselines

We manipulated the configurations of the BN layers for the existing TTA baselines that update the BN layers [6,29]. NOTE [6] updated the normalization statistics and the learnable parameters with the input target data while Tent [29] estimated the batch statistics and updated the learnable parameters with the input target data. In addition, CoTTA [30] updated all parameters in the model with the input target data, where the BN layers initialized the pre-trained normalization statistics but normalized with the input batch statistics for both adaptation and prediction.

As shown in Fig. 3, the overall performance increased significantly after manipulation with our proposed configuration of the BN layers. In particular, Tent [29] and CoTTA [30] not only significantly improved their average F1-scores, but also outperformed the average F1-score of the source baseline model. Ultimately, our results demonstrate that employing fixed normalization statistics for normalization enhances robustness against domain shifts, surpassing the performance of existing BN layer configurations.

5 Conclusions

In this paper, we introduce a novel online brain-computer interface (BCI) framework for electroencephalogram (EEG)-based driver drowsiness classification, leveraging test-time adaptation (TTA) methods. Our approach, *test-time entropy minimization with prototype learning for EEG signals* (TEMPLE), effectively addresses the critical challenges within online BCI frameworks. TEMPLE stands out by preserving pre-trained statistics of the batch normalization layers while updating their learnable parameters, significantly enhancing its robustness against the inherent noise and variability in EEG signals. Our proposed memory bank effectively captures and adapts to the evolving patterns of the EEG signals using a novel sampling technique considering the energy score and timeliness. Moreover, we introduce prototype learning, which continually updates the model's understanding with each new instance. Our comprehensive experiments show the superiority of our proposed methods, achieving the highest performance among all existing TTA baselines. This demonstrates the effectiveness and reliability of the TTA methods within the EEG-based driver drowsiness classification framework.

Acknowledgment. This work was supported by the Institute of Information & Communications Technology Planning & Evaluation (IITP) grant, funded by the Korea government (MSIT) (No. 2019-0-00079, Artificial Intelligence Graduate School Program (Korea University); No. 2021-0-02068, Artificial Intelligence Innovation Hub; No. 2021-0-00866, Development of BMI application technology based on multiple bio-signals for autonomous vehicle drivers).

References

1. Bartler, A., Bender, F., Wiewel, F., Yang, B.: TTAPS: test-time adaption by aligning prototypes using self-supervision. In: International Joint Conference on Neural Networks (IJCNN), pp. 1–8 (2022)
2. Cao, Z., Chuang, C.-H., King, J.-K., Lin, C.-T.: Multi-channel EEG recordings during a sustained-attention driving task. Sci. Data **6**, 19 (2019)
3. Cui, J., Lan, Z., Sourina, O., Müller-Wittig, W.: EEG-based cross-subject driver drowsiness recognition with an interpretable convolutional neural network. IEEE Trans. Neural Netw. Learn. Syst. 7921–7933 (2022)

4. Cui, Y., Xu, Y., Wu, D.: EEG-based driver drowsiness estimation using feature weighted episodic training. IEEE Trans. Neural Syst. Rehabil. Eng. **27**(11), 2263–2273 (2019)

5. Djurisic, A., Bozanic, N., Ashok, A., Liu, R.: Extremely simple activation shaping for out-of-distribution detection. In: International Conference on Learning Representations (ICLR), pp. 1–12 (2023)

6. Gong, T., et al.: Note: robust continual test-time adaptation against temporal correlation. In: Advances in Neural Information Processing Systems (NeurIPS), pp. 27253–27266 (2022)

7. Hwang, S., Park, S., Kim, D., Lee, J., Byun, H.: Mitigating inter-subject brain signal variability for EEG-based driver fatigue state classification. In: IEEE International Conference on Acoustics, Speech and Signal Processing (ICASSP), pp. 990–994 (2021)

8. Ioffe, S., Szegedy, C.: Batch normalization: accelerating deep network training by reducing internal covariate shift. In: International Conference on Machine Learning (ICML), pp. 448–456 (2015)

9. Iwasawa, Y., Matsuo, Y.: Test-time classifier adjustment module for model-agnostic domain generalization. In: Advances in Neural Information Processing Systems (NeurIPS), pp. 2427–2440 (2021)

10. Jiang, X., Zhao, J., Du, B., Yuan, Z.: Self-supervised contrastive learning for EEG-based sleep staging. In: International Joint Conference on Neural Networks (IJCNN), pp. 1–8 (2021)

11. Jin, L., Kim, E.-Y.: E-emoticonnet: EEG-based emotion recognition with context information. In: International Joint Conference on Neural Networks (IJCNN), pp. 1–8 (2022)

12. Kim, D.-Y., Han, D.-K., Jeong, J.-H., Lee, S.-W.: EEG-based driver drowsiness classification via calibration-free framework with domain generalization. In: IEEE International Conference on Systems, Man, and Cybernetics (SMC), pp. 2293–2298 (2022)

13. Kingma, D.-P., Ba, J.: Adam: a method for stochastic optimization. In: International Conference on Learning Representations (ICLR), pp. 1–11 (2015)

14. Lawhern, V.-J., et al.: EEGNet: a compact convolutional neural network for EEG-based brain-computer interfaces. J. Neural Eng. **15**(5), 056013 (2018)

15. Lee, S.-H., Lee, M.-J., Jeong, J.-H., Lee, S.-W.: Towards an EEG-based intuitive BCI communication system using imagined speech and visual imagery. In: 2019 IEEE International Conference on Systems, Man and Cybernetics (SMC), pp. 4409–4414 (2019)

16. Lee, S.-H., Lee, M., Lee, S.-W.: Neural decoding of imagined speech and visual imagery as intuitive paradigms for BCI communication. IEEE Trans. Neural Syst. Rehabil. Eng. **28**(12), 2647–2659 (2020)

17. Lee, S.-B., et al.: Comparative analysis of features extracted from EEG spatial, spectral and temporal domains for binary and multiclass motor imagery classification. Inf. Sci. **502**, 190–200 (2019)

18. Li, G., et al.: Adaptive prototype learning and allocation for few-shot segmentation. In: Proceedings of the IEEE/CVF Conference on Computer Vision and Pattern Recognition (CVPR), pp. 8334–8343 (2021)

19. Li, R., Gao, R., Suganthan, P.-N.: A decomposition-based hybrid ensemble CNN framework for driver fatigue recognition. Inf. Sci. **624**, 833–848 (2023)

20. Lin, C.-T., et al.: A driving performance forecasting system based on brain dynamic state analysis using 4-D convolutional neural networks. IEEE Trans. Cybern. **51**(10), 4959–4967 (2020)

21. Liu, W., Wang, X., Owens, J., Li, Y.: Energy-based out-of-distribution detection. In: Advances in Neural Information Processing Systems (NeurIPS), pp. 21464–21475 (2020)
22. Mane, R., et al.: FBCNet: a multi-view convolutional neural network for brain-computer interface. arXiv preprint arXiv:2104.01233 (2021)
23. Niu, S., et al.: Towards stable test-time adaptation in dynamic wild world. In: International Conference on Learning Representations (ICLR), pp. 1–14 (2023)
24. Paulo, J.-R., Pires, G., Nunes, U.-J.: Cross-subject zero calibration driver's drowsiness detection: exploring spatiotemporal image encoding of EEG signals for convolutional neural network classification. IEEE Trans. Neural Syst. Rehabil. Eng. **29**, 905–915 (2021)
25. Ray, A.-M., et al.: A subject-independent pattern-based brain-computer interface. Front. Behav. Neurosci. **9**, 1–15 (2015)
26. Schirrmeister, R.-T., et al.: Deep learning with convolutional neural networks for EEG decoding and visualization. Hum. Brain Mapp. **38**(11), 5391–5420 (2017)
27. Snell, J., Swersky, K., Zemel, R.: Prototypical networks for few-shot learning. In: Advances in Neural Information Processing Systems (NeurIPS), pp. 1–11 (2017)
28. Suk, H.-I., Fazli, S., Mehnert, J., Müller, K.-R., Lee, S.-W.: Predicting BCI subject performance using probabilistic spatio-temporal filters. PLoS ONE **9**(2), e87056 (2014)
29. Wang, D., Shelhamer, E., Liu, S., Olshausen, B., Darrell, T.: Tent: fully test-time adaptation by entropy minimization. In: International Conference on Learning Representations (ICLR), pp. 1–12 (2021)
30. Wang, Q., Fink, O., Van Gool, L., Dai, D.: Continual test-time domain adaptation. In: Proceedings of the IEEE/CVF Conference on Computer Vision and Pattern Recognition (CVPR), pp. 7201–7211 (2022)
31. Wei, C.-S., Wang, Y.-T., Lin, C.-T., Jung, T.-P.: Toward drowsiness detection using non-hair-bearing EEG-based brain-computer interfaces. IEEE Trans. Neural Syst. Rehabil. Eng. **26**(2), 400–406 (2018)
32. Yuan, L., Xie, B., Li, S.: Robust test-time adaptation in dynamic scenarios. In: Proceedings of the IEEE/CVF Conference on Computer Vision and Pattern Recognition (CVPR), pp. 15922–15932 (2023)
33. Zhang, X., et al.: Fatigue detection with covariance manifolds of electroencephalography in transportation industry. IEEE Trans. Industr. Inf. **17**(5), 3497–3507 (2020)
34. Zhou, K., Yang, Y., Qiao, Y., Xiang, T.: Domain generalization with mixstyle. In: International Conference on Learning Representations (ICLR), pp. 1–12 (2021)

Poster Session

A Novel Post-Hoc Explanation Comparison Metric and Applications

Shreyan Mitra[1]($\boxtimes$) and Leilani Gilpin[2]

[1] Paul G. Allen School of Computer Science and Engineering,
University of Washington at Seattle, Seattle, USA
`s99s42m@uw.edu`
[2] Baskin School of Engineering, University of California at Santa Cruz,
Santa Cruz, USA

Abstract. Explanatory systems ("explainers") make the behavior of blackbox machine learning models more transparent. However, the results of different explainers ("explanations") are often inconsistent with each other. To measure such differences, we propose a novel metric, the Shreyan Distance d_S. This paper uses d_S to compare two explanatory systems, SHAP and LIME, for both regression and classification learning tasks on tabular data. We find that the linearly weighted mean d_S value varies significantly between these two tasks. This leads us to conclude that consistency between explainers depends not only on inherent properties of the explainers themselves, but also on the type of learning task. In the hopes that more accurately quantifying differences between existing explainers will lead to better explanations in the future, we demonstrate a way to integrate our novel metric into existing machine learning pipelines via the XAISuite library.

1 Introduction

From self-driving cars to customer support chat-bots, machine learning models have become pervasive in our daily lives [1]. The problem is that these machine learning models are opaque; the underlying model processes are not known by humans. When these opaque systems are being entrusted with human-level decisions, e.g., sentencing convicts or driving a car, they will need to be able to explain themselves to justify their behavior [2].

This is especially pertinent when such opaque models fail. In 2016, a ProPublica article revealed that Northpointe, a widely used criminal risk assessment tool, was racially biased. It incorrectly rated incarcerated African Americans as more likely to commit future crimes than Caucasians [3]. And in 2018, a self-driving car hit and tragically killed a cyclist [4]. The machine learning model in the car was unable to reconcile contrasting information from various sensors, and thus failed to make the right decision [5].

Explanatory systems produce explanations, also known as model-dependent justifications [6]. They provide one way to understand machine learning models.

C. Wallraven et al. (Eds.): ICPRAI 2024, LNCS 14892, pp. 427–446, 2025.
https://doi.org/10.1007/978-981-97-8702-9_29

However, for explanations to be trustworthy, it is essential that they are consistent and accurate [7]. Currently, there is no standard definition of explainer consistency and accuracy. Therefore, we define consistency as having two components. The first part is reproducibility - applying explanation methods repeatedly should yield the same results. Secondly, the results of different explanatory methods in similar scenarios should be similar. By accurate, we mean that the justifications provided by explanation systems are correct.

In this paper, we focus on interexplanatory consistency among two state of the art explanatory systems - SHAP [8], based on the game theory concept of Shapley values and LIME [9], which stands for local interpretable model-agnostic explanations. Specifically, we propose an approach to compare SHAP and LIME and to automatically detect cases where they are inconsistent. The underlying process demonstrated here for comparing two explainers can be extended to any number of them.

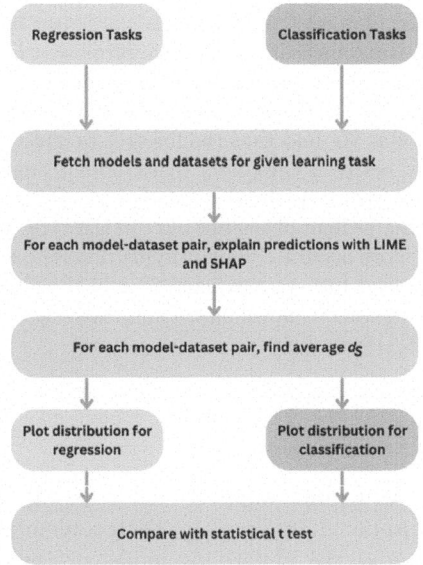

Fig. 1. An overview of the comparison methodology used in this paper to compare explanation differences in regression and classification tasks

By highlighting the inconsistencies between explanatory systems, this paper lays the groundwork for future work in getting explainers to converge on consistent, accurate justifications of model behavior. More consistent explanations will provide users and stakeholders a supported reason behind system malfunctions. In addition, system debugging and diagnosis will be more efficient when there are no disagreements about the reason for a particular behavior.

Consistent explanations are the first step towards trustworthy explanations. Without trustworthy explanations, users are effectively blind to the operation of machine learning models and cannot mitigate model flaws. Our work therefore answers the following research questions:

1) How can consistency between explanatory systems be measured?
2) How can the metric calculated in (1) be used to draw generalized conclusions about the consistency of explanatory systems for a given dataset and learning task?
3) How can comparison of explanatory systems be integrated into conventional machine learning pipelines for use in larger scales?

In this paper, we present the Shreyan Distance and the XAISuite Library, both of which attempt to answer these questions. The Shreyan Distance measures consistency between explainers by comparing ranked feature importance lists from each explainer. This is a potential solution to Question 1. In addition, by using the Shreyan Distance to identify patterns in explainer similarities across various datasets and learning tasks, we seek to answer Question 2. And finally, the XAISuite library offers a seamless way to integrate the Shreyan Distance with other common machine learning utilities through wide-ranging compatibility and a comprehensive model-selection-to-explanation framework. This is our response to Question 3.

2   Background/Related Work

Our paper builds on previous work on vector comparison, explanations, failure analysis, and machine learning error.

2.1   Vector Comparison

In this paper, we compare vectors containing features ordered by importance. Several methods to compare vectors ("distance metrics") exist.

The Euclidean distance is the length of the line segment between two points. Previous research has shown the ineffectiveness of the Euclidean distance for high-dimensional spaces [10], rendering it a poor comparison metric for explainers, especially in learning tasks with a large number of features. The Spearman's Distance is the square of the Euclidean distance between two ranked vectors, and is often used as a measure of disarray [11]. However, it cannot be easily applied to comparing ordered feature importance lists produced by explainers. This is because Spearman's Distance does not weigh differences in certain vector dimensions more than differences in others. However, in explanation comparison, differences in what the explainers detect as the most important feature are more significant than disagreements about less important features. d_S rectifies this by assigning a weightage to each vector dimension.

Both the Pearson's correlation coefficient and Kendall's rank correlation coefficient (also referred to as Kendall's Tau) pose the same problem as Spearman's Distance, i.e. they fail to take into account weight differences between different vector dimensions. While Kendall's Tau is specifically less sensitive to variations in data than other metrics, it is affected equally by equal changes in different vector dimensions. A weighted Kendall's Tau statistic [12] has been proposed. However, there are important differences between a weighted Kendall's Tau and d_S. The lowest value of the weighted Kendall's Tau metric is -1, which indicates a perfect negative relationship between two variables. However, the lowest value of d_S, 0, does not necessarily indicate a perfect negative relationship, but the highest cumulative weighted difference. In this paper, we make a key assumption regarding user expectations, namely that two explainers are perceived to share some similarity if they share a feature-rank pair in common, even if they are negatively correlated overall. The emphasis of d_S on weighted difference over correlation reflects this.

2.2   Metrics for Explanation Accuracy

Recall from the introduction that explainer accuracy is how similar the justifications produced by explanation systems are to reality. In this section, we provide an overview of existing explanatory accuracy baselines.

A research paper published by DeepMind [13] suggests that machine learning is analogous to human thought and can be explained through similar processes. The paper explores the use of cognitive psychology to explain the decisions of machine learning models, drawing parallels between biases humans develop during their maturation and those acquired by machine learning. By likening machine learning models to humans, the paper provides a framework to determine which explanations have a higher probability of being accurate. Since explanations are ultimately meant for human understanding, we find the use of psychology in explanation generation promising and perhaps capable of resolving the discrepancies between explanatory systems found in this paper.

Gilpin et al. [7] state that what is defined as accurate might depend on user requirements. They note a tradeoff between completeness and interpretability that all explanatory systems must follow - the more accurate explanations are, the less likely they are to be understandable by humans. This tradeoff may affect the discrepancies between different explanatory models. Thus, a key part of future explanatory system research is creating explainers that gain the user's trust [14]. We see our work in quantifying explainer consistency as integral to that effort. Research on user requirements for explanations is elaborated on further later in this section.

Han et al. [15] propose that different explanatory systems are optimal for different scenarios, and an "adversarial" sample exists that will lead to a large error for any given explanatory system. For example, while SHAP and LIME are both based on local function approximation (LFA), they differ in their optimal intervals due to their noise functions. This can help explain the discrepancies between SHAP and LIME that we observe in our research. Prior work on explanation comparison is explored later in this section.

2.3   On User Requirements for Meaningful Explanations

Numerous papers [16–18] have highlighted the importance of user expectations in explanation utility. Since user expectations are often implicit, determining what type of explanations users are looking for is difficult. The XAISuite library described later in this paper alleviates this problem by providing users with the option to use multiple explanatory systems, compare them, and choose the explanations most suitable to their scenario.

Chazette et al. [19] previously created a framework for explanatory systems embedded in user trust. Consistency was a key factor in their analysis, and the XAISuite library is designed keeping the requirements outlined in the paper in mind.

Machine learning models need to be safe and trustworthy, especially when entrusted with human-level decision making. [20]. One way to ensure safety is to have stricter requirements and guarantees. In 2021, Nadia Burkart and Marco Huber [21] laid out the requirements of explainable supervised machine learning models. Our paper implements two of their requirements: (1) We make explanation of machine learning models more easily available through our open source XAISuite library and (2) By highlighting inconsistencies between explanatory systems, we set the scene for more consistent and trustworthy explainers.

User requirements for explanations may vary in specialized fields. Ghassemi et al. [22] argue against the use of explainers in the medical profession, claiming that the many failures and contradictions of explanatory systems endanger the trust of healthcare professionals and the lives of patients. They propose that machine learning models be rigorously tested instead. However, we believe that the solution to explainer error is not abandoning explanatory systems altogether, but to improve them until they are trustworthy. Our analysis of explainer consistency is a step in this direction because it highlights contradictions among different explanatory systems and identifies particular test cases that lead to explainer inconsistency.

2.4   Explaining Machine Learning Failure

Examples of machine learning failure abound, but Gilpin et al. [7] specifically note several cases where machine learning systems fail, including racially biased criminal-assessment tools and flawed categorization due to the introduction of noise. For users to trust ML systems, they need to be able to understand the rationale behind mistakes made by machine learning models on such cases where the input leads to machine learning errors [23]. A user of the XAISuite library has the ability to consult different explainers, a key part of gaining more insight about such "adversarial" cases.

2.5   On Comparing Explanatory Systems

Comparing explanatory models is an open area of research. Differences between the explanations generated by different explainers is sometimes known as the "disagreement problem" [24].

In their paper, Covert et al. [25] point out that while there are many different explanatory methods, it remains unknown how "most methods are related or when one method is preferable to another." The authors propose a new class of similar explanations supported by cognitive psychology called removal-based explanations. These systems determine the importance of a feature by analyzing the impact of its removal. The paper specifically highlights that as SHAP and LIME are both part of the removal-based explanatory framework, they share a resemblance. The discrepancies between SHAP and LIME shown in our paper are markers of where two very similar explanatory systems with related internal mechanisms can differ.

Roy et al. [26] in "Why Don't XAI Techniques Agree?" acknowledged that SHAP and LIME explanations often disagree and that users do not know which method to trust. They proposed an aggregate explainer that focuses on the similarities between SHAP and LIME and disregarded discrepancies. But the authors of that paper do not set forth a way to find and resolve the discrepancies. We contribute a method to empower users to better identify points of disagreement between SHAP and LIME and come to a decision.

Van der Waa et al. [27] extended explanatory system comparison further with a detailed analysis of rule-based versus example-based explanations, with implications on user trust and accuracy. Our contribution allows users to validate this analysis by highlighting the differences between explanatory systems rather than trusting only one of them.

Duell et al. [28] specifically compares the results of explanatory systems such as SHAP and LIME on electronic health records. They note significant differences in importance scores between the explanatory systems, stating that "studied XAI methods circumstantially generate different top features; their aberrations in shared feature importance merit further exploration from domain-experts to evaluate human trust towards XAI." While this aligns with the results of our paper, we extend the study to different types of data outside of health records. We also create a generalized machine learning pipeline to help in the "further exploration" Duell et al. deemed necessary.

The in-depth comparison that we perform between two explanatory systems has been previously explored. A paper published by Lee et al. [29] compares breakDown (BD) and SHAP explainers in the specific case of classification of multi-principal element alloys. However, their work is not generalizable to all data and all machine learning models, which our contribution is. That paper also does not propose a systematic way to compare explainers, which we do. In our work, we use various models on data of different types to allow us to have a better picture of exactly what factors affect explainer consistency. Furthermore, we compare multiple commonly used machine learning models in the field, and thus our results are more applicable to different machine learning tasks.

2.6   Related Software

Various tools similar to XAISuite also exist. However, the contribution of a novel explanation comparison metric is unique to XAISuite.

1) Agarwal et al. [30] created a tool, OpenXAI, for evaluating and benchmarking post-hoc explanation systems, comparable in functionality and user interface to our XAISuite. While OpenXAI focuses more on accuracy of explanatory systems over one another in specific tasks, we put a heavier emphasis on consistency for all tasks. Furthermore, we integrate explanatory comparison into XAISuite.
2) Yang et al. [31] created the OmniXAI library for explainable AI that allows easy access to numerous explainers for a particular machine learning model. The OmniXAI library serves as part of the backend of the XAISuite library by helping to fetch explanatory systems that the user requests. The XAISuite library's data visualization and explanation comparison abilities build on the core functionality offered by OmniXAI.
3) Captum, similar to OmniXAI, was proposed by Kohklikyan et al. [32]. In their implementation of the XAISuite library, the authors believed that OmniXAI was easier to work with.

3 Methods

We take a theoretical, experimental, and a software developmental approach in this paper. Therefore, we divide the methodology into three parts: (1) developing the Shreyan Distance metric (2) using the metric to compare the results of SHAP and LIME across a variety of datasets and learning tasks, and (3) building an adaptable software system using the XAISuite Framework.

3.1 The Shreyan Distance

The Shreyan Distance d_S is defined as:

Definition 3.1 (Shreyan Distance): $d_S = 1 - \frac{\sum_{n=1}^{x} P(n,x) \cdot |r(n) - r*(n)|}{\sum_{n=1}^{\alpha} P(n,x)(x-2n+1) + \sum_{n=\alpha+1}^{x} P(n,x) \cdot \alpha}$
where $\alpha = \lfloor x/2 \rfloor$ and $P(n,x)$ is the weighting function for elements of rank n in vectors r and $r*$ of equal size x

Weighting Functions
Below, we include a table (see Table 1) of various weightings and the corresponding value of P. We also graph out the various weighting functions for $x = 5$ (see Fig. 2):

Table 1. .

Weighting	Weighting Function
Linear	$x - n + 1$
Hyperbolic	x/n
Exponential	$x \cdot e^{n-1}$

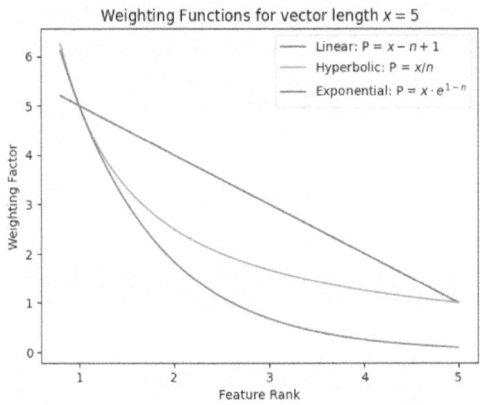

Fig. 2. Weighting functions for $x = 5$

Simplistically, d_S can be thought of as

$$1 - \frac{\text{sum of weighted differences between vectors}}{\text{maximum possible sum of weighted difference between vectors}}$$

The d_{max} Value

The expression for the denominator of the fractional term in the definition of d_S is

$$d_{max} = \sum_{n=1}^{\alpha} P(n, x)(x - 2n + 1) + \sum_{n=\alpha+1}^{x} P(n, x) \cdot \alpha,$$

It is derived by noting the fact that for any ordered vector of length x : $[1, 2, 3, ...x]$, the maximum cumulative weighted difference (for a monotonically decreasing, positive weighting function) between elements of this vector and another occurs when we compare it to the vector $[x, x - 1, ..., \lfloor x/2 \rfloor + 1] + [1, 2, ..., \lfloor x/2 \rfloor]$. A brief proof outline of this follows:

Proof outline of value of d_{max}

Consider the vector $a = [1, 2, 3, ...x]$ of length x. Let b be the vector which will give us the maximum cumulative weighted difference with a for a monotonically decreasing, positive weighting function.

   Observe the following:

1) Since the weighted function is always positive across its domain, the cumulative weighted difference is positively related to the cumulative nonweighted difference. (By nonweighted here, we mean weight $P = 1$). Therefore we must seek to maximize the difference between the two elements at the same index position of a and b, i.e. we must optimize $| a[i] - b[i] |$ for an index i
2) Since the weighted function is monotonically decreasing, differences in earlier indices matter more. We must prioritize maximizing the difference between the elements of a and b at these indices.

   Observations 1 and 2 lead to the following algorithm for determining b:

1) Start at the first index (with rank value 1 in vector a) and repeat the following steps for all indices i from 1 to x.
2) Find an element in a with which the current element has the maximum difference. This element is the ith element of b.
3) Once an element has been put in b, it is eliminated from further consideration for the previous step for all future indices.

This algorithm gives us the first element of b is x, since that has the largest difference with 1. Similarly, the second element of b is $x - 1$, assuming $x > 1$. However, when we reach the "middle element" of a, which is $\lfloor \frac{x}{2} \rfloor + 1$, all the elements in a in the next indices have already been used in b and all the elements before haven't. So, we reverse the direction of the difference and the element of b at the same index as $\lfloor \frac{x}{2} \rfloor + 1$ in a is 1. For $\lfloor \frac{x}{2} \rfloor + 2$ in a, b has 2, and so on.

To illustrate this concept, we construct a diagram (see Fig. 3) for $x = 9$. The arrows depict the direction of the difference (from larger to smaller element). The red arrows represent the element pairings before reaching the "middle element" of a, and the blue arrows, after. Notice that each element has exactly one arrow going into and out of it. This represents the fact that all element in a are in b and all elements in b are in a.

Now, the cumulative weighted difference between a and b, where b is derived in the manner detailed in this outline, can easily be proved to be d_{max} as defined before.

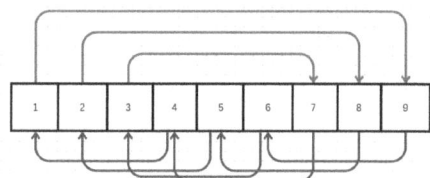

Fig. 3. A visualization of how vector b is derived for $x = 9$. Here, $b = [9, 8, 7, 6, 1, 2, 3, 4, 5]$

Properties of d_S

In this section, we present 5 properties of d_S. Where applicable, we include concrete examples illustrating each property.

1) Commutative Property: It can be shown that the Shreyan Distance is commutative. That is, the distance between two vectors a and b is equal to the distance between b and a for all a, b.
2) Different Weightings Give Similar Results: Different weightings of d_S produce similar distance measurements even though they have different probability distributions, allowing the Shreyan Distance algorithm to generate an illustrative number which can be used to draw conclusions about the similarity between two explainers.

Take the following feature importance lists produced by two explainers, Explainer 1 and Explainer 2. The lists have already been enumerated for simplicity, i.e. the features have been assigned corresponding numbers.

Explainer 1: [1, 2, 3, 4, 5]

Explainer 2: [2, 1, 3, 5, 4]

Using linear weighting, the Shreyan Distance between these two explainer results is $d_S = 0.7$. For this case, using the hyperbolic or exponential weightings also gives approximately 0.7, rounded to two significant figures. We take a Shreyan Distance value of 0.7 to indicate moderate similarity.

3) Rank Matters: Shreyan's Distance is catered specifically to the comparison of explanatory features and other ranked vectors because it puts greater emphasis on differences among elements at higher rank positions. This reflects our previously discussed key assumption that users care more about consistency in the most important feature detected by different explainers than consistency is less important features

Here are three vectors:

Vector 1: [1, 2, 3, 4, 5]

Vector 2: [1, 2, 3, 5, 4]

Vector 3: [2, 1, 3, 4, 5]

The Spearman's Distance between Vector 1 and Vector 2 and the Spearman's Distance between Vector 1 and Vector 3 are the same (the value is 2 for both). But this is not realistic in an explainer importance context, since we would expect Vector 1 and Vector 2 to be more similar. The vector elements are ordered by descending importance, and so Vector 1 and Vector 2's differences are comparatively smaller than those between Vector 1 and Vector 3. This is reflected by the Shreyan Distances (again, we use linear weighting):

d_S between Vector 1 and Vector 2: ≈ 0.987

d_S between Vector 1 and Vector 3: ≈ 0.734

4) Negative Correlation $\neq$ **Maximum Difference**: Two vectors that are negatively correlated do not have the lowest Shreyan Distance value.

Take the following feature importance lists produced by two explainers, Explainer 1 and Explainer 2.

Explainer 1: [1, 2, 3, 4, 5]

Explainer 2: [5, 4, 3, 2, 1]

The two vectors are perfectly negatively correlated. They have a Kendall's Tau value of −1.

We might expect the Shreyan Distance to similarly be the lowest possible value: 0. But linear-weighted d_S between these two vectors is 0.05, not 0. Again, the 0.05, however small, is an acknowledgement of key assumptions made about user expectations in this paper.

5) Bimodality and Skew of Density Distributions: Shreyan Distance distributions are bimodal, while other distance metrics are unimodal. Furthermore, d_S distributions have a definite positive skew. A detailed examination of these properties and their implications is left for future research. But, more generally, the authors posit that these two properties are a result of (1) *alertness*, the tendency of d_S to mark two vectors as more dissimilar compared to other metrics, and (2) the observation that, given an explanation, there are two classes of explainers: those whose output matches closely with the results, and those whose output has very little similarity with the result. *Alertness* is especially important in the field of explanations, where even the slightest discrepancy can negatively affect user trust.

As an example, we include overlaid kernel density plots (see Fig. 4) of the distribution of distances returned by various weightings of the Shreyan Distance and other metrics for the vector [1,2,3,4,5] (notice $x = 5$) and all 5! possible permutations of this vector (e.g. [5,4,3,2,1], [1,2,3,5,4], etc.) The Shreyan Distance distributions are filled, while the others are marked with dashed lines.

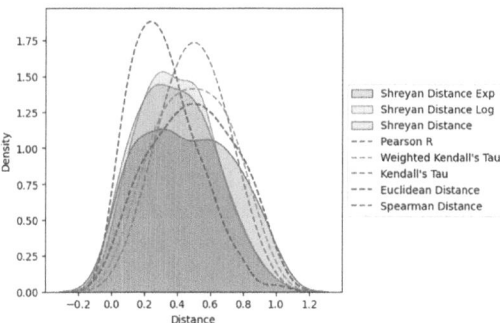

Fig. 4. Density Plots for Shreyan Distance and Other Distance Metrics, $x = 5$

3.2   Comparing Explainers Across Tasks and Models

The models we use in our analysis, along with the task for which they will be used, are listed in Table 2.

Table 2. Machine learning models used for regression and classification tasks. All models were used with default, non-optimized parameters.

Task	Models
Regression	ARDRegression, AdaBoostRegressor, BaggingRegressor, Bayesian-Ridge, DecisionTreeRegressor, DummyRegressor, ElasticNet, ElasticNetCV, ExtraTreeRegressor, ExtraTreesRegressor, GaussianProcessRegressor, GradientBoostingRegressor, HistGradientBoostingRegressor, HuberRegressor, KNeighborsRegressor, KernelRidge, Lars, LarsCV, Lasso, LassoCV, LassoLars, LassoLarsCV, LinearSVR, MLPRegressor, NuSVR, OrthogonalMatchingPursuit, OrthogonalMatchingPursuitCV, PLSRegression, PassiveAggressiveRegressor, PoissonRegressor, QuantileRegressor, RandomForestRegressor, Ridge, RidgeCV, SGDRegressor, SVR, TheilSenRegressor, TransformedTargetRegressor, TweedieRegressor
Classification	AdaBoostClassifier, BaggingClassifier, BernoulliNB, CalibratedClassifierCV, DecisionTreeClassifier, DummyClassifier, ExtraTreeClassifier, ExtraTreesClassifier, GaussianNB, GaussianProcessClassifier, GradientBoostingClassifier, HistGradientBoostingClassifier, KNeighborsClassifier, LinearDiscriminantAnalysis, LinearSVC, LogisticRegressionCV, MLPClassifier, NuSVC, Perceptron, QuadraticDiscriminantAnalysis, RandomForestClassifier, RidgeClassifier, RidgeClassifierCV, SGDClassifier, SVC

While we focus only on SHAP and LIME explanations for tabular data, we hope further work will consider other explanatory methods and widen the scope of our research to image and textual data. Furthermore, only supervised learning tasks are studied in this paper, unsupervised learning methods (like clustering, for example) can also be explained and should be the focus of future research. Finally, although specific examples are provided, this paper does *not* demonstrate empirical proof of d_S being a better measure of explanation difference than other similar metrics, like Kendall's Tau or Spearman's Distance. This is due to time and space constraints. However, we hope to show this in future papers. See more information in the paragraph on future work in the Conclusion section.

For the remainder of the paper, note that "Shreyan Distance" or "d_S" refers to the linear weighting of our metric, as opposed to a hyperbolic or exponential weighting.

To compare SHAP and LIME for 64 models across both regression and classification tasks, we follow the procedure below. This procedure is also briefly outlined in Fig. 1

1) Install the XAISuite library (to be discussed in Section C) from the Python Package Index.

2) Install the SciKit-Learn library from the Python Package Index if it is not already automatically installed through XAISuite.
3) Install the SciPy library from the Python Package Index.
4) Let *regData* be an array holding data from the regression tasks and *classData* be an array holding data from the classification tasks.
5) Regression Tasks: For each regression model in Table 2,
   - Use the XAISuite library to calculate the average Shreyan Distance scores on a regression dataset of size n generated by SciKit-Learn. In our research, we take $n = 100$. Regenerate the dataset for each iteration.
   - Repeat this three times for each model. Append all three Shreyan Distance results to *regData*
6) Classification Tasks: For each classification model in Table 2,
   - Use the XAISuite library to calculate the average Shreyan Distance scores on a classification dataset of size n generated by SciKit-Learn. In our research, we take $n = 100$. Regenerate the dataset for each iteration.
   - Repeat this three times for each model. Append all three Shreyan Distance results to *classData*
7) Use the stats package of SciPy to perform a 2-sample t-test for difference in population means using *regData* and *classData* as the two samples. We assume that the scores in *regData* and *classData* are independent and have equal variance. Use a $\alpha = 0.05$ or 5% significance level.

   For the t-test, use the following hypotheses:

   Null Hypothesis H_o: There is no difference between the true mean LIME and SHAP similarity (as measured using the Shreyan Distance) between classification and regression tasks.

   Alternate Hypothesis H_a: There is a difference between the true mean LIME and SHAP similarity (as measured using the Shreyan Distance) between classification and regression tasks.
8) Interpret the results of the statistical test to determine whether there is significant evidence that the true SHAP and LIME similarity, as measured by the Shreyan Distance, is different for regression and classification tasks.

Below, in Listing 1 we include setup code that implements the procedure above:

```
from xaisuite import*
import seaborn as sns
import scipy.stats as stats
#The variable definitions for reg_models and class_models are
    not included here for the sake of space. See Table 1.
regData = []
classData = []
for model in reg_models:
  for i in range(3):
      corr = InsightGenerator(ModelTrainer(model,
    DataProcessor(DataLoader(make_regression) , processor =
    ''TabularTransform"), explainers = {"lime": {"
    feature_selection": ''none"}, ''shap":{}}).
    getExplanationsFor([])).calculateExplainerSimilarity("
    lime", ''shap")
```

```
        regData.append(corr)
for model in class_models:
  for i in range(3):
      corr = InsightGenerator(ModelTrainer(model,
      DataProcessor(DataLoader(make_classification) , processor
      = ``TabularTransform"), explainers = {"lime": {"
      feature_selection": ``none"}, ``shap":{}}).
      getExplanationsFor([])).calculateExplainerSimilarity("
      lime", ``shap")
        classData.append(corr)
sns.kdeplot(regData, label = 'Regression Distribution')
sns.kdeplot(classData, label = 'Classification Distribution')
stats.ttest_ind(a=regData, b=classData, equal_var=True)
```

Listing 1. Setup script for SHAP and LIME comparison

3.3   The XAISuite Library and Framework

We now present the XAISuite framework, a unified tool for comparing explanatory systems. It forms the basis of the XAISuite library, which enables users to train and explain models with minimal input. It also answers one of our primary research questions by integrating the Shreyan Distance metric into machine learning pipelines. In constructing this library, we build on OmniXAI [31], which allows direct access to different explainers. An earlier version of XAISuite was first proposed by the authors in a separate paper [33].

A brief overview of the XAISuite framework is presented in Fig. 5. The framework consists of four components: data loading and processing, machine learning model training and explanation, and explanation generation.

We contribute the XAISuite framework with the intention for it to be a standard platform for training, explaining, and analyzing models. The framework was constructed based on five key factors:

1) **Simplicity:** Containing just three parts which depend on data retrieval, function calls, and writing to output files, XAISuite provides guiding principles for any implementation to enhance code changes and user convenience.
2) **Integratablity:** A library is limited if it cannot be used with other libraries. Core functionalities, like model training, explanation generation, and graphics creation, are designed to use external libraries. However, the framework is flexible and not based on any specific external dependency, so there is flexibility in the way in which the model is trained or explanations are generated.
3) **Flexibility:** A key feature of XAISuite is flexibility. This is enabled by the lack of specifics and the use of general terms. Note that *any* dataset can be used, *any* model can be trained, *any* explanatory system can be initialized, depending on the implementation. The templates have no fixed form, nor is the form of data storage specified. As mentioned in the previous point, the XAISuite framework is compatible with any potential provider of its constituent parts, whether they be model libraries(sk-learn, XGBoost, etc.),

transform function types (Logarithmic, Exponential, etc.), or different data storage options (Dataframe, Numpy, Files, etc.).

4) **Usability:** Users are the center of explainability research [16], and so any interface that facilitates interactions between the user and explanatory system must be user-centric. XAISuite achieves this by ensuring that results are understandable in a readable table or graphical format. Again, individual implementations of data or graph generation may vary, but by enforcing the requirement of converting data into a portable and visualizable medium, XAISuite reinforces the human-centric approach that is a hallmark of explainability research.

5) **Expandability:** XAISuite is not designed to be a closed system. There are opportunities for users to extend existing functionalities or link XAISuite with other existing frameworks.

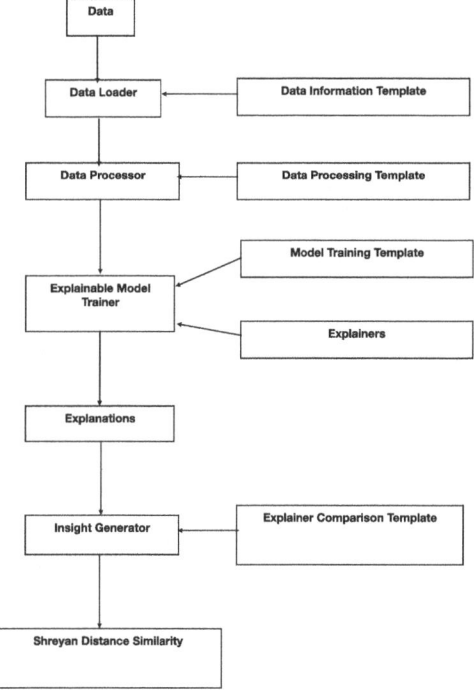

Fig. 5. The XAISuite Framework: Integrating the Shreyan Distance in to a comprehensive machine learning pipeline. The library can be found at github.com/11301858/XAISuite

Algorithms and code for the implementation of the XAISuite Framework's machine learning model training and explanation utilities is included in the XAISuite codebase.

4   Results

The Shreyan Distance is a novel way to quantify the differences between the results of explanatory systems. We used the average Shreyan distance to evaluate explainer similarity across several models and datasets for regression and classification tasks. Shown below in Fig. 6 is a bar graph representing the calculated explainer similarities for each instance of an autogenerated dataset used to train an AdaBoostClassifier model. The calculated average is also shown as a red line.

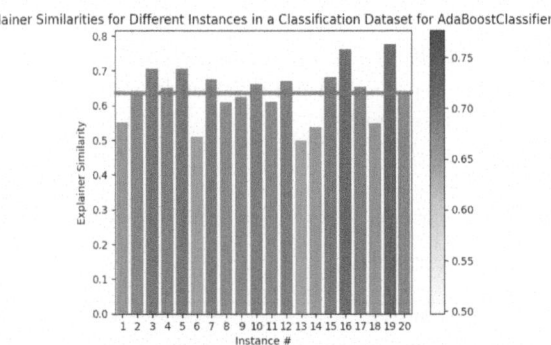

Fig. 6. The model was trained on a classification dataset with 20 features and 2 classes.

We then conducted a 2-sample t-test for difference between population means to determine whether there is a statiscally significant difference between the average LIME-SHAP similarity (as measured by the Shreyan Distance) for regression and classification tasks. The test yielded a test statistic of -2.58 and a p-value of 0.01. Because $0.01 < 0.05$, we can reject the null hypothesis. There is convincing evidence that there is a difference between the true mean LIME and SHAP similarity (as measured using the Shreyan Distance) between classification and regression tasks.

Figure 7 is a density plot showing the distribution of the Shreyan Distance values for the regression and classification models.

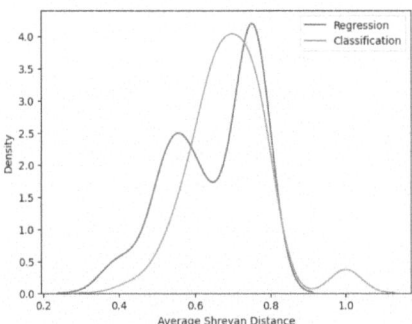

Fig. 7. Distributions of Shreyan Distance for regression and classification tasks

The data in Table 3 contains summary statistics about the average Shreyan Distances for the regression and classification tasks.

Table 3. Summary data from the study

	Regression	Classification
minmax	(0.37273575413884535, 0.7773132717460898)	(0.4242825607064017, 1.0)
mean	0.649809	0.692116
variance	0.013377	0.010448
skewness	−0.590239	0.560591
kurtosis	−0.839749	1.85009

The Shreyan Distances were calculated by the XAISuite library, which we developed in the Methodology section. This supports the claim that explainer comparison can be integrated into machine learning pipelines.

5 Discussion

The results showed that similarity between SHAP and LIME importance scores differ significantly for regression and classification tasks. While previous studies have shown that explainers are inconsistent, our work shows that the level of inconsistency is different for different types of learning tasks. Therefore, any explainer inconsistency is not just an inherent property of the explainers themselves, but it depends also on the training data and type of model being explained.

The Shreyan Distance by itself also represents an advancement in the field of machine learning explainability. By taking into account user-expectations and offering advantages over other metrics like Spearman's Footrule or Kendall's Tau to measure explainer similarity, the Shreyan Distance provides a way to accurately differentiate varying accounts of what the ground truth is. We lay the groundwork for progress towards greater explainer consistency by quantifying these explainer inconsistencies through our experimental results and by proposing Shreyan's Distance.

In addition to the XAISuite Framework and the results of our study, we would also like to briefly mention several related projects that we believe have relevance to a discussion about the XAISuite library. XAISuiteCLI is a comprehensive machine learning explainability command-line tool keeping with the XAISuite framework's emphasis on usability. This utility allows users to train and explain machine learning models using shell commands. XAISuiteGUI is a comprehensive graphical user interface that allows users without coding experience to train, explain, and compare machine learning models. XAISuiteBlock is a block-based site inspired by Scratch for machine learning model training and explanation. This offers machine learning utilities to those without coding experience. This is a great step forward in making machine learning explainability available to everyone regardless of age or coding experience. We envision it as a potential educational tool.

6   Conclusion

Explanatory systems allow users to look through the "black box" of machine learning models. This is not only useful in understanding the internal mechanisms of machine learning models but also is essential in diagnosing model malfunctions. However, when multiple explanatory systems differ, users do not know which one to trust. By arming users of machine learning with the information they need to make decisions, XAISuite increases trust. Furthermore, through its contribution of several interfaces catered to people regardless of age or coding experience, XAISuite empowers the use of machine learning among those that would be previously unable to do so. Finally, by setting the example for a comprehensive framework on machine learning explainability, XAISuite makes the entire process of machine learning more transparent and understandable.

Our work opens up new areas of possible research in this regard. While we performed our analysis with two types of tasks and 64 models, we encourage others to replicate our work with more models, more learning tasks, larger datasets, and more explainers to confirm our results. With regards to the Shreyan Distance, we look forward to future work evaluating it in comparison with other existing comparison algorithms and exploring new applications. In addition, we understand that SHAP and LIME are inherently mathematical models, and we look forward to a mathematical basis for the results of our study. Our goal is that the results of this paper, along with the XAISuite framework and algorithm we outline, will facilitate further efforts to resolve discrepancies between explanatory systems so that humans can gain a clearer understanding of how machine learning models work. This will lead, in turn, to a greater ability to fine tune these models to prevent error.

References

1. Nirmal, D.: Machine learning is everywhere: Preparing for the future July 2017.   https://www.datanami.com/2017/07/03/machine-learning-everywhere-preparing-future/
2. Lakshmanan, L.: Why you need to explain machine learning models google cloud blog (2021). https://cloud.google.com/blog/products/ai-machine-learning/why-you-need-to-explain-machine-learning-models
3. Angwin, J., Larson, J., Kirchner, L., Mattu, S.: Machine bias, May 2016. https://www.propublica.org/article/machine-bias-risk-assessments-in-criminal-sentencing
4. Wakabayashi, D.: Self-driving uber car kills pedestrian in arizona, where robots roam, The New York Times, vol. 19, no. 03 (2018)

5. Jones, R.: Report: Uber's self-driving car sensors ignored cyclist in fatal accident, May 2018. https://gizmodo.com/report-ubers-self-driving-car-sensors-ignored-cyclist-1825832504

6. Rose, C., McLaughlin, E., Liu, R., Koedinger, K.: Explanatory learner models: why machine learning (alone) is not the answer, BERA https://doi.org/10.1111/bjet.12858 (2019)

7. Gilpin, B., Yuan, S., Kagal.: Explaining explanations: an overview of interpretability of machine learning. In: 2018 IEEE 5th International Conference on Data Science and Advanced Analytics (DSAA) (2019)

8. Lundberg, S.M., Lee, S.-I.: A unified approach to interpreting model predictions. In: Guyon, I., et al. (eds.) Advances in Neural Information Processing Systems 30, Curran Associates, Inc., pp. 4765–4774 (2017). http://papers.nips.cc/paper/7062-a-unified-approach-to-interpreting-model-predictions.pdf

9. Ribeiro, M.T., Singh, S., Guestrin, C.: Why should I trust you?: explaining the predictions of any classifier. In: Proceedings of the 22nd ACM SIGKDD International Conference on Knowledge Discovery and Data Mining, San Francisco, CA, USA, 13–17 August 2016, pp. 1135–1144 (2016)

10. Xia, S., Xiong, Z., Luo, Y., WeiXu, Zhang, G.: Effectiveness of the euclidean distance in high dimensional spaces, Optik, vol. 126, no. 24, pp. 5614–5619 (2015). https://www.sciencedirect.com/science/article/pii/S0030402615011493

11. Diaconis, P., Graham, R.L.: Spearman's footrule as a measure of disarray. J. Royal Stat. Soc. Ser. B (Methodological) **39**(2), 262–268 (2018). https://doi.org/10.1111/j.2517-6161.1977.tb01624.x

12. Shieh, G.S.: A weighted kendall's tau statistic. Stat. Probab. Lett. **39**(1), 17–24 (1998). https://www.sciencedirect.com/science/article/pii/S0167715298000066

13. Ritter, S., Barrett, D.G.T., Santoro, A., Botvinick, M.M.: Cognitive psychology for deep neural networks: a shape bias case study (2017). 1706.08606

14. Goel, K., Sindhgatta, R., Kalra, S., Goel, R., Mutreja, P.: The effect of machine learning explanations on user trust for automated diagnosis of covid-19, July 2022. https://www.ncbi.nlm.nih.gov/pmc/articles/PMC9080676/

15. Han, T., Srinivas, S., Lakkaraju, H.: Which explanation should i choose? a function approximation perspective to characterizing post hoc explanations, *arXiv preprint*arXiv: 2206.01254pdf (2022)

16. Riveiro, M., Thill, S.: That's (not) the output i expected! on the role of end user expectations in creating explanations of AI systems (2021). https://doi.org/10.1016/j.artint.2021.103507

17. Ehrlich, K., Kirk, S.E., Patterson, J., Rasmussen, J.C., Ross, S.I., Gruen, D.M.: Taking advice from intelligent systems: the double-edged sword of explanations. In: Proceedings of the 16th International Conference on Intelligent User Interfaces, ser. IUI 2011, pp. 125–134. New York, NY, USA, Association for Computing Machinery (2011). https://doi.org/10.1145/1943403.1943424

18. Riveiro, M., Thill, S.: The challenges of providing explanations of AI systems when they do not behave like users expect. In: Proceedings of the 30th ACM Conference on User Modeling, Adaptation and Personalization, ser. UMAP 2022. New York, NY, USA, Association for Computing Machinery, pp. 110–120 (2022). https://doi.org/10.1145/3503252.3531306

19. Chazette, L., Klös, V., Herzog, F., Schneider, K.: Requirements on explanations: a quality framework for explainability. In: 2022 IEEE 30th International Requirements Engineering Conference (RE), pp. 140–152 (2022)

20. Otte, C.: Safe and interpretable machine learning: a methodological review. In: Moewes, C., Nürnberger, A. (eds.) Computational Intelligence in Intelligent Data Analysis, Springer, Berlin, Heidelberg, pp. 111–122 (2013)
21. Burkart and Huber, A survey on the explainability of supervised machine learning, January 2021. https://doi.org/10.1613/jair.1.12228
22. Ghassemi, M., Oakden-Rayner, L., Beam, A.L.: The false hope of current approaches to explainable artificial intelligence in health care. The Lancet Digital Health **3**(11), e745–e750 (2021). https://doi.org/10.1016/s2589-7500(21)00208-9
23. Szegedy, C., et al.: Intriguing properties of neural networks (2013). 1312.6199
24. Krishna, S., et al.: The disagreement problem in explainable machine learning: a practitioner's perspective (2022). 2202.01602
25. Covert, I., Lundberg, S., Lee, S.-I.: Explaining by removing: a unified framework for model explanation. arXiv preprintarXiv:2011.14878pdf (2022)
26. Roy, S., Laberge, G., Roy, B., Khomh, F., Nikanjam, A., Mondal, S.: Why don't xai techniques agree? characterizing the disagreements between post-hoc explanations of defect predictions. In: IEEE International Conference on Software Maintenance and Evolution (ICSME), vol. 2022, pp. 444–448 (2022)
27. van der Waa, J., Nieuwburg, E., Cremers, A., Neerincx, M.: Evaluating xai: a comparison of rule-based and example-based explanations. Artif. Intell. **291**, 103404 (2021). https://www.sciencedirect.com/science/article/pii/S0004370220301533
28. Duell, J., Fan, X., Burnett, B., Aarts, G., Zhou, S.-M.: A comparison of explanations given by explainable artificial intelligence methods on analysing electronic health records. In: IEEE EMBS International Conference on Biomedical and Health Informatics (BHI), vol. 2021, pp. 1–4 (2021)
29. Lee, K., Ayyasamy, M.V., Ji, Y., Balachandran, P.V.: A comparison of explainable artificial intelligence methods in the phase classification of multi-principal element alloys. Sci. Rep. **12**(1), 11591 (2022). https://doi.org/10.1038/s41598-022-15618-4
30. Agarwal, C., et al.: Openxai: towards a transparent evaluation of model explanations. arXiv preprintarXiv:2206.11104 (2022)
31. Yang, W., Le, H., Savarese, S., Hoi, S.: Omnixai: a library for explainable AI (2022). Available: 2206.01612
32. Kokhlikyan, N., et al.: Captum: a unified and generic model interpretability library for pytorch (2020)
33. Mitra, S., Gilpin, L.: The xaisuite framework and the implications of explanatory system dissonance (2023)

Time Series Anomaly Detection via Reconstruction-Limited Probability Estimation

Yuye Feng[1] and Yongfeng Niu[2](✉)

[1] Hikvision Institute, Hangzhou 310051, China
fengyuye@hikvision.com
[2] School of Computer Science and Artificial Intelligence, Changzhou University,
Changzhou 213164, China
yongfengniu@cczu.edu.cn.com

Abstract. Time series anomaly detection is a pervasive task in cyber-physical system. Due to the intricate dynamics of multivariate time series (MTS), unsupervised anomaly detection has always been a research hot-pot. Common methods are mainly based on achieving accurate reconstruction or maximizing probability estimation, but these optimization objectives may not be sufficient to distinguish abnormal from normal. In our work, we introduce a learnable uncertainty factor to connect reconstruction and probability estimation, which can reflect the uncertainties of the reconstructed results and facilitate more precise probability estimates. Meanwhile, a novel Reconstruction-Limited Probability (RLP) loss is proposed, its core is to reduce the estimated probabilities of suspicious time segments, while weakly influence the estimation of other points. Based on Transformer, we propose a modified framework TRLP to improve the effectiveness of probability estimation, which realizes reasonable uncertainty factor estimation through some elaborate modules. Extensive experiments and visual analyses are conducted on four real-world datasets, the results under different evaluation metrics demonstrate that our method outperforms existing state-of-the-art frameworks.

Keywords: Anomaly Detection · Multivariate Time Series · Uncertainty Estimation

1 Introduction

As an emerging product of Industrial 4.0 era, the cyber-physical system (CPS), is committed to conduct proper management and control on industrial mechanisms [1]. During the operation process, vast quantities of time series data are collected by multiple sensors in real time, and the deviations from normal patterns may imply operational failures (i.e., anomalies) or even potential risks. To prevent such risks, some deep learning algorithms for anomaly detection have witnessed a rosy picture of prosperity [2–4].

Due to the rarity of anomalies and the high cost of manual labeling, unsupervised networks have been the foci in recent researches for anomaly detection. In

C. Wallraven et al. (Eds.): ICPRAI 2024, LNCS 14892, pp. 447–461, 2025.
https://doi.org/10.1007/978-981-97-8702-9_30

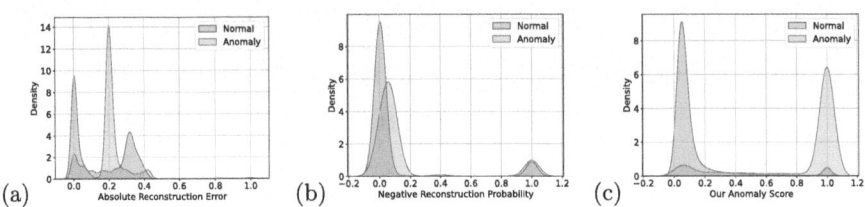

Fig. 1. The anomaly score distributions of normal and abnormal are compared under different optimization objectives. The horizontal coordinate of each subfigure is the anomaly score under particular optimization objective, and the vertical ordinate reflects the density value of normal samples and anomalies. We use the format of "{Optimization Objective}: {Anomaly Score}" to illustrate how each subfigure is acquired. (a) Minimizing reconstruction error: the mean reconstruction error of different sensors; (b) maximizing probability estimation: the negative logarithmic probability; (c) our RLP: the negative logarithmic probability. The tested dataset is SWaT.

a sense, these methods aim to capture the generalized patterns of normal data via accurate reconstruction, forecasting or probability density estimation [5,6]. Although these methods have made some progress, their optimization targets may not be sufficient to spot anomalies. For instance, when the reconstruction error is minimized as optimization goal, the error of normal points is expected to be minimized, while the error of anomalies is relatively large. However, this optimization target does not meet our expectation. As illustrated in Fig. 1(a), there is no clear dividing line between normal and abnormal when the reconstruction error is used as anomaly score. Besides, the reconstruction error ignores the fact that each sensor has different reconstruction difficulty due to its own dynamics, and the reconstruction difficulty may be time-varying. These different levels of difficulty reflect the **uncertainty factor** that need to be considered in the optimization process. There are some probability-based methods that take the uncertainty factor into account. These methods aim to provide adaptive uncertainty factors for different timestamps and sensors, and use the estimation probability as anomaly score [7,8]. However, as shown in Fig. 1(b), under the objective of maximizing the estimation probability, most anomalies share a high probability with normal points. The above shows that the current optimization goals may not be sufficient to achieve the separation of normal and abnormal.

To address the above issues, our main idea is to find an optimization objective that conforms to the intention of isolating anomalies from normal points. By introducing the uncertainty prediction, we propose a novel Reconstruction-Limited Probability (RLP) loss. Instead of fully maximizing the observed probability, our objective focuses more on reducing the estimated probability of suspicious segments, while weakly influences the probability evaluation of other points. The core idea of RLP is to mutually restrict the objectives of reconstruction and probability estimation, and further make the model reduce the estimated probability of certain points by reasonable prediction of uncertainty. Moreover, we propose a Transformer-based framework (named as TRLP) to instruct the optimization process. The distribution of estimated probability acquired by our method is shown in Fig. 1(c), which sufficiently demonstrates the effectiveness of our framework. In summary, our main contributions are listed as follows.

- We propose RLP loss by mutually limiting the objectives of reconstruction and probability estimation, it can not only achieve effective probability estimation but also reduce the estimated probability of those suspicious segments.
- Based on Transformer, we design TRLP to instruct the optimization process. This framework can prevent self-information leakage for reconstruction, and utilize the attention score to fine-tune the uncertainty factor estimation.
- Extensive experiments are conducted on four real-world datasets with different evaluation metrics. Our empirical studies show that the proposed model achieves state-of-the-art performance on anomaly detection task.

2   Related Work

2.1   Time Series Anomaly Detection

There are a considerable amount of algorithms for unsupervised anomaly detection, the core idea of which is to learn generalized patterns from normal data. With the development of deep learning, Recurrent Neural Networks (RNNs) [19,24] and Graph Neural Networks (GNNs) [14,25] have been widely employed to model the intrinsic correlations behind the time series. More recently, Transformer has also shown great power in extracting broad contextual information and significantly improve the performance of anomaly detection [12,13,18]. The optimization targets of these deep learning methods are mainly based on reconstruction, forecasting and probability density estimation [7,14,20], in which reconstruction has attracted much attention. It defaults that normal samples can be accurately reconstructed due to their normal patterns but anomalies cannot. For instance, LSTM-VAE [19] integrates LSTM with VAE to model the temporal dependencies and minimize the reconstruction error. However, the single objective of minimizing reconstruction error may be untenable for anomaly detection task [12,18]. A few researches argued to skillfully amplify the reconstruction errors of those suspicious subsequences in an adversarial manner, such as USAD [16]. Besides, some probability-based methods [7,8,21] attempted to implement probability estimation by maximizing the observed probability, which improve the discrimination between normal and abnormal points somewhat. More recently, Anomaly Transformer [13] derived a new criterion called association discrepancy. It is based on that when reconstructing the abnormal timestamps, it is difficult to establish a strong association with the whole series from these timestamps, which achieves some breakthroughs.

2.2   Uncertainty Estimation

Uncertainty estimation or prediction mainly aims to assess the confidence level and validity for the predicted results of a model [9]. It has been investigated in a variety of applications, like image processing and natural language processing [10]. Existing methods tend to automatically extract desirable representations for uncertainty quantification. Some methods directly integrate uncertainty into the loss function to implement forecasting and uncertainty estimation simultaneously, like DUQ [11]. Analog to this operation, we propose a novel RLP loss and utilize the diagonal attention score in Transformer to efficiently implement the uncertainty factor estimation.

3 Reconstruction-Limited Probability Loss

In this section, we introduce our RLP loss, which restricts both the objectives of reconstruction and probability estimation. First, we show that the traditional reconstruction loss can be understood as a probability density loss with fixed uncertainty factor. By assigning different uncertainty factor to different sensors and timestamps, the reconstruction loss evolves into a standard probability density loss. In order to make the optimization process proceed in the direction of reducing the probability values of anomalies, a subsidiary condition is proposed to skillfully constrain the reconstruction and probability estimation.

Throughout the paper, denote T, S as the number of all timestamps and sensors from MTS respectively. From temporal perspective, MTS can be formulated as:

$$\mathcal{X} = \{x_1, \cdots, x_T\}, \tag{1}$$

and x_{ts} denote the value of the $s - th$ sensor at the t timestamp.

Reconstruction Loss. Denote $\hat{x}_{ts}$ as the reconstructed result of x_{ts}, $\ddot{x}_{ts} = \hat{x}_{ts} - x_{ts}$, and $\ddot{X} = \{\ddot{x}_{ts} | t = 1, \cdots, K; s = 1, \cdots, S\}$. The commonly used reconstruction loss can be formulated by Mean Squared Error (MSE):

$$\mathcal{L}_{rec}(\ddot{X}) = \sum_{t=1}^{K} \sum_{s=1}^{S} (\ddot{x}_{ts})^2. \tag{2}$$

From probabilistic perspective, it is equivalent to the following assumptions:

$$\ddot{x}_{ts} \sim \mathcal{N}(0, a^2), \quad t = 1, \cdots K; \ s = 1, \cdots, S, \tag{3}$$

where $a > 0$ is a constant, $\mathcal{N}$ denotes Gaussian distribution. Denote $f(\cdot)$ as the probability density function, we have $-\ln f(\ddot{x}_{ts}) = \frac{1}{2} \ln(2\pi a^2) + \frac{1}{2a^2}(\ddot{x}_{ts})^2$. To maximize the probability density value of $\ddot{x}_{ts}$, it is equivalent to minimize $(\ddot{x}_{ts})^2$. After computing the empirical mean, the probabilistic density loss with fixed variance a^2 is apparently equivalent to $\mathcal{L}_{rec}$ in (2).

As noted above, the reconstruction loss can be interpreted as a probability density loss with fixed uncertainty factor. By adaptively assigning a, the probability density loss can consider the varying difficulty of reconstruction for different t and s.

Probability Density Loss. We assume that

$$\ddot{x}_{ts} \sim \mathcal{N}(0, \sigma_{ts}^2) \quad t = 1, \cdots K; \ s = 1, \cdots, S, \tag{4}$$

Denote $\hat{\sigma}_{ts} = \frac{1}{\sigma_{ts}^2}, \hat{\Sigma} = \{\hat{\sigma}_{ts} | t = 1, \cdots, K; s = 1, \cdots, S\}$. To maximize the observed probability density of $\ddot{X}$, by taking the negative logarithm of $f(\ddot{x}_{ts})$, the loss function can be formulated as

$$\mathcal{L}_p(\ddot{X}, \hat{\Sigma}) = \sum_{t=1}^{K} \sum_{s=1}^{S} (\hat{\sigma}_{ts} \cdot (\ddot{x}_{ts})^2 - \ln \hat{\sigma}_{ts}), \tag{5}$$

Intuitively, $\mathcal{L}_p$ includes two targets: reducing reconstruction error $\ddot{x}_{ts}^2$ and providing the optimal $\hat{\sigma}_{ts}$ that reflects the reconstruction uncertainty of x_{ts}. However, due to the characteristic of Gaussian distribution, $f(\ddot{x}_{ts})$ goes to $+\infty$ when σ_{ts} and $\ddot{x}_{ts}$ both approach to 0. When most of x_{ts} can be accurately reconstructed, the model is biased to reduce the errors $(\ddot{x}_{ts})^2$ and output the corresponding σ_{ts} approaching 0 inevitably. Thus, we argue to put more emphasis on providing proper variance $\hat{\sigma}_{ts}$ for each $\ddot{x}_{ts}$, rather than relying primarily on reducing reconstruction error. Specifically, a detached strategy is proposed to make the estimation of $\hat{\sigma}_{ts}$ more credible. The detached form of probability density loss is

$$\mathcal{L}_{dp}(\ddot{X}, \hat{\Sigma}) = \sum_{t=1}^{K} \sum_{s=1}^{S} (\hat{\sigma}_{ts} \cdot (\ddot{x}_{ts}.detach)^2 - \ln \hat{\sigma}_{ts}), \tag{6}$$

where *detach* denotes stop-gradient. Obviously, $\mathcal{L}_{dp}$ only focuses on the optimal estimation of uncertainty $\hat{\sigma}_{ts}$, thus completely ignoring the effects of reconstruction error. To enable both the capabilities of uncertainty estimation and reconstruction, based on $\mathcal{L}_{rec}$ and $\mathcal{L}_{dp}$, we propose Error-Limited probability loss that combining both the two objectives.

RLP Loss. The Reconstruction-Limited Probability loss is expressed as

$$\mathcal{L}_{rlp} = |\mathcal{L}_{dp} + \lambda \mathcal{L}_{rec}| + c * \mathcal{L}_{dp}, \tag{7}$$

where c is a postive constant. In a sense, the RLP loss can be interpreted as the following optimization problem. Since the accurate reconstruction of most points may weaken the validity of uncertainty estimation, the overall reconstruction error needs to be limited within a certain range such that a large error can be assigned to the suspicious segments. In order to achieve reasonable uncertainty estimation and reduce the predicted probabilities of suspicious segments, a novel constraint term is introduced to adaptively limit the overall reconstruction error and the estimated probability:

$$\min_{\ddot{X}, \hat{\Sigma}} \quad \mathcal{L}_{dp}(\ddot{X}, \hat{\Sigma}),$$
$$s.t. \quad |\mathcal{L}_{dp}(\ddot{X}, \hat{\Sigma}) + \lambda \mathcal{L}_{rec}(\ddot{X})| \leq \epsilon, \tag{8}$$

where $\lambda > 0$ is a constant and $\epsilon \to 0$ is a small value. This can be simply understood as two targets: **1)** providing the optimal estimation of reconstruction uncertainty $\hat{\sigma}_{ts}$; **2)** forcing a balance between the reconstruction error and the detached probability density of it. Overall, by matching the optimal uncertainty estimate and enlarging the reconstruction error of suspicious segments, the estimated probability of anomalies will be reduced significantly.

4 Proposed Framework

The overview of our model is shown in Fig. 2. The framework of TRLP is based on Transformer, and the RLP loss is employed as the optimization target to achieve both reconstruction and uncertainty prediction. It consists of two main components: **1)** a modified Self-Masked Temporal Encoders (SMTEs) based on Transformer to extract bidirectional contextual features, which can prevent self-information leakage of original features; **2)** uncertainty factor estimation based on both the hidden features and the diagonal self-attention score in SMTEs.

4.1 Self-Masked Temporal Encoder

It has recently been pointed out that, the reconstruction based frameworks may fall into an "identical shortcut" problem, where both normal and abnormal samples can be well reconstructed. Due to the self-information leakage, the model tends to copy the original input features rather than learning the contextual representation [12], making the extracted representations meaningless. Aiming at the above problem, it is observed that some potential paths may cause self-information leakage in the following two operations of vanilla Transformer (considering one-head attention for simplicity):

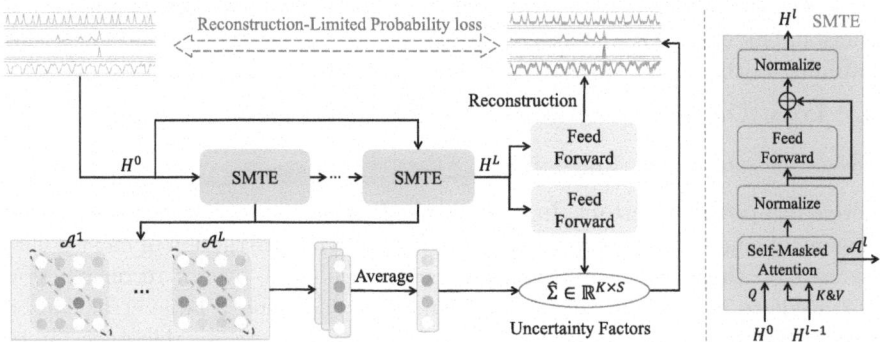

Fig. 2. Overview of TRLP, where H^0 is representation of input time window, SMTE denotes the Self-Masked Temporal Encoder, $\mathcal{A}^l$ is the self-attention score of the l_{th} SMTE, H^l denotes the output of the l_{th} SMTE, and $\hat{\Sigma} = \{\frac{1}{\sigma_{ts}^2} | t = 1, \cdots, K; s = 1, \cdots, S\}$ quantifies the inverse of uncertainty factors. The right part shows the specific architecture of SMTE.

$$\begin{cases} \text{Attn}(X) = \text{Softmax}[\frac{(XW_{\mathcal{Q}})(XW_{\mathcal{K}})'}{\sqrt{S}}](XW_{\mathcal{V}}), \\ \widetilde{H}^1 = \text{LayerNorm}[X + \text{Attn}(X)], \end{cases} \tag{9}$$

where $X \in \mathbb{R}^{K \times S}$ are the input features, $W_{\mathcal{Q}}, W_{\mathcal{K}}, W_{\mathcal{V}} \in \mathbb{R}^{S \times S}$ are learnable parameters. For the first operation in (9), if Softmax[·] and $W_{\mathcal{V}}$ approximate to identity matrix $\mathcal{I}$, then $\text{Attn}(X) \approx X$. For the second operation, if $W_{\mathcal{V}} \to \mathbf{0}$, $\widetilde{H}^1 \approx \text{LayerNorm}(X)$. In both cases, there is a high probability that the model can simply copy original features, but fails to obtain meaningful representations.

We propose a novel Self-Masked Temporal Encoder by eliminating the above possibility, as visualized in the right part of Fig. 2. Compared with vanilla Transformer, there are three improvements : **1)** Similar to UniAD [12], the self information will be masked after performing attention calculation; **2)** In SMTEs, the first residual connection is removed directly, which can avoid self-information leakage in the second operation of (9). **3)** The representation of query in $\text{Attn}(H^l)$ is kept as the initial representation H^0 in each SMTE. The operation aims at preserving part of the original features to ensure the effectiveness of attention mechanism. Integrating these modifications, our model can only focus on fusing the contextual representations for reconstruction. The l-th SMTE can be expressed as:

$$\begin{cases} \text{Attn}(H^l) = \text{Softmax}[\text{Mask}(\frac{(H^0 W_{\mathcal{Q}}^l)(H^l W_{\mathcal{K}}^l)'}{\sqrt{S}})](H^l W_{\mathcal{V}}^l), \\ \widetilde{H}^{l+1} = \text{LayerNorm}[\text{Attn}(H^l)], \end{cases} \tag{10}$$

where $\text{Mask}(\cdot)$ sets the diagonal elements of a matrix to $-\infty$.

4.2 Estimation of Uncertainty Factor

As shown in the left part of Fig. 2, the final hidden features H^L is fed into two FeedForward layer to obtain reconstruction and uncertainty estimation respectively. Since it has observed that anomalies are usually hard to build strong associations with the whole series [13]. To further amplify the discrepancy between abnormal and normal points, it is expected that our model could present relatively high values of uncertainty factors for those suspicious segments, as this will reduce their estimated probabilities according to Eq. (5). We experimentally observe that the diagonal self-attention score regarding the same timestamp is exactly capable of reflecting the associations. If the diagonal self-attention score is relatively low, it implies that the representation of current timestamp is strongly similar with those of other timestamps. Thus, as shown in Fig. 2, we exploit the diagonal self-attention score in SMTEs to get the coarse-grained prediction of uncertainty factors, which are further quantified by the final hidden variables. It can be formulated as:

$$\begin{cases} \mathcal{A} = \frac{1}{L} \sum_{l=1}^{L} \text{Softmax}[\frac{(H^0 W_{\mathcal{Q}}^l)(H^l W_{\mathcal{K}}^l)'}{\sqrt{S}}], \\ \sigma_{ts} = \beta \exp(\gamma \mathcal{A}_{tt}) \cdot [\text{FeedForward}(H^L)]_{ts}, \end{cases} \tag{11}$$

where L is the number of SMTEs, H^L is the final variables and $[\text{FeedForward}(H^L)] \succ 0$, $\mathcal{A}_{tt}$ is the t_{th} diagonal element of $\mathcal{A}$, and β, γ are rescale hyper-parameters.

4.3 Anomaly Score

The logarithm of the estimated probability density value is treated as anomaly score for each data x_{ts}:

$$\text{Score}(t, s) = \hat{\sigma}_{ts} \cdot (\ddot{x}_{ts})^2 - \ln \hat{\sigma}_{ts}. \tag{12}$$

As the characteristics of different sensors are discrepant, similar to the approach in [14], the $\text{Score}(t, s)$ will be normalized. For each timestamp t, we use the largest value of sensors to quantify its anomaly score.

5 Experiments

We implement experiments on four real-world MTS datasets. Extensive experimental results are presented to cover following questions:

- **Q1**: Under rigorous evaluation, how does our framework perform on different datasets compared to existing state-of-the-art methods?
- **Q2**: Does each of the introduced modules in our approach have positive effect on detection performance?
- **Q3**: How does our method work on detecting diverse anomalies?
- **Q4**: How does our framework perform on robustness and complexity?

Table 1. Detailed statistics of different datasets used in experiments. AR denotes anomaly rate of test set.

Dataset	Train	Test	Dimensions	Entities	AR(%)
SWaT	99360	89984	51	1	11.99
WADI	241921	34560	123	1	5.75
MSL	58317	73729	55	27	10.72
SMD	708405	708420	38	28	4.16

5.1 Datasets, Metrics and Baseline Methods

Four public datasets are adopted to evaluate the performance of different anomaly detection frameworks. The detailed statistical information of the datasets are shown in Table 1. Towards a rigorous evaluation, we use the following metrics to evaluate the performance: **1)** F1-score. **2)** F1-score after point adjustment (i.e. F1_{PA}) [15]. Point adjustment (PA) can be illustrated as that, if at least one timestamp in a successive anomalous sequence $\mathcal{X}_A$ is detected, all timestamps in that sequence are considered to be correctly detected. F1_{PA} is widely used for evaluation of detection tasks [8, 13, 16].

Ten prevalent methods for anomaly detection are selected for comparison. BeatGAN [17], USAD [16], GDN [14] and TranAD [18] belong to error-based approaches, LSTM-VAE [19], DAGMM [20] and OmniAnomaly [7] are probabilistic models. NSIBF [21] is a specialized architecture based on dynamical state-space model. In training phase, it focus on minimizing both the reconstruction and prediction error, but for inference, the Bayesian Filtering is employed to evaluate the probability density of observed measurements. Anomaly Transformer [13] presents an Association Discrepancy based criterion to distinguish anomalies. Besides, TranAD, LSTM-VAE, OmniAnomaly, NSIBF and Anomaly Transformer mainly aim to capture temporal associations of MTS data, while GDN is a GNN-based framework to model spatial dependencies. A classical method called Isolation Forest [22] is also compared in this paper.

5.2 Experimental Setup

All of the experiments are conducted in Pytorch 1.7 with one TITAN X Pascal 12 GB GPU. For all of the tested methods, the best threshold is obtained through equispaced search.

Hyper-parameter Setting. Each dataset used for training will be divided into training set and valid set, and the ratio is 9 : 1 for WADI and 4 : 1 for other datasets. During training, Adam [23] with an initial learning rate of $5e^{-4}$ is leveraged as the optimizer, and early stop strategy is used with patience 10. For all of the datasets, the batch size is set to 64. Besides, the rescale hyperparameter β, γ in Eq. (11) are set to $\exp(-\frac{1}{K-1})$ and $1 - \frac{1}{K}$ respectively, where K is the window length. K is 12 for SWaT and WADI, while 60 for SMD and MSL.

Implementation of Baselines. For implementation of IsolationForest[1], DAGMM[2], OmniAnomaly[3], NSIBF[4], TranAD[5], GDN[6] and Anomaly Transformer(noted as ATransformer)[7], the source codes are directly utilized to obtain the experimental results.

5.3 Experimental Results

Q1: Overall Performance. As shown in Table 2, our framework achieves the best $F1_{PA}$ on all of the tested datasets and surpasses the baselines a large margin. As our optimization objective is to reduce the estimated probabilities of potential anomalies, which makes it easier to distinguish between normal and abnormal compared to other baselines. We also notice that USAD performs better than approaches based on $\mathcal{L}_{rec}$ like BeatGAN, since this method also attempts to magnify the reconstruction errors of suspicious segments.

---

[1] https://scikit-learn.org/stable/modules/generated/sklearn.ensemble. IsolationForest.html.

[2] https://github.com/tnakae/DAGMM.

[3] https://github.com/NetManAIOps/OmniAnomaly.

[4] https://github.com/NSIBF/NSIBF.

[5] https://github.com/imperial-qore/TranAD.

[6] https://github.com/d-ailin/GDN.

[7] https://github.com/thuml/Anomaly-Transformer.

Table 2. Performance of different models under $F1_{PA}$. P, R denote precision (%) and recall (%) respectively. The best results are highlighted in bold, and the second best are underlined.

Model	SWaT			WADI			SMD			MSL		
	P	R	$F1_{PA}$	P	R	$F1_{PA}$	P	R	$F1_{PA}$	P	R	$F1_{PA}$
IsolationForest	93.06	80.27	86.19	80.42	61.00	69.38	90.37	88.89	89.62	77.05	90.69	83.31
LSTM-VAE	96.51	84.54	90.13	91.87	61.45	73.64	90.54	96.91	93.61	76.60	95.31	84.94
DAGMM	87.17	84.25	85.69	90.46	46.75	61.65	79.81	91.99	87.13	84.77	88.77	86.77
BeatGAN	99.84	69.84	82.19	55.35	29.69	38.65	85.16	89.19	87.13	89.75	85.42	87.53
OmniAnomaly	81.42	84.30	82.83	68.10	39.76	50.21	95.12	93.21	94.15	91.11	88.01	89.53
USAD	98.70	74.02	84.60	64.51	32.20	42.96	93.14	96.17	93.82	88.10	97.86	91.09
NSIBF	98.20	86.30	91.90	17.01	38.14	23.64	77.93	86.11	81.82	62.14	94.67	75.03
GDN	94.46	90.74	92.56	88.91	91.19	90.01	88.38	94.93	91.53	84.73	83.26	83.99
TranAD	89.10	77.31	82.79	71.07	25.97	38.04	87.97	91.38	89.64	56.77	96.34	71.44
ATransformer	91.55	96.73	94.07	87.56	90.69	89.10	89.40	95.45	92.33	92.09	95.15	93.59
TRLP	96.27	94.69	95.47	92.22	93.66	92.93	94.90	96.06	95.48	92.31	100.00	96.00

Table 3. Performance of different models under F1. P, R denote precision (%) and recall (%) respectively. What are highlighted in bold indicate the best results, and the second best are underlined.

Model	SWaT			WADI		
	P	R	F1	P	R	F1
IsolationForest	91.32	63.02	74.57	24.59	38.60	30.04
LSTM-VAE	65.73	76.96	70.91	36.14	36.24	36.19
DAGMM	39.60	69.55	50.47	73.25	8.96	15.96
BeatGAN	83.65	56.91	67.73	85.59	14.95	25.45
OmniAnomaly	98.25	64.97	78.22	99.47	12.98	22.96
USAD	98.51	66.18	79.17	99.47	13.18	23.28
NSIBF	96.21	65.27	77.78	7.13	84.76	13.16
GDN	98.11	67.52	80.00	90.22	35.28	50.71
TranAD	94.86	61.49	74.61	88.76	15.50	26.39
ATransformer	7.31	6.91	7.10	5.79	43.43	10.21
TRLP	90.84	78.89	84.44	70.78	55.46	62.19

In Table 3, our framework surpasses the other approaches by far on both datasets. Compared to the best of these methods (e.g. GDN), our method improves the F1-score from 80.00% to 84.44% on SWaT dataset, and from 50.71% to 62.19% on WADI dataset. This demonstrates the great superiority of our proposed framework, by focusing more on reducing the estimated probabilities of suspicious segments, TRLP could detect more anomalies consistently in an anomalous sequence.

Q2: Ablation Study. Table 4 exhibits the performance of our framework with different optimization objectives, including $\mathcal{L}_{rec}$, $\mathcal{L}_p$ and our RLP loss: $\mathcal{L}_{rlp}$. They were detailed in Sect. 3. Among these loss functions, our $\mathcal{L}_{rlp}$ achieves the best performance. Table 5 shows the effect of different parts in our framework:

- SMTEs denotes the Self-Masked Temporal Encoders, which will be replaced by the encoders of vanilla Transformer without ✓.

Table 4. Ablation study in terms of optimization objective on different datasets. What are highlighted in bold indicate the best results.

Optimization Objective	SWaT		WADI		SMD	MSL
	F1	$F1_{PA}$	F1	$F1_{PA}$	$F1_{PA}$	$F1_{PA}$
$\mathcal{L}_{rec}$	81.57	91.12	47.11	73.56	**95.84**	86.14
$\mathcal{L}_p$	80.19	94.50	51.10	73.56	94.51	94.36
$\mathcal{L}_{rlp}$	**84.44**	**95.47**	**62.19**	**88.72**	95.48	**96.00**

Table 5. Ablation study in terms of module design on different datasets. What are highlighted in bold indicate the best results.

SMTEs	$\mathcal{A}_{self}$	SWaT		WADI		SMD	MSL
		F1	$F1_{PA}$	F1	$F1_{PA}$	$F1_{PA}$	$F1_{PA}$
–	–	83.85	94.95	59.60	87.29	90.74	93.11
✓	–	82.58	**95.80**	**62.27**	**88.96**	92.47	87.44
✓	✓	**84.44**	95.47	62.19	88.72	**95.48**	**96.00**

- $\mathcal{A}_{self}$ indicates that uncertainty factor prediction is implemented via Eq. (11). It will be replaced by only a FeedForward network without ✓.

We can conclude that: **1)** Even with a vanilla Transformer, TRLP could achieve excellent performance with our proposed objective. **2)** With the incorporation of SMTEs, better performances on WADI and SMD datasets can be achieved. Meanwhile, it shows that the combination of both SMTEs and $\mathcal{A}_{self}$ is necessary to further instruct reconstruction and probability estimation. As shown in Table 5, the performance is further improved by the combination of the two modules.

Q3: Case Visualization. To explain the significance of uncertainty estimation and the operation mechanism of our framework, we visualize some representative cases from distinct datasets in Fig. 3. **1)** Based on $\mathcal{L}_{rlp}$, the reconstruction error of anomalous segments could be magnified, but for normal sequences, the errors are relatively small (e.g., SWaT and MSL). This demonstrates that TRLP can not only reconstruct the normal points well, but also remains sensitive to suspicious subsequences, which are essential for anomaly detection in MTS. **2)** With the help of uncertainty factor estimates, the anomaly scores of abnormal segments will be further amplified, while for those normal points with fluctuations that may be hard to reconstruct (e.g. WADI), their scores will be reduced clearly. In summary, the visualized cases fully illustrates the necessity of uncertainty estimation for reconstruction-based methods.

Q4: Robustness and Complexity. In Fig. 4, we present TRLP's sensitivity to part of the parameters on SWaT dataset. The parameters include the value of λ in RLP loss and the number of SMTEs. **1)** With the increase of λ, the perfor-

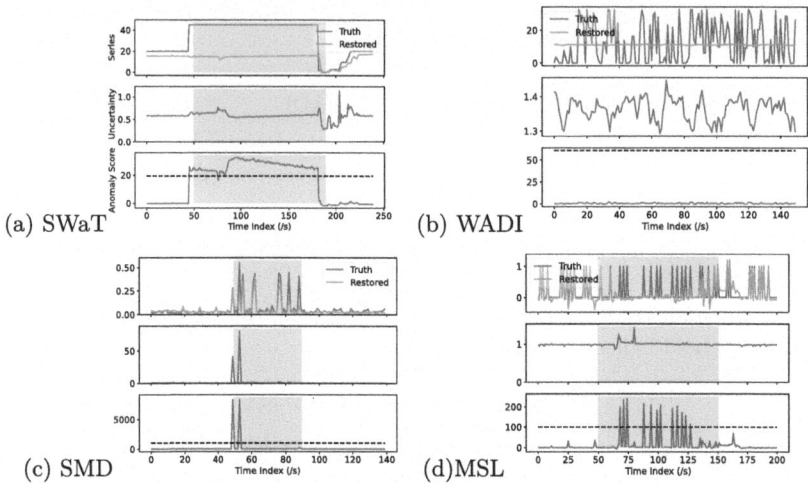

(a) SWaT   (b) WADI

(c) SMD   (d) MSL

Fig. 3. Four cases in which the anomalous behaviours are detected by TRLP. For clarity, time series with only one dimension is selected for visualization here. From top to bottom of each graph, the subplots represent the time series (ground truth VS restored results), the estimated uncertainty of reconstruction and the anomaly scores respectively. For the bottom subplots, the black dotted lines are the thresholds. We highlight the anomalous segments with orange shadows. (Color figure online)

Table 6. Complexity comparison of different methods. AT is the abbreviation of Anomaly Transformer.

	GDN	LSTM-VAE	AT	Transformer	TRLP
Params (K)	8.5	83.1	4854.9	43.2	43.3
Inference (s)	14.2	26.6	41.0	4.8	4.8

mance is stable and it can even be further improved for both F1 ($81.07 \rightarrow 84.44$) and $F1_{PA}$ ($94.02 \rightarrow 95.47$). **2)** The number of SMTEs has a mild impact on the performance of our framework. When stacking multiple layers, both F1 and $F1_{PA}$ improve marginally. The above results sufficiently validate the robustness of TRLP. Our framework has almost no increase in time and space complexity compared with vanilla Transformer. As shown in Table 6, the number of learnable parameters and inference time of TRLP are almost the same as those of Transformer. Also, it is able to perform a faster execution of anomaly detection than other approaches, which is critical for practical deployment.

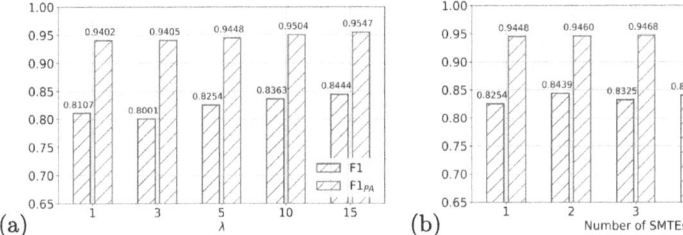

Fig. 4. Parameter sensitivity of TRLP on SWaT dataset: (a) Value of λ; (b) Number of SMTEs.

6   Conclusion

In this work, we focus on reducing the estimated probabilities of anomalous segments while weakly influence the probability estimation of normal points. Meanwhile, TRLP consisting of self-masked temporal encoders is proposed to prevent self-information leakage, and diagonal attention scores are used to guide the estimation of uncertainty factor. Extensive experimental results and the analysis have been given which demonstrate the superiority of our framework on four real-world datasets, and it is also verified that TRLP exhibits good characteristics of robustness and convergence.

Acknowledgments. This paper are supported by the National Natural Science Foundation of China (Grant No. 12301665), the Basic Science (Natural Science) Research Projects of Universities in Jiangsu Province under Grant Agreement (Grant No. 22KJB110009), and Applied Basic Research Support Project of Changzhou Science and Technology (Grant No. CJ20235031).

References

1. J. Lee, B. Bagheri, and H. A. Kao, A cyber-physical systems architecture for industry 4.0-based manufacturing systems. Manuf. Lett. **3**, 18–23 (2015)
2. Liu, H., Xu, X., Li, E., Zhang, S., Li, X.: Anomaly detection with representative neighbors. IEEE Trans. Neural Netw. Learn. Syst. **34**(6), 2831–2841 (2023)
3. Tu, B., Yang, X., He, W., Li, J., Plaza, A.: Hyperspectral anomaly detection using reconstruction fusion of quaternion frequency domain analysis. IEEE Trans. Neural Netw. Learn. Syst. 1–15 (2023)
4. Kim, M., Yu, J., Kim, J., Oh, T.-H., Choi, J.K.: An iterative method for unsupervised robust anomaly detection under data contamination. IEEE Trans. Neural Netw. Learn. Syst. 1–13 (2023)
5. Huang, Z., Zhang, B., Hu, G., Li, L., Xu, Y., Jin, Y.: Enhancing unsupervised anomaly detection with score-guided network. IEEE Trans. Neural Netw. Learn. Syst. 1–16 (2023)
6. Xie, Q., Zhang, P., Yu, B., Choi, J.: Semisupervised training of deep generative models for high-dimensional anomaly detection. IEEE Trans. Neural Netw. Learn. Syst. **33**(6), 2444–2453 (2022)

7. Su, Y., Zhao, Y., Niu, C., Liu, R., Sun, W., Pei, D.: Robust anomaly detection for multivariate time series through stochastic recurrent neural network. In: Proceedings of the 25th ACM SIGKDD Conference on Knowledge Discovery Data Mining, pp. 2828–2837 (2019)
8. Li, Z., Zhao, Y., Han, J., Su, Y., Jiao, R., Wen, X., Pei, D.: Multivariate time series anomaly detection and interpretation using hierarchical intermetric and temporal embedding. In: Proceedings of the 27th ACM SIGKDD Conference on Knowledge Discovery Data Mining, pp. 3220–3230. Association for Computing Machinery (2021)
9. Kiureghian, A.D., Ditlevsen, O.: Aleatory or epistemic? does it matter?. Struct. Saf. **31**(2), 105–112 (2009)
10. Wang, H., Yeung, D.Y.: Towards bayesian deep learning: a framework and some existing methods. IEEE Trans. Knowl. Data Eng. **28**(12), 3395–3408 (2016)
11. Wang, B., Lu, J., Yan, Z., Luo, H., Li, T., Zheng, Y., Zhang, G.: Deep uncertainty quantification: a machine learning approach for weather forecasting. In: Proceedings of the 25th ACM SIGKDD International Conference on Knowledge Discovery Data Mining, pp. 2087–2095 (2019)
12. You, Z., et al.: A unified model for multi-class anomaly detection. In: Proceedings of the 36th International Conference on Neural Information Processing Systems (2022)
13. Xu, J., Wu, H., Wang, J., Long, M.: Anomaly transformer: Time series anomaly detection with association discrepancy. In: Proceedings of the 10th International Conference on Learning Representations (2022)
14. Deng, A., Hooi, B.: Graph neural network-based anomaly detection in multivariate time series. Proc. AAAI Conf. Artif. Intell. **35**, 4027–4035 (2021)
15. Xu, H., et al.: Unsupervised anomaly detection via variational auto-encoder for seasonal kpis in web applications. In: Proceedings of the 2018 World Wide Web Conference, pp. 187-196, International World Wide Web Conferences Steering Committee (2018)
16. Audibert, J., Michiardi, P., Guyard, F., Marti, S., Zuluaga, M.A.: Usad: unsupervised anomaly detection on multivariate time series. In: Proceedings of the 26th ACM SIGKDD Conference on Knowledge Discovery Data Mining, pp. 3395–3404 (2020)
17. Zhou, B., Liu, S.H., Hooi, B., Cheng, X., Ye, J.: BeatGAN: anomalous rhythm detection using adversarially generated time series. In: International Joint Conference on Artificial Intelligence (2019)
18. Tuli, S., Casale, G., Jennings, N.R.: TranAD: deep transformer networks for anomaly detection in multivariate time series data. Proc. Very Large Data Bases **15**, 1201–1214 (2022)
19. Park, D., Hoshi, Y., Kemp, C.C.: A multimodal anomaly detector for robot-assisted feeding using an lstm-based variational autoencoder. IEEE Robot. Autom. Lett. **3**(3), 1544–1551 (2018)
20. Zong, B., et al.: Deep autoencoding gaussian mixture model for unsupervised anomaly detection. In: International Conference on Learning Representations (2018)
21. Feng, C., Tian, P.: Time series anomaly detection for cyber-physical systems via neural system identification and bayesian filtering. In: Proceedings of the 27th ACM SIGKDD Conference on Knowledge Discovery Data Mining, pp. 2858–2867 (2021)
22. Liu, F.T., Ting, K.M., Zhou, Z.H.: Isolation forest. In: Proceedings of the 8th IEEE International Conference on Data Mining (ICDM), pp. 413–422 (2008)

23. Kingma, D.P., Ba, J.: Adam: a method for stochastic optimization (2014)
24. Hochreiter, S., Schmidhuber, J.: Long short-term memory. Neural Comput. **9**(8), 1735–1780 (1997)
25. Shuman, D.I., Narang, S.K., Frossard, P., Ortega, A., Van- dergheynst, P.: The emerging field of signal processing on graphs: ex- tending high-dimensional data analysis to networks and other irregular domains. IEEE Signal Process. Mag. **30**(3), 83–98 (2013)

Cloth-Independent Feature Learning from Multi-perspective for Cloth-Changing Person Re-Identification

Wajahat Khalid[1], Bin Liu[1]([✉]), Xulin Li[1],
and Muhammad Ali Qureshi[2]

[1] University of Science and Technology of China, Hefei, China
{wajahat28,lxlkw}@mail.ustc.edu.cn, flowice@ustc.edu.cn
[2] The Islamia University of Bahawalpur, Bahawalpur, Pakistan
ali.qureshi@iub.edu.pk

Abstract. Cloth-independent features are the main core of Cloth-Changing Person Re-Identification (CCReID), such as the face, hairstyle, gaits, body structure, shape, etc. Most current CCReID models exploit multi-modality information (e.g., contour, skeleton, and silhouette) to estimate the body shape for target matching. However, the performance and complexity of these methods are highly dependent on the additional multi-modality models (e.g., accuracy, and computational cost). This paper explores cloth-independent features directly from the original images through a multi-perspective of identity analysis. To this end, we propose a novel Cloth-Independent feature learning from Multi-Perspective for Cloth-Changing Person Re-Identification (CIMP-CCReID) model. Specifically, we introduce View Classification Learning (VCL) and Cloth Classification Learning (CCL) along with identity classification, which force the model to mine cloth-independent features from different perspectives of identity in RGB images. Since no view ground truths are available in the current cloth-changing datasets, we propose a new View Predictor (VP) module that predicts the identity view in the image with respect to the capturing camera. Extensive experiments on three benchmarked cloth-changing datasets, including LTCC, PRCC, and VC-Clothes, demonstrate the effectiveness of our model against state-of-the-art CCReID methods.

Keywords: Cloth-Changing · Person Re-Identification · Multi-Perspective · Cloth-independent features

1 Introduction

Person Re-IDentification (Re-ID) goal is to find a person of interest across multiple non-overlapping cameras. In particular, person Re-ID identifies a target person by comparing the specific features of the probe image with other gallery images to determine whether this is the same person. Moreover, initial studies in person Re-IDs are classified as short-term person Re-ID, which assumes that

C. Wallraven et al. (Eds.): ICPRAI 2024, LNCS 14892, pp. 462–477, 2025.
https://doi.org/10.1007/978-981-97-8702-9_31

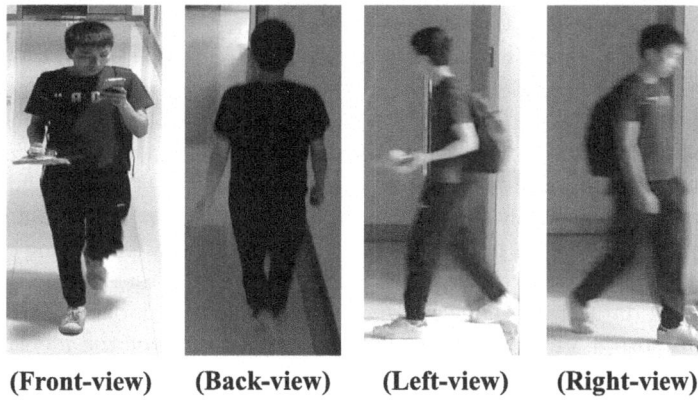

(Front-view)   (Back-view)   (Left-view)   (Right-view)

Fig. 1. The illustration of the same person images with different views w.r.t the capturing camera. The same person looks differently in all four images, although he wears the same clothes. The reason is that the same person's body shape reflects differently in different points of view.

the targeted person is wearing the same clothes and moving with respect to a short period in a multi-camera system.

Short-term person Re-ID methods leverage visual appearance features such as colors, clothes, shoes, etc., to identify a specific person and simplify various challenges such as illumination [11], occlusions [18], image resolutions [26], misalignment [23], background bias [24], etc. On the contrary, visual appearance information can also vary for the same person with different clothes/outfits, e.g., in criminal cases suspect may try to change outfits and hide his identity, or under long-term person tracking normal person also change the clothes. Hence, it is challenging for existing short-term person Re-ID models to identify the same person with different clothes. Therefore, a new direction named Cloth-Changing Person Re-Identification (CCreID) is initiated to counter this challenge.

In general, CCreID methods mitigate the influence of cloth variations by estimating body shape and gait through multi-modality information, e.g., human key points [19], contour sketches [27], radio signals [3], silhouettes [7,13], human parsing [21] and 3D shape [1,28]. However, multi-modality-based methods not only enhance the complexity but also estimate the body shape, which usually depends upon image quality that is actually degraded in real-world CCTV applications. On the other hand, the original RGB images contain rich cloth-independent information such as the face, hairstyle, body structure, shape, gaits, etc., especially when studied from a multi-perspective. In particular, identity body shape reflects differently in RGB images when observed from different perspectives (front, back, left, and right views). Thus, front or back views highlight the face, torso shape, body width information, etc., and side views reflect hairstyle, arm shape, belly shape, gaits information, etc., as shown in Fig. 1.

In this paper, we leverage the alteration of body shapes and structure from different perspectives and explore cloth-independent features directly from the RGB image by proposing View Classification Learning (VCL) and Cloth

Classification Learning (CCL). Specifically, we introduce view and cloth classifiers along with identity classifier after the backbone of the Re-ID model and exploit a multi-class classification learning strategy, where we further divide identity images into view and cloth classes. The core idea is to force the backbone to inspect each identity from different perspectives and extract cloth-independent features such as face, hairstyle, body shape, structure, etc. To this end, we design view-based and cloth-based adversarial loss functions to disentangle cloth-independent features from multi-perspective of identity by penalizing the identifying power of backbone relative to views and clothes. Moreover, image-based cloth-changing datasets do not contain view ground truth labels. To tackle this issue, we propose a View Predictor (VP) module to predict the identity views in RGB images w.r.t the capturing camera.

In summary, our main contributions to this paper are the following:

- We propose a novel CCreID method, called CIMP-CCreID, which directly explores cloth-independent features from RGB images through multi-perspective of identity. To the best of our knowledge, CIMP is the first CCreID model that studies body shape reflection in images from different perspectives and explores cloth-independent features.
- To implement the CIMP-CCreID, we propose the VP module to predict the identity views in the image with respect to the capturing camera and introduce VCL and CCL to extract cloth-independent features from multi-perspective of identity in RGB images for CCreID.
- CIMP outperforms significantly on three famous cloth-changing benchmarks: LTCC, PRCC, and VC-Clothes. Moreover, comprehensive ablation studies demonstrate the effectiveness of our proposed module and strategies.

2   Related Work

Short-term Person Re-ID. Many short-term person Re-ID methods have been proposed to tackle various challenges such as illumination [11], occlusions [18], image resolutions [26], pose variations [8], misalignment [17,23], background bias [24], etc. Due to the high reliance on visual appearance information, these methods are unable to perform under cloth change scenarios where the target changes their outfits.

Cloth-Changing Person Re-ID. In long-term person tracking, variation of outfits alters the visual appearance of the same person, which increases the intraclass distance and becomes a most significant challenge for person Re-ID. Some CCreID methods use extra multi-modality information to reduce the cloth variation influence and force the model to learn cloth-irrelevant features. Specifically, Qian et al. [19] exploit the pose estimation model to extract human joints/key points and then estimate body structure and shape with the help of joint information. However, Partial body or occluded images affect the human joints/key points information. Yang et al. [27] used a contour sketch of the person's body and applied a spatial polar transformation to extract discriminative body shape information, but this method assumed that cloth thickness and sizes were consistent. Fan et al. [3] used Radio Frequency (RF) signals to extract intrinsic features such as body shape, size, etc., but RF signals require additional devices that limit their practical applications.

Hong et al. [7] and Jin et al. [13] extracted body shapes and gait information from human silhouettes and transferred them to appearance stream features by mutual learning. However, this requires an additional stream to extract the body shapes or gaits information. Shu et al. [21] shuffled clothes pixels of different identity images with the help of human parsing for data augmentation. This method increases the cloth variation but not cloth textures (new outfits). Chen et al. [1] and Yu et al. [28] explored cloth texture-insensitive 3D shape features directly from 2D images by the 3D human body reconstruction approach. Similarly, Han et al. [5] extracted 3D human shape features from video frames, but the 3D body reconstruction approach increases the complexity and provides estimated body shape information.

Huang et al. [10] regularized identity descriptions by assessing clothing status in RGB images, aiming to effectively handle both scenarios of cloth changing and cloth consistency. Gu et al. [4] proposed a Cloth-based Adversarial Loss (CAL) for only RGB modality, which works as a multi-positive-class classification loss, where all cloth classes under the same person are categorized into mutual-positive classes. Inspired by CAL, in this paper, we decouple cloth-independent features using a multi-class classification learning approach. However, our method explores features from different identity perspectives in the image and focuses on body shape and structure along with other cloth-independent information such as the face, arm, hairstyle, etc., which enhances its effectiveness more than CAL.

Multi-perspective. A person's body structure reflects differently under different viewpoints, which is a considerable challenge for person Re-ID. Many methods [12,14,20,22] have been proposed to tackle the view variation issue. Specifically, Karanam et al. [14] introduce viewpoint invariant dictionaries that match the person's image captured from different perspectives. Sun et al. [22] investigate the consequence of viewpoint on person Re-ID accuracy. Sarfraz et al. [20] incorporate body joints and viewpoint information to train a robust person Re-ID. Jia et al. [12] proposed a semi-supervised learning approach to learn projections of different views. While in this paper, we use view information to train the Re-ID backbone to focus and explore cloth-independent features such as face, body shape, structure, etc., from different perspectives.

3   Proposed Method

3.1   CIMP-CCreID Framework

CIMP-CCreID framework aims to explore cloth-independent features from input identity images based on multi-perspective. The main structure of our proposed CIMP-CCreID model is shown in Fig. 2, where initially, the proposed VP module predicts the person's view in the image relative to the capturing camera (see

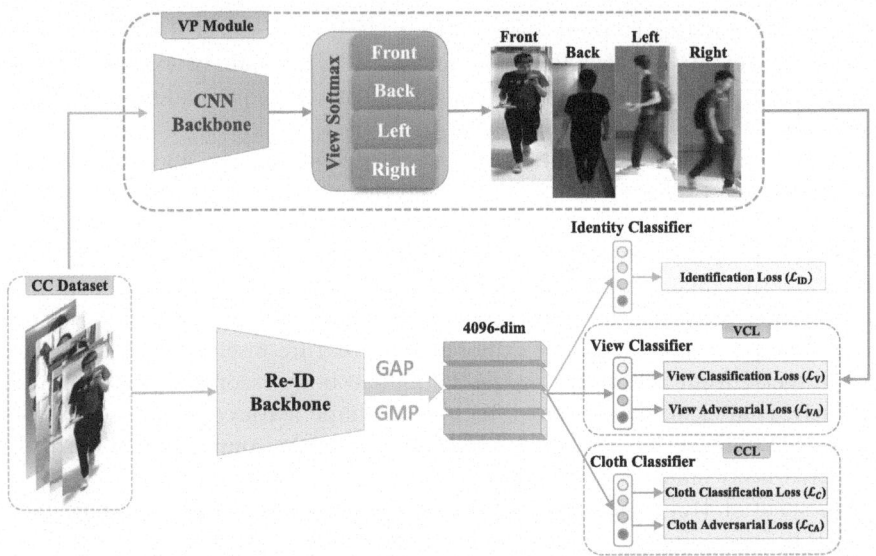

Fig. 2. The framework of the proposed CIMP-CCreID. The View Predictor (VP) module aims to predict the person's view w.r.t the capturing camera. View Classification Learning (VCL) mines identity-relevant cues by analyzing each identity from multiple perspectives. Cloth Classification Learning (CCL) disentangles cloth-independent cues by penalizing the identifying power of backbone to clothes. VCL and CCL jointly explore the cloth-independent features from different viewpoints over a single identity in RGB images.

Sect. 3.2). Subsequently, the input images are fed into the backbone of the Re-ID model for feature extraction. In the next step, the model applies Global Average Pooling (GAP) and Global Max Pooling (GMP) to the backbone's output features and concatenates them. Next, these features move through a bottleneck layer composed of a batch normalization layer, and lastly, the view classifier (in Sect. 3.3) and cloth classifier (in Sect. 3.4) are used with the identity classifier. The identity classifier explores the discriminative identity features. Specifically, let $C_{ID}(.|y)$ is an identity classifier with parameters ϕ and given an input image x_i with identity annotation y_i, the identification loss $\mathcal{L}_{ID}$ can be defined as:

$$\mathcal{L}_{ID} = -\sum_{i=1}^{N} \log \left(\frac{p\,(x_i, y_i)}{\sum_{j=1}^{N_{ID}} p\,(x_i, y_j)} \right), \qquad (1)$$

$$p\,(x_i, y) = C_{ID}\,(\phi\,(x_i; \theta)\mid y), \qquad (2)$$

where N and N_{ID} represent the number of images and identity classes, respectively, and $(x_i; \theta)$ is the output of the backbone with parameters θ, and $p(x_i, y)$ the predicted probability of x_i for identity label y.

3.2 View Predictor

Person views with respect to the camera play a vital role in the person Re-ID model because the variation of the view alters the visual information. We aim to train the model to explore cloth-independent cues from different viewpoints over a single person in RGB images. In this work, we use four view annotations (front, back, left, and right), but unfortunately, no view annotations are available in current cloth-changing datasets. To tackle this issue, we propose a View Predictor (VP) module that predicts identity views in images w.r.t the capturing camera. The VCL leverages this view information and compels the model to learn cloth-independent features from multiple perspectives of identity.

Concretely, we use DenseNet-121 [9] pre-trained on the ImageNet [2] dataset as the backbone of the VP module and fine-tune the view classifier of the VP module on the RAP [16] dataset, which contains 84,928 images with 72 types of attributes, including viewpoints.

3.3 View Classification Learning

The core idea of CIMP-CCreID is to explore cloth-independent features directly from RGB images. However, it is difficult for the Re-ID model to neglect visual appearance and focus on cloth-independent features. Therefore, we aim to force the model to analyze each identity from multiple perspectives. To achieve this goal, we proposed View Classification Learning (VCL) to explore cloth-independent features, especially body shape and structure, from multi-view in RGB images. We design a view-based adversarial loss function that leverages view information to study each identity's body shape and structure from diverse perspectives. More specifically, we classify each identity image further into view classes, and different identity view classes are assigned differently from each other, which depends upon the identity label plus view information. By view classification under each identity, VCL compels the Re-ID backbone to scrutinize each individual from four perspectives (front, back, left, and right views) as shown in Fig. 3.

Concretely, let $C_v(.|v)$ is a view classifier with parameters φ and given an input image x_i with view annotation v_i, VCL consists of two phases: in the first phase view classification loss $\mathcal{L}_V$ are utilized to train the view classifier by classifying identity images further into view classes as follows in equation (3):

$$\mathcal{L}_V = -\sum_{i=1}^{N} \log \left(\frac{p(x_i, v_i)}{\sum_{j=1}^{N_v} p(x_i, v_j)} \right), \tag{3}$$

$$p(x_i, v) = C_v(\varphi(x_i; \theta) \mid v), \tag{4}$$

where N_v represent the number of view classes, and $p(x_i, v)$ is the predicted probability of x_i for identity view label v.

In the second phase, we introduce a view-based adversarial loss $\mathcal{L}_{VA}$ function to learn the identity-relevant features from multi-perspective by multi-positive-class learning strategy, which treats all view classes under the same identity as

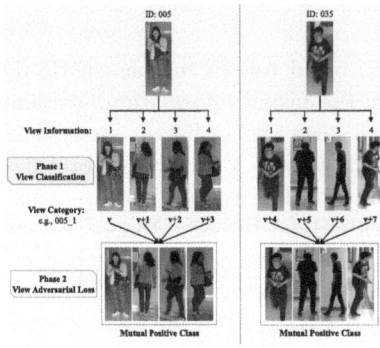 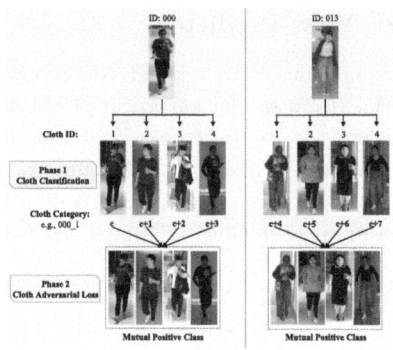

Fig. 3. The illustration of VCL, which consists of two phases: 1) View Classification that classifies each individual further into view categories ('v' represents the view class number). 2) Multi-positive-class classification, which treats all view classes under the same identity as a mutual positive class.

Fig. 4. The illustration of CCL, which consists of two phases: 1) Cloth Classification that classifies each individual further into cloth categories ('c' represents the cloth class number). 2) Multi-positive-class classification, which treats all cloth classes under the same identity as a mutual positive class

a mutual positive class and can be defined as:

$$\mathcal{L}_{VA} = -\sum_{i=1}^{N}\sum_{v=1}^{N_v} w(v)\log\left(\frac{p\left(x_i,v\right)}{p\left(x_i,v\right)+\sum_{j\in y_i^{v-}} p\left(x_i,j\right)}\right), \tag{5}$$

$$w(v) = \begin{cases} \frac{\rho^2}{M} & ,v\in y_i^{v+} \\ 0 & ,otherwise \end{cases}, \tag{6}$$

where y_i^{v+} is a set of view classes that belong to the same identity and y_i^{v-} is a set of view classes that belong to different identities. M represents the total number of view classes in y_i^{v+}. $w(v)$ is the weight of cross-entropy loss for v^{th} view class and ρ is a hyper-parameter.

3.4 Cloth Classification Learning

To further disentangle cloth-irrelevant features, we introduce Cloth Classification Learning (CCL), where we divide each identity image into cloth classes. The cloth classes depend upon identity labels plus cloth information, and every identity has different cloth classes even though they wear the same clothes. The illustration of CCL is shown in Fig. 4.

Concretely, let $C_{cl}(.|c)$ is a cloth classifier with parameters ϑ, and given an input image x_i with cloth annotation c_i, CCL is divided into two phases: In the first phase, cloth classification loss $\mathcal{L}_C$ is used to optimize the cloth classifier that can be expressed as:

$$\mathcal{L}_C = -\sum_{i=1}^{N} \log \left(\frac{p(x_i, c_i)}{\sum_{j=1}^{N_c} p(x_i, c_j)} \right), \tag{7}$$

$$p(x_i, c) = C_{cl}(\vartheta(x_i; \theta) \mid c), \tag{8}$$

where N_c represent the number of cloth classes, and $p(x_i, c)$ is the predicted probability of x_i for identity cloth label c.

In the second phase, following CAL [4], we introduce a cloth-based adversarial loss $\mathcal{L}_{CA}$ function to learn the cloth-independent features by penalizing the identifying power of backbone relative to clothes and can be defined as:

$$\mathcal{L}_{CA} = -\sum_{i=1}^{N} \sum_{c=1}^{N_c} w(c) \log \left(\frac{p(x_i, c)}{p(x_i, c) + \sum_{j \in y_i^{c-}} p(x_i, j)} \right), \tag{9}$$

$$w(c) = \begin{cases} 1 - \rho + \frac{\rho}{K} & , c = c_i \\ \frac{\rho}{K} & , c \neq c_i \text{ and } c \in y_i^{c+}, \\ 0 & , c \in y_i^{c-} \end{cases} \tag{10}$$

where y_i^{c+} is a set of cloth classes that belong to the same identity, and y_i^{c-} is a set of cloth classes that belong to different identities. K represents the total number of cloth classes in y_i^{c+}. $w(c)$ represents the weight of cross-entropy loss for c^{th} cloth class and gives high weight $(1 - \rho + \frac{\rho}{K})$ in equation (10) to positive cloth class (with the same outfits under the same identity) compared to the weights $(\frac{\rho}{K})$ of the positive cloth classes (with different outfits under the same identity) for better cloth-consistent accuracy under cloth-changing Re-ID. ρ is a hyper-parameter.

3.5 Optimization

During training, each iteration comprises the following two-stage optimization.

In the first stage, we optimize the view and cloth classifier by minimizing the view classification loss $\mathcal{L}_V$ and cloth classification loss $\mathcal{L}_C$. In the second stage, we fix the parameters of the view and cloth classifier and optimize the backbone by minimizing the view-based adversarial loss $\mathcal{L}_{VA}$, cloth-based adversarial loss $\mathcal{L}_{CA}$, and identification loss $\mathcal{L}_{ID}$.

The total loss function is computed as follows:

$$\mathcal{L}_{TOTAL} = \mathcal{L}_{ID} + \mathcal{L}_V + \mathcal{L}_{VA} + \mathcal{L}_C + \mathcal{L}_{CA} \tag{11}$$

4 Experiments

4.1 Datasets and Evaluation Protocol

We evaluate our proposed CIMP method on three widely used image-based cloth-changing datasets: LTCC [19], PRCC [27], and VC-Clothes [25].

LTCC [19] dataset comprises 17,119 images of 152 identities with 477 outfits captured by 12 different cameras, and each identity has outfits in the range of 2–14. **PRCC** [27] dataset comprises 33,698 images of 221 identities with 442 outfits captured by three different cameras, and each identity has two outfits. **VC-Clothes** [25] is a synthetic dataset captured through the GTA5 game, which comprises 19,060 images of 512 identities with 1,241 outfits captured by four different cameras.

Evaluation Protocol: The cumulative matching characteristics of top K results (CMC@K) and mean average precision (mAP) are used as the evaluation metrics. To ensure a fair comparison with existing methods, we evaluate our method under three different test settings: 1) **Standard Setting:** All query and test images are used for evaluation, which includes cloth-change and cloth-consistent identity images. 2) **Cloth-Change Setting:** Only cloth-changing query and test identity images are used in the evaluation, and cloth-consistent images are discarded in this setting. 3) **Same-Clothes Setting:** Only cloth-consistent query and test images are used in the evaluation. For LTCC and VC-Clothes datasets, evaluate the accuracy using standard and cloth-change settings. As for the PRCC dataset, evaluate the accuracy using same-clothes and cloth-change settings [27].

4.2   Implementation Details

We implemented our method on the PyTorch framework. For a fair comparison, we use ResNet-50 [6] pre-trained on the ImageNet [2] dataset as the backbone of the Re-ID model. The last downsampling of ResNet-50 is removed to boost the granularity. We selected an image size of 384×192 [19] for data augmentation, with random cropping, random horizontal flipping, and random erasing [29]. The batch size is 32, with four identities and 8 images per identity. The model is trained for 80 epochs with Adam optimizer [15], and the learning rate is initialized to 3.5×10^{-4} and dropped by 10% of the original rate after every 20 epochs. Hyper-parameter ρ is empirically set to 0.1. Following [4], the $\mathcal{L}_V + \mathcal{L}_{VA} + \mathcal{L}_C + \mathcal{L}_{CA}$ are introduced after 25th epoch for training.

4.3   Comparison with State-of-the-Art Methods

We compare our proposed CIMP method with state-of-the-art general Re-ID methods (HACNN [17], PCB [23], IANet [8]) and cloth-changing Re-ID methods (SPT+ASE [27], GI-ReID [13], CESD [19], RCSANet [10], 3DSL [1], FSAM [7], CAL [4]) as shown in Table 1. Our method achieves significant performance in all three cloth-changing datasets under cloth-change settings.

Compared with FSAM [7], a state-of-the-art multi-modality-based CCreID method, our method surpasses by 4.1%/3.1%/6.8% in Rank@1 accuracy on LTCC/PRCC/VC-Clothes datasets, respectively. FSAM [7] utilizes two additional modalities (pose + silhouettes) with a double-stream network for its approach. In contrast, our proposed CIMP method achieves superior performance with less complexity, leveraging only extra view labels for view classification.

Table 1. Comparison of rank@1 and mAP accuracy (%) with state-of-the-art methods on LTCC, PRCC, and VC-Clothes datasets under the cloth-change setting. 'Sil.', 'Pose', and '3D' refer to the silhouettes, human body poses, and 3D body shape information, respectively. The best results are represented in bold.

Methods	Modalities	LTCC Dataset		PRCC Dataset		VC-Clothes	
		Rank@1	mAP	Rank@1	mAP	Rank@1	mAP
HACNN [17]	RGB	21.6	9.3	21.8	–	–	–
PCB [23]	RGB	23.5	10.0	41.8	38.7	62.0	62.2
IANet [8]	RGB	25.0	12.6	46.3	45.9	–	–
SPT+ASE [27]	Contour sketch	–	–	34.4	–	–	–
GI-ReID [13]	RGB + Sil.	23.7	10.4	33.3	–	64.5	57.8
CESD [19]	RGB + Pose	26.2	12.4	–	–	–	–
RCSANet [10]	RGB	–	–	50.2	48.6	–	–
3DSL [1]	RGB+Pose+Sil.+3D	31.2	14.8	51.3	–	79.9	**81.2**
FSAM [7]	RGB+Pose+Sil.	38.5	16.2	54.5	–	78.6	78.9
CAL [4]	RGB	40.1	18.0	55.2	55.8	84.7	78.9
CIMP (Our)	RGB	**42.6**	**19.1**	**57.6**	**56.7**	**85.4**	80.3

Table 2. Comparison of rank@1 and mAP accuracy (%) with state-of-the-art methods under standard and same-clothes settings. The best results are represented in bold.

Methods	LTCC Dataset		PRCC Dataset		VC-Clothes	
	Standard Setting		Same-Clothes Setting		Standard Setting	
	Rank@1	mAP	Rank@1	mAP	Rank@1	mAP
PCB [23]	65.1	30.6	99.8	97.0	94.7	94.3
FSAM [7]	73.2	35.4	98.8	–	94.7	94.8
CAL [4]	74.2	40.8	100	99.8	94.5	95.1
Baseline	65.3	29.3	99.7	97.7	93.4	92.9
CIMP (Our)	**75.5**	**41.3**	**100**	**99.9**	**95.7**	**95.6**

Compared with the existing state-of-the-art CCreID method CAL [4], which only uses RGB modality, our method outperforms by 2.5%/2.4%/0.7% in Rank@1 accuracy on LTCC/PRCC/VC-Clothes datasets, respectively. The main reason for the absolute improvement in performance is that our method more competently explores cloth-independent features, especially body shape and structure, through multi-perspective analysis of identity in RGB images. CAL and our approach are based on multi-class classification learning, but the CAL method is clueless regarding body shape and structure, which is the essential cue for CCreID. The experimental results demonstrate our proposed CIMP model's effectiveness and superiority over existing CCreID methods.

The experiment results under the standard and same-clothes settings are shown in Table 2. Our CIMP method achieves consistent performance compared to the baseline, improving by 10.2%/0.3%/2.3% in Rank@1 accuracy on LTCC/PRCC/VC-Clothes datasets, respectively. Compared with state-of-the-art Re-ID methods, our proposed method also rendered significant results under the standard and same-clothes settings, demonstrating its strong generalizability.

Table 3. Ablation studies of each component of the proposed CIMP method on the LTCC dataset under standard and cloth-change settings.

Baseline	VCL		CCL		LTCC Dataset			
					Standard Setting		Cloth-Change Setting	
$\mathcal{L}_{ID}$	$\mathcal{L}_V$	$\mathcal{L}_{VA}$	$\mathcal{L}_C$	$\mathcal{L}_{CA}$	Rank@1	mAP	Rank@1	mAP
✓					65.3	29.3	27.8	11.0
✓	✓	✓			75.0	38.5	41.6	17.5
✓			✓	✓	74.2	40.8	40.1	18.0
✓	✓	✓	✓	✓	**75.5**	**41.3**	**42.6**	**19.1**

5   Ablation Studies

In this section, we perform an ablation study on the widely-used cloth-changing dataset LTCC [19] to verify the effectiveness of different modules of the proposed CIMP model, such as VCL, CCL, and VP modules.

Component Analysis. To verify the validity of each component of the proposed CIMP method, we conducted an ablation study, shown in Table 3. First, we reproduce the baseline model which only utilizes identification loss $\mathcal{L}_{ID}$ during training. Next, we introduce the VCL by incorporating a view classifier following the Re-ID backbone and optimize the view classifier using the view classification loss $\mathcal{L}_V$, and simultaneously optimize the backbone by minimizing view-based adversarial loss $\mathcal{L}_{VA}$ and identification loss $\mathcal{L}_{ID}$. VCL outperformed the baseline by achieving a 9.7%/13.8% improvement in Rank@1 accuracy under standard/cloth-change settings on the LTCC dataset, respectively. The reason is that VCL forces the backbone to analyze each identity's body shape and structure from a multi-perspective. Subsequently, we only incorporate CCL and train the backbone model by minimizing cloth-based adversarial loss $\mathcal{L}_{CA}$, and identification loss $\mathcal{L}_{ID}$. Additionally, we employ the cloth classification loss $\mathcal{L}_C$ to optimize the cloth classifier. CCL surpasses the baseline by a considerable margin under standard and cloth-change settings, primarily because CCL guides the backbone to learn cloth-independent features by penalizing the identifying power of backbone to clothes. When both VCL and CCL are introduced together, they achieve the best performance and surpass the baseline with an impressive 10.2%/14.8% absolute improvement in Rank@1 accuracy under standard/cloth-change settings on the LTCC dataset, respectively. One plausible explanation for this improvement is that VCL and CCL jointly force the backbone to thoroughly explore cloth-independent features under multi-perspective cues, which enhances the Re-ID model's robustness against cloth variation.

The Backbone of VP Module. We evaluate the performance of our proposed CIMP with different backbone selections of the VP module, as shown in Table 4. In this ablation study, we testify the influence of VP module prediction on CIMP model performance by using different backbones (e.g., ResNet-50 [6], DenseNet-121 [9]) of VP module. ResNet-50 [6] shows slightly low performance compared to DenseNet-121 [9] as a backbone of the VP module. Thus, we choose DenseNet-121 [9] as the backbone of our proposed VP module.

Table 4. Ablation studies of the backbone of the proposed VP module on the LTCC dataset under standard and cloth-change settings.

Backbone	LTCC Dataset			
	Standard Setting		Cloth-Change Setting	
	Rank@1	mAP	Rank@1	mAP
ResNet-50 [6]	74.6	41.1	42.1	18.9
DenseNet-121 [9]	**75.5**	**41.3**	**42.6**	**19.1**

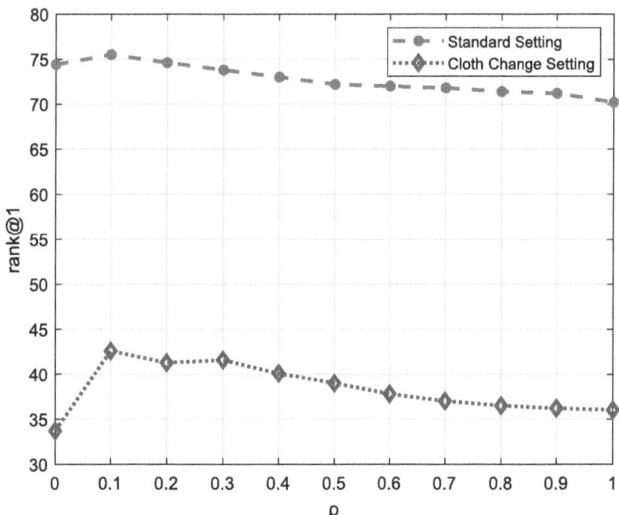

Fig. 5. Hyperparameter sensitivity analysis: we report the rank@1 accuracy of the proposed CIMP method under different values of ρ on the LTCC dataset.

Hyperparameter Sensitivity Analysis. To further investigate the robustness of our CIMP method, we analyze the influence of ρ in view-based and cloth-based adversarial losses under standard and cloth-change settings on LTCC dataset, as shown in Fig. 5. In Eqs. (6) and (10), we use the same ρ hyperparameter but assign different weights to enhance joint learning between VCL and CCL. When $\rho = 0$ both $\mathcal{L}_{VA}$ and $\mathcal{L}_{CA}$ turn into simple view and cloth classification losses, which confuses the backbone between multiple classifications without proper identity supervision. Thus, it leads to sub-optimal outcomes under cloth-change settings. As ρ increases, the weight difference also increases among the same clothes, different clothes, and views under identity. Consequently, accuracy under cloth-change settings exhibits an initial rapid increase, followed by oscillations and degradation, ultimately indicating signs of overfitting. Therefore, we find a trade-off and set ρ to 0.1 for all experiments.

Visualization. We visualize the feature activation maps through different perspectives (front, back, left, and right views) on three cloth-changing datasets (LTCC, PRCC, and VC-Clothes), as shown in Fig. 6. Compared to the baseline, our proposed CIMP method thoroughly explores cloth-independent features, especially more focused on body shape and structure. In front view images, our method almost covers all identity front body parts such as the face, torso, legs, etc. Similarly, in back and side views, our method focused specifically on body structure (e.g., back body, arms, gait) compared to the baseline. Therefore, with the help of a multi-perspective analysis of identity, the CIMP method learns cloth-independent features more effectively under cloth variations.

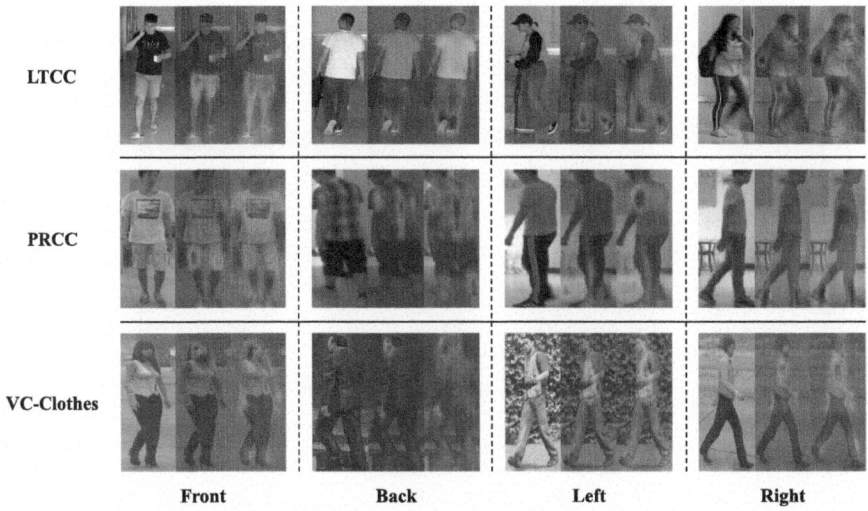

Fig. 6. The visualization of feature activation maps from different perspectives (front, back, left, and right views) on LTCC, PRCC, and VC-Clothes datasets. In each triplet of images, the first column represents the original RGB image, while the second and third columns represent the baseline and our CIMP method, respectively.

6   Conclusion

This paper proposes a novel Cloth-Changing Person Re-Identification method, termed Cloth-Independent feature learning from Multi-Perspective (CIMP), which directly explores cloth-independent features from RGB images. We introduce View Classification Learning (VCL) and Cloth Classification Learning (CCL), which jointly compel the backbone model to learn cloth-independent features through multi-perspective identity analysis in RGB images using a multi-class classification learning approach. Moreover, current image-based cloth-changing datasets do not contain view ground truth labels. To tackle this issue, we propose a View Predictor (VP) module to predict the identity views in RGB images w.r.t the capturing camera. Extensive experiments on three benchmarked cloth-changing datasets demonstrate the effectiveness of our proposed CIMP method.

In the next phase, to further disentangle the cloth-independent features under the cloth-change scenarios, especially for the body shape and structure information, the CIMP-CCreID can be improved by considering the body rotation angle ($0°$- $360°$) cues along with viewpoints information. However, the existing cloth-changing dataset doesn't have enough training data with complete identity body rotation images. To this end, a cloth-changing dataset containing identity images with complete $360°$ body rotation is required.

Acknowledgements. This work is supported by the National Natural Science Foundation of China (Grant No. 62272430).

References

1. Chen, J., Jiang, X., Wang, F., Zhang, J., Zheng, F., Sun, X., Zheng, W.S.: Learning 3d shape feature for texture-insensitive person re-identification. In: Proceedings of the IEEE/CVF Conference on Computer Vision and Pattern Recognition, pp. 8146–8155 (2021)
2. Deng, J., Dong, W., Socher, R., Li, L.J., Li, K., Fei-Fei, L.: ImageNet: a large-scale hierarchical image database. In: 2009 IEEE Conference on Computer Vision and Pattern Recognition, pp. 248–255. IEEE (2009)
3. Fan, L., Li, T., Fang, R., Hristov, R., Yuan, Y., Katabi, D.: Learning longterm representations for person re-identification using radio signals. In: Proceedings of the IEEE/CVF Conference on Computer Vision and Pattern Recognition, pp. 10699–10709 (2020)
4. Gu, X., Chang, H., Ma, B., Bai, S., Shan, S., Chen, X.: Clothes-changing person re-identification with rgb modality only. In: Proceedings of the IEEE/CVF Conference on Computer Vision and Pattern Recognition, pp. 1060–1069 (2022)
5. Han, K., Huang, Y., Gong, S., Wang, L., Tan, T.: 3d shape temporal aggregation for video-based clothing-change person re-identification. In: Proceedings of the Asian Conference on Computer Vision, pp. 2371–2387 (2022)
6. He, K., Zhang, X., Ren, S., Sun, J.: Deep residual learning for image recognition. In: Proceedings of the IEEE Conference on Computer Vision and Pattern Recognition, pp. 770–778 (2016)

7. Hong, P., Wu, T., Wu, A., Han, X., Zheng, W.S.: Fine-grained shape-appearance mutual learning for cloth-changing person re-identification. In: Proceedings of the IEEE/CVF Conference on Computer Vision and Pattern Recognition, pp. 10513–10522 (2021)
8. Hou, R., Ma, B., Chang, H., Gu, X., Shan, S., Chen, X.: Interaction-and-aggregation network for person re-identification. In: Proceedings of the IEEE/CVF Conference on Computer Vision and Pattern Recognition, pp. 9317–9326 (2019)
9. Huang, G., Liu, Z., Van Der Maaten, L., Weinberger, K.Q.: Densely connected convolutional networks. In: Proceedings of the IEEE Conference on Computer Vision and Pattern Recognition, pp. 4700–4708 (2017)
10. Huang, Y., Wu, Q., Xu, J., Zhong, Y., Zhang, Z.: Clothing status awareness for long-term person re-identification. In: Proceedings of the IEEE/CVF International Conference on Computer Vision, pp. 11895–11904 (2021)
11. Huang, Y., Zha, Z.J., Fu, X., Zhang, W.: Illumination-invariant person re-identification. In: Proceedings of the 27th ACM International Conference on Multimedia, pp. 365–373 (2019)
12. Jia, J., Ruan, Q., Jin, Y., An, G., Ge, S.: View-specific subspace learning and re-ranking for semi-supervised person re-identification. Pattern Recogn. **108**, 107568 (2020)
13. Jin, X., et al.: Cloth-changing person re-identification from a single image with gait prediction and regularization. In: Proceedings of the IEEE/CVF Conference on Computer Vision and Pattern Recognition, pp. 14278–14287 (2022)
14. Karanam, S., Li, Y., Radke, R.J.: Person re-identification with discriminatively trained viewpoint invariant dictionaries. In: Proceedings of the IEEE International Conference on Computer Vision, pp. 4516–4524 (2015)
15. Kingma, D., Ba, J.: Adam: a method for stochastic optimization. In: International Conference on Learning Representations (ICLR), San Diega, CA, USA (2015)
16. Li, D., Zhang, Z., Chen, X., Huang, K.: A richly annotated pedestrian dataset for person retrieval in real surveillance scenarios. IEEE Trans. Image Process. **28**(4), 1575–1590 (2018)
17. Li, W., Zhu, X., Gong, S.: Harmonious attention network for person re-identification. In: Proceedings of the IEEE Conference on Computer Vision and Pattern Recognition, pp. 2285–2294 (2018)
18. Miao, J., Wu, Y., Liu, P., Ding, Y., Yang, Y.: Pose-guided feature alignment for occluded person re-identification. In: Proceedings of the IEEE/CVF International Conference on Computer Vision, pp. 542–551 (2019)
19. Qian, X., et al.: Long-term cloth-changing person re-identification. In: Proceedings of the Asian Conference on Computer Vision (2020)
20. Sarfraz, M.S., Schumann, A., Eberle, A., Stiefelhagen, R.: A pose-sensitive embedding for person re-identification with expanded cross neighborhood re-ranking. In: Proceedings of the IEEE Conference on Computer Vision and Pattern Recognition, pp. 420–429 (2018)
21. Shu, X., Li, G., Wang, X., Ruan, W., Tian, Q.: Semantic-guided pixel sampling for cloth-changing person re-identification. IEEE Signal Process. Lett. **28**, 1365–1369 (2021)
22. Sun, X., Zheng, L.: Dissecting person re-identification from the viewpoint of viewpoint. In: Proceedings of the IEEE/CVF Conference on Computer Vision and Pattern Recognition, pp. 608–617 (2019)
23. Sun, Y., Zheng, L., Yang, Y., Tian, Q., Wang, S.: Beyond part models: person retrieval with refined part pooling (and a strong convolutional baseline). In: Pro-

ceedings of the European Conference on Computer Vision (ECCV), pp. 480–496 (2018)

24. Tian, M., et al.: Eliminating background-bias for robust person re-identification. In: Proceedings of the IEEE Conference on Computer Vision and Pattern Recognition, pp. 5794–5803 (2018)

25. Wan, F., Wu, Y., Qian, X., Chen, Y., Fu, Y.: When person re-identification meets changing clothes. In: Proceedings of the IEEE/CVF Conference on Computer Vision and Pattern Recognition Workshops, pp. 830–831 (2020)

26. Wang, Y., et al.: Resource aware person re-identification across multiple resolutions. In: Proceedings of the IEEE Conference on Computer Vision and Pattern Recognition, pp. 8042–8051 (2018)

27. Yang, Q., Wu, A., Zheng, W.S.: Person re-identification by contour sketch under moderate clothing change. IEEE Trans. Pattern Anal. Mach. Intell. **43**(6), 2029–2046 (2019)

28. Yu, H., Liu, B., Lu, Y., Chu, Q., Yu, N.: Multi-view geometry distillation for cloth-changing person reid. In: Chinese Conference on Pattern Recognition and Computer Vision (PRCV), pp. 29–41. Springer (2022)

29. Zhong, Z., Zheng, L., Kang, G., Li, S., Yang, Y.: Random erasing data augmentation. In: Proceedings of the AAAI Conference on Artificial Intelligence, vol. 34, pp. 13001–13008 (2020)

Calibration Misalignment as a Post-Hoc Approach for Out-of-Distribution Detection in Deep Neural Networks

Felip Guimerà Cuevas[1]($\boxtimes$) and Helmut Schmid[2]

[1] BMW Group, Munich, Germany
`felip.guimera-cuevas@bmw.de`
[2] Center for Information and Language Processing at LMU, Munich, Germany
`schmid@cis.lmu.de`

Abstract. This paper presents a post-hoc method for detecting out-of-distribution (OOD) examples in deep neural networks by utilizing multi-class output calibration misalignment. OOD detection is an essential subfield of outlier detection, which aims to classify new instances as either conforming to the training set distribution or being anomalous. Our method quantifies the difference in output probability calibration for individual classes by utilizing a one-vs-rest approach to the normalized total probability mass over all class calibrations. Furthermore, we leverage the magnitude of the probability mass misalignment between that of the combined probabilities of class pairs over the expected sum of their individual calibrated probabilities. Our results show that this discrepancy and probability misalignment can effectively be used to identify OOD examples for neural networks, as calibration alignment trained on in-distribution examples behaves anomalously when presented with outliers. Additionally, our prediction-based OOD approach can outperform common embedding-based anomaly detection methods on standard computer vision datasets.

Keywords: Out-of-distribution · Outlier · Deep Learning · Calibration

1 Introduction

Adjusting the predictions of a statistical or machine learning (ML) model to more closely match the true probabilities of the predicted events is a common practice known as calibration, which can improve the overall accuracy of the model [2,34]. The goal is to achieve a "well-calibrated" model that reflects the observed distributions in the data, ensuring reliable and trustworthy predictions by mitigating both overconfidence and underconfidence. Modern neural network models often exhibit poor calibration [10], with increasing classification accuracy corresponding to worsening probability error and miscalibration. Calibrating the probabilities produced by predictive ML models can thus be a valuable technique for improving their accuracy. Nonetheless, it is important to consider that the

C. Wallraven et al. (Eds.): ICPRAI 2024, LNCS 14892, pp. 478–492, 2025.
https://doi.org/10.1007/978-981-97-8702-9_32

calibration procedure may be time-consuming and may not always be required, depending on the specific application of the model.

Model calibration in predictive models can fail in various scenarios, but various methods are available to assess and monitor calibration quality [16]. Overfitting the training data can cause poor calibration, so data is divided into training, development, and test sets. Inadequate calibration can occur if test data has a different distribution than the training data, and a small sample size can lead to inadequate calibration. It's important to note that statistical calibration provides an average measure of confidence, not determining the confidence level for a specific instance based on the model.

Traditional evaluation measures like accuracy, precision, and recall help assess a model's predictive capabilities. However, achieving good overall performance is often insufficient. It's crucial to identify cases where the model is prone to making inaccurate predictions, such as dealing with outlier instances from different distributions, known as out-of-distribution (OOD) samples. Model calibration adjusts output probabilities to align with classification accuracy, but assumes new samples originate from the same distribution as the calibration set. State-of-the-art machine learning models perform well on test data but often assume real-world data is from the same distribution. This assumption, known as the closed-world assumption [28,35], poses a challenge when encountering OOD data, which refers to atypical samples.

Different tasks fall under OOD detection, such as outlier, anomaly, novelty, multi-class, and open-set recognition [28]. These terms are sometimes used inconsistently, so care should be taken when referring to them. Outlier detection involves modeling concentrated regions while training with contaminated data and ignoring these anomalous observations. On the other hand, novelty detection assumes clean data and aims to determine if new observations belong to the same distribution as the training data. Outlier detection methods can be categorized into clustering, classification, neighbor-based, statistical, information-theoretic, and spectral methods [1]. A more general distinction between approaches can be made as either embedding- or prediction-based. Embedding-based approaches transform data into lower dimensions and identify anomalies, while prediction-based approaches make predictions on new data points using a trained model. Choosing an approach depends on various assumptions, factors, and trade-offs. Outlier detection is crucial in applications like fraud detection, anomaly detection, data cleaning, and quality control [32,33].

This work introduces a prediction-based method for identifying OOD instances using a weighted one-vs-rest approach. It adjusts multi-class classification probabilities by training separate calibration models for each class, addressing the imbalance between positive and negative classes. The discrepancy vector is used to estimate confidence in output predictions, enhancing OOD instance recognition and novelty detection. The approach focuses on reliability and certainty, determining a level of mismatch. "Novelty" quantifies the discrepancy between reliability and certainty across all classes, aiding in detecting outliers and identifying instances deviating from the model's established patterns.

2   Related Work

Model calibration in machine learning helps to align the output probabilities of a model with the true probabilities of the data. There are various model calibration methods, including histogram binning [36], Platt scaling [27], isotonic regression [37], beta calibration [18], temperature scaling [10], matrix and vector scaling [10], Dirichlet calibration [17], Bayesian methods [8], and maximum-likelihood calibration [29]. Histogram binning is effective for already somewhat well-calibrated probabilities. Platt scaling transforms the outputs by fitting a logistic regression. Beta calibration is an improvement in logistic calibration. Isotonic regression corrects monotonic distortions but is prone to overfitting. Temperature scaling adjusts logits by dividing them by a learned scalar parameter, while Matrix and Vector scaling is a multi-class extension of Platt scaling.

Outlier detection is the identification of unusual data within a dataset that deviates from the norm. This can be considered a one-class classification problem where a model is trained exclusively on normal data and subsequently used to detect abnormal data based on a distance measure and threshold [26]. For novelty detection, various methods and techniques exist, including statistical approaches, neural networks, support vector machines, and clustering [21,23]; usually categorized into probabilistic methods, linear models, proximity-based approaches, outlier ensembles, or graph-based methods. The efficacy of each method varies depending on the data characteristics and distribution, data assumptions, and application domain. Challenges include handling high dimensional data, concept drifts, imbalanced data, and noise [9,31].

Overall, these approaches can further be categorized as [4,28]: one-class classification, probability and generative models, statistical methods, reconstruction methods, model consistency methods, and auxiliary task methods. These approaches differ in how they define and measure the similarity between new examples and the in-distribution data. One-class classification trains a classifier to distinguish between in-distribution and out-of-distribution examples. Probability and generative models fit a probability distribution to the in-distribution data and classify examples with low probability as out-of-distribution. Statistical methods compare the statistics of the input example to those of the in-distribution data and classify examples with anomalous statistics as out-of-distribution. Reconstruction methods train an autoencoder to encode and decode the in-distribution data and classify examples with poor reconstruction quality as out-of-distribution. Model consistency methods train (multiple) models or ensembles on the in-distribution data and classify examples where the models disagree as OOD. Auxiliary task methods train a model to perform a secondary task on the in-distribution data and classify examples where the performance on this task is as low as OOD.

Outlier detection in neural networks can be achieved through two main methods: ad-hoc and post-hoc. Ad-hoc methods involve integrating outlier detection into the model training process, while post-hoc methods analyze the model's output to detect outliers without modifying the training. Examples of ad-hoc methods include methods based on temperature scaling, noise, and decomposition [14,19], or the membership loss [25]. On the other hand, post-hoc methods include OpenMax [3,7], or methods based on density, e.g. Local Outlier Factor (LOF) [5], Local Correlation Integral (LOCI) [24], Global-Local Outlier Scores from Hierarchies (GLOSH) [6], clustering membership strengths [22], etc. Additional methods include One-Class-SVM [30] and Isolation Forests [20]. One-Class-SVM uses kernel functions and parameters to map data into a nonlinear space, while Isolation Forests use random feature space partitions to separate anomalies. A comprehensive benchmark of numerous outlier detection algorithms and techniques is provided by [11].

In this paper, we focus on post-hoc OOD detection which does not influence the original training of the model and is applied directly to the model outputs.

3 Methods

The objective is to calibrate the output probability estimates of a model for a multi-class classification problem with k classes, such that the calibrated probabilities reflect the model's prediction confidence both statistically and on a per-instance basis. Notice, how conventional calibration focuses on statistical "on-average" calibration. Given an instance i in a dataset, let $\vec{p}_i \in \mathbb{R}^k$ denote the learned output probability vector of the model, where $\sum_{j=0}^{k-1} p_i^{[j]} = 1$. So for each class index j, we define the corresponding one-vs-rest binary classification probabilities as $p_i^{[j]}$, representing the probability of instance i belonging to class j, and $\neg p_i^{[j]} = 1 - p_i^{[j]}$, representing the complement probability of instance i not belonging to class j. Note that $\neg p_i^{[j]} = \sum_{j' \neq j} p_i^{[j']}$, implying that $\neg p_i^{[j]}$ is equal to the sum of probabilities of instance i belonging to all other classes except class j. This observation will be used later to quantify the level of novelty in the discrepancy between the calibrated probabilities and the original probabilities. Hence, we consider two vectors: $\vec{p}_i$ and $\neg \vec{p}_i \triangleq \mathbb{1} - \vec{p}_i$, where $\mathbb{1}$ is a vector of ones of the corresponding size.

To calibrate the model, we fit k separate class-weighted one-vs-rest calibration models, denoted as Ξ_j, where each calibration model is responsible for calibrating the probability estimates of the original model for a specific class j. Class weighting is essential to address the inherent imbalance in binary one-vs-rest models. Calibration is performed on a distinct development set that does not overlap with the training set used for the original model, ensuring that the calibration models are not biased toward the training set. Ξ_j calibrates the probability estimate of the original model for class j, ensuring it accurately reflects the true probability of an instance belonging to class j or not. In essence, it calibrates the probability estimate to make decisions about whether an instance belongs to class j or not. Since each calibration model Ξ_j is trained independently, they result in different calibration adjustments for each class. While the goal is usually to maintain class-prediction rankings during calibration, we are particularly interested in examining these differences in calibration among the classes. To capture this, we construct the weight vector

$\vec{w}_i := [\Xi_0(p_i^{[0]}), \Xi_1(p_i^{[1]}), \ldots, \Xi_{k-1}(p_i^{[k-1]})]^T$, representing the calibrated positive scores for all classes. As it does not form a probability vector, we normalize it to $\vec{p}_i^* = \vec{w}_i/(\mathbb{1}^T\vec{w}_i)$. The final calibrated class prediction $\hat{y}$ is then simply the class index with the highest probability.

Considering the following difference $\epsilon_i^{[\hat{y}]} := p_i^{*[\hat{y}]} - \Xi_{\hat{y}}(p_i^{[\hat{y}]})$, which is the difference in the calibrated binary class probability over the transformed probability across all other calibrated predictions, we have:

$$\epsilon_i^{[\hat{y}]} = \frac{w_i^{[\hat{y}]}}{\mathbb{1}^T\vec{w}_i} - w_i^{[\hat{y}]} = \frac{w_i^{[\hat{y}]}(1 - \mathbb{1}^T\vec{w}_i)}{\mathbb{1}^T\vec{w}_i} \tag{1}$$

and following, with $\vec{\epsilon}_i := \vec{p}_i^* - \vec{w}_i$, then:

$$\mathbb{1}^T\vec{\epsilon}_i = \sum_{j=0}^{k-1} \epsilon_i^{[j]} = \sum_{j=0}^{k-1} \frac{w_i^{[j]}(1 - \mathbb{1}^T\vec{w}_i)}{\mathbb{1}^T\vec{w}_i} = \frac{(1 - \mathbb{1}^T\vec{w}_i)}{\mathbb{1}^T\vec{w}_i}\mathbb{1}^T\vec{w}_i = 1 - \mathbb{1}^T\vec{w}_i \tag{2}$$

With $\mathbb{1}^T\vec{p}_i \triangleq 1$, it immediately follows that in a perfectly calibrated model $\vec{p}_i = \vec{w}_i \implies \mathbb{1}^T\vec{\epsilon}_i = 0$; however, the converse is *not* true, i.e. $\mathbb{1}^T\vec{\epsilon}_i = 0 \not\Longrightarrow \vec{p}_i = \vec{w}_i$, since $1 - \mathbb{1}^T\vec{w}_i = 0 \iff 1 = \mathbb{1}^T\vec{w}_i \iff \mathbb{1}^T\vec{w}_i = \mathbb{1}^T\vec{p}_i \not\iff \vec{w}_i = \vec{p}_i$.

Knowing that $\forall j : 0 \le w_i^{[j]} \le 1$, an alternative is to calculate the sum of absolute error differences (the L_1 vector norm), which also eliminates the possibility of positive and negative $\epsilon_i^{[j]}$ values canceling each other out:

$$\|\vec{\epsilon}_i\|_1 = \mathbb{1}^T|\vec{\epsilon}_i| \triangleq \sum_{j=0}^{k-1} |\epsilon_i^{[j]}| = \sum_{j=0}^{k-1} \left|\frac{w_i^{[j]}(1 - \mathbb{1}^T\vec{w}_i)}{\mathbb{1}^T\vec{w}_i}\right| = \frac{|1 - \mathbb{1}^T\vec{w}_i|}{\mathbb{1}^T w_i} \sum_{j=0}^{k-1} \vec{w}_i^{[j]} = |1 - \mathbb{1}^T\vec{w}_i| \tag{3}$$

We may also consider the L_2 norm (i.e. Euclidean distance) $\|\vec{\epsilon}_i\|_2$ instead:

$$\|\vec{\epsilon}_i\|_2 = \sqrt{\sum_{j=0}^{k-1}(\epsilon_i^{[j]})^2} = \sqrt{\sum_{j=0}^{k-1}\left(\frac{w_i^{[j]}(1 - \mathbb{1}^T\vec{w}_i)}{\mathbb{1}^T\vec{w}_i}\right)^2} = \sqrt{\left(\frac{1 - \mathbb{1}^T\vec{w}_i}{\mathbb{1}^T\vec{w}_i}\right)^2}\sqrt{\sum_{j=0}^{k-1}(\vec{w}_i^{[j]})^2}$$
$$= \frac{|1 - \mathbb{1}^T\vec{w}_i|}{\mathbb{1}^T\vec{w}_i}\|\vec{w}_i\|_2 = \underbrace{\|\vec{\epsilon}_i\|_1}_{\text{novelty}} \frac{\|\vec{w}_i\|_2}{\mathbb{1}^T\vec{w}_i} = \|\vec{\epsilon}_i\|_1 \underbrace{\frac{\|\vec{w}_i\|_2}{\|\vec{w}_i\|_1}}_{\text{confidence}} \tag{4}$$

Formula 4 breaks down the magnitude of the error into two components. The first component is the magnitude of the difference between 1 and the sum of the calibrated probabilities, $\|\vec{\epsilon}_i\|_1 = |1 - \mathbb{1}^T\vec{w}_i|$, and measures how well the independently calibrated outputs align to a probability distribution. Given a perfect alignment, the sum of the calibrated probabilities is 1, and the component will yield 0. The second component, $\frac{\|\vec{w}_i\|_2}{\|\vec{w}_i\|_1}$, represents how "spread out" the elements of $\vec{w}_i$ are. In general, a vector with a higher quotient (magnitude divided by the sum of its components) will have more "spread out" components, while a vector with a lower quotient will have more concentrated components. Increased variance in the probability predictions indicates that certain predictions carry more probability weight, which in turn implies higher confidence in the model. Conversely, in the absence of variance, such as when output probabilities are evenly or equally predicted, there is a lack of confidence as all outputs have comparable probabilities. The spread is minimal, when all predictions are equal, and maximal when all predictions are zero except one (with then $p_i^{[\hat{y}]} = 1$); due to the square term dominating the sum term. Consequently, if all components have the same prediction confidence w, i.e. $\forall_{0 \leq j < k} w_i^{[j]} \triangleq w$, then we have $\|\vec{w}_i\|_2 = \sqrt{\sum_{j=0}^{k-1} (w_i^{[j]})^2} = \sqrt{kw^2} = \sqrt{k} w_i$. Also, $\not{k}^T \vec{w}_i = \sum_{j=0}^{k-1} w_i^{[j]} = \sum_{j=0}^{k-1} w_i = kw$. Therefore, we get $\frac{\|\vec{w}_i\|_2}{\|\vec{w}_i\|_1} = \frac{w\sqrt{k}}{kw} = \frac{1}{\sqrt{k}}$. If all classes except one have a zero prediction and the remaining one a prediction of one, then we have $\|\vec{w}_i\|_2 = 1$ and $\|\vec{w}_i\|_1 = 1$. Therefore, $\frac{\|\vec{w}_i\|_2}{\|\vec{w}_i\|_1} = 1$. Hence, we have a boundary of $\frac{\|\vec{w}_i\|_2}{\|\vec{w}_i\|_1} \in [\frac{1}{\sqrt{k}}, 1]$. On the other hand, the novelty score $\|\vec{w}_i\|_1$ is in the range of $[0, k]$, since $\epsilon_i^{[j]} \in [0, 1]$. Therefore, $\|\vec{\epsilon}_i\|_2 \in [0 \cdot \frac{1}{\sqrt{k}}, 1 \cdot 1] = [0, 1]$ is automatically guaranteed, i.e. $\|\vec{\epsilon}_i\|_2$ is bounded between zero and one; and increases proportionally with both the level of novelty and confidence.

Novelty measures the degree of unexpectedness, with higher values indicating greater novelty. Confidence represents the level of certainty or assurance, with higher values indicating greater model certainty. Multiplying these two components yields a measure of the magnitude or impact of an (unexpected) prediction. In particular, ϵ_i is an instance-specific measure of calibration quality for a class. If the value of $\epsilon_i^{[j]}$ is positive, it indicates that the model has a higher level of confidence in predicting class j than the calibration, and the corresponding calibration model Ξ_j needs to be adjusted. Conversely, if $\epsilon_i^{[j]}$ is negative, the model is less confident in predicting class j than the calibration, and the adjustment made by the corresponding calibration model Ξ_j is too strong. If $\epsilon_i^{[j]}$ is near zero, the model is well-calibrated for class j. The value of ϵ_i reflects the extent of miscalibration, with higher magnitudes indicating greater miscalibration; hence ϵ_i can be perceived as a degree of "novelty". The average value of ϵ_i offers insight into the model's confidence across all classes. However, its vector magnitude $\|\vec{\epsilon}_i\|_2$ represents the confidence-weighted novelty, which considers both novelty and confidence in the prediction. This helps identify areas where unexpected errors occur with high confidence.

Equation 4 also holds true for any arbitrary L_ρ norm $\|\vec{\epsilon}_i\|_\rho := \left(\sum_{j=1}^{k-1} |\epsilon_i^{[j]}|^\rho\right)^{1/\rho} = \left(|\frac{1 - \not{k}^T \vec{w}_i}{\not{k}^T \vec{w}_i}|^\rho\right)^{1/\rho} \|\vec{w}_i\|_\rho = \|\vec{\epsilon}_i\|_1 \frac{\|\vec{w}_i\|_\rho}{\|\vec{w}_i\|_1}$. In particular, the L_∞ norm corresponds per definition to the maximum value in a vector, and therefore:

$$\|\vec{\epsilon}_i\|_\infty = \|\vec{\epsilon}_i\|_1 \frac{\|\vec{w}_i\|_\infty}{\|\vec{w}_i\|_1} = \|\vec{\epsilon}_i\|_1 \frac{\vec{w}_i^{[\hat{y}]}}{\|\vec{w}_i\|_1} = \underbrace{\|\vec{\epsilon}_i\|_1}_{\text{novelty}} \overbrace{p_i^{*[\hat{y}]}}^{\text{max. confidence}} \tag{5}$$

Thus, in the L_∞ norm, the second term is the maximum confidence value (i.e. output probability of its prediction $\hat{y}$).

3.1 Score Adjustment

To calculate the error norm $\|\vec{\epsilon}\|$, we need to consider the impact of calibration mismatches on low probability class scores compared to high scores. Larger scores have a diminishing effect on smaller scores in the probability distribution. For example, if the predicted class has no mismatch but other classes do, the contribution from those mismatches will be limited if the main class has a high probability. To address this issue, we can assign weights based on the (normalized) complement probability.

$$\|\vec{\epsilon_i}\|_\rho^\propto := \left\| \frac{k(\not{\mathbb{1}} - \vec{p_i}^*)}{\not{\mathbb{1}}^T(\not{\mathbb{1}} - \vec{p_i}^*)} \circ \vec{\epsilon_i} \right\|_\rho = \left\| \frac{k(\not{\mathbb{1}} - \vec{p_i}^*)}{k-1} \circ \vec{\epsilon_i} \right\|_\rho \triangleq \|\vec{\propto_i} \circ \vec{\epsilon_i}\|_\rho \qquad (6)$$

where $\circ$ is the Hadamard product and $\vec{\propto_i}$ be the proportional normalized complement weight vector. Multiplying by the class size k is a common practice when working with sample weights. It ensures that the weighted average of the samples is equal to the unweighted average. Yet, given a closer look, we can realize that $\|\vec{\epsilon_i}\|_\rho^\propto$ is proportional to:

$$\|\vec{\epsilon_i}\|_\rho^\propto \triangleq \|\vec{\propto_i} \circ \vec{\epsilon_i}\|_\rho = \frac{k}{k-1} \|\neg\vec{p_i}^* \circ \vec{\epsilon_i}\|_\rho \sim \|\neg\vec{p_i}^* \circ \vec{\epsilon_i}\|_\rho \qquad (7)$$

where k is the number of classes. Considering mismatches for low probability classes leverages "dark knowledge" [13], i.e. knowledge encoded in the relative probabilities of incorrect outputs, which we can use for mismatch scoring.

3.2 Calibration Discrepancy with Label Aggregations

Let $\mathcal{C}$ be a set of k distinct classes. Our aim is to measure the calibration error discrepancies for each class. To do so, we propose expanding the error vector $\vec{\epsilon}$ to higher dimensions by combining pairwise labels using a subset or all $\binom{k}{2}$ label pairs under a single label and evaluating calibration accuracy. Let i be an arbitrary instance and $\vec{p_i}$ its corresponding probability vector with $p_i^{[j]}$ representing the probability assigned to class j. Given that the prediction is determined by the class index with the highest probability, $p_i^{[j]}$ and $p_i^{[j']}$ are mutually exclusive for $j \neq j'$; making their joint-conditional probability zero for any pair of classes: $P(\hat{y} = j \cap \hat{y} = j') = 0 \implies P(\hat{y} = j | \hat{y} = j') = 0$. Let $P_i(j)$ denote the probability of the predicted class being j for instance i. We can express the probability $P_i(j \cup j') \triangleq P_i(j) + P_i(j') - P_i(j \cap j') \equiv P_i(j) + P_i(j')$ for $j \neq j'$. Hence, $0 = P_i(j \cup j') - P_i(j) - P_i(j')$. We define an indexing function $\chi(j, j') \mapsto \{1, \cdots, k\}$ to uniquely identify each pair by an index. Without loss of generality, we consider $j < j'$ and define the difference:

$$\epsilon_i^{\bullet \, [\chi(j,j')]} = \Theta[P_i(j \cup j')] - \Theta[P_i(j)] - \Theta[P_i(j')] \tag{8}$$

where $\Theta[\cdot]$ is the calibration function. Ideally, $\epsilon_i^{[\chi(j,j')]} = 0$, indicating that the aggregated pairwise labels do not exhibit any calibration discrepancy. Similar to Eq. 7, we can incorporate the normalized complement weight vector $\vec{\alpha}_i^{\bullet}$ with components $\vec{\alpha}_i^{\bullet \, [\chi(j,j')]} := \frac{\binom{k}{2}(1-\Theta[P_i(j \cup j')])}{\sum_{\kappa \neq \kappa'} 1 - \Theta[P_i(\kappa \cup \kappa')]}$. Analogously, let λ be an integer such that $1 < \lambda < k$. We can generalize the formula for multiple different sized λ-tuple class pairs J_λ of size λ as:

$$\epsilon_{i/\lambda}^{\bullet \, [\chi(J_\lambda)]} = \Theta[P_i(\bigcup_{j \in J_\lambda} j)] - \sum_{j \in J_\lambda} \Theta[P_i(j)] \tag{9}$$

The total loss is then the magnitude of the concatenated class error discrepancies and all λ_n-pair aggregations for each instance:

$$\|\vec{\epsilon}_i\|_\rho^\alpha = \| \underbrace{(\vec{\alpha}_i \circ \vec{\epsilon}_i)}_{k \text{ class errors}} \overset{H}{\oplus} \underbrace{\left(\vec{\alpha}_{i/\lambda_1}^{\bullet} \circ \vec{\epsilon}_{i/\lambda_1}^{\bullet}\right)}_{\binom{k}{\lambda_1} \text{ class-pair errors}} \overset{H}{\oplus} \cdots \overset{H}{\oplus} \underbrace{\left(\vec{\alpha}_{i/\lambda_n}^{\bullet} \circ \vec{\epsilon}_{i/\lambda_n}^{\bullet}\right)}_{\binom{k}{\lambda_n} \text{ class-pair errors}} \|_\rho \tag{10}$$

where $\overset{H}{\oplus}$ represents the horizontal-concatenation operation. Since the number of pairs scales binomially, but we have the identity $\binom{k}{\lambda} = \binom{k}{k-\lambda}$, one simple choice for the values of λ would be to use $\lambda_1 := 2, \lambda_2 := k - 2$. Alternatively, we could choose any two distinct values for λ_1 and λ_2 such that $1 < \lambda_1 < \lambda_2 < k$. However, choosing larger values for λ increases the number of pairs considerably due to the rapid growth of the binomial coefficient.

3.3   Hybrid ODD: Embedding and Prediction-Based

We can make OOD decisions by combining the results of multiple models, such as averaging or selecting the maximum value. This allows us to create a hybrid OOD outlier score function for a new instance z_i, using the maximum of the base model and the calibration mismatch over their unified probability scores. Unified scores [15] are necessary because raw scores from different models may not be directly comparable. We define $\Phi_j^{\mathcal{X}}$ as the unifying score function for a model Π_j over instances in $\mathcal{X}$. The hybrid outlier score π is then given by:

$$\pi(z_i) = \max\{\Phi_0^{\mathcal{X}}\left(\Pi_0(z_i)\right), \cdots, \Phi_j^{\mathcal{X}}\left(\Pi_j(z_i)\right), \Phi_{j+1}^{\mathcal{X}}\left(\|\vec{\epsilon}_i\|_\rho^\alpha\right)\} \tag{11}$$

where $\Phi_j^{\mathcal{X}}$ is the "unifying score function" for Π_j over $\mathcal{X}$ [15], with:

$$\mathrm{erf}(x) := \frac{2}{\sqrt{\pi}} \int_0^x e^{-t^2} dt \; ; \; \Phi_j^{\mathcal{X}}(z_i) := \frac{1}{2}\left[1 + \mathrm{erf}\left(\frac{\Pi_j(z_i) - \mu_{\mathcal{X}}}{\sigma_{\mathcal{X}} \sqrt{2}}\right)\right] \tag{12}$$

$\mu_{\mathcal{X}}, \sigma_{\mathcal{X}}$ are respectively the mean and standard deviation of $\Pi_j(\mathcal{X})$; The Gauss error, $\mathrm{erf}(x)$, represents the likelihood that a single measurement's error

$x > 0$ falls within a fixed range. It is known that, for a normal distribution with zero mean and standard deviation of $\frac{1}{\sqrt{2}}$, $\mathrm{erf}(x)$ gives the probability of the variable being within the symmetric range of $[-x, x]$. However, if the variable conforms to a normal distribution with a standard deviation σ (and mean zero), the probability is given by $\mathrm{erf}(\frac{x\sqrt{2}}{\sigma})$. Overall, by dividing the result by 2 and adding 1, we ensure that the probability falls between 0 and 1.

4   Percentile Ranked Scores

To handle uneven distributions of raw probability scores, we suggest calibrating scores based on their percentiles relative to other scores. Outliers will here deviate more likely from the reference data distribution, making it easier to detect anomalies. When calibrating probabilities, an outlier's class probability may draw mass from other predictions, leading to significant percentile variations due to ranking changes. We use the formula $\Xi_{\hat{y}}^{\Psi}(p_i^{[j]}) := \Xi_j\big(\Psi(p_i^{[\hat{y}]})\big)$, where $\Psi(.)$ is the percentile transformation that converts probability data into percentiles using reference data; the other formulas are updated accordingly. The percentile transformation finds the left and right indices of the input probabilities in sorted reference data and calculates the percentiles as their average.

5   Experimental Methods

For evaluation, we focused on DL scenarios that produce both: embedding representations and classification probabilities. We took three approaches: (1) We fine-tuned a pre-trained ResNet18 model [12] on a specific dataset (inliers) and forwarded a different OOD dataset (outliers) through the model. The goal was to identify elements as either an inlier or an outlier, respectively. The penultimate layer vector representation was used as the feature representation for the baseline algorithms. (2) Given one dataset, we trained only half of the classes and regarded the other half as outliers. (3) We conducted experiments against synthetically generated data in form of cluster groups (inliers) and uniformly sampled points outside the clusters (outliers). Here the raw features (instead of deep embeddings) were used by the baseline outlier detection algorithms.

All results represent the average of 15 independent runs. We used the score adjusted formula 10 (with $\lambda_1 = 2, \lambda_2 = k - 2$) and compared it against multiple different common outlier detection algorithms [11,38]: ECOD, SAMPLING, QMCD, ABOD, OCSVM, MCD, COF, LOF, HBOS, LODA, IFOREST, INNE, SUOD, HDBSCAN; as well as against an ensemble method which was the maximum unified score [15] from these models. Additionally, we considered hybrid models, which represented the highest combined score achieved by pairing a particular baseline algorithm with our proposed OOD approach (for all baselines respectively). Evaluation was done using the "Area Under the Curve" (AUC) metric since it works well for binary classification problems (outlier or not); measuring the entire area underneath the ROC curve from (0,0) to (1,1). AUC provides an aggregated measure of performance across all possible classification thresholds. We chose BetaCalibration over Isotonic regression to prevent plateaus; and performed percentile-wise calibration using $\Xi_{\hat{y}}^{\Phi}(p_i^{[j]})$.

6 Results and Discussion

We compared the calibration discrepancy's OOD detection on synthetic clusters (Table 1) and real data (Table 2) using class-weighted percentile-based calibrations $\Xi_{\hat{y}}^{\Phi}(p_i^{[j]})$. Real data used specific classes or entire datasets as training sets with outliers regarded as classes not included in the training set or from a completely different dataset; while synthetic data had synthesized clusters. For real data, experiments utilized large deep neural networks; for synthetic data, smaller simple models such as linear perceptrons and decision trees were employed.

Table 1. Average Out-of-Distribution Area Under the Receiver Operating Characteristic Curve (ROC AUC) scores on *trivial* synthetic clusters for multiple simple classifiers.

algorithm	ROC AUC	algorithm	ROC AUC
ECOD	0.70 ($\pm$ 0.01)	$\lVert \epsilon\, Perceptron \rVert_1^{\infty}$	0.72 ($\pm$ 0.22)
Sampling	0.97 ($\pm$ 0.03)	$\lVert \epsilon\, Perceptron \rVert_2^{\infty}$	0.81 ($\pm$ 0.21)
QMCD	0.53 ($\pm$ 0.07)	$\lVert \epsilon\, Perceptron \rVert_{\infty}^{\infty}$	0.99 ($\pm$ 0.01)
ABOD	1.00 ($\pm$ 0.00)	$\lVert \epsilon\, SVC \rVert_1^{\infty}$	0.82 ($\pm$ 0.22)
OCSVM	1.00 ($\pm$ 0.00)	$\lVert \epsilon\, SVC \rVert_2^{\infty}$	0.91 ($\pm$ 0.15)
MCD	0.89 ($\pm$ 0.04)	$\lVert \epsilon\, SVC \rVert_{\infty}^{\infty}$	1.00 ($\pm$ 0.00)
COF	0.44 ($\pm$ 0.01)	$\lVert \epsilon\, DecisionTreeClassifier \rVert_1^{\infty}$	0.50 ($\pm$ 0.08)
LOF	1.00 ($\pm$ 0.00)	$\lVert \epsilon\, DecisionTreeClassifier \rVert_2^{\infty}$	0.50 ($\pm$ 0.08)
HBOS	1.00 ($\pm$ 0.00)	$\lVert \epsilon\, DecisionTreeClassifier \rVert_{\infty}^{\infty}$	0.53 ($\pm$ 0.07)
LODA	0.91 ($\pm$ 0.03)	$\lVert \epsilon\, KNeighborsClassifier \rVert_1^{\infty}$	0.50 ($\pm$ 0.03)
IForest	1.00 ($\pm$ 0.00)	$\lVert \epsilon\, KNeighborsClassifier \rVert_2^{\infty}$	0.50 ($\pm$ 0.03)
INNE	0.99 ($\pm$ 0.01)	$\lVert \epsilon\, KNeighborsClassifier \rVert_{\infty}^{\infty}$	0.61 ($\pm$ 0.03)
hdbscan	1.00 ($\pm$ 0.00)	$\lVert \epsilon\, GaussianProcessClassifier] \rVert_1^{\infty}$	0.76 ($\pm$ 0.31)
ENSEMBLE	1.00 ($\pm$ 0.00)	$\lVert \epsilon\, GaussianProcessClassifier] \rVert_2^{\infty}$	0.80 ($\pm$ 0.29)
		$\lVert \epsilon\, GaussianProcessClassifier] \rVert_{\infty}^{\infty}$	0.99 ($\pm$ 0.01)

Table 1 demonstrates interesting characteristics of the $\lVert \epsilon \rVert$ score and its dependence on the classifier chosen. $\lVert \epsilon \rVert$ is dependent on the classifier because each classifier has a different accuracy and output distribution, meaning that they assign confidence scores differently. This is important to consider when performing outlier detection, as the effectiveness of the method may vary depending on the classifier used. For instance, it is not sensible to perform outlier detection if the model is not even able to perform well on the training or test set.

Table 2. Average Out-of-Distribution Area Under the Receiver Operating Characteristic Curve (ROC AUC) scores on real-world data. The column "alg_log" represents the application of the outlier-detection algorithm on the logits, while "alg_pred" its application on the predictions. The columns "max[alg_log, ϵ]" and "max[alg_pred, ϵ]" represent the ROC AUC scores computed based on the maximum of the algorithm and ϵ, using either the logits or the predictions, respectively.

	Trainset: CIFAR10 - Outlier: MNIST				Trainset: MNIST - Outlier: CIFAR10			
	alg_log	alg_pred	max[alg_log, ϵ]	max[alg_pred,ϵ]	alg_log	alg_pred	max[alg_log, ϵ]	max[alg_pred,ϵ]
ECOD	0.31 (± 0.03)	0.31 (± 0.02)	**0.78 (± 0.06)**	**0.78 (± 0.06)**	0.15 (± 0.02)	0.20 (± 0.02)	**0.98 (± 0.01)**	**0.98 (± 0.01)**
Sampling	0.56 (± 0.11)	0.58 (± 0.08)	**0.79 (± 0.03)**	**0.79 (± 0.05)**	0.84 (± 0.07)	0.85 (± 0.09)	**0.98 (± 0.02)**	**0.98 (± 0.02)**
QMCD	0.55 (± 0.04)	0.51 (± 0.09)	**0.81 (± 0.06)**	0.80 (± 0.07)	0.48 (± 0.09)	0.39 (± 0.10)	**0.99 (± 0.01)**	0.98 (± 0.02)
ABOD	0.81 (± 0.04)	0.80 (± 0.04)	**0.83 (± 0.04)**	**0.83 (± 0.04)**	**0.99 (± 0.01)**	**0.99 (± 0.01)**	**0.99 (± 0.01)**	**0.99 (± 0.01)**
OCSVM	0.77 (± 0.06)	0.72 (± 0.07)	**0.82 (± 0.03)**	**0.82 (± 0.03)**	**0.99 (± 0.00)**	**0.99 (± 0.01)**	**0.99 (± 0.00)**	**0.99 (± 0.00)**
MCD	0.55 (± 0.09)	0.43 (± 0.08)	**0.78 (± 0.06)**	0.77 (± 0.06)	0.60 (± 0.01)	0.51 (± 0.01)	**0.98 (± 0.02)**	**0.98 (± 0.02)**
COF	0.49 (± 0.01)	0.50 (± 0.01)	**0.80 (± 0.05)**	**0.80 (± 0.05)**	0.52 (± 0.01)	0.52 (± 0.01)	**0.98 (± 0.01)**	**0.98 (± 0.01)**
LOF	0.66 (± 0.08)	0.65 (± 0.07)	**0.82 (± 0.03)**	0.81 (± 0.03)	0.88 (± 0.06)	0.92 (± 0.05)	**0.99 (± 0.01)**	**0.99 (± 0.01)**
HBOS	0.26 (± 0.07)	0.36 (± 0.08)	0.76 (± 0.06)	**0.77 (± 0.06)**	0.55 (± 0.19)	0.50 (± 0.19)	**0.98 (± 0.01)**	**0.98 (± 0.01)**
LODA	0.20 (± 0.07)	0.18 (± 0.05)	**0.76 (± 0.07)**	**0.76 (± 0.07)**	0.06 (± 0.05)	0.16 (± 0.12)	**0.98 (± 0.02)**	**0.98 (± 0.02)**
IForest	0.24 (± 0.06)	0.26 (± 0.06)	**0.76 (± 0.06)**	**0.76 (± 0.06)**	0.45 (± 0.19)	0.35 (± 0.17)	**0.98 (± 0.01)**	**0.98 (± 0.01)**
INNE	0.21 (± 0.06)	0.23 (± 0.07)	**0.76 (± 0.06)**	**0.76 (± 0.06)**	0.18 (± 0.08)	0.23 (± 0.10)	**0.98 (± 0.01)**	**0.98 (± 0.01)**
hdbscan	0.73 (± 0.03)	0.72 (± 0.03)	**0.83 (± 0.04)**	0.82 (± 0.04)	0.97 (± 0.02)	0.97 (± 0.01)	**0.99 (± 0.01)**	**0.99 (± 0.01)**
Ensemble	0.69 (± 0.08)	0.69 (± 0.08)	**0.77 (± 0.03)**	**0.77 (± 0.03)**	0.97 (± 0.01)	0.97 (± 0.01)	**0.99 (± 0.01)**	**0.99 (± 0.01)**
$\|\epsilon\|_1^\alpha$	**0.84 (± 0.04)**				**0.99 (± 0.01)**			
$\|\epsilon\|_2^\alpha$	0.83 (± 0.05)				**0.99 (± 0.01)**			
$\|\epsilon\|_{inf}^\alpha$	0.82 (± 0.06)				**0.99 (± 0.01)**			

	Trainset: FashionMNIST - Outlier: KMNIST				Trainset: CIFAR10 - Outlier: FashionMNIST			
	alg_log	alg_pred	max[alg_log, ϵ]	max[alg_pred,ϵ]	alg_log	alg_pred	max[alg_log, ϵ]	max[alg_pred,ϵ]
ECOD	0.23 (± 0.02)	0.28 (± 0.02)	**0.93 (± 0.02)**	**0.93 (± 0.02)**	0.33 (± 0.02)	0.33 (± 0.02)	**0.79 (± 0.04)**	0.78 (± 0.04)
Sampling	0.69 (± 0.08)	0.67 (± 0.11)	**0.94 (± 0.02)**	0.93 (± 0.02)	0.56 (± 0.07)	0.57 (± 0.06)	**0.80 (± 0.04)**	**0.80 (± 0.04)**
QMCD	0.56 (± 0.07)	0.41 (± 0.06)	**0.96 (± 0.01)**	0.94 (± 0.02)	0.53 (± 0.04)	0.48 (± 0.09)	**0.83 (± 0.04)**	0.81 (± 0.04)
ABOD	0.94 (± 0.01)	0.94 (± 0.01)	**0.96 (± 0.01)**	**0.96 (± 0.01)**	0.77 (± 0.04)	0.77 (± 0.04)	**0.83 (± 0.03)**	**0.83 (± 0.03)**
OCSVM	0.92 (± 0.02)	0.92 (± 0.02)	**0.95 (± 0.01)**	**0.95 (± 0.01)**	0.74 (± 0.04)	0.69 (± 0.04)	**0.81 (± 0.03)**	**0.81 (± 0.03)**
MCD	0.55 (± 0.02)	0.49 (± 0.03)	**0.93 (± 0.02)**	**0.93 (± 0.02)**	0.46 (± 0.06)	0.44 (± 0.11)	**0.78 (± 0.04)**	**0.78 (± 0.04)**
COF	0.49 (± 0.01)	0.49 (± 0.01)	**0.94 (± 0.02)**	**0.94 (± 0.02)**	0.53 (± 0.01)	0.52 (± 0.01)	**0.81 (± 0.03)**	**0.81 (± 0.03)**
LOF	0.81 (± 0.02)	0.85 (± 0.03)	**0.95 (± 0.01)**	**0.95 (± 0.02)**	0.64 (± 0.04)	0.65 (± 0.04)	**0.81 (± 0.03)**	**0.81 (± 0.03)**
HBOS	0.40 (± 0.09)	0.50 (± 0.15)	**0.93 (± 0.02)**	**0.93 (± 0.02)**	0.25 (± 0.04)	0.35 (± 0.07)	0.76 (± 0.04)	**0.78 (± 0.04)**
LODA	0.05 (± 0.02)	0.15 (± 0.09)	**0.92 (± 0.02)**	**0.92 (± 0.02)**	0.18 (± 0.03)	0.20 (± 0.06)	**0.76 (± 0.05)**	**0.76 (± 0.04)**
IForest	0.19 (± 0.06)	0.36 (± 0.10)	**0.93 (± 0.02)**	0.92 (± 0.02)	0.22 (± 0.03)	0.23 (± 0.07)	**0.76 (± 0.04)**	**0.76 (± 0.04)**
INNE	0.12 (± 0.03)	0.35 (± 0.07)	**0.93 (± 0.02)**	**0.93 (± 0.02)**	0.21 (± 0.04)	0.24 (± 0.04)	**0.76 (± 0.04)**	**0.76 (± 0.05)**
hdbscan	0.85 (± 0.05)	0.86 (± 0.04)	**0.95 (± 0.01)**	**0.95 (± 0.01)**	0.70 (± 0.04)	0.69 (± 0.04)	**0.82 (± 0.03)**	**0.82 (± 0.03)**
Ensemble	0.85 (± 0.04)	0.85 (± 0.04)	**0.92 (± 0.02)**	**0.92 (± 0.02)**	0.67 (± 0.04)	0.67 (± 0.04)	**0.77 (± 0.03)**	**0.77 (± 0.03)**
$\|\epsilon\|_1^\alpha$	**0.96 (± 0.01)**				**0.84 (± 0.03)**			
$\|\epsilon\|_2^\alpha$	0.95 (± 0.01)				0.83 (± 0.04)			
$\|\epsilon\|_{inf}^\alpha$	0.95 (± 0.01)				0.82 (± 0.04)			

	Trainset: KMNIST Classes 1-5 - Outlier: KMNIST Classes 6-10				Trainset: CIFAR Classes 1-5 - Outlier: CIFAR Classes 6-10			
	alg_log	alg_pred	max[alg_log, ϵ]	max[alg_pred,ϵ]	alg_log	alg_pred	max[alg_log, ϵ]	max[alg_pred,ϵ]
ECOD	0.28 (± 0.01)	0.31 (± 0.02)	0.74 (± 0.04)	**0.75 (± 0.04)**	0.43 (± 0.01)	0.44 (± 0.01)	0.61 (± 0.02)	**0.67 (± 0.02)**
Sampling	0.73 (± 0.11)	0.82 (± 0.06)	0.82 (± 0.05)	**0.85 (± 0.04)**	0.55 (± 0.04)	0.54 (± 0.04)	**0.64 (± 0.03)**	0.63 (± 0.03)
QMCD	0.51 (± 0.05)	0.38 (± 0.14)	**0.80 (± 0.03)**	0.78 (± 0.04)	0.55 (± 0.08)	0.47 (± 0.09)	**0.68 (± 0.04)**	0.63 (± 0.05)
ABOD	0.91 (± 0.01)	**0.91 (± 0.01)**	0.84 (± 0.02)	0.84 (± 0.02)	0.59 (± 0.02)	0.59 (± 0.01)	**0.66 (± 0.02)**	**0.66 (± 0.02)**
OCSVM	0.89 (± 0.02)	**0.90 (± 0.02)**	0.89 (± 0.02)	**0.90 (± 0.02)**	0.57 (± 0.01)	0.57 (± 0.01)	**0.64 (± 0.02)**	**0.64 (± 0.01)**
MCD	0.59 (± 0.02)	0.54 (± 0.03)	**0.77 (± 0.03)**	0.75 (± 0.03)	0.51 (± 0.03)	0.47 (± 0.04)	**0.62 (± 0.03)**	0.60 (± 0.02)
COF	0.51 (± 0.01)	0.50 (± 0.01)	**0.80 (± 0.03)**	**0.80 (± 0.03)**	0.49 (± 0.01)	0.49 (± 0.01)	**0.63 (± 0.02)**	**0.63 (± 0.02)**
LOF	0.73 (± 0.05)	0.75 (± 0.05)	**0.82 (± 0.03)**	**0.82 (± 0.03)**	0.53 (± 0.02)	0.53 (± 0.02)	**0.63 (± 0.02)**	**0.63 (± 0.02)**
HBOS	0.72 (± 0.09)	0.74 (± 0.07)	**0.82 (± 0.04)**	**0.82 (± 0.04)**	0.45 (± 0.02)	0.50 (± 0.03)	0.59 (± 0.03)	**0.61 (± 0.02)**
LODA	0.17 (± 0.07)	0.59 (± 0.22)	0.74 (± 0.04)	**0.81 (± 0.07)**	0.33 (± 0.02)	0.34 (± 0.03)	**0.57 (± 0.03)**	**0.57 (± 0.03)**
IForest	0.68 (± 0.06)	0.70 (± 0.08)	0.77 (± 0.04)	**0.78 (± 0.04)**	0.43 (± 0.03)	0.42 (± 0.03)	**0.59 (± 0.02)**	**0.59 (± 0.02)**
INNE	0.78 (± 0.06)	0.81 (± 0.07)	0.83 (± 0.04)	**0.85 (± 0.05)**	0.44 (± 0.03)	0.45 (± 0.03)	**0.59 (± 0.03)**	**0.59 (± 0.02)**
hdbscan	0.87 (± 0.03)	0.85 (± 0.02)	**0.90 (± 0.02)**	0.89 (± 0.02)	0.58 (± 0.01)	0.57 (± 0.02)	**0.65 (± 0.02)**	**0.65 (± 0.01)**
Ensemble	0.85 (± 0.02)	0.85 (± 0.02)	**0.87 (± 0.02)**	**0.87 (± 0.02)**	0.56 (± 0.03)	0.56 (± 0.03)	**0.61 (± 0.03)**	**0.61 (± 0.03)**
$\|\epsilon\|_1^\alpha$	0.83 (± 0.03)				**0.67 (± 0.02)**			
$\|\epsilon\|_2^\alpha$	0.85 (± 0.03)				**0.67 (± 0.02)**			
$\|\epsilon\|_{inf}^\alpha$	**0.91 (± 0.02)**				0.65 (± 0.02)			

On simple synthetic data with well-defined clusters and random noise outside the clusters, most of the conventional methods tested performed (extremely) well with about perfect outlier detection scores. However, the $\|\epsilon\|$ score struggled in this setting. One possible explanation for this is that noise was defined as random points in the embedding space outside the clusters. In deep neural networks, however, noise may instead be mapped/embedded using a specific logic; and its intermediate representations may not be simply random. I.e., even though the input noise to the model may be random, after passing through multiple deep layers, the output is not as random anymore. For example, if data is generated from a multivariate Gaussian distribution and passed through a deep neural network to retrieve the embeddings, the value distributions of the embedding features will not follow a Gaussian distribution any more (neural networks are heavily non-linear); i.e. the neural network model has the ability to transform the input data in a manner that can produce embeddings with a distribution that differs from the original input data. The exact (distributional) mapping of inputs to embeddings is non-trivial and highly dependent on the model, training objective, input data, etc. The model itself defines this mapping.

However, the success of the $||\epsilon||$ score on complex real-world input data in a deep neural network setting, where identifying outliers in the deep embedding space is challenging, can possibly be attributed to the "non-random" and "non-trivial" mapping of neural networks. This is because the embedding now relies on the latent manifold of the model, and outliers are represented by points that lie outside the corresponding (local) manifolds. Notably, the $||\epsilon||$ score outperformed most traditional methods in this context. In contrast, random outlier points in the input data are, on the other hand, determined e.g. solely by large Euclidean distances or drawn from the tail distributions of the feature values.

Moreover, we noticed that the infinity norm exhibited better performance for deep neural networks on the synthetic data compared to its overall performance on the real-world data sets (Table 2). The infinity norm represents the maximum absolute difference between the features of two vectors. In this particular case, the maximum difference proved to be more informative for outlier detection, possibly due to the outliers being generated by Euclidean distant points initially. This implies that different norms can be more effective in specific scenarios.

Naively, one approach to outlier detection is to train one-versus-rest classifiers for all classes and use the difference between 1 and the sum of probabilities as an outlier measure (similar to membership loss [25]). This assumes that if an example does not fit any class, it is an outlier. However, it is not a post-hoc method (but ad-hoc) and requires modifying the training process, which can be computationally expensive for large datasets or models. In our approach, we identify outliers as those instances where the model prediction significantly deviates from calibration, such as overconfident predictions that fall outside the distribution of the training set. The greater the deviation from in-distribution calibration across all classes, the more likely an instance is to be considered OOD. When applying the L2 norm, then instances are more likely to be classified as outliers if also the one-versus-rest probabilities are unevenly distributed. This is helpful for identifying instances where the outputs are especially uncertain and misaligned. E.g., a uniform probability distribution suggests that the model recognizes the example as not belonging to any class. Thus, using the L2 norm we can apply a weight penalty on instances where the model's confidence in its prediction of a particular class is high but incorrect (i.e. OOD), and such instances are identified as more severe outliers.

7   Conclusion

We introduced a novel post-hoc method for identifying out-of-distribution (OOD) examples in deep neural networks (DNNs). Our approach analyzes discrepancies in model calibration alignment to detect anomalies that result in unexpected prediction patterns. OOD detection is a challenging task, as the effectiveness of different algorithms depends on the structure and distribution of the data, as well as the nature of the outliers. Our method is based on the premise that anomalies are more likely to exhibit irregular behavior that diverges from a model's expectations based on its training data distribution. Specifically, models calibrated on in-distribution examples may react differently to OOD samples, causing more noticeable calibration misalignments. We demonstrate that the extent of this calibration discrepancy can serve as a useful indicator for OOD detection. For DNNs in particular, empirical results show that our calibration-based method performs effectively, matching or surpassing other common outlier detection algorithms.

References

1. Belhaouari, S.B., et al.: Unsupervised outlier detection in multidimensional data. J. Big Data **8**(1), 1–27 (2021)
2. Bella, A., Ferri, C., Hernández-Orallo, J., Ramírez-Quintana, M.J.: Calibration of machine learning models. In: Handbook of Research on Machine Learning Applications and Trends: Algorithms, Methods, and Techniques, pp. 128–146. IGI Global (2010)
3. Bendale, A., Boult, T.E.: Towards open set deep networks. In: Proceedings of the IEEE Conference on Computer Vision and Pattern Recognition, pp. 1563–1572 (2016)
4. Boukerche, A., Zheng, L., Alfandi, O.: Outlier detection: methods, models, and classification. ACM Comput. Surv. (CSUR) **53**(3), 1–37 (2020)
5. Breunig, M.M., Kriegel, H.P., Ng, R.T., Sander, J.: Lof: identifying density-based local outliers. In: Proceedings of the 2000 ACM SIGMOD International Conference on Management of Data, pp. 93–104 (2000)
6. Campello, R.J., Moulavi, D., Zimek, A., Sander, J.: Hierarchical density estimates for data clustering, visualization, and outlier detection. ACM Trans. Knowl. Disc. Data (TKDD) **10**(1), 1–51 (2015)
7. Ge, Z., Demyanov, S., Chen, Z., Garnavi, R.: Generative openmax for multi-class open set classification. arXiv preprintarXiv:1707.07418 (2017)
8. Gelman, A., Carlin, J.B., Stern, H.S., Rubin, D.B.: Bayesian data analysis. Chapman and Hall/CRC (1995)
9. Gruhl, C., Sick, B., Tomforde, S.: Novelty detection in continuously changing environments. Futur. Gener. Comput. Syst. **114**, 138–154 (2021)
10. Guo, C., Pleiss, G., Sun, Y., Weinberger, K.Q.: On calibration of modern neural networks. In: International Conference on Machine Learning, pp. 1321–1330. PMLR (2017)
11. Han, S., Hu, X., Huang, H., Jiang, M., Zhao, Y.: Adbench: anomaly detection benchmark. Adv. Neural. Inf. Process. Syst. **35**, 32142–32159 (2022)

12. He, K., Zhang, X., Ren, S., Sun, J.: Deep residual learning for image recognition. In:Proceedings of the IEEE Conference on Computer Vision and Pattern Recognition, pp. 770–778 (2016)
13. Hinton, G., Vinyals, O., Dean, J.: Distilling the knowledge in a neural network. arXiv preprintarXiv:1503.02531 (2015)
14. Hsu, Y.-C., Shen, Y., Jin, H., Kira, Z.: Generalized odin: detecting out-of-distribution image without learning from out-of-distribution data. In: Proceedings of the IEEE/CVF Conference on Computer Vision and Pattern Recognition, pp. 10951–10960 (2020)
15. Kriegel, H.-P., Kroger, P., Schubert, E., Zimek, A.: Interpreting and unifying outlier scores. In: Proceedings of the 2011 SIAM International Conference on Data Mining, pp. 13–24. SIAM (2011)
16. Kuhn, M., Johnson, K., et al.: Applied predictive modeling, vol. 26. Springer (2013)
17. Kull, M., Perello Nieto, M., Kängsepp, M., Silva Filho, T., Song, H., Flach, P.: Beyond temperature scaling: obtaining well-calibrated multi-class probabilities with dirichlet calibration. In: Advances in Neural Information Processing Systems, vol. 32 (2019)
18. Kull, M., Silva Filho, T., Flach, P.: Beta calibration: a well-founded and easily implemented improvement on logistic calibration for binary classifiers. In: Artificial Intelligence and Statistics, pp. 623–631. PMLR (2017)
19. Liang, S., Li, Y., Srikant, R.: Enhancing the reliability of out-of-distribution image detection in neural networks. arXiv preprintarXiv:1706.02690 (2017)
20. Liu, F.T., Ting, K.M., Zhou, Z.-H.: Isolation forest. In: 2008 Eighth IEEE International Conference on Data Mining, pp. 413–422. IEEE (2008)
21. Markou, M., Singh, S.: Novelty detection: a review–part 1: statistical approaches. Signal Process. **83**(12), 2481–2497 (2003)
22. McInnes, L., Healy, J., Astels, S.: hdbscan: hierarchical density based clustering. J. Open Source Softw. **2**(11), 205 (2017)
23. Pang, G., Shen, C., Cao, L., Hengel, A.V.D.: Deep learning for anomaly detection: a review. ACM Comput. Surv. (CSUR) **54**(2), 1–38 (2021)
24. Papadimitriou, S., Kitagawa, H., Gibbons, P.B., Faloutsos, C.: Loci: fast outlier detection using the local correlation integral. In: Proceedings 19th International Conference on Data Engineering (Cat. No. 03CH37405), pp. 315–326. IEEE (2003)
25. Perera, P., Patel, V.M.: Deep transfer learning for multiple class novelty detection. In: Proceedings of the IEEE/CVF Conference on Computer Vision and Pattern Recognition, pp. 11544–11552 (2019)
26. Pimentel, M.A., Clifton, D.A., Clifton, L., Tarassenko, L.: A review of novelty detection. Signal Process. **99**, 215–249 (2014)
27. Platt, J., et al.: Probabilistic outputs for support vector machines and comparisons to regularized likelihood methods. Adv. Large Margin Classifiers **10**(3), 61–74 (1999)
28. Prince, S.: Out-of-distribution detection i: anomaly detection. Borealis AI, June 2022
29. Saerens, M., Latinne, P., Decaestecker, C.: Adjusting the outputs of a classifier to new a priori probabilities: a simple procedure. Neural Comput. **14**(1), 21–41 (2002)
30. Schölkopf, B., Platt, J.C., Shawe-Taylor, J., Smola, A.J., Williamson, R.C.: Estimating the support of a high-dimensional distribution. Neural Comput. **13**(7), 1443–1471 (2001)

31. Seliya, N., Abdollah Zadeh, A., Khoshgoftaar, T.M.: A literature review on one-class classification and its potential applications in big data. J. Big Data **8**(1), 1–31 (2021)
32. Singh, K., Upadhyaya, S.: Outlier detection: applications and techniques. Int. J. Comput. Sci. Issues (IJCSI) **9**(1), 307 (2012)
33. Smiti, A.: A critical overview of outlier detection methods. Comput. Sci. Rev. **38**, 100306 (2020)
34. Vaicenavicius, J., Widmann, D., Andersson, C., Lindsten, F., Roll, J., Schön, T.: Evaluating model calibration in classification. In: The 22nd International Conference on Artificial Intelligence and Statistics, pp. 3459–3467. PMLR (2019)
35. Yang, J., et al.:Openood: benchmarking generalized out-of-distribution detection. arXiv preprintarXiv:2210.07242 (2022)
36. Zadrozny, B., Elkan, C.: Obtaining calibrated probability estimates from decision trees and naive bayesian classifiers. In Icml **1**, 609–616 (2001)
37. Zadrozny, B., Elkan, C.: Transforming classifier scores into accurate multiclass probability estimates. In: Proceedings of the eighth ACM SIGKDD International Conference on Knowledge Discovery and Data Mining, pp. 694–699 (2002)
38. Zhao, Y., Nasrullah, Z., Li, Z.: Pyod: a python toolbox for scalable outlier detection. J. Mach. Learn. Res. **20**(96), 1–7 (2019)

Examining Policy Entropy
of Reinforcement Learning Agents
for Personalization Tasks

Anton Dereventsov$^{(\boxtimes)}$ ⓘ, Andrew Starnes ⓘ, and Clayton Webster ⓘ

Lirio AI Research, Lirio LLC, Knoxville, TN 37830, USA
{adereventsov,astarnes,cwebster}@lirio.com

Abstract. This paper examines the behavior of reinforcement learning systems in personalization environments and details the differences in policy entropy associated with the type of learning algorithm utilized. We observe that as agents evolve towards the optimal policy, the trajectory of the learned policy is intricately linked to the chosen learning paradigm. Through a series of numerical experiments, we consistently observe differences in policy entropy values between Policy Optimization and Q-Learning agents during the training process. Our empirical findings are complimented by a theoretical analysis that sheds light on this phenomenon, which has not yet been explored in existing literature.

Keywords: Reinforcement Learning · Policy Optimization · Q-Learning · Recommender System · Personalization · Entropy

1 Introduction

Recommendation and personalization are commonly misconstrued as interchangeable concepts in the context of tailoring content suggestions to individual interests. While both are intricate methods for customer and patient engagement, they differ subtly. Typically, recommendations are based on a user's historical preferences, whereas personalization focuses on a user's personal attributes.

Recommender systems are crucial for customer retention in industries like retail, e-commerce, media apps, and healthcare, see e.g. [6,34,46,50]. Corporations like Netflix, Spotify, and Amazon use advanced collaborative filtering and content-based recommendation systems for tailored suggestions [4,14,20,37], where the next recommendation is determined by the similarity between users and/or content items.

In contrast, personalization focuses on personal, transactional, demographic, and health-related information, such as age, location, employment, purchases, and medical history. Applications include web content personalization [11,33],

Supplementary Information The online version contains supplementary material available at https://doi.org/10.1007/978-981-97-8702-9_33.

C. Wallraven et al. (Eds.): ICPRAI 2024, LNCS 14892, pp. 493–504, 2025.
https://doi.org/10.1007/978-981-97-8702-9_33

customer-centric interaction with healthcare providers [17,23,24,43,47,55], and personalized medical treatments [5,13,16].

Reinforcement learning (RL) has been increasingly exploited in personalized recommendation systems that continually interact with users, see e.g. [18] and the references therein. In this work we consider the two most commonly employed-in-practice types of RL techniques: Policy Optimization (PO) and Q-Learning (QL). While both approaches strive to learn the optimal policy, the trajectories they follow are different, which results in different behaviors during the training process. We numerically and theoretically explore this phenomenon throughout this effort and explain that its source stems from the learning objectives that each approach utilizes. Our main contributions are:

- Formalization of the phenomenon of different behaviors of the PO and QL agents;
- Empirical demonstration of this phenomenon on a wide variety of personalization tasks;
- Theoretical explanation of the driving factors behind this phenomenon.

Related Work. Our research aims to understand the fundamental behavior of reinforcement learning agents, focusing on the impact of learning types on policy entropy, particularly within policy optimization (PO) and Q-learning (QL) algorithm families, aligned with the Alberta Plan for AI Research [40].

Our theoretical analysis explore policy dynamics under PO and QL update rules, previously examined in various settings [2,48]. While entropy regularization is commonly used to address undesirable policy behavior [3,53], our work does not consider regularization techniques, emphasizing understanding over issue resolution.

Some of our experiments transform image classification tasks into contextual bandit environments, as it has been proposed in [10] and employed in [7,12,42]. Due to limited availability of personalized data, we use simulated environments that replicate real-world personalization applications, similarly to [8,19,35].

In [12,27] the authors address sub-optimal action selection of RL agents. Similarly, in [30] a unification approach for PO and QL is proposed, addressing similar distinctions. Our work prioritizes understanding root causes of such behavior over providing remedies.

2   Preliminaries

In this paper we consider a contextual bandit setting, defined in [22], with discrete action space, which is the standard setting for recommendation and personalization tasks, see e.g. [25,44]. Throughout this paper we use the notational standard MDPNv1 [45]. Namely, $S \subset \mathcal{R}^d$ denotes the state (context) space, $\mathcal{A} = \{1, 2, \ldots, K\}$ denotes the action space consisting of K available actions, and $r : S \times \mathcal{A} \to \mathcal{R}$ denotes the reward function.

The main metric of performance of a reinforcement learning agent is the value V of its policy π, which is defined as the expected return under the policy, i.e.

$$V(\pi) = \mathbb{E}\Big[r(s,a) \mid s \sim \mathcal{S}, a \sim \pi(s)\Big]. \tag{2.1}$$

In addition to the agent's performance, the distribution of the agent's policy π is often critical in practical applications as it directly translates to the actions the agent is taking throughout the training process. A conventional way to quantify the policy distribution is via its entropy $\mathcal{H}(\pi)$ that indicates how distributed the actions over the policy is, with more localized policies having lower entropy values, which is known to lead to undesirable results [9]. As we are interested in an aggregate distribution of the actions selected over the population of users, we introduce the *batch-entropy* $\mathcal{H}_b(\pi; \mathcal{S}_0)$, which is computed on the evaluation set $\mathcal{S}_0 \subset \mathcal{S}$ as

$$\mathcal{H}_b(\pi; \mathcal{S}_0) = - \sum_{a \in \mathcal{A}} \mathbb{E}\big[\pi(a|s) \mid s \sim \mathcal{S}_0\big] \log \mathbb{E}\big[\pi(a|s) \mid s \sim \mathcal{S}_0\big]. \tag{2.2}$$

Unlike the regular entropy $\mathcal{H}(\pi)$, the batch-entropy $\mathcal{H}_b(\pi; \mathcal{S}_0)$ is computed on the average distribution over the evaluation set $\mathcal{S}_0$ and thus serves as a more reliable representation of the distribution of the policy π. In particular, low values of $\mathcal{H}_b(\pi; \mathcal{S}_0)$ indicate that the distribution of π is localized on the whole evaluation set $\mathcal{S}_0$ rather than its individual elements.

In this work we focus on the distinction between Policy Optimization (PO) and Q-Learning (QL) approaches. PO methods, see e.g. [15], attempt to directly maximize the expected return of the policy, while QL methods, see, e.g. [21], attempt to learn the reward signal, which implicitly leads to higher returns. Despite being commonly used in practical RL environments, see e.g. [26,31, 38,49,52], and sharing the same goal of learning the optimal policy, PO and QL methods employ fundamentally different solution strategies which result in drastically different behaviors in terms of the policy entropy. In this work we provide a detailed explanation of this phenomenon, showing that the primary cause comes from the learning objective that each approach utilizes. In the next section we showcase this point on a variety of numerical examples.

3   Numerical Experiments

In this section we deploy reinforcement learning algorithms on a variety of personalization tasks. The presented experiments are performed in Python3.8 with the use of publicly available libraries. The datasets are either publicly available or included in the repository so that the results can be reproduced. The source code will be made available at the time of publication.

The reinforcement learning agents utilized in our examples are implemented via Stable-Baselines3[1] library [32]. Specifically, we deploy Advantage Actor

---
[1] https://github.com/DLR-RM/stable-baselines3.

Critic [28], Deep Q Network [29], and Proximal Policy Optimization [36]. These algorithms were selected because they are widely used in practice and support discrete action spaces and both continuous and discrete state spaces, as such environments best model our setting.

The performance of the agents is measured in terms of policy value (2.1) and policy batch-entropy (2.2), which are computed over the evaluation set that is fixed throughout the training. Additionally, for each agent we provide the stochastic action selection histogram that represents the agent's policy distribution over the evaluation set S_0. For the simplicity of presentation the histograms are sorted, though the unmodified histograms for each experiment are provided in Appendix B. In all the plots presented in Figs. 1–4 the x-axis shows the number of unique agent-environment interactions. The main point of our numerical experiments is to substantiate the claim that, with all else equal, throughout the training process the policy optimization agents tend to have policies of low entropy, while q-learning agents maintain a higher entropy on a wide range of tasks.

3.1 Image Classification Experiment

In this experiment we train reinforcement learning agents to classify the images from CIFAR10[2] dataset. Specifically, we rewrite the image classification task as a contextual problem, the same way it is proposed in [7,10,42].

The state space S consists of $32 \times 32 \times 3$ train/test images. The action space $A = \{0, 1, \ldots, 9\}$ consists of the available labels. On each interaction an agent observes a state (a training image) $s \in S$ and takes an action (makes a prediction) $a \in A$, and receives a reward $r(s, a)$. The reward function $r : S \times A \to \mathbb{R}$ is given

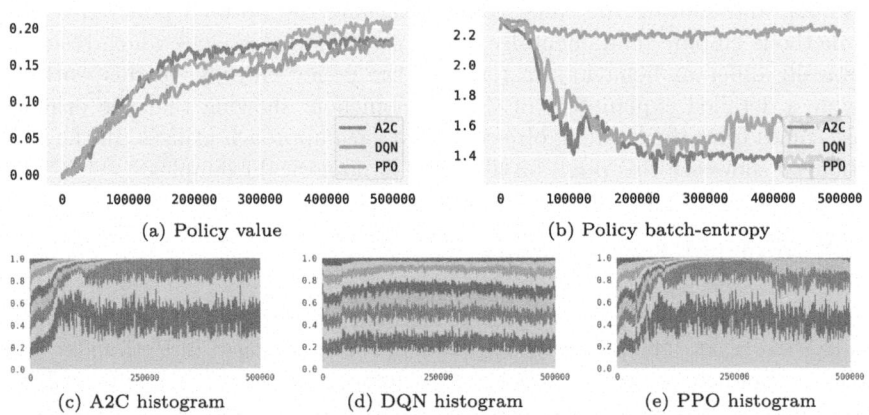

(a) Policy value   (b) Policy batch-entropy

(c) A2C histogram   (d) DQN histogram   (e) PPO histogram

Fig. 1. Results of the Image Classification Experiment on CIFAR10 dataset.

---

[2] https://www.cs.toronto.edu/~kriz/cifar.html.

as

$$r(s,a) = \begin{cases} 1 & \text{if } a \text{ is the correct label for } s, \\ -1/9 & \text{if } a \text{ is an incorrect label for } s. \end{cases}$$

In this setting a random policy has the value of 0 and the optimal policy has the value of 1.

Each agent's policy value, batch-entropy, and action selection histogram are presented in Fig. 1. The hyperparameter choices for each agent are listed in Appendix B in Table 6 and any unspecified parameters are kept at their default values. The unsorted action selection histograms are presented in Fig. 10 respectively in Appendix B.

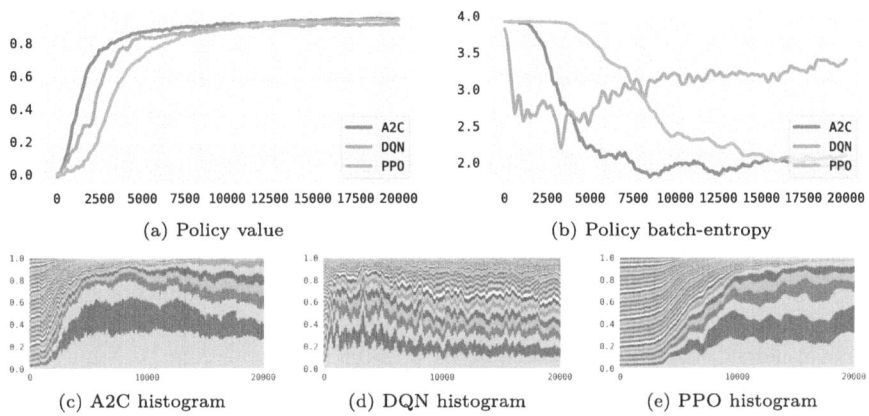

(a) Policy value

(b) Policy batch-entropy

(c) A2C histogram

(d) DQN histogram

(e) PPO histogram

Fig. 2. Results of the Music Recommendation Experiment.

3.2 Music Recommendation Experiment

In this experiment we train a music recommendation agent on the Spotify[3] platform. We obtain data using Spotify Web API[4] that we use to train agents to provide personalized recommendations from 'Top 50 - Global' playlist based on the user's preferences for musical genres.

The state space $\mathcal{S} = \{0,1\}^{20} \subset \mathbb{R}^{20}$ consists of vectors of user preferences for musical genres from Table 3 in Appendix B. Numerically, each coordinate of s is either 0 or 1, indicating whether the user likes a particular musical genre or not. The sparsity of user's preference vectors is between 5% and 25%, i.e. each user has a preference to 1–5 out of 20 available musical genres.

The action space $\mathcal{A} = \{0,1,\ldots,49\}$ is a discrete set of tracks to recommend to users. The available tracks are taken from 'Top 50 - Global' playlist presented in Table 5 in Appendix B. Each track is represented by the vector of 10 audio features obtained with Spotify Web API, see Fig. 8 in Appendix B. The available

---

[3] https://www.spotify.com/.
[4] https://developer.spotify.com/documentation/web-api/.

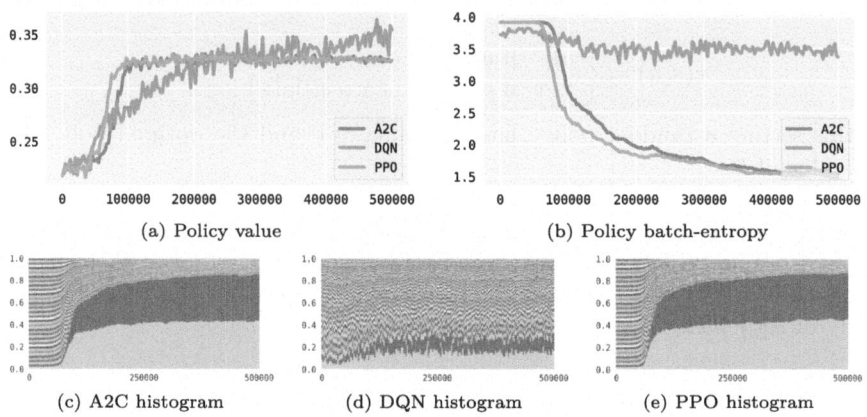

(a) Policy value

(b) Policy batch-entropy

(c) A2C histogram

(d) DQN histogram

(e) PPO histogram

Fig. 3. Results of the Online Advertisement Experiment.

features are the following: acousticness, danceability, energy, instrumentalness, liveness, loudness, mode, speechiness, tempo, valence. Each audio feature is represented by a number from the interval $[0, 1]$, indicating how prominent it is in a given track.

For a user $s \in \mathcal{S}$ the suitability of a track $a \in \mathcal{A}$ is determined by its audio features and their relevance to the audio features associated with the user's preferred musical genres displayed in Table 4 in Appendix B. Namely, we compute a user's s preference p for a given track a as

$$p(s, a) = \underbrace{s}_{1 \times 20} \times \underbrace{\mathcal{F}_{\mathcal{S}}}_{20 \times 10} \times \underbrace{\mathcal{F}_a}_{10 \times 1} \in \mathbb{R},$$

where $\mathcal{F}_{\mathcal{S}} \in \mathbb{R}^{20 \times 10}$ and $\mathcal{F}_a \in \mathbb{R}^{10}$ are the mean-normalized audio features of the musical genres and the track a respectively.

The reward for each interaction is determined by how relevant the audio features of the recommended track are to the audio features corresponding to the user's preferred musical genres. Specifically, in the reward function $r : \mathcal{S} \times \mathcal{A} \to \mathbb{R}$ is given as

$$r(s, a) = \begin{cases} -1 \text{ if } & p(s, a) < -\varepsilon, \\ 0 \text{ if } & -\varepsilon \leq p(s, a) \leq \varepsilon, \\ 1 \text{ if } & p(s, a) > \varepsilon, \end{cases}$$

where parameter $\varepsilon > 0$ indicates a threshold for providing feedback. The values $r(s, a) \in \{-1, 1\}$ indicate that the user s liked/disliked the track a, and the reward value of 0 indicates the absence of user feedback. We use the value $\varepsilon = 0.1$, which results in about 50% average feedback sparsity.

Each agent's policy value, batch-entropy, and action selection histogram are presented in Fig. 2. The evaluations are performed on the set of 10,000 users sampled before the training. The unsorted action selection histograms for this experiment are presented in Fig. 9 in Appendix B. We note that the data used in this experiment, presented in Tables 3–5 in Appendix B, was obtained on 16 August 2023 and, since Spotify playlists are not stationary, will likely differ if obtained at a later date.

3.3   Online Advertisement Experiment

In this experiment we train reinforcement learning agents to provide product recommendations based on users' preferences. We use the RecoGym[5] environment [35] to simulate the interactions between users and the recommended products. We set the numbers of available products to 50 and add a user preference simulation to form a proper contextual bandit environment, and otherwise use the default parameters set by the authors.

The state space $\mathcal{S} = \mathbb{R}^{50}$ represents users' shopping preferences, which determine the likelihood of clicking on an advertised product. These preferences are sampled from the normal distribution, i.e.

$$s = [s_1, \ldots, s_{50}] \in \mathcal{S} \text{ is such that } s_i \sim \mathcal{N}(0,1) \text{ for any } 1 \le i \le 50.$$

The action space $\mathcal{A} = \{0, 1, \ldots, 49\}$ consists of 50 products that are being shown to users. The order of the available products $\mathcal{A}$ is then permuted in accordance with the user's preferences to ensure variety in users' feedback to different products. The reward function $r : \mathcal{S} \times \mathcal{A} \to \{0, 1\}$ represents the user's $s \in \mathcal{S}$ response to observing an advertisement for the product $a \in \mathcal{A}$, where the reward value of 1 indicates that the user clicked on the advertisement, and the reward value of 0 indicates the absence of the user's reaction. The reward function $r : \mathcal{S} \times \mathcal{A} \to \mathbb{R}$ is given as

$$r(s, a) = \begin{cases} 1 & \text{if the user } s \text{ clicked the product } a, \\ 0 & \text{if the user } s \text{ didn't click the product } a. \end{cases}$$

We note that the exact mechanics by which the reward is assigned is established by the RecoGym's developers and is outside the scope of this work.

Each agent's policy value, batch-entropy, and action selection histogram are presented in Fig. 3. The evaluations are performed on the set of 10,000 users sampled before the training. The hyperparameter choices for each agent are listed in Table 6 in Appendix B and any unspecified parameters are kept at their default values. The unsorted action selection histograms for each agent are presented in Fig. 10 in Appendix B.

3.4   Behavioral Preference Experiment

In this experiment we deploy reinforcement learning agents on Synthetic Personalization Environment[6] [8] to learn users' behavioral preferences from the available data. We use the default environment parameters set by the authors and train agents on an unmodified reward signal.

---

[5] https://github.com/criteo-research/reco-gym.
[6] https://github.com/sukiboo/personalization_wain21.

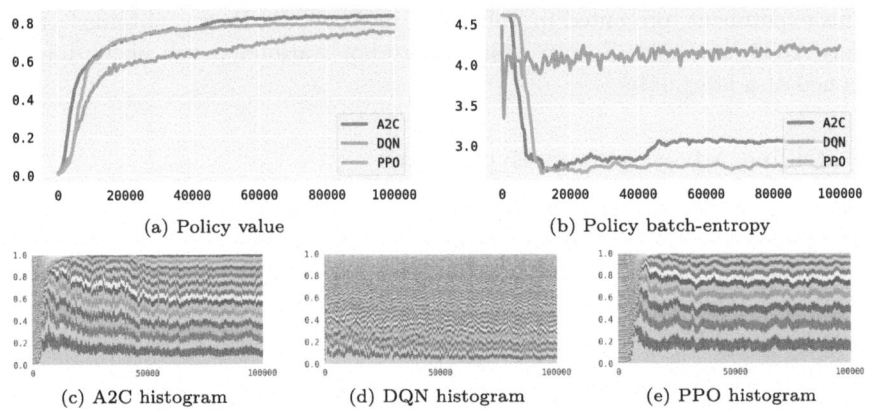

(a) Policy value

(b) Policy batch-entropy

(c) A2C histogram

(d) DQN histogram

(e) PPO histogram

Fig. 4. Results of the Behavioral Preference Experiment.

The state space $\mathcal{S} = \mathbb{R}^{100}$ describes the user's behavior, which determines how the user will respond to the provided recommendation. The action space $\mathcal{A} = \{0, 1, \ldots, 99\}$ consists of 100 behavioral recommendations that can be offered to users. The reward function $r : \mathcal{S} \times \mathcal{A} \to \mathbb{R}$ represents the user's $s \in \mathcal{S}$ response to the behavioral recommendation $a \in \mathcal{A}$, where the higher reward indicates the higher chance of the behavioral adoption. The calculation of the reward signal is established by the Synthetic Personalization Environment's developers and schematically demonstrated in Fig. 11 in Appendix B, though the exact formulation is outside of the scope of this work.

Each agent's policy value, batch-entropy, and action selection histogram for this experiment are presented in Fig. 4. The evaluations are performed on the set of 10,000 users sampled before the training. The hyperparameter choices for each agent are listed in Table 7 in Appendix B and any unspecified parameters are kept at their default values. The unsorted action selection histograms for each agent are presented in Fig. 12 in Appendix B.

4   Conclusion

In this paper, we explore the behavior of reinforcement learning agents employing different learning paradigms in personalization contextual bandit tasks. Our findings reveal that the trajectory of the learned policy is significantly influenced by the type of learning algorithm used. Specifically, we observe that Policy Optimization agents tend to develop low-entropy policies during training, leading them to prioritize certain actions over others. In contrast, Q-Learning agents maintain higher-entropy policies throughout training, which may be more beneficial in diverse real-world applications. These observations are supported by numerical experiments and are further analyzed theoretically in Appendix C, providing new insights into the dynamics of policy entropy in reinforcement learning systems.

Restrictions and Limitations. While our study provides both practical and analytical insights into the behavior of reinforcement learning agents, it does have certain limitations. One significant limitation is the absence of entropy regularization or other optimization relaxation techniques in our experimental setup. We selected this approach to focus on understanding the fundamental behaviors of RL agents without the influence of these techniques; however, this choice may limit the direct applicability of our findings to real-world scenarios where such techniques are commonly employed to enhance performance and ensure robustness.

Future Work. The findings from this study open several avenues for future research. One immediate area of interest is the integration of entropy regularization techniques into the training of RL agents. Investigating how these techniques affect policy entropy and overall agent performance could provide deeper insights and potentially lead to more effective RL applications. Additionally, expanding this research to include other types of reinforcement learning algorithms and comparing their behavior in similar tasks could further enrich our understanding of the dynamics at play. We intend to pursue these research directions to not only address the limitations of the current study but also to expand the scope of our understanding of reinforcement learning in complex environments.

Disclosure of Interests. The authors have no competing interests to declare that are relevant to the content of this article.

References

1. Abel, D., MacGlashan, J., Littman, M.L.: Reinforcement learning as a framework for ethical decision making. In: Workshops at the thirtieth AAAI Conference on Artificial Intelligence (2016)
2. Agarwal, A., Kakade, S.M., Lee, J.D., Mahajan, G.: On the theory of policy gradient methods: optimality, approximation, and distribution shift. J. Mach. Learn. Res. **22**(1), 4431–4506 (2021)
3. Ahmed, Z., Le Roux, N., Norouzi, M., Schuurmans, D.: Understanding the impact of entropy on policy optimization. In: International Conference on Machine Learning, pp. 151–160. PMLR (2019)
4. Amatriain, X., Basilico, J.: Recommender systems in industry: a netflix case study, pp. 385–419. Springer US, Boston, MA (2015). https://doi.org/10.1007/978-1-4899-7637-6_11
5. Aspinall, M., Hamermesh, R.: Realizing the promise of personalized medicine. Harvard Business Rev. **85**, 108–17, 165 (2007)
6. Burke, R., Felfernig, A., Göker, M.H.: Recommender systems: an overview. AI Mag. **32**(3), 13–18 (2011). https://doi.org/10.1609/aimag.v32i3.2361
7. Chen, M., Gummadi, R., Harris, C., Schuurmans, D.: Surrogate objectives for batch policy optimization in one-step decision making. In: Advances in Neural Information Processing Systems, vol. 32 (2019)

8. Dereventsov, A., Vatsavai, R., Webster, C.G.: On the unreasonable efficiency of state space clustering in personalization tasks. In: 2021 International Conference on Data Mining Workshops (ICDMW), pp. 742–749. IEEE (2021)

9. Dou, Z., Song, R., Wen, J.R., Yuan, X.: Evaluating the effectiveness of personalized web search. IEEE Trans. Knowl. Data Eng. **21**(8), 1178–1190 (2008)

10. Dudík, M., Langford, J., Li, L.: Doubly robust policy evaluation and learning. In: Proceedings of the 28th International Conference on International Conference on Machine Learning, pp. 1097–1104 (2011)

11. Ferretti, S., Mirri, S., Prandi, C., Salomoni, P.: Automatic web content personalization through reinforcement learning. J. Syst. Softw. **121**, 157–169 (2016). https://doi.org/10.1016/j.jss.2016.02.008, https://www.sciencedirect.com/science/article/pii/S0164121216000443

12. Garg, S., Tosatto, S., Pan, Y., White, M., Mahmood, A.R.: An alternate policy gradient estimator for softmax policies. arXiv preprint arXiv:2112.11622 (2021)

13. Ginsburg, G.S., McCarthy, J.J.: Personalized medicine: revolutionizing drug discovery and patient care. Trends Biotechnol. **19**(12), 491–496 (2001)

14. Gomez-Uribe, C.A., Hunt, N.: The netflix recommender system: Algorithms, business value, and innovation. ACM Trans. Manage. Inf. Syst. (TMIS) **6**(4) (2016). https://doi.org/10.1145/2843948

15. Grondman, I., Busoniu, L., Lopes, G.A., Babuska, R.: A survey of actor-critic reinforcement learning: standard and natural policy gradients. IEEE Trans. Syst. Man Cybern. Part C (Appl. Rev.) **42**(6), 1291–1307 (2012)

16. Harrison, R.M., Dereventsov, A., Bibin, A.: Zero-shot recommendations with pre-trained large language models for multimodal nudging. In: 2023 IEEE International Conference on Data Mining Workshops (ICDMW), pp. 1535–1542. IEEE (2023)

17. Hassouni, A.e., Hoogendoorn, M., Otterlo, M.v., Barbaro, E.: Personalization of health interventions using cluster-based reinforcement learning. In: International Conference on Principles and Practice of Multi-Agent Systems, pp. 467–475. Springer (2018)

18. den Hengst, F., Grua, E., el Hassouni, A., Hoogendoorn, M.: Reinforcement learning for personalization: a systematic literature review. Data Sci. **3**, 1–41 (2020). https://doi.org/10.3233/DS-200028

19. Ie, E., et al.: Recsim: a configurable simulation platform for recommender systems. arXiv preprint arXiv:1909.04847 (2019)

20. Jacobson, K., Murali, V., Newett, E., Whitman, B., Yon, R.: Music personalization at spotify. In: Proceedings of the 10th ACM Conference on Recommender Systems, RecSys 2016, p. 373. Association for Computing Machinery, New York, NY, USA (2016). https://doi.org/10.1145/2959100.2959120

21. Jang, B., Kim, M., Harerimana, G., Kim, J.W.: Q-learning algorithms: a comprehensive classification and applications. IEEE Access **7**, 133653–133667 (2019)

22. Langford, J., Zhang, T.: The epoch-greedy algorithm for multi-armed bandits with side information. In: Advances in Neural Information Processing Systems, vol. 20 (2007)

23. Lasalvia, L.: Personalization and standardization: Can we have it all? J. Precis. Med. **6**(1) (2020)

24. Lei, H., Tewari, A., Murphy, S.A.: An actor-critic contextual bandit algorithm for personalized mobile health interventions. arXiv preprint arXiv:1706.09090 (2017)

25. Li, L., Chu, W., Langford, J., Schapire, R.E.: A contextual-bandit approach to personalized news article recommendation. In: Proceedings of the 19th International Conference on World Wide Web, pp. 661–670 (2010)

26. Li, S., Yan, Y., Ren, J., Zhou, Y., Zhang, Y.: A sample-efficient actor-critic algorithm for recommendation diversification. Chin. J. Electron. **29**(1), 89–96 (2020)
27. Mei, J., Xiao, C., Dai, B., Li, L., Szepesvári, C., Schuurmans, D.: Escaping the gravitational pull of softmax. Adv. Neural. Inf. Process. Syst. **33**, 21130–21140 (2020)
28. Mnih, V., et al.: Asynchronous methods for deep reinforcement learning. In: International Conference on Machine Learning, pp. 1928–1937. PMLR (2016)
29. Mnih, V., et al.: Playing atari with deep reinforcement learning. arXiv preprint arXiv:1312.5602 (2013)
30. Nachum, O., Norouzi, M., Xu, K., Schuurmans, D.: Bridging the gap between value and policy based reinforcement learning. In: Advances in Neural Information Processing Systems, vol. 30 (2017)
31. Pan, F., Cai, Q., Tang, P., Zhuang, F., He, Q.: Policy gradients for contextual recommendations. In: The World Wide Web Conference, pp. 1421–1431 (2019)
32. Raffin, A., Hill, A., Gleave, A., Kanervisto, A., Ernestus, M., Dormann, N.: Stable-baselines3: reliable reinforcement learning implementations. J. Mach. Learn. Res. (2021)
33. Ricci, F., Rokach, L., Shapira, B.: Introduction to recommender systems handbook. In: Recommender Systems Handbook (2011)
34. Ricci, F., Rokach, L., Shapira, B.: Recommender systems: introduction and challenges, pp. 1–34. Springer US, Boston, MA (2015). https://doi.org/10.1007/978-1-4899-7637-6_1
35. Rohde, D., Bonner, S., Dunlop, T., Vasile, F., Karatzoglou, A.: Recogym: a reinforcement learning environment for the problem of product recommendation in online advertising. arXiv preprint arXiv:1808.00720 (2018)
36. Schulman, J., Wolski, F., Dhariwal, P., Radford, A., Klimov, O.: Proximal policy optimization algorithms. arXiv preprint arXiv:1707.06347 (2017)
37. Smith, B., Linden, G.: Two decades of recommender systems at amazon.com. IEEE Internet Comput. **21**(3), 12–18 (2017). https://doi.org/10.1109/MIC.2017.72
38. Srivihok, A., Sukonmanee, P.: E-commerce intelligent agent: personalization travel support agent using q learning. In: Proceedings of the 7th International Conference on Electronic Commerce, pp. 287–292 (2005)
39. Sutton, R.S., Barto, A.G.: Reinforcement Learning: An Introduction. MIT Press (2018)
40. Sutton, R.S., Bowling, M.H., Pilarski, P.M.: The alberta plan for AI research. arXiv preprint arXiv:2208.11173 (2022)
41. Sutton, R.S., McAllester, D., Singh, S., Mansour, Y.: Policy gradient methods for reinforcement learning with function approximation. In: Advances in Neural Information Processing Systems, vol. 12 (1999)
42. Swaminathan, A., Joachims, T.: Counterfactual risk minimization: learning from logged bandit feedback. In: International Conference on Machine Learning, pp. 814–823. PMLR (2015)
43. Tan, C., Han, R., Ye, R., Chen, K.: Adaptive learning recommendation strategy based on deep q-learning. Appl. Psychol. Meas. **44**(4), 251–266 (2020)
44. Tang, L., Jiang, Y., Li, L., Zeng, C., Li, T.: Personalized recommendation via parameter-free contextual bandits. In: Proceedings of the 38th International ACM SIGIR Conference on Research and Development in Information Retrieval, pp. 323–332 (2015)
45. Thomas, P.S., Okal, B.: A notation for markov decision processes. arXiv preprint arXiv:1512.09075 (2015)

46. Tran, T.N.T., Felfernig, A., Trattner, C., Holzinger, A.: Recommender systems in the healthcare domain: state-of-the-art and research issues. J. Intell. Inf. Syst. **57**(1), 171–201 (2021). https://doi.org/10.1007/s10844-020-00633-6

47. Vatian, A., et al.: Design patterns for personalization of healthcare process. In: Proceedings of the 2019 2nd International Conference on Geoinformatics and Data Analysis, pp. 83–88. ICGDA 2019, Association for Computing Machinery, New York, NY, USA (2019). https://doi.org/10.1145/3318236.3318249

48. Wang, L., Cai, Q., Yang, Z., Wang, Z.: Neural policy gradient methods: global optimality and rates of convergence. arXiv preprint arXiv:1909.01150 (2019)

49. Wang, P., Rowe, J.P., Min, W., Mott, B.W., Lester, J.C.: Interactive narrative personalization with deep reinforcement learning. In: IJCAI, pp. 3852–3858 (2017)

50. Wang, X., Wang, Y., Hsu, D., Wang, Y.: Exploration in interactive personalized music recommendation: a reinforcement learning approach. ACM Trans. Multimedia Comput. Commun. Appl. **11**(1) (2014). https://doi.org/10.1145/2623372

51. Whittlestone, J., Arulkumaran, K., Crosby, M.: The societal implications of deep reinforcement learning. J. Artif. Intell. Res. **70**, 1003–1030 (2021)

52. Xin, X., Karatzoglou, A., Arapakis, I., Jose, J.: Supervised advantage actorcritic for recommender systems. In: ACM International WSDM Conference, vol. 15 (2022)

53. Yang, W., Li, X., Zhang, Z.: A regularized approach to sparse optimal policy in reinforcement learning. In: Advances in Neural Information Processing Systems, vol. 32 (2019)

54. Zahavy, T., et al.: A self-tuning actor-critic algorithm. Adv. Neural. Inf. Process. Syst. **33**, 20913–20924 (2020)

55. Zhu, F., Guo, J., Li, R., Huang, J.: Robust actor-critic contextual bandit for mobile health (mhealth) interventions. In: Proceedings of the 2018 ACM International Conference on Bioinformatics, Computational Biology, and Health Informatics, pp. 492–501 (2018)

Arbitrary-Shape Text Spotting Based on Global, Pixel and Sequence Semantics

Chunhu Zhang[1,2] , Mayire Ibrayim[1,2](✉) , Askar Hamdulla[2,3] ,
and Qilin Deng[1,2]

[1] Xinjiang Key Laboratory of Signal Detection and Processing, Urumqi, China
mydear1949@163.com
[2] Xinjiang University School of Information Science and Engineering, Urumqi, China
[3] Xinjiang University College of Future Technology, Urumqi, China

Abstract. The field of end-to-end text spotting has garnered significant interest in recent years, propelled by the revealed intrinsic synergies between scene text detection and recognition. While advancements have been made, the challenge of arbitrarily shaped scene text spotting persists. This paper introduces an innovative feature augmentation module that addresses the issues of limited receptive fields and weak representation typical of lightweight backbone networks, while also enhancing multi-scale information more effectively and reducing information loss during feature aggregation. Furthermore, to extract a richer set of backbone features, we propose a dual information attention mechanism that enables the backbone network to neuronally focus on salient information.

Keywords: Deep Learning · Text Spotting · Feature Pyramids · Information Focus

1 Introduction

End-to-end text spotter has received extensive attention in recent years, but how to more accurately recognize arbitrary-shaped scene text is still a big problem. Li et al. [13] is the first end-to-end model to support text recognition in horizontal scenes, but this model cannot be applied to the recognition of curved text. S. Qin et al. [23] removed the rectification module designed for straight text, and let the attention decoder directly operate on the cropped and masked text instance features. FOTS [19] proposed the ROI Rotate method, which combines the two supervisions of text detection and text recognition to complement each other. PAN++ [3] uses a way of reformulating text lines as text kernels surrounded by peripheral pixels to detect and recognize arbitrary-shaped text in natural scenes.

In ABCNet v2 [5], a Bezier curve is innovatively adapted to arbitrary-shaped text with coordinate convolution encoding position. Dai et al. [11] harness Transformer for node dependency modeling, enhancing disambiguation via global marker information exchange. Kittenplon et al. [8] pioneer a framework flexible for both fully-supervised and weakly-supervised training regimes. Text

C. Wallraven et al. (Eds.): ICPRAI 2024, LNCS 14892, pp. 505–519, 2025.
https://doi.org/10.1007/978-981-97-8702-9_34

recognition in [4] leverages a streamlined Transformer model, eschewing complex processing steps. SwinTextSpotter [21] integrates detection within a Transformer encoder, synergizing tasks through a transformative recognition mechanism guided by localization loss.

Inspired by the work of PAN++ [3], this study proposes a refined technique for text spotting of arbitrary shapes, enhancing the feature extraction efficacy of the lightweight ResNet18 [17] network. This enhancement ensures multiple captures of critical information, and our developed feature augmentation network exploits this to refine multi-scale features, significantly mitigating information loss during fusion. The paper's key contributions are outlined subsequently:

1) We propose a Dual Information Attention Mechanism (DIAM) and meticulously design an Upsampling Pyramid Module (USPM), which synergistically enhance the backbone network's ability to prioritize relevant information in the form of neuronal activations. The USPM facilitates a refined spatial and channel-wise focus on the extracted backbone features, enabling a secondary extraction of pertinent information.
2) We have engineered a highly effective Multi-scale Bidirectional Feature Enhancement Module (MBFM), which is adept at capturing diverse receptive fields for high-level features. This approach facilitates the acquisition of richer high-level semantic information, whilst concurrently minimizing information loss during multi-scale feature amalgamation.
3) It can effectively spot adjacent text instances and small text instances.

2   Related Work

Text processing in natural scenes primarily encompasses three core tasks: detection, recognition, and spotting. Spotting integrates the former two, leveraging a shared convolutional neural network feature extractor. Initially, a two-stage algorithm was employed, serializing detection and recognition models, which led to dependency on detection accuracy and frequent mispredictions. Recognizing the synergy between detection and recognition, a one-stage end-to-end methodology emerged, enabling simultaneous text instance detection and recognition within a unified network architecture. We will discuss related work from the perspectives of text detection, text recognition and text spotting.

2.1   Text Detection

Text detection is how to discover and predict areas from natural images that may contain text, but without prior identification. The early image backgrounds were simple and the form of the text was relatively simple, so the text detection task achieved good results. In the wave of deep learning, a large number of excellent text detection models have gradually emerged, and the problems they solve are becoming more and more difficult. PSENet [20] uses a progressive scale expansion algorithm to segment text, effectively solving the problem of curved text detection. PAN [14] further innovated this and finally obtained a detector that can detect arbitrary-shaped text. DBNet [34] is different from the above two algorithms. It simplifies the post-processing process and performs text segmentation by predicting the threshold of each pixel position in the image.

2.2   Text Recognition

According to actual scenarios, text recognition tasks are usually divided into two categories: regular text recognition and irregular text recognition. The mainstream algorithms for rule text recognition include the algorithm based on CTC (Conectionist Temporal Classification) [32] and the Seq2Seq [35] algorithm. The difference between the two is mainly in the decoding stage. Due to the limitations of network design, this type of method is difficult to solve the bending and rotating irregular text recognition task. Irregular text recognition algorithms usually have correction-based methods [33], which have better transferability. Attention-based methods [36] mainly focus on the correlation between parts of the sequence. Segmentation-based methods [37] identify each character of a text line as an independent individual. And Transformer-based methods [28].

2.3   End-To-End Text Spotting

Boundary TextSpotter [22] proposes an end-to-end trainable network for text recognition. Different from existing methods that use bounding boxes or shape templates to describe the shape of text instances, it represents the shape of text instances as a set of boundary points. CharNet [12] successfully solved the two problems of text detection and recognition in one forward propagation. PGNet [1] converts polygonal text boundaries into centerlines, boundary offsets, and orientation offsets, and performs multi-task learning for these objectives. Mask TextSpotter v3 [29] uses the Segmentation Proposal Network to generate polygon Proposals, and calculates hard ROI features based on these Proposals, which better characterizes the text area. With the widespread application of Transformer in the field of CV, a standard Transformer-based encoder-decoder model was adopted for text recognition in [40] without relying on any complex pre- (or post-) processing steps. While SPTS v2 [2] treats all position information as the center point, and autoregressively predicts the coordinate mark and word transcription mark of the center point. And ABINet++ [28], were proposed in response to the shortcomings of existing methods in terms of internal interaction, feature representation, and execution methods, based on the guiding principles of autonomy, bidirectionalness, and iteration. By repeatedly inputting the output into the language model, the prediction is gradually refined, which alleviates the problem of length misalignment to a certain extent.

3 Methods

3.1 General Architecture

The model in this paper is shown in Fig. 1. It includes a dual information attention mechanism composed of a lightweight backbone network based on non-parametric attention SimAM [10] and an upsampling pyramid module; a multiscale bidirectional feature fusion module; and a detection and identification module inherited from the baseline [3] model.

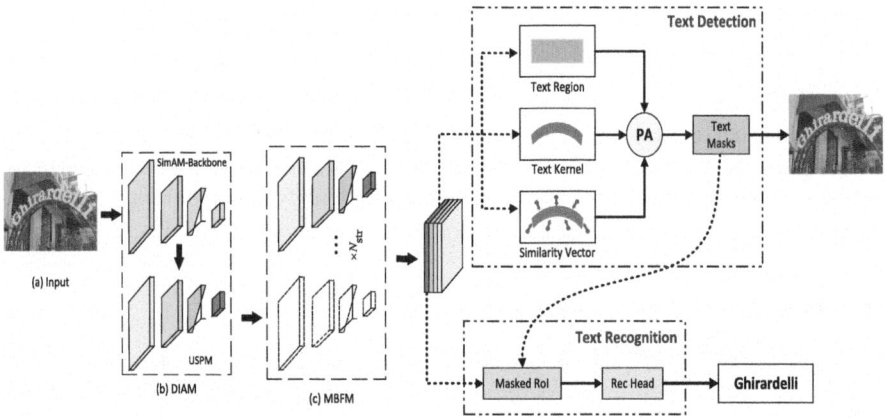

Fig. 1. The overall structure of the model.

3.2 Dual Information Attention Mechanism

We found that using irregular convolution to expand the receptive field in different directions before feature extraction on the image can obtain more refined information and help detect and recognize small-sized text. The 3D parameter-free attention SimAM [10] is integrated into the residual block, which determines the importance of each key to the query vector by calculating the similarity between the query vector and each key. The entire residual structure can be formally defined as $y = S_{im}[\mathcal{F}(x, \{W_i\})] + x$ (S_{im} refers to SimAM Operation, $\mathcal{F}(x, \{W_i\})$ refers to the fitted residual mapping, W_i represents two weight layers). Compared with other traditional attention mechanisms, it is more flexible and does not require the calculation of attention weights between elements. This enables the backbone network to focus on effective information in a neuron-like manner, and its extracted features can better focus on the main target without introducing additional parameters. To achieve the first capture of key information, the multi-scale feature map extracted by the backbone network is $h_i = layer_i(h_{i-1})$ (Fig. 2).

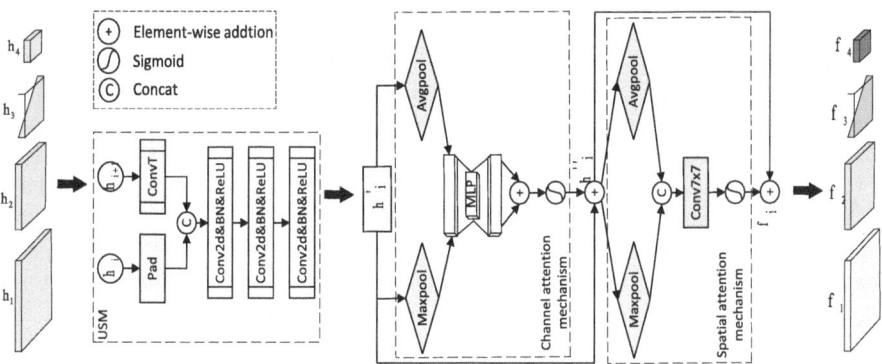

Fig. 2. Upsampling Pyramid Module (USPM). This module mainly includes the upsampling module (USM) and channel and spatial attention modules [6].

USPM mainly consists of two parts: an upsampling module and a channel and spatial attention serial module. Different from general upsampling, using inverse convolution to replace the interpolation method for upsampling not only avoids the dependence on the input target size but also distributes the pixel information to the expanded area well, avoiding information scatter to a certain extent. Considering the specificity of channels, channel attention is used to assign a weight equivalent to its importance to each channel. However, text instances in natural scene pictures are often small, and spatial attention can well focus on this target area in the entire area. The two attention mechanisms are sorted in a serial manner with the best performance [6], and the features of secondary information attention through the attention mechanism are more abundant and delicate. In order to reduce the interference of useless channel information, the number of channels is uniformly operated, and a more suitable 128 is selected. The module formula can be expressed as follows:

$$h_i' = C_{br}^{\ 3}(C_{at}(C_{onvT}\left(h_{i+1}\right), P_{ad}(h_i))) \tag{1}$$

$$h_i'' = \sigma\left(M_{lp}\left(A_{Pool}(h_i')\right) + M_{lp}\left(M_{Pool}\left(h_i'\right)\right)\right) + h_i' \tag{2}$$

$$f_i = \sigma\left(C_{onv}(C_{at}(A_{Pool}\left(h_i''\right), M_{Pool}\left(h_i''\right)))\right) + h_i'' \tag{3}$$

Here $C_{br}^{\ 3}(\cdot)$ represents the three-dimensional convolution operation, $\sigma(\cdot)$ represents the Sigmoid activation operation, $A_{Pool}(\cdot)$ represents the global average pooling, and $M_{Pool}(\cdot)$ represents the global Max pooling.

3.3 Multi-scale Bi-directional Feature Enhancement Module

MBFM is the basic unit of a feature enhancement network, which is U-shaped. Multi-scale information enhancement is performed on the features generated by

DIAM. It includes upper-scale semantic information enhancement, contextual information capture and lower-scale detail information enhancement, and residual connection stages. Upscaling is applied to the input feature pyramid, which iteratively augments the input feature map with a stride of 32, 16, 8, and 4 pixels. The context information capture mainly captures the global context information of the upper layer features through the hole convolution with the hole rate of 18, 12, 6, and 1. In the downscale enhancement stage, the input is the feature pyramid generated by upscale enhancement and contextual information capture, and the enhancement is performed in an iterative manner from 4 steps to 32 steps. The final output feature pyramid is the result of element-wise addition of the input feature pyramid and the feature pyramid produced by downscaling augmentation. And the module can be stacked. As the number of stacks increases, the feature map will be more fully integrated, and the network will be deepened with a small computational overhead. This is due to the fact that we use separable convolutions instead of regular volumes. Product to realize the connection part of MBFM. This part can be summarized as follows:

$$f'_{i+1} = S_{ien}(f_i, f_{i+1}) \qquad i = 3, 2, 1 \tag{4}$$

$$f''_i = C_{icn}(f_i) \qquad i = 3, 4 \tag{5}$$

$$f'''_i = D_{ien}\left(f''_{i+1}, f''_i\right) \qquad i = 2, 3, 4 \tag{6}$$

$$f_i = f'''_i + f_i \qquad i = 1, 2, 3, 4 \tag{7}$$

Here $S_{ien}(\cdot)$, $C_{icn}(\cdot)$, and $D_{ien}(\cdot)$ respectively represent the semantic information enhancement network, context information capture network and detail information enhancement network operations (Fig. 3).

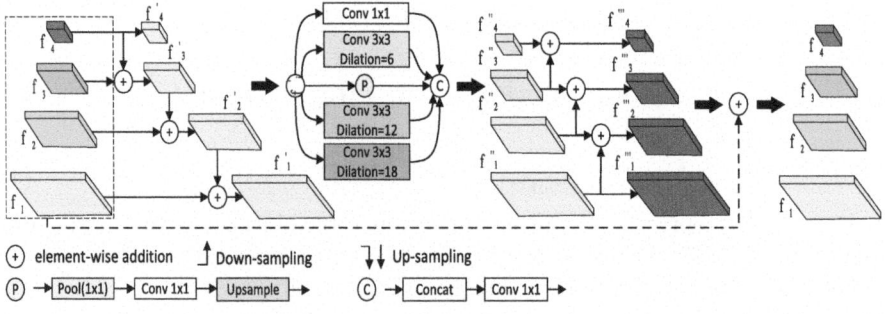

Fig. 3. Multi-scale bi-directional feature enhancement module(MBFM).

3.4   Detection and Recognition Module

The detection head consists of only two convolutions, outputting text regions, text kernels, and similarity vectors. The text area can maintain the complete shape of the text line, but when there are multiple parallel texts, there will be area overlap, and the kernel can well distinguish adjacent text instances. The similarity vector can point the pixels in the text region to the corresponding text kernel, which successfully combines the advantages of the text region and the text kernel. These three can effectively complement each other, and for the text instance with an incomplete kernel, the pixels in the text area are gathered into the kernel by pixel aggregation (PA) to reconstruct a complete text instance. And assemble the output of the detection head through it.

The loss functions of the detection part are text area segmentation loss $\mathcal{L}_{tex}$, text kernel segmentation loss $\mathcal{L}_{ker}$, and $\mathcal{L}_{agg}$ and $\mathcal{L}_{dis}$ comprises together:

$$\mathcal{L}_{dec} = \mathcal{L}_{tex} + \alpha \mathcal{L}_{ker} + \beta(\mathcal{L}_{agg} + \mathcal{L}_{dis}) \tag{8}$$

α and β here are used to balance $\mathcal{L}_{tex}$, $\mathcal{L}_{ker}$, $\mathcal{L}_{agg}$, and $\mathcal{L}_{dis}$ For importance, α and β were set to 0.5 and 0.25 respectively in all experiments.

Calculate the minimum bounding rectangle of the target text line through Masked RoI, and perform a binary mask to filter noise features and extract feature blocks of fixed size. The recognition head is a seq2seq model equipped with multi-head attention, which has no encoder and only consists of an enabler and a decoder. The initiator is used to find the start of a string, which is not necessarily the leftmost region of an arbitrarily shaped line of text. The starter contains only the embedding layer and the multi-head attention layer. The decoder consists of only two LSTM layers and one attention layer. Furthermore, this attention layer is based on multi-head attention, which can effectively fuse temporal (LSTM) features and visual (CNN) features. The loss function of the recognition part is:

$$\mathcal{L}_{rec} = \frac{1}{|\omega|} \sum_{i=0}^{|\omega|} CrossEntropy(y_i, \omega_i) \tag{9}$$

where ω is the ground truth transcript (text content) containing EOS symbols. $|\omega|$ represents the number of characters in the transcription. ω_i is the ith character in the transcription.The total loss is $\mathcal{L} = \mathcal{L}_{tex} + \mathcal{L}_{rec}$, details about this part can be found in [3].

4   Experiment

4.1   Dataset and Experimental Setup

All selected are public benchmark data sets. The task role of each data set in the experiment as well as its annotation form and the number of images for training and testing are shown in Table 1. Use SynthText, ICDAR2017-MLT, COCO-Text, Total-Text (only used for pre-training of the IC15 data set), ICDAR2015 (only used for pre-training of the Total-Text data set) and other data sets for joint training to fine-tune and test text recognition performance. Use SynthText and ICDAR2017-MLT separately as additional data sets for the detection model to pre-train the model. In the experiment, we set the batch-size to 4, the initial learning rate was 0.001, selected the Adam optimizer, and used Python versions 3.7 and 1.7 of Pytorch. Pre-training for 3 epochs on 4 GPUs with 24G video memory: RTX 3090 takes about 12 days. Use the comprehensive index F-measure (F) to evaluate the performance of the model.

Table 1. Basic properties of the dataset.

Dataset	Marker	Missions	Train	Test
Total-Text [30]	Word level	Detection/Spotting	1255	300
COCO-Text [26]	Character level/Text line	Pre-training	63686	–
ICDAR 2015 [27]	Character and word level	Detection/Spotting	1000	500
ICDAR 2017-MLT [15]	Character and word level	Pre-training	7200	1800
SynthText [9]	Character and word level	Pre-training	800k	–
MSRA-TD500 [43]	Character and word level	Detection	300	200
CTW1500 [26]	Character and word level	Detection	1000	500

Table 2. Text spotting ablation experiments at IC15. The results are all F values.

DIEM	MBFM	N	G	W	S	DIEM	MBFM	N	G	W	S
N	N	65.57	66.07	74.71	79.42	N	Y	66.97	67.43	76.87	81.59
Y	N	66.18	67.06	76.98	81.47	Y	Y	67.33	67.92	77.52	82.19

"N" means the module is not enabled, while "Y" means the module is enabled.

4.2   Ablation Experiments

In order to verify the effectiveness of the module, ResNet18 is used as the backbone network to conduct ablation experiments for text positioning. The image size is set to 736 × 736, and four dictionary methods of S (strong), W (weak), G (generic), and N (none) are used for experiments. As shown in Table 2, this paper has achieved good performance improvements when using DIEM or MBFM alone. When DIEM+MBFM is used, it has achieved excellent improvements of 2.77%, which further proves that In order to ensure that MBFM can fully utilize the useful information captured by DIEM and further enhance it, the two strategies achieve complementary performance.

We also conducted ablation studies for text detection with different input sizes on the Total-Text and CTW1500 datasets to further verify the detection performance of the network model on small-scale text after using all modules, and after pre-training the model, the detection performance obtained is more superior, further reflecting the effectiveness of our model. as shown in Table 3.

Table 3. Ablation study on text detection with different input sizes on Total-Text and CTW1500 datasets.

Img-size	Total-Text			CTW1500		
	P	R	F	P	R	F
320	86.67	77.26	81.69	85.67	76.60	80.88
512	87.48	82.67	85.01	85.89	80.84	83.29
640	91.17	81.90	86.24	86.77	82.82	84.75
320-SynthText	87.84	82.55	82.55	86.67	78.30	82.27
512-SynthText	91.74	81.85	86.51	88.02	82.10	84.96
640-SynthText	92.70	82.76	87.45	90.53	82.83	86.51

Table 4. Text detection results on MSRA-TD1500 and ICDAR2015 datasets.

Model	Ext.	MSRA-TD500			ICDAR 2015		
		P	R	F	P	R	F
PSENet* [20]	N	–	–	–	81.49	79.68	80.57
PAN++* [3]	N	81.60	80.30	80.90	85.50	77.20	81.20
TextPMs* [9]	N	82.43	78.30	80.31	84.53	79.89	82.14
PAN* [14]	N	80.70	77.30	78.60	82.55	77.50	79.94
CentripetalText [42]	N	87.10	79.30	83.00	87.10	79.30	83.00
ContourNet [7]	N	–	–	–	86.10	87.60	86.90
CRAFT [16]	Y	88.20	78.20	82.90	89.80	84.30	86.90
DBNet [34]	Y	90.40	76.30	82.80	86.80	78.40	82.30
DBNet++ [18]	Y	87.90	82.50	85.10	90.10	77.20	83.10
PAN++* [3]	Y	85.30	84.00	84.70	85.90	80.40	83.10
TextBPN [24]	Y	86.62	84.54	85.57	-	-	-
FAST-T-736 [25]	Y	88.10	81.90	84.90	86.30	79.80	82.90
PGNet [1]	Y	–	–	–	85.60	83.60	84.60
Tang et al. [47]	Y	91.60	84.80	88.10	91.10	86.70	88.80
DB+TCM [31]	Y	–	–	88.80	–	–	89.40
CentripetalText [42]	Y	-	-	-	90.00	82.50	86.10
BTS'22 [39]	Y	–	–	–	88.70	84.60	86.60
PCR [38]	Y	90.80	83.50	87.00	–	–	–
Long et al. [45]	Y	88.04	87.44	87.70	–	–	–
Our	N	85.91	83.89	84.89	88.03	79.83	83.73
	SynthText	91.80	86.70	89.18	89.53	82.72	85.99
	IC17-MLT	92.40	87.32	89.79	92.36	84.66	88.34

* indicates that the comparison data are repeated values. N means no additional data set is used, while Y means additional data set is used.

4.3 Experimental Results for Text Detection

Experimental results of text detection As can be seen from Table 4, the detection results on the MSRA-TD500 and ICDAR 2015 data sets achieved excellent detection performances of 89.79% and 88.34% respectively. In Table 5, the detection results on the Toatl-Text and CTW1500 datasets achieved detection performances of 87.45% and 86.51% respectively. And it has achieved the best detection accuracy on these four data sets, and the detection performance on the MSRA-TD500 and CTW1500 data sets has also achieved the best results. These excellent detection results can fully prove that the detection performance of our model for arbitrary-shaped text has reached the ranks of the most advanced algorithms.

Table 5. Text detection results on Total-Text and CTW1500 datasets.

Model	Ext.	Total-Text			CTW1500		
		P	R	F	P	R	F
PSENet* [20]	N	81.77	75.11	78.30	80.60	75.60	78.00
PAN++* [3]	N	89.20	80.30	84.50	85.20	81.10	83.10
TextPMs* [9]	N	83.61	80.03	81.78	76.49	75.49	75.98
PAN* [14]	N	80.70	87.15	83.15	84.78	77.35	80.89
CentripetalText [42]	N	88.80	81.40	84.90	85.50	79.20	82.20
ContourNet [7]	N	86.90	83.90	85.40	83.70	84.10	83.90
FCE [41]	N	89.30	82.50	85.80	87.60	83.40	85.50
CRAFT [16]	Y	87.60	79.90	83.60	86.00	81.10	83.90
DBNet++ [18]	Y	87.40	79.60	83.30	86.70	81.30	81.00
DBNet [34]	Y	88.30	77.90	82.80	84.80	77.50	84.51
TextBPN [24]	Y	90.27	84.65	87.37	87.81	81.45	84.51
FAST-T-736 [25]	Y	89.60	82.40	85.80	84.80	77.50	81.00
PAN++* [3]	Y	89.90	81.00	85.30	87.10	81.10	84.00
PGNet [1]	Y	84.60	85.00	84.60	–	–	–
CentripetalText [42]	Y	90.60	82.50	86.30	88.30	79.90	83.90
Tang et al. [47]	Y	90.70	85.70	88.10	88.10	82.40	85.20
DB+TCM [31]	Y	–	–	85.90	–	–	85.10
BTS'22 [39]	Y	89.60	81.20	85.20	88.10	78.20	82.90
PCR [38]	Y	88.50	82.00	85.20	87.20	82.30	84.70
Long et al. [45]	Y	84.96	91.06	87.90	83.92	85.87	84.88
Our	N	89.59	81.32	85.26	86.77	82.82	84.75
	SynthText	92.70	82.76	87.45	90.53	82.83	86.51

* indicates that the comparison data are repeated values. N means no additional data set is used, while Y means additional data set is used.

Table 6. Text Spotting results on the ICDAR2015 and Total-Text datasets.

Model	Backbone	Training Strategy	ICDAR2015				Total-Text	
			N	G	W	S	None	Full
SPTS [48]	Transformer	Finetune	–	65.80	70.20	77.50	74.20	82.40
PGNet [1]	ResNet50	Finetune	–	63.50	78.30	83.30	63.10	–
ABCNet [53]	ResNet50	Finetune	–	–	–	–	64.20	75.70
BTS'22 [39]	ResNet50	Finetune	–	71.70	77.40	82.50	66.20	78.40
P Wang et al. [50]	ResNet50	Finetune	–	65.53	78.04	84.23	58.56	–
BTS [44]	ResNet50	Finetune	–	64.10	75.20	79.42	65.00	76.10
Text Perceptron [52]	ResNet50	Finetune	–	65.10	76.60	80.50	69.70	78.30
MANGO [46]	ResNet50	Finetune	–	67.30	78.90	81.80	71.70	82.60
ABCNet v2 [5]	ResNet50	Finetune	–	73.00	78.50	82.70	70.40	78.10
SwinTextSpotter [21]	Transformer	Finetune	–	70.50	77.30	83.90	74.30	84.10
SPTS v2 [2]	Transformer	Finetune	–	68.00	74.30	81.20	75.00	82.60
PAN++ [3]	ResNet50|18	Finetune	67.58	68.78	77.32	82.61	68.60	78.60
Our	ResNet18	Finetune	68.81	69.07	79.02	82.90	71.00	80.60
	ResNet50	Finetune	70.68	71.26	80.24	84.54	71.46	81.32
Qinet et al. [49]	ResNet50	Jointly	–	68.00	79.90	83.40	67.80	–
Mask TextSpotter [51]	ResNet50	Jointly	–	60.30	69.90	77.30	52.90	71.80
Mask TextSpotter v2 [54]	ResNet50	Jointly	–	63.50	69.20	74.20	65.30	77.40
Mask TextSpotter v3 [29]	ResNet50	Jointly	–	74.20	78.10	83.30	71.20	78.40
P Wang et al. [50]	ResNet50	Jointly	–	63.55	77.14	82.21	58.72	–
SPTS v2 [2]	ResNet50	Jointly	–	–	–	–	68.50	81.40
PAN++ [3]	ResNet50|18	Jointly	67.99	69.31	77.64	82.10	68.64	78.56
Our	ResNet18	Jointly	68.50	69.46	79.02	83.34	71.02	80.71
	ResNet50	Jointly	70.03	71.44	80.31	84.68	71.83	81.65

None means no lexicon is used. Full means the lexicon contains all words in test set is used.

4.4 Experimental Results for Text Spotting

The end-to-end text positioning results of IC15 and Total-Text data sets are shown in Table 6. "Finetune" is to load the pre-trained model and then train the target data set separately for 100 epochs. "Jointly" directly uses the pre-trained model to test the target data set. It can be seen that under the "Finetune" strategy of the IC15 data set, compared with SwinTextSpotter [21], the algorithm in this paper is more accurate and detailed in extracting information, which is 2.94 (W) percentage points higher than it. The "Jointly" strategy achieved an excellent result of 84.68% (S). On Total-Text, compared with the 81.4% (Full) positioning result of SPTS v2 [2] when using the same backbone network, this result is undoubtedly more advantageous. These results show that the model has excellent detection and recognition performance for both curved and straight text.

5   Conclusion

Extensive experiments on these benchmark data sets show that compared with previous state-of-the-art text localization algorithms, this model has similar or even better robustness. But there are still some shortcomings. For example, when text instances are in extremely dark, blurry, and bright scenes, it is impossible to accurately locate the contents of all text instances. and error detection and recognition of special characters with consistent fonts and colors. These are also common challenges in current natural scene text positioning tasks, and they are also focus issues that need to be solved urgently. We believe that if the Transformer encoder and the CNN network are used to share the feature extraction work, better results can be achieved. Specifically, CNN can extract low-level and fine-grained features of the image through the convolution kernel, retain the spatial structure information of the image, and have translation invariance. Transformer can capture the long-distance dependencies of images through the self-attention mechanism, model the global semantic information of images, handle inputs of variable length, and adapt to multi-scale features.

Acknowledgments. This article was submitted on Dec 5, 2023. This work was supported by the National Natural Science Foundation of China (No. 62166043, U2003207).

Disclosure of Interests. The authors have no competing interests to declare that are relevant to the content of this article.

References

1. Wang, P., Zhang, C., et al.: Pgnet: real-time arbitrarily-shaped text spotting with point gathering network. In: Proceedings of the AAAI, vol. 35, no. 4, pp. 2782–2790 (2021)
2. Liu, Y., Zhang, J., et al.: SPTS v2: single-point scene text spotting (2023)
3. Wang, W., et al.: PAN++: towards efficient and accurate end-to-end spotting of arbitrarily-shaped text. In: IEEE TPAMI, vol. 44, no. 9, pp. 5349–5367, 1 September 2022. https://doi.org/10.1109/TPAMI.2021.3077555
4. Xu, Y., Xu, W., Cheung, D., Tu, Z.: Line segment detection using transformers without edges. In: 2021 IEEE/CVF Conference on Computer Vision and Pattern Recognition (CVPR), Nashville, TN, USA, pp. 4255–4264 (2021). https://doi.org/10.1109/CVPR46437.2021.00424
5. Liu, Y., Shen, L.C., et al.: ABCNet v2: adaptive bezier-curve network for real-time end-to end text spotting. IEEE Trans. Pattern Anal. Mach. Intell. **44**(11), 8048–8064 (2022)
6. Woo, S., Park, J., Lee, J.Y., et al.: CBAM: Convolutional Block Attention Module. Springer, Cham (2018)

7. Wang, Y., Xie, H.Z.-J., et al.: Contournet: taking a further step toward accurate arbitrary-shaped scene text detection. In: Proceedings of the IEEE/CVF Conference on Computer Vision and Pattern Recognition (CVPR), pp. 11 753–11 762 (2020)

8. Kittenplon, Y., Lavi, I., Fogel, S., Bar, Y., Manmatha, R., Perona, P.: Towards weakly-supervised text spotting using a multi-task transformer (2022)

9. Zhang, S. -X., Zhu, X.L., et al.: Arbitrary shape text detection via segmentation with probability maps. In: IEEE TPAMI, vol. 45, no. 3, pp. 2736–2750, 1 March 2023. https://doi.org/10.1109/TPAMI.2022.3176122

10. Yang, L., Zhang, R., et al.: SimAM: a simple, parameter-free attention module for convolutional neural networks. In: Proceedings of the 38th International Conference on Machine Learning, in Proceedings of Machine Learning Research, vol. 139, pp. 11863–11874 (2021)

11. Dai, W., et al.: An end-to-end chinese text normalization model based on rule-guided flat-lattice transformer. In: ICASSP 2022, Singapore, pp. 7122–7126 (2022). https://doi.org/10.1109/ICASSP43922.2022.9747316

12. Xing, L., Tian, Z., Huang, W., Scott, M.: Convolutional character networks. In: 2019 IEEE/CVF International Conference on Computer Vision (ICCV), Seoul, Korea (South), pp. 9125–9135 (2019). https://doi.org/10.1109/ICCV.2019.00922

13. Peng, D., Wang, X.Y., et al.: SPTS: single-point text spotting. In: Proceedings of the 30th ACM International Conference on Multimedia, pp. 4272–4281 (2022)

14. Wang, W., Xie, E., Song, X., et al.: Efficient and accurate arbitrary-shaped text detection with pixel aggregation network. In: Proceedings of the IEEE/CVF International Conference on Computer Vision, pp. 8440–8449 (2019)

15. Nayef, N., et al.: ICDAR2017 robust reading challenge on multilingual scene text detection and script identification-RRC-MLT. In: Proceedings of International Conference on Document Analysis and Recognition, pp. 1454–1459 (2017)

16. Baek, Y., Lee, B., Han, D., et al.: Character region awareness for text detection. In: Proceedings of the IEEE/CVF Conference on Computer Vision and Pattern Recognition, pp. 9365–9374 (2019)

17. He, K., Zhang, X., Ren, S., Sun, J.: Deep residual learning for image recognition. In: Proceedings of IEEE Conference on Computer Vision and Pattern Recognition, pp. 770–778 (2016)

18. Liao, M., Zou, Z.Z., et al.: Real-time scene text detection with differentiable binarization and adaptive scale fusion. In: IEEE TPAMI (2022)

19. Liu, X., Liang, D.S., et al.: FOTS: fast oriented text spotting with a unified network. In: 2018 IEEE/CVF Conference on Computer Vision and Pattern Recognition, Salt Lake City, UT, USA, pp. 5676–5685 (2018). https://doi.org/10.1109/CVPR.2018.00595

20. Wang, W., Xie, E., Li, X., et al.: Shape robust text detection with progressive scale expansion network. In: Proceedings of the IEEE/CVF Conference on Computer Vision and Pattern Recognition, pp. 9336–9345 (2019)

21. Huang, M., et al.: SwinTextSpotter: scene text spotting via better synergy between text detection and text recognition. In: 2022 IEEE/CVF Conference on Computer Vision and Pattern Recognition (CVPR), New Orleans, LA, USA, pp. 4583–4593 (2022). https://doi.org/10.1109/CVPR52688.2022.00455

22. Lu, P., Wang, H., Zhu, S., et al.: Boundary TextSpotter: toward arbitrary-shaped scene text spotting. IEEE TIP **31**, 6200–6212 (2022)

23. Qin, S., Bissacco, A.M., et al.: Towards unconstrained end-to-end text spotting. In: Proceedings of IEEE International Conference on Computer Vision, pp. 4703–4713 (2019)

24. Zhang, S.-X., Zhu, X., et al.: Adaptive boundary proposal network for arbitrary shape text detection. In: Proceedings of the IEEE/CVF International Conference on Computer Vision (ICCV), pp. 1305–1314, October 2021
25. Chen, Z., Wang, W., Xie, E., et al.: FAST: Searching for a faster arbitrarily-shaped text detector with minimalist kernel representation (2021)
26. Yuliang, L., Lianwen, J.Z., et al.: Detecting curve text in the wild: new dataset and new solution (2017) arXiv:1712.02170
27. Karatzas, D., et al.: ICDAR 2015 competition on robust reading. In: Proceedings of International conference on Document Analysis Recognition, pp. 1156–1160 (2015)
28. Fang, S., Mao, Z., Xie, H., et al.: Abinet++: autonomous, bidirectional and iterative language modeling for scene text spotting. In: IEEE TPAMI (2022)
29. Liao, M., Pang, G., et al.: Mask TextSpotter v3: segmentation proposal network for robust scene text spotting. In: Vedaldi, A., Bischof, H., Brox, T., Frahm, JM. (eds.) Computer Vision – ECCV 2020, LNCS, vol. 12356. Springer, Cham (2020). https://doi.org/10.1007/978-3-030-58621-8-41
30. Ch'ng, C.K., Chan, C.S.: Total-text: a comprehensive dataset for scene text detection and recognition. In: Proceedings of International Conference on Document Analysis Recognition, pp. 935–942 (2017)
31. Yu, W., Liu, Y., Hua, W., et al.: Turning a CLIP model into a scene text detector. In: Proceedings of the IEEE/CVF Conference on Computer Vision and Pattern Recognition, pp. 6978–6988 (2023)
32. Shi, B., Bai, X., Yao, C.: An end-to-end trainable neural network for image-based sequence recognition and its application to scene text recognition. IEEE TPAMI **39**(11), 2298–2304 (2016)
33. Jaderberg, S.-N.M., et al. Spatial transformer networks. In: Advances in Neural Information Processing Systems, pp. 2017–2025 (2015)
34. Liao, M., Wan, Z., Yao, C., et al.: Real-time scene text detection with differentiable binarization. In: Proceedings of the AAAI Conference on Artificial Intelligence, vol. 34, pp. 11474–11481 (2020)
35. Shi, B, Wang, X, et al.: Robust scene text recognition with automatic rectification. In: Proceedings of the CVPR, pp. 4168–4176 (2016)
36. Li, H., Wang, P., et al.: Show, attend and read: a simple and strong baseline for irregular text recognition. In: Proceedings of the AAAI Conference on Artificial Intelligence, vol. 33, no. 01, pp. 8610–8617, July 2019
37. Liao, M., Zhang, J., et al.: Scene text recognition from two-dimensional perspective. In: Proceedings of the AAAI Conference on Artificial Intelligence, vol. 33, no. 01, pp. 8714–8721, July 2019
38. Dai, P., Zhang, S., et al.: Progressive contour regression for arbitrary-shape scene text detection. In: Proceedings of the IEEE/CVF Conference on Computer Vision and Pattern Recognition (CVPR), pp. 7393–7402, June 2021
39. Lu, P., Wang, H., S., et al.: Boundary TextSpotter: toward arbitrary-shaped scene text spotting. In: IEEE TIP, vol. 31, pp. 6200–6212 (2022). https://doi.org/10.1109/TIP.2022.3206615
40. Li, M., et al.: TrOCR: transformer-based optical character recognition with pre-trained models (2021)
41. Zhu, Y., Chen, J., et al.: Fourier contour embedding for arbitrary-shaped text detection. In: Proceedings of the IEEE/CVF Conference on Computer Vision and Pattern Recognition (CVPR), pp. 3123–3131, June 2021
42. Sheng, T., Chen, J., et al.: Centripetaltext: an efficient text instance representation for scene text detection. In: Advances in Neural Information Processing Systems, vol. 34 (2021)

43. Yao, C., et al.: Detecting texts of arbitrary orientations in natural images. In: Proceedings of IEEE Conference on Computer Vision and Pattern Recognition, pp. 1083–1090 (2012)
44. Wang, H., et al.: All you need is boundary: toward arbitrary-shaped text spotting. In: AAAI, vol. 34, pp. 12160–12167 (2020)
45. Long, S., Qin, S., Panteleev, D., et al.: Towards end-to-end unified scene text detection and layout analysis (2022)
46. Qiao, L., et al.: Mango: a mask at tention guided one-stage scene text spotter. In: AAAI, vol. 35, pp. 2467–2476 (2021)
47. Tang., J., Few could be better than all: feature sampling and grouping for scene text detection (2022). https://doi.org/10.48550/arXiv.2203.15221
48. Peng, D., et al.: Spts: single-point text spotting. In: Proceedings of the 30th ACM International Conference on Multimedia, pp. 4272–4281 (2022)
49. Qin, S., et al.: Towards unconstrained end-to-end text spotting. In: CVPR, pp. 4704–4714 (2019)
50. Wang, P., Li, H., Shen, C.: Towards end to-end text spotting in natural scenes. IEEE TPAMI **44**(10), 7266–7281 (2021)
51. Lyu, P., etal.: Mask textspotter: an end-to-end trainable neural network for spotting text with arbitrary shapes. In: ECCV, pp. 67–83 (2018)
52. Qiao, L., et al.: Text perceptron: Towards end-to end arbitrary-shaped text spotting. In: AAAI, vol. 34, pp. 11899–11907 (2020)
53. Liu, Y., et al.: Abcnet: real-time scene text spotting with adaptive bezier-curve network. In: CVPR, pp. 9809–9818 (2020)
54. Liao, M., et al.: Mask textspotter: an end-to-end trainable neural network for spotting text with arbitrary shapes. In: IEEE TPAMI, vol. 43, no. 2, pp. 532–548 (2021)

Author Index

The manufacturer's authorised representative in the EU is Springer
Nature Customer Service Centre GmbH, Europaplatz 3, 69115 Heidelberg,
Germany. If you have any concerns regarding our products, please
contact ProductSafety@springernature.com

Printed and bound by CPI Group (UK) Ltd, Croydon, CR0 4YY
27/04/2026
02097586-0020